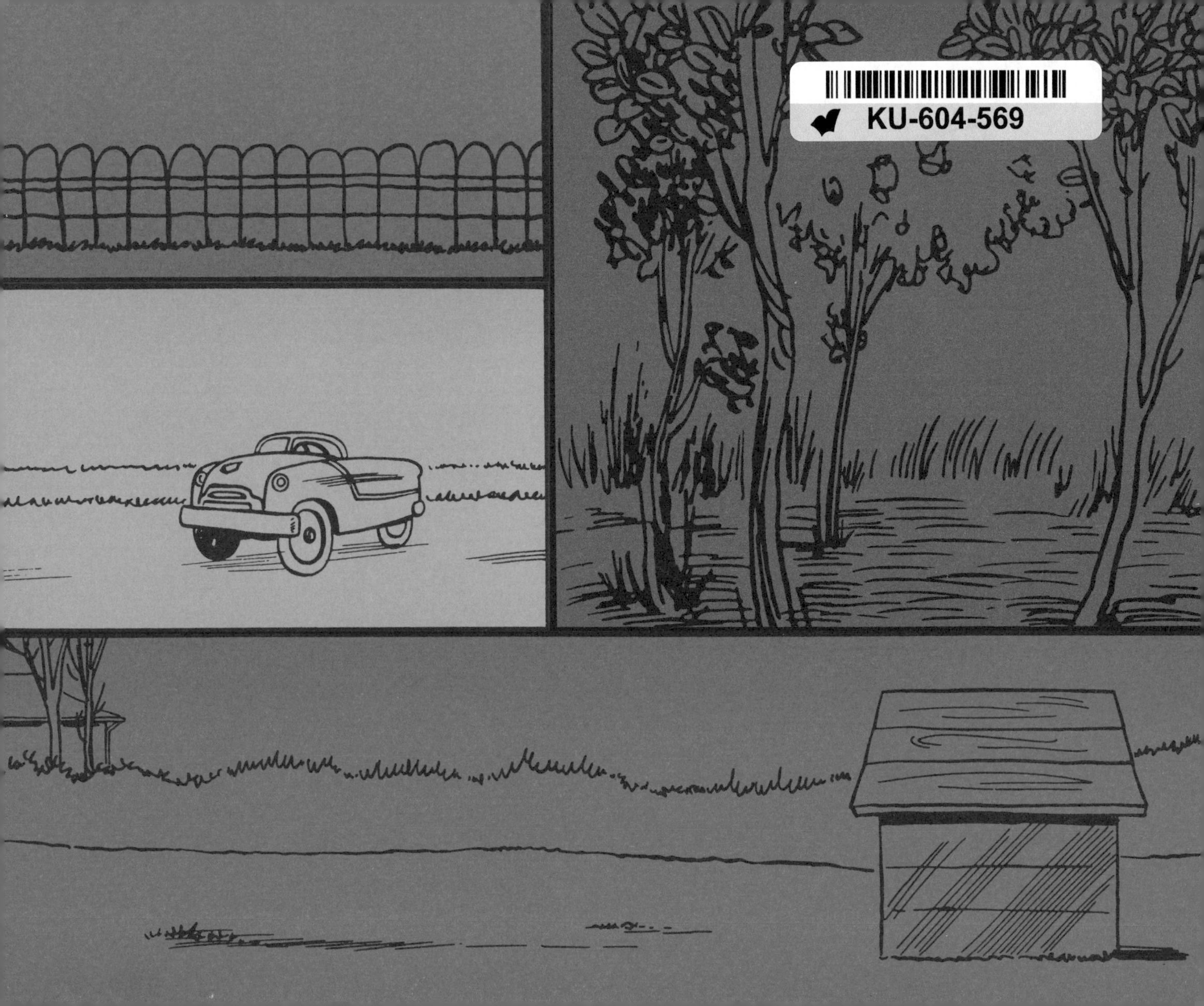

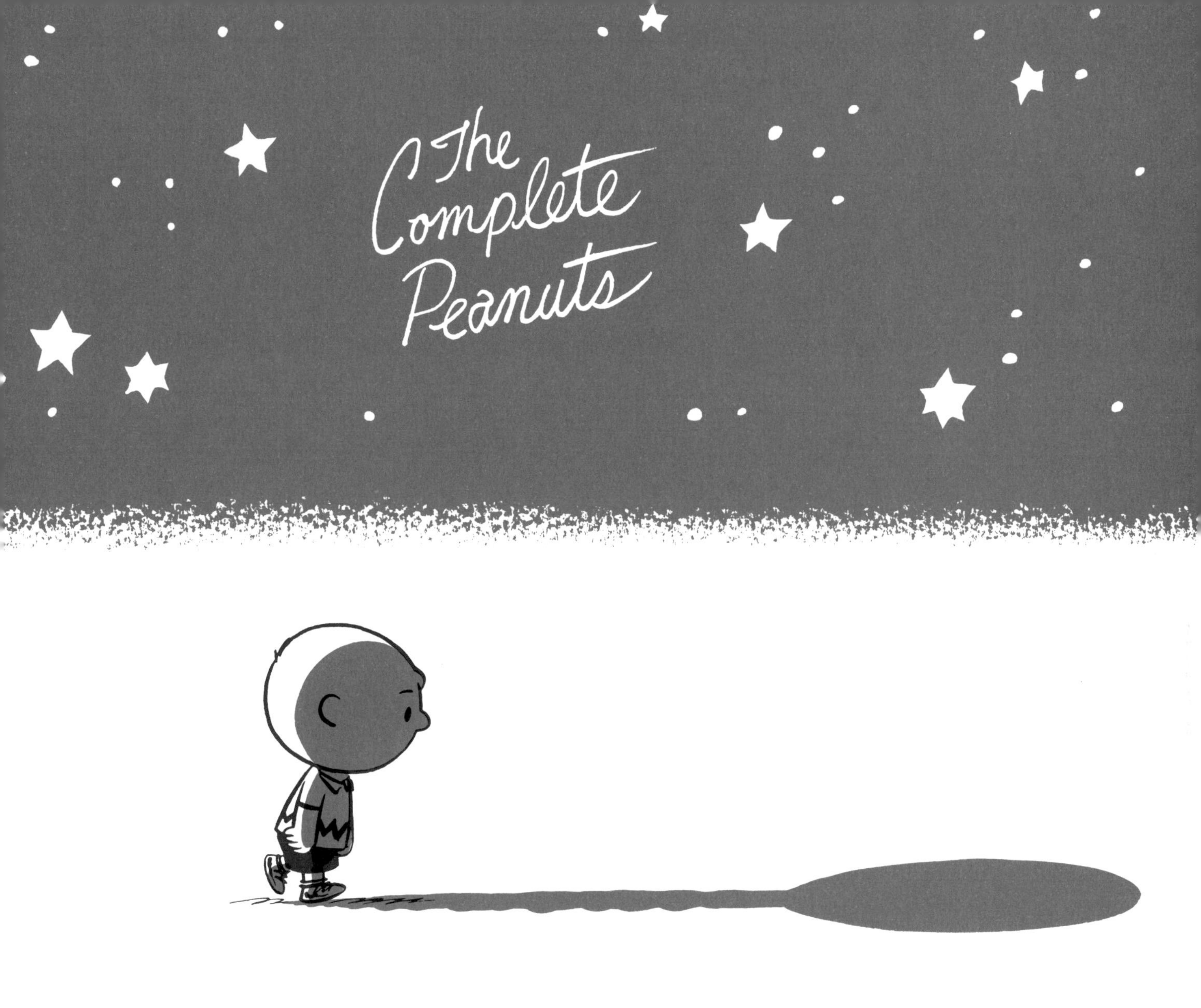
The Complete Peanuts

with love

from
franny and grandpa

~~~~~~

London, 25. November 2007
DRAGON SCHOOL EXEAT

THE COMPLETE PEANUTS
by Charles M. Schulz

Publishers: Gary Groth & Kim Thompson
Designer: Seth

Special thanks to Jeannie Schulz, without whom this project would not have come to fruition. Thanks to
Charles M. Schulz Creative Associates, especially Paige Braddock, Heather Orosco, and Kim Towner.
Thanks for special support from United Media.

First published in America in 2004 by Fantagraphics Books, 7563 Lake City Way, Seattle, WA 98115, USA

First published in Great Britain in 2007 by Canongate Books Ltd, 14 High Street, Edinburgh EH1 1TE

1

British Library Cataloguing-in-Publication Data
A catalogue record for this book is available on
request from the British Library

ISBN 978 1 84767 031 1

Printed and bound in China

www.canongate.net

CHARLES M. SCHULZ

THE COMPLETE PEANUTS

1950 TO 1952

"IT'S RISKY, BUT I GET MY LAUGHS!"

CANONGATE BOOKS

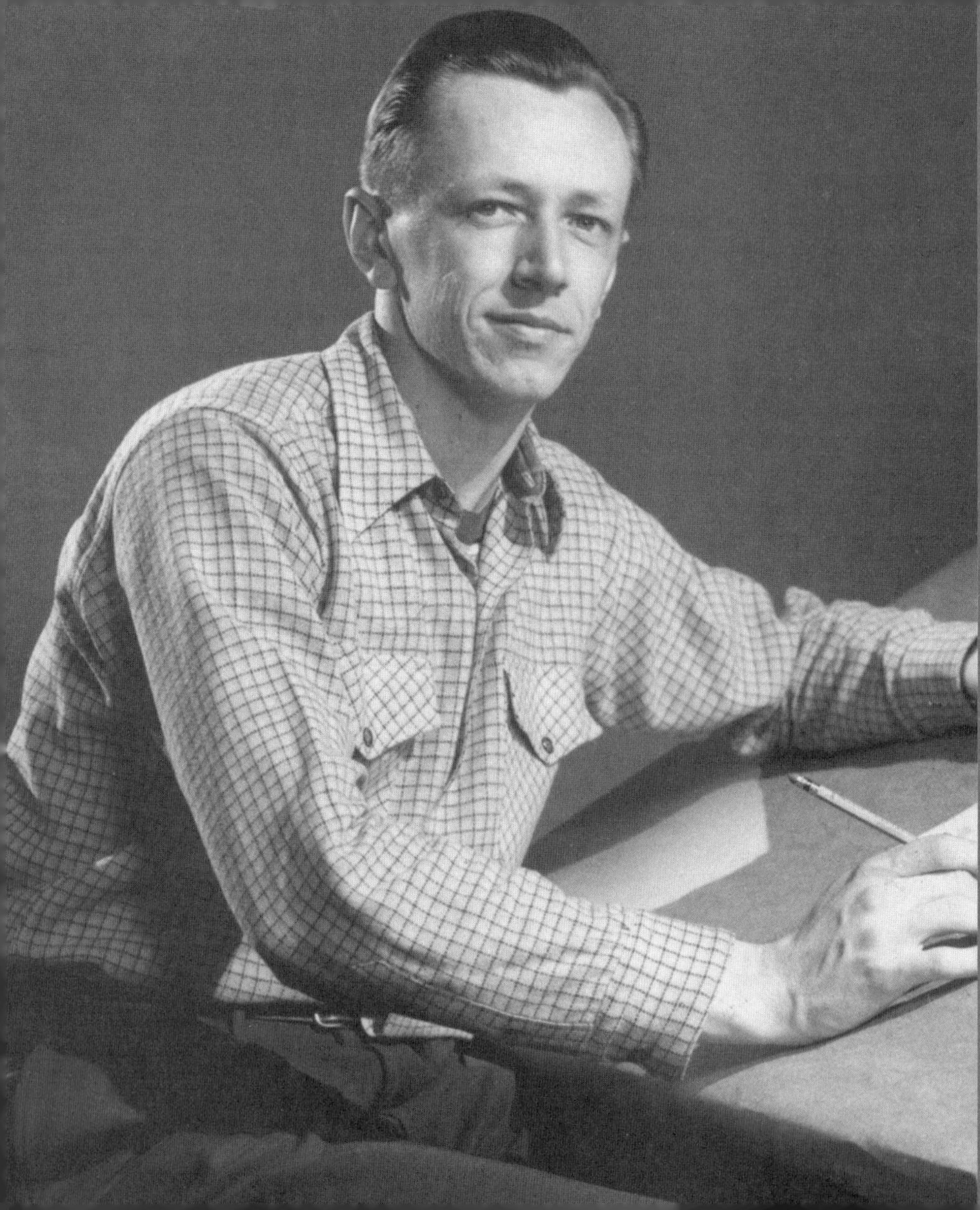

Charles Schulz
circa 1950.

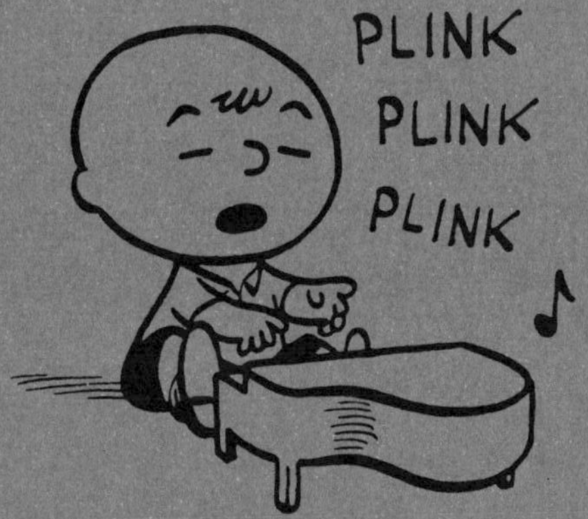
PLINK
PLINK
PLINK

INTRODUCTION by GARRISON KEILLOR

Sparky Schulz (b. 11/26/22) was a shy, self-conscious kid with bad skin, too light to play football, not tall enough for basketball, the only child of Carl and Dena Schulz of St. Paul, a painful student at St. Paul Central High School, failing at everything, wanting to talk to girls and not knowing how, tormented by teachers and other bullies, finding solace at the movies, sitting in the lovely dark and watching Victor McLaglen in *Lost Patrol* and Gary Cooper in *Beau Geste* and Laurel and Hardy and Tarzan, and reading the funny papers, *Popeye* and *Captain Easy* and *Wash Tubbs*. Hundreds of other St. Paul boys were in the same boat, whether Sparky knew it or not, and negotiated the white waters of adolescence and came out into the calm pond of Actuarial or Home Loans or Homiletics, but Sparky had a good hand for drawing with a pencil, at least compared to other kids at Central High he did, and when his mom saw an ad for a University of Minnesota extension class in cartooning, he enrolled in it, and that, as they say, was that. The boy got a notion that he had a Gift and found an endeavor that quickened his heart and might be his Calling and this miraculous turn of events steadied him through the travails of the Nineteen Forties. He was drafted by the Army in 1943, about the time his mom was diagnosed with cancer. She looked up at him from her bed and said, "I suppose that we should say goodbye" and died the next day. After training at Camp Campbell, Kentucky, he shipped off to Europe with the infantry, the leader of a machine gun squad, a serious soldier, and put aside cartooning until he returned home. He hung around St. Paul for a few years, taught at the commercial art correspondence school in Minneapolis where he had formerly been a student, got good at cartoon lettering, sold some gag cartoons to *The Saturday Evening Post*, and then, encouraged by a fellow instructor named Frank Wing, focused on drawing little kids and created a strip cartoon called *Li'l Folks* which he sold to the *St. Paul Pioneer Press* which ran it in the women's section. It was an odd strip, no adults present, only kids, who were not little rascals like the Katzenjammers or Little Iodine, but contemplative creatures capable of long brooding thoughts and comic pathos. He drew the strip for two years for $10 a week and then went in to the paper and asked for a raise and for a better location in the paper and was turned down. "Then I better quit," said Sparky. "All right," said the editor. That was in the spring of 1950. Schulz was 27. He got on the train to New York and took his strip to Jim Freeman, the editorial director of United Feature Syndicate, who snapped it up and the first *Peanuts* strip appeared on October 2, 1950. And that is the St. Paul chapter of the legend of Charles Schulz. Good grief.

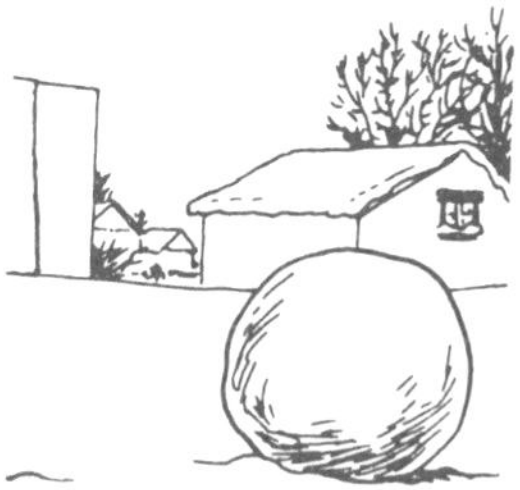

We St. Paulites wish we could make it up to Sparky and since his death the city has gone through waves of *Peanuts* sculptures, polyurethane Charlie Browns and Lucys and Linuses and Snoopys, hanging out in Rice Park and on Selby Avenue near Sparky's dad's old barbershop and all over town. We'd give anything if we could go back to 1950 and say the right thing and not drive him away to Santa Rosa, California. I would mention in my city's defense that Sparky took up golf here and that gave him pleasure and he became active in the Church of God and found a spiritual home there. He became a serious reader here after the war, riding the streetcar back and forth to his job in downtown Minneapolis, reading Tolstoy and Thomas Wolfe and Fitzgerald, and he loved his time at the correspondence school. So he did find a degree of happiness here. We weren't a gulag in his life. He learned a lot about pen technique here that helped him get Linus's hair right and the zigzags on Charlie Brown's sweater and Snoopy sitting on the doghouse writing on the typewriter. And *Peanuts* is more about St. Paul than it is about Santa Rosa, I'd say. Snow falls on Snoopy's doghouse. The beautiful modesty and understatement of the strip strike us as Midwestern. Charlie Brown is a stoic like us. He doesn't imagine that some magical book or herb or 12-step program is going to turn him into Charles Green. And it's the Great Pumpkin who comes at Halloween, not the Blissful Artichoke or the Sacred Asparagus.

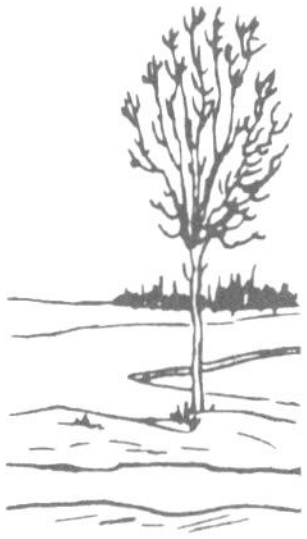

Charles Schulz was an innovative genius of American comics and also the marathon man, drawing strip after four-panel strip, batch after batch, writing the storyboards for the TV specials, year after year, creating a fantasy world that connected to kids as well as adults and all based on powerful iconic characters who express deep feelings of loneliness and resentment and despair. The feeling that everything is against us. The craving for love. An enormous earnestness about doing the right thing. There is not much in *Peanuts* that is shallow or heedless. Schroeder puts everything he has into those notes of Beethoven's and Sparky Schulz put everything he had into the strip. He didn't live to see the rise of graphic novels but he would have admired them as he admired all true artists, R. Crumb or George Herriman or Flannery O'Connor or Fitzgerald, all the class acts. Like Fitzgerald, he left St. Paul wounded and realized his greatness elsewhere and we remember him here with love and admiration and gratitude for his gifts and his heroic endurance. If you stand on Selby Avenue in the late afternoon, just east of Snelling where Carl's barbershop stood, you will see any number of shy, self-conscious 14-year-olds walk past and in Sparky's memory, wish them a good and glorious life like his.

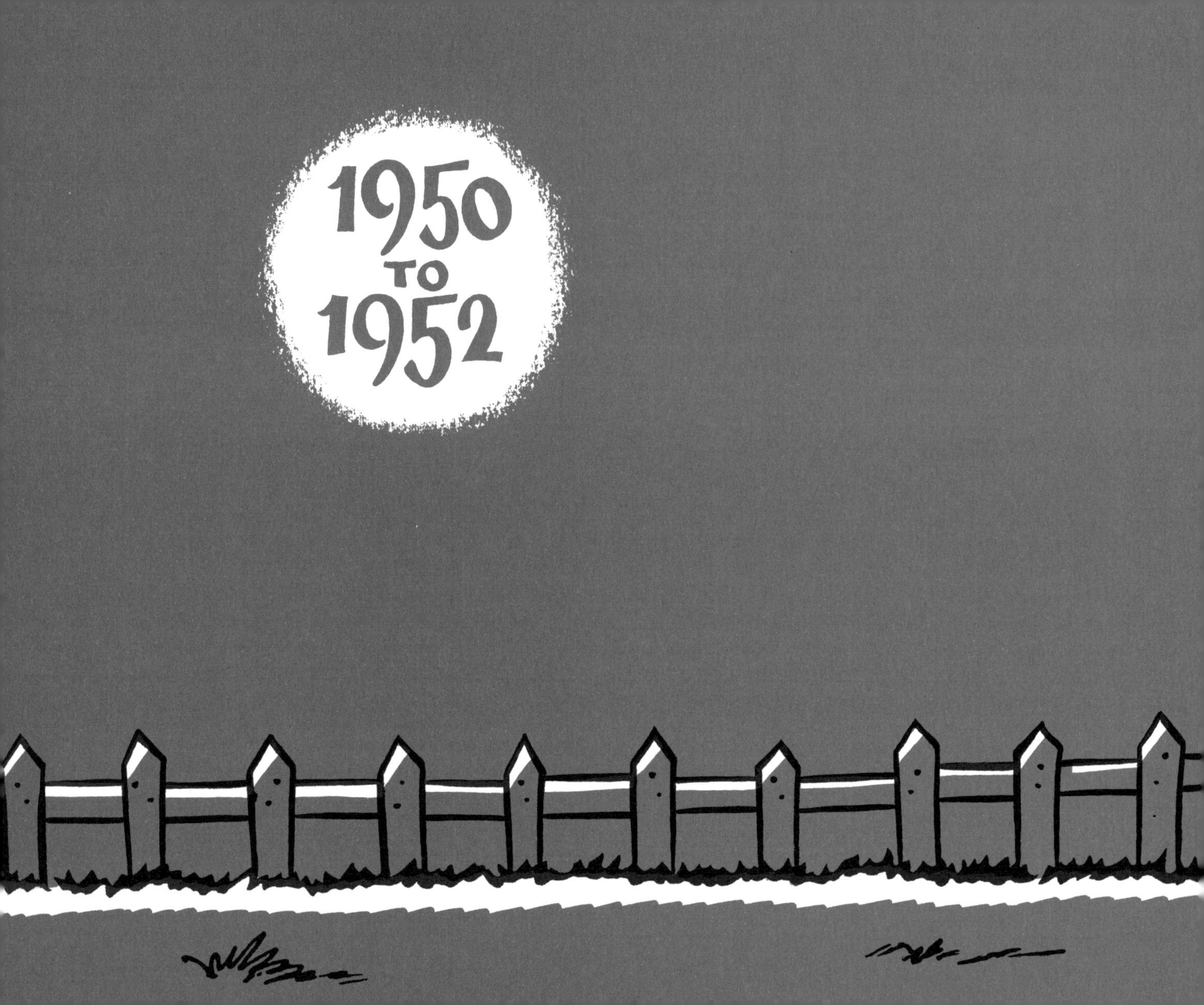
1950
TO
1952

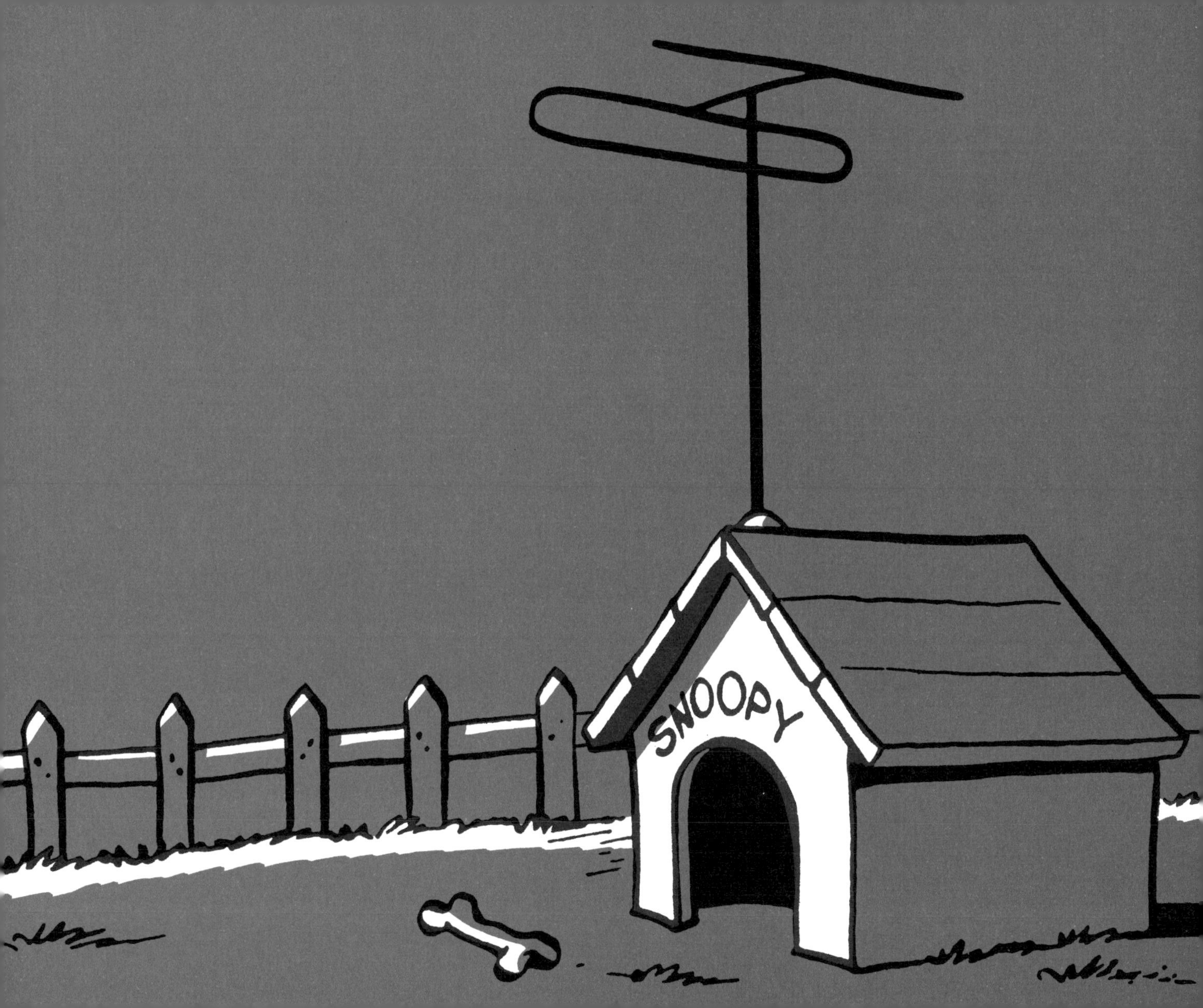
SNOOPY

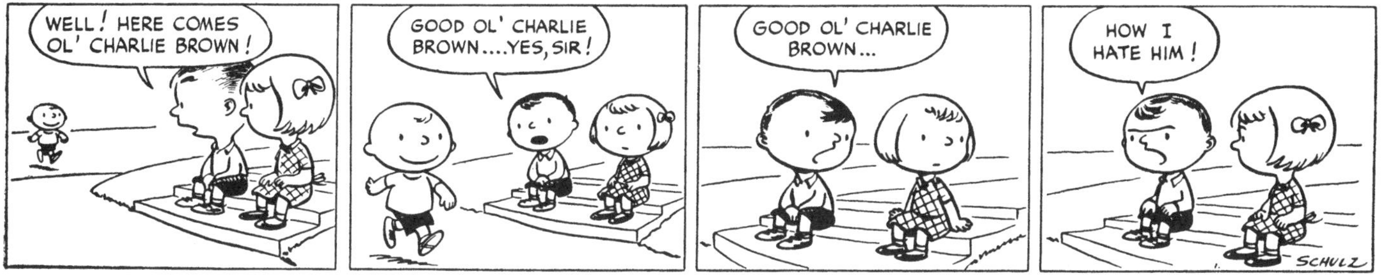
WELL! HERE COMES OL' CHARLIE BROWN!
GOOD OL' CHARLIE BROWN....YES, SIR!
GOOD OL' CHARLIE BROWN...
HOW I HATE HIM!
SCHULZ

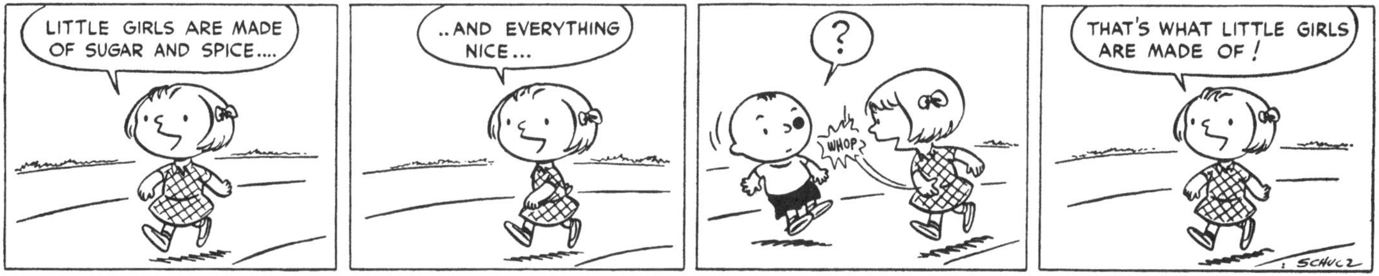
LITTLE GIRLS ARE MADE OF SUGAR AND SPICE....
..AND EVERYTHING NICE...
?
WHOP
THAT'S WHAT LITTLE GIRLS ARE MADE OF!
SCHULZ

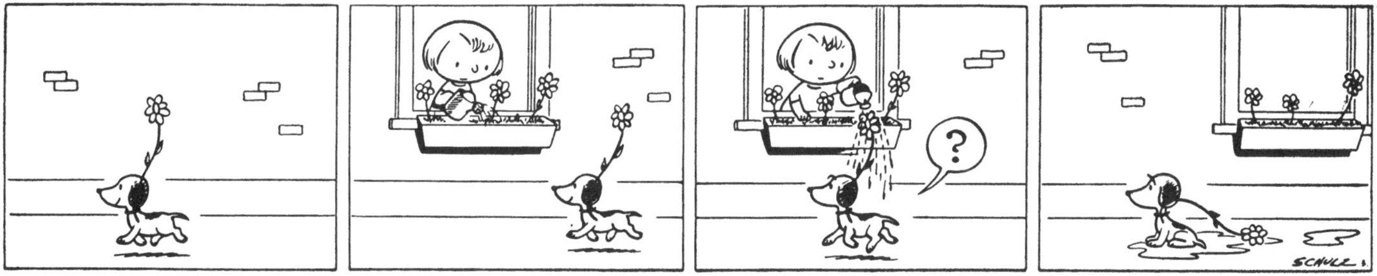
?
SCHULZ

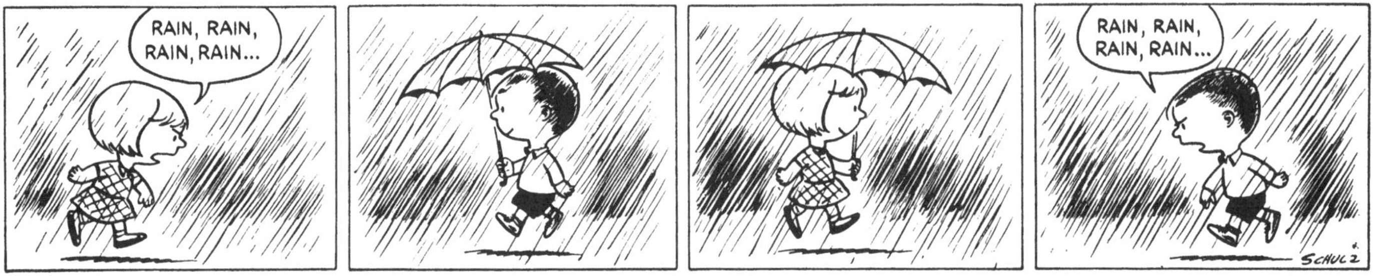
RAIN, RAIN, RAIN, RAIN...
RAIN, RAIN, RAIN, RAIN...
SCHULZ

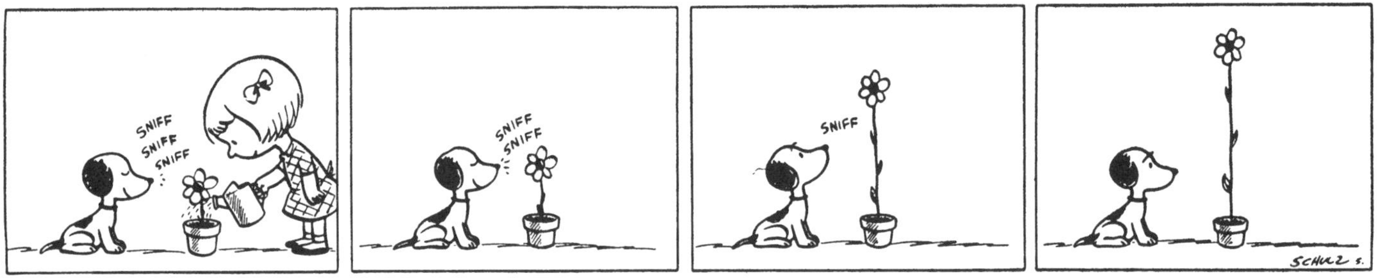
SNIFF SNIFF SNIFF
SNIFF SNIFF
SNIFF
SCHULZ

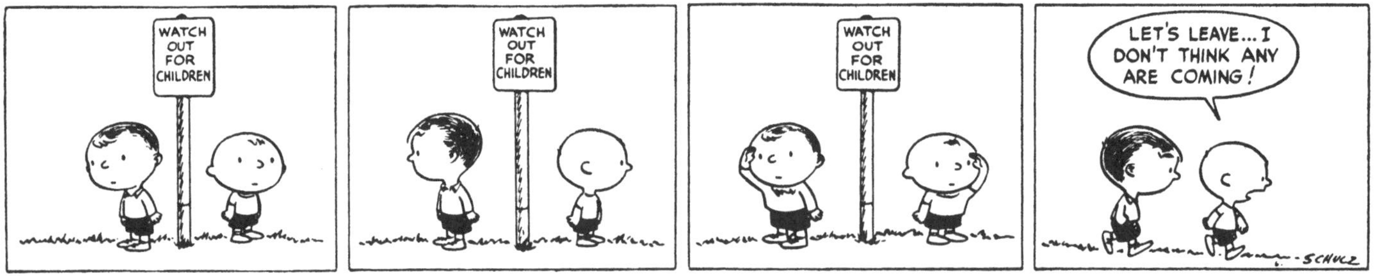
WATCH OUT FOR CHILDREN
WATCH OUT FOR CHILDREN
WATCH OUT FOR CHILDREN
LET'S LEAVE... I DON'T THINK ANY ARE COMING!
SCHULZ

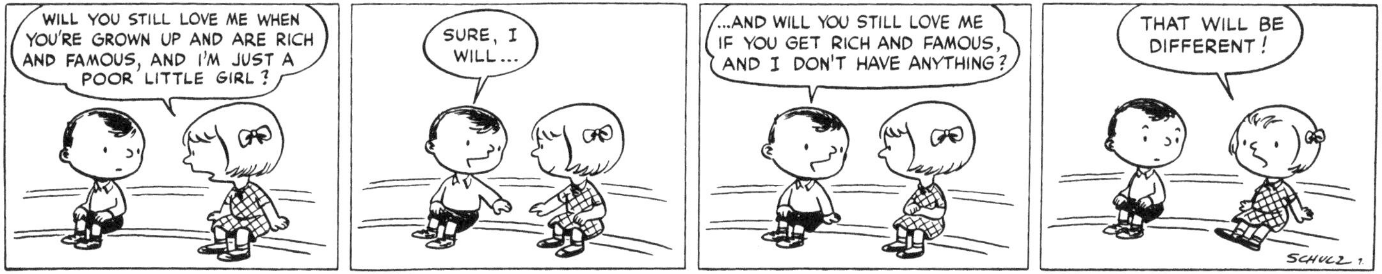
WILL YOU STILL LOVE ME WHEN YOU'RE GROWN UP AND ARE RICH AND FAMOUS, AND I'M JUST A POOR LITTLE GIRL?
SURE, I WILL...
...AND WILL YOU STILL LOVE ME IF YOU GET RICH AND FAMOUS, AND I DON'T HAVE ANYTHING?
THAT WILL BE DIFFERENT!
SCHULZ

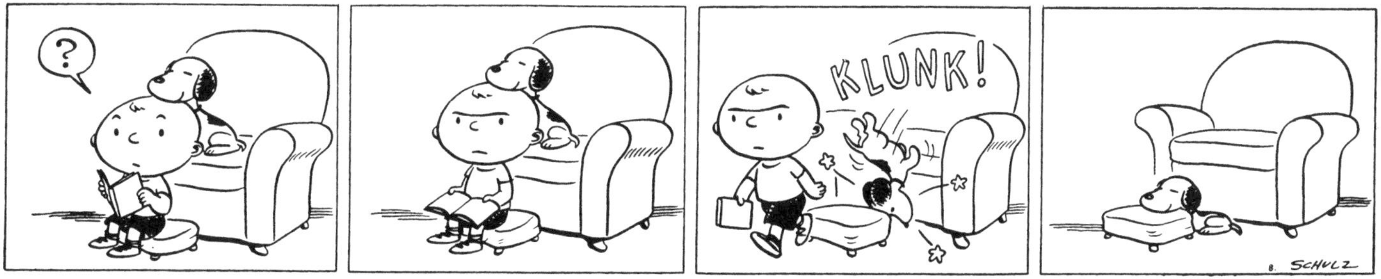
?
KLUNK!
SCHULZ

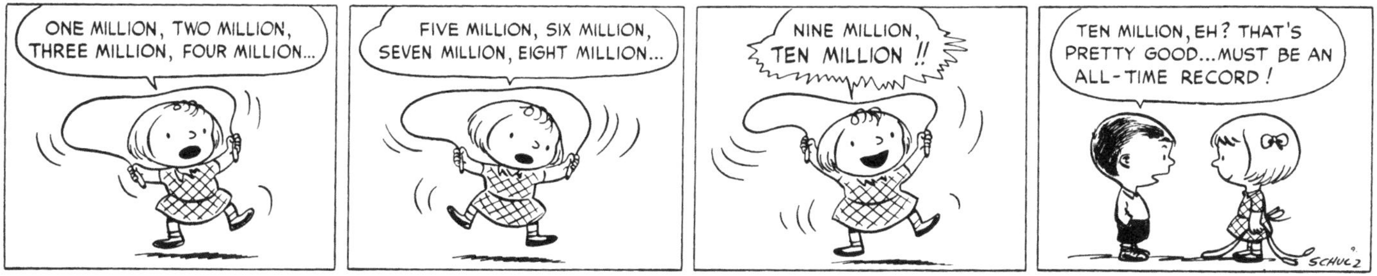
ONE MILLION, TWO MILLION, THREE MILLION, FOUR MILLION...
FIVE MILLION, SIX MILLION, SEVEN MILLION, EIGHT MILLION...
NINE MILLION, TEN MILLION !!
TEN MILLION, EH? THAT'S PRETTY GOOD...MUST BE AN ALL-TIME RECORD!
SCHULZ

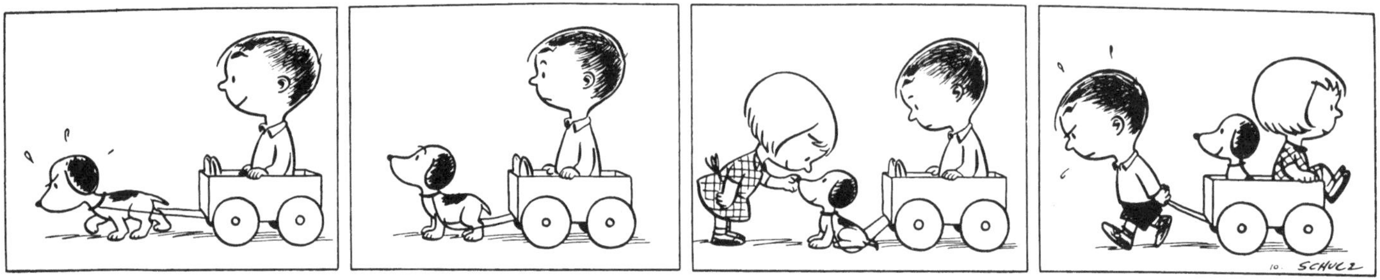

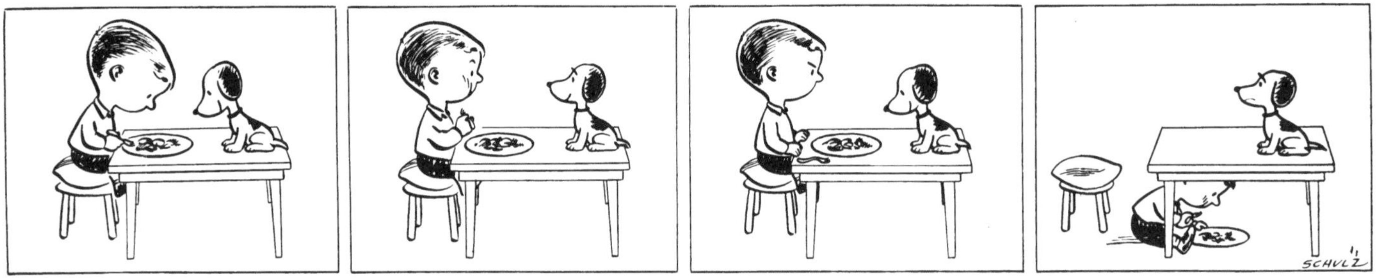

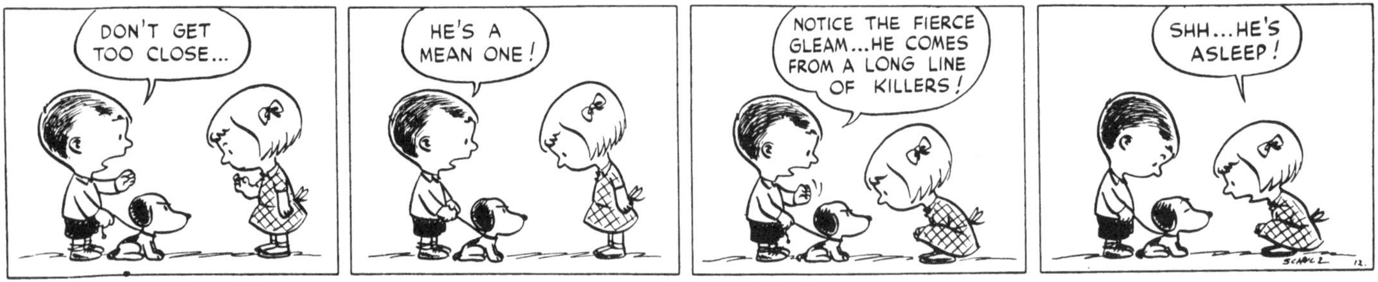
DON'T GET TOO CLOSE...
HE'S A MEAN ONE!
NOTICE THE FIERCE GLEAM...HE COMES FROM A LONG LINE OF KILLERS!
SHH...HE'S ASLEEP!

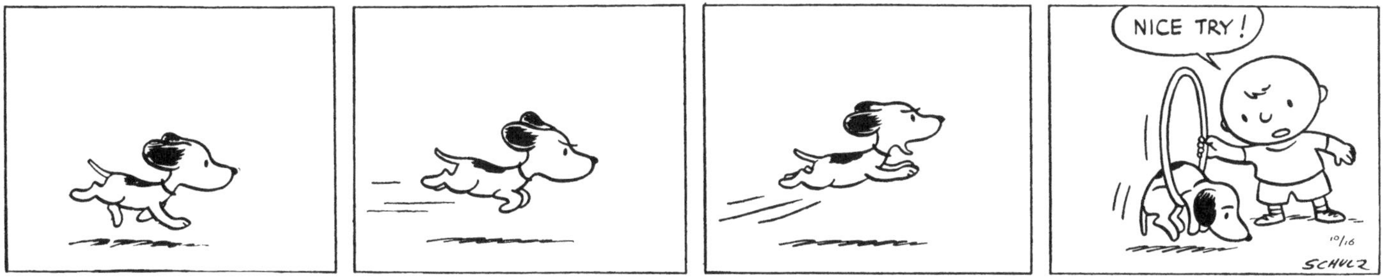
NICE TRY!
10/16
SCHULZ

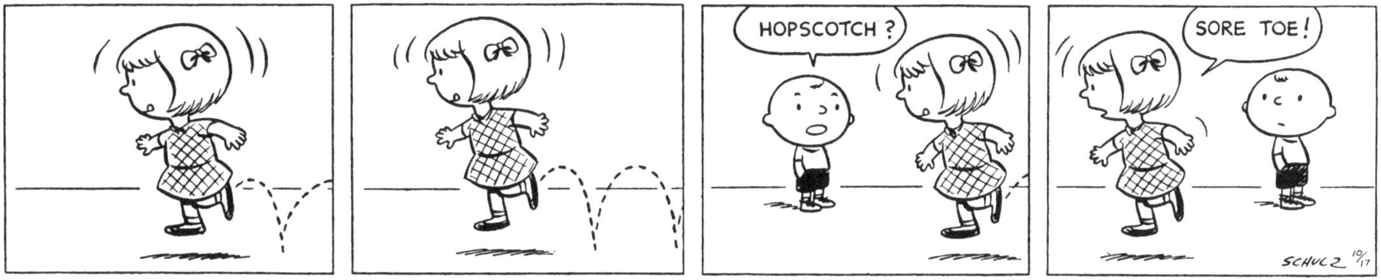
HOPSCOTCH?
SORE TOE!
SCHULZ 10/17

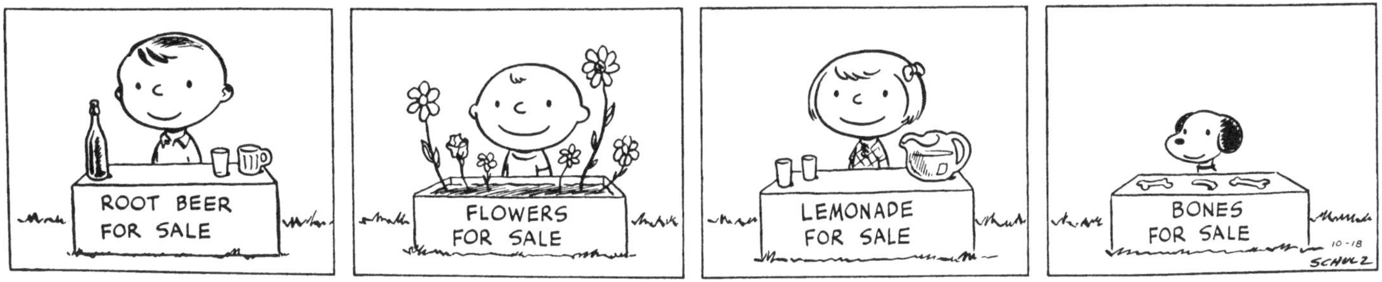
ROOT BEER FOR SALE
FLOWERS FOR SALE
LEMONADE FOR SALE
BONES FOR SALE
10-18
SCHULZ

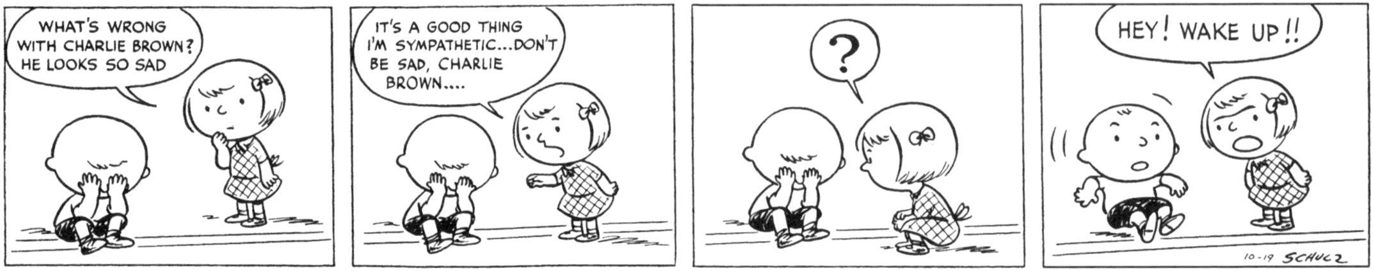
WHAT'S WRONG WITH CHARLIE BROWN? HE LOOKS SO SAD
IT'S A GOOD THING I'M SYMPATHETIC...DON'T BE SAD, CHARLIE BROWN....
?
HEY! WAKE UP!!
10-19 SCHULZ

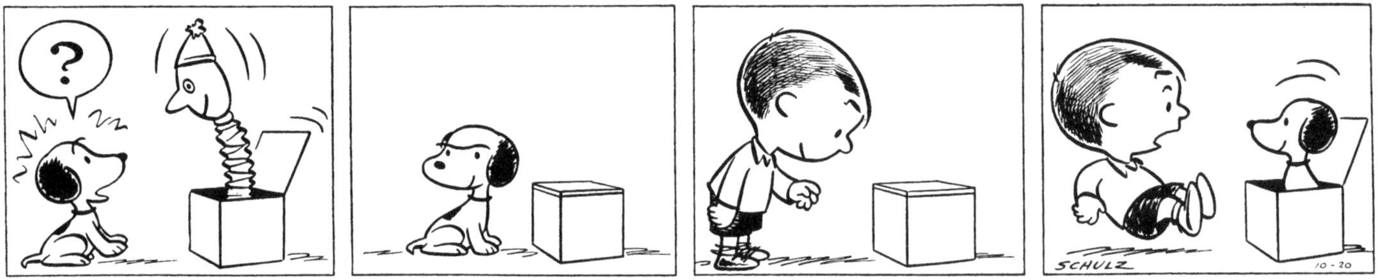
?
SCHULZ
10-20

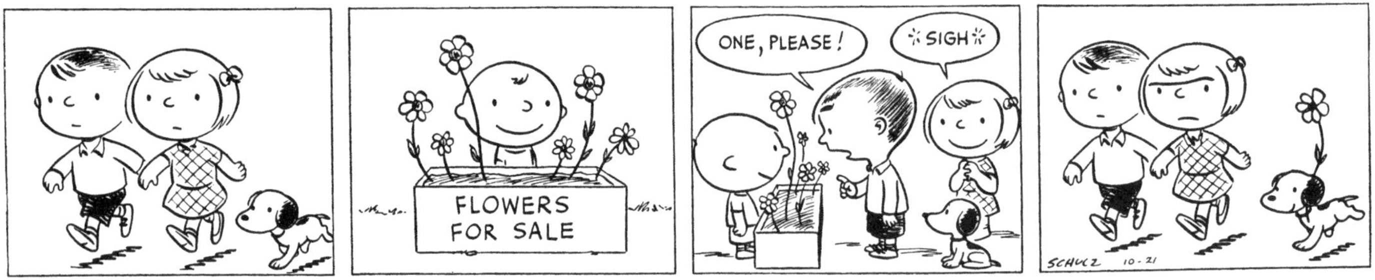
FLOWERS FOR SALE
ONE, PLEASE!
SIGH
SCHULZ 10-21

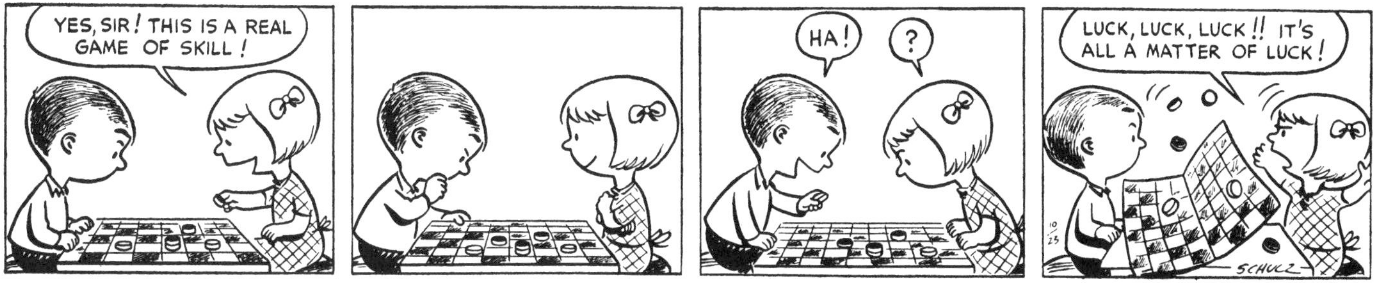
YES, SIR! THIS IS A REAL GAME OF SKILL!
HA!
?
LUCK, LUCK, LUCK!! IT'S ALL A MATTER OF LUCK!
10/23
SCHULZ

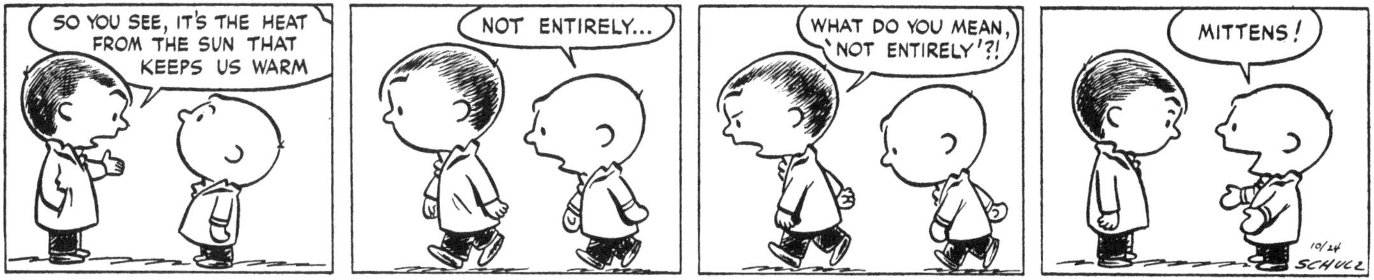
SO YOU SEE, IT'S THE HEAT FROM THE SUN THAT KEEPS US WARM
NOT ENTIRELY...
WHAT DO YOU MEAN, 'NOT ENTIRELY'?!
MITTENS!
10/24
SCHULZ

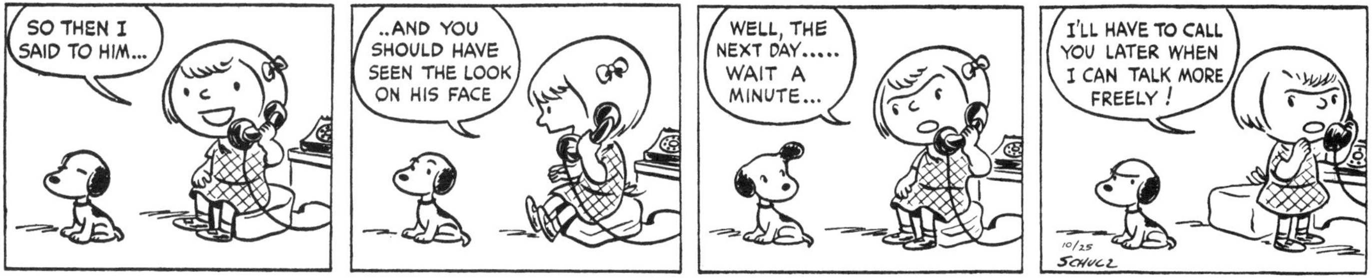
SO THEN I SAID TO HIM...
..AND YOU SHOULD HAVE SEEN THE LOOK ON HIS FACE
WELL, THE NEXT DAY..... WAIT A MINUTE...
I'LL HAVE TO CALL YOU LATER WHEN I CAN TALK MORE FREELY!
10/25
SCHULZ

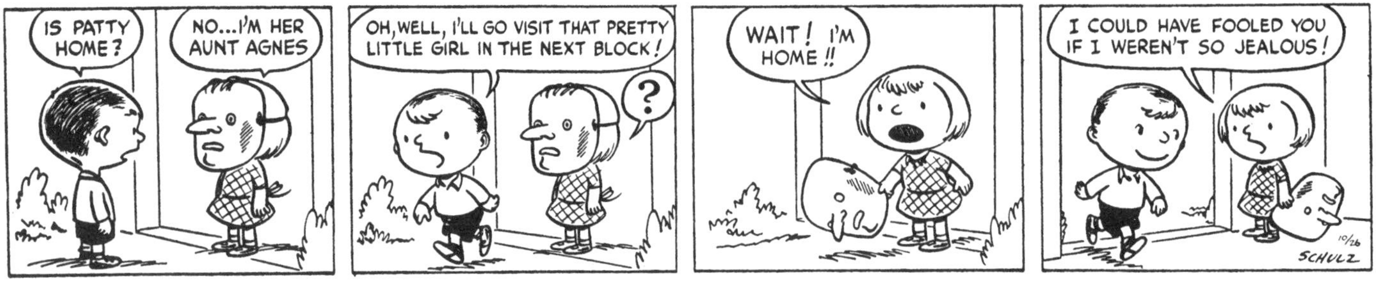
IS PATTY HOME?
NO...I'M HER AUNT AGNES
OH, WELL, I'LL GO VISIT THAT PRETTY LITTLE GIRL IN THE NEXT BLOCK!
?
WAIT! I'M HOME!!
I COULD HAVE FOOLED YOU IF I WEREN'T SO JEALOUS!
10/26
SCHULZ

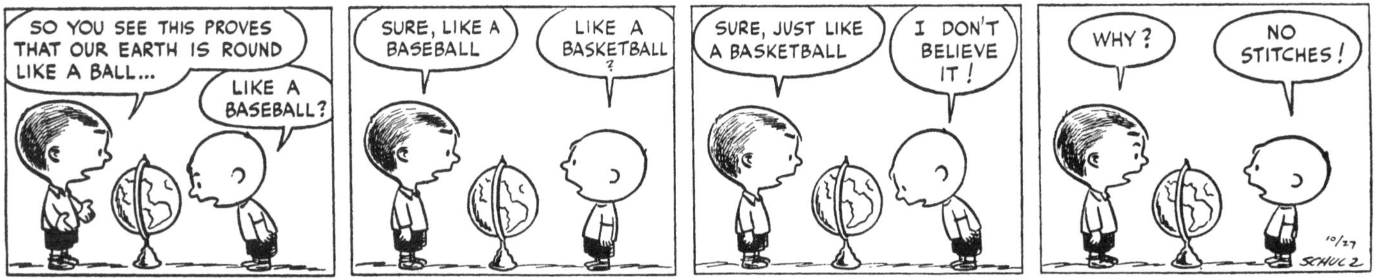
SO YOU SEE THIS PROVES THAT OUR EARTH IS ROUND LIKE A BALL...
LIKE A BASEBALL?
SURE, LIKE A BASEBALL
LIKE A BASKETBALL?
SURE, JUST LIKE A BASKETBALL
I DON'T BELIEVE IT!
WHY?
NO STITCHES!
10/27
SCHULZ

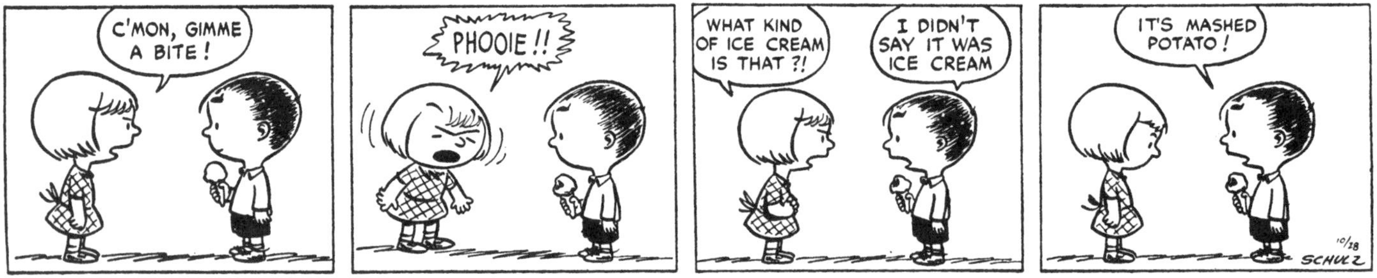
C'MON, GIMME A BITE!
PHOOIE!!
WHAT KIND OF ICE CREAM IS THAT?!
I DIDN'T SAY IT WAS ICE CREAM
IT'S MASHED POTATO!
10/28
SCHULZ

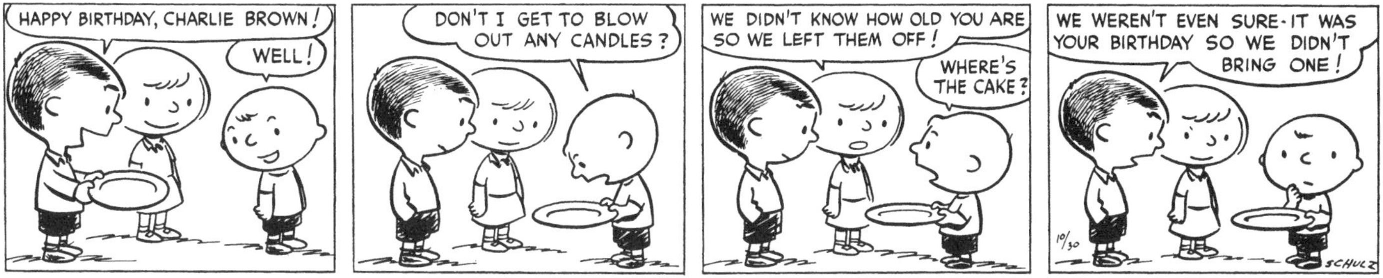
HAPPY BIRTHDAY, CHARLIE BROWN!
WELL!
DON'T I GET TO BLOW OUT ANY CANDLES?
WE DIDN'T KNOW HOW OLD YOU ARE SO WE LEFT THEM OFF!
WHERE'S THE CAKE?
WE WEREN'T EVEN SURE IT WAS YOUR BIRTHDAY SO WE DIDN'T BRING ONE!
10/30
SCHULZ

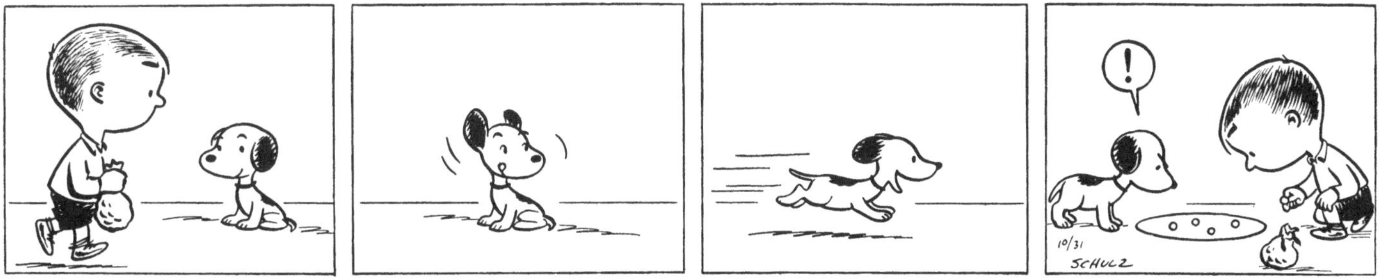
!
10/31
SCHULZ

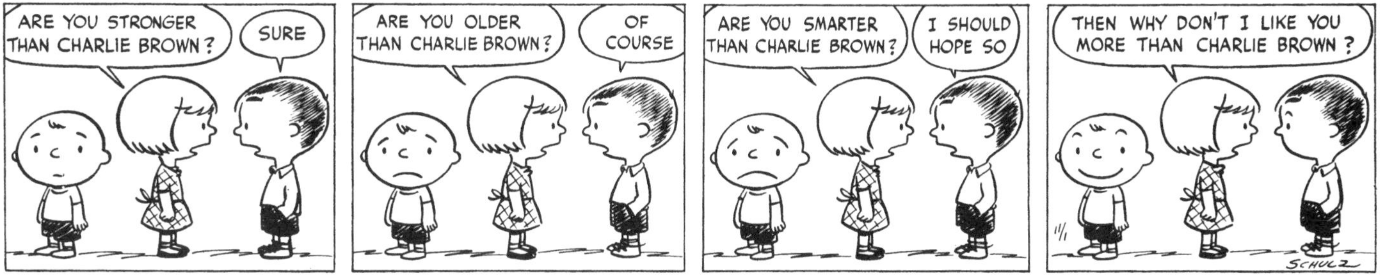
ARE YOU STRONGER THAN CHARLIE BROWN?
SURE
ARE YOU OLDER THAN CHARLIE BROWN?
OF COURSE
ARE YOU SMARTER THAN CHARLIE BROWN?
I SHOULD HOPE SO
THEN WHY DON'T I LIKE YOU MORE THAN CHARLIE BROWN?
11/1
SCHULZ

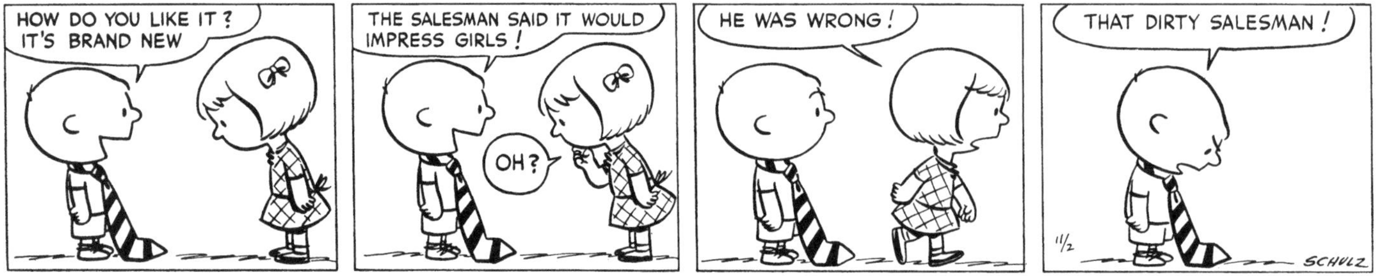
HOW DO YOU LIKE IT ? IT'S BRAND NEW
THE SALESMAN SAID IT WOULD IMPRESS GIRLS !
OH ?
HE WAS WRONG !
THAT DIRTY SALESMAN !
11/2
SCHULZ

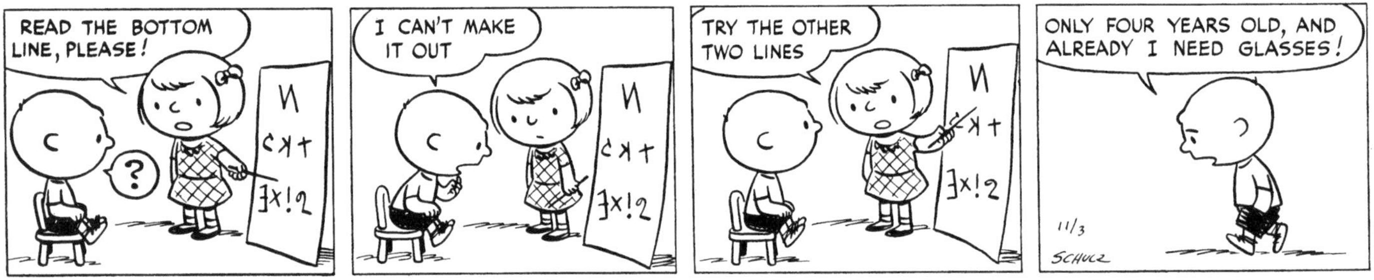
READ THE BOTTOM LINE, PLEASE !
?
I CAN'T MAKE IT OUT
TRY THE OTHER TWO LINES
ONLY FOUR YEARS OLD, AND ALREADY I NEED GLASSES !
11/3
SCHULZ

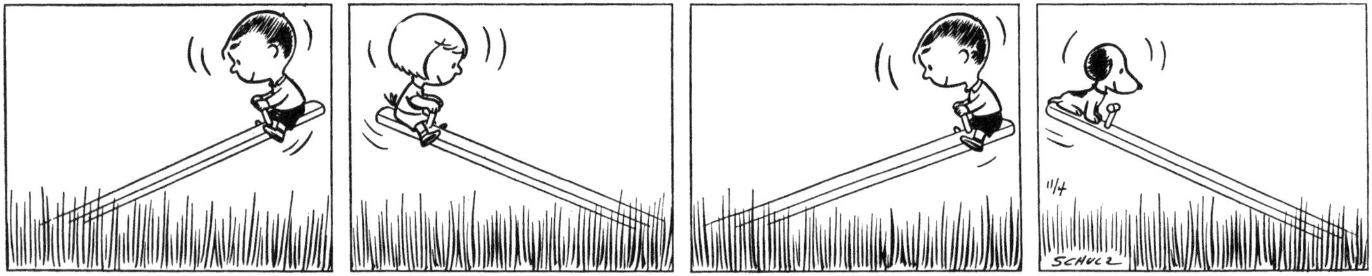
11/4
SCHULZ

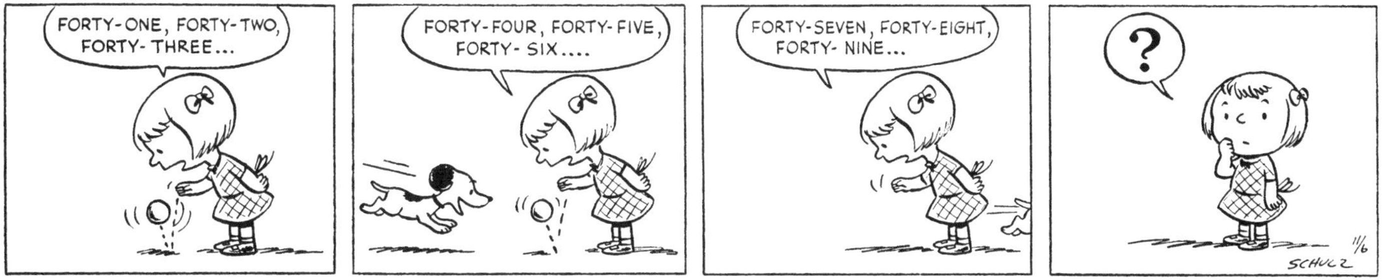
FORTY-ONE, FORTY-TWO, FORTY- THREE...
FORTY-FOUR, FORTY-FIVE, FORTY- SIX....
FORTY-SEVEN, FORTY-EIGHT, FORTY- NINE...
?
11/6
SCHULZ

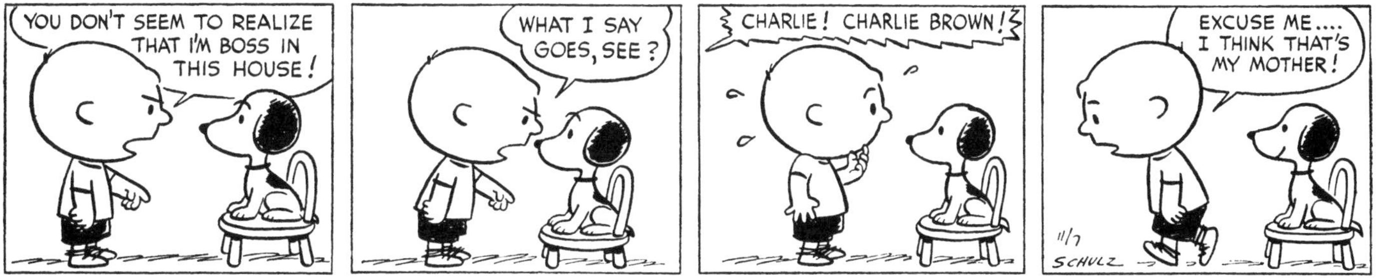
YOU DON'T SEEM TO REALIZE THAT I'M BOSS IN THIS HOUSE!
WHAT I SAY GOES, SEE?
CHARLIE! CHARLIE BROWN!
EXCUSE ME.... I THINK THAT'S MY MOTHER!
11/7
SCHULZ

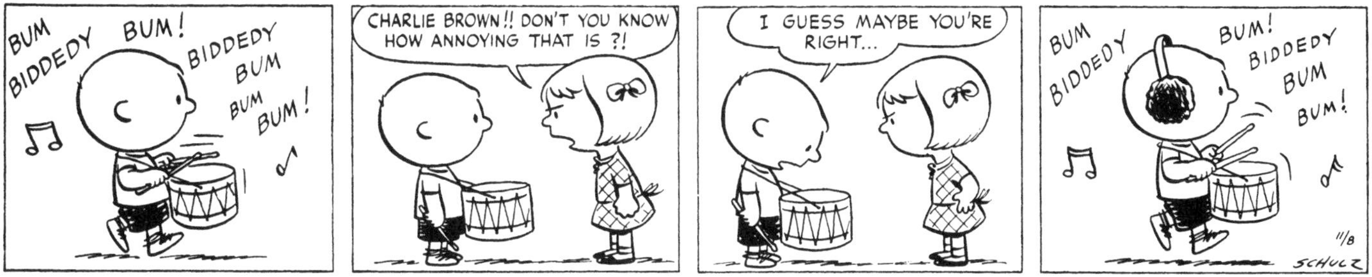
BUM BIDDEDY BUM! BIDDEDY BUM BUM BUM!
CHARLIE BROWN!! DON'T YOU KNOW HOW ANNOYING THAT IS ?!
I GUESS MAYBE YOU'RE RIGHT...
BUM BIDDEDY BUM! BIDDEDY BUM BUM!
11/8
SCHULZ

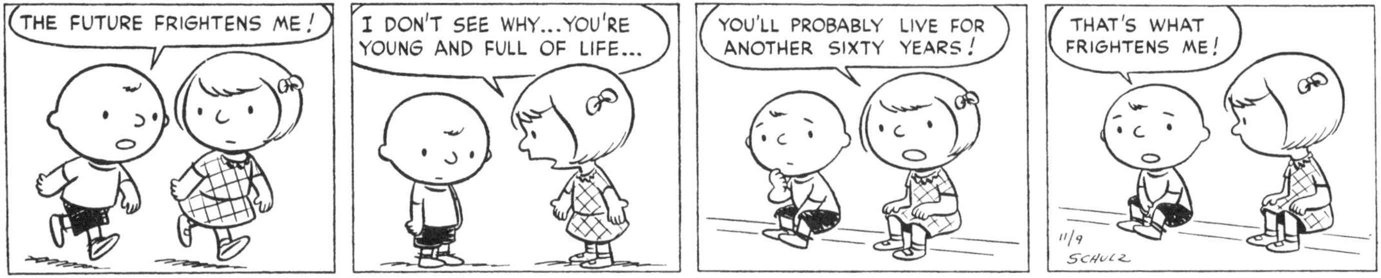
THE FUTURE FRIGHTENS ME!
I DON'T SEE WHY...YOU'RE YOUNG AND FULL OF LIFE...
YOU'LL PROBABLY LIVE FOR ANOTHER SIXTY YEARS!
THAT'S WHAT FRIGHTENS ME!
11/9
SCHULZ

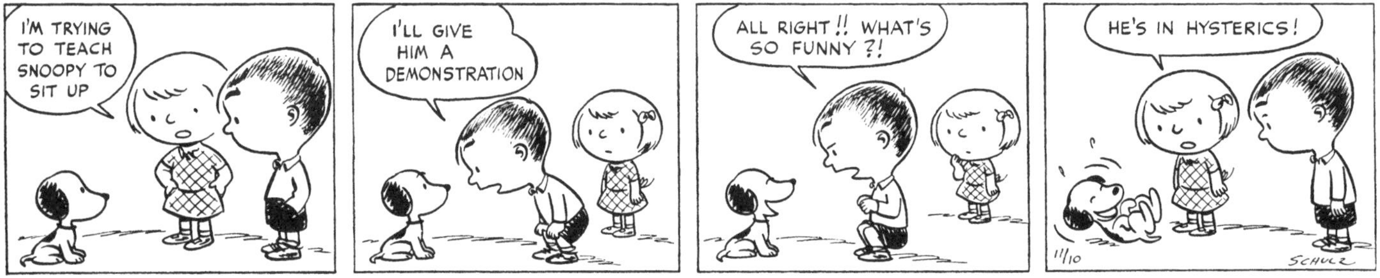
I'M TRYING TO TEACH SNOOPY TO SIT UP
I'LL GIVE HIM A DEMONSTRATION
ALL RIGHT!! WHAT'S SO FUNNY?!
HE'S IN HYSTERICS!
11/10
SCHULZ

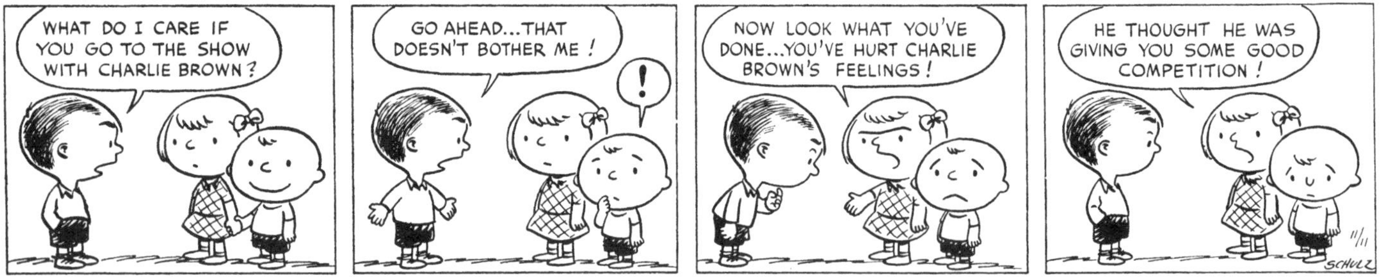
WHAT DO I CARE IF YOU GO TO THE SHOW WITH CHARLIE BROWN?
GO AHEAD...THAT DOESN'T BOTHER ME!
!
NOW LOOK WHAT YOU'VE DONE...YOU'VE HURT CHARLIE BROWN'S FEELINGS!
HE THOUGHT HE WAS GIVING YOU SOME GOOD COMPETITION!
11/11
SCHULZ

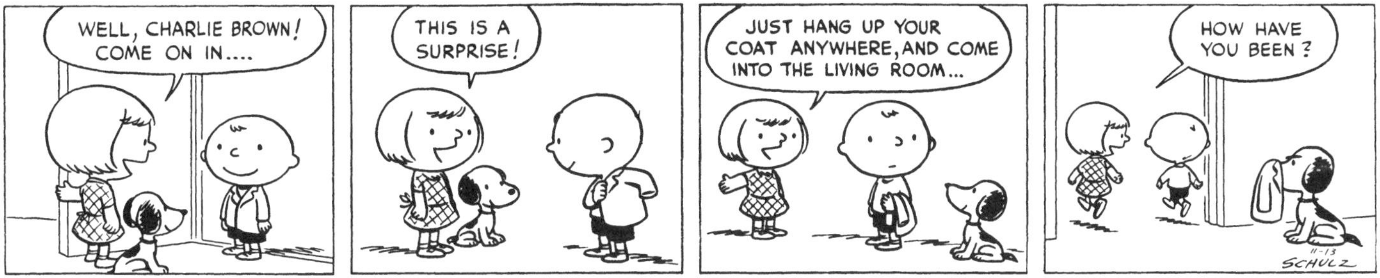
WELL, CHARLIE BROWN! COME ON IN....
THIS IS A SURPRISE!
JUST HANG UP YOUR COAT ANYWHERE, AND COME INTO THE LIVING ROOM...
HOW HAVE YOU BEEN?
11-13
SCHULZ

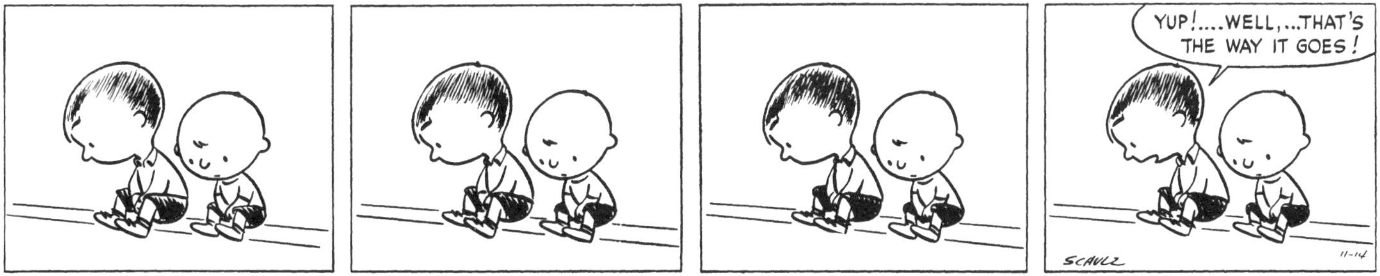
YUP!....WELL,...THAT'S THE WAY IT GOES!
SCHULZ
11-14

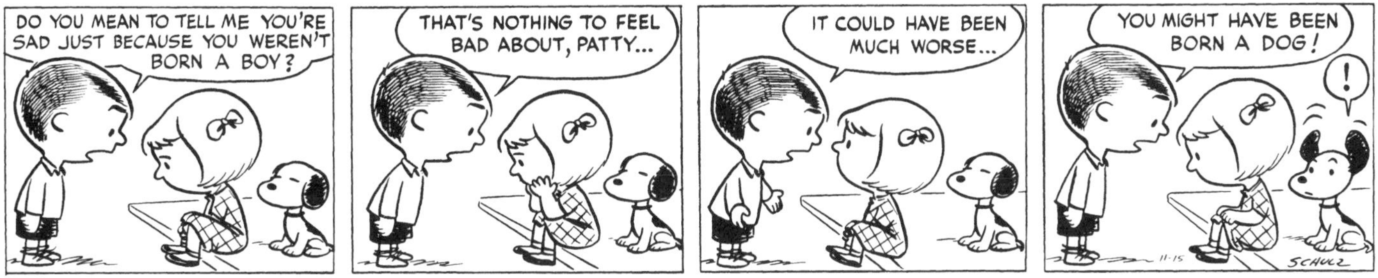
DO YOU MEAN TO TELL ME YOU'RE SAD JUST BECAUSE YOU WEREN'T BORN A BOY?
THAT'S NOTHING TO FEEL BAD ABOUT, PATTY...
IT COULD HAVE BEEN MUCH WORSE...
YOU MIGHT HAVE BEEN BORN A DOG!
!
11-15
SCHULZ

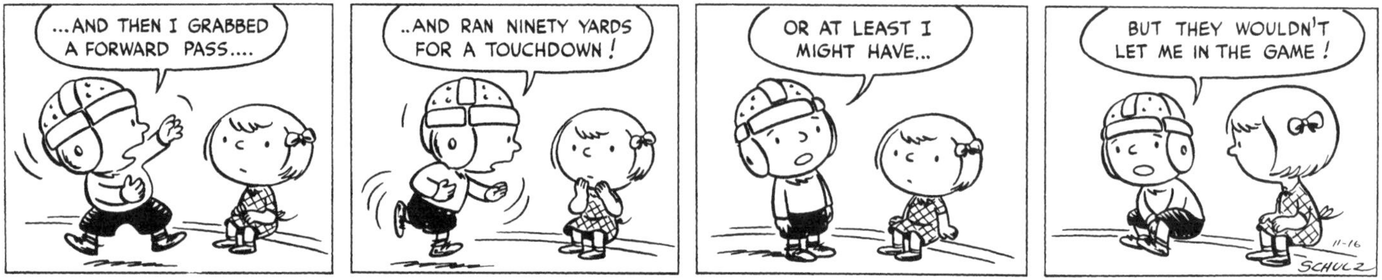
...AND THEN I GRABBED A FORWARD PASS....
..AND RAN NINETY YARDS FOR A TOUCHDOWN!
OR AT LEAST I MIGHT HAVE...
BUT THEY WOULDN'T LET ME IN THE GAME!
11-16
SCHULZ

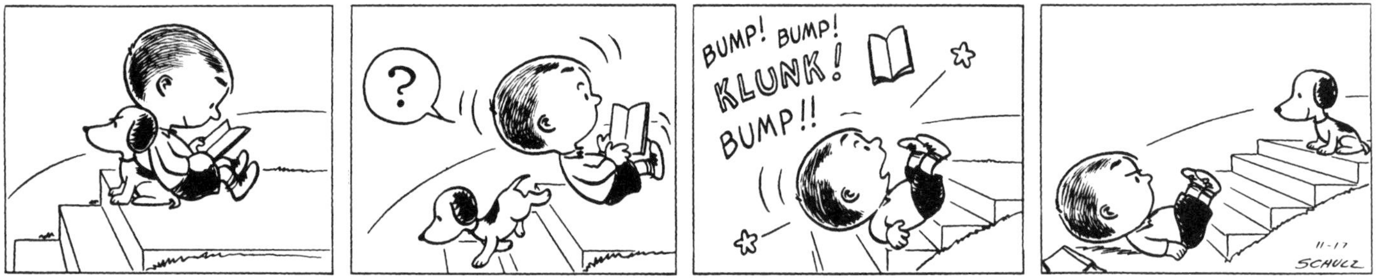
?
BUMP! BUMP!
KLUNK!
BUMP!!
11-17
SCHULZ

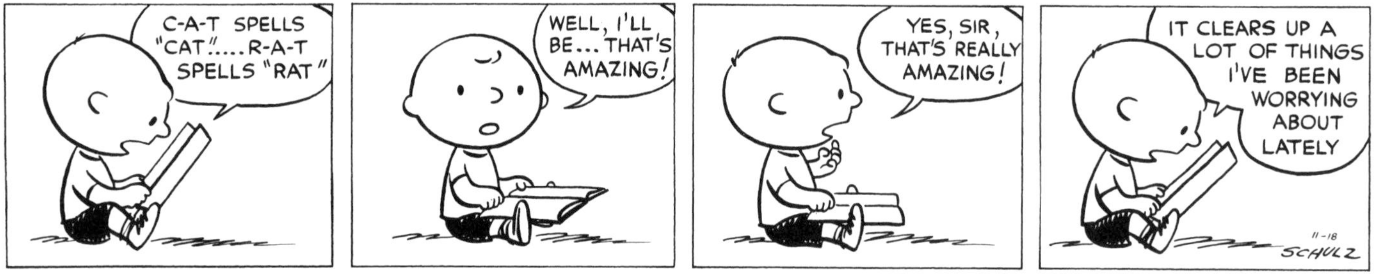
C-A-T SPELLS "CAT"!..... R-A-T SPELLS "RAT"
WELL, I'LL BE... THAT'S AMAZING!
YES, SIR, THAT'S REALLY AMAZING!
IT CLEARS UP A LOT OF THINGS I'VE BEEN WORRYING ABOUT LATELY
11-18
SCHULZ

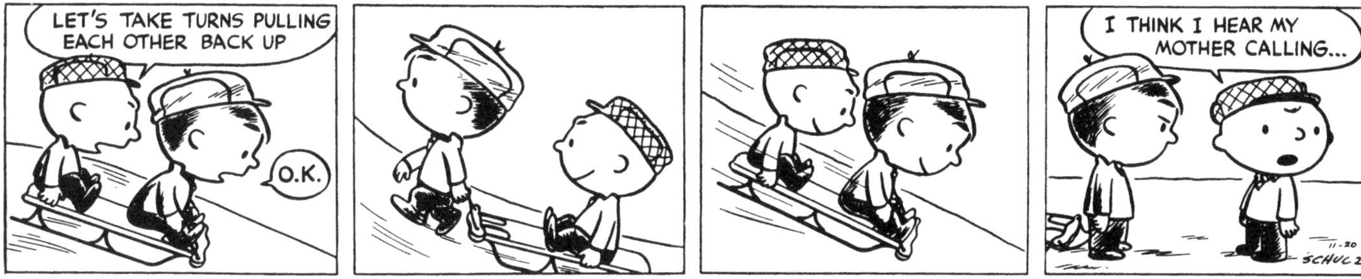
LET'S TAKE TURNS PULLING EACH OTHER BACK UP
O.K.
I THINK I HEAR MY MOTHER CALLING...
11-20
SCHULZ

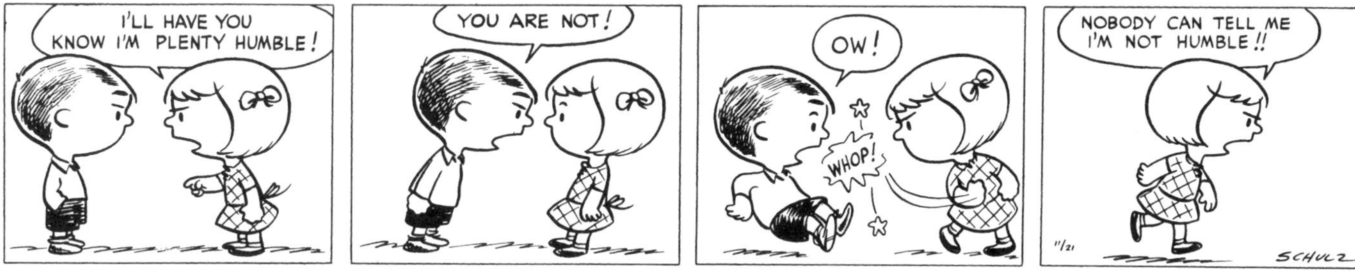
I'LL HAVE YOU KNOW I'M PLENTY HUMBLE!
YOU ARE NOT!
OW!
WHOP!
NOBODY CAN TELL ME I'M NOT HUMBLE!!
11/21
SCHULZ

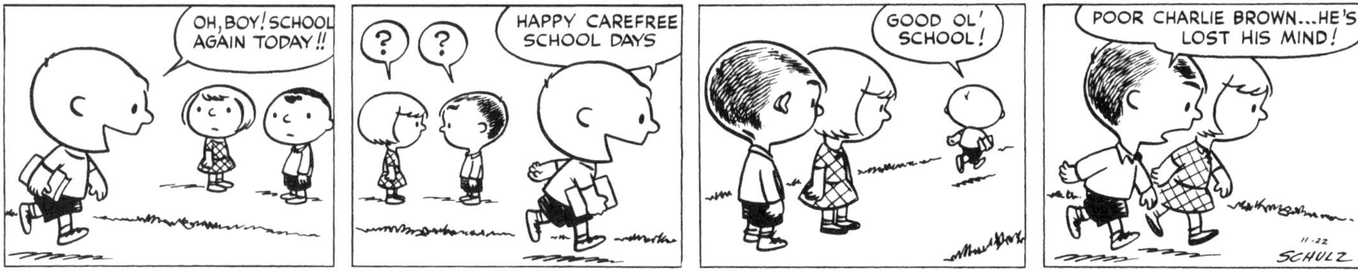
OH, BOY! SCHOOL AGAIN TODAY!!
?
?
HAPPY CAREFREE SCHOOL DAYS
GOOD OL' SCHOOL!
POOR CHARLIE BROWN...HE'S LOST HIS MIND!
11-22
SCHULZ

YES, SIR! ABRAHAM LINCOLN WAS A GREAT MAN!
WOULD YOU LIKE TO HAVE BEEN ABRAHAM LINCOLN?
I DOUBT IT
I HAVE A HARD ENOUGH TIME BEING JUST PLAIN CHARLIE BROWN!
11-23
SCHULZ

MY JOINTS SQUEAK WHEN I WALK!
SQUEAK
SQUEAK
THAT'S NOT YOUR JOINTS... THAT'S YOUR SHOES!
WHAT A RELIEF!
I THOUGHT I WAS GETTING OLD
SCHULZ
11-24
SQUEAK
SQUEAK!

SO LONG, OL' PAL...I'M GONNA MISS YOU...
BUT DON'T BE SAD... TRY TO KEEP YOUR CHIN UP!
IT WON'T BE FOR LONG...
IN FACT, I'LL SEE YOU IN THE MORNING!
11-25
SCHULZ

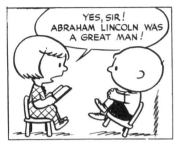

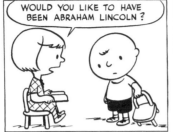

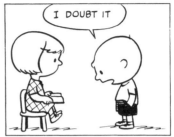

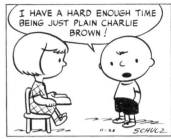

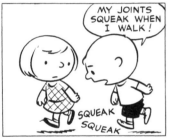

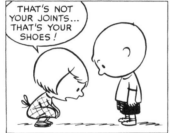

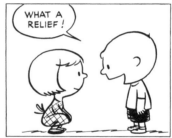

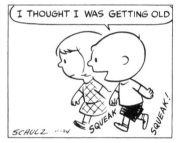

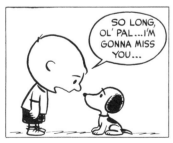

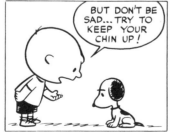

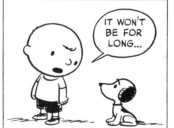

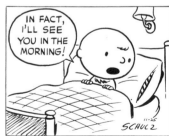

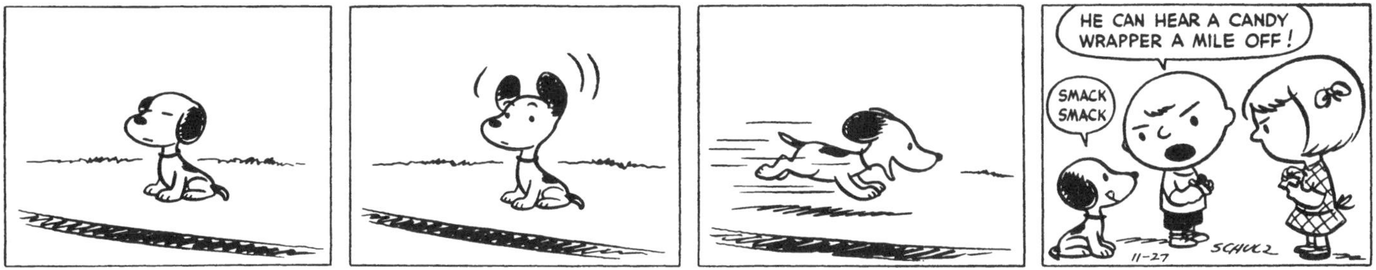
SMACK SMACK
HE CAN HEAR A CANDY WRAPPER A MILE OFF!
11-27
SCHULZ

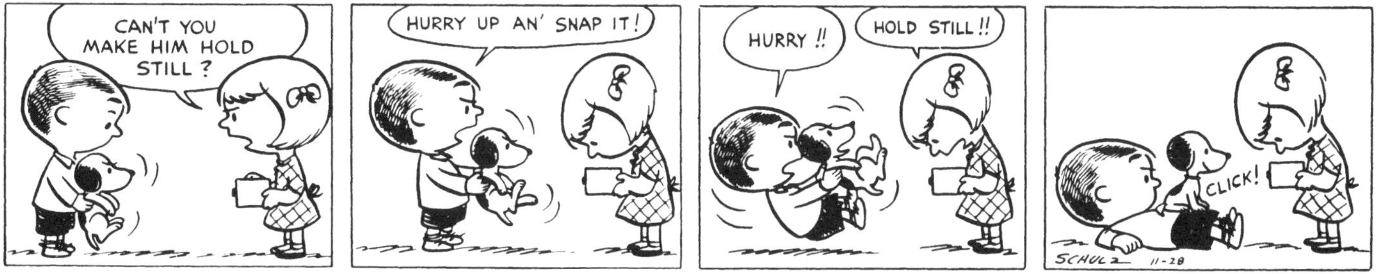
CAN'T YOU MAKE HIM HOLD STILL?
HURRY UP AN' SNAP IT!
HURRY!!
HOLD STILL!!
CLICK!
SCHULZ
11-28

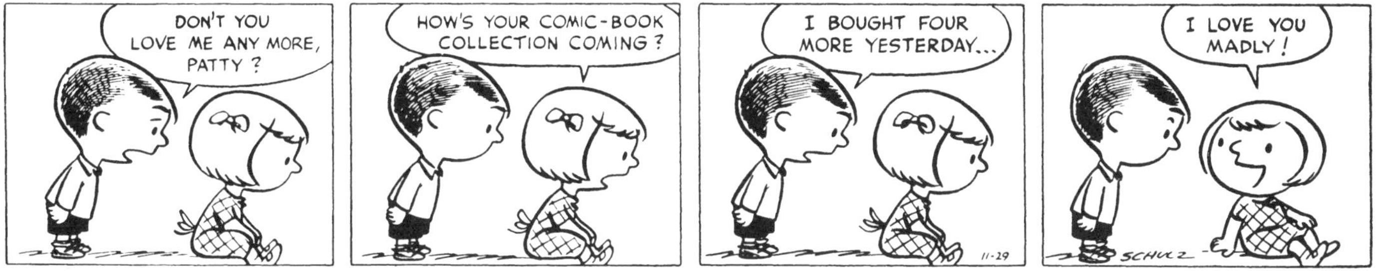
DON'T YOU LOVE ME ANY MORE, PATTY?
HOW'S YOUR COMIC-BOOK COLLECTION COMING?
I BOUGHT FOUR MORE YESTERDAY...
11-29
I LOVE YOU MADLY!
SCHULZ

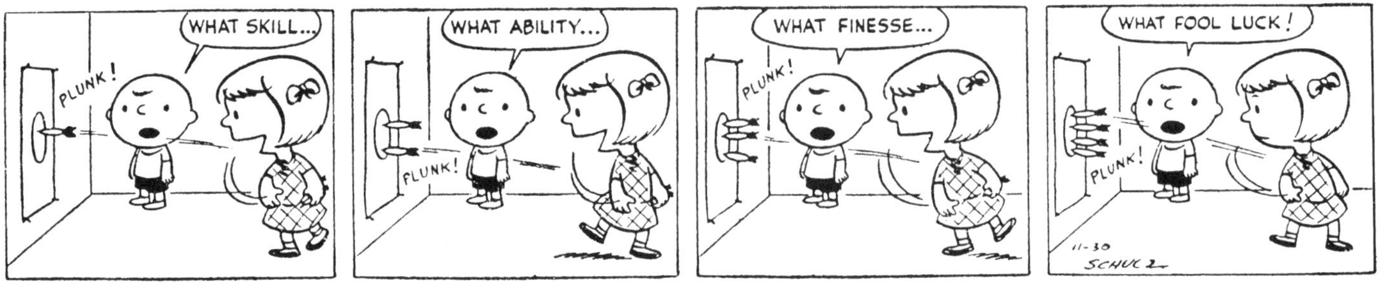
WHAT SKILL...
PLUNK!
WHAT ABILITY...
PLUNK!
WHAT FINESSE...
PLUNK!
WHAT FOOL LUCK!
PLUNK!
11-30
SCHULZ

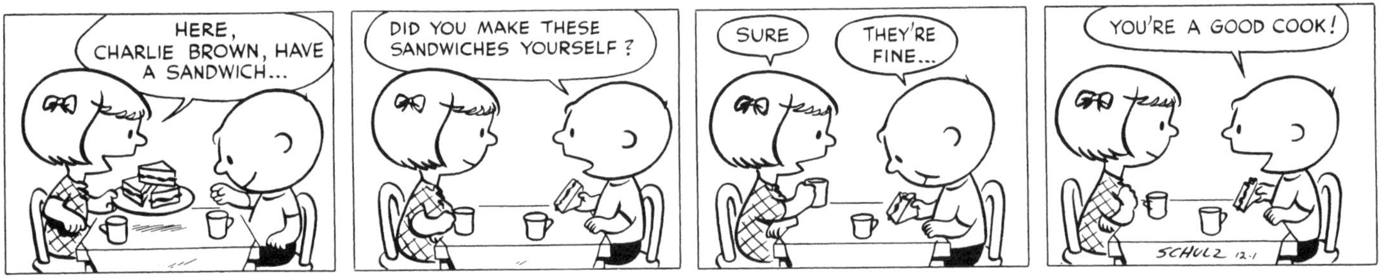
HERE, CHARLIE BROWN, HAVE A SANDWICH...
DID YOU MAKE THESE SANDWICHES YOURSELF?
SURE
THEY'RE FINE...
YOU'RE A GOOD COOK!
SCHULZ 12-1

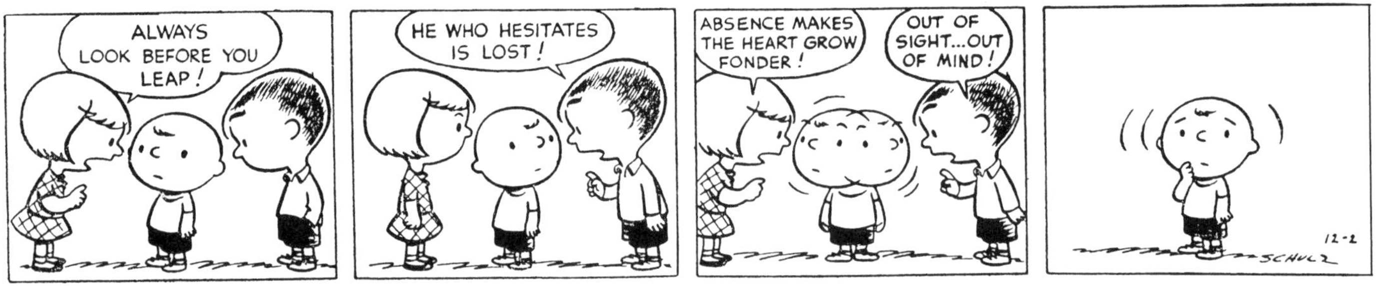
ALWAYS LOOK BEFORE YOU LEAP!
HE WHO HESITATES IS LOST!
ABSENCE MAKES THE HEART GROW FONDER!
OUT OF SIGHT...OUT OF MIND!
12-2
SCHULZ

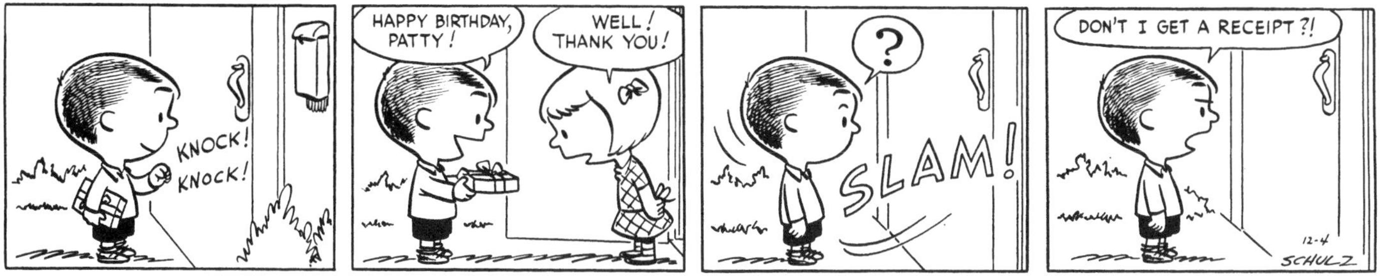
KNOCK! KNOCK!
HAPPY BIRTHDAY, PATTY!
WELL! THANK YOU!
?
SLAM!
DON'T I GET A RECEIPT?!
12-4
SCHULZ

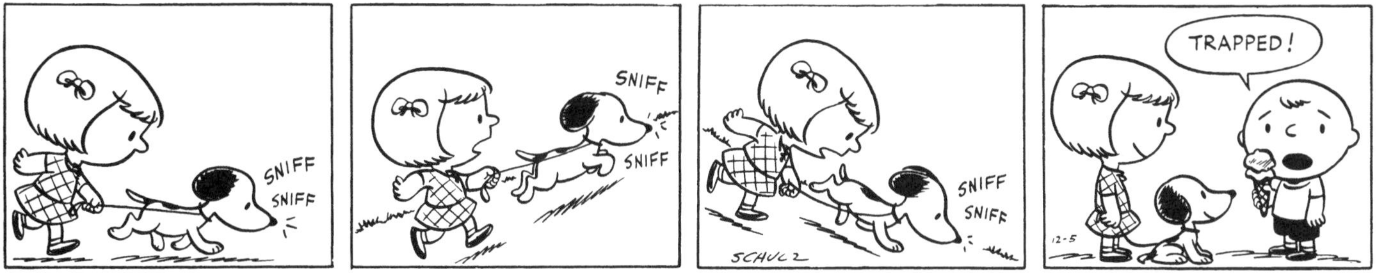
SNIFF SNIFF
SNIFF SNIFF
SNIFF SNIFF
SCHULZ
TRAPPED!
12-5

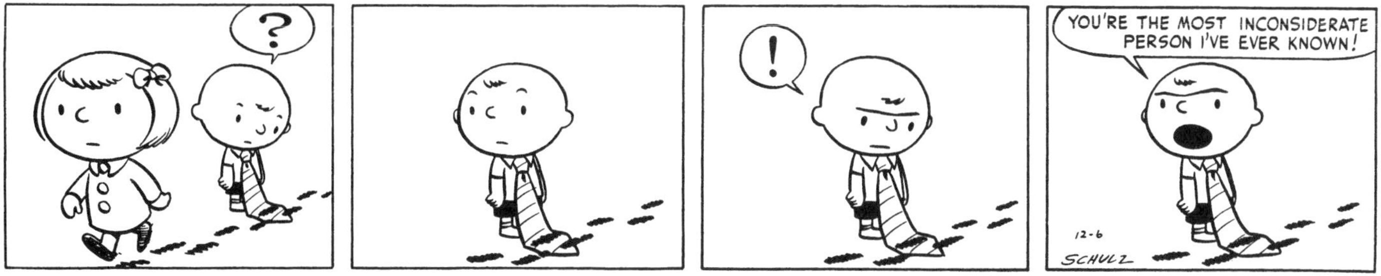
?
!
YOU'RE THE MOST INCONSIDERATE PERSON I'VE EVER KNOWN!
12-6
SCHULZ

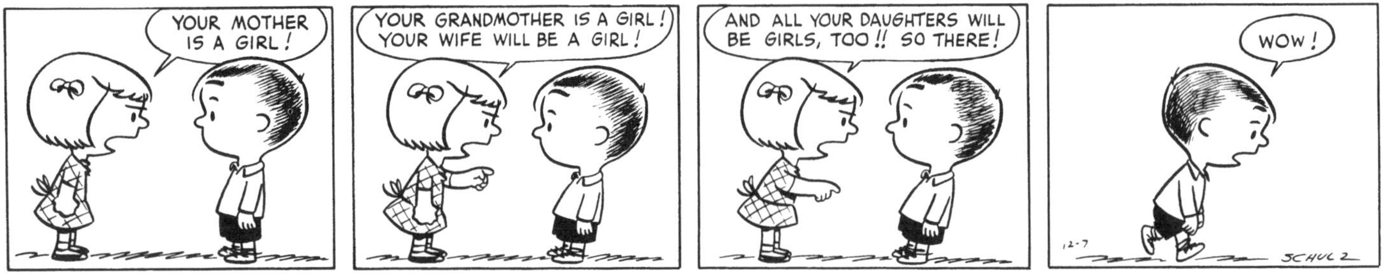
YOUR MOTHER IS A GIRL!
YOUR GRANDMOTHER IS A GIRL! YOUR WIFE WILL BE A GIRL!
AND ALL YOUR DAUGHTERS WILL BE GIRLS, TOO!! SO THERE!
WOW!
12-7
SCHULZ

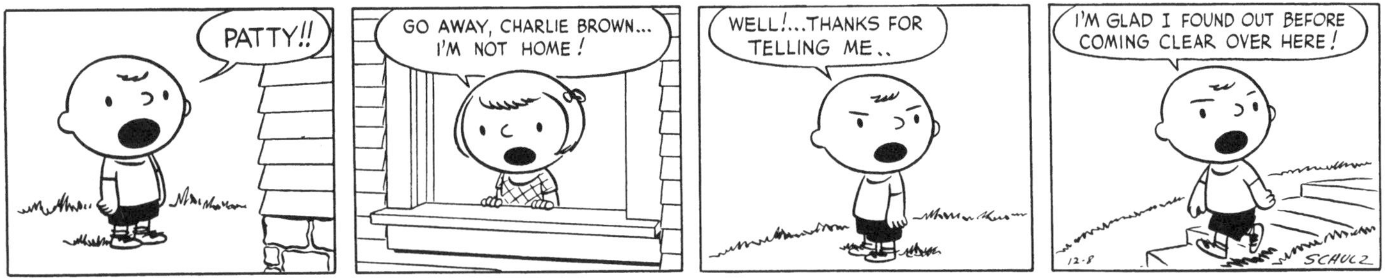
PATTY!!
GO AWAY, CHARLIE BROWN... I'M NOT HOME!
WELL!...THANKS FOR TELLING ME..
I'M GLAD I FOUND OUT BEFORE COMING CLEAR OVER HERE!
12-8
SCHULZ

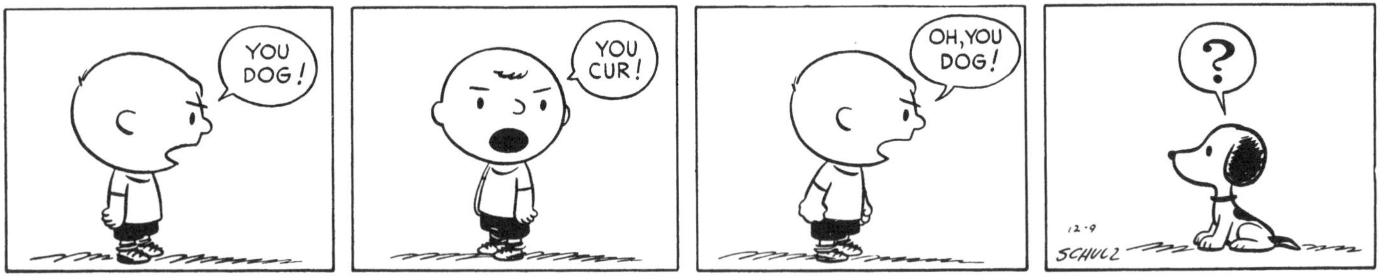
YOU DOG!
YOU CUR!
OH, YOU DOG!
?
12-9
SCHULZ

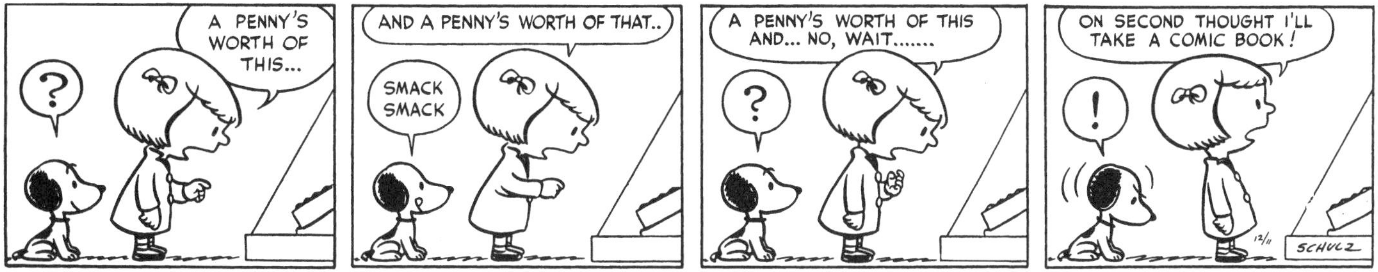
?
A PENNY'S WORTH OF THIS...
AND A PENNY'S WORTH OF THAT..
SMACK SMACK
?
A PENNY'S WORTH OF THIS AND... NO, WAIT.......
!
ON SECOND THOUGHT I'LL TAKE A COMIC BOOK!
12/11
SCHULZ

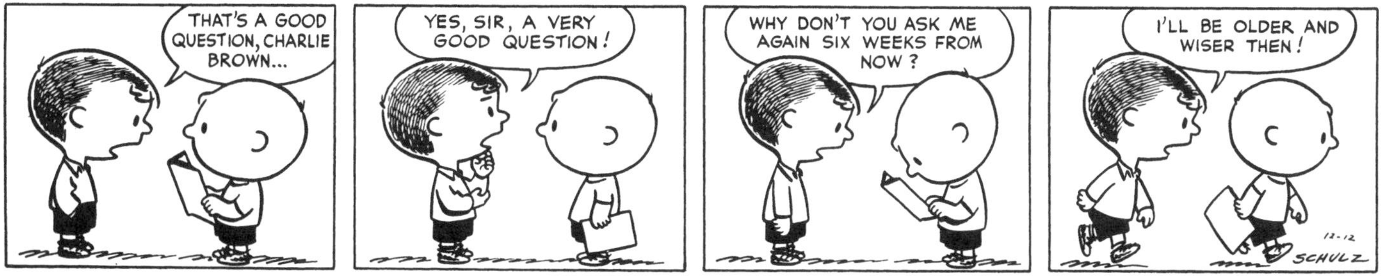
THAT'S A GOOD QUESTION, CHARLIE BROWN...
YES, SIR, A VERY GOOD QUESTION!
WHY DON'T YOU ASK ME AGAIN SIX WEEKS FROM NOW?
I'LL BE OLDER AND WISER THEN!
12-12
SCHULZ

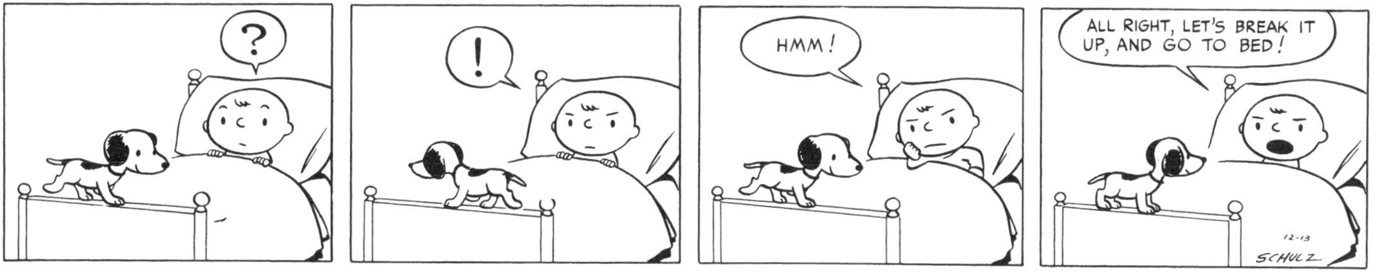
?
!
HMM!
ALL RIGHT, LET'S BREAK IT UP, AND GO TO BED!
12-13
SCHULZ

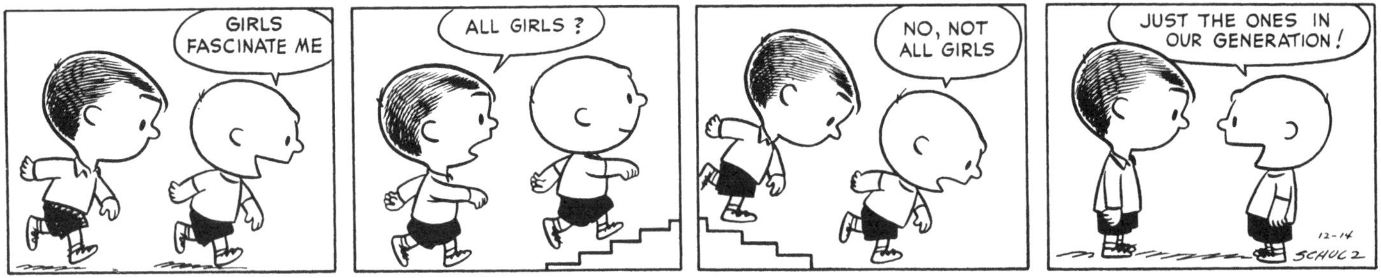
GIRLS FASCINATE ME
ALL GIRLS ?
NO, NOT ALL GIRLS
JUST THE ONES IN OUR GENERATION !
12-14
SCHULZ

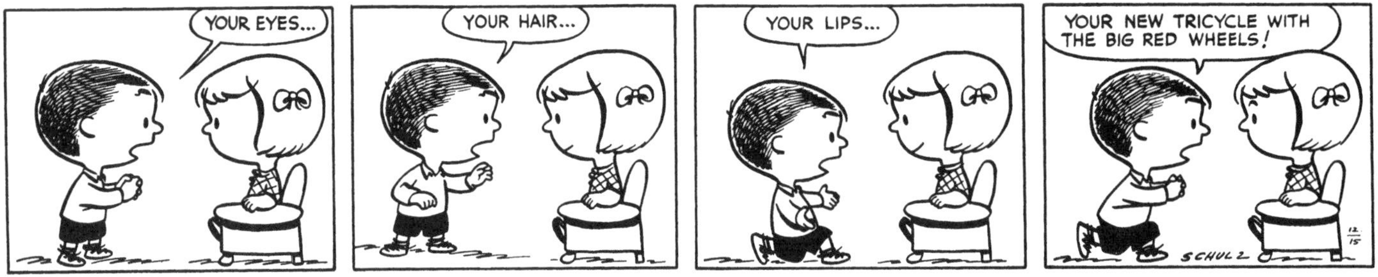
YOUR EYES...
YOUR HAIR...
YOUR LIPS...
YOUR NEW TRICYCLE WITH THE BIG RED WHEELS !
12/15
SCHULZ

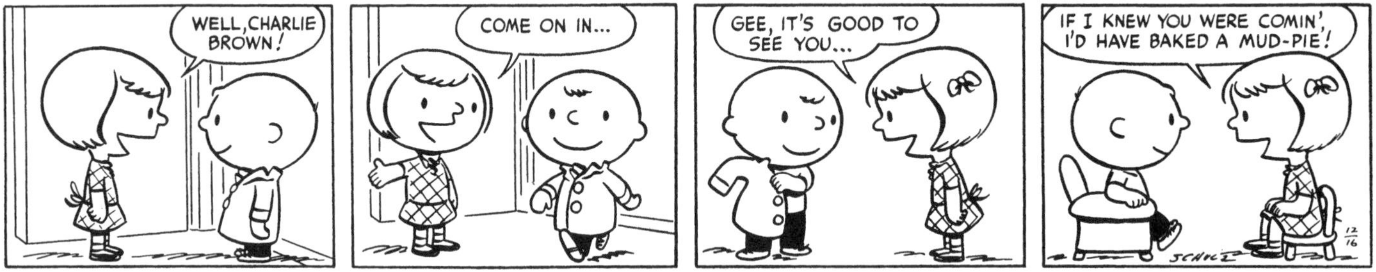
WELL, CHARLIE BROWN !
COME ON IN...
GEE, IT'S GOOD TO SEE YOU...
IF I KNEW YOU WERE COMIN', I'D HAVE BAKED A MUD-PIE !
12/16
SCHULZ

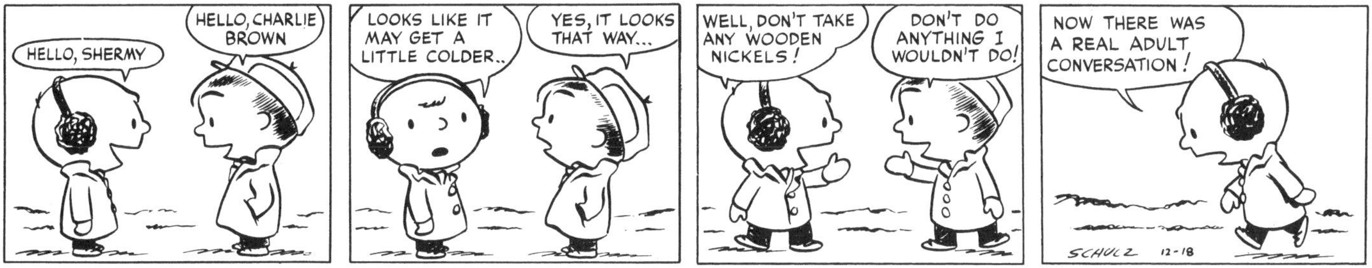
HELLO, SHERMY
HELLO, CHARLIE BROWN
LOOKS LIKE IT MAY GET A LITTLE COLDER..
YES, IT LOOKS THAT WAY...
WELL, DON'T TAKE ANY WOODEN NICKELS!
DON'T DO ANYTHING I WOULDN'T DO!
NOW THERE WAS A REAL ADULT CONVERSATION!
SCHULZ 12-18

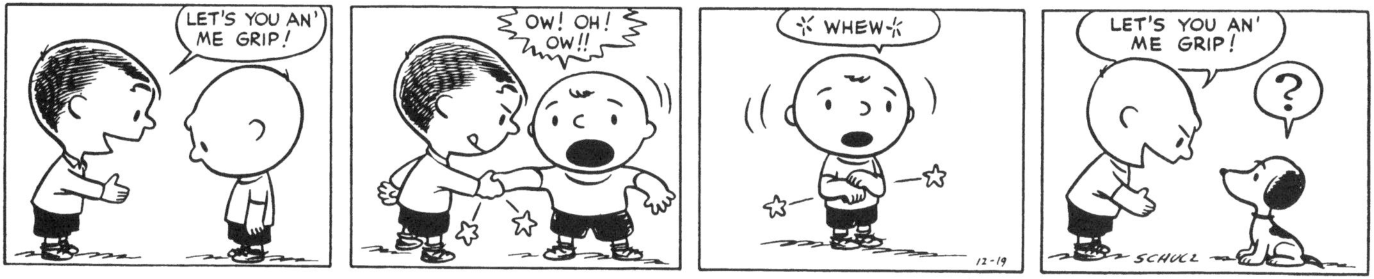
LET'S YOU AN' ME GRIP!
OW! OH! OW!!
WHEW
12-19
LET'S YOU AN' ME GRIP!
?
SCHULZ

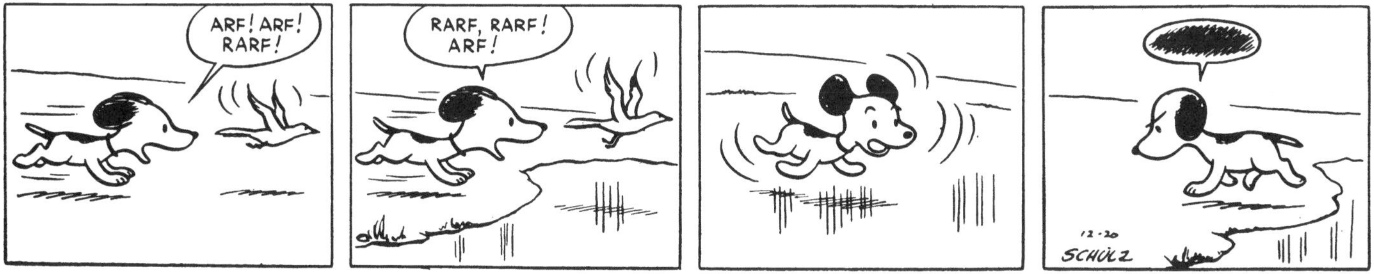
ARF! ARF! RARF!
RARF, RARF! ARF!
12-20
SCHULZ

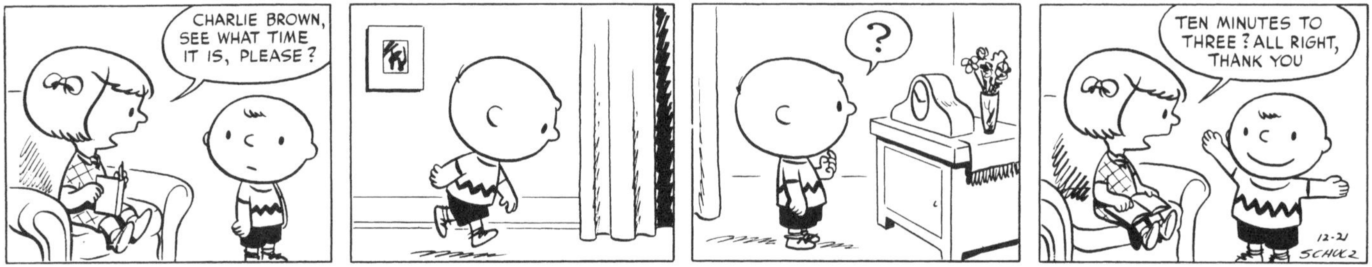
CHARLIE BROWN, SEE WHAT TIME IT IS, PLEASE?
?
TEN MINUTES TO THREE? ALL RIGHT, THANK YOU
12-21 SCHULZ

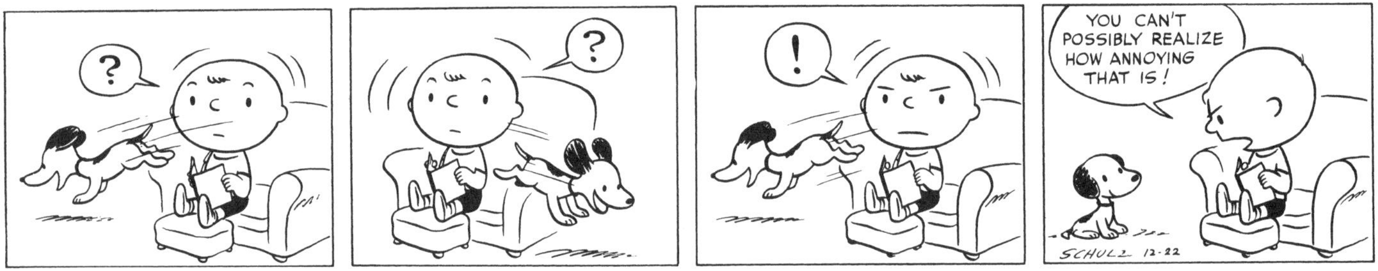
?
?
!
YOU CAN'T POSSIBLY REALIZE HOW ANNOYING THAT IS!
SCHULZ 12-22

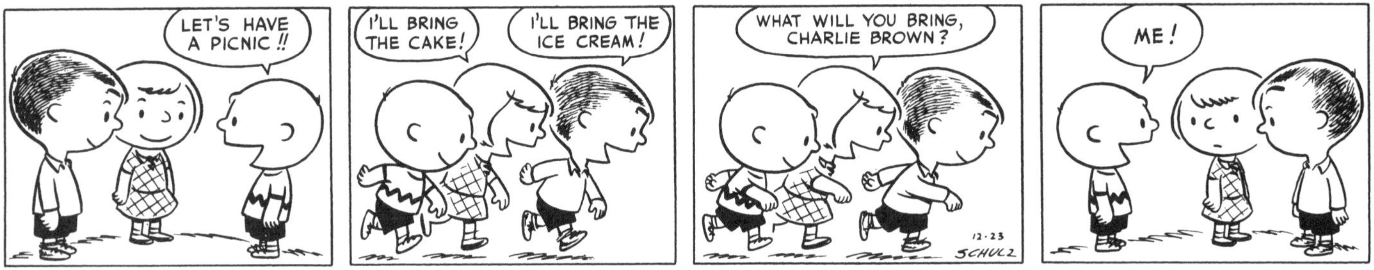
LET'S HAVE A PICNIC!!
I'LL BRING THE CAKE!
I'LL BRING THE ICE CREAM!
WHAT WILL YOU BRING, CHARLIE BROWN?
12-23 SCHULZ
ME!

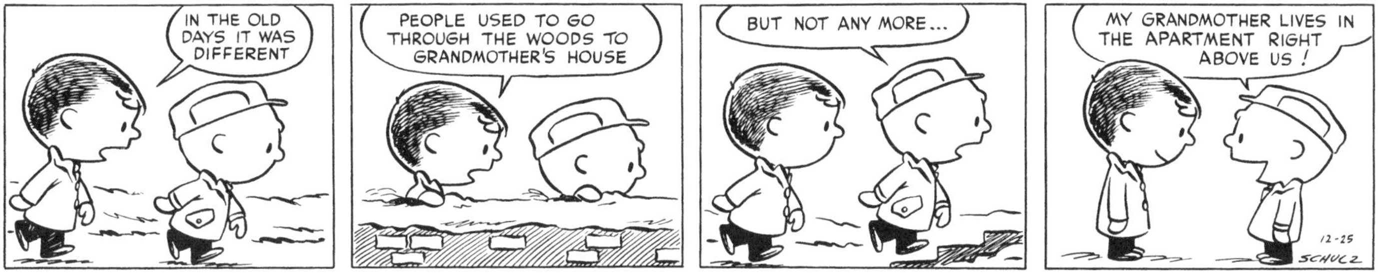
IN THE OLD DAYS IT WAS DIFFERENT
PEOPLE USED TO GO THROUGH THE WOODS TO GRANDMOTHER'S HOUSE
BUT NOT ANY MORE...
MY GRANDMOTHER LIVES IN THE APARTMENT RIGHT ABOVE US!
12-25
SCHULZ

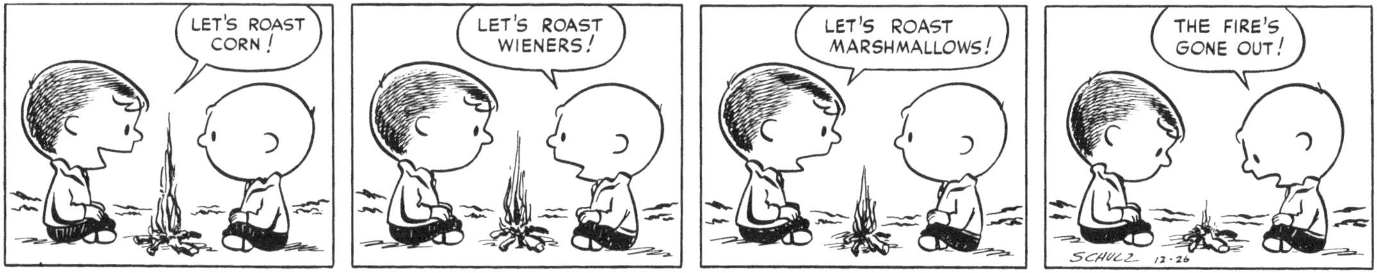
LET'S ROAST CORN!
LET'S ROAST WIENERS!
LET'S ROAST MARSHMALLOWS!
THE FIRE'S GONE OUT!
SCHULZ 12-26

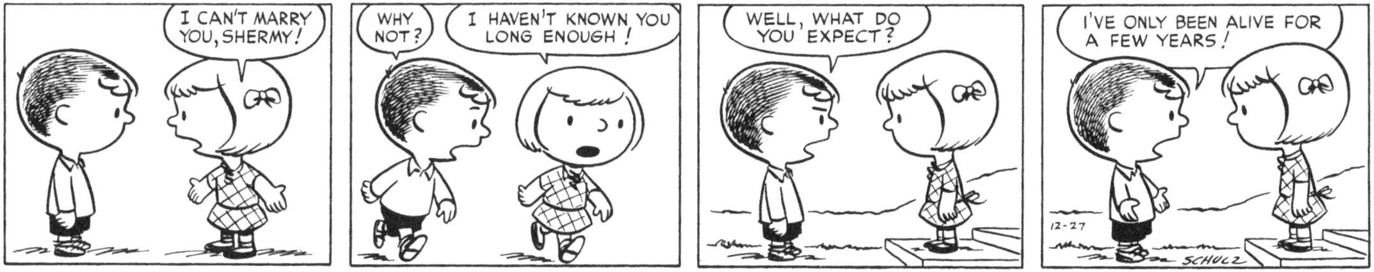
I CAN'T MARRY YOU, SHERMY!
WHY NOT?
I HAVEN'T KNOWN YOU LONG ENOUGH!
WELL, WHAT DO YOU EXPECT?
I'VE ONLY BEEN ALIVE FOR A FEW YEARS!
12-27
SCHULZ

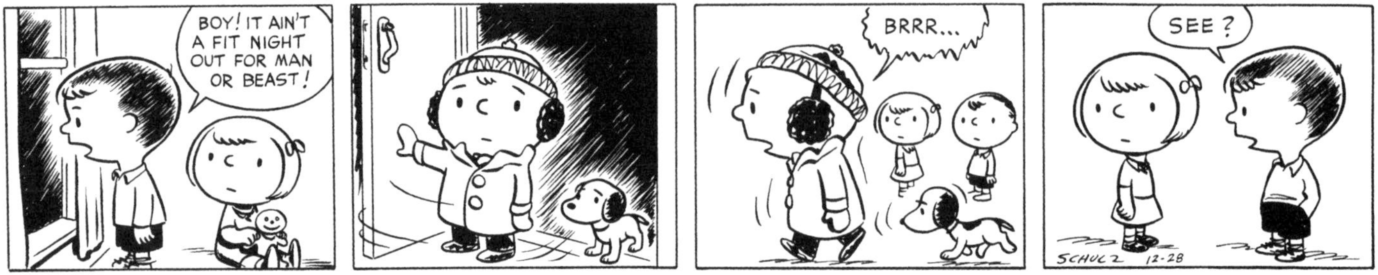
BOY! IT AIN'T A FIT NIGHT OUT FOR MAN OR BEAST!
BRRR...
SEE?
SCHULZ 12-28

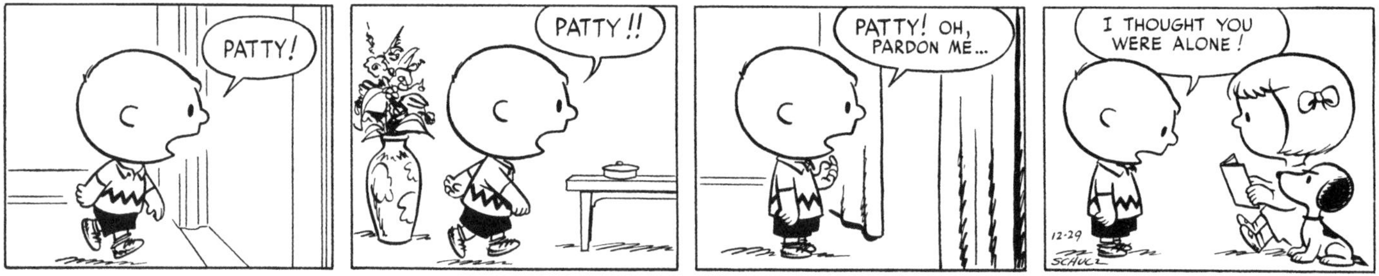
PATTY!
PATTY!!
PATTY! OH, PARDON ME...
I THOUGHT YOU WERE ALONE!
12-29
SCHULZ

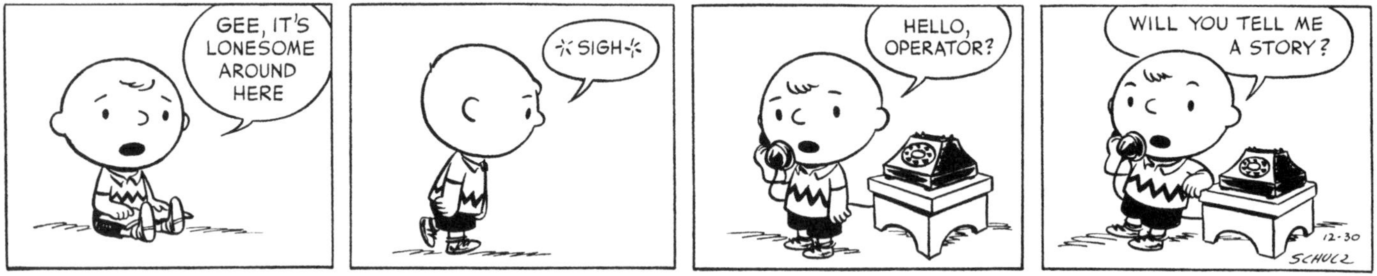
GEE, IT'S LONESOME AROUND HERE
SIGH
HELLO, OPERATOR?
WILL YOU TELL ME A STORY?
12-30
SCHULZ

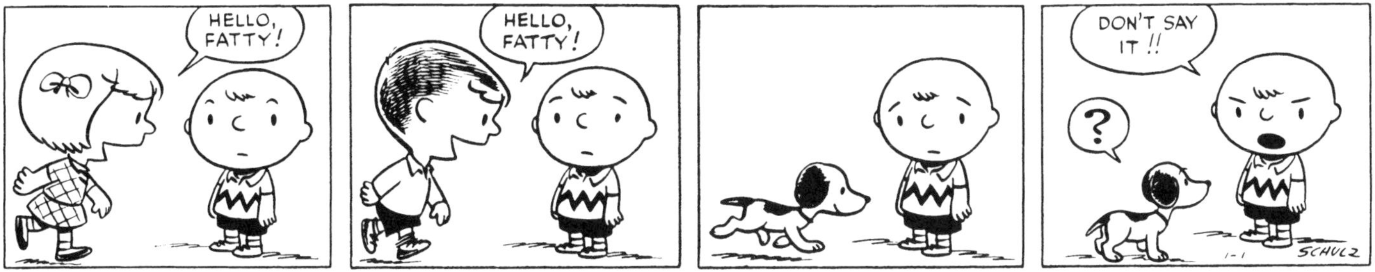
HELLO, FATTY!
HELLO, FATTY!
?
DON'T SAY IT !!
1-1
SCHULZ

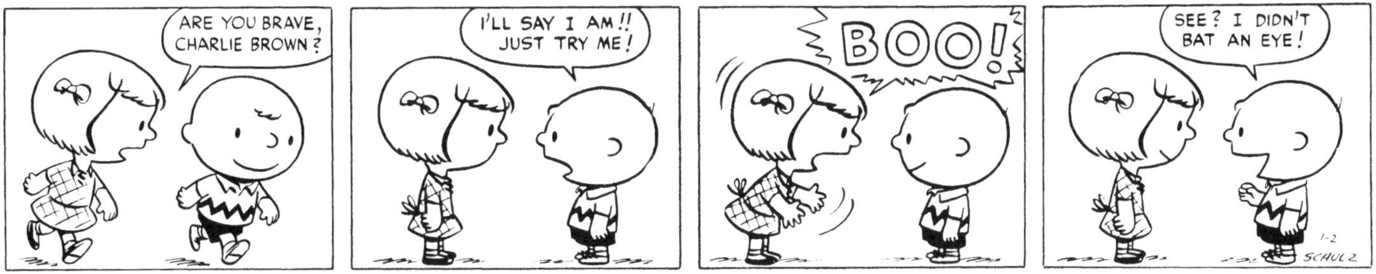
ARE YOU BRAVE, CHARLIE BROWN?
I'LL SAY I AM!! JUST TRY ME!
BOO!
SEE? I DIDN'T BAT AN EYE!
1-2
SCHULZ

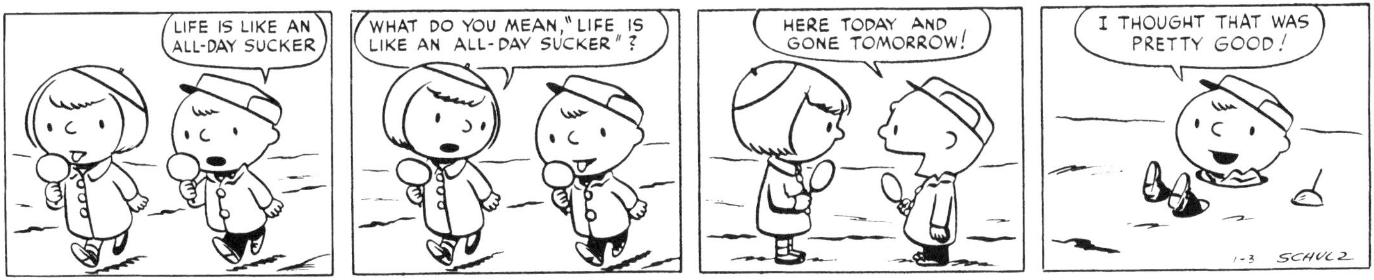
LIFE IS LIKE AN ALL-DAY SUCKER
WHAT DO YOU MEAN, "LIFE IS LIKE AN ALL-DAY SUCKER"?
HERE TODAY AND GONE TOMORROW!
I THOUGHT THAT WAS PRETTY GOOD!
1-3
SCHULZ

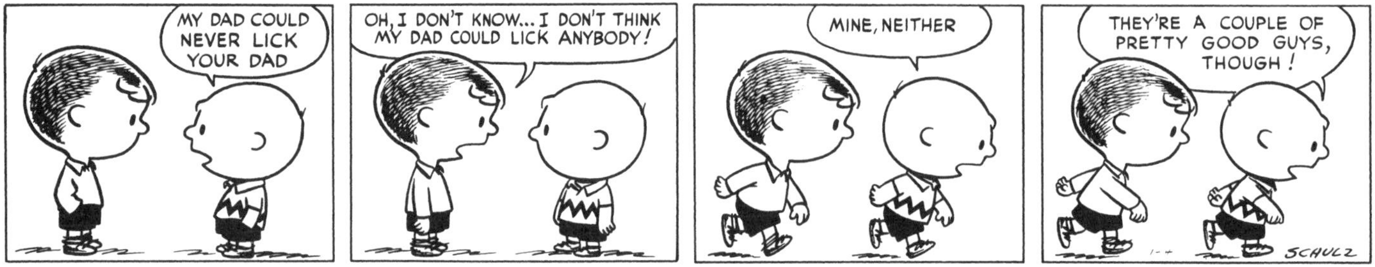
MY DAD COULD NEVER LICK YOUR DAD
OH, I DON'T KNOW... I DON'T THINK MY DAD COULD LICK ANYBODY!
MINE, NEITHER
THEY'RE A COUPLE OF PRETTY GOOD GUYS, THOUGH!
SCHULZ

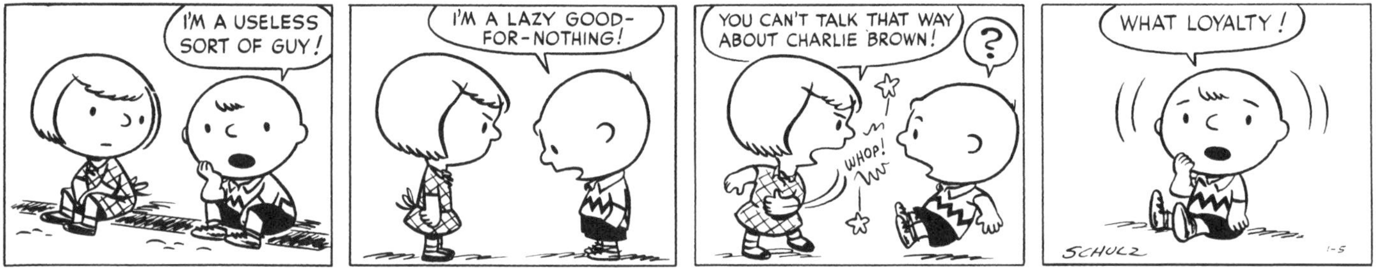
I'M A USELESS SORT OF GUY!
I'M A LAZY GOOD-FOR-NOTHING!
YOU CAN'T TALK THAT WAY ABOUT CHARLIE BROWN!
?
WHOP!
WHAT LOYALTY!
SCHULZ

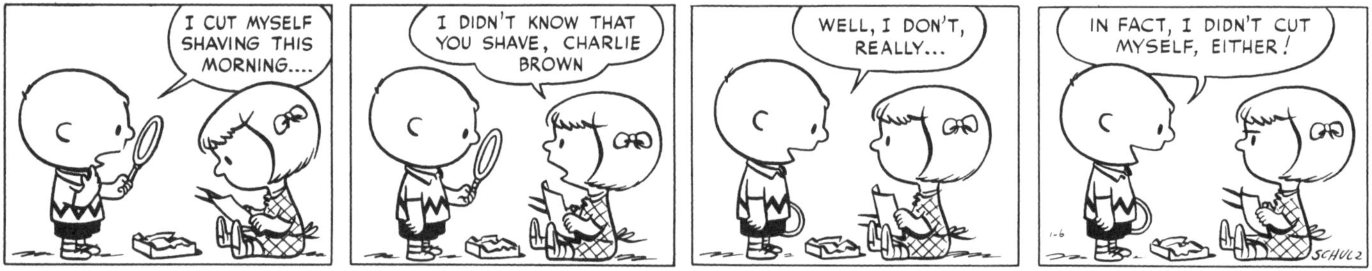
I CUT MYSELF SHAVING THIS MORNING....
I DIDN'T KNOW THAT YOU SHAVE, CHARLIE BROWN
WELL, I DON'T, REALLY...
IN FACT, I DIDN'T CUT MYSELF, EITHER!
SCHULZ

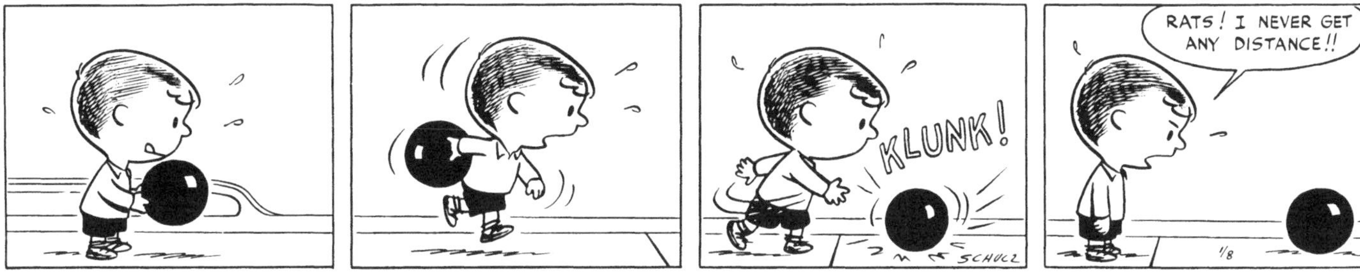
KLUNK!
RATS! I NEVER GET ANY DISTANCE!!

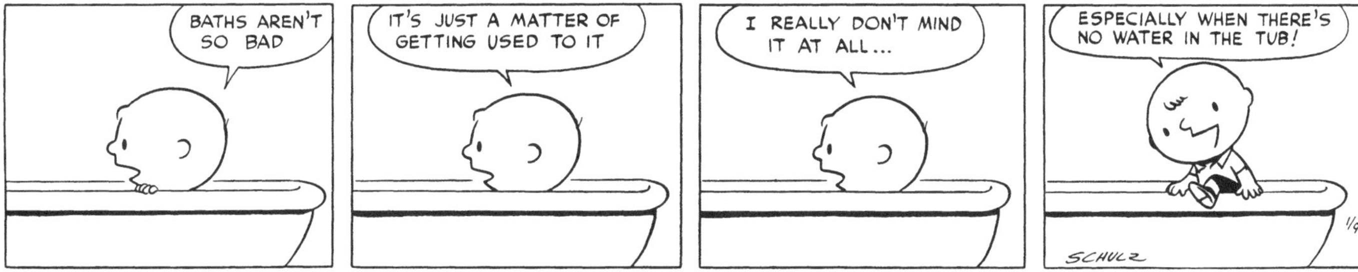
BATHS AREN'T SO BAD
IT'S JUST A MATTER OF GETTING USED TO IT
I REALLY DON'T MIND IT AT ALL...
ESPECIALLY WHEN THERE'S NO WATER IN THE TUB!

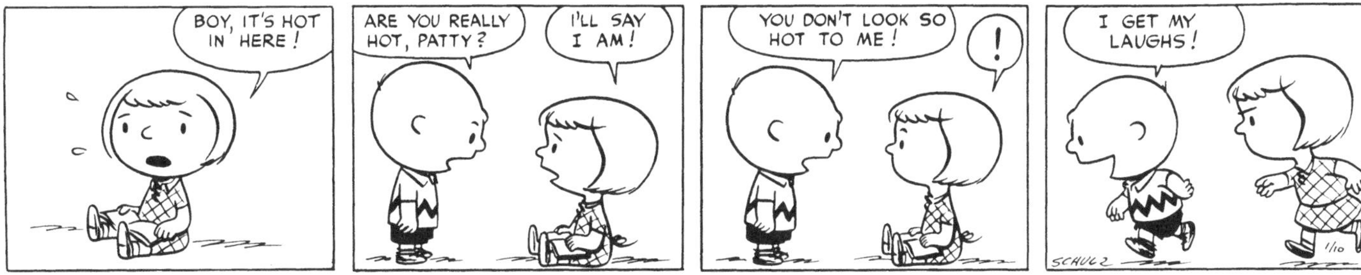
BOY, IT'S HOT IN HERE!
ARE YOU REALLY HOT, PATTY?
I'LL SAY I AM!
YOU DON'T LOOK SO HOT TO ME!
!
I GET MY LAUGHS!

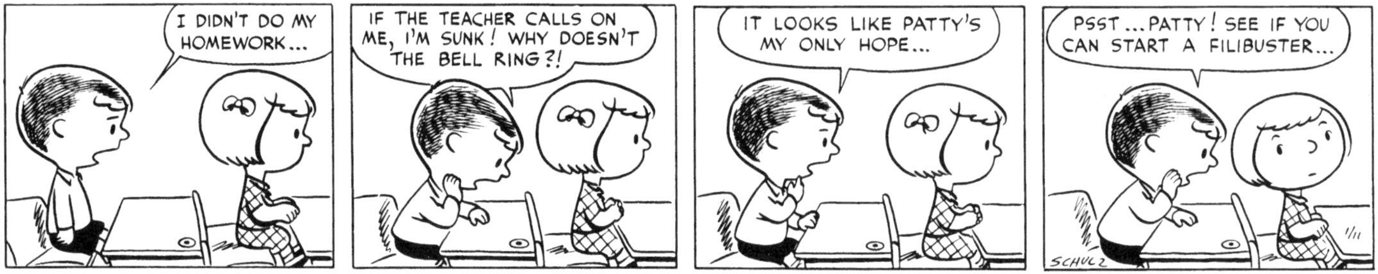
I DIDN'T DO MY HOMEWORK...
IF THE TEACHER CALLS ON ME, I'M SUNK! WHY DOESN'T THE BELL RING?!
IT LOOKS LIKE PATTY'S MY ONLY HOPE...
PSST... PATTY! SEE IF YOU CAN START A FILIBUSTER...
1/11
SCHULZ

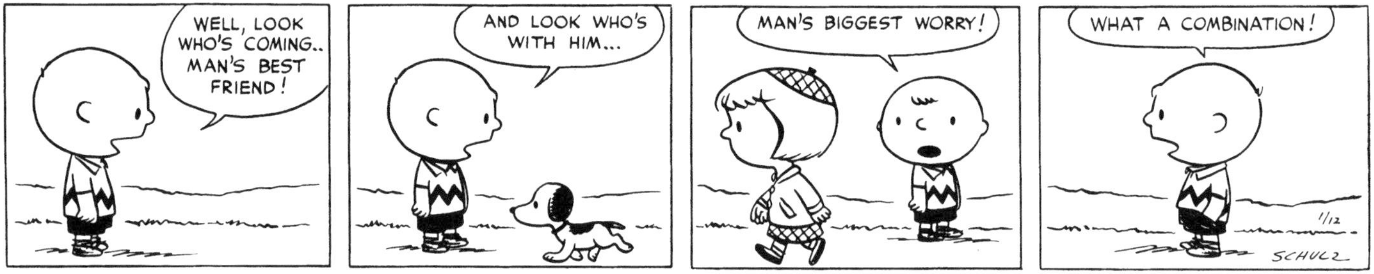
WELL, LOOK WHO'S COMING.. MAN'S BEST FRIEND!
AND LOOK WHO'S WITH HIM...
MAN'S BIGGEST WORRY!
WHAT A COMBINATION!
1/12
SCHULZ

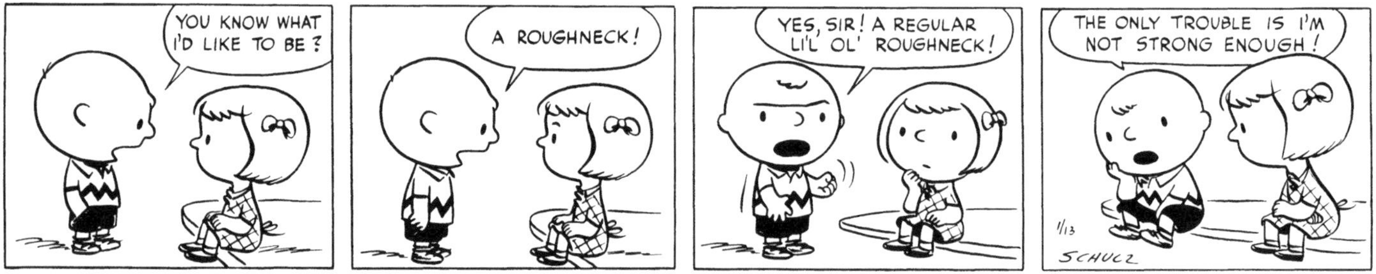
YOU KNOW WHAT I'D LIKE TO BE?
A ROUGHNECK!
YES, SIR! A REGULAR LI'L OL' ROUGHNECK!
THE ONLY TROUBLE IS I'M NOT STRONG ENOUGH!
1/13
SCHULZ

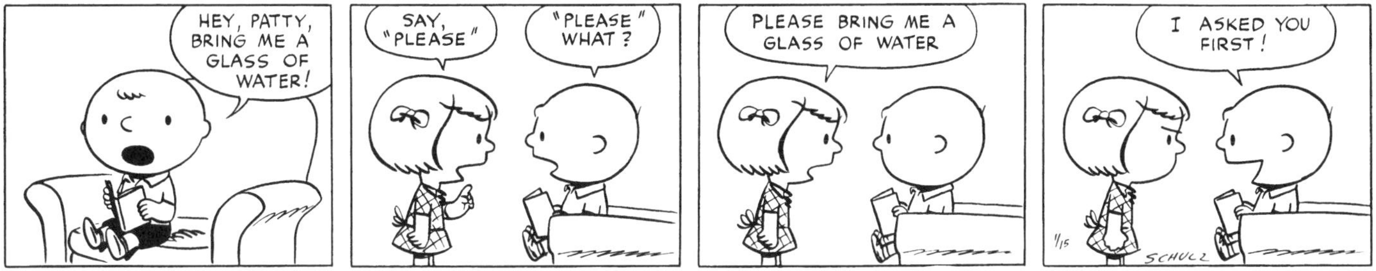
HEY, PATTY, BRING ME A GLASS OF WATER!
SAY, "PLEASE"
"PLEASE" WHAT?
PLEASE BRING ME A GLASS OF WATER
I ASKED YOU FIRST!
SCHULZ

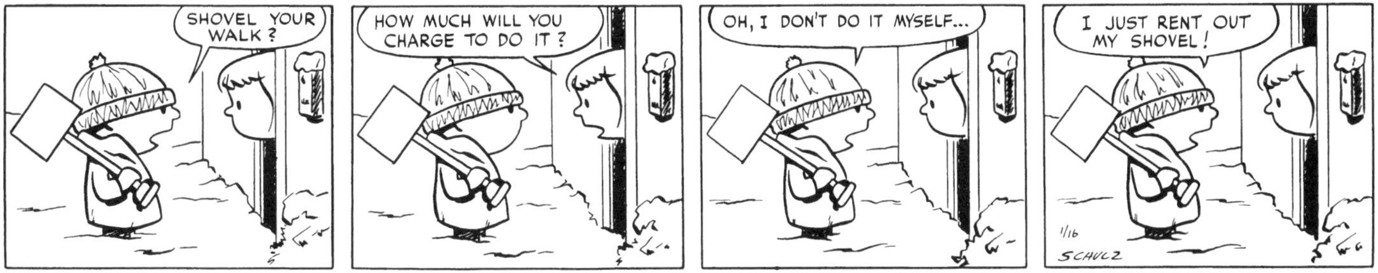
SHOVEL YOUR WALK?
HOW MUCH WILL YOU CHARGE TO DO IT?
OH, I DON'T DO IT MYSELF...
I JUST RENT OUT MY SHOVEL!
SCHULZ

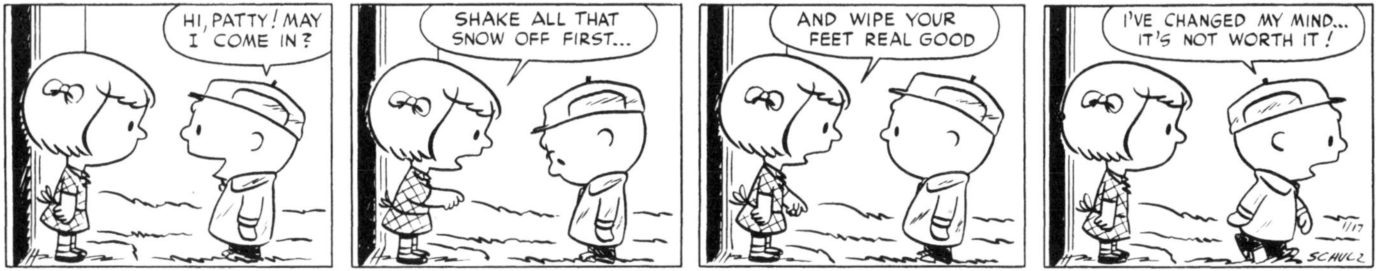
HI, PATTY! MAY I COME IN?
SHAKE ALL THAT SNOW OFF FIRST...
AND WIPE YOUR FEET REAL GOOD
I'VE CHANGED MY MIND... IT'S NOT WORTH IT!
SCHULZ

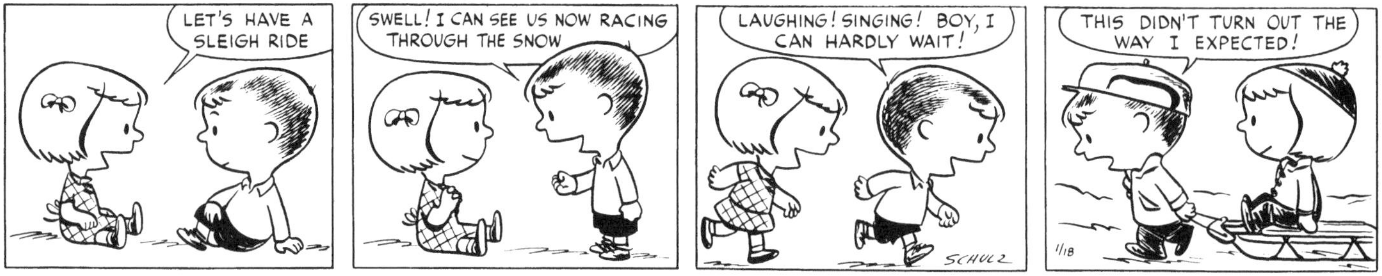
LET'S HAVE A SLEIGH RIDE
SWELL! I CAN SEE US NOW RACING THROUGH THE SNOW
LAUGHING! SINGING! BOY, I CAN HARDLY WAIT!
SCHULZ
THIS DIDN'T TURN OUT THE WAY I EXPECTED!
1/18

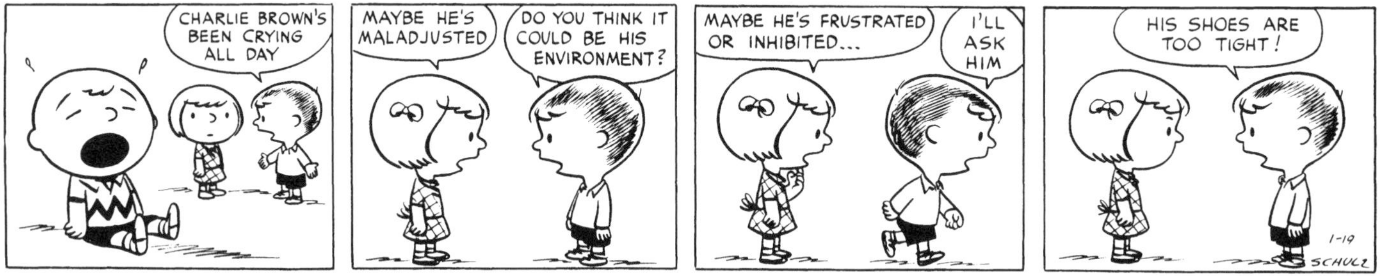
CHARLIE BROWN'S BEEN CRYING ALL DAY
MAYBE HE'S MALADJUSTED
DO YOU THINK IT COULD BE HIS ENVIRONMENT?
MAYBE HE'S FRUSTRATED OR INHIBITED...
I'LL ASK HIM
HIS SHOES ARE TOO TIGHT!
1-19
SCHULZ

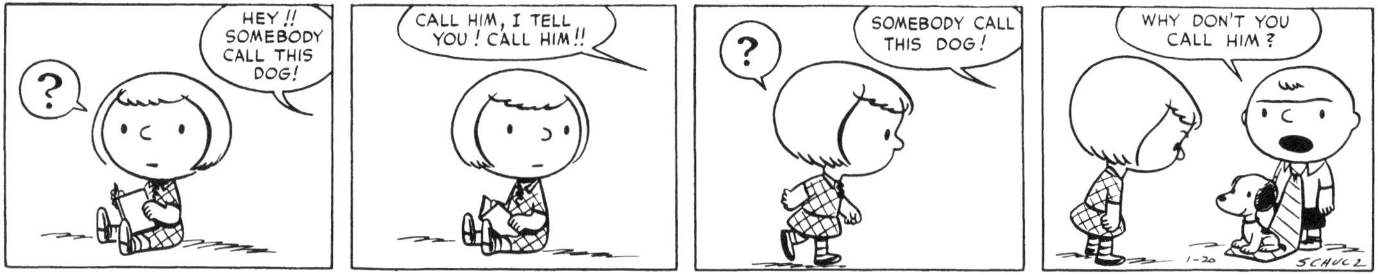
?
HEY!! SOMEBODY CALL THIS DOG!
CALL HIM, I TELL YOU! CALL HIM!!
?
SOMEBODY CALL THIS DOG!
WHY DON'T YOU CALL HIM?
1-20
SCHULZ

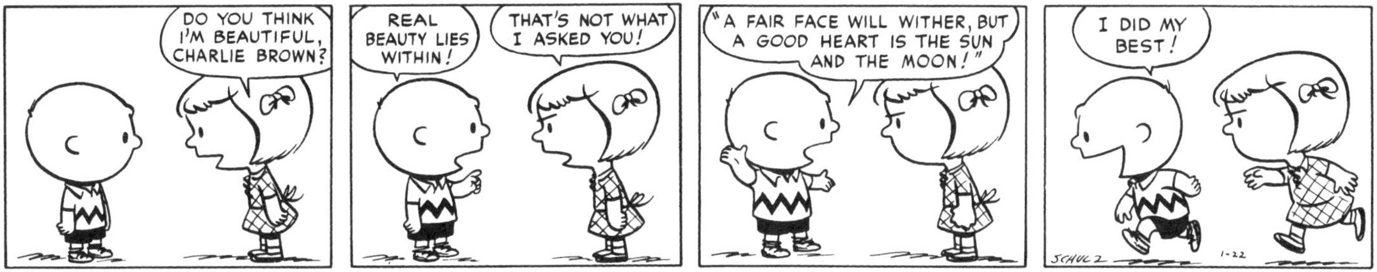
DO YOU THINK I'M BEAUTIFUL, CHARLIE BROWN?
REAL BEAUTY LIES WITHIN!
THAT'S NOT WHAT I ASKED YOU!
"A FAIR FACE WILL WITHER, BUT A GOOD HEART IS THE SUN AND THE MOON!"
I DID MY BEST!
SCHULZ
1-22

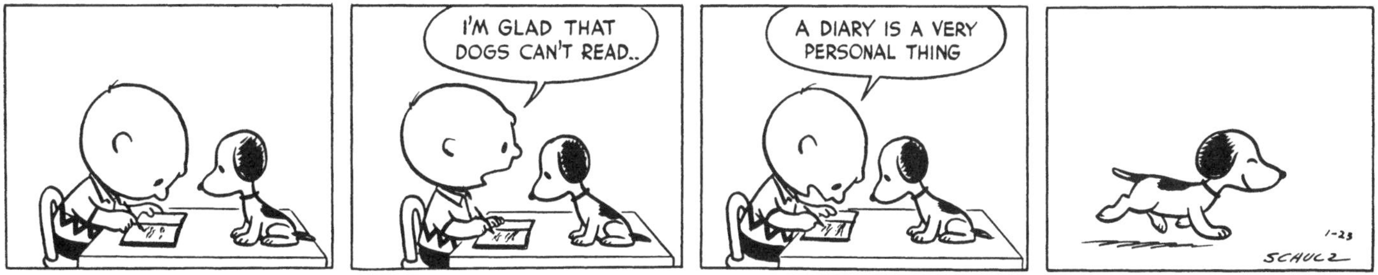
I'M GLAD THAT DOGS CAN'T READ..
A DIARY IS A VERY PERSONAL THING
1-23
SCHULZ

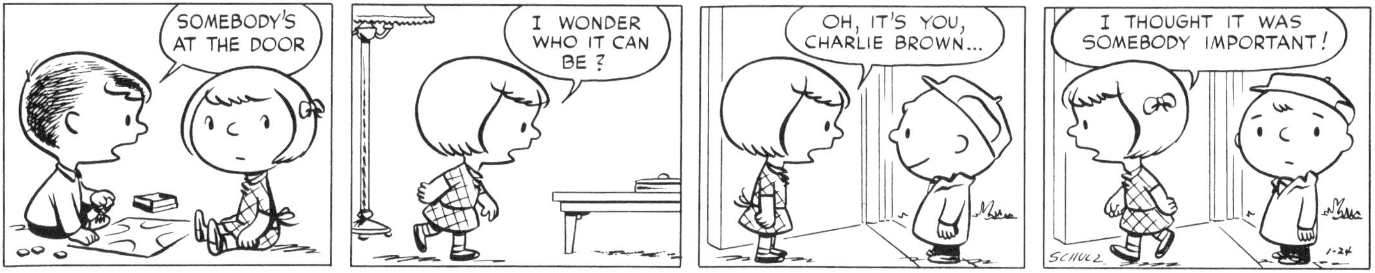
SOMEBODY'S AT THE DOOR
I WONDER WHO IT CAN BE?
OH, IT'S YOU, CHARLIE BROWN...
I THOUGHT IT WAS SOMEBODY IMPORTANT!
SCHULZ
1-24

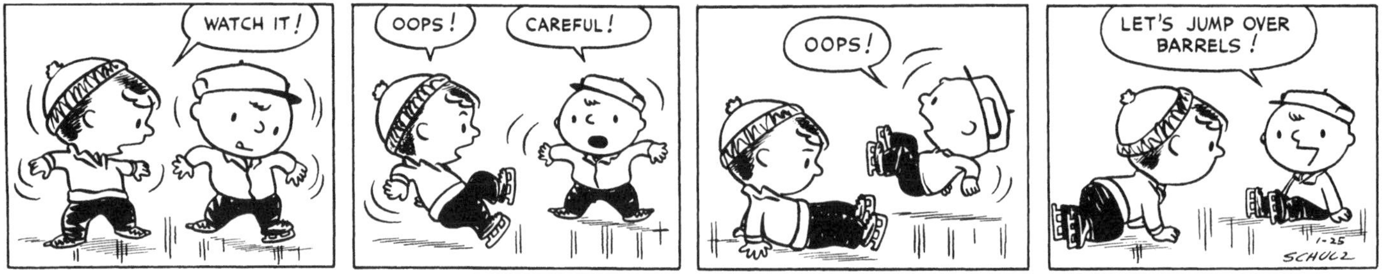
WATCH IT!
OOPS!
CAREFUL!
OOPS!
LET'S JUMP OVER BARRELS!
1-25
SCHULZ

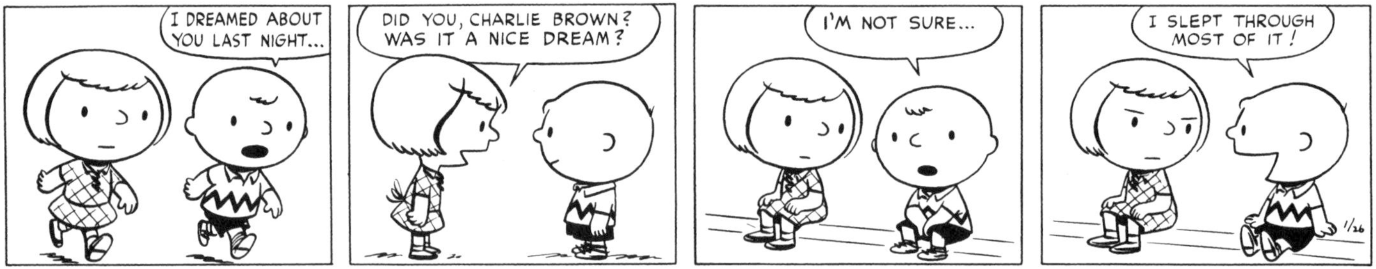
I DREAMED ABOUT YOU LAST NIGHT...
DID YOU, CHARLIE BROWN? WAS IT A NICE DREAM?
I'M NOT SURE...
I SLEPT THROUGH MOST OF IT!
1/26

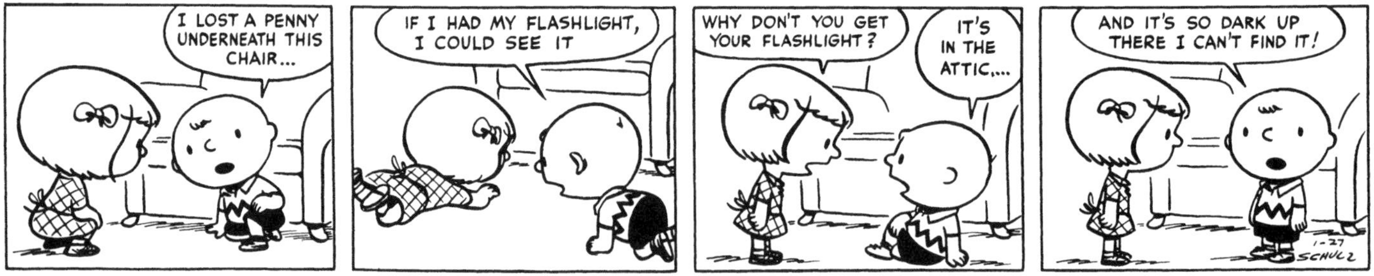
I LOST A PENNY UNDERNEATH THIS CHAIR...
IF I HAD MY FLASHLIGHT, I COULD SEE IT
WHY DON'T YOU GET YOUR FLASHLIGHT?
IT'S IN THE ATTIC,...
AND IT'S SO DARK UP THERE I CAN'T FIND IT!
1-27
SCHULZ

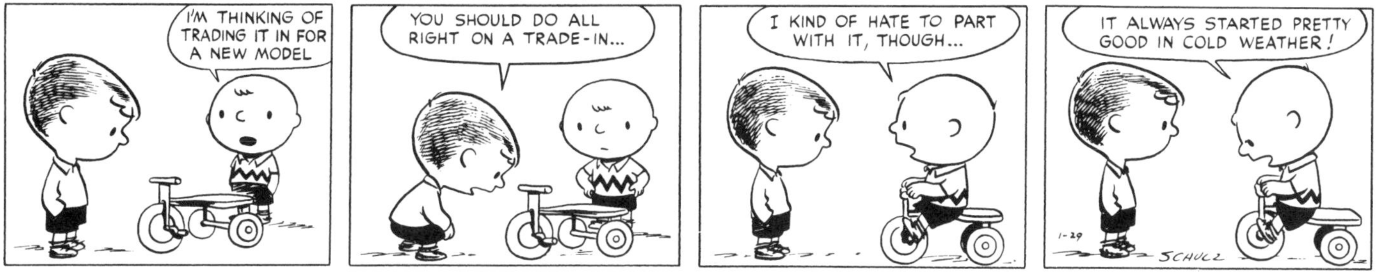
I'M THINKING OF TRADING IT IN FOR A NEW MODEL
YOU SHOULD DO ALL RIGHT ON A TRADE-IN...
I KIND OF HATE TO PART WITH IT, THOUGH...
IT ALWAYS STARTED PRETTY GOOD IN COLD WEATHER!
1-29
SCHULZ

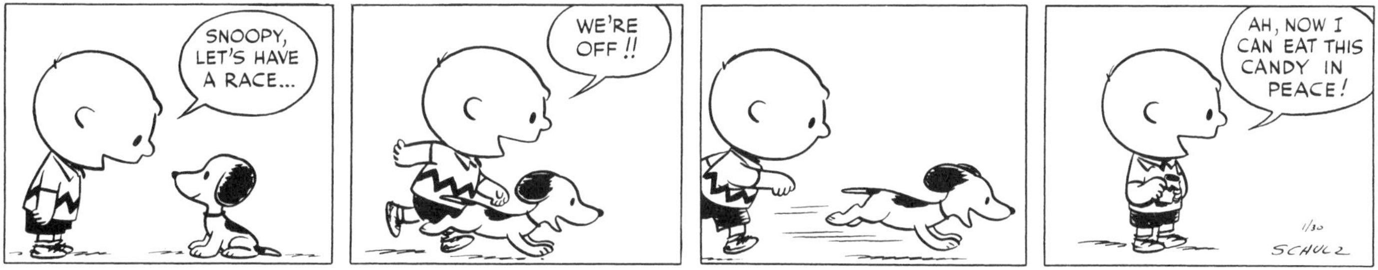
SNOOPY, LET'S HAVE A RACE...
WE'RE OFF!!
AH, NOW I CAN EAT THIS CANDY IN PEACE!
1/30
SCHULZ

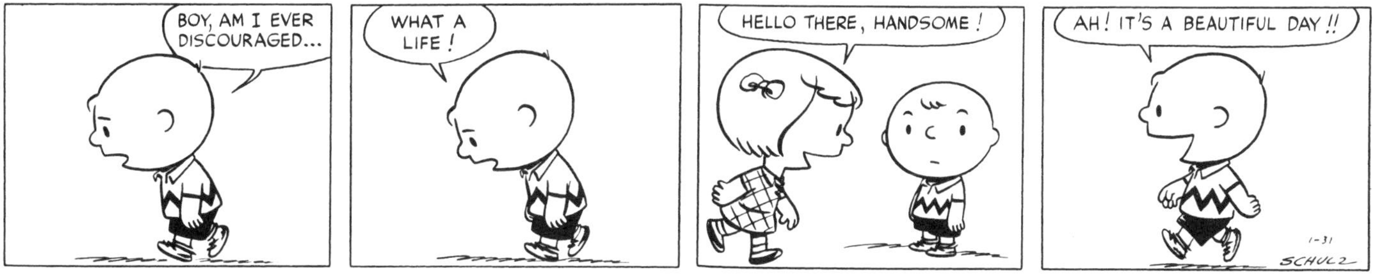
BOY, AM I EVER DISCOURAGED...
WHAT A LIFE!
HELLO THERE, HANDSOME!
AH! IT'S A BEAUTIFUL DAY!!
1-31
SCHULZ

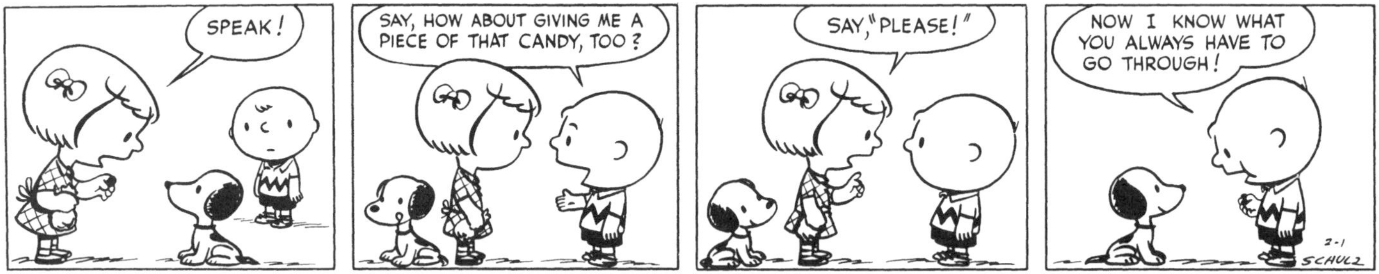
SPEAK!
SAY, HOW ABOUT GIVING ME A PIECE OF THAT CANDY, TOO?
SAY, "PLEASE!"
NOW I KNOW WHAT YOU ALWAYS HAVE TO GO THROUGH!
2-1
SCHULZ

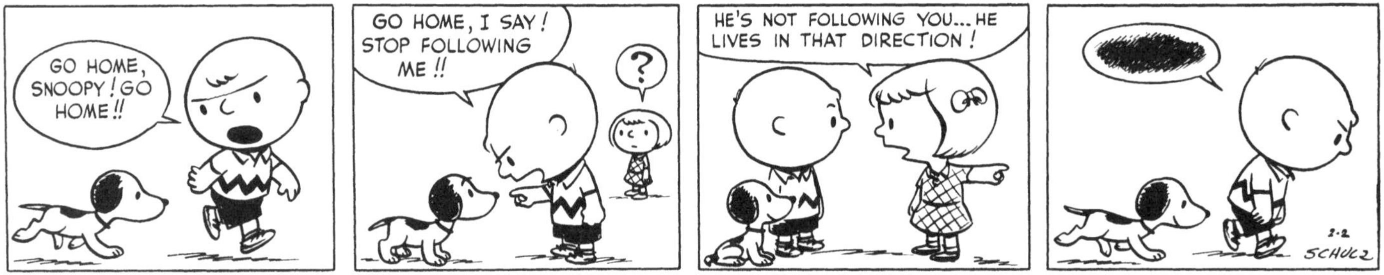
GO HOME, SNOOPY! GO HOME!!
GO HOME, I SAY! STOP FOLLOWING ME!!
?
HE'S NOT FOLLOWING YOU...HE LIVES IN THAT DIRECTION!
2-2
SCHULZ

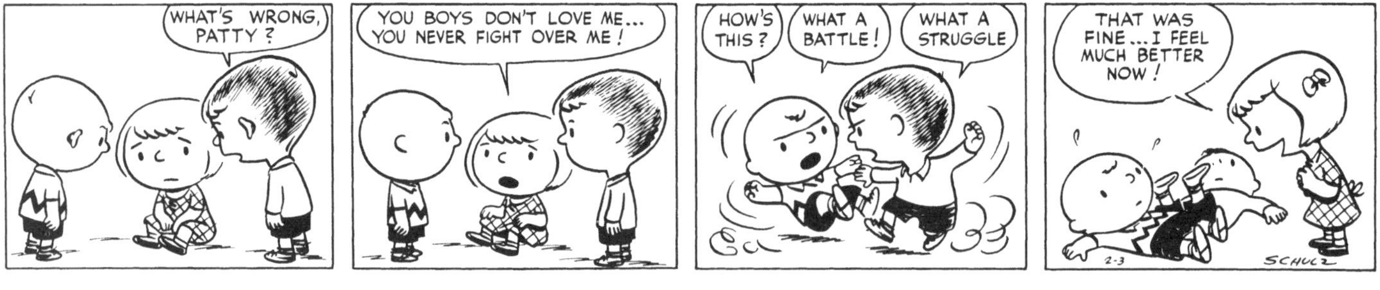
WHAT'S WRONG, PATTY?
YOU BOYS DON'T LOVE ME... YOU NEVER FIGHT OVER ME!
HOW'S THIS?
WHAT A BATTLE!
WHAT A STRUGGLE
THAT WAS FINE...I FEEL MUCH BETTER NOW!
2-3
SCHULZ

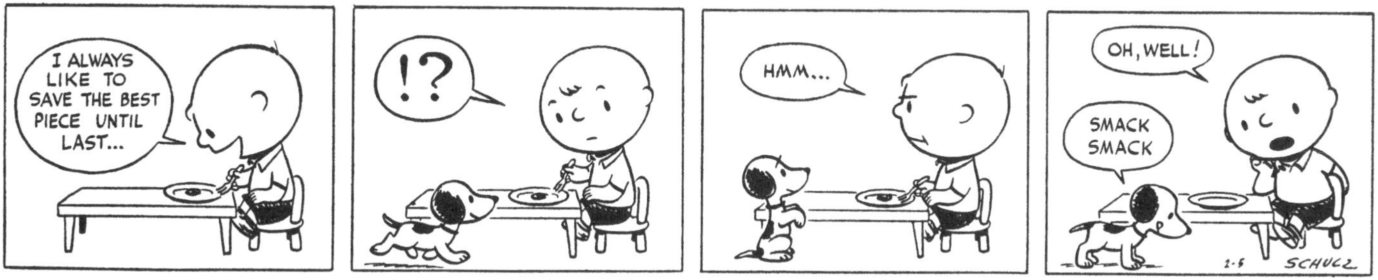
I ALWAYS LIKE TO SAVE THE BEST PIECE UNTIL LAST...
!?
HMM...
OH, WELL!
SMACK SMACK
2-5 SCHULZ

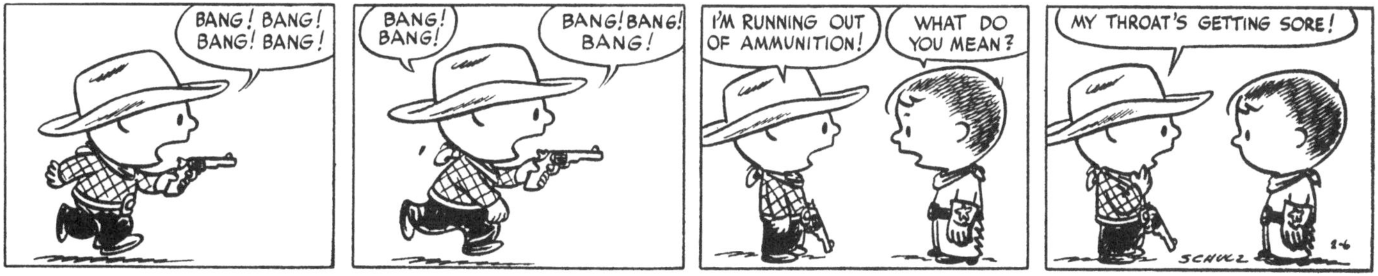
BANG! BANG! BANG! BANG!
BANG! BANG!
BANG! BANG! BANG!
I'M RUNNING OUT OF AMMUNITION!
WHAT DO YOU MEAN?
MY THROAT'S GETTING SORE!
SCHULZ 2-6

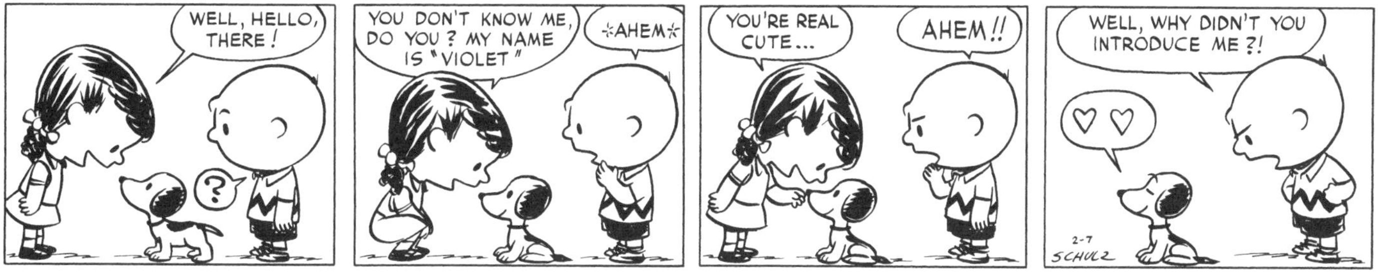
WELL, HELLO, THERE!
?
YOU DON'T KNOW ME, DO YOU? MY NAME IS "VIOLET"
AHEM
YOU'RE REAL CUTE...
AHEM!!
WELL, WHY DIDN'T YOU INTRODUCE ME?!
♡ ♡
2-7 SCHULZ

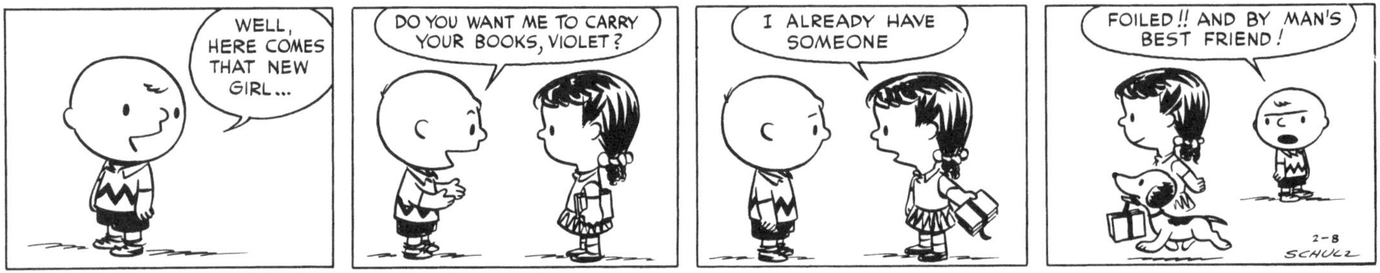
WELL, HERE COMES THAT NEW GIRL...
DO YOU WANT ME TO CARRY YOUR BOOKS, VIOLET?
I ALREADY HAVE SOMEONE
FOILED!! AND BY MAN'S BEST FRIEND!
2-8
SCHULZ

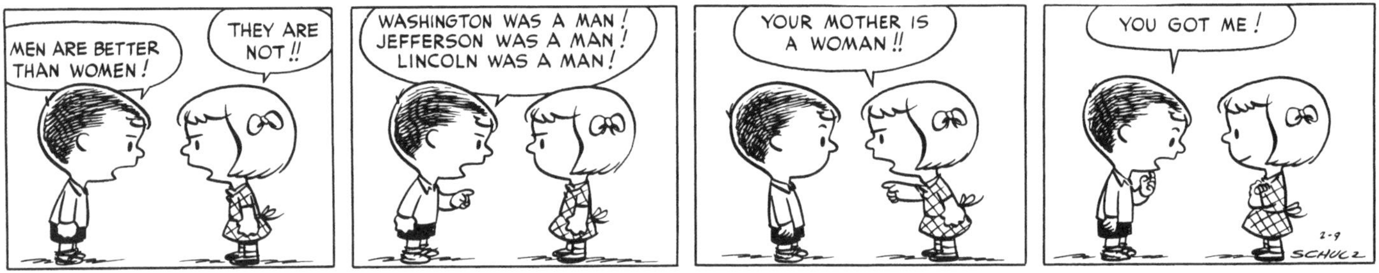
MEN ARE BETTER THAN WOMEN!
THEY ARE NOT!!
WASHINGTON WAS A MAN! JEFFERSON WAS A MAN! LINCOLN WAS A MAN!
YOUR MOTHER IS A WOMAN!!
YOU GOT ME!
2-9
SCHULZ

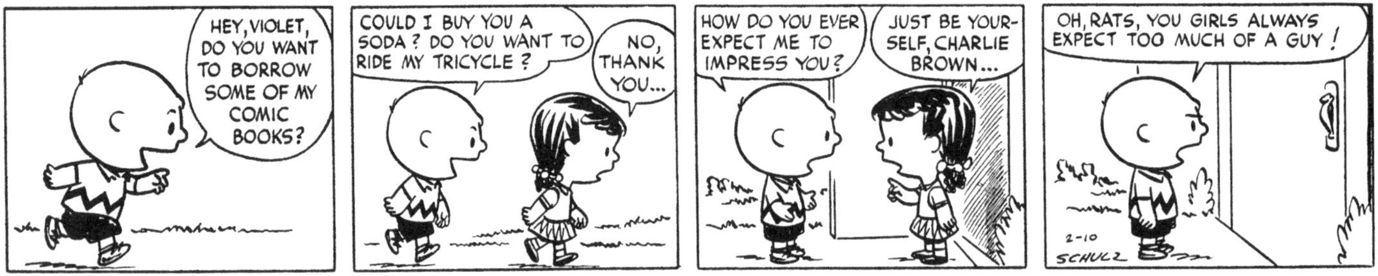
HEY, VIOLET, DO YOU WANT TO BORROW SOME OF MY COMIC BOOKS?
COULD I BUY YOU A SODA? DO YOU WANT TO RIDE MY TRICYCLE?
NO, THANK YOU...
HOW DO YOU EVER EXPECT ME TO IMPRESS YOU?
JUST BE YOURSELF, CHARLIE BROWN...
OH, RATS, YOU GIRLS ALWAYS EXPECT TOO MUCH OF A GUY!
2-10
SCHULZ

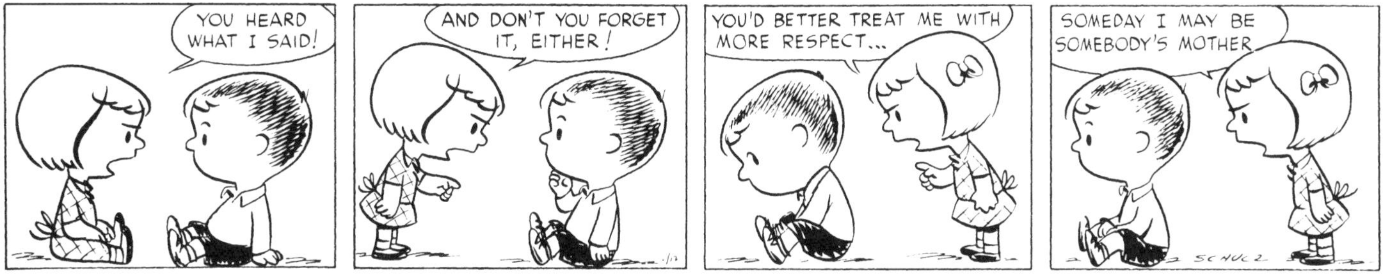
YOU HEARD WHAT I SAID!
AND DON'T YOU FORGET IT, EITHER!
YOU'D BETTER TREAT ME WITH MORE RESPECT...
SOMEDAY I MAY BE SOMEBODY'S MOTHER
SCHULZ

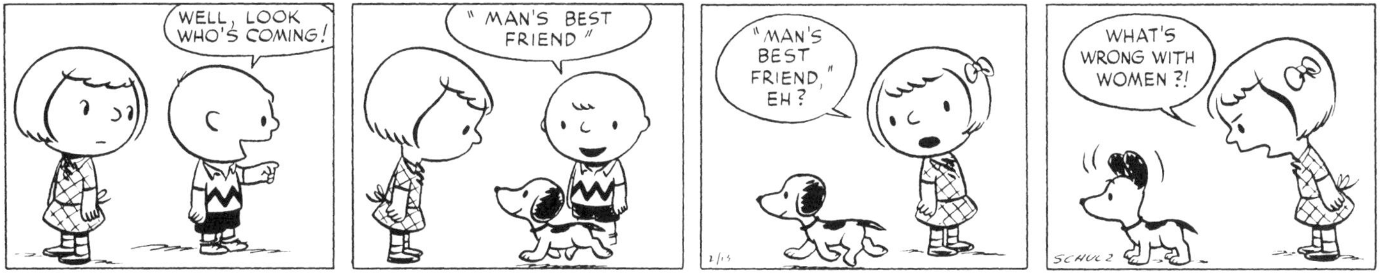
WELL, LOOK WHO'S COMING!
" MAN'S BEST FRIEND "
"MAN'S BEST FRIEND," EH?
WHAT'S WRONG WITH WOMEN ?!
SCHULZ

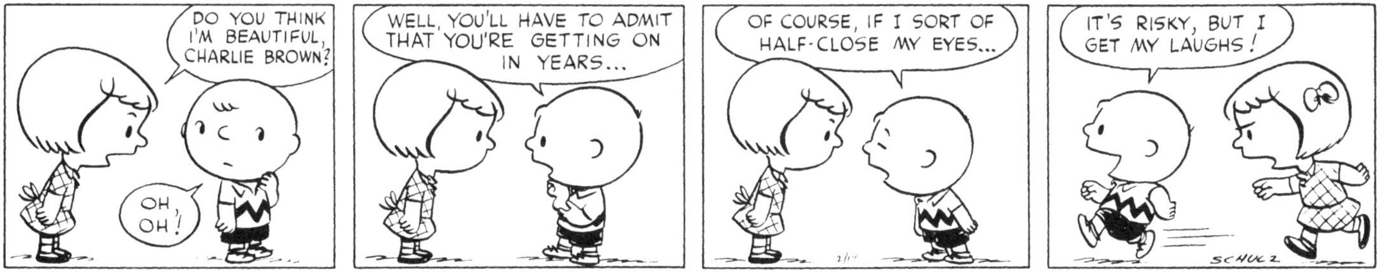
DO YOU THINK I'M BEAUTIFUL, CHARLIE BROWN?
OH, OH!
WELL, YOU'LL HAVE TO ADMIT THAT YOU'RE GETTING ON IN YEARS...
OF COURSE, IF I SORT OF HALF-CLOSE MY EYES...
IT'S RISKY, BUT I GET MY LAUGHS!
SCHULZ

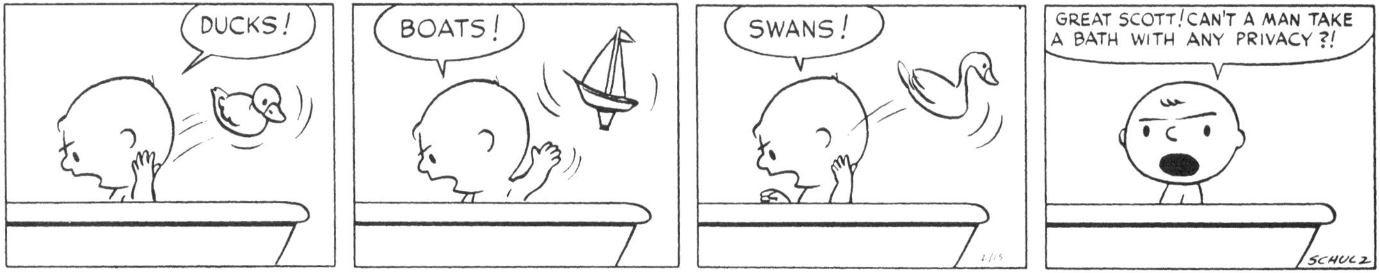
DUCKS!
BOATS!
SWANS!
GREAT SCOTT! CAN'T A MAN TAKE A BATH WITH ANY PRIVACY ?!

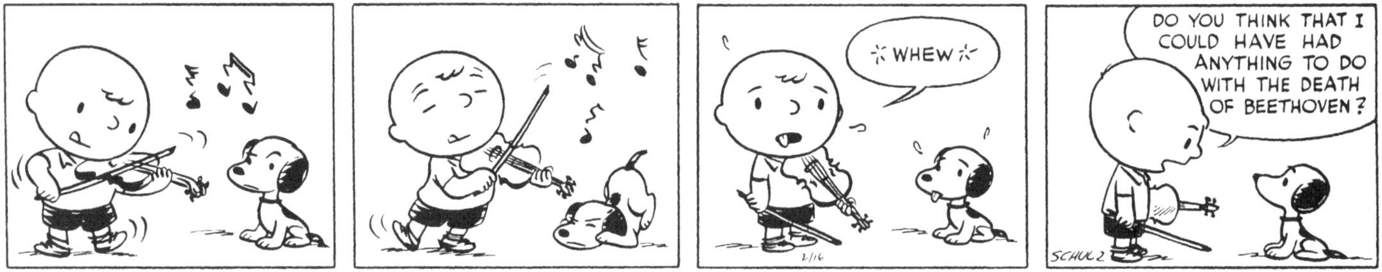
WHEW
DO YOU THINK THAT I COULD HAVE HAD ANYTHING TO DO WITH THE DEATH OF BEETHOVEN ?

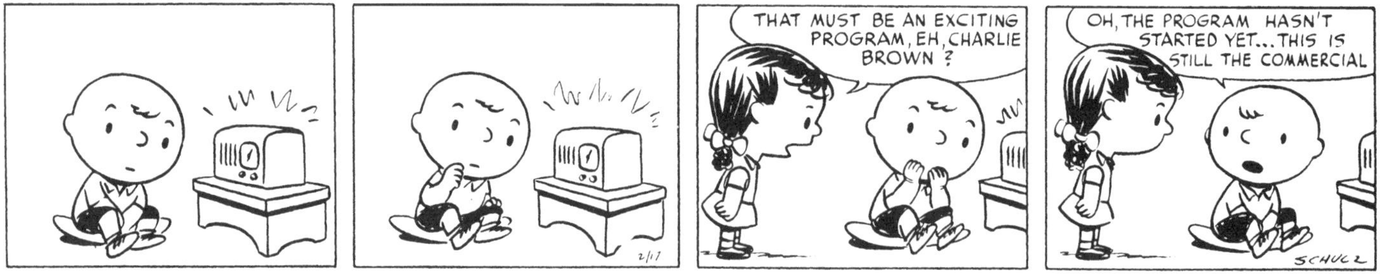
THAT MUST BE AN EXCITING PROGRAM, EH, CHARLIE BROWN ?
OH, THE PROGRAM HASN'T STARTED YET... THIS IS STILL THE COMMERCIAL

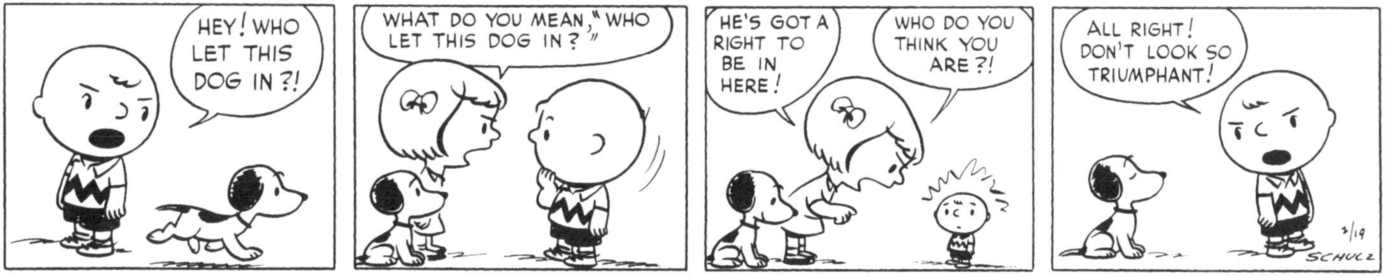
HEY! WHO LET THIS DOG IN?!
WHAT DO YOU MEAN, "WHO LET THIS DOG IN?"
HE'S GOT A RIGHT TO BE IN HERE!
WHO DO YOU THINK YOU ARE?!
ALL RIGHT! DON'T LOOK SO TRIUMPHANT!
2/19
SCHULZ

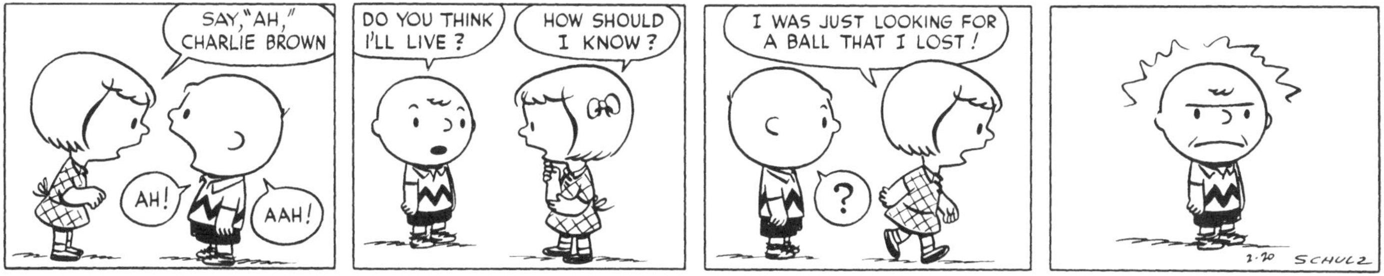
SAY, "AH," CHARLIE BROWN
AH!
AAH!
DO YOU THINK I'LL LIVE?
HOW SHOULD I KNOW?
I WAS JUST LOOKING FOR A BALL THAT I LOST!
?
2·20
SCHULZ

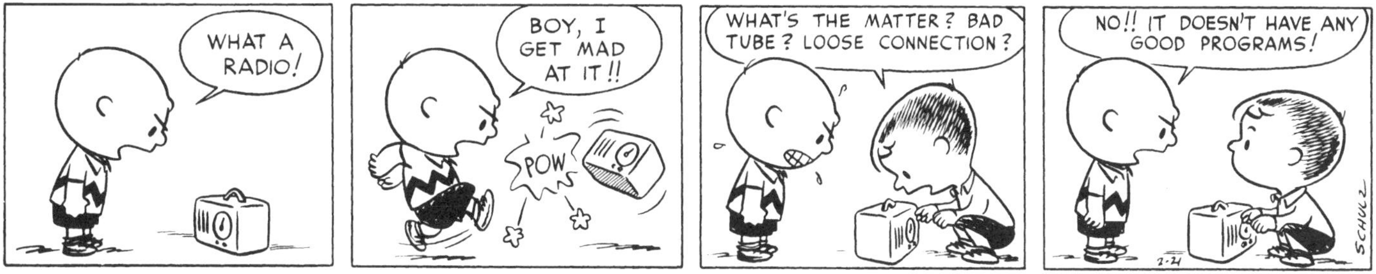
WHAT A RADIO!
BOY, I GET MAD AT IT!!
POW
WHAT'S THE MATTER? BAD TUBE? LOOSE CONNECTION?
NO!! IT DOESN'T HAVE ANY GOOD PROGRAMS!
SCHULZ
2·21

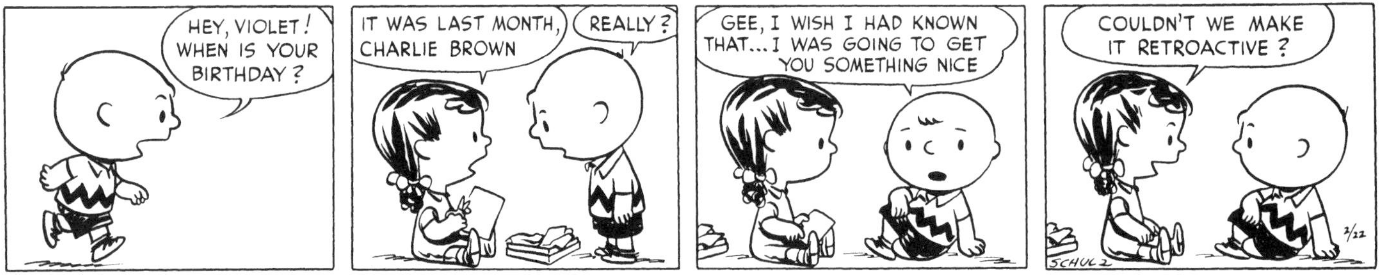
HEY, VIOLET! WHEN IS YOUR BIRTHDAY?
IT WAS LAST MONTH, CHARLIE BROWN
REALLY?
GEE, I WISH I HAD KNOWN THAT... I WAS GOING TO GET YOU SOMETHING NICE
COULDN'T WE MAKE IT RETROACTIVE?

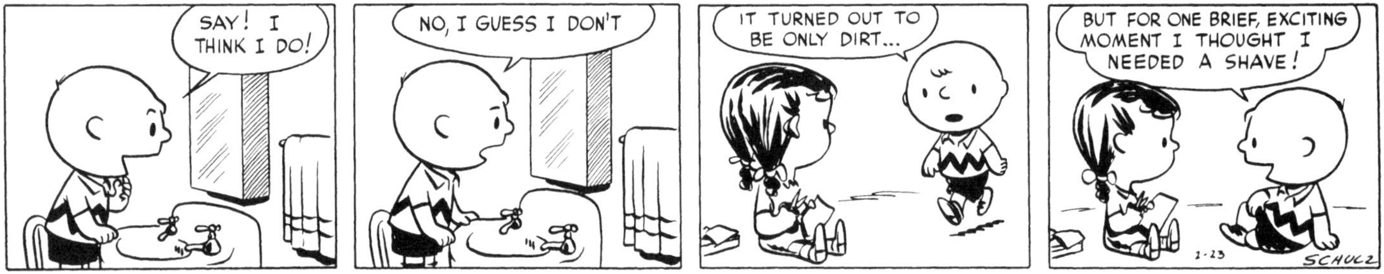
SAY! I THINK I DO!
NO, I GUESS I DON'T
IT TURNED OUT TO BE ONLY DIRT...
BUT FOR ONE BRIEF, EXCITING MOMENT I THOUGHT I NEEDED A SHAVE!

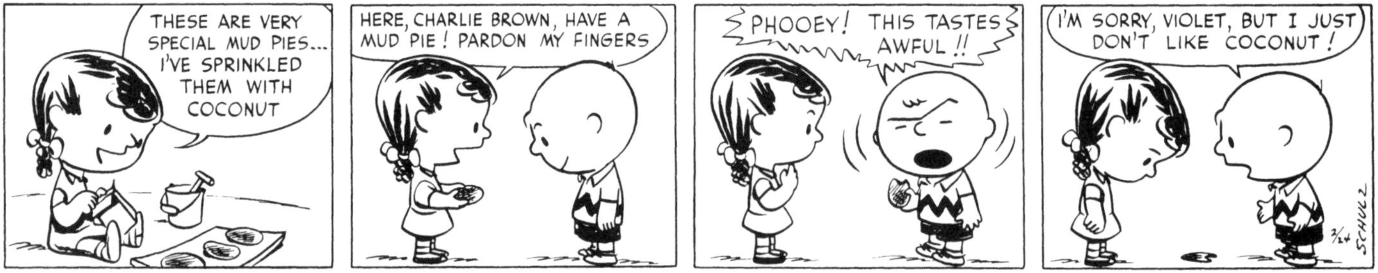
THESE ARE VERY SPECIAL MUD PIES... I'VE SPRINKLED THEM WITH COCONUT
HERE, CHARLIE BROWN, HAVE A MUD PIE! PARDON MY FINGERS
PHOOEY! THIS TASTES AWFUL!!
I'M SORRY, VIOLET, BUT I JUST DON'T LIKE COCONUT!

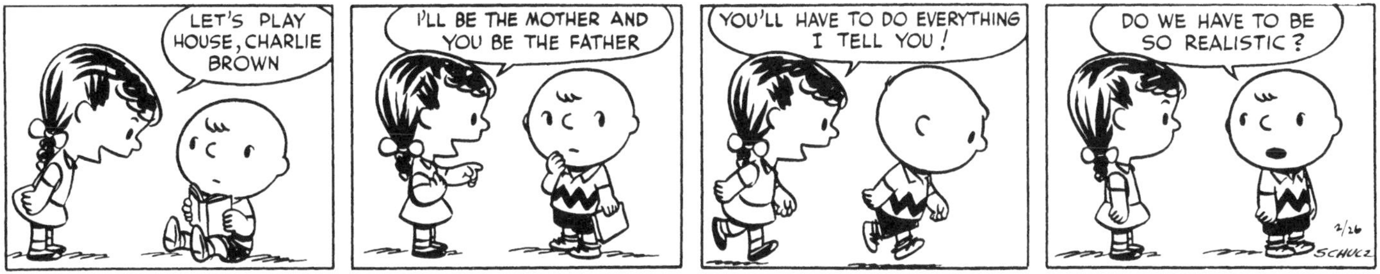
LET'S PLAY HOUSE, CHARLIE BROWN
I'LL BE THE MOTHER AND YOU BE THE FATHER
YOU'LL HAVE TO DO EVERYTHING I TELL YOU!
DO WE HAVE TO BE SO REALISTIC?
2/26
SCHULZ

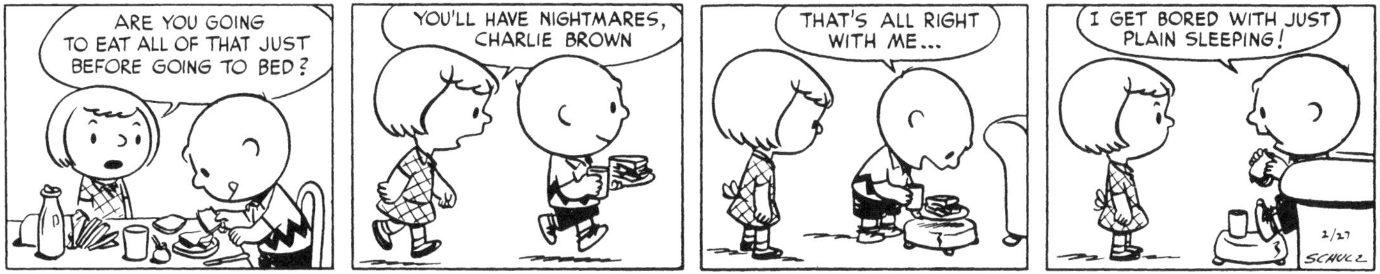
ARE YOU GOING TO EAT ALL OF THAT JUST BEFORE GOING TO BED?
YOU'LL HAVE NIGHTMARES, CHARLIE BROWN
THAT'S ALL RIGHT WITH ME...
I GET BORED WITH JUST PLAIN SLEEPING!
2/27
SCHULZ

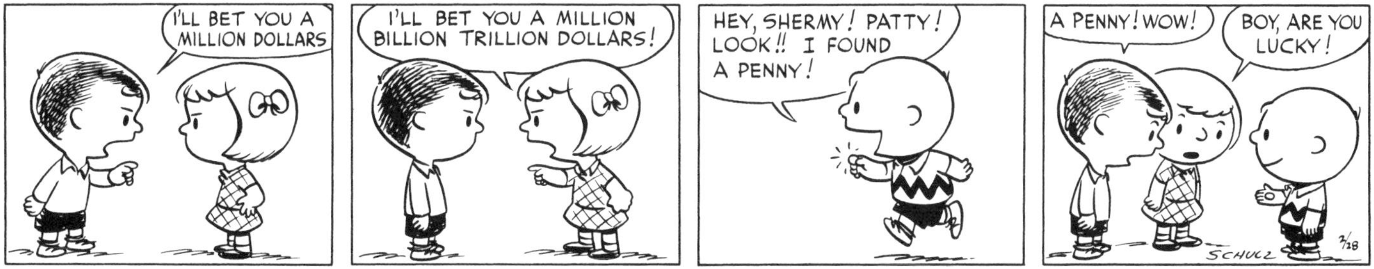
I'LL BET YOU A MILLION DOLLARS
I'LL BET YOU A MILLION BILLION TRILLION DOLLARS!
HEY, SHERMY! PATTY! LOOK!! I FOUND A PENNY!
A PENNY! WOW!
BOY, ARE YOU LUCKY!
SCHULZ
2/28

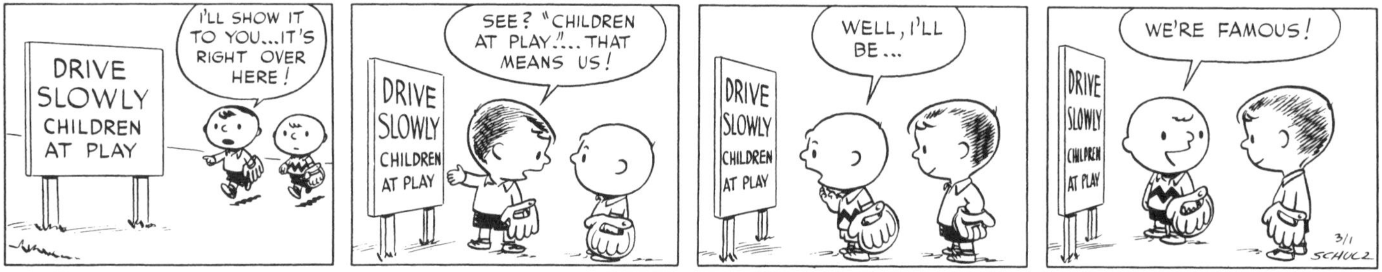
DRIVE SLOWLY CHILDREN AT PLAY
I'LL SHOW IT TO YOU...IT'S RIGHT OVER HERE!
SEE? "CHILDREN AT PLAY!"... THAT MEANS US!
WELL, I'LL BE...
WE'RE FAMOUS!
3/1
SCHULZ

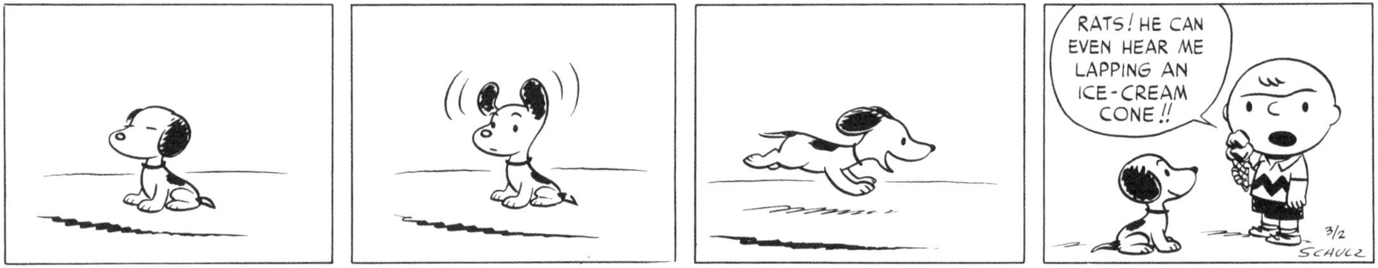
RATS! HE CAN EVEN HEAR ME LAPPING AN ICE-CREAM CONE!!
3/2
SCHULZ

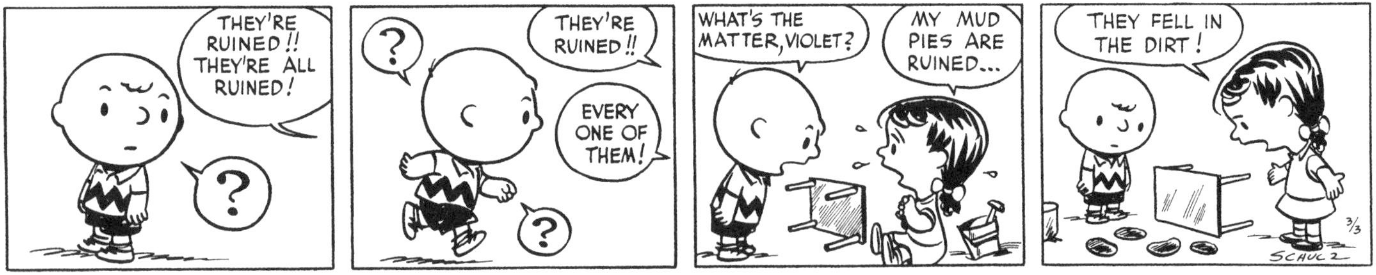
THEY'RE RUINED!! THEY'RE ALL RUINED!
?
?
THEY'RE RUINED!!
EVERY ONE OF THEM!
?
WHAT'S THE MATTER, VIOLET?
MY MUD PIES ARE RUINED...
THEY FELL IN THE DIRT!
3/3
SCHULZ

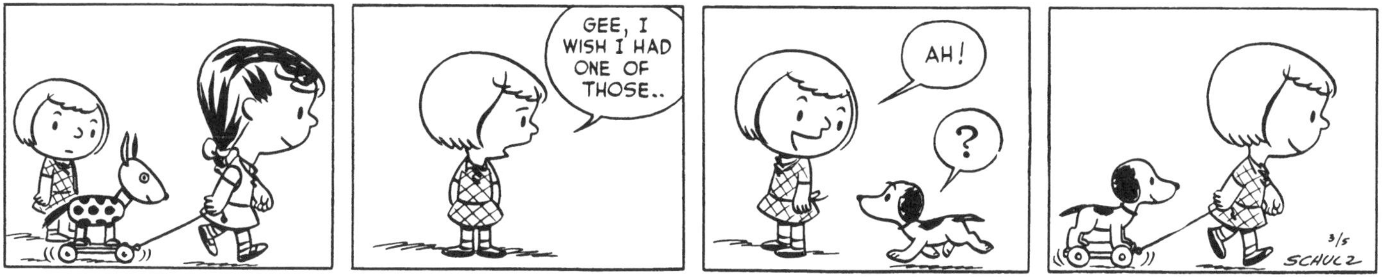
GEE, I WISH I HAD ONE OF THOSE..
AH!
?
3/5
SCHULZ

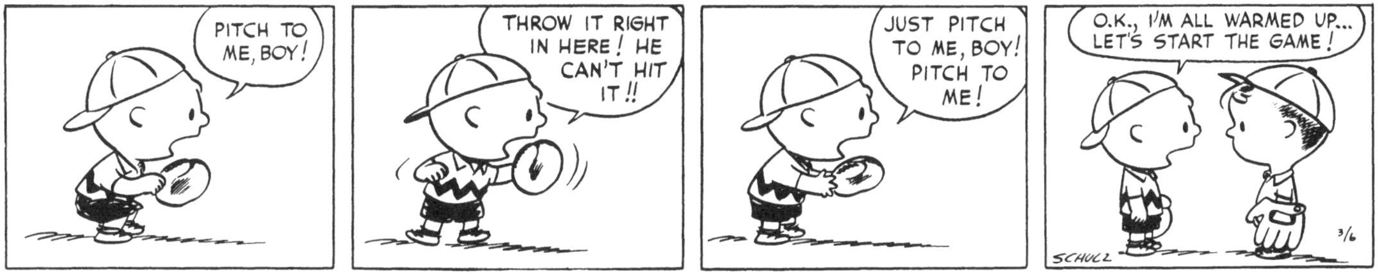
PITCH TO ME, BOY!
THROW IT RIGHT IN HERE! HE CAN'T HIT IT!!
JUST PITCH TO ME, BOY! PITCH TO ME!
O.K., I'M ALL WARMED UP... LET'S START THE GAME!
3/6
SCHULZ

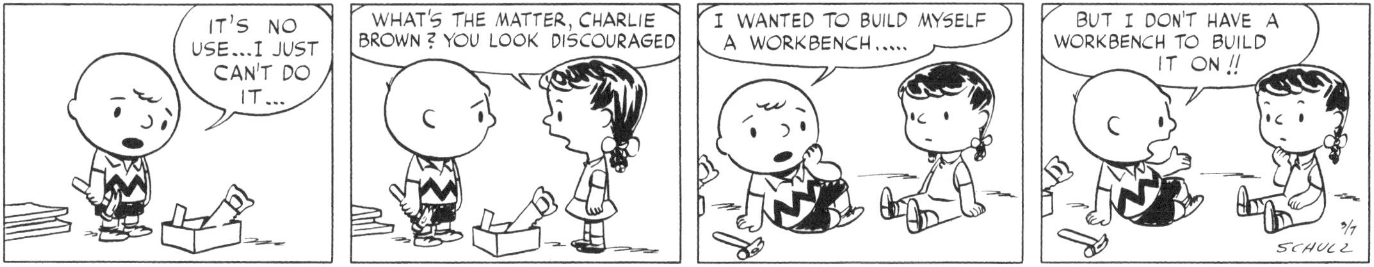
IT'S NO USE...I JUST CAN'T DO IT...
WHAT'S THE MATTER, CHARLIE BROWN? YOU LOOK DISCOURAGED
I WANTED TO BUILD MYSELF A WORKBENCH.....
BUT I DON'T HAVE A WORKBENCH TO BUILD IT ON!!
3/7
SCHULZ

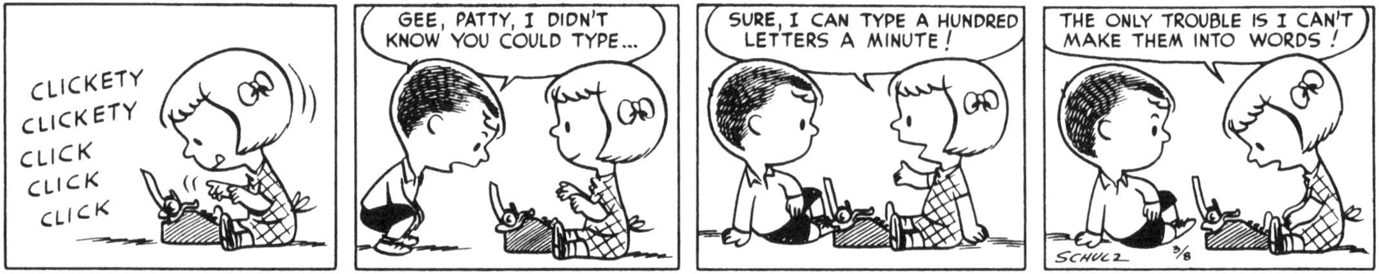
CLICKETY
CLICKETY
CLICK
CLICK
CLICK
GEE, PATTY, I DIDN'T KNOW YOU COULD TYPE...
SURE, I CAN TYPE A HUNDRED LETTERS A MINUTE!
THE ONLY TROUBLE IS I CAN'T MAKE THEM INTO WORDS!
SCHULZ 3/8

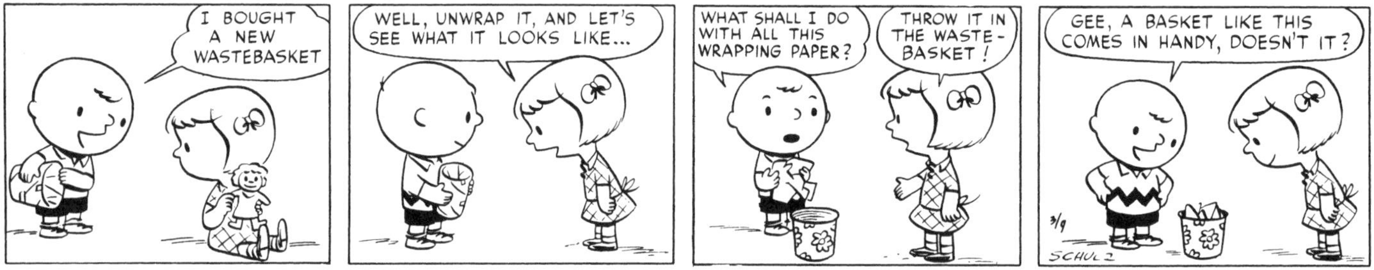
I BOUGHT A NEW WASTEBASKET
WELL, UNWRAP IT, AND LET'S SEE WHAT IT LOOKS LIKE...
WHAT SHALL I DO WITH ALL THIS WRAPPING PAPER?
THROW IT IN THE WASTE-BASKET!
GEE, A BASKET LIKE THIS COMES IN HANDY, DOESN'T IT?
3/9
SCHULZ

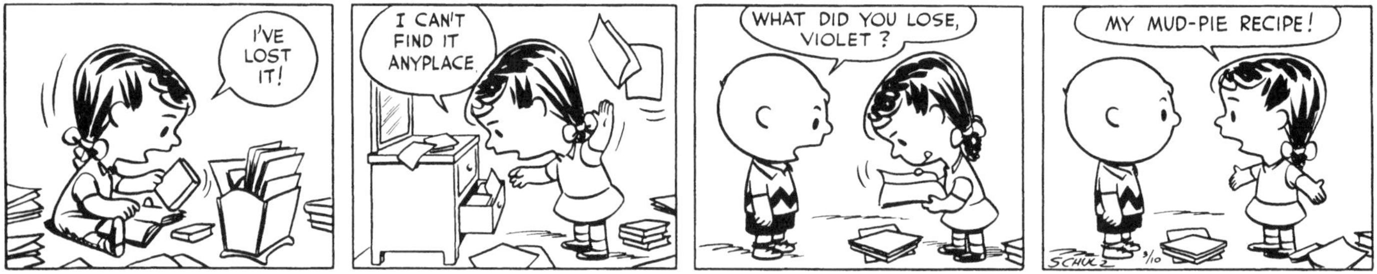
I'VE LOST IT!
I CAN'T FIND IT ANYPLACE
WHAT DID YOU LOSE, VIOLET?
MY MUD-PIE RECIPE!
SCHULZ 3/10

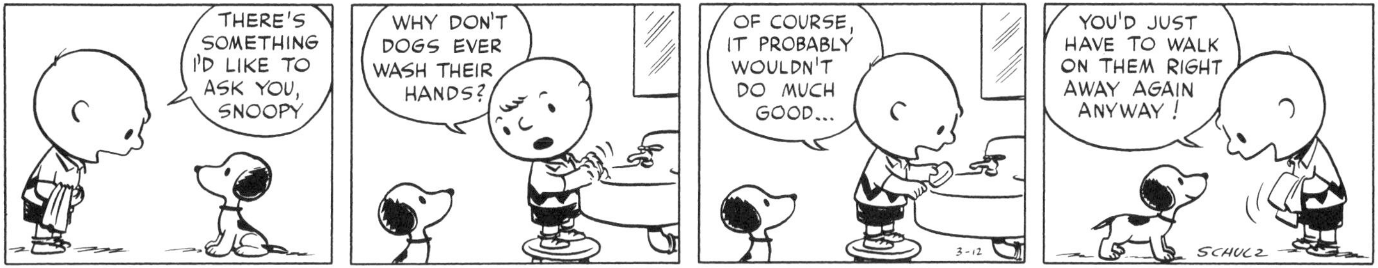
THERE'S SOMETHING I'D LIKE TO ASK YOU, SNOOPY
WHY DON'T DOGS EVER WASH THEIR HANDS?
OF COURSE, IT PROBABLY WOULDN'T DO MUCH GOOD...
YOU'D JUST HAVE TO WALK ON THEM RIGHT AWAY AGAIN ANYWAY!
3-12
SCHULZ

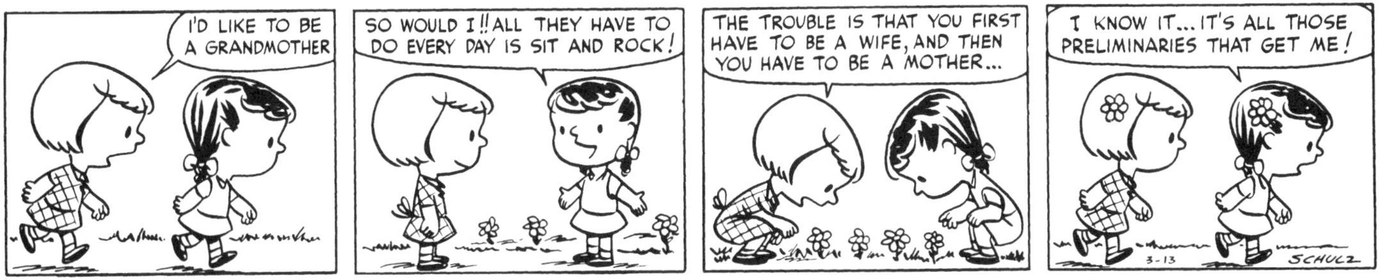
I'D LIKE TO BE A GRANDMOTHER
SO WOULD I!! ALL THEY HAVE TO DO EVERY DAY IS SIT AND ROCK!
THE TROUBLE IS THAT YOU FIRST HAVE TO BE A WIFE, AND THEN YOU HAVE TO BE A MOTHER...
I KNOW IT... IT'S ALL THOSE PRELIMINARIES THAT GET ME!
3-13
SCHULZ

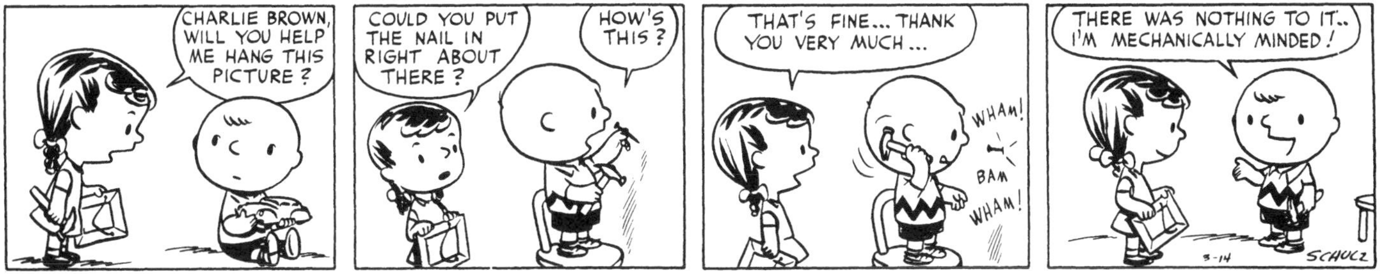
CHARLIE BROWN, WILL YOU HELP ME HANG THIS PICTURE?
COULD YOU PUT THE NAIL IN RIGHT ABOUT THERE?
HOW'S THIS?
THAT'S FINE... THANK YOU VERY MUCH...
WHAM!
BAM
WHAM!
THERE WAS NOTHING TO IT.. I'M MECHANICALLY MINDED!
3-14
SCHULZ

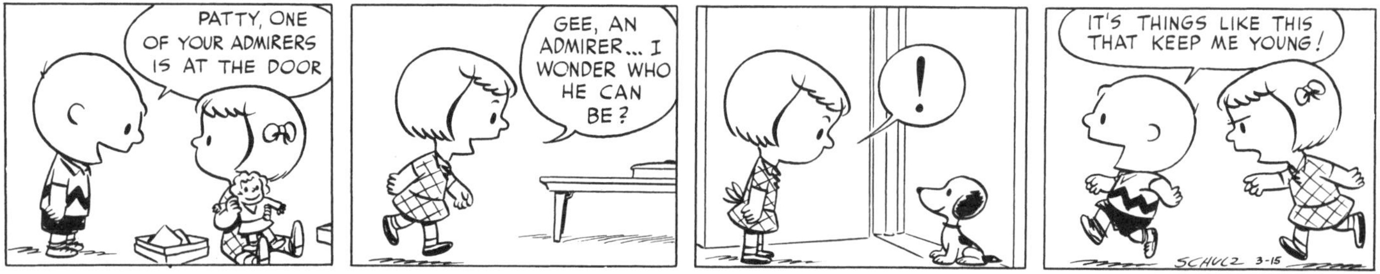
PATTY, ONE OF YOUR ADMIRERS IS AT THE DOOR
GEE, AN ADMIRER... I WONDER WHO HE CAN BE?
!
IT'S THINGS LIKE THIS THAT KEEP ME YOUNG!
SCHULZ 3-15

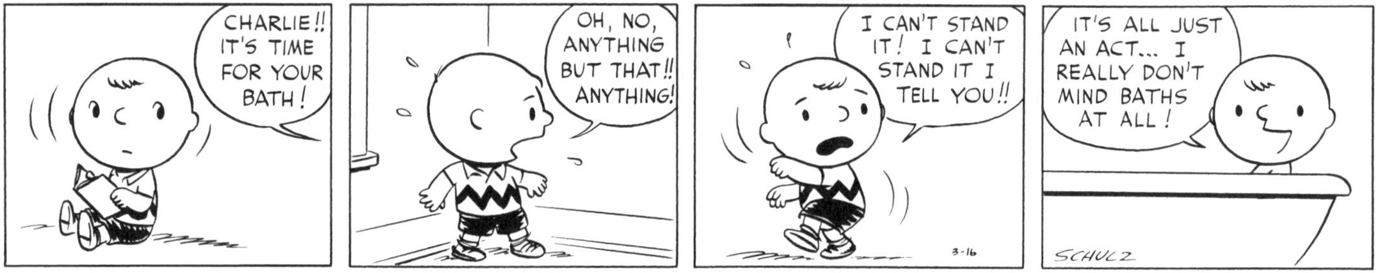
CHARLIE!! IT'S TIME FOR YOUR BATH!
OH, NO, ANYTHING BUT THAT!! ANYTHING!
I CAN'T STAND IT! I CAN'T STAND IT I TELL YOU!!
3-16
IT'S ALL JUST AN ACT... I REALLY DON'T MIND BATHS AT ALL!
SCHULZ

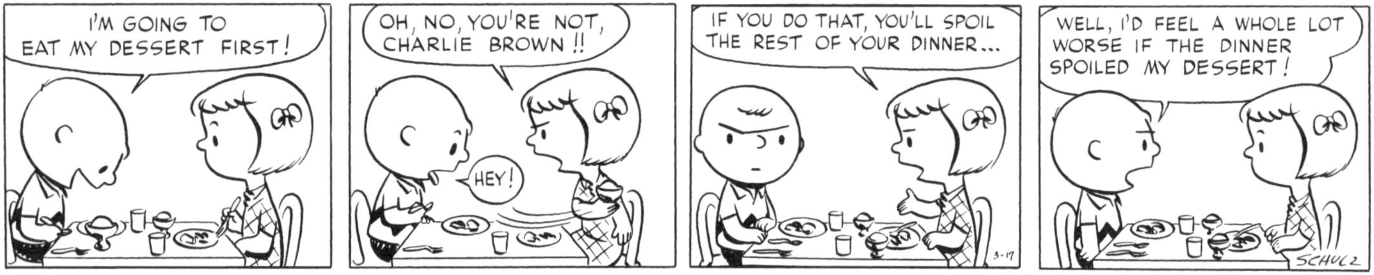
I'M GOING TO EAT MY DESSERT FIRST!
OH, NO, YOU'RE NOT, CHARLIE BROWN!!
HEY!
IF YOU DO THAT, YOU'LL SPOIL THE REST OF YOUR DINNER...
3-17
WELL, I'D FEEL A WHOLE LOT WORSE IF THE DINNER SPOILED MY DESSERT!
SCHULZ

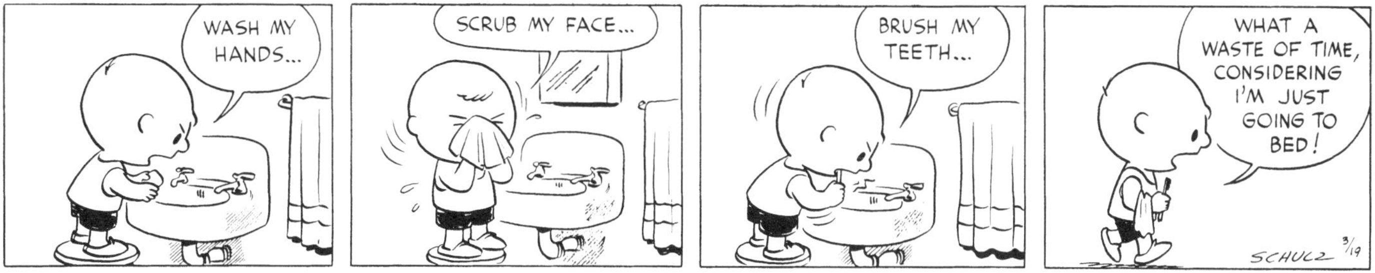
WASH MY HANDS...
SCRUB MY FACE...
BRUSH MY TEETH...
WHAT A WASTE OF TIME, CONSIDERING I'M JUST GOING TO BED!
SCHULZ 3/19

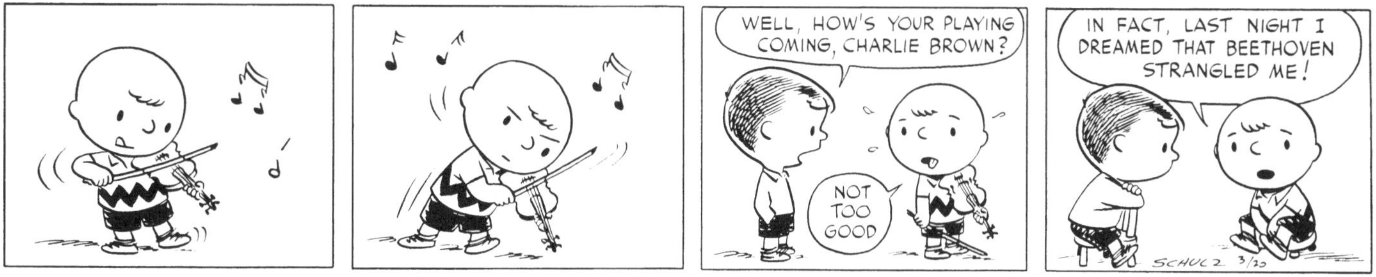
WELL, HOW'S YOUR PLAYING COMING, CHARLIE BROWN?
NOT TOO GOOD
IN FACT, LAST NIGHT I DREAMED THAT BEETHOVEN STRANGLED ME!
SCHULZ 3/20

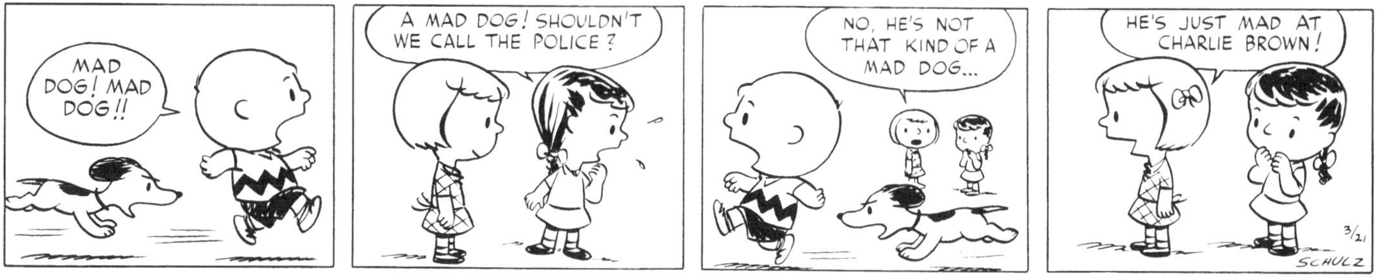
MAD DOG! MAD DOG!!
A MAD DOG! SHOULDN'T WE CALL THE POLICE?
NO, HE'S NOT THAT KIND OF A MAD DOG...
HE'S JUST MAD AT CHARLIE BROWN!
3/21
SCHULZ

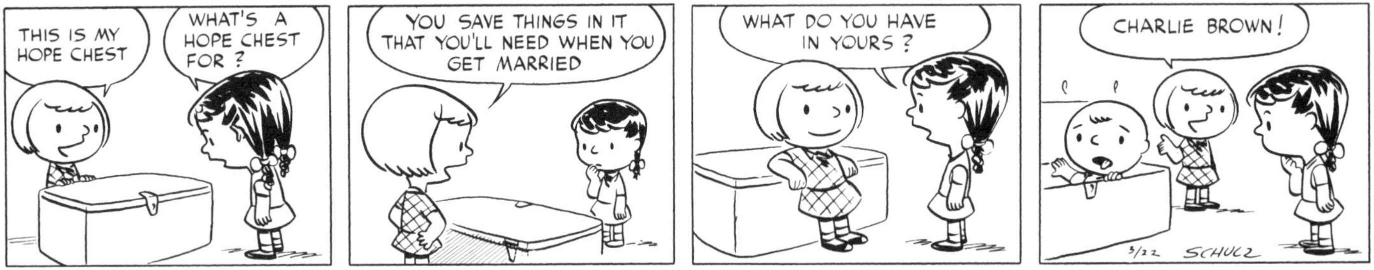
THIS IS MY HOPE CHEST
WHAT'S A HOPE CHEST FOR ?
YOU SAVE THINGS IN IT THAT YOU'LL NEED WHEN YOU GET MARRIED
WHAT DO YOU HAVE IN YOURS ?
CHARLIE BROWN !
3/22 SCHULZ

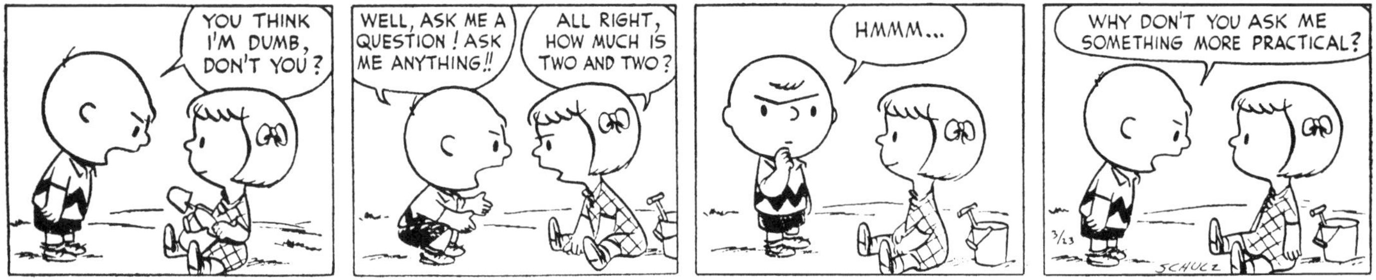
YOU THINK I'M DUMB, DON'T YOU ?
WELL, ASK ME A QUESTION ! ASK ME ANYTHING !!
ALL RIGHT, HOW MUCH IS TWO AND TWO ?
HMMM...
WHY DON'T YOU ASK ME SOMETHING MORE PRACTICAL ?
3/23
SCHULZ

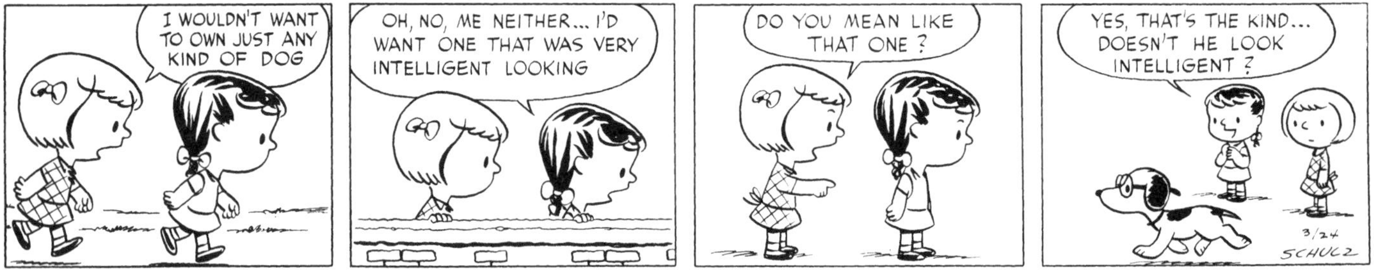
I WOULDN'T WANT TO OWN JUST ANY KIND OF DOG
OH, NO, ME NEITHER... I'D WANT ONE THAT WAS VERY INTELLIGENT LOOKING
DO YOU MEAN LIKE THAT ONE ?
YES, THAT'S THE KIND... DOESN'T HE LOOK INTELLIGENT ?
3/24
SCHULZ

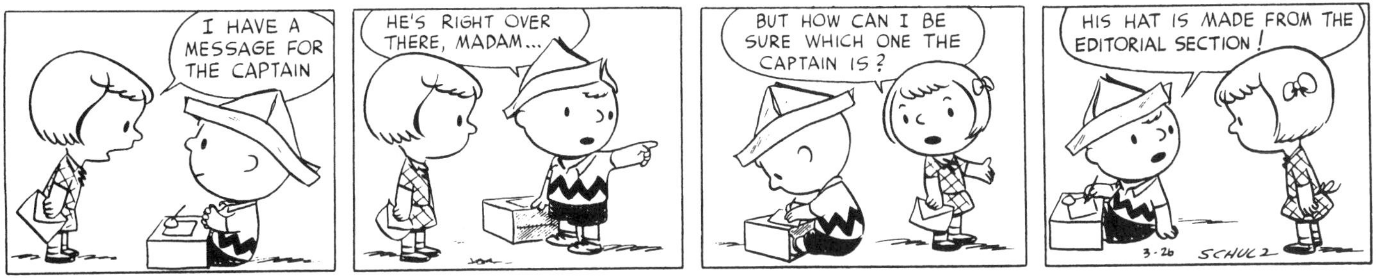
I HAVE A MESSAGE FOR THE CAPTAIN
HE'S RIGHT OVER THERE, MADAM...
BUT HOW CAN I BE SURE WHICH ONE THE CAPTAIN IS?
HIS HAT IS MADE FROM THE EDITORIAL SECTION!
3-26
SCHULZ

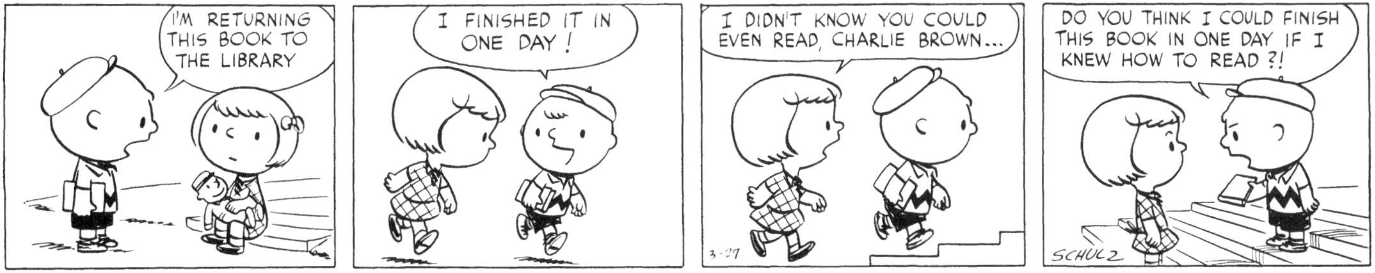
I'M RETURNING THIS BOOK TO THE LIBRARY
I FINISHED IT IN ONE DAY!
I DIDN'T KNOW YOU COULD EVEN READ, CHARLIE BROWN...
3-27
DO YOU THINK I COULD FINISH THIS BOOK IN ONE DAY IF I KNEW HOW TO READ?!
SCHULZ

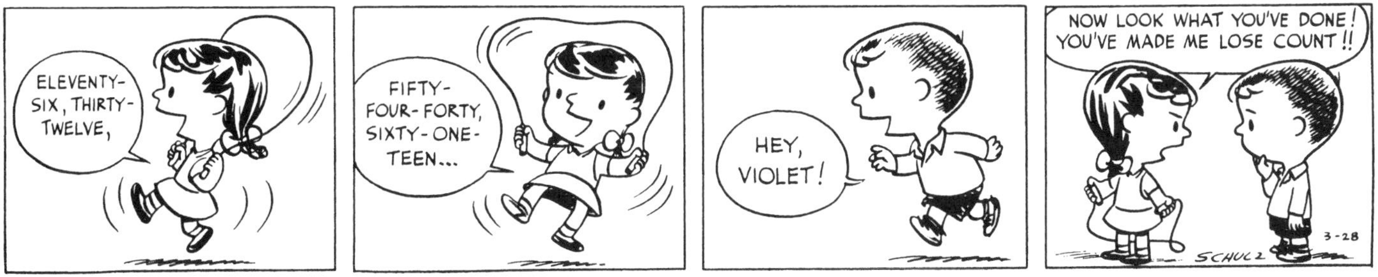
ELEVENTY-SIX, THIRTY-TWELVE,
FIFTY-FOUR-FORTY, SIXTY-ONE-TEEN...
HEY, VIOLET!
NOW LOOK WHAT YOU'VE DONE! YOU'VE MADE ME LOSE COUNT!!
3-28
SCHULZ

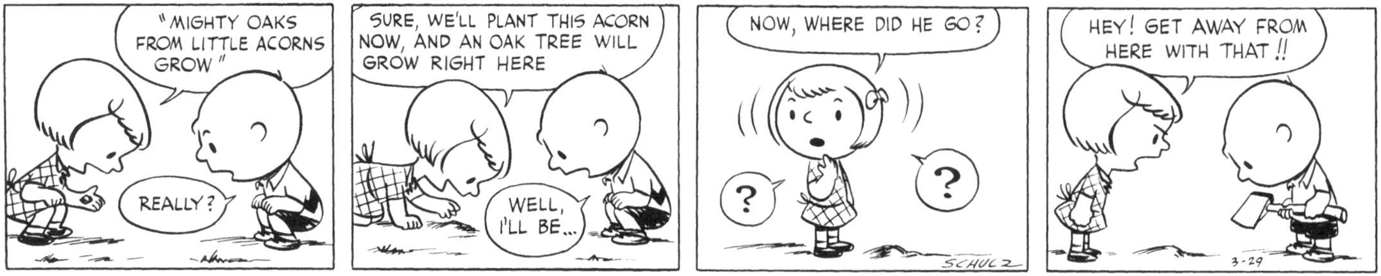
"MIGHTY OAKS FROM LITTLE ACORNS GROW"
REALLY?
SURE, WE'LL PLANT THIS ACORN NOW, AND AN OAK TREE WILL GROW RIGHT HERE
WELL, I'LL BE...
NOW, WHERE DID HE GO?
?
?
HEY! GET AWAY FROM HERE WITH THAT!!
SCHULZ
3-29

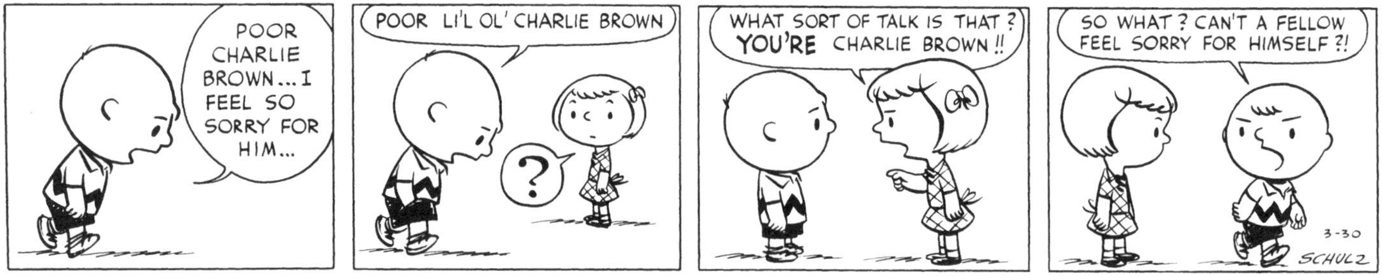
POOR CHARLIE BROWN... I FEEL SO SORRY FOR HIM...
POOR LI'L OL' CHARLIE BROWN
?
WHAT SORT OF TALK IS THAT? **YOU'RE** CHARLIE BROWN!!
SO WHAT? CAN'T A FELLOW FEEL SORRY FOR HIMSELF?!
3-30
SCHULZ

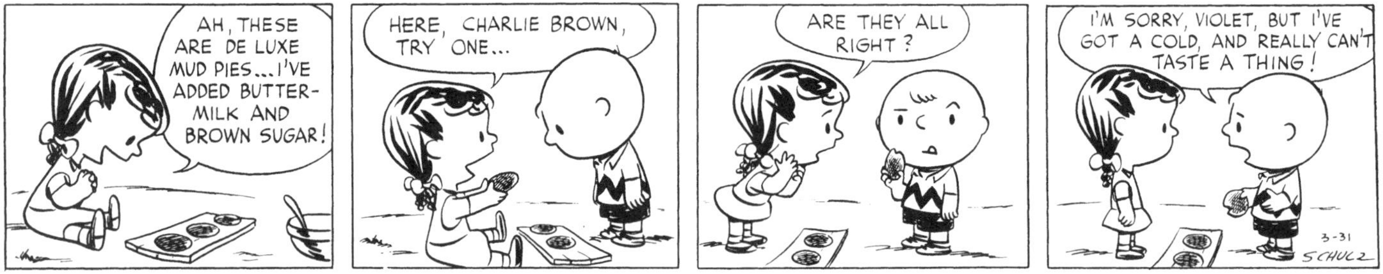
AH, THESE ARE DE LUXE MUD PIES... I'VE ADDED BUTTER-MILK AND BROWN SUGAR!
HERE, CHARLIE BROWN, TRY ONE...
ARE THEY ALL RIGHT?
I'M SORRY, VIOLET, BUT I'VE GOT A COLD, AND REALLY CAN'T TASTE A THING!
3-31
SCHULZ

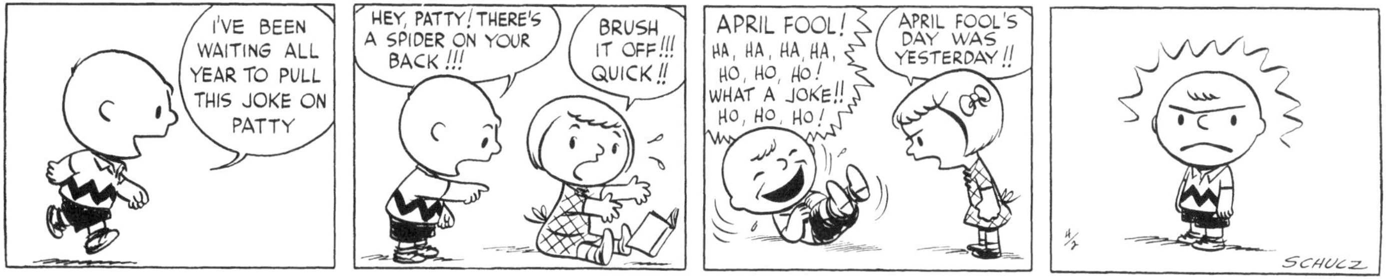
I'VE BEEN WAITING ALL YEAR TO PULL THIS JOKE ON PATTY
HEY, PATTY! THERE'S A SPIDER ON YOUR BACK!!!
BRUSH IT OFF!!! QUICK!!
APRIL FOOL! HA, HA, HA, HA, HO, HO, HO! WHAT A JOKE!! HO, HO, HO!
APRIL FOOL'S DAY WAS YESTERDAY!!
4/2
SCHULZ

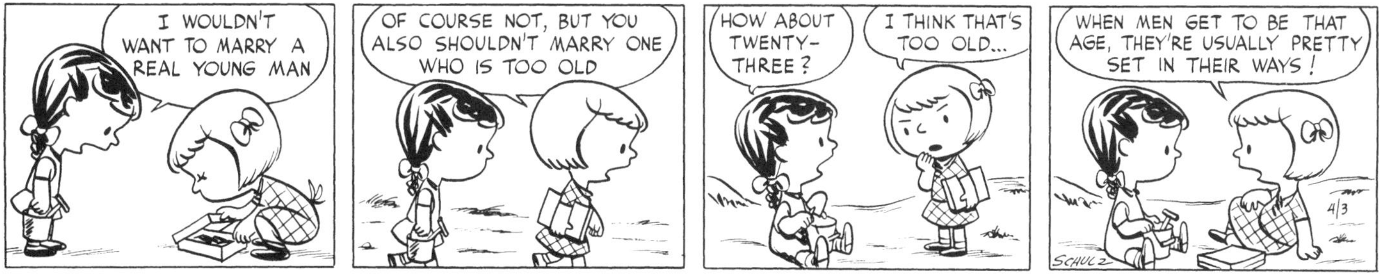
I WOULDN'T WANT TO MARRY A REAL YOUNG MAN
OF COURSE NOT, BUT YOU ALSO SHOULDN'T MARRY ONE WHO IS TOO OLD
HOW ABOUT TWENTY-THREE?
I THINK THAT'S TOO OLD...
WHEN MEN GET TO BE THAT AGE, THEY'RE USUALLY PRETTY SET IN THEIR WAYS!
4/3
SCHULZ

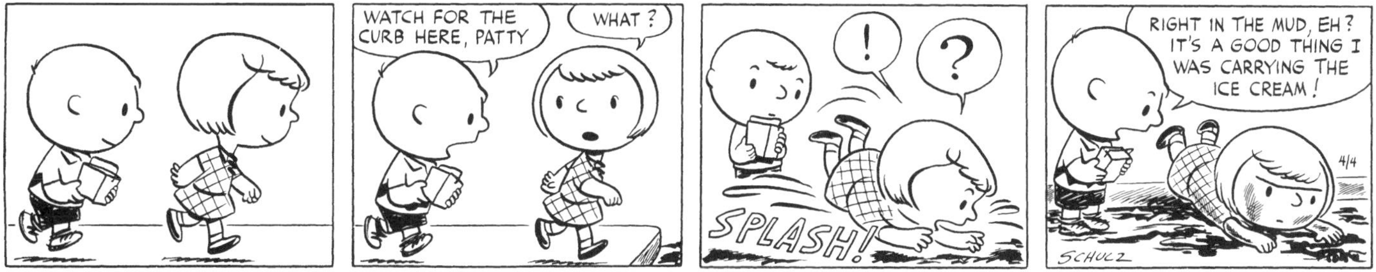
WATCH FOR THE CURB HERE, PATTY
WHAT?
!
?
SPLASH!
RIGHT IN THE MUD, EH? IT'S A GOOD THING I WAS CARRYING THE ICE CREAM!
4/4
SCHULZ

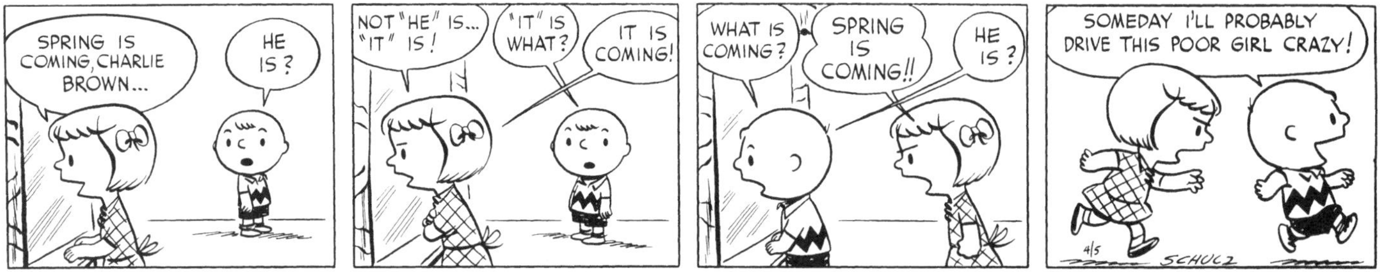
SPRING IS COMING, CHARLIE BROWN...
HE IS?
NOT "HE" IS... "IT" IS!
"IT" IS WHAT?
IT IS COMING!
WHAT IS COMING?
SPRING IS COMING!!
HE IS?
SOMEDAY I'LL PROBABLY DRIVE THIS POOR GIRL CRAZY!
4/5
SCHULZ

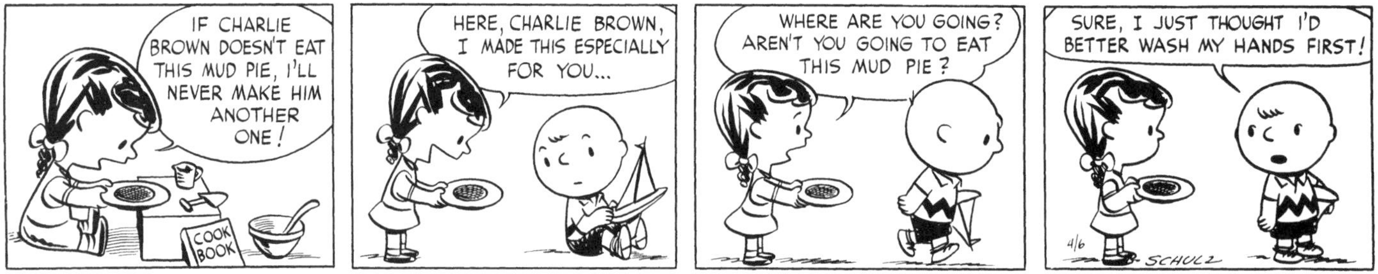
IF CHARLIE BROWN DOESN'T EAT THIS MUD PIE, I'LL NEVER MAKE HIM ANOTHER ONE!
COOK BOOK
HERE, CHARLIE BROWN, I MADE THIS ESPECIALLY FOR YOU...
WHERE ARE YOU GOING? AREN'T YOU GOING TO EAT THIS MUD PIE?
SURE, I JUST THOUGHT I'D BETTER WASH MY HANDS FIRST!
4/6
SCHULZ

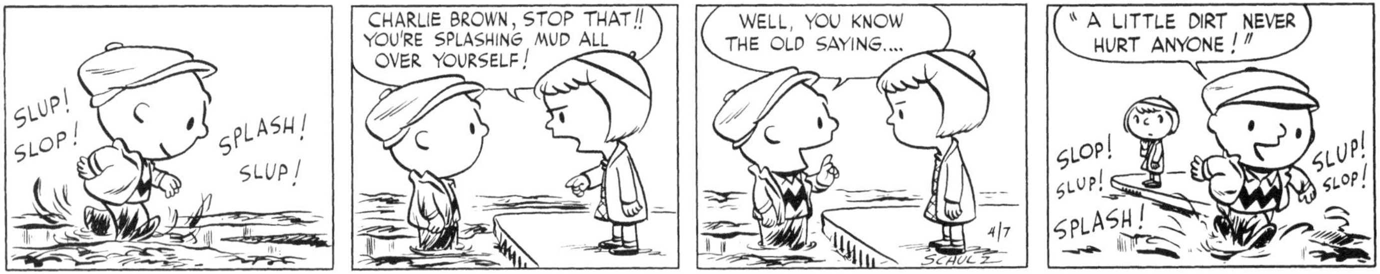
SLUP!
SLOP!
SPLASH!
SLUP!
CHARLIE BROWN, STOP THAT!! YOU'RE SPLASHING MUD ALL OVER YOURSELF!
WELL, YOU KNOW THE OLD SAYING....
4/7
SCHULZ
" A LITTLE DIRT NEVER HURT ANYONE! "
SLOP!
SLUP!
SPLASH!
SLUP!
SLOP!

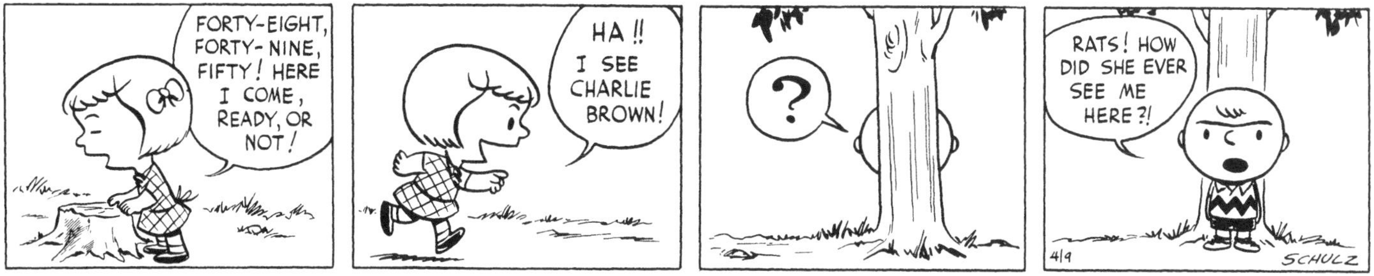
FORTY-EIGHT, FORTY-NINE, FIFTY! HERE I COME, READY, OR NOT!
HA !! I SEE CHARLIE BROWN!
?
RATS! HOW DID SHE EVER SEE ME HERE?!
4/9
SCHULZ

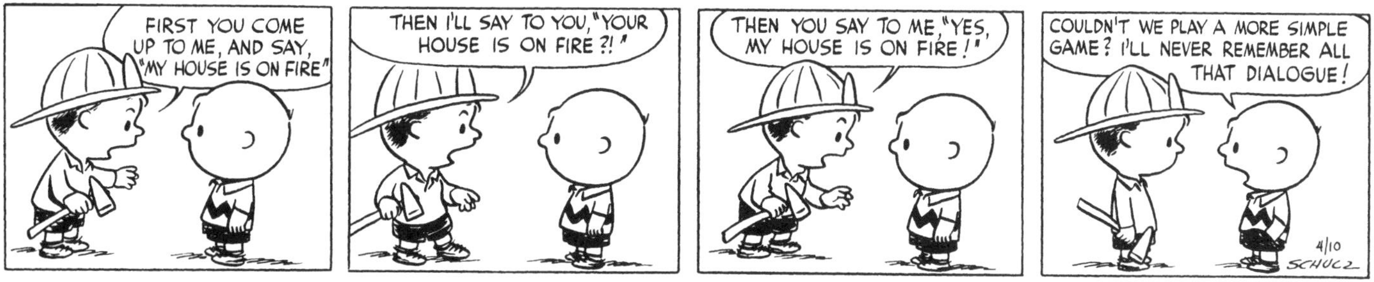
FIRST YOU COME UP TO ME, AND SAY, "MY HOUSE IS ON FIRE"
THEN I'LL SAY TO YOU, "YOUR HOUSE IS ON FIRE?!"
THEN YOU SAY TO ME, "YES, MY HOUSE IS ON FIRE!"
COULDN'T WE PLAY A MORE SIMPLE GAME? I'LL NEVER REMEMBER ALL THAT DIALOGUE!
4/10
SCHULZ

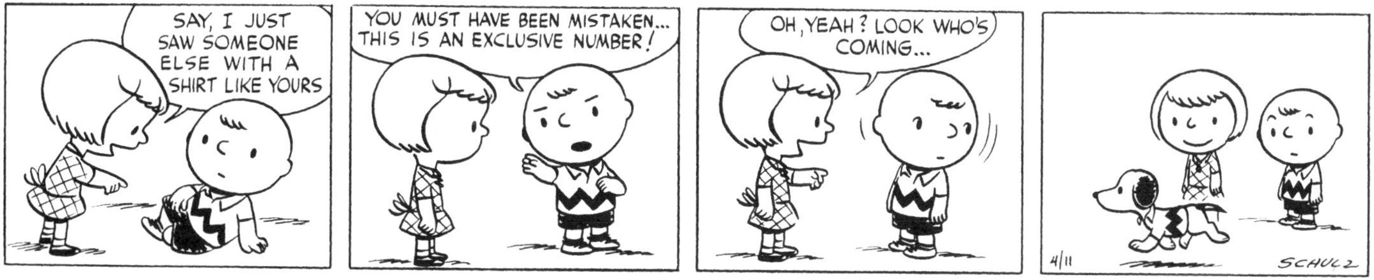
SAY, I JUST SAW SOMEONE ELSE WITH A SHIRT LIKE YOURS
YOU MUST HAVE BEEN MISTAKEN... THIS IS AN EXCLUSIVE NUMBER!
OH, YEAH? LOOK WHO'S COMING...
4/11
SCHULZ

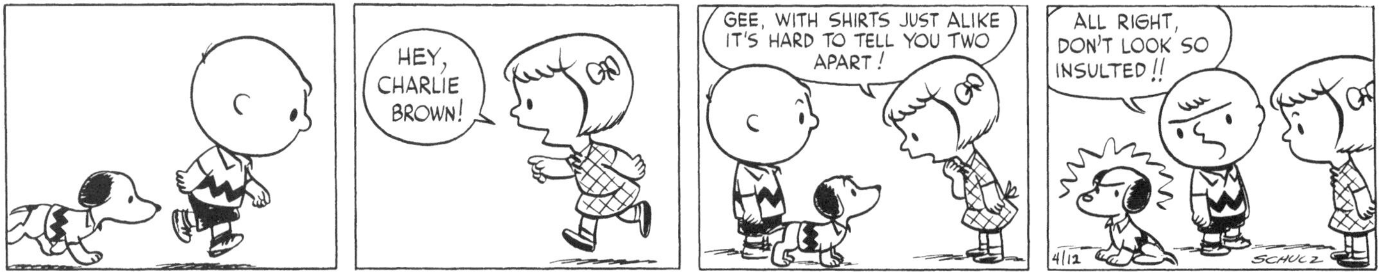
HEY, CHARLIE BROWN!
GEE, WITH SHIRTS JUST ALIKE IT'S HARD TO TELL YOU TWO APART!
ALL RIGHT, DON'T LOOK SO INSULTED!!
4/12
SCHULZ

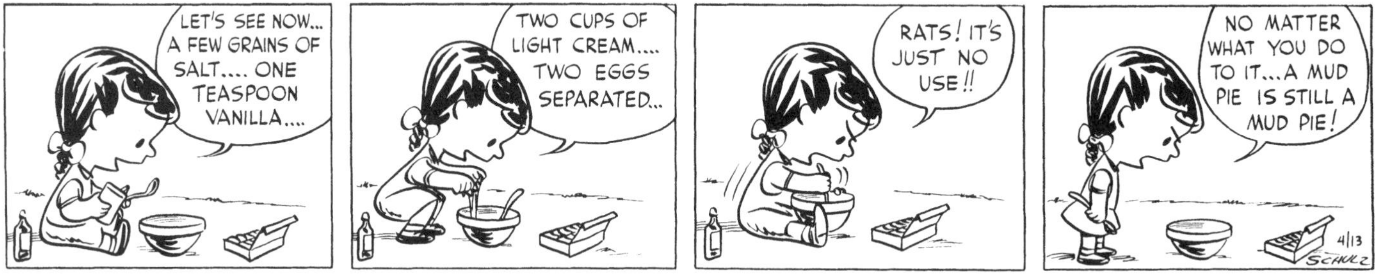
LET'S SEE NOW... A FEW GRAINS OF SALT.... ONE TEASPOON VANILLA....
TWO CUPS OF LIGHT CREAM.... TWO EGGS SEPARATED...
RATS! IT'S JUST NO USE!!
NO MATTER WHAT YOU DO TO IT...A MUD PIE IS STILL A MUD PIE!
4/13
SCHULZ

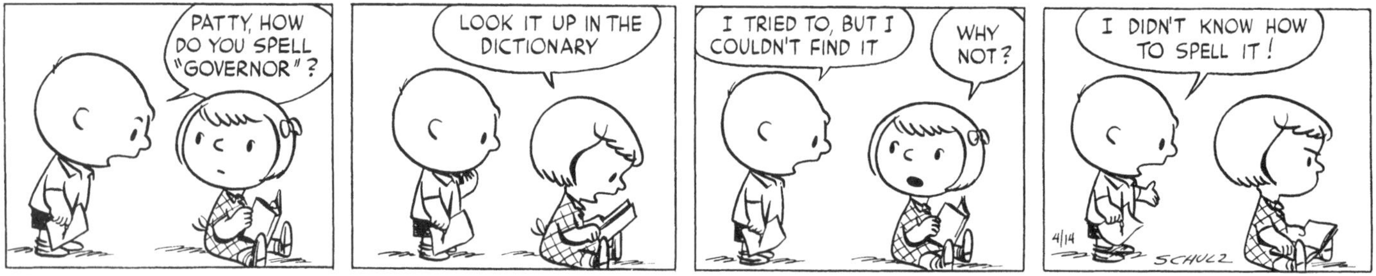
PATTY, HOW DO YOU SPELL "GOVERNOR"?
LOOK IT UP IN THE DICTIONARY
I TRIED TO, BUT I COULDN'T FIND IT
WHY NOT?
I DIDN'T KNOW HOW TO SPELL IT!
4/14
SCHULZ

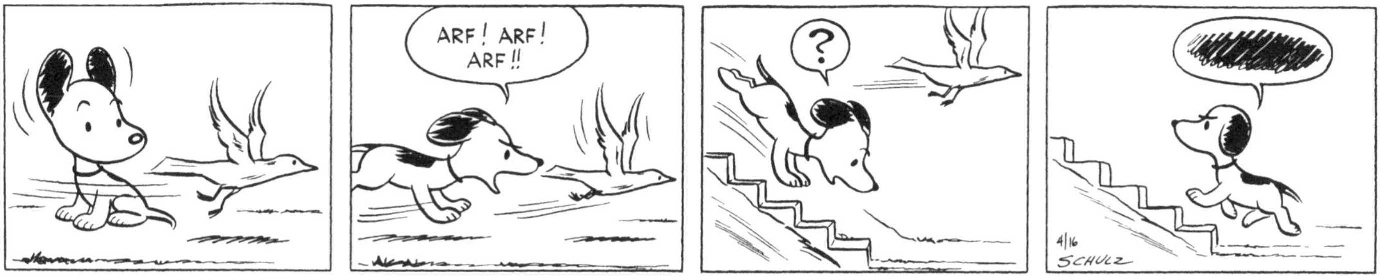
ARF! ARF! ARF!!
?
4/16
SCHULZ

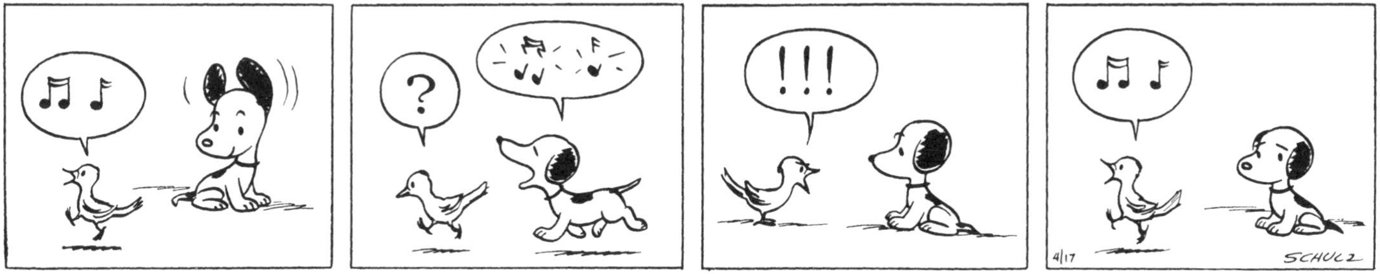
?
!!!
4/17
SCHULZ

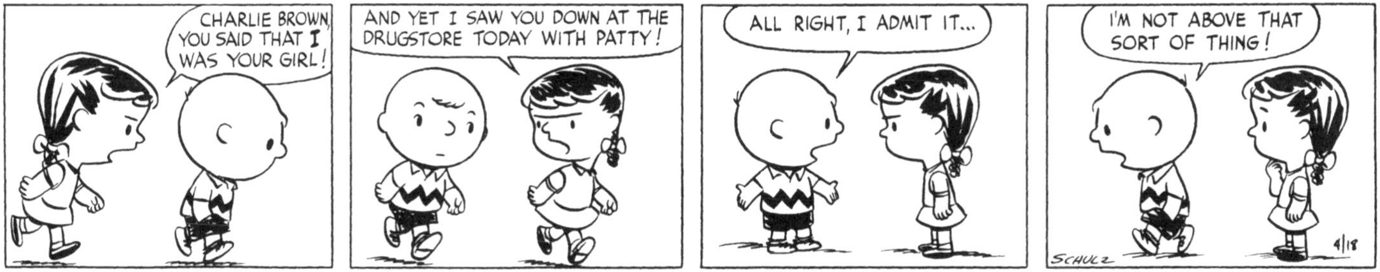
CHARLIE BROWN, YOU SAID THAT I WAS YOUR GIRL!
AND YET I SAW YOU DOWN AT THE DRUGSTORE TODAY WITH PATTY!
ALL RIGHT, I ADMIT IT...
I'M NOT ABOVE THAT SORT OF THING!
SCHULZ
4/18

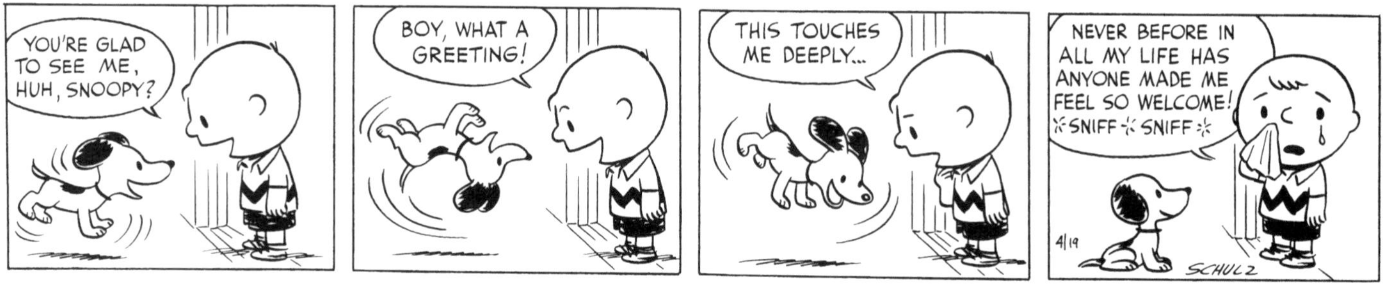
YOU'RE GLAD TO SEE ME, HUH, SNOOPY?
BOY, WHAT A GREETING!
THIS TOUCHES ME DEEPLY...
NEVER BEFORE IN ALL MY LIFE HAS ANYONE MADE ME FEEL SO WELCOME! *SNIFF* *SNIFF*
4/19
SCHULZ

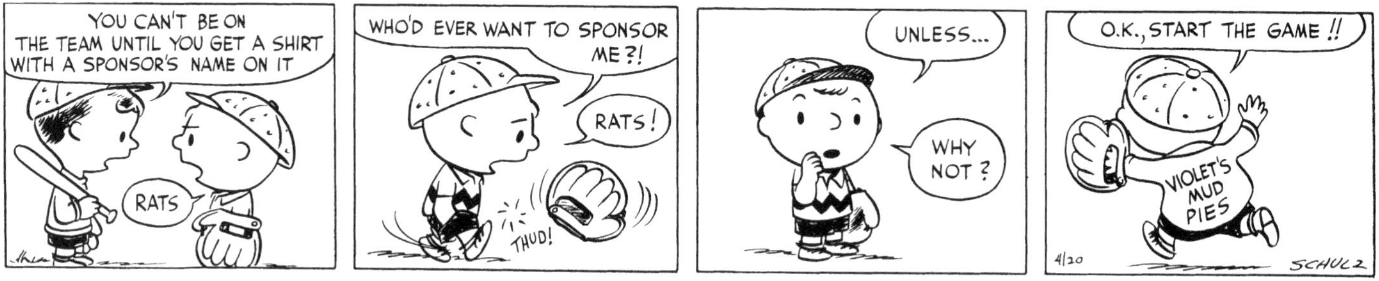
YOU CAN'T BE ON THE TEAM UNTIL YOU GET A SHIRT WITH A SPONSOR'S NAME ON IT
RATS
WHO'D EVER WANT TO SPONSOR ME?!
RATS!
THUD!
UNLESS...
WHY NOT?
O.K., START THE GAME!!
VIOLET'S MUD PIES
4/20
SCHULZ

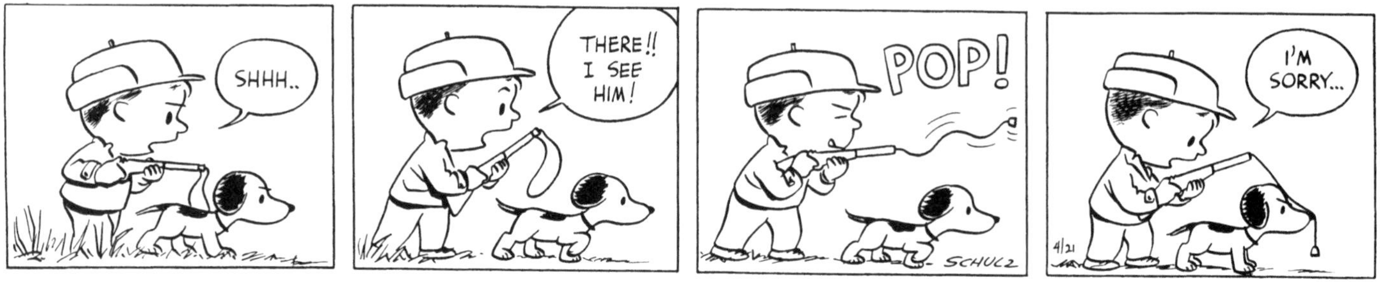
SHHH..
THERE!! I SEE HIM!
POP!
SCHULZ
I'M SORRY...
4/21

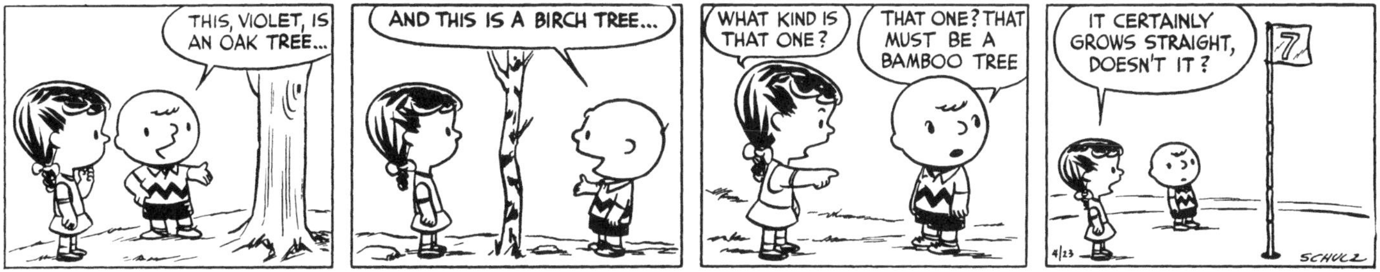
THIS, VIOLET, IS AN OAK TREE...
AND THIS IS A BIRCH TREE...
WHAT KIND IS THAT ONE?
THAT ONE? THAT MUST BE A BAMBOO TREE
IT CERTAINLY GROWS STRAIGHT, DOESN'T IT?
7
4/23
SCHULZ

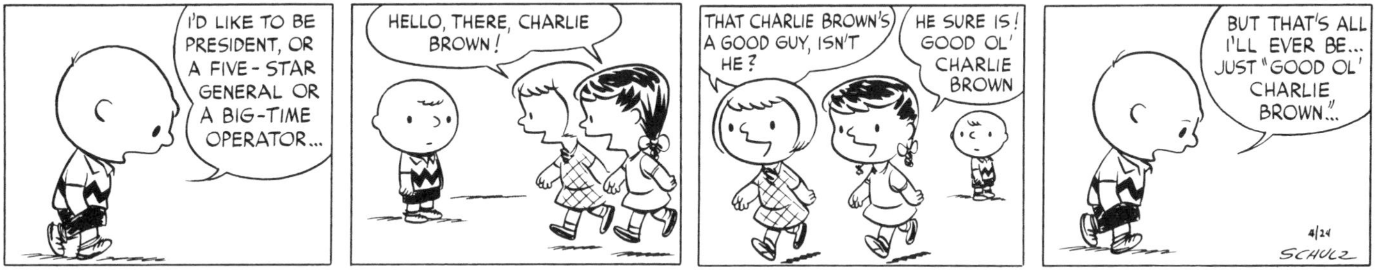
I'D LIKE TO BE PRESIDENT, OR A FIVE-STAR GENERAL OR A BIG-TIME OPERATOR...
HELLO, THERE, CHARLIE BROWN!
THAT CHARLIE BROWN'S A GOOD GUY, ISN'T HE?
HE SURE IS! GOOD OL' CHARLIE BROWN
BUT THAT'S ALL I'LL EVER BE... JUST "GOOD OL' CHARLIE BROWN."
4/24
SCHULZ

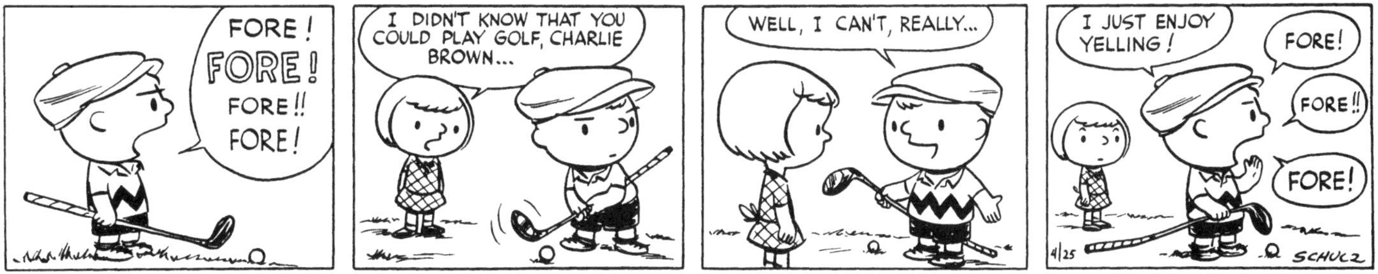
FORE! FORE! FORE!! FORE!
I DIDN'T KNOW THAT YOU COULD PLAY GOLF, CHARLIE BROWN...
WELL, I CAN'T, REALLY...
I JUST ENJOY YELLING!
FORE!
FORE!!
FORE!
4/25
SCHULZ

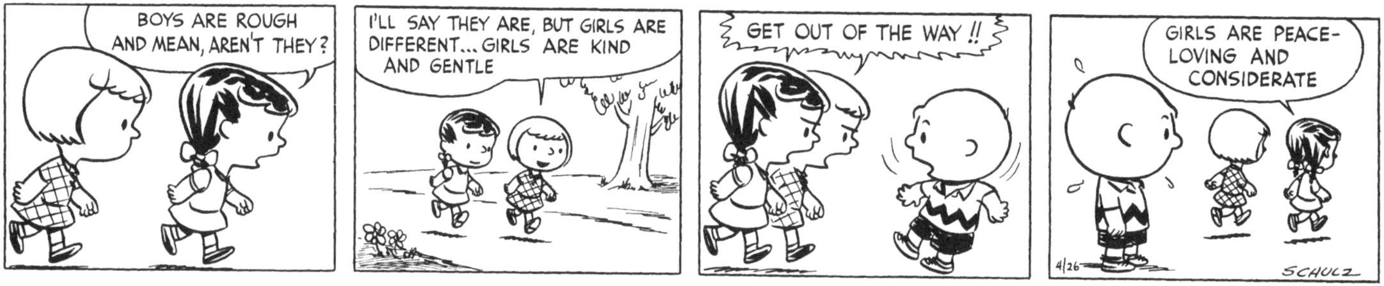
BOYS ARE ROUGH AND MEAN, AREN'T THEY?
I'LL SAY THEY ARE, BUT GIRLS ARE DIFFERENT... GIRLS ARE KIND AND GENTLE
GET OUT OF THE WAY!!
GIRLS ARE PEACE-LOVING AND CONSIDERATE
4/26
SCHULZ

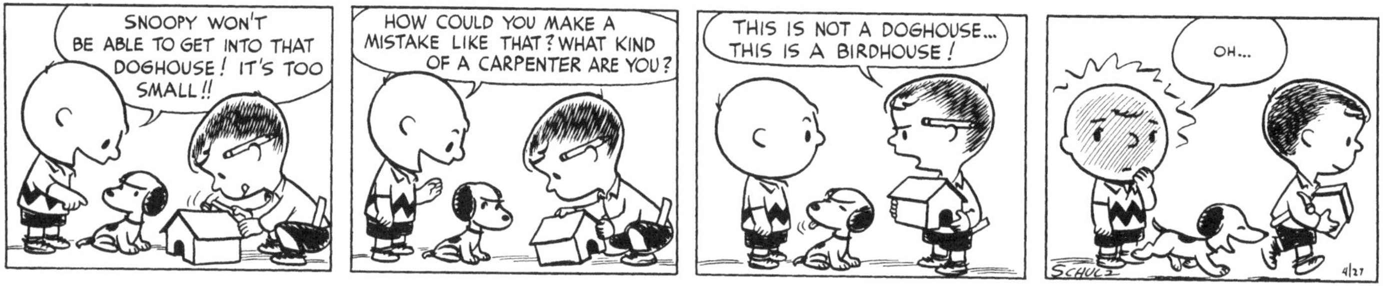
SNOOPY WON'T BE ABLE TO GET INTO THAT DOGHOUSE! IT'S TOO SMALL!!
HOW COULD YOU MAKE A MISTAKE LIKE THAT? WHAT KIND OF A CARPENTER ARE YOU?
THIS IS NOT A DOGHOUSE... THIS IS A BIRDHOUSE!
OH...
SCHULZ
4/27

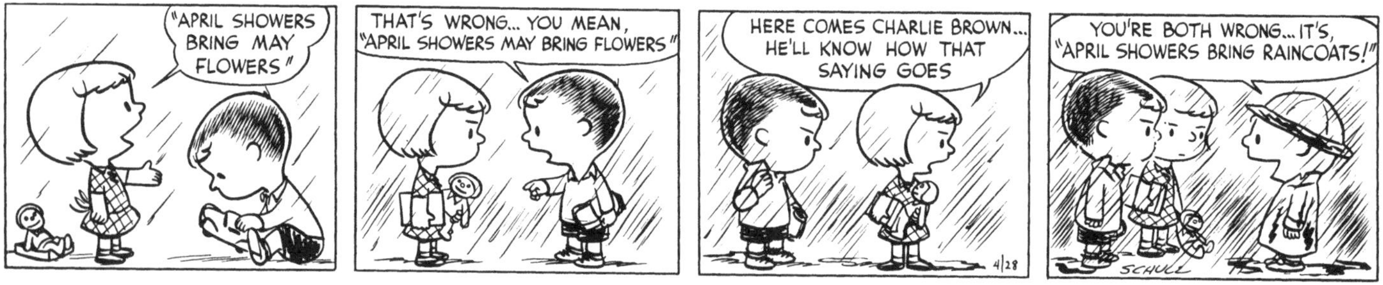
"APRIL SHOWERS BRING MAY FLOWERS"
THAT'S WRONG... YOU MEAN, "APRIL SHOWERS MAY BRING FLOWERS"
HERE COMES CHARLIE BROWN... HE'LL KNOW HOW THAT SAYING GOES
4/28
YOU'RE BOTH WRONG... IT'S, "APRIL SHOWERS BRING RAINCOATS!"
SCHULZ

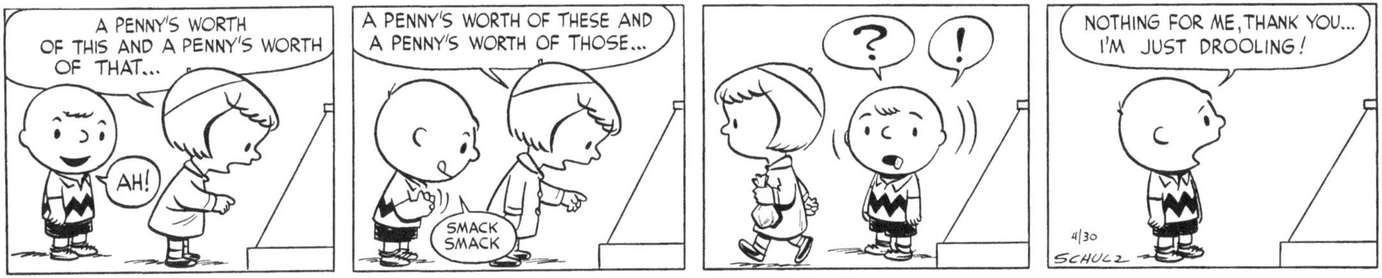
A PENNY'S WORTH OF THIS AND A PENNY'S WORTH OF THAT...
AH!
A PENNY'S WORTH OF THESE AND A PENNY'S WORTH OF THOSE...
SMACK SMACK
?
!
NOTHING FOR ME, THANK YOU... I'M JUST DROOLING!
4/30
SCHULZ

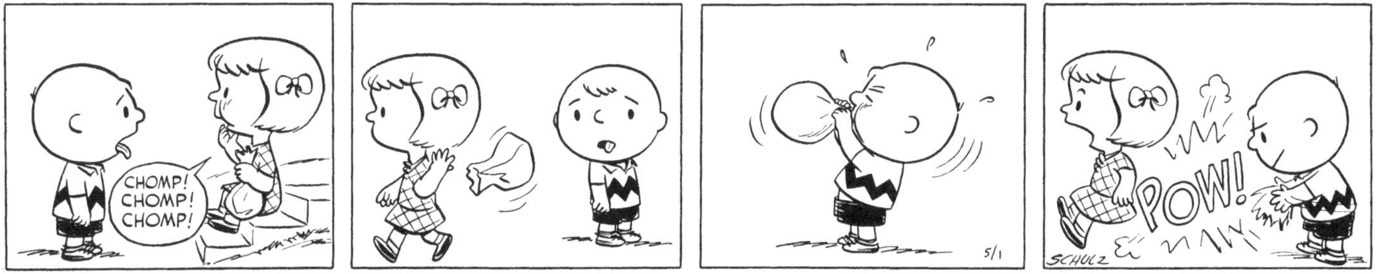
CHOMP! CHOMP! CHOMP!
5/1
POW!
SCHULZ

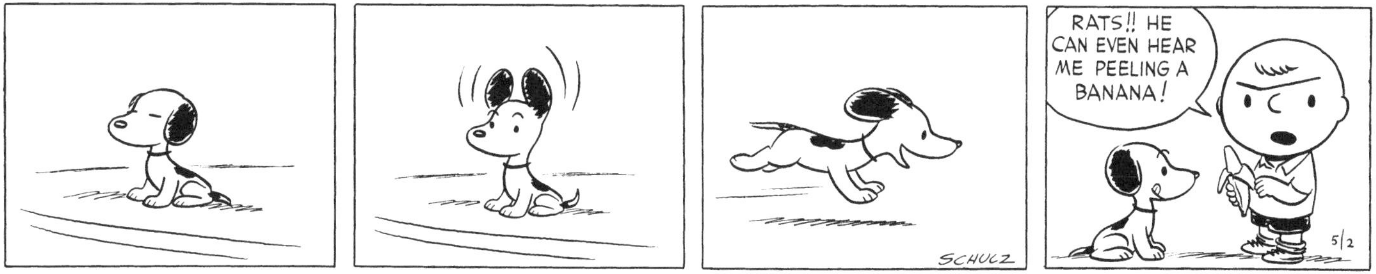
SCHULZ
RATS!! HE CAN EVEN HEAR ME PEELING A BANANA!
5/2

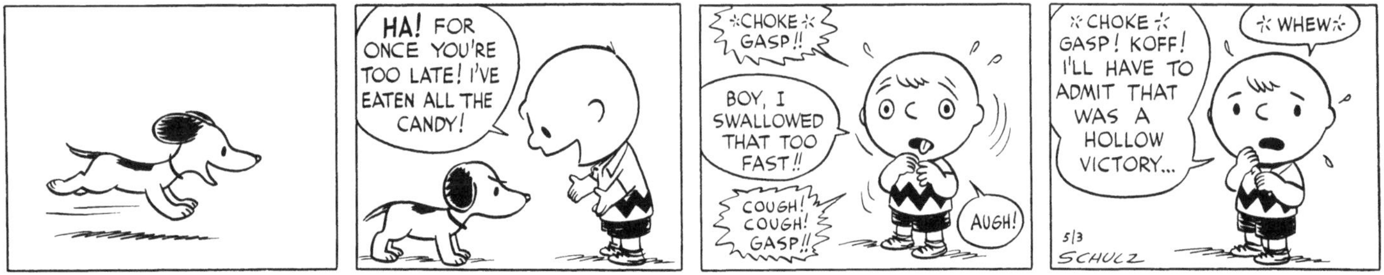
HA! FOR ONCE YOU'RE TOO LATE! I'VE EATEN ALL THE CANDY!
CHOKE GASP!!
BOY, I SWALLOWED THAT TOO FAST!!
COUGH! COUGH! GASP!!
AUGH!
CHOKE GASP! KOFF! I'LL HAVE TO ADMIT THAT WAS A HOLLOW VICTORY...
WHEW
5/3
SCHULZ

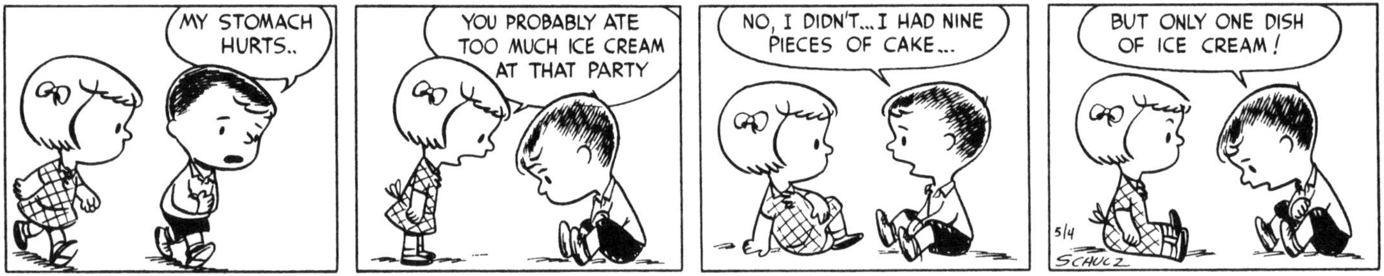
MY STOMACH HURTS..
YOU PROBABLY ATE TOO MUCH ICE CREAM AT THAT PARTY
NO, I DIDN'T... I HAD NINE PIECES OF CAKE...
BUT ONLY ONE DISH OF ICE CREAM!
5/4
SCHULZ

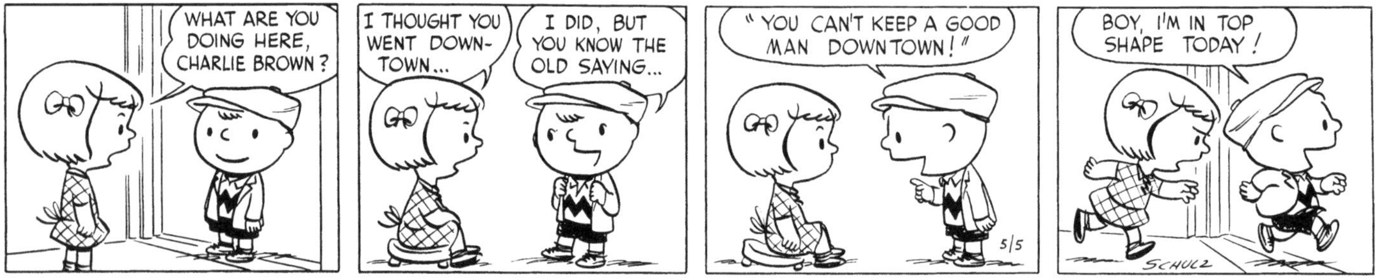
WHAT ARE YOU DOING HERE, CHARLIE BROWN?
I THOUGHT YOU WENT DOWN-TOWN...
I DID, BUT YOU KNOW THE OLD SAYING...
"YOU CAN'T KEEP A GOOD MAN DOWNTOWN!"
5/5
BOY, I'M IN TOP SHAPE TODAY!
SCHULZ

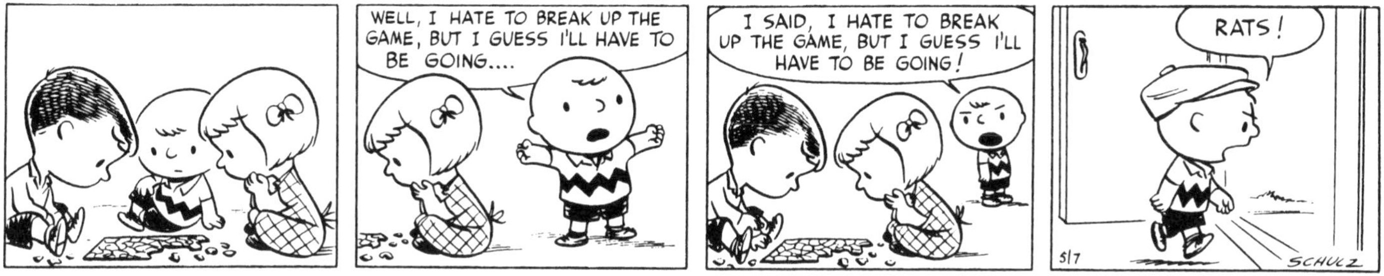
WELL, I HATE TO BREAK UP THE GAME, BUT I GUESS I'LL HAVE TO BE GOING....
I SAID, I HATE TO BREAK UP THE GAME, BUT I GUESS I'LL HAVE TO BE GOING!
RATS!
5/7
SCHULZ

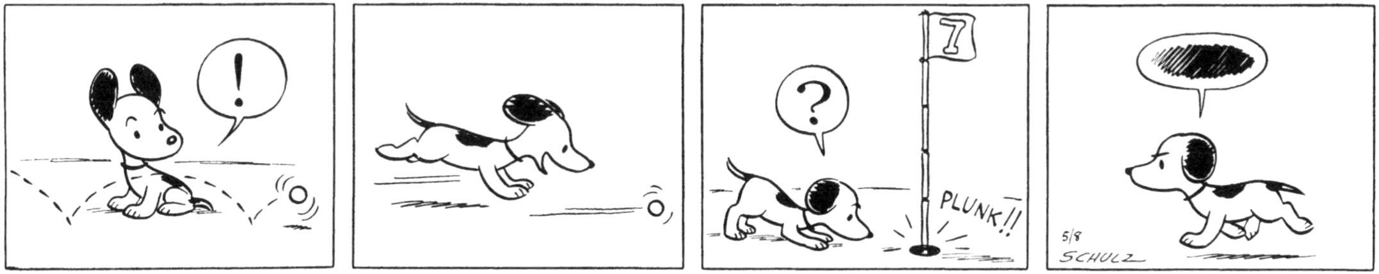
!
?
7
PLUNK!!
5/8
SCHULZ

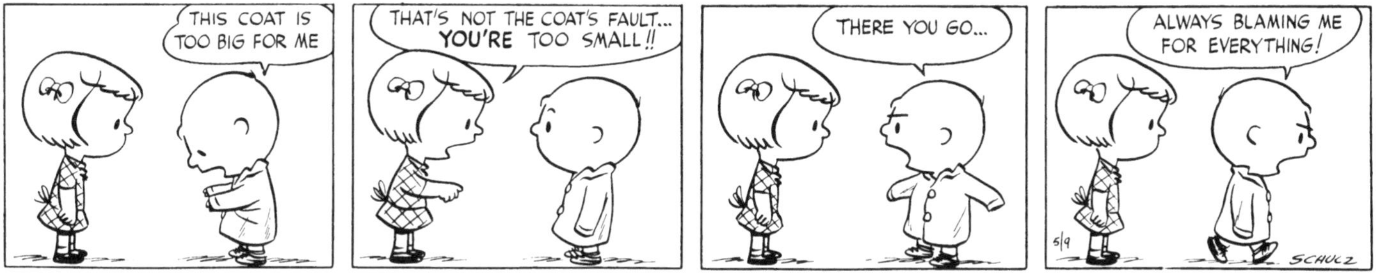
THIS COAT IS TOO BIG FOR ME
THAT'S NOT THE COAT'S FAULT... YOU'RE TOO SMALL!!
THERE YOU GO...
ALWAYS BLAMING ME FOR EVERYTHING!
5/9
SCHULZ

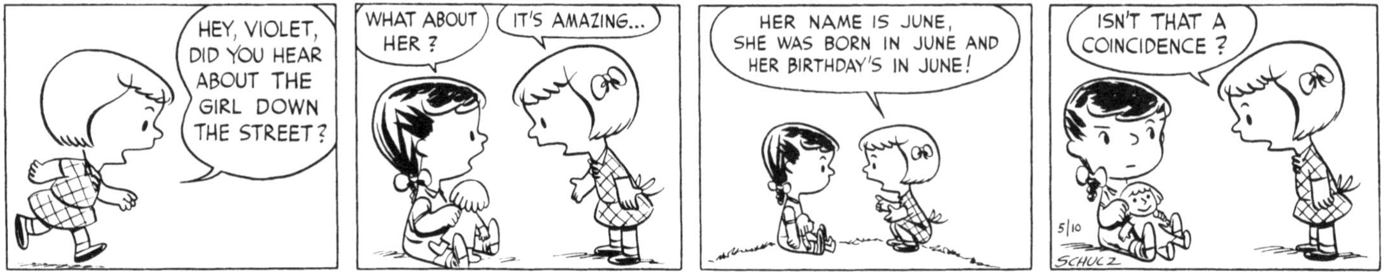
HEY, VIOLET, DID YOU HEAR ABOUT THE GIRL DOWN THE STREET?
WHAT ABOUT HER?
IT'S AMAZING...
HER NAME IS JUNE, SHE WAS BORN IN JUNE AND HER BIRTHDAY'S IN JUNE!
ISN'T THAT A COINCIDENCE?
5/10
SCHULZ

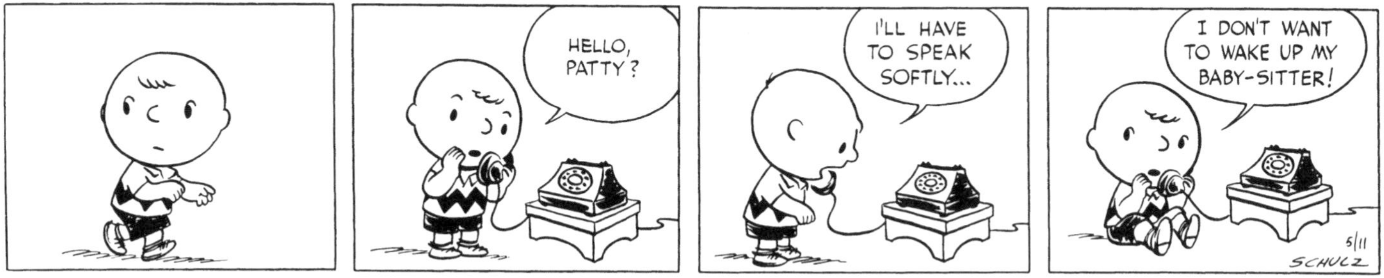
HELLO, PATTY?
I'LL HAVE TO SPEAK SOFTLY...
I DON'T WANT TO WAKE UP MY BABY-SITTER!
5/11
SCHULZ

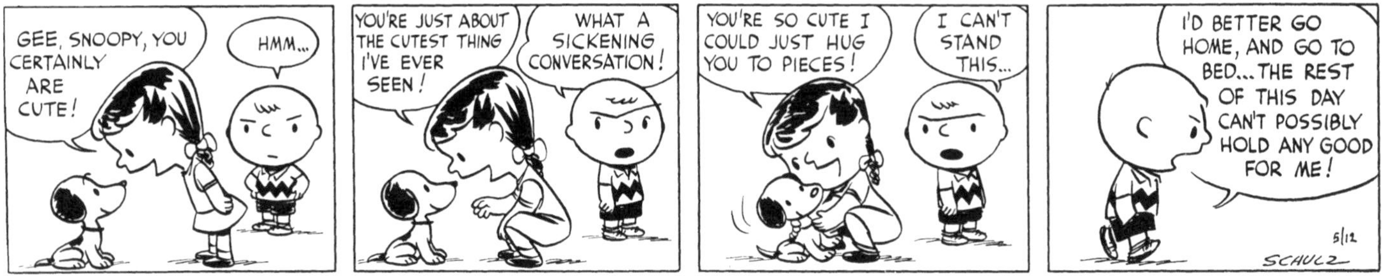
GEE, SNOOPY, YOU CERTAINLY ARE CUTE!
HMM...
YOU'RE JUST ABOUT THE CUTEST THING I'VE EVER SEEN!
WHAT A SICKENING CONVERSATION!
YOU'RE SO CUTE I COULD JUST HUG YOU TO PIECES!
I CAN'T STAND THIS...
I'D BETTER GO HOME, AND GO TO BED... THE REST OF THIS DAY CAN'T POSSIBLY HOLD ANY GOOD FOR ME!
5/12
SCHULZ

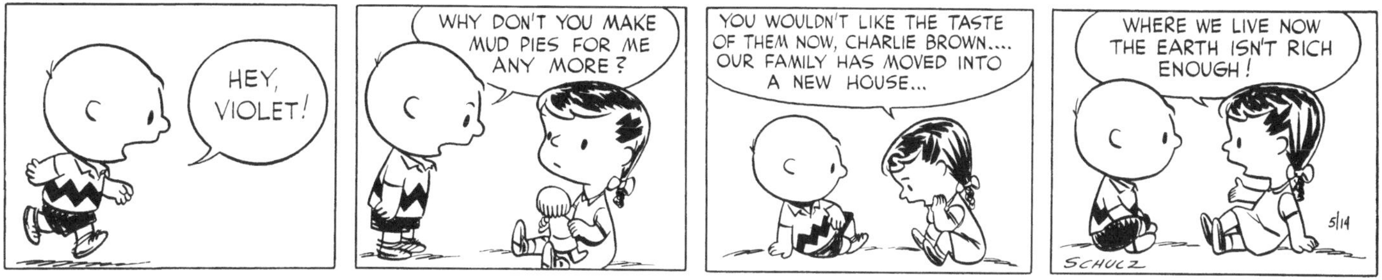
HEY, VIOLET!
WHY DON'T YOU MAKE MUD PIES FOR ME ANY MORE?
YOU WOULDN'T LIKE THE TASTE OF THEM NOW, CHARLIE BROWN.... OUR FAMILY HAS MOVED INTO A NEW HOUSE...
WHERE WE LIVE NOW THE EARTH ISN'T RICH ENOUGH!
5/14
SCHULZ

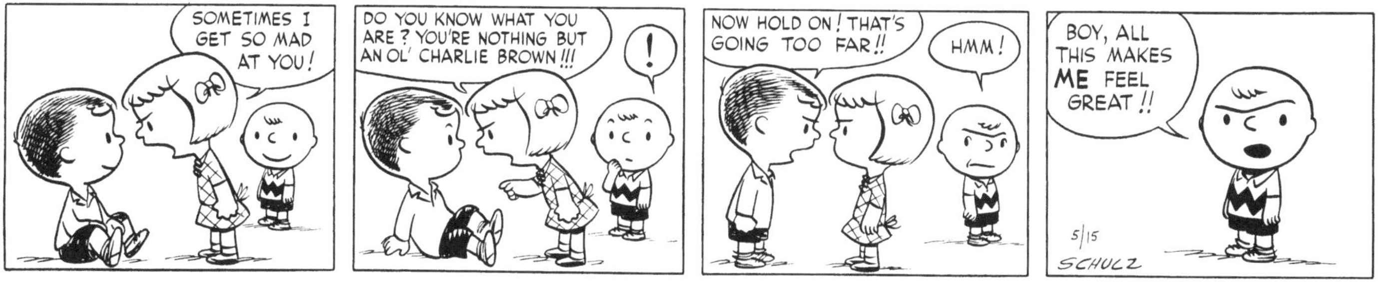
SOMETIMES I GET SO MAD AT YOU!
DO YOU KNOW WHAT YOU ARE? YOU'RE NOTHING BUT AN OL' CHARLIE BROWN!!!
!
NOW HOLD ON! THAT'S GOING TOO FAR!!
HMM!
BOY, ALL THIS MAKES ME FEEL GREAT!!
5/15
SCHULZ

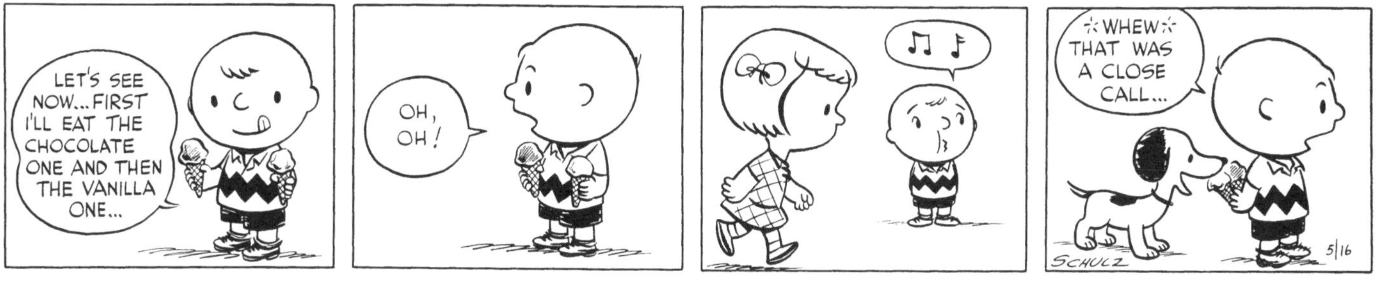
LET'S SEE NOW...FIRST I'LL EAT THE CHOCOLATE ONE AND THEN THE VANILLA ONE...
OH, OH!
WHEW THAT WAS A CLOSE CALL...
SCHULZ
5/16

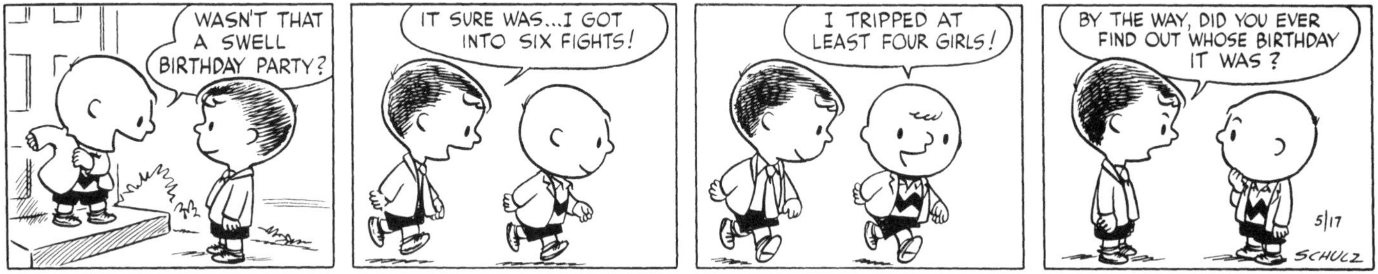
WASN'T THAT A SWELL BIRTHDAY PARTY?
IT SURE WAS...I GOT INTO SIX FIGHTS!
I TRIPPED AT LEAST FOUR GIRLS!
BY THE WAY, DID YOU EVER FIND OUT WHOSE BIRTHDAY IT WAS?
5/17
SCHULZ

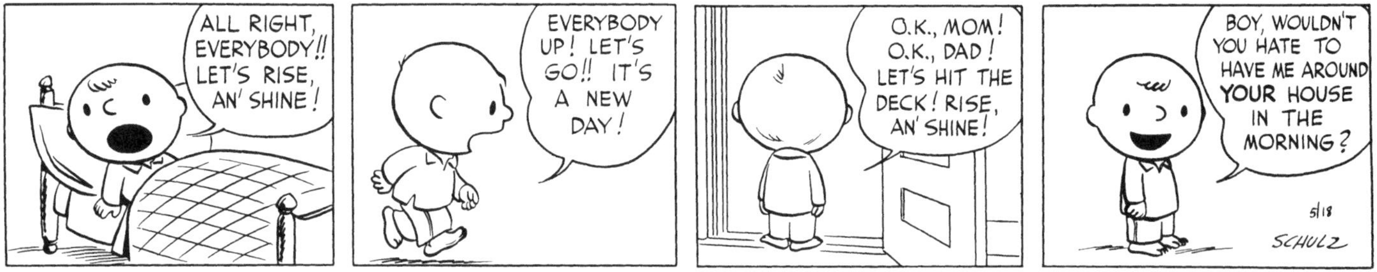
ALL RIGHT, EVERYBODY!! LET'S RISE, AN' SHINE!
EVERYBODY UP! LET'S GO!! IT'S A NEW DAY!
O.K., MOM! O.K., DAD! LET'S HIT THE DECK! RISE, AN' SHINE!
BOY, WOULDN'T YOU HATE TO HAVE ME AROUND YOUR HOUSE IN THE MORNING?
5/18
SCHULZ

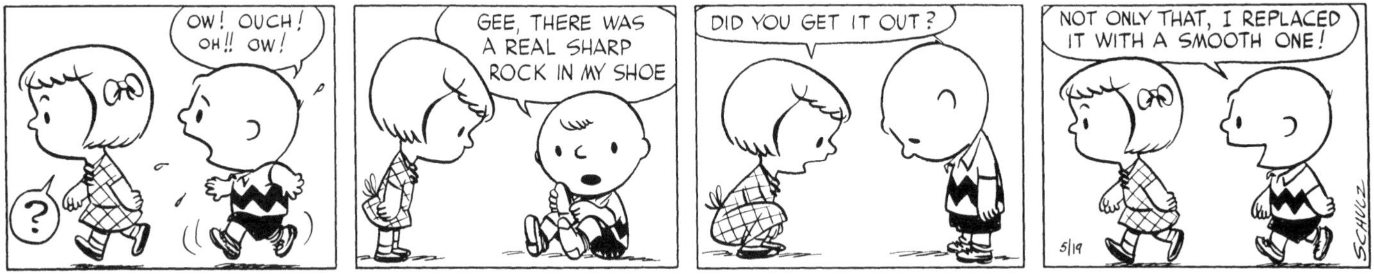
OW! OUCH! OH!! OW!
?
GEE, THERE WAS A REAL SHARP ROCK IN MY SHOE
DID YOU GET IT OUT?
NOT ONLY THAT, I REPLACED IT WITH A SMOOTH ONE!
5/19
SCHULZ

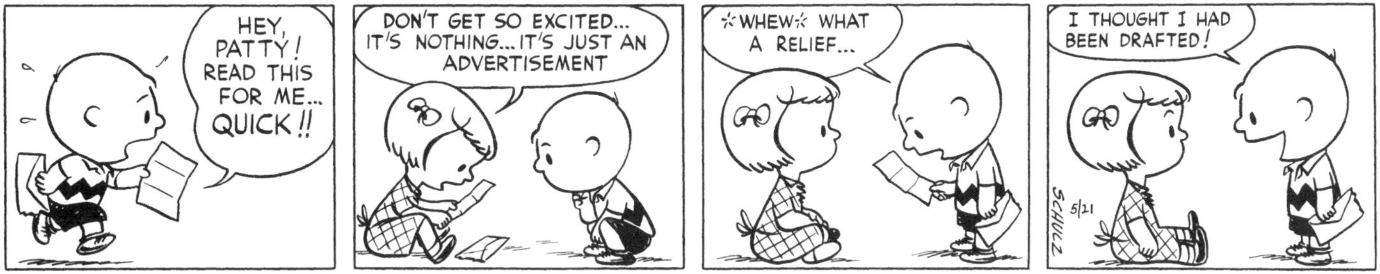
HEY, PATTY! READ THIS FOR ME... QUICK!!
DON'T GET SO EXCITED... IT'S NOTHING... IT'S JUST AN ADVERTISEMENT
WHEW WHAT A RELIEF...
I THOUGHT I HAD BEEN DRAFTED!
SCHULZ 5/21

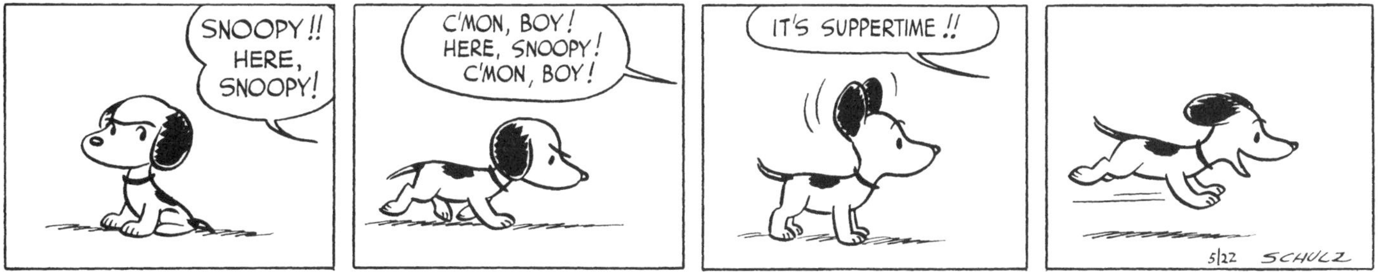
SNOOPY!! HERE, SNOOPY!
C'MON, BOY! HERE, SNOOPY! C'MON, BOY!
IT'S SUPPERTIME!!
5/22 SCHULZ

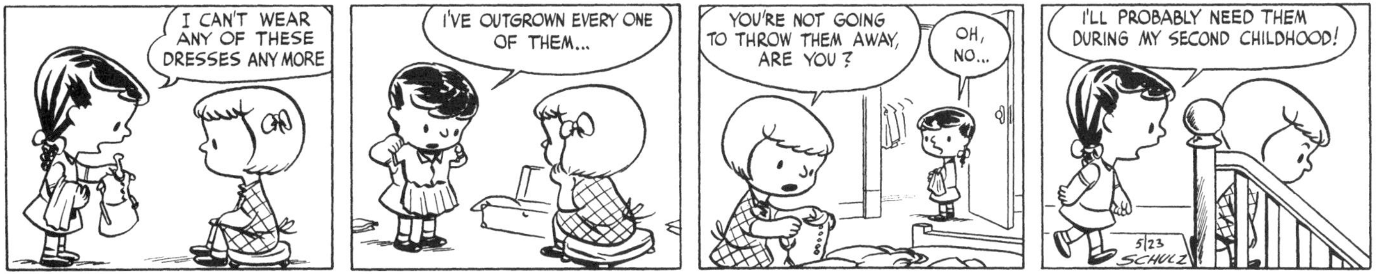
I CAN'T WEAR ANY OF THESE DRESSES ANY MORE
I'VE OUTGROWN EVERY ONE OF THEM...
YOU'RE NOT GOING TO THROW THEM AWAY, ARE YOU?
OH, NO...
I'LL PROBABLY NEED THEM DURING MY SECOND CHILDHOOD!
5/23 SCHULZ

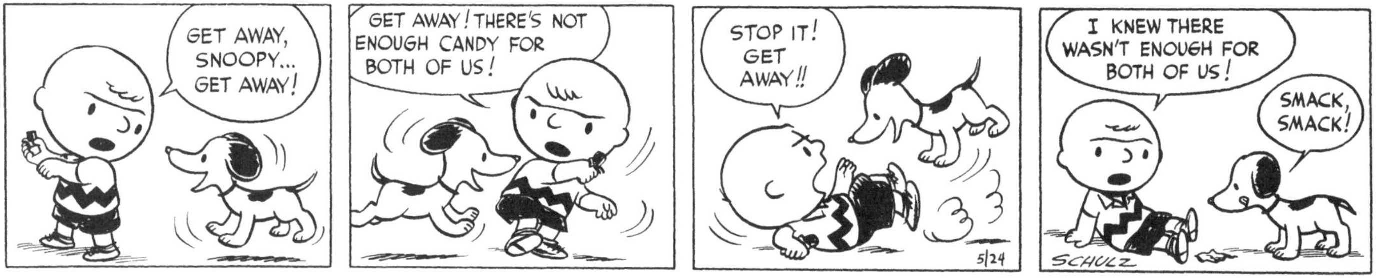
GET AWAY, SNOOPY... GET AWAY!
GET AWAY! THERE'S NOT ENOUGH CANDY FOR BOTH OF US!
STOP IT! GET AWAY!!
5/24
I KNEW THERE WASN'T ENOUGH FOR BOTH OF US!
SMACK, SMACK!
SCHULZ

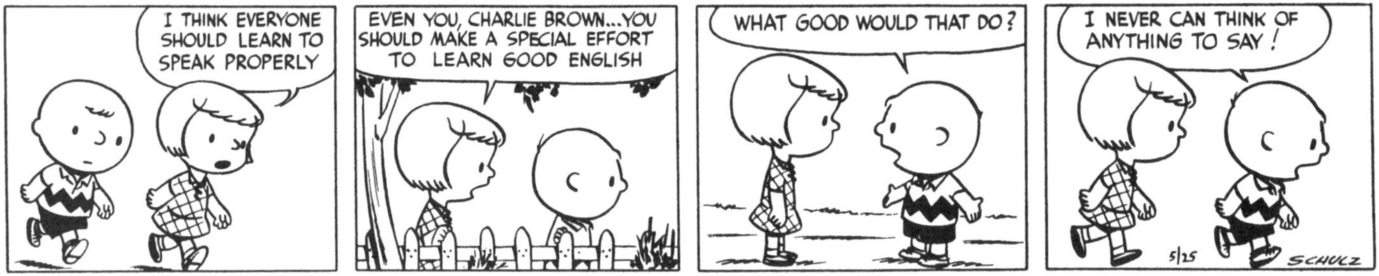
I THINK EVERYONE SHOULD LEARN TO SPEAK PROPERLY
EVEN YOU, CHARLIE BROWN...YOU SHOULD MAKE A SPECIAL EFFORT TO LEARN GOOD ENGLISH
WHAT GOOD WOULD THAT DO?
I NEVER CAN THINK OF ANYTHING TO SAY!
5/25
SCHULZ

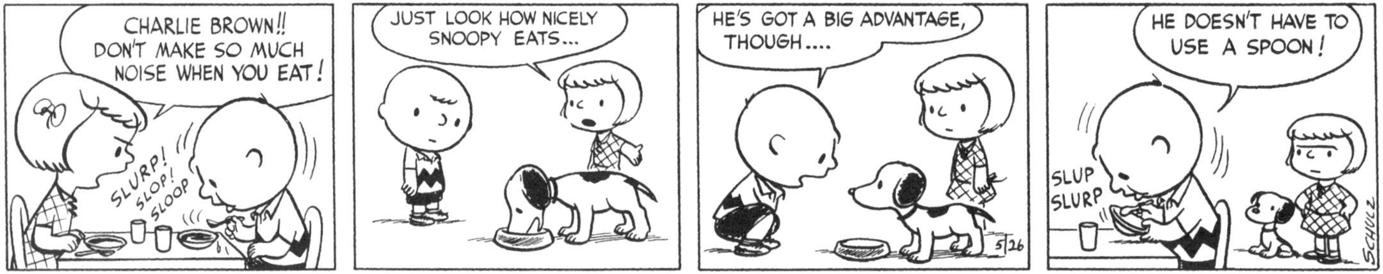
CHARLIE BROWN!! DON'T MAKE SO MUCH NOISE WHEN YOU EAT!
SLURP! SLOP! SLOOP
JUST LOOK HOW NICELY SNOOPY EATS...
HE'S GOT A BIG ADVANTAGE, THOUGH....
5/26
HE DOESN'T HAVE TO USE A SPOON!
SLUP SLURP
SCHULZ

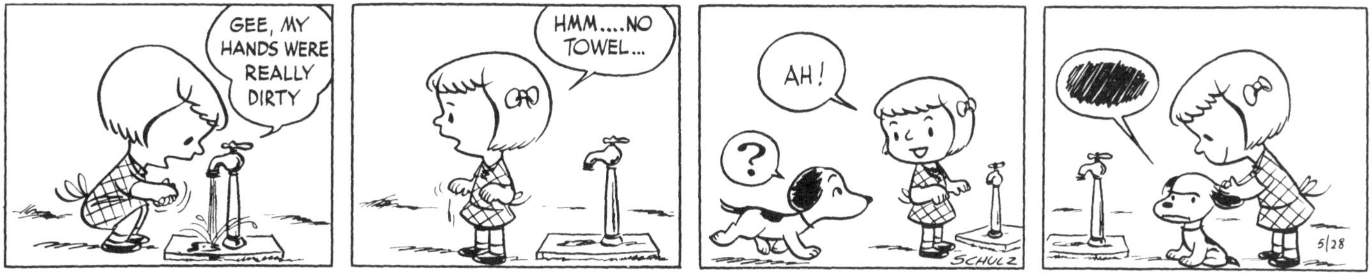
GEE, MY HANDS WERE REALLY DIRTY
HMM....NO TOWEL...
AH!
?
SCHULZ
5/28

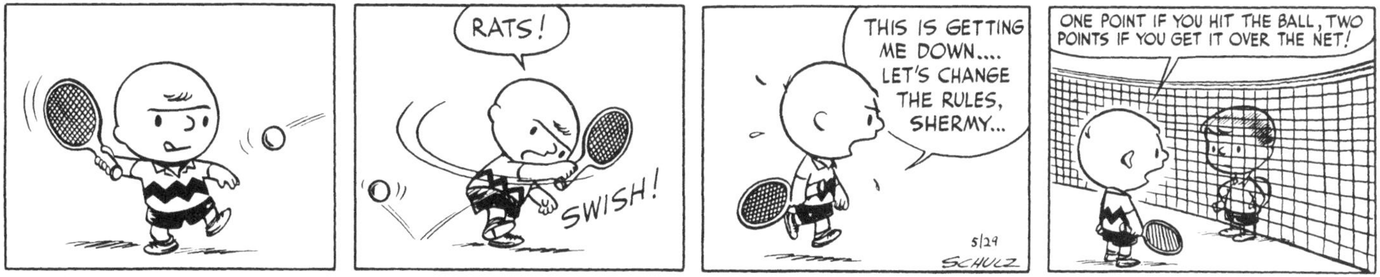
RATS!
SWISH!
THIS IS GETTING ME DOWN.... LET'S CHANGE THE RULES, SHERMY...
5/29
SCHULZ
ONE POINT IF YOU HIT THE BALL, TWO POINTS IF YOU GET IT OVER THE NET!

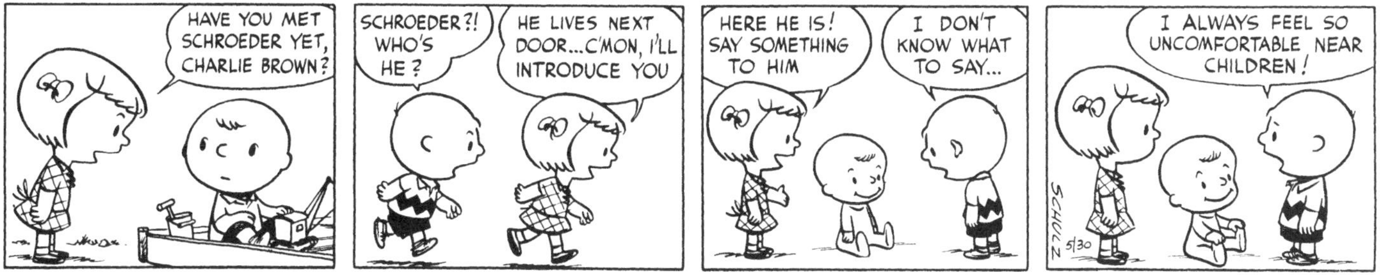
HAVE YOU MET SCHROEDER YET, CHARLIE BROWN?
SCHROEDER?! WHO'S HE?
HE LIVES NEXT DOOR...C'MON, I'LL INTRODUCE YOU
HERE HE IS! SAY SOMETHING TO HIM
I DON'T KNOW WHAT TO SAY...
SCHULZ
5/30
I ALWAYS FEEL SO UNCOMFORTABLE NEAR CHILDREN!

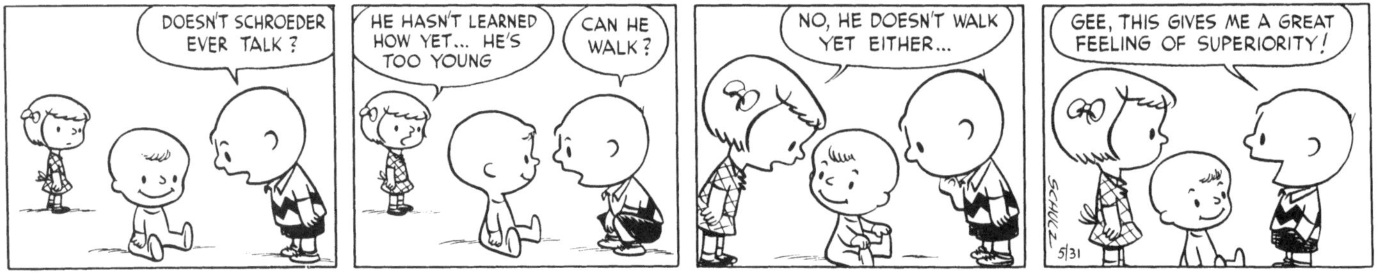
DOESN'T SCHROEDER EVER TALK ?
HE HASN'T LEARNED HOW YET... HE'S TOO YOUNG
CAN HE WALK ?
NO, HE DOESN'T WALK YET EITHER...
GEE, THIS GIVES ME A GREAT FEELING OF SUPERIORITY!
SCHULZ
5/31

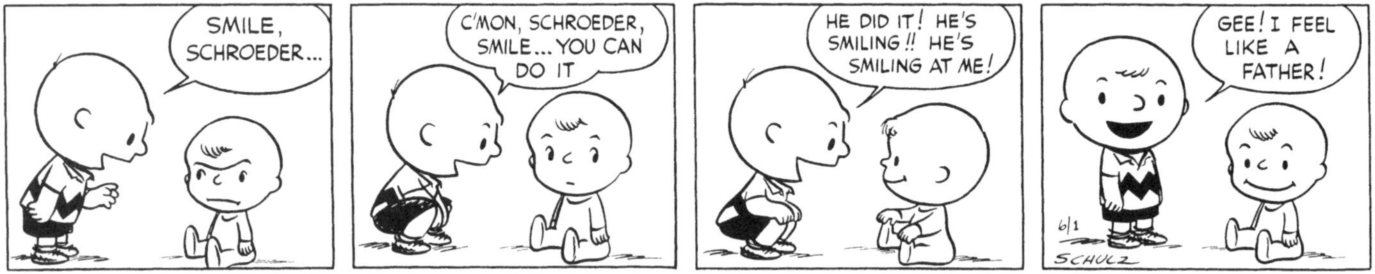
SMILE, SCHROEDER...
C'MON, SCHROEDER, SMILE... YOU CAN DO IT
HE DID IT! HE'S SMILING!! HE'S SMILING AT ME!
GEE! I FEEL LIKE A FATHER!
6/1
SCHULZ

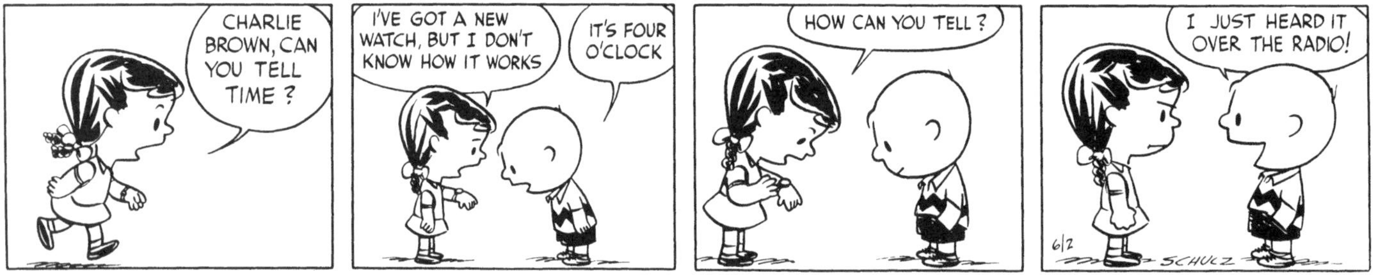
CHARLIE BROWN, CAN YOU TELL TIME ?
I'VE GOT A NEW WATCH, BUT I DON'T KNOW HOW IT WORKS
IT'S FOUR O'CLOCK
HOW CAN YOU TELL ?
I JUST HEARD IT OVER THE RADIO!
6/2
SCHULZ

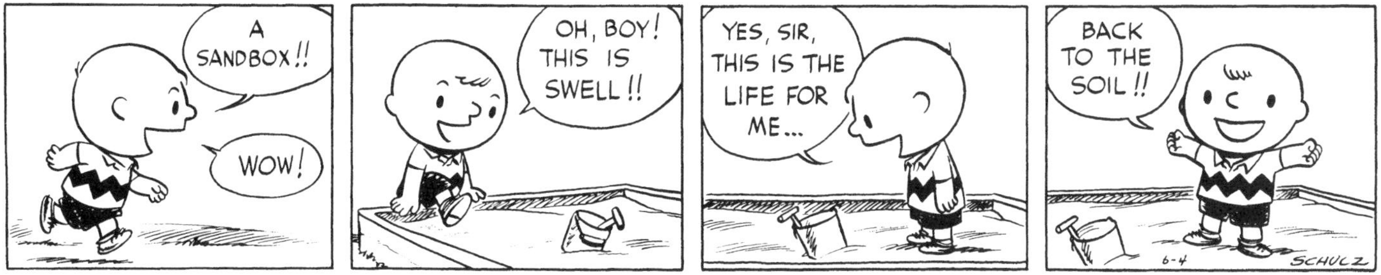
A SANDBOX!!
WOW!
OH, BOY! THIS IS SWELL!!
YES, SIR, THIS IS THE LIFE FOR ME...
BACK TO THE SOIL!!
6-4
SCHULZ

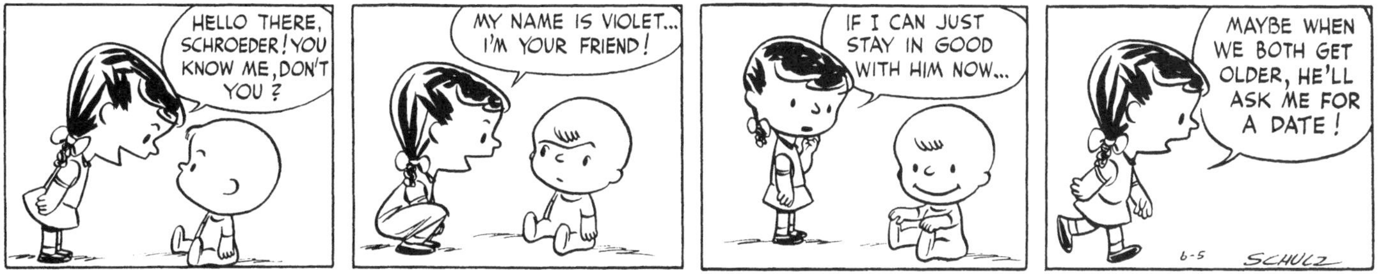
HELLO THERE, SCHROEDER! YOU KNOW ME, DON'T YOU?
MY NAME IS VIOLET... I'M YOUR FRIEND!
IF I CAN JUST STAY IN GOOD WITH HIM NOW...
MAYBE WHEN WE BOTH GET OLDER, HE'LL ASK ME FOR A DATE!
6-5
SCHULZ

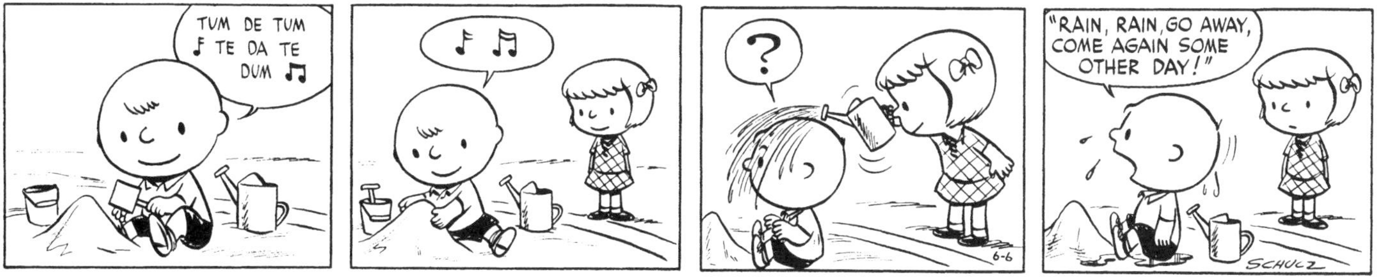
TUM DE TUM
TE DA TE
DUM
?
6-6
"RAIN, RAIN, GO AWAY, COME AGAIN SOME OTHER DAY!"
SCHULZ

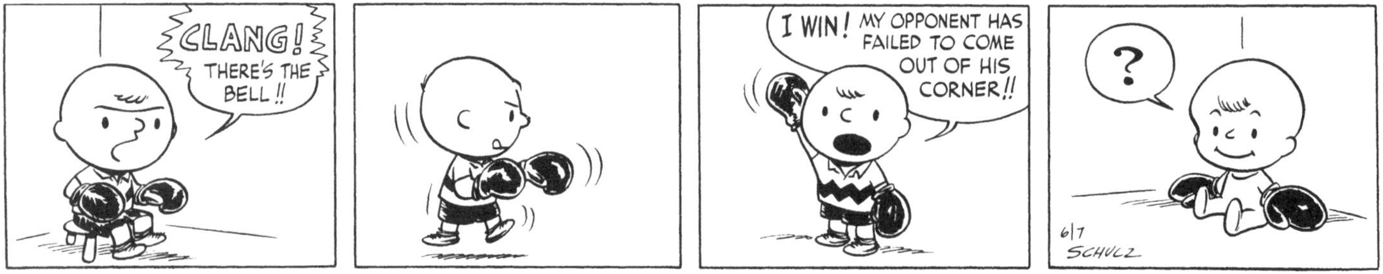
CLANG! THERE'S THE BELL !!
I WIN! MY OPPONENT HAS FAILED TO COME OUT OF HIS CORNER!!
?
6/7
SCHULZ

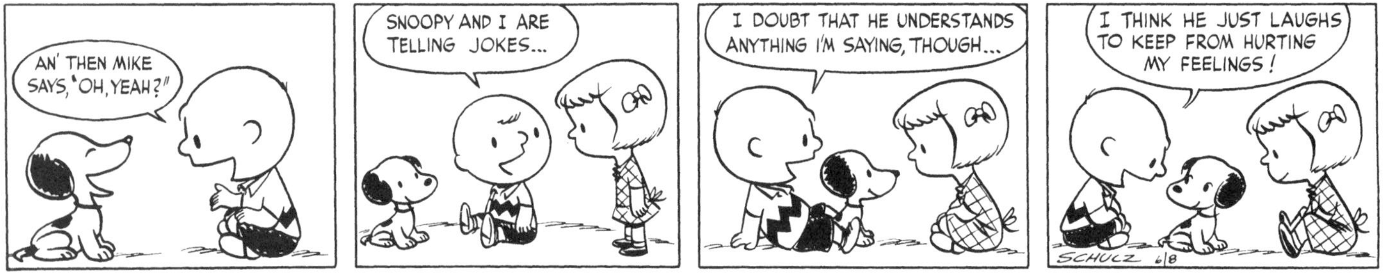
AN' THEN MIKE SAYS, "OH, YEAH?"
SNOOPY AND I ARE TELLING JOKES...
I DOUBT THAT HE UNDERSTANDS ANYTHING I'M SAYING, THOUGH...
I THINK HE JUST LAUGHS TO KEEP FROM HURTING MY FEELINGS!
SCHULZ 6/8

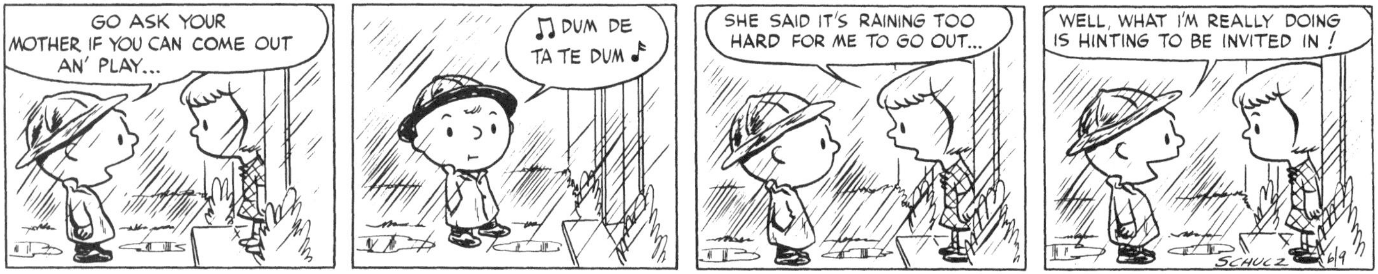
GO ASK YOUR MOTHER IF YOU CAN COME OUT AN' PLAY...
DUM DE TA TE DUM
SHE SAID IT'S RAINING TOO HARD FOR ME TO GO OUT...
WELL, WHAT I'M REALLY DOING IS HINTING TO BE INVITED IN!
SCHULZ 6/9

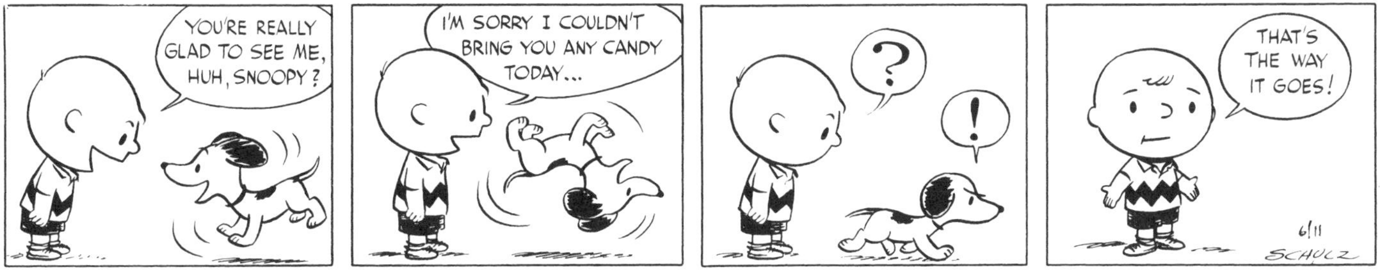
YOU'RE REALLY GLAD TO SEE ME, HUH, SNOOPY?
I'M SORRY I COULDN'T BRING YOU ANY CANDY TODAY...
?
!
THAT'S THE WAY IT GOES!
6/11
SCHULZ

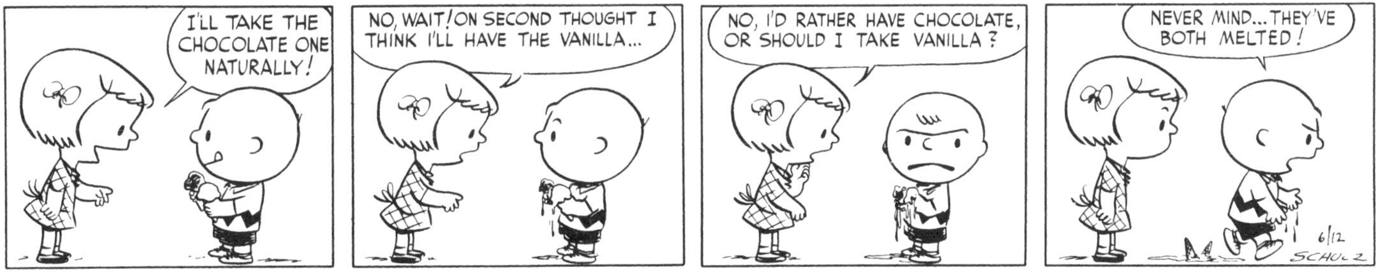
I'LL TAKE THE CHOCOLATE ONE NATURALLY!
NO, WAIT! ON SECOND THOUGHT I THINK I'LL HAVE THE VANILLA...
NO, I'D RATHER HAVE CHOCOLATE, OR SHOULD I TAKE VANILLA?
NEVER MIND...THEY'VE BOTH MELTED!
6/12
SCHULZ

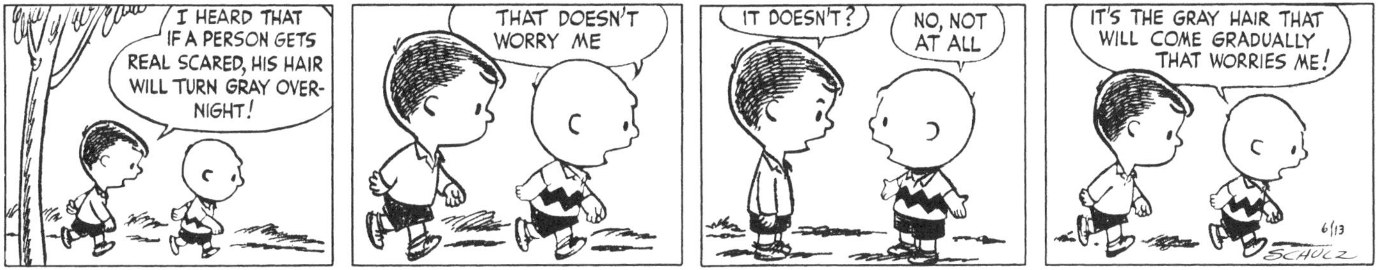
I HEARD THAT IF A PERSON GETS REAL SCARED, HIS HAIR WILL TURN GRAY OVER-NIGHT!
THAT DOESN'T WORRY ME
IT DOESN'T?
NO, NOT AT ALL
IT'S THE GRAY HAIR THAT WILL COME GRADUALLY THAT WORRIES ME!
6/13
SCHULZ

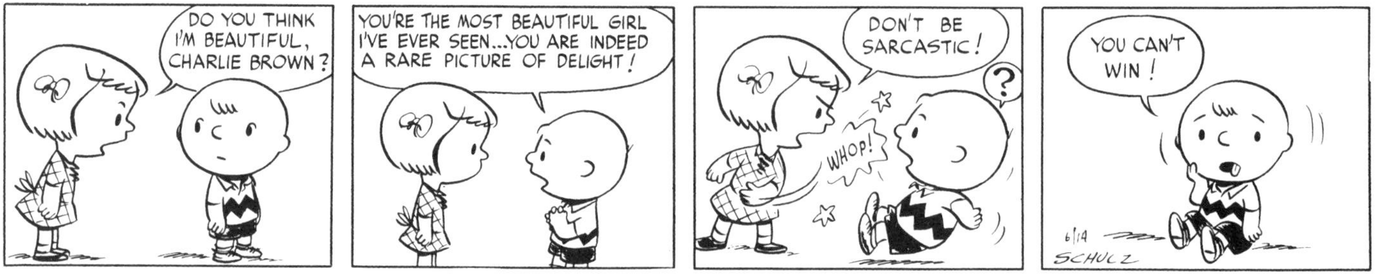
DO YOU THINK I'M BEAUTIFUL, CHARLIE BROWN?
YOU'RE THE MOST BEAUTIFUL GIRL I'VE EVER SEEN...YOU ARE INDEED A RARE PICTURE OF DELIGHT!
DON'T BE SARCASTIC!
?
WHOP!
YOU CAN'T WIN!
6/14
SCHULZ

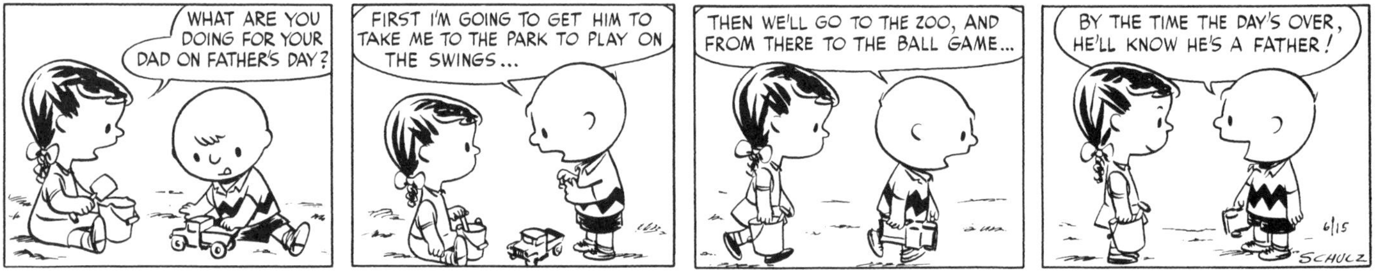
WHAT ARE YOU DOING FOR YOUR DAD ON FATHER'S DAY?
FIRST I'M GOING TO GET HIM TO TAKE ME TO THE PARK TO PLAY ON THE SWINGS...
THEN WE'LL GO TO THE ZOO, AND FROM THERE TO THE BALL GAME...
BY THE TIME THE DAY'S OVER, HE'LL KNOW HE'S A FATHER!
6/15
SCHULZ

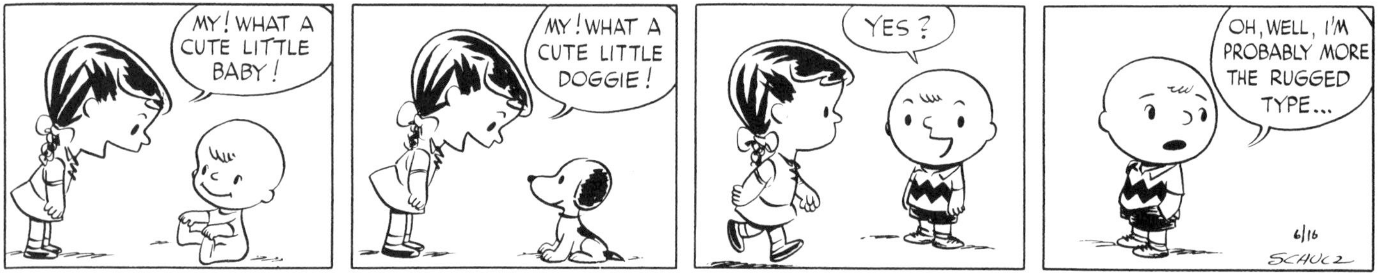
MY! WHAT A CUTE LITTLE BABY!
MY! WHAT A CUTE LITTLE DOGGIE!
YES?
OH, WELL, I'M PROBABLY MORE THE RUGGED TYPE...
6/16
SCHULZ

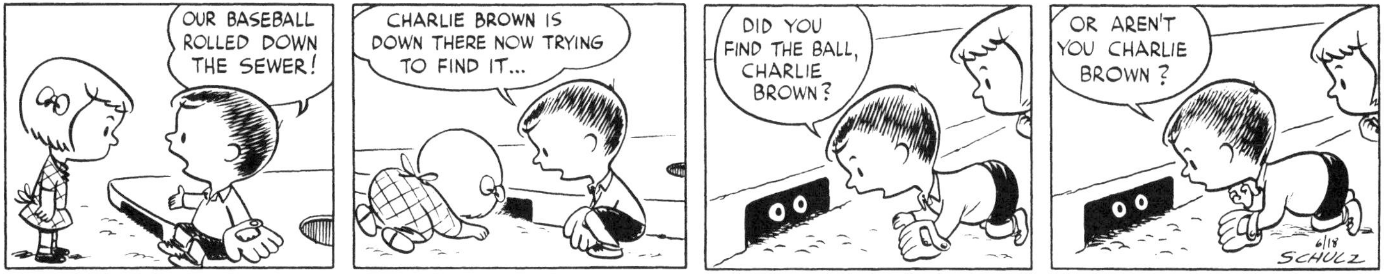
OUR BASEBALL ROLLED DOWN THE SEWER!
CHARLIE BROWN IS DOWN THERE NOW TRYING TO FIND IT...
DID YOU FIND THE BALL, CHARLIE BROWN?
OR AREN'T YOU CHARLIE BROWN?
6/18
SCHULZ

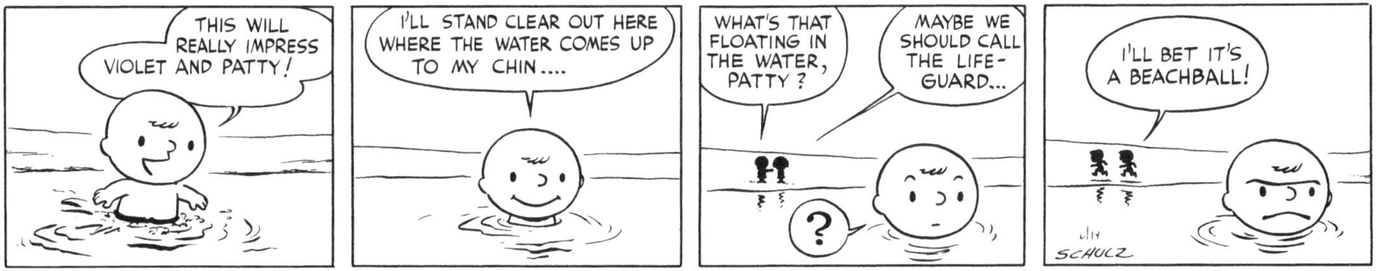
THIS WILL REALLY IMPRESS VIOLET AND PATTY!
I'LL STAND CLEAR OUT HERE WHERE THE WATER COMES UP TO MY CHIN....
WHAT'S THAT FLOATING IN THE WATER, PATTY?
MAYBE WE SHOULD CALL THE LIFE-GUARD...
?
I'LL BET IT'S A BEACHBALL!
SCHULZ

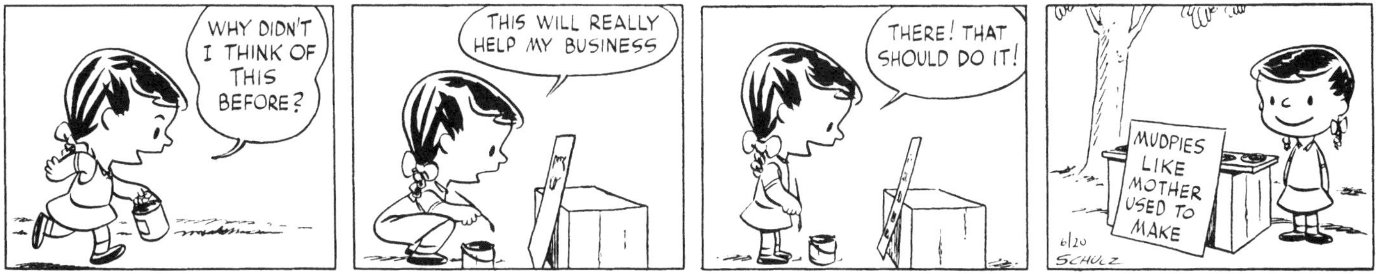
WHY DIDN'T I THINK OF THIS BEFORE?
THIS WILL REALLY HELP MY BUSINESS
THERE! THAT SHOULD DO IT!
MUDPIES LIKE MOTHER USED TO MAKE
6/20
SCHULZ

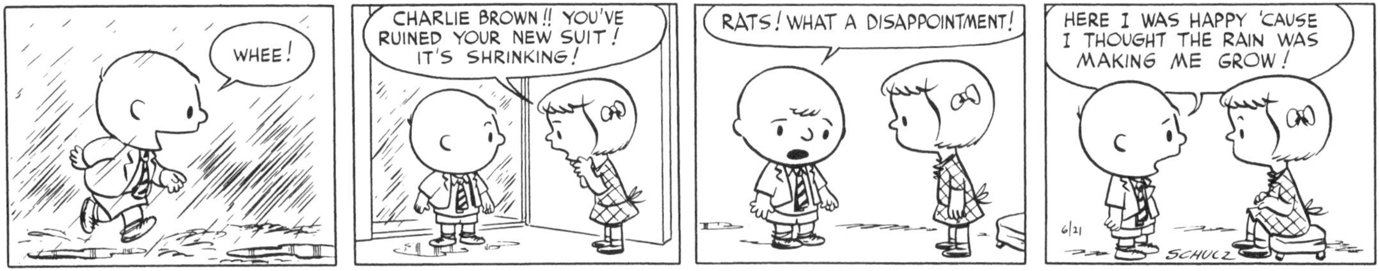
WHEE!
CHARLIE BROWN!! YOU'VE RUINED YOUR NEW SUIT! IT'S SHRINKING!
RATS! WHAT A DISAPPOINTMENT!
HERE I WAS HAPPY 'CAUSE I THOUGHT THE RAIN WAS MAKING ME GROW!
6/21
SCHULZ

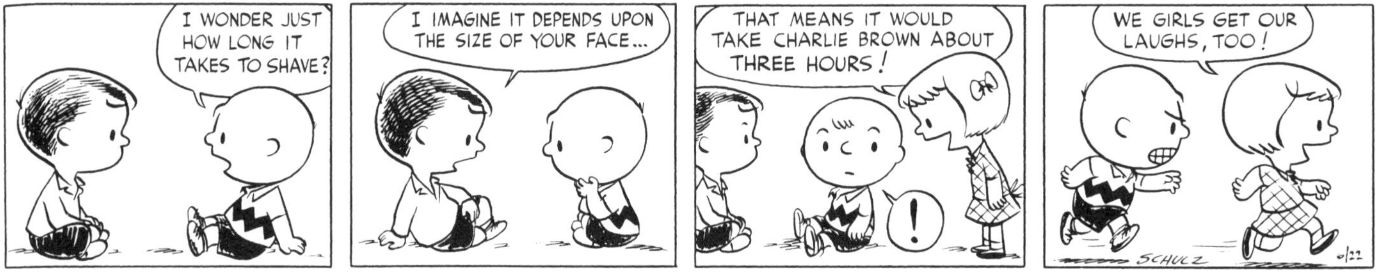
I WONDER JUST HOW LONG IT TAKES TO SHAVE?
I IMAGINE IT DEPENDS UPON THE SIZE OF YOUR FACE...
THAT MEANS IT WOULD TAKE CHARLIE BROWN ABOUT THREE HOURS!
!
WE GIRLS GET OUR LAUGHS, TOO!
SCHULZ
6/22

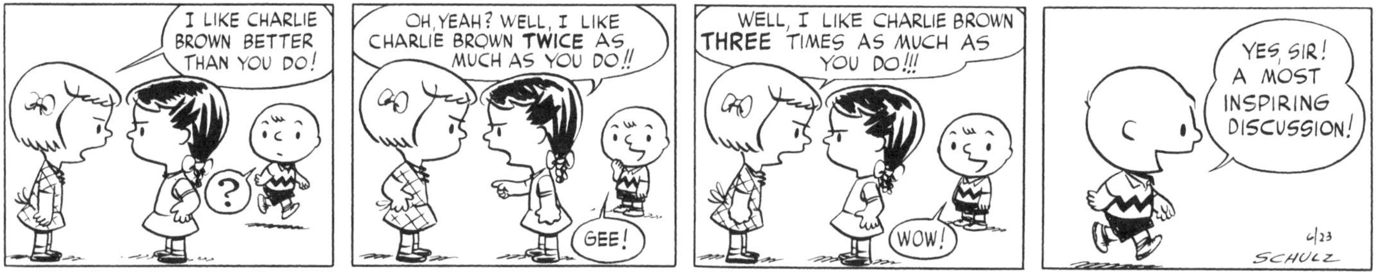
I LIKE CHARLIE BROWN BETTER THAN YOU DO!
?
OH, YEAH? WELL, I LIKE CHARLIE BROWN TWICE AS MUCH AS YOU DO!!
GEE!
WELL, I LIKE CHARLIE BROWN THREE TIMES AS MUCH AS YOU DO!!!
WOW!
YES, SIR! A MOST INSPIRING DISCUSSION!
6/23
SCHULZ

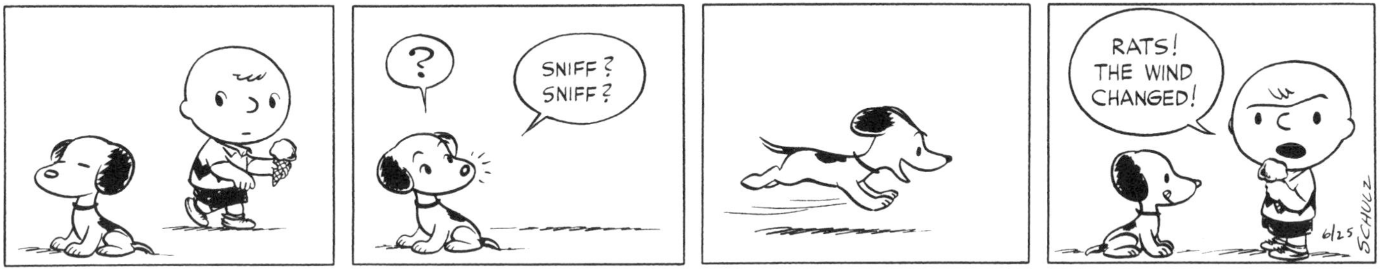
?
SNIFF? SNIFF?
RATS! THE WIND CHANGED!
6/25
SCHULZ

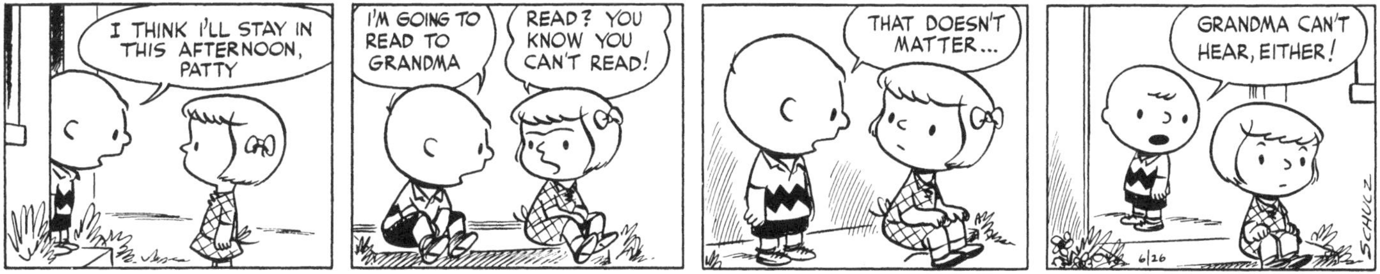
I THINK I'LL STAY IN THIS AFTERNOON, PATTY
I'M GOING TO READ TO GRANDMA
READ? YOU KNOW YOU CAN'T READ!
THAT DOESN'T MATTER...
GRANDMA CAN'T HEAR, EITHER!
6/26
SCHULZ

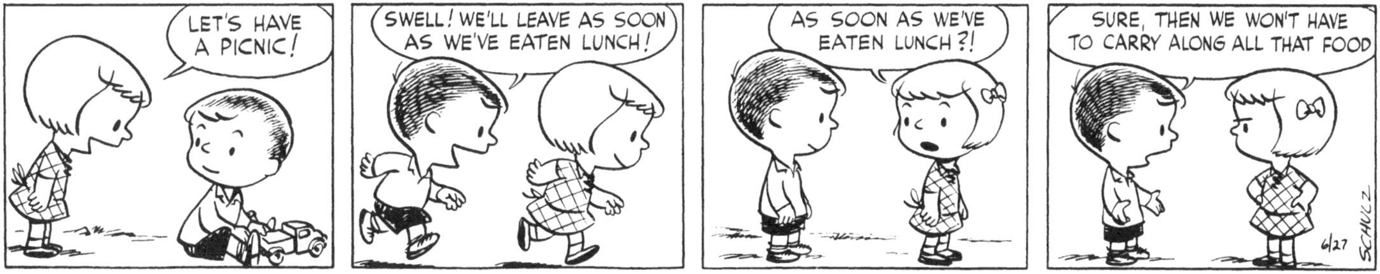
LET'S HAVE A PICNIC!
SWELL! WE'LL LEAVE AS SOON AS WE'VE EATEN LUNCH!
AS SOON AS WE'VE EATEN LUNCH?!
SURE, THEN WE WON'T HAVE TO CARRY ALONG ALL THAT FOOD
6/27
SCHULZ

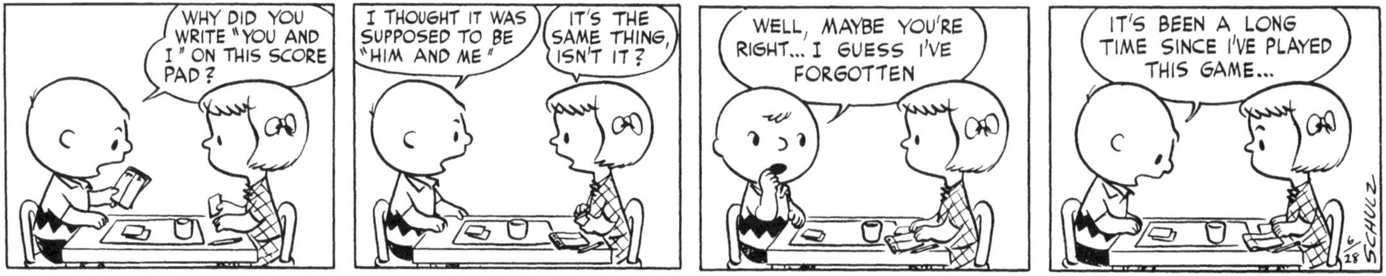
WHY DID YOU WRITE "YOU AND I" ON THIS SCORE PAD?
I THOUGHT IT WAS SUPPOSED TO BE "HIM AND ME"
IT'S THE SAME THING, ISN'T IT?
WELL, MAYBE YOU'RE RIGHT... I GUESS I'VE FORGOTTEN
IT'S BEEN A LONG TIME SINCE I'VE PLAYED THIS GAME...
6/28 SCHULZ

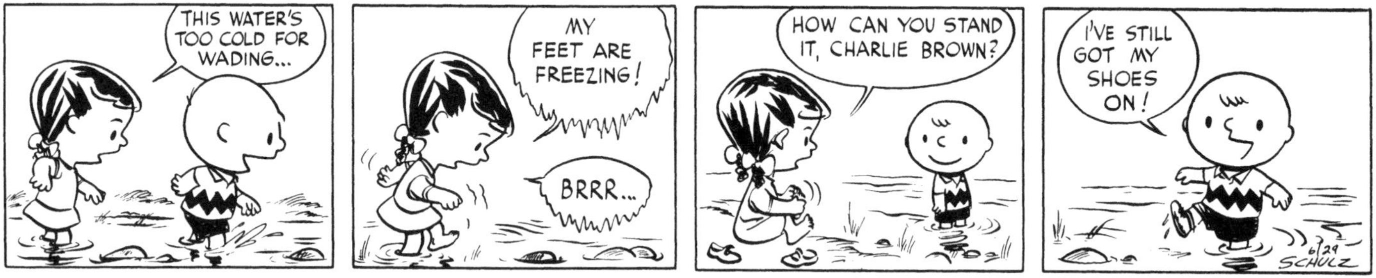
THIS WATER'S TOO COLD FOR WADING...
MY FEET ARE FREEZING!
BRRR...
HOW CAN YOU STAND IT, CHARLIE BROWN?
I'VE STILL GOT MY SHOES ON!
6/29 SCHULZ

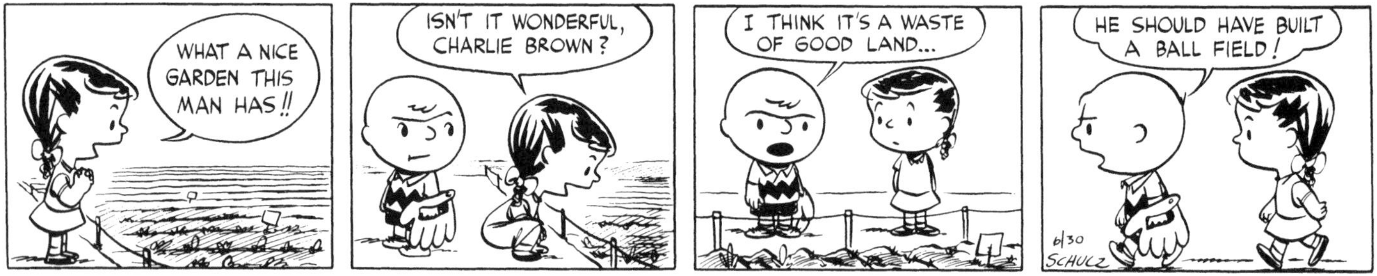
WHAT A NICE GARDEN THIS MAN HAS!!
ISN'T IT WONDERFUL, CHARLIE BROWN?
I THINK IT'S A WASTE OF GOOD LAND...
HE SHOULD HAVE BUILT A BALL FIELD!
6/30 SCHULZ

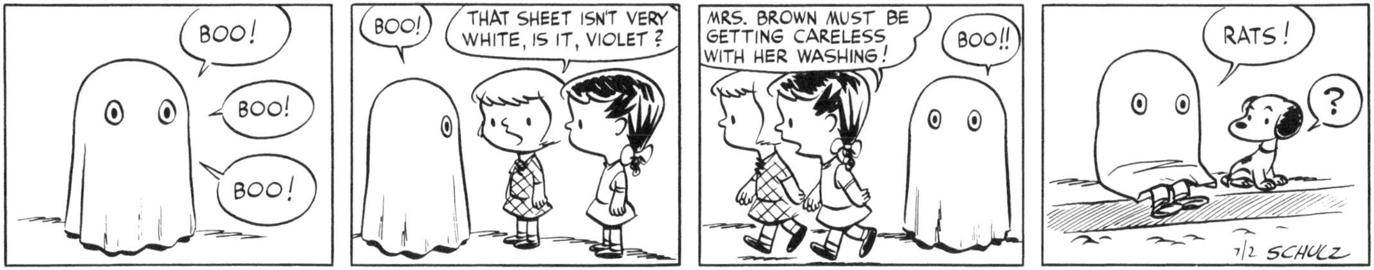
BOO!
BOO!
BOO!
BOO!
THAT SHEET ISN'T VERY WHITE, IS IT, VIOLET?
MRS. BROWN MUST BE GETTING CARELESS WITH HER WASHING!
BOO!!
RATS!
?
7/2 SCHULZ

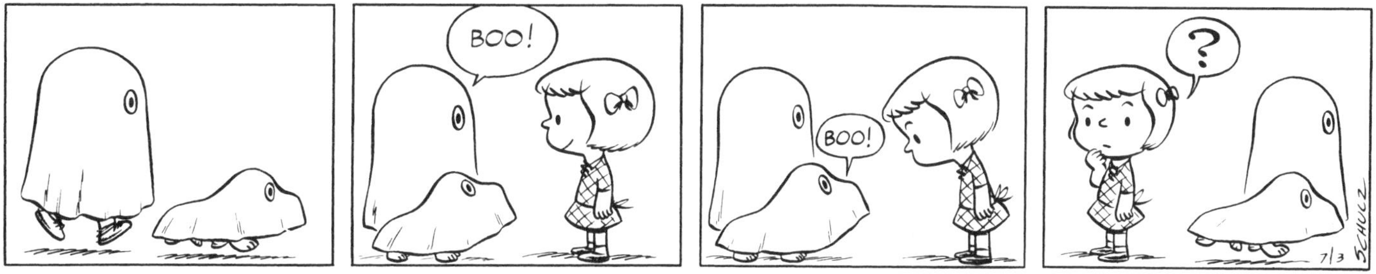
BOO!
BOO!
?
7/3 SCHULZ

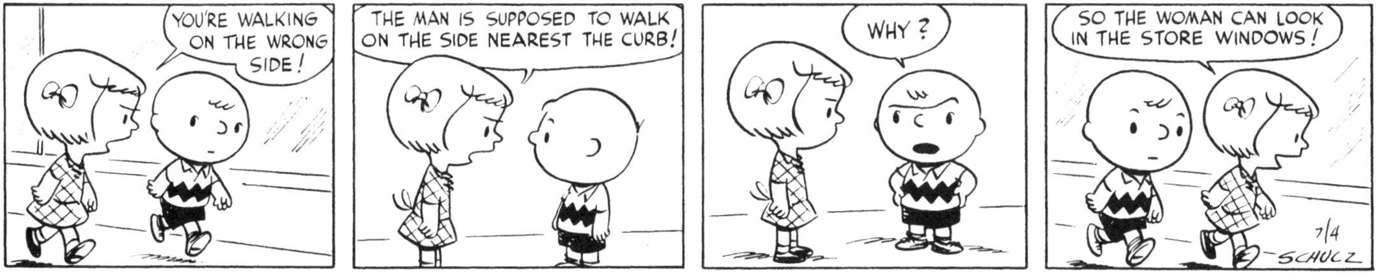
YOU'RE WALKING ON THE WRONG SIDE!
THE MAN IS SUPPOSED TO WALK ON THE SIDE NEAREST THE CURB!
WHY?
SO THE WOMAN CAN LOOK IN THE STORE WINDOWS!
7/4 SCHULZ

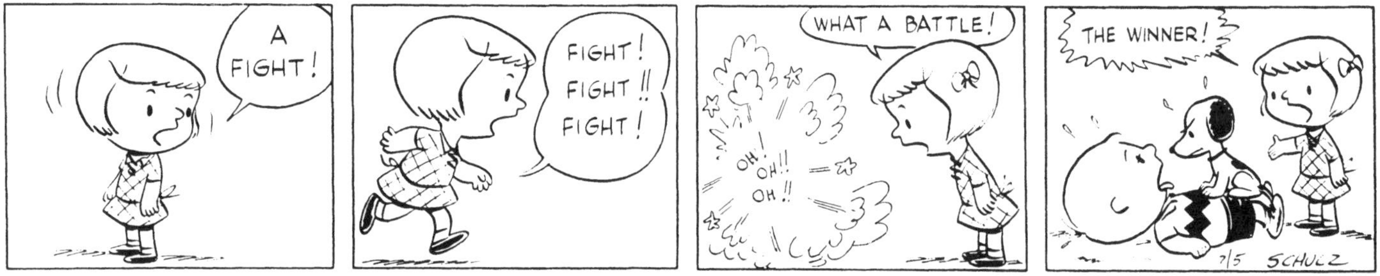
A FIGHT!
FIGHT! FIGHT!! FIGHT!
WHAT A BATTLE!
OH! OH!! OH!!
THE WINNER!
7/5 SCHULZ

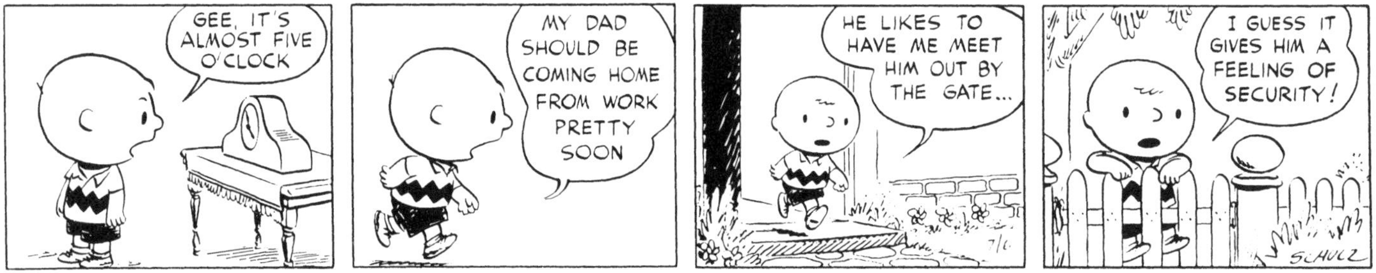
GEE, IT'S ALMOST FIVE O'CLOCK
MY DAD SHOULD BE COMING HOME FROM WORK PRETTY SOON
HE LIKES TO HAVE ME MEET HIM OUT BY THE GATE...
7/6
I GUESS IT GIVES HIM A FEELING OF SECURITY!
SCHULZ

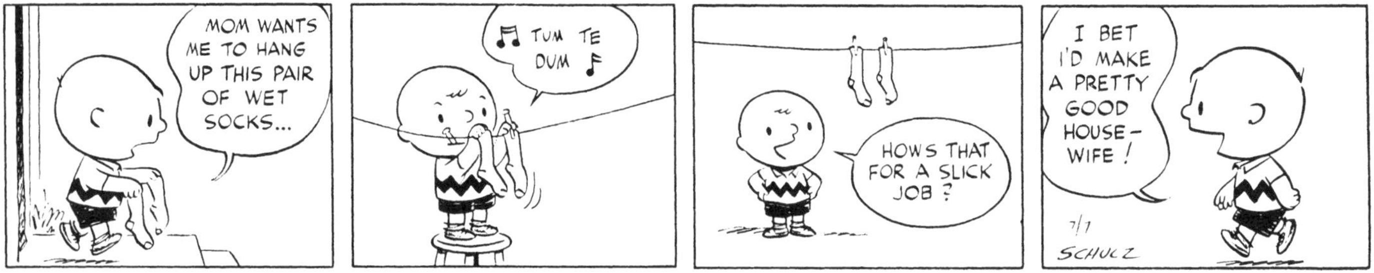
MOM WANTS ME TO HANG UP THIS PAIR OF WET SOCKS...
TUM TE DUM
HOWS THAT FOR A SLICK JOB?
I BET I'D MAKE A PRETTY GOOD HOUSE-WIFE!
7/7
SCHULZ

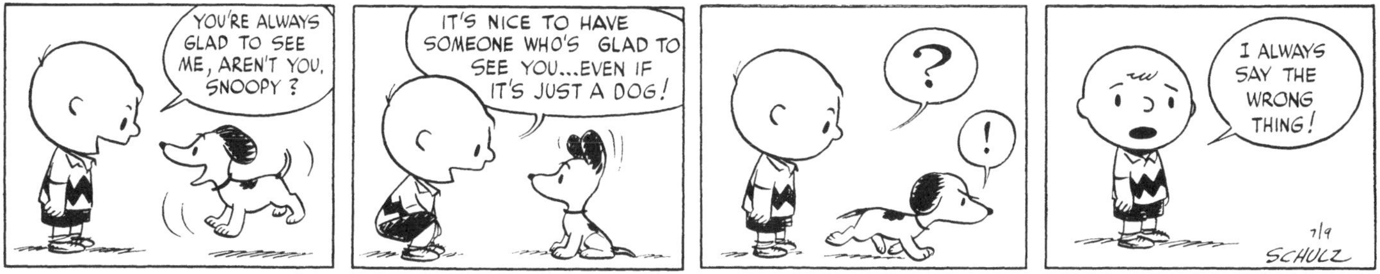
YOU'RE ALWAYS GLAD TO SEE ME, AREN'T YOU, SNOOPY ?
IT'S NICE TO HAVE SOMEONE WHO'S GLAD TO SEE YOU...EVEN IF IT'S JUST A DOG!
?
!
I ALWAYS SAY THE WRONG THING!
7/9
SCHULZ

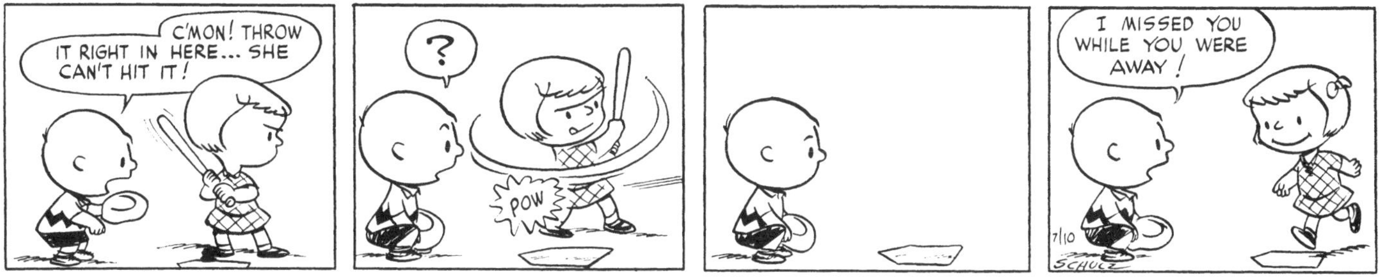
C'MON! THROW IT RIGHT IN HERE... SHE CAN'T HIT IT!
?
POW
I MISSED YOU WHILE YOU WERE AWAY!
7/10
SCHULZ

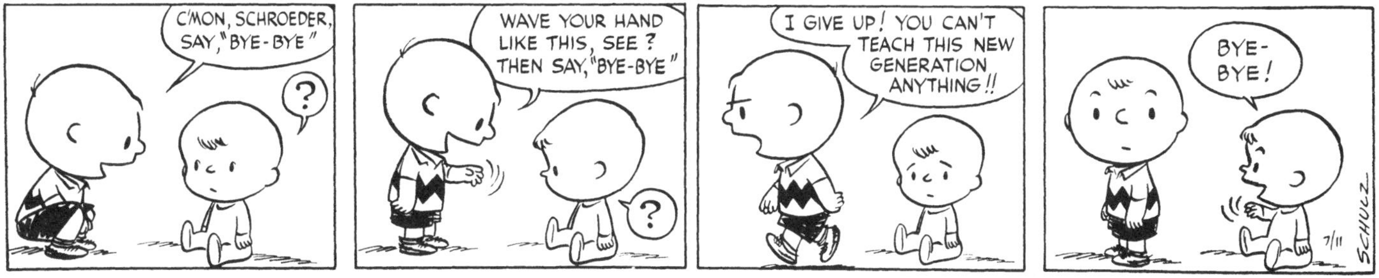
C'MON, SCHROEDER, SAY, "BYE-BYE"
?
WAVE YOUR HAND LIKE THIS, SEE ? THEN SAY, "BYE-BYE"
?
I GIVE UP! YOU CAN'T TEACH THIS NEW GENERATION ANYTHING!!
BYE-BYE!
7/11
SCHULZ

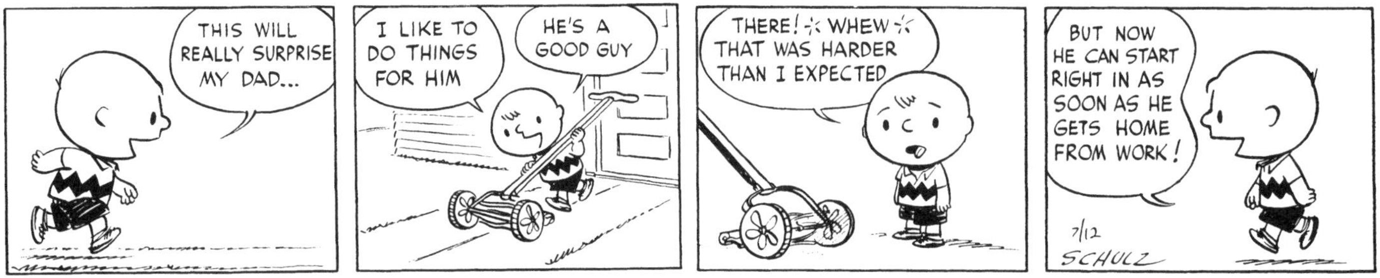
THIS WILL REALLY SURPRISE MY DAD...
I LIKE TO DO THINGS FOR HIM
HE'S A GOOD GUY
THERE! WHEW THAT WAS HARDER THAN I EXPECTED
BUT NOW HE CAN START RIGHT IN AS SOON AS HE GETS HOME FROM WORK!
7/12
SCHULZ

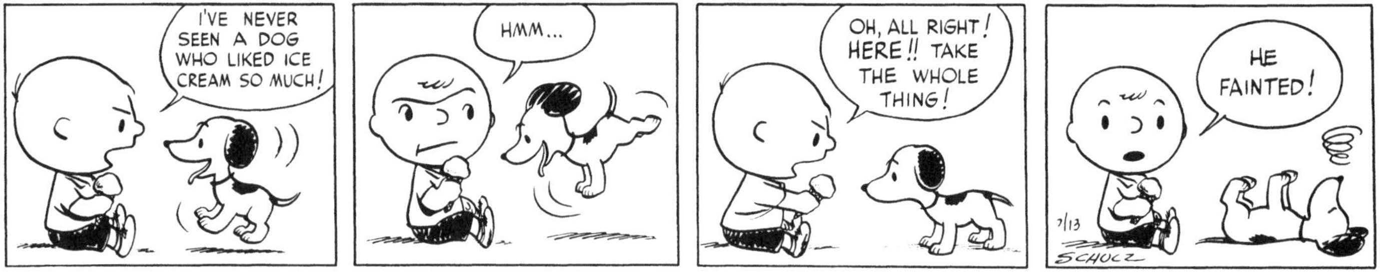
I'VE NEVER SEEN A DOG WHO LIKED ICE CREAM SO MUCH!
HMM...
OH, ALL RIGHT! HERE!! TAKE THE WHOLE THING!
HE FAINTED!
7/13
SCHULZ

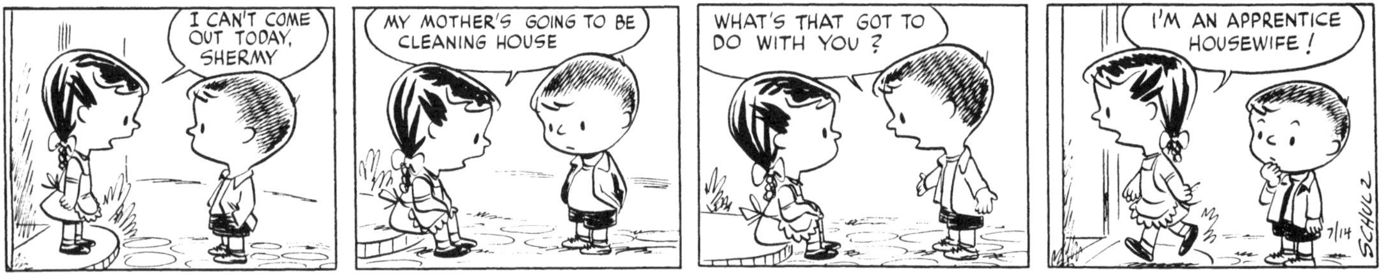
I CAN'T COME OUT TODAY, SHERMY
MY MOTHER'S GOING TO BE CLEANING HOUSE
WHAT'S THAT GOT TO DO WITH YOU?
I'M AN APPRENTICE HOUSEWIFE!
7/14
SCHULZ

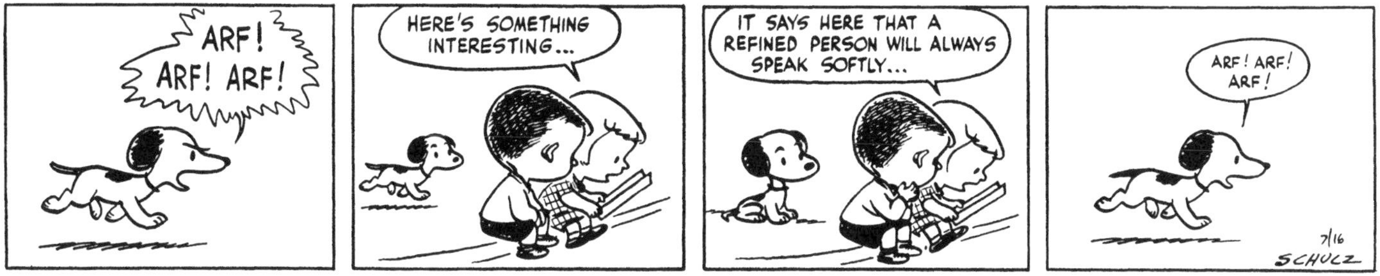
ARF! ARF! ARF!
HERE'S SOMETHING INTERESTING...
IT SAYS HERE THAT A REFINED PERSON WILL ALWAYS SPEAK SOFTLY...
ARF! ARF! ARF!
7/16
SCHULZ

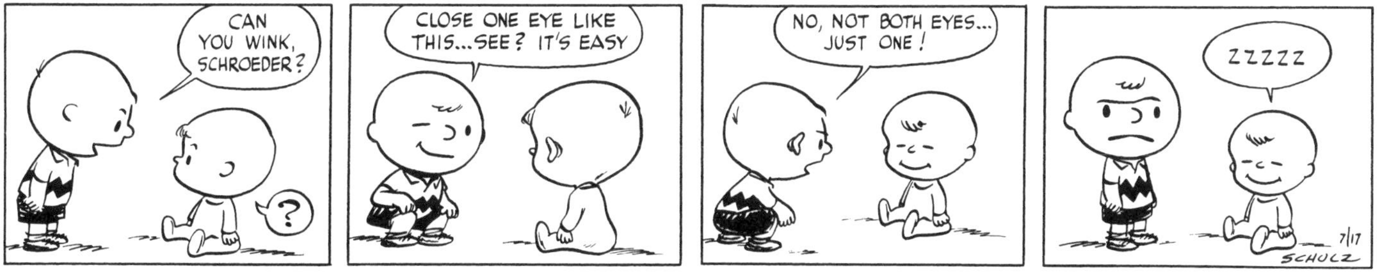
CAN YOU WINK, SCHROEDER?
?
CLOSE ONE EYE LIKE THIS...SEE? IT'S EASY
NO, NOT BOTH EYES... JUST ONE!
ZZZZZ
7/17
SCHULZ

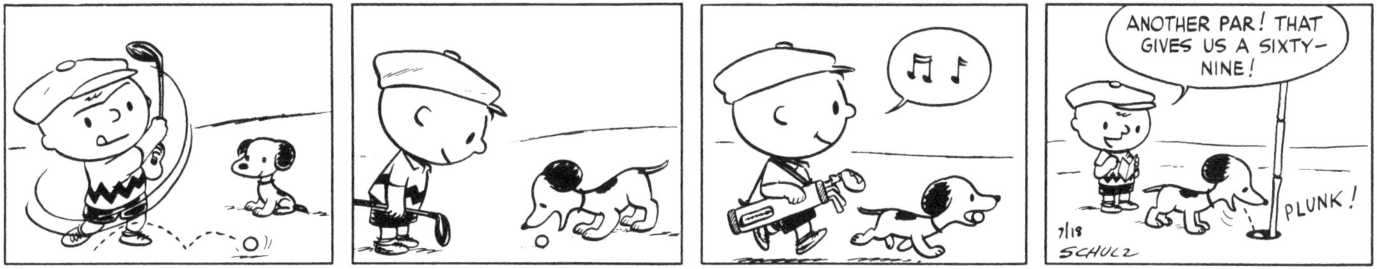
ANOTHER PAR! THAT GIVES US A SIXTY-NINE!
PLUNK!
7/18
SCHULZ

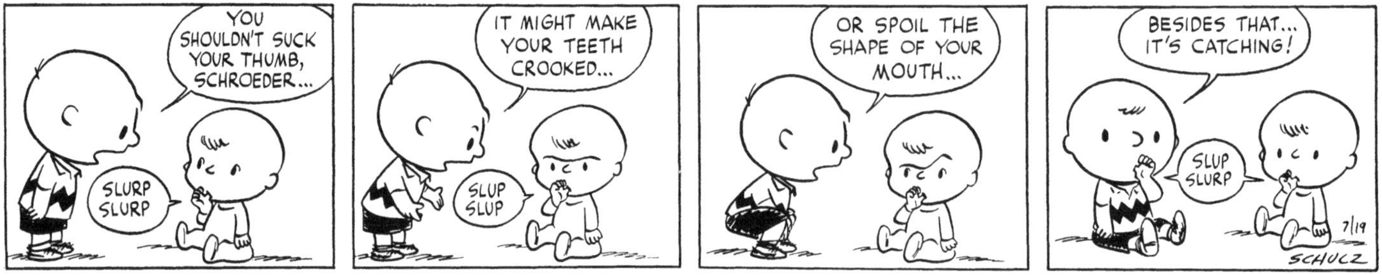
YOU SHOULDN'T SUCK YOUR THUMB, SCHROEDER...
SLURP SLURP
IT MIGHT MAKE YOUR TEETH CROOKED...
SLUP SLUP
OR SPOIL THE SHAPE OF YOUR MOUTH...
BESIDES THAT... IT'S CATCHING!
SLUP SLURP
7/19
SCHULZ

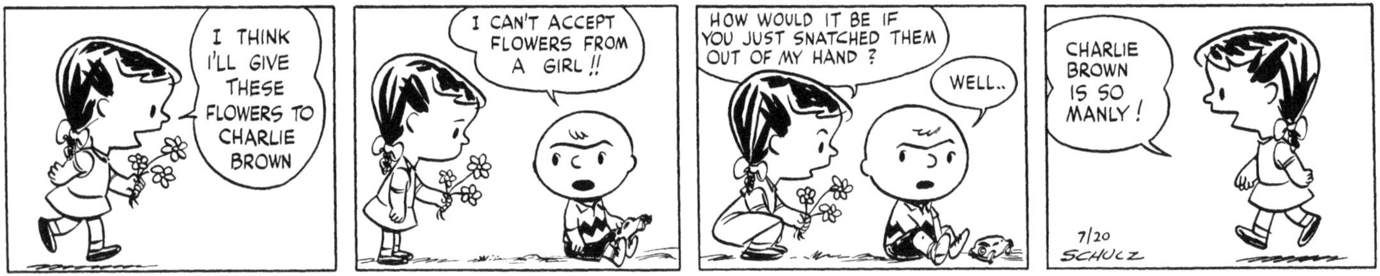
I THINK I'LL GIVE THESE FLOWERS TO CHARLIE BROWN
I CAN'T ACCEPT FLOWERS FROM A GIRL!!
HOW WOULD IT BE IF YOU JUST SNATCHED THEM OUT OF MY HAND ?
WELL..
CHARLIE BROWN IS SO MANLY!
7/20
SCHULZ

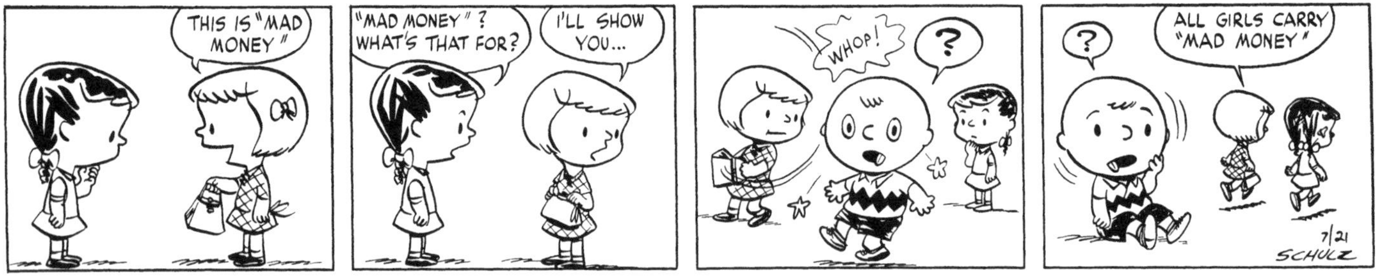
THIS IS "MAD MONEY"
"MAD MONEY"? WHAT'S THAT FOR?
I'LL SHOW YOU...
WHOP!
?
?
ALL GIRLS CARRY "MAD MONEY"
7/21
SCHULZ

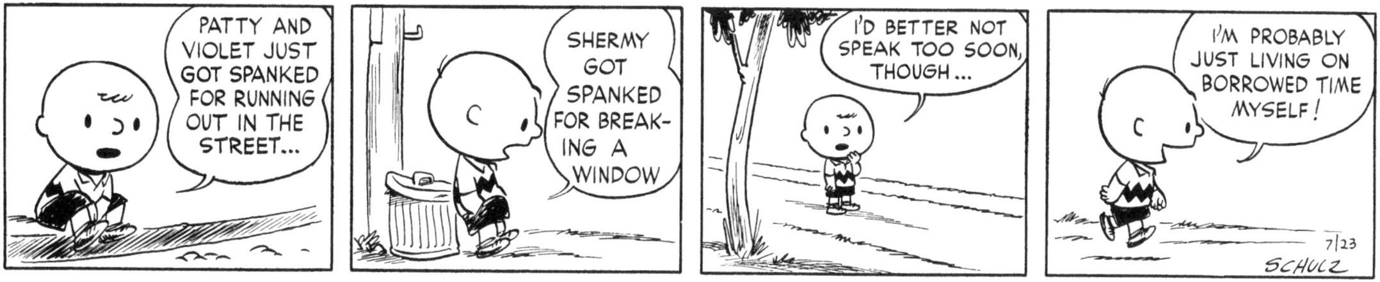
PATTY AND VIOLET JUST GOT SPANKED FOR RUNNING OUT IN THE STREET...
SHERMY GOT SPANKED FOR BREAK-ING A WINDOW
I'D BETTER NOT SPEAK TOO SOON, THOUGH...
I'M PROBABLY JUST LIVING ON BORROWED TIME MYSELF!
7/23
SCHULZ

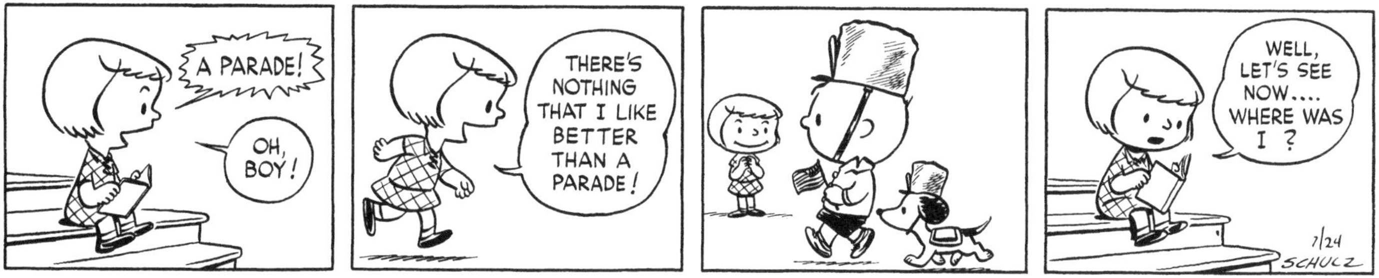
A PARADE!
OH, BOY!
THERE'S NOTHING THAT I LIKE BETTER THAN A PARADE!
WELL, LET'S SEE NOW.... WHERE WAS I ?
7/24
SCHULZ

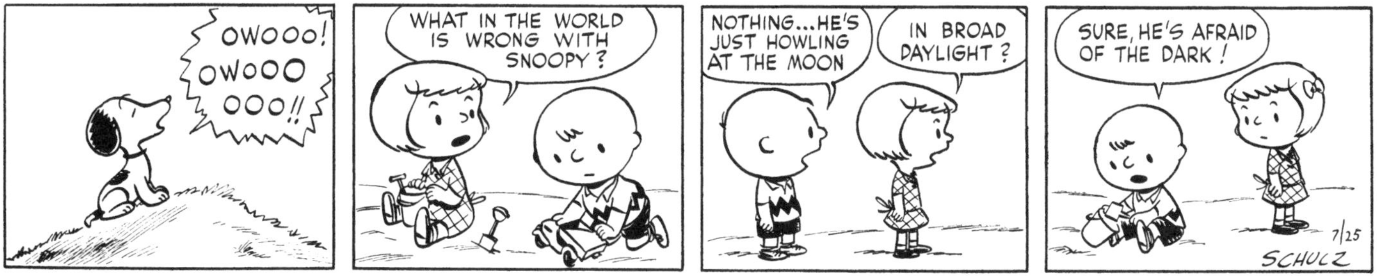
OWOOO! OWOOO OOO!!
WHAT IN THE WORLD IS WRONG WITH SNOOPY ?
NOTHING...HE'S JUST HOWLING AT THE MOON
IN BROAD DAYLIGHT ?
SURE, HE'S AFRAID OF THE DARK!
7/25
SCHULZ

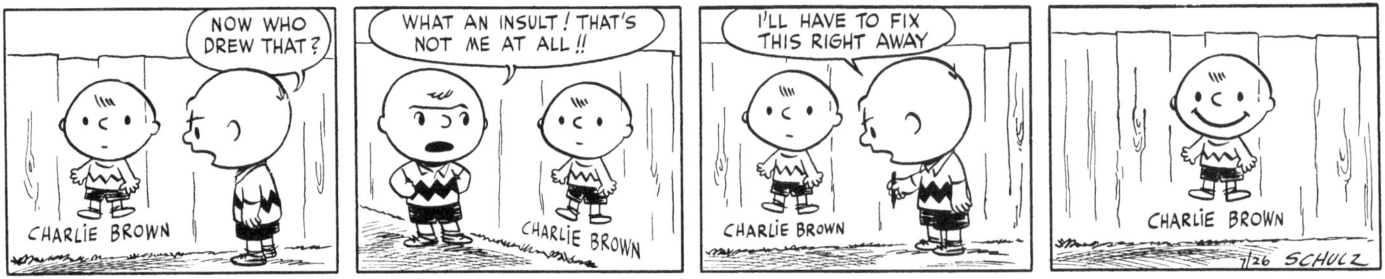
NOW WHO DREW THAT?
CHARLIE BROWN
WHAT AN INSULT! THAT'S NOT ME AT ALL!!
CHARLIE BROWN
I'LL HAVE TO FIX THIS RIGHT AWAY
CHARLIE BROWN
CHARLIE BROWN
7/26 SCHULZ

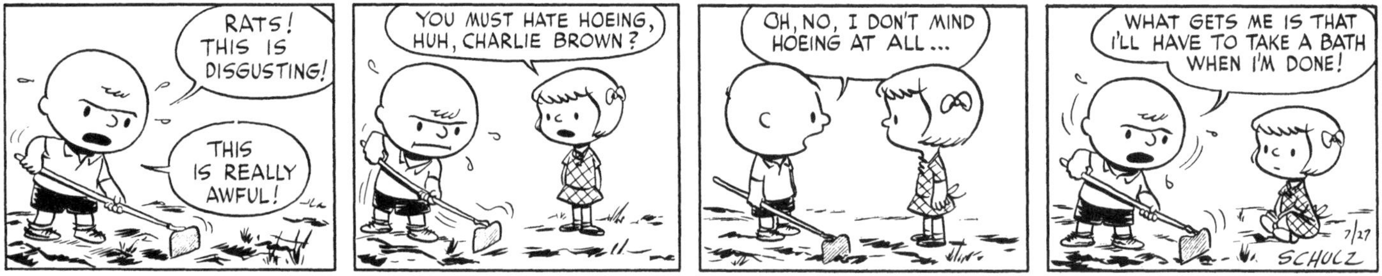
RATS! THIS IS DISGUSTING!
THIS IS REALLY AWFUL!
YOU MUST HATE HOEING, HUH, CHARLIE BROWN?
OH, NO, I DON'T MIND HOEING AT ALL...
WHAT GETS ME IS THAT I'LL HAVE TO TAKE A BATH WHEN I'M DONE!
7/27 SCHULZ

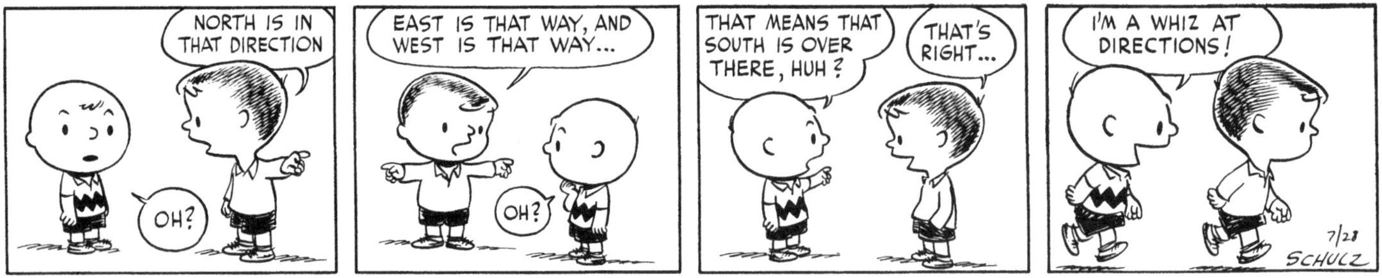
NORTH IS IN THAT DIRECTION
OH?
EAST IS THAT WAY, AND WEST IS THAT WAY...
OH?
THAT MEANS THAT SOUTH IS OVER THERE, HUH?
THAT'S RIGHT...
I'M A WHIZ AT DIRECTIONS!
7/28 SCHULZ

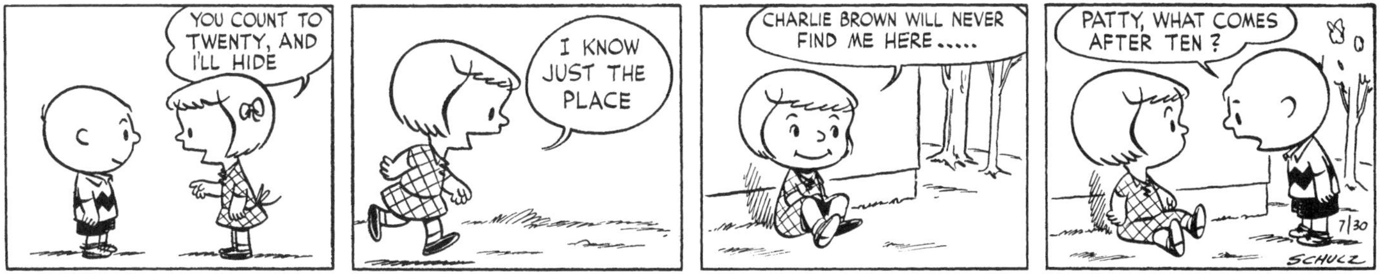
YOU COUNT TO TWENTY, AND I'LL HIDE
I KNOW JUST THE PLACE
CHARLIE BROWN WILL NEVER FIND ME HERE.....
PATTY, WHAT COMES AFTER TEN ?
7/30
SCHULZ

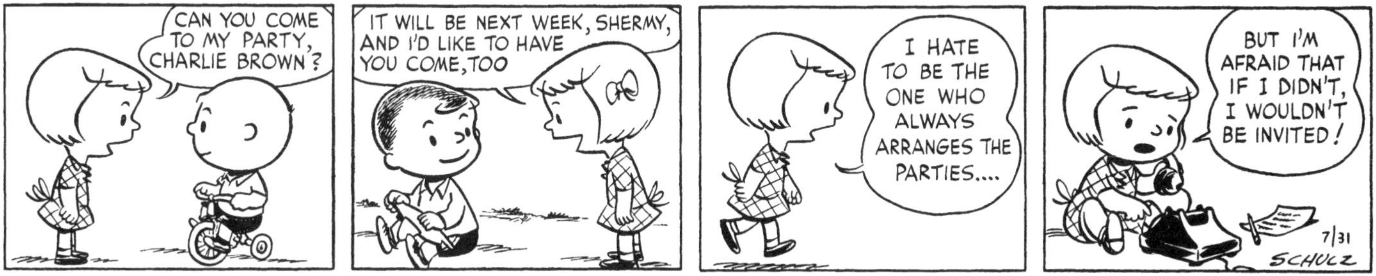
CAN YOU COME TO MY PARTY, CHARLIE BROWN ?
IT WILL BE NEXT WEEK, SHERMY, AND I'D LIKE TO HAVE YOU COME, TOO
I HATE TO BE THE ONE WHO ALWAYS ARRANGES THE PARTIES....
BUT I'M AFRAID THAT IF I DIDN'T, I WOULDN'T BE INVITED !
7/31
SCHULZ

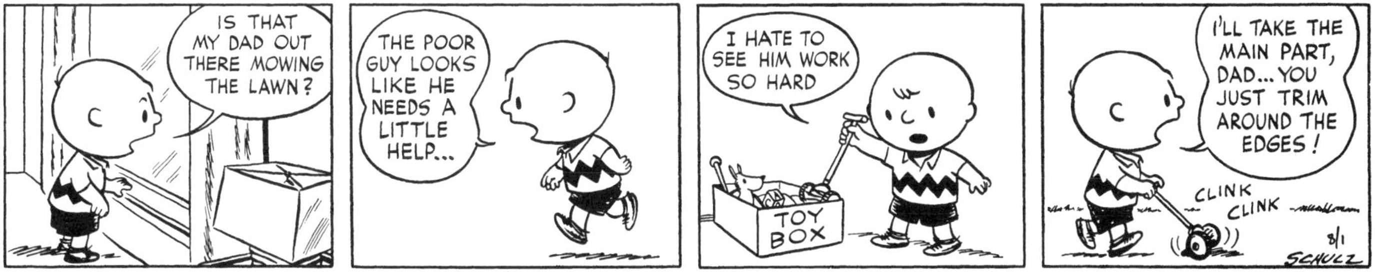
IS THAT MY DAD OUT THERE MOWING THE LAWN ?
THE POOR GUY LOOKS LIKE HE NEEDS A LITTLE HELP...
I HATE TO SEE HIM WORK SO HARD
TOY BOX
I'LL TAKE THE MAIN PART, DAD... YOU JUST TRIM AROUND THE EDGES !
CLINK
CLINK
8/1
SCHULZ

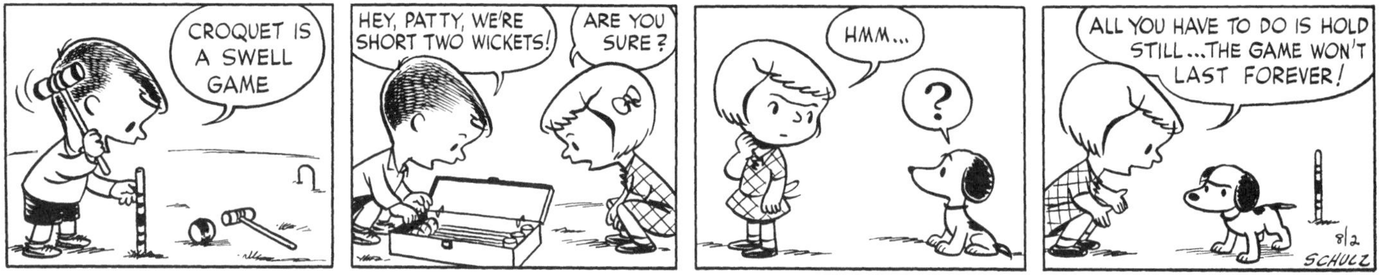
CROQUET IS A SWELL GAME
HEY, PATTY, WE'RE SHORT TWO WICKETS!
ARE YOU SURE?
HMM...
?
ALL YOU HAVE TO DO IS HOLD STILL...THE GAME WON'T LAST FOREVER!
8/2
SCHULZ

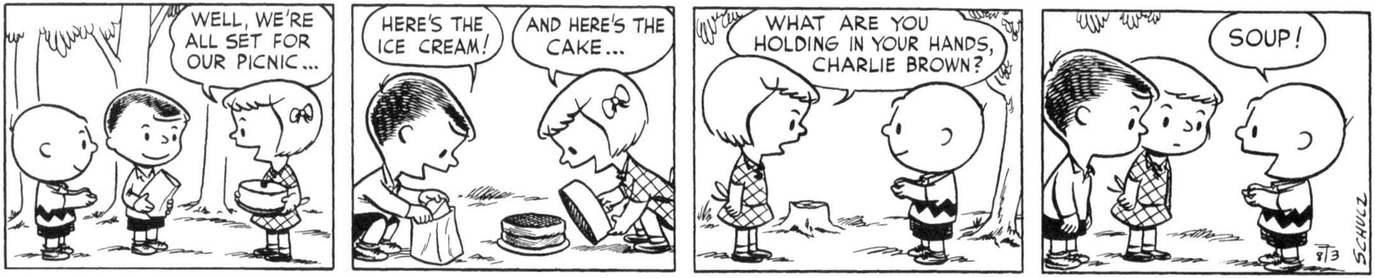
WELL, WE'RE ALL SET FOR OUR PICNIC...
HERE'S THE ICE CREAM!
AND HERE'S THE CAKE...
WHAT ARE YOU HOLDING IN YOUR HANDS, CHARLIE BROWN?
SOUP!
8/3
SCHULZ

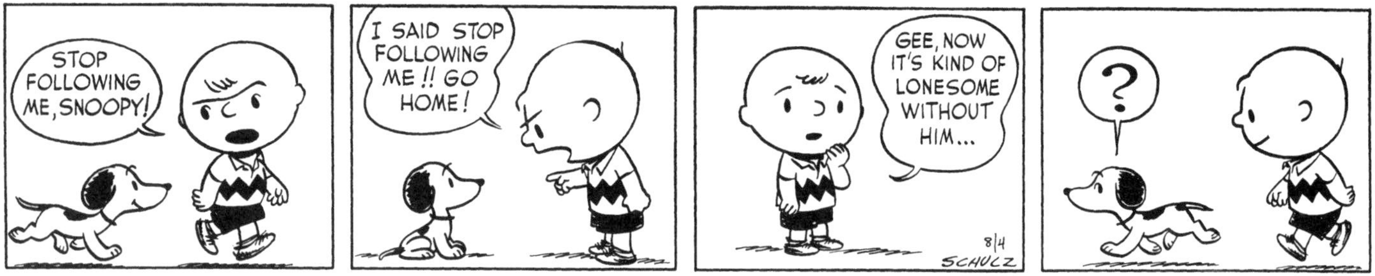
STOP FOLLOWING ME, SNOOPY!
I SAID STOP FOLLOWING ME!! GO HOME!
GEE, NOW IT'S KIND OF LONESOME WITHOUT HIM...
8/4
SCHULZ
?

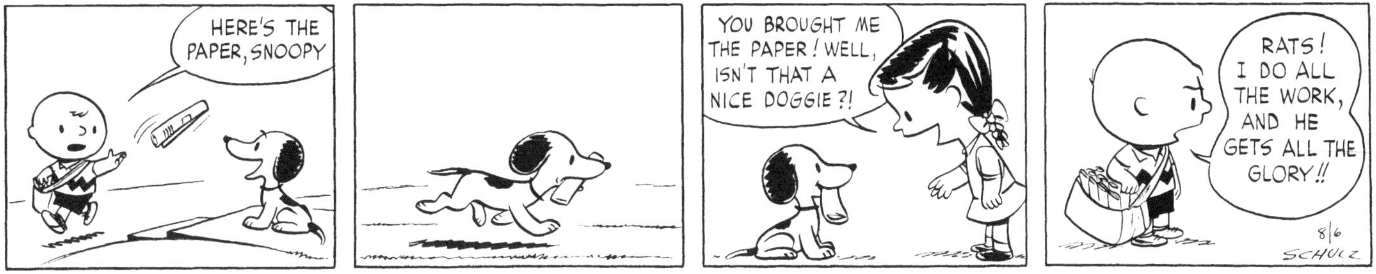
HERE'S THE PAPER, SNOOPY
YOU BROUGHT ME THE PAPER! WELL, ISN'T THAT A NICE DOGGIE?!
RATS! I DO ALL THE WORK, AND HE GETS ALL THE GLORY!!
8/6
SCHULZ

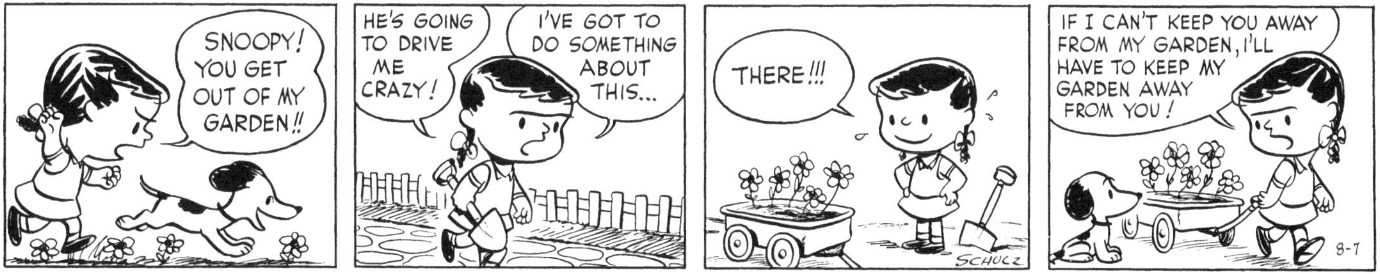
SNOOPY! YOU GET OUT OF MY GARDEN!!
HE'S GOING TO DRIVE ME CRAZY!
I'VE GOT TO DO SOMETHING ABOUT THIS...
THERE!!!
SCHULZ
IF I CAN'T KEEP YOU AWAY FROM MY GARDEN, I'LL HAVE TO KEEP MY GARDEN AWAY FROM YOU!
8-7

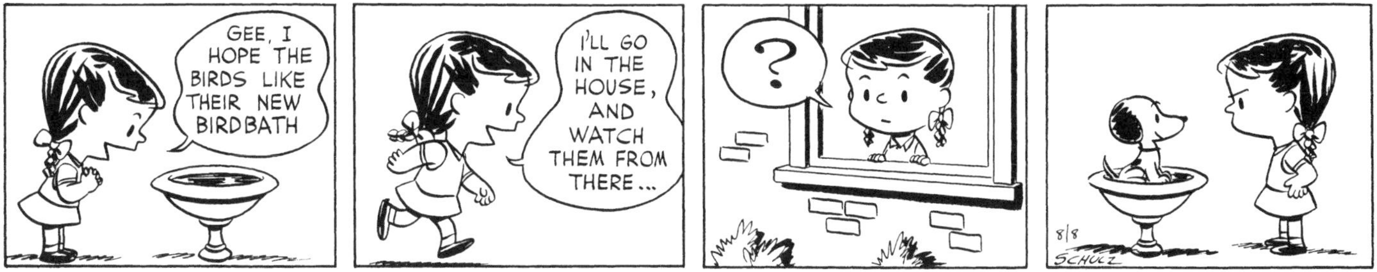
GEE, I HOPE THE BIRDS LIKE THEIR NEW BIRDBATH
I'LL GO IN THE HOUSE, AND WATCH THEM FROM THERE...
?
8/8
SCHULZ

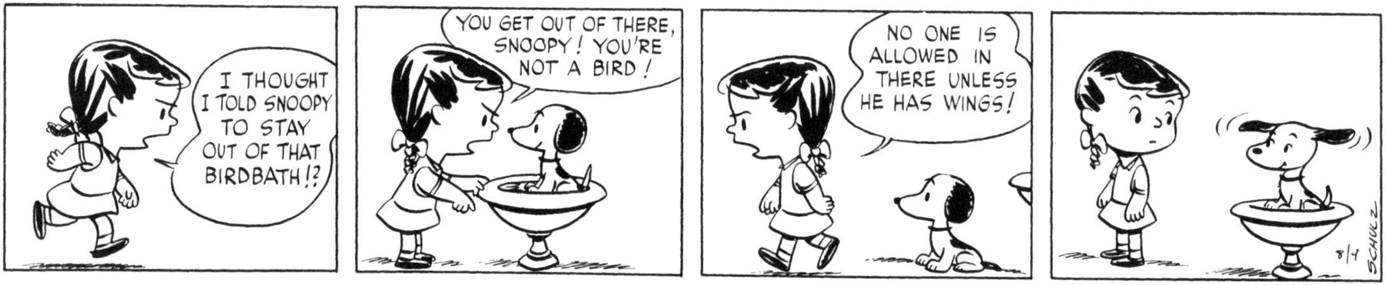
I THOUGHT I TOLD SNOOPY TO STAY OUT OF THAT BIRDBATH!?
YOU GET OUT OF THERE, SNOOPY! YOU'RE NOT A BIRD!
NO ONE IS ALLOWED IN THERE UNLESS HE HAS WINGS!
8/4
SCHULZ

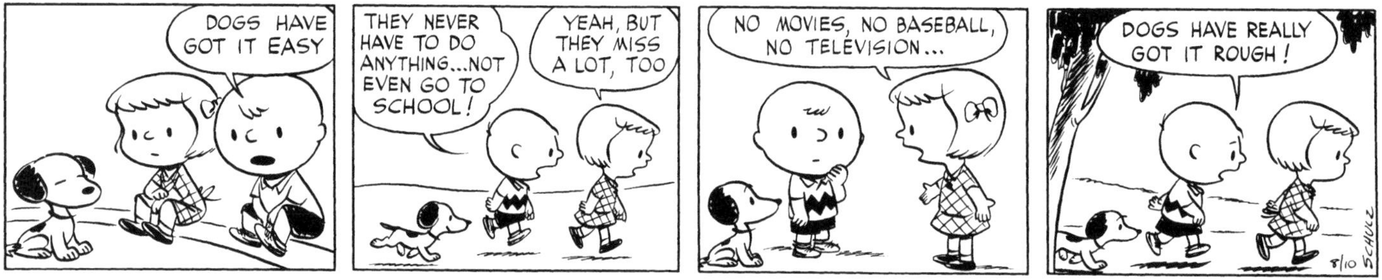
DOGS HAVE GOT IT EASY
THEY NEVER HAVE TO DO ANYTHING...NOT EVEN GO TO SCHOOL!
YEAH, BUT THEY MISS A LOT, TOO
NO MOVIES, NO BASEBALL, NO TELEVISION...
DOGS HAVE REALLY GOT IT ROUGH!
8/10
SCHULZ

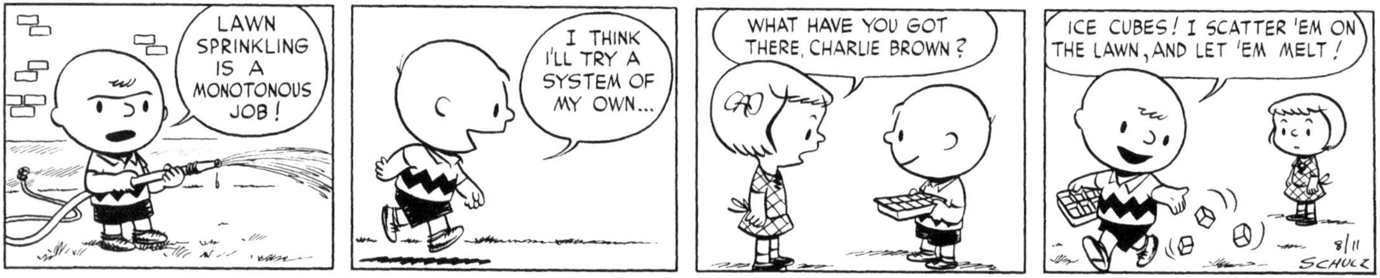
LAWN SPRINKLING IS A MONOTONOUS JOB!
I THINK I'LL TRY A SYSTEM OF MY OWN...
WHAT HAVE YOU GOT THERE, CHARLIE BROWN?
ICE CUBES! I SCATTER 'EM ON THE LAWN, AND LET 'EM MELT!
8/11
SCHULZ

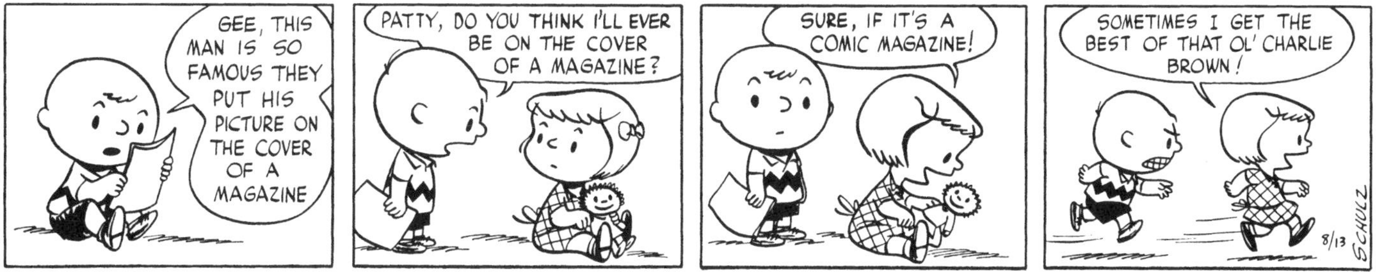
GEE, THIS MAN IS SO FAMOUS THEY PUT HIS PICTURE ON THE COVER OF A MAGAZINE
PATTY, DO YOU THINK I'LL EVER BE ON THE COVER OF A MAGAZINE?
SURE, IF IT'S A COMIC MAGAZINE!
SOMETIMES I GET THE BEST OF THAT OL' CHARLIE BROWN!
8/13
SCHULZ

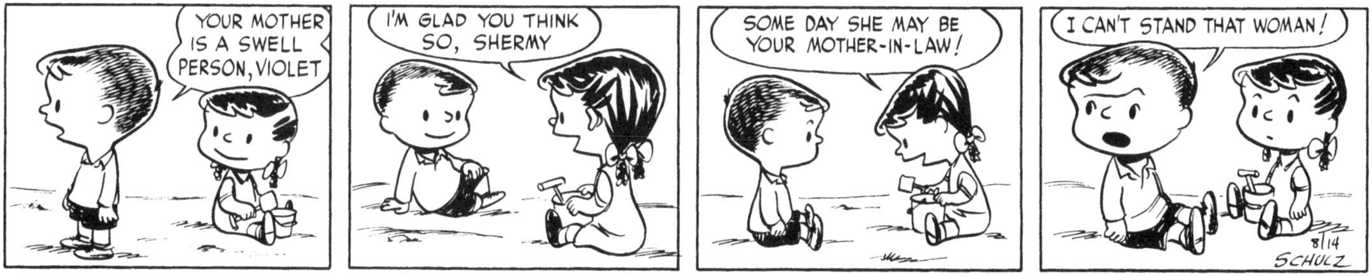
YOUR MOTHER IS A SWELL PERSON, VIOLET
I'M GLAD YOU THINK SO, SHERMY
SOME DAY SHE MAY BE YOUR MOTHER-IN-LAW!
I CAN'T STAND THAT WOMAN!
8/14
SCHULZ

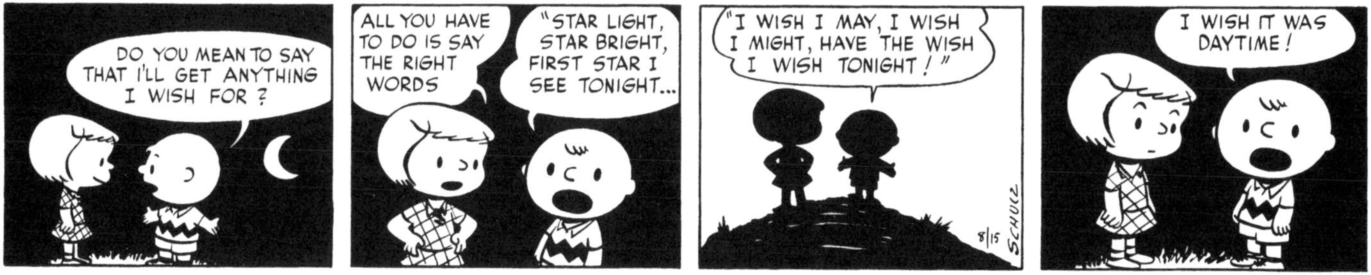
DO YOU MEAN TO SAY THAT I'LL GET ANYTHING I WISH FOR?
ALL YOU HAVE TO DO IS SAY THE RIGHT WORDS
"STAR LIGHT, STAR BRIGHT, FIRST STAR I SEE TONIGHT...
"I WISH I MAY, I WISH I MIGHT, HAVE THE WISH I WISH TONIGHT!"
8/15
SCHULZ
I WISH IT WAS DAYTIME!

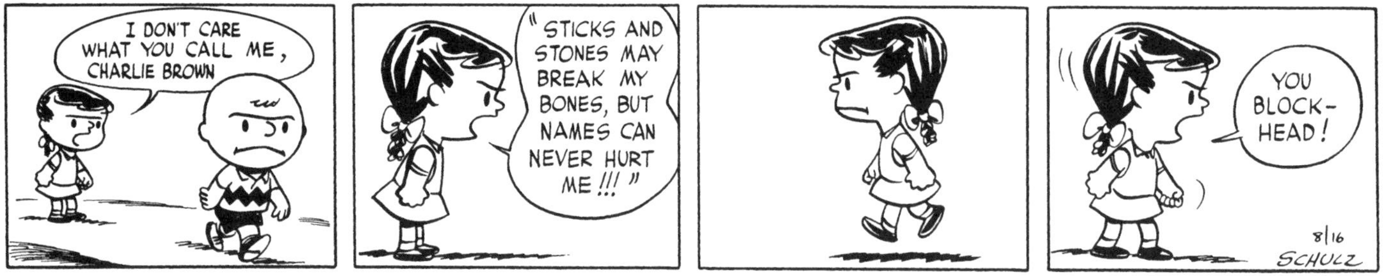
I DON'T CARE WHAT YOU CALL ME, CHARLIE BROWN
"STICKS AND STONES MAY BREAK MY BONES, BUT NAMES CAN NEVER HURT ME!!!"
YOU BLOCK-HEAD!
8/16
SCHULZ

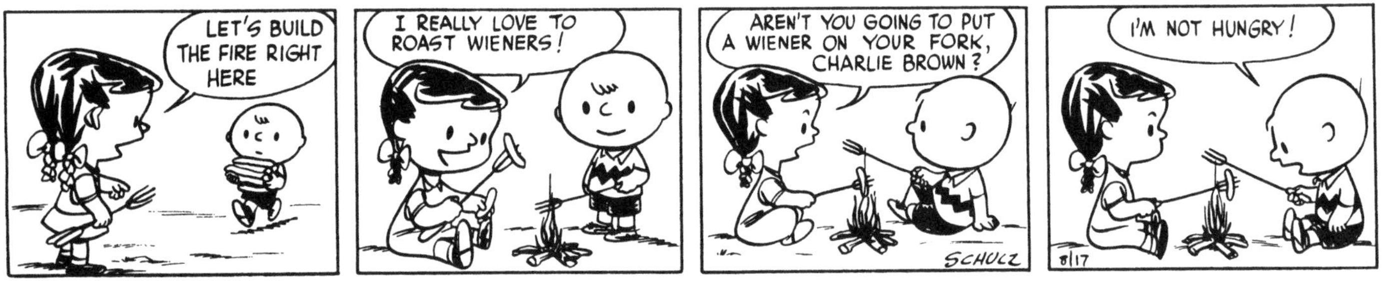
LET'S BUILD THE FIRE RIGHT HERE
I REALLY LOVE TO ROAST WIENERS!
AREN'T YOU GOING TO PUT A WIENER ON YOUR FORK, CHARLIE BROWN?
SCHULZ
I'M NOT HUNGRY!
8/17

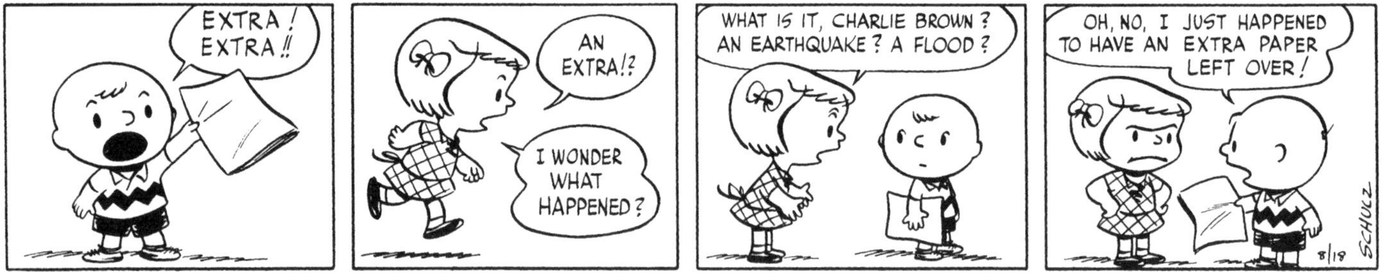
EXTRA! EXTRA!!
AN EXTRA!?
I WONDER WHAT HAPPENED?
WHAT IS IT, CHARLIE BROWN? AN EARTHQUAKE? A FLOOD?
OH, NO, I JUST HAPPENED TO HAVE AN EXTRA PAPER LEFT OVER!
SCHULZ
8/18

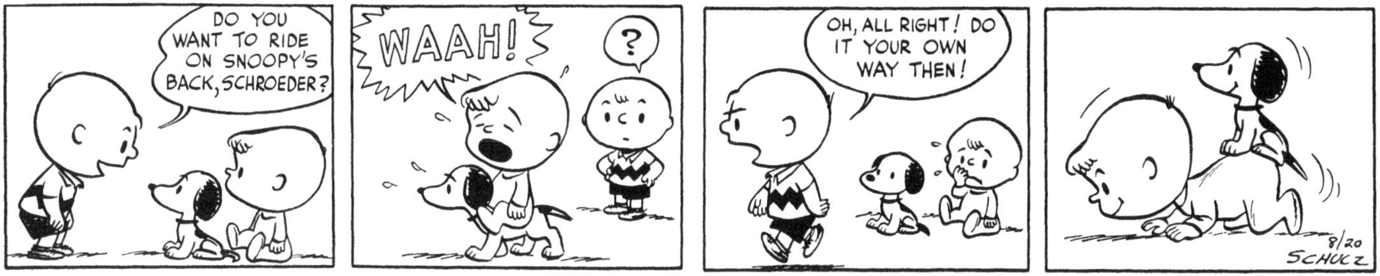
DO YOU WANT TO RIDE ON SNOOPY'S BACK, SCHROEDER?
WAAH!
?
OH, ALL RIGHT! DO IT YOUR OWN WAY THEN!
8/20
SCHULZ

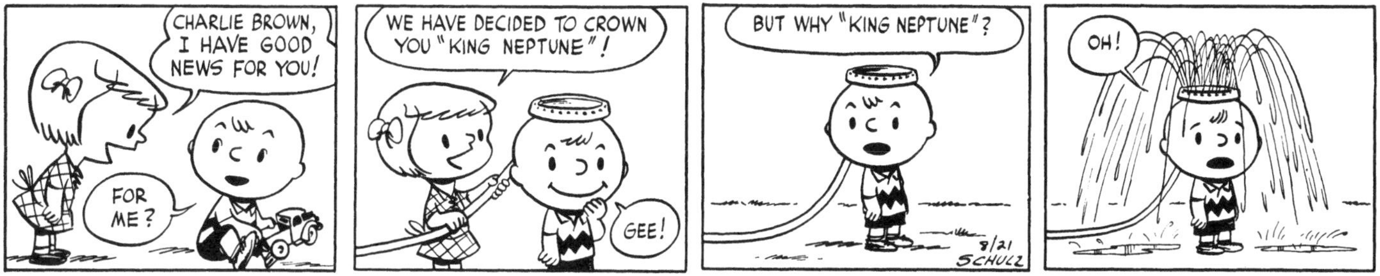
CHARLIE BROWN, I HAVE GOOD NEWS FOR YOU!
FOR ME?
WE HAVE DECIDED TO CROWN YOU "KING NEPTUNE"!
GEE!
BUT WHY "KING NEPTUNE"?
8/21
SCHULZ
OH!

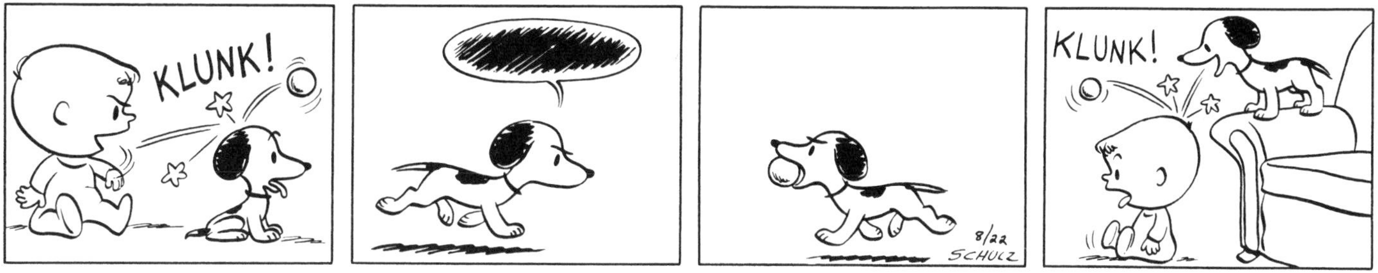
KLUNK!
8/22
SCHULZ
KLUNK!

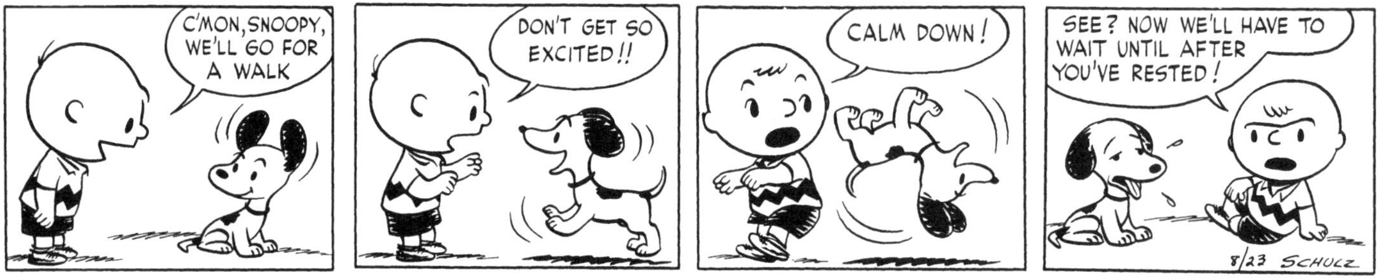
C'MON, SNOOPY, WE'LL GO FOR A WALK
DON'T GET SO EXCITED!!
CALM DOWN!
SEE? NOW WE'LL HAVE TO WAIT UNTIL AFTER YOU'VE RESTED!
8/23 SCHULZ

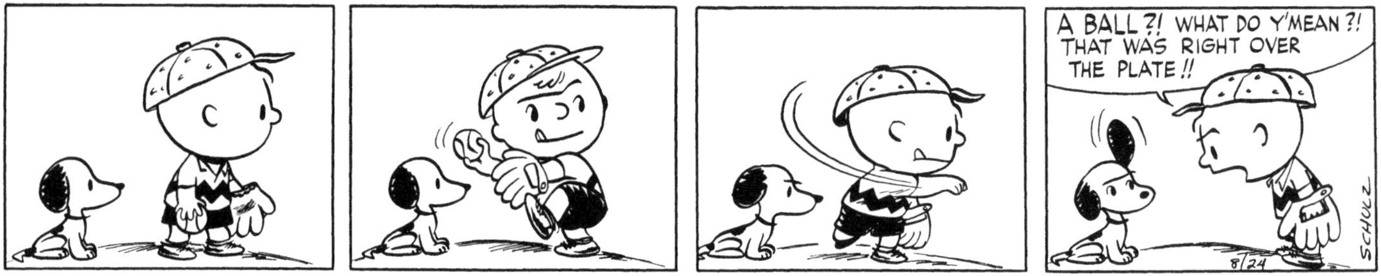
A BALL?! WHAT DO Y'MEAN?! THAT WAS RIGHT OVER THE PLATE!!
8/24
SCHULZ

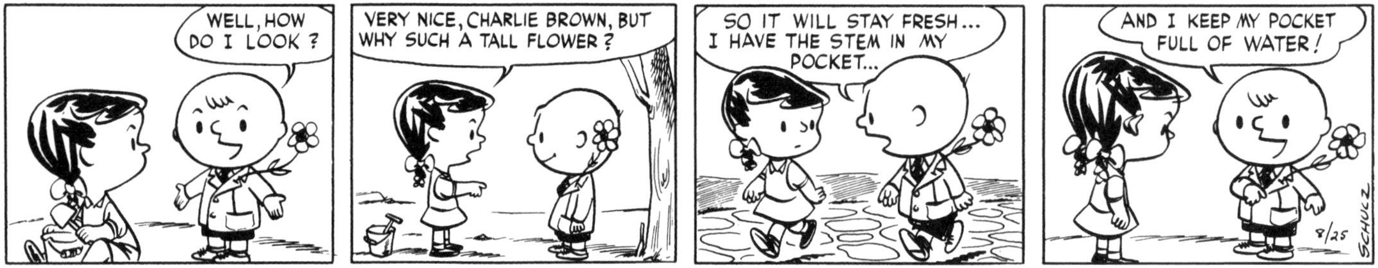
WELL, HOW DO I LOOK?
VERY NICE, CHARLIE BROWN, BUT WHY SUCH A TALL FLOWER?
SO IT WILL STAY FRESH... I HAVE THE STEM IN MY POCKET...
AND I KEEP MY POCKET FULL OF WATER!
8/25
SCHULZ

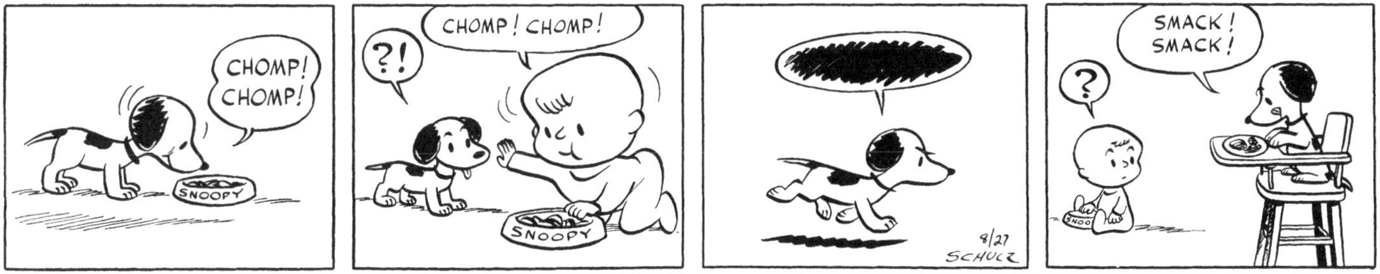
CHOMP!
CHOMP!
SNOOPY
?!
CHOMP! CHOMP!
SNOOPY
8/27
SCHULZ
?
SMACK!
SMACK!

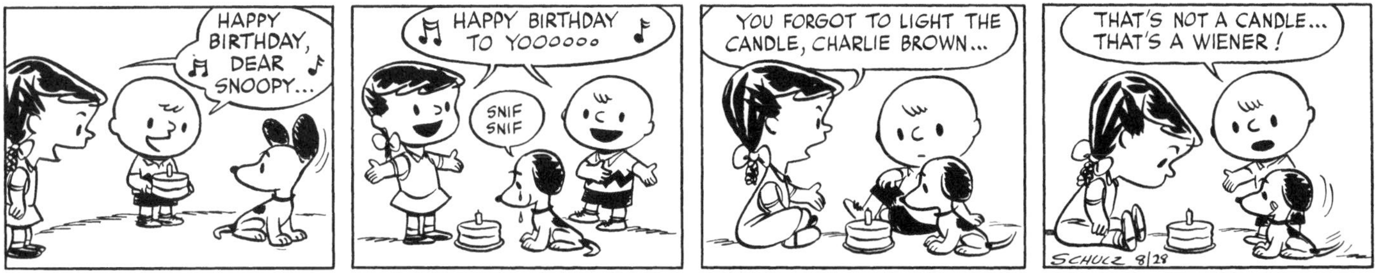
HAPPY BIRTHDAY, DEAR SNOOPY...
HAPPY BIRTHDAY TO YOOOOOO
SNIF SNIF
YOU FORGOT TO LIGHT THE CANDLE, CHARLIE BROWN...
THAT'S NOT A CANDLE... THAT'S A WIENER!
SCHULZ 8/28

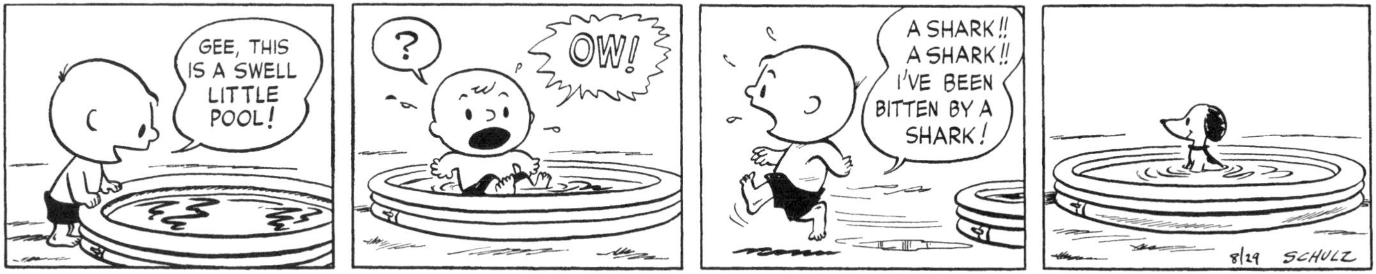
GEE, THIS IS A SWELL LITTLE POOL!
?
OW!
A SHARK!! A SHARK!! I'VE BEEN BITTEN BY A SHARK!
8/29 SCHULZ

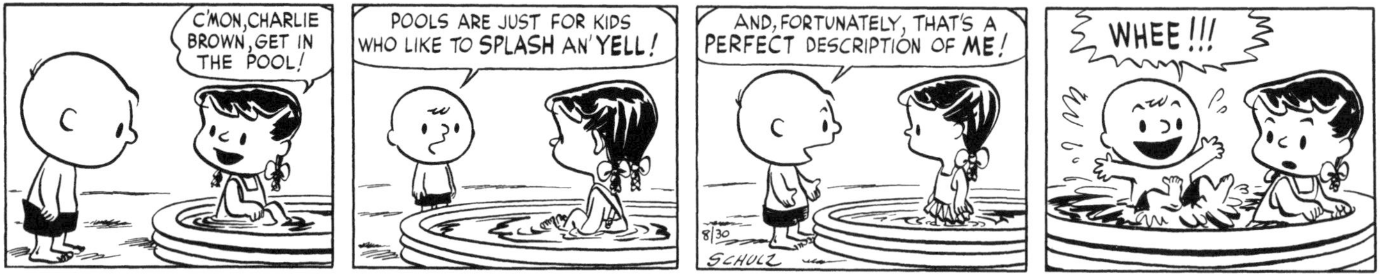
C'MON, CHARLIE BROWN, GET IN THE POOL!
POOLS ARE JUST FOR KIDS WHO LIKE TO SPLASH AN' YELL!
AND, FORTUNATELY, THAT'S A PERFECT DESCRIPTION OF ME!
8/30
SCHULZ
WHEE!!!

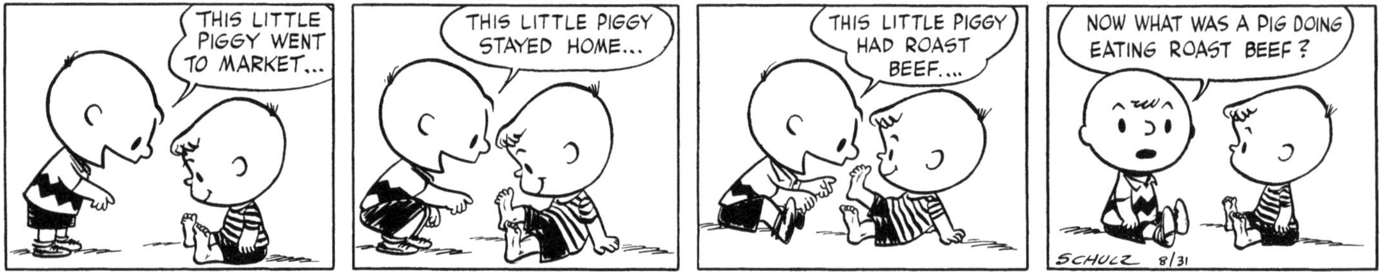
THIS LITTLE PIGGY WENT TO MARKET...
THIS LITTLE PIGGY STAYED HOME...
THIS LITTLE PIGGY HAD ROAST BEEF....
NOW WHAT WAS A PIG DOING EATING ROAST BEEF?
SCHULZ 8/31

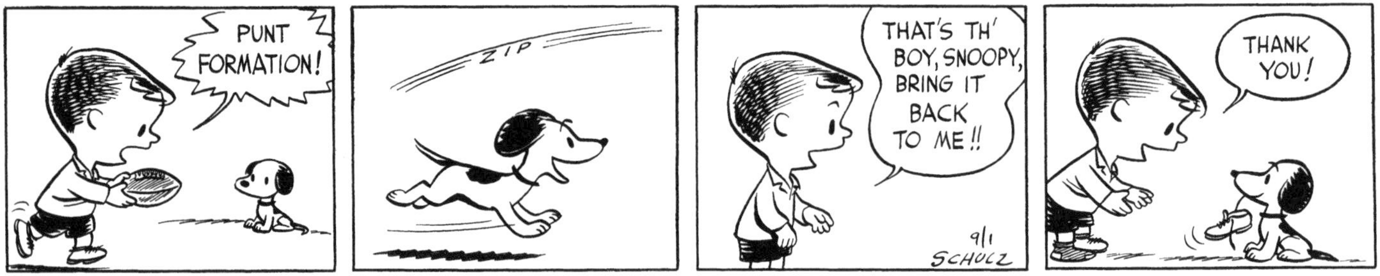
PUNT FORMATION!
ZIP
THAT'S TH' BOY, SNOOPY, BRING IT BACK TO ME!!
9/1
SCHULZ
THANK YOU!

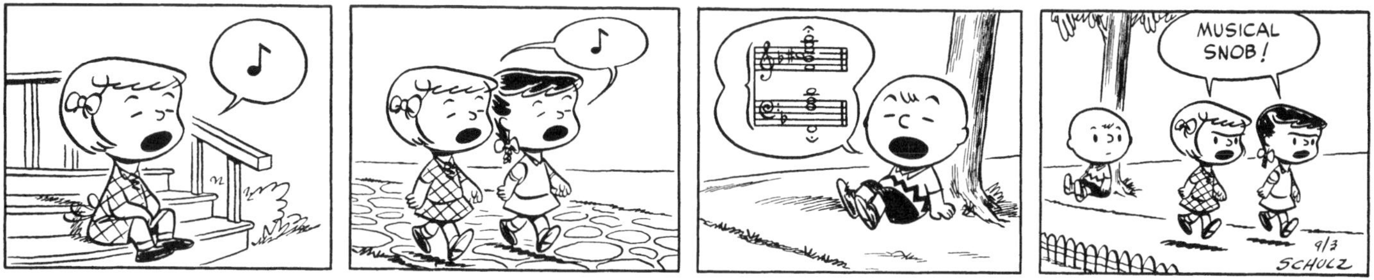
MUSICAL SNOB!
9/3
SCHULZ

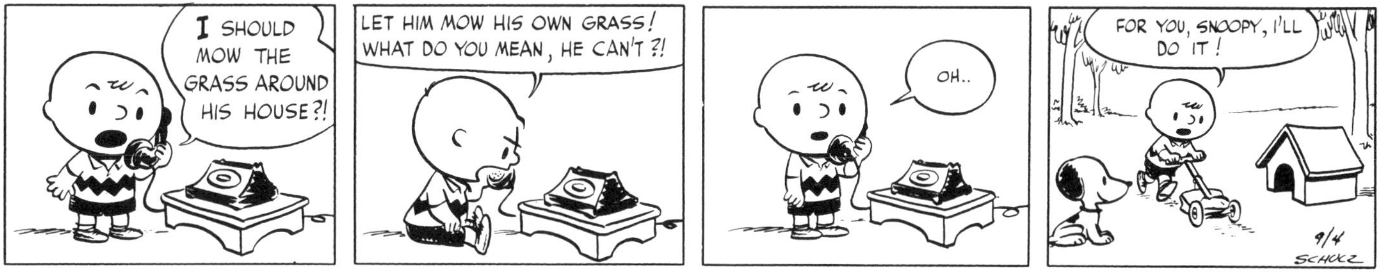
I SHOULD MOW THE GRASS AROUND HIS HOUSE?!
LET HIM MOW HIS OWN GRASS! WHAT DO YOU MEAN, HE CAN'T?!
OH..
FOR YOU, SNOOPY, I'LL DO IT!
9/4
SCHULZ

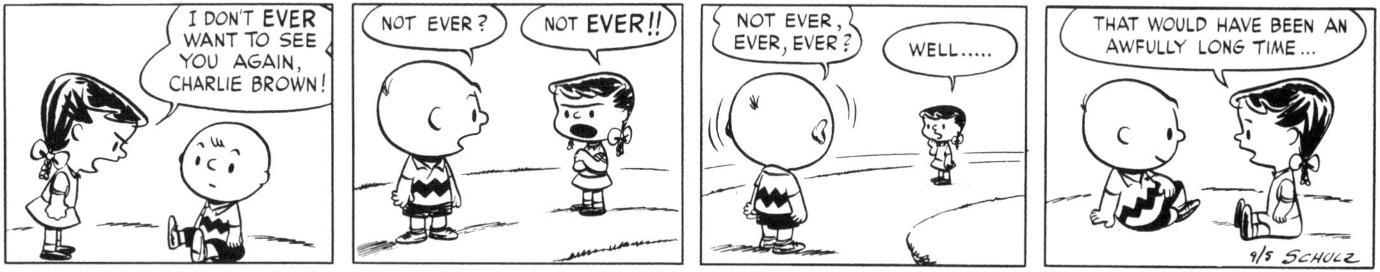
I DON'T EVER WANT TO SEE YOU AGAIN, CHARLIE BROWN!
NOT EVER?
NOT EVER!!
NOT EVER, EVER, EVER?
WELL.....
THAT WOULD HAVE BEEN AN AWFULLY LONG TIME...
9/5 SCHULZ

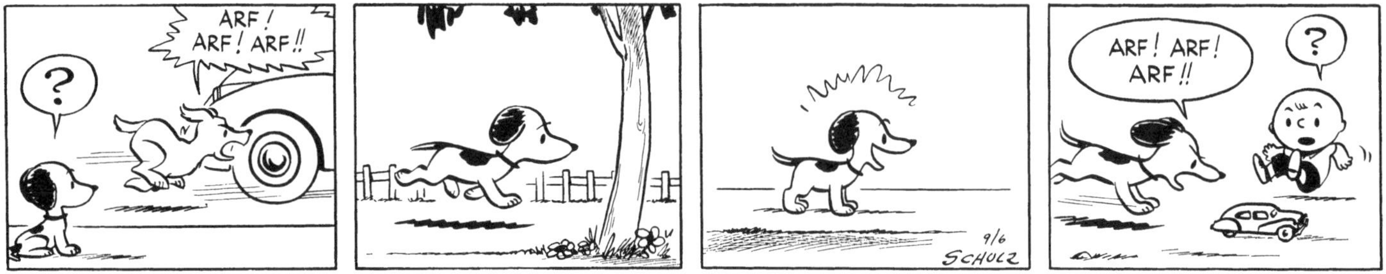
?
ARF! ARF! ARF!!
9/6
SCHULZ
ARF! ARF! ARF!!
?

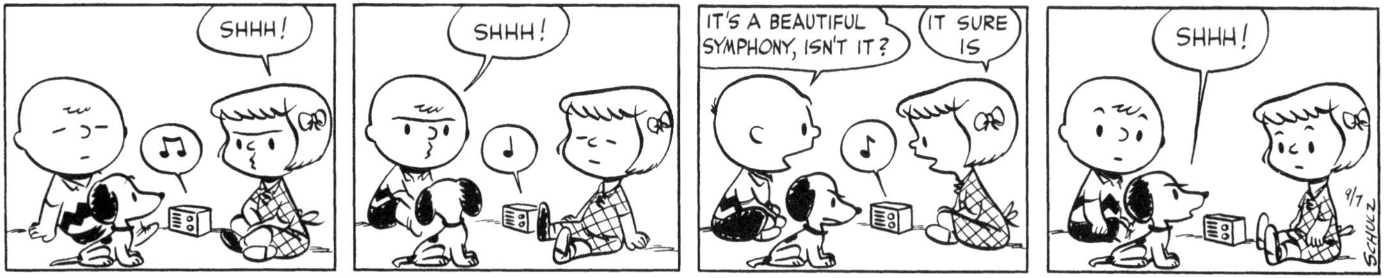
SHHH!
SHHH!
IT'S A BEAUTIFUL SYMPHONY, ISN'T IT?
IT SURE IS
SHHH!
9/7
SCHULZ

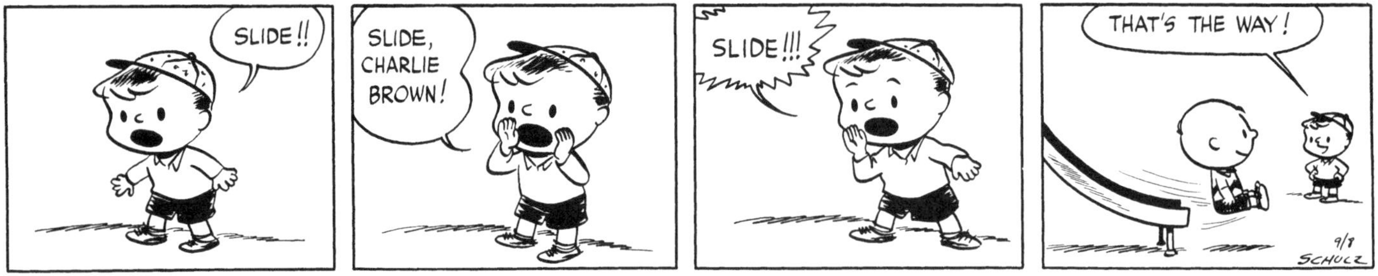
SLIDE!!
SLIDE, CHARLIE BROWN!
SLIDE!!!
THAT'S THE WAY!
9/8
SCHULZ

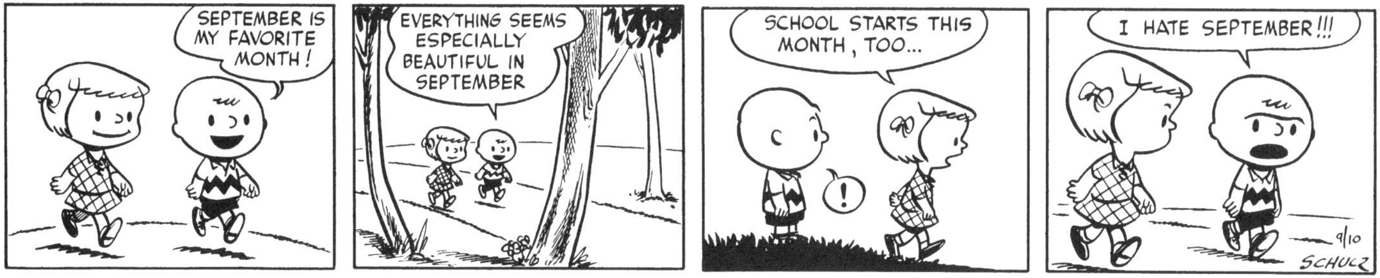
SEPTEMBER IS MY FAVORITE MONTH!
EVERYTHING SEEMS ESPECIALLY BEAUTIFUL IN SEPTEMBER
SCHOOL STARTS THIS MONTH, TOO...
!
I HATE SEPTEMBER!!!
9/10
SCHULZ

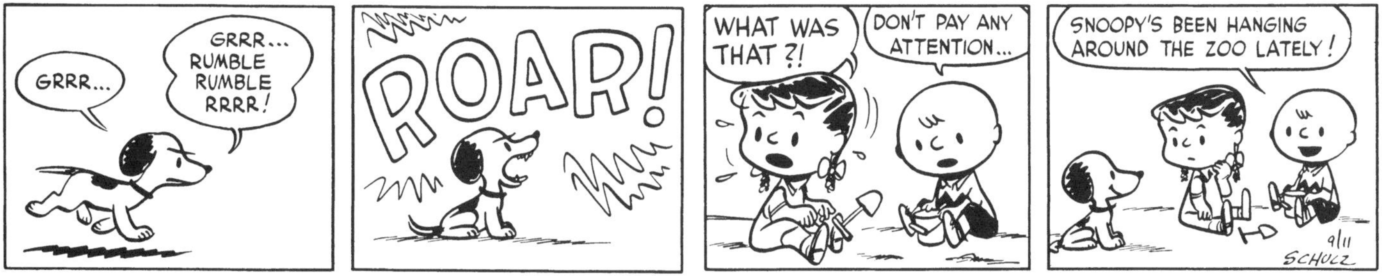
GRRR...
GRRR... RUMBLE RUMBLE RRRR!
ROAR!
WHAT WAS THAT?!
DON'T PAY ANY ATTENTION...
SNOOPY'S BEEN HANGING AROUND THE ZOO LATELY!
9/11
SCHULZ

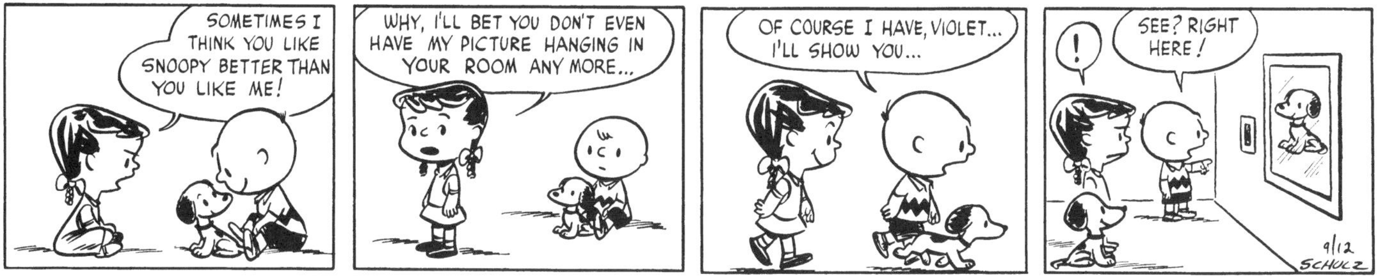
SOMETIMES I THINK YOU LIKE SNOOPY BETTER THAN YOU LIKE ME!
WHY, I'LL BET YOU DON'T EVEN HAVE MY PICTURE HANGING IN YOUR ROOM ANY MORE...
OF COURSE I HAVE, VIOLET... I'LL SHOW YOU...
!
SEE? RIGHT HERE!
9/12
SCHULZ

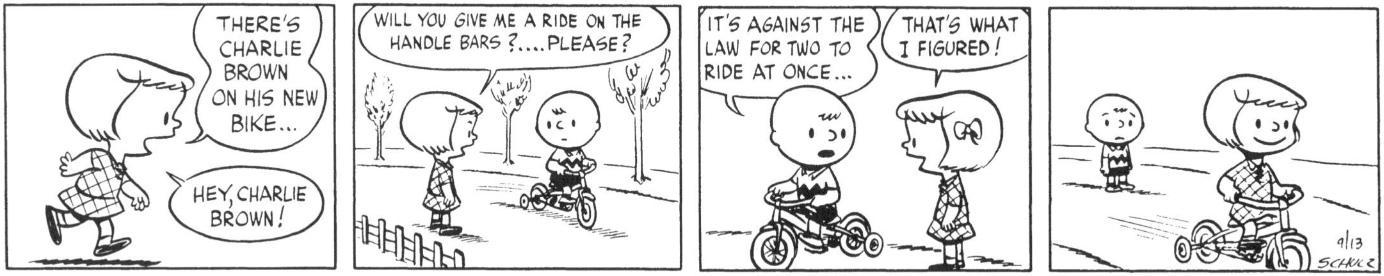
THERE'S CHARLIE BROWN ON HIS NEW BIKE...
HEY, CHARLIE BROWN!
WILL YOU GIVE ME A RIDE ON THE HANDLE BARS?....PLEASE?
IT'S AGAINST THE LAW FOR TWO TO RIDE AT ONCE...
THAT'S WHAT I FIGURED!
9/13
SCHULZ

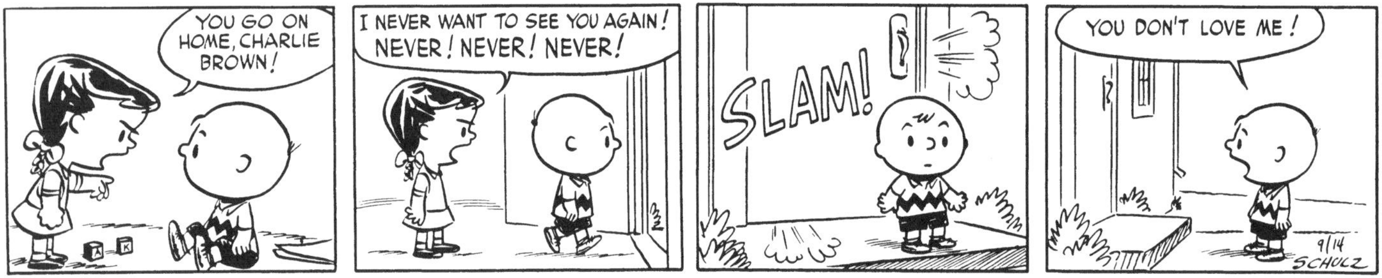
YOU GO ON HOME, CHARLIE BROWN!
I NEVER WANT TO SEE YOU AGAIN! NEVER! NEVER! NEVER!
SLAM!
YOU DON'T LOVE ME!
9/14
SCHULZ

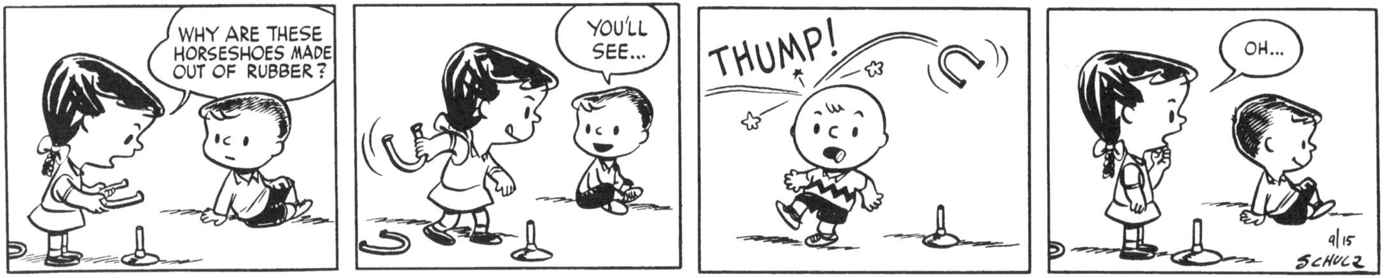
WHY ARE THESE HORSESHOES MADE OUT OF RUBBER?
YOU'LL SEE...
THUMP!
OH...
9/15
SCHULZ

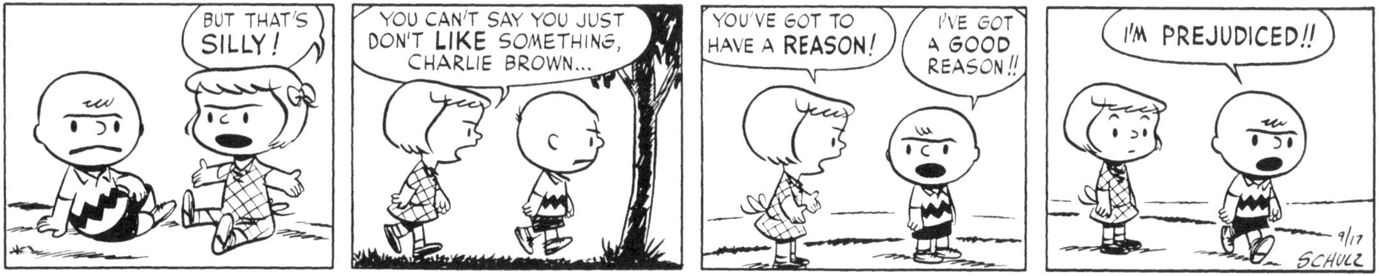

BUT THAT'S SILLY!
YOU CAN'T SAY YOU JUST DON'T LIKE SOMETHING, CHARLIE BROWN...
YOU'VE GOT TO HAVE A REASON!
I'VE GOT A GOOD REASON!!
I'M PREJUDICED!!
9/17
SCHULZ

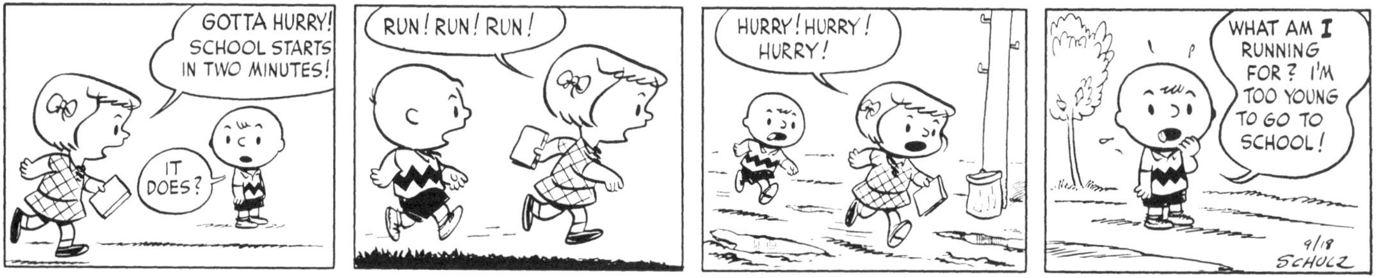

GOTTA HURRY! SCHOOL STARTS IN TWO MINUTES!
IT DOES?
RUN! RUN! RUN!
HURRY! HURRY! HURRY!
WHAT AM I RUNNING FOR? I'M TOO YOUNG TO GO TO SCHOOL!
9/18
SCHULZ

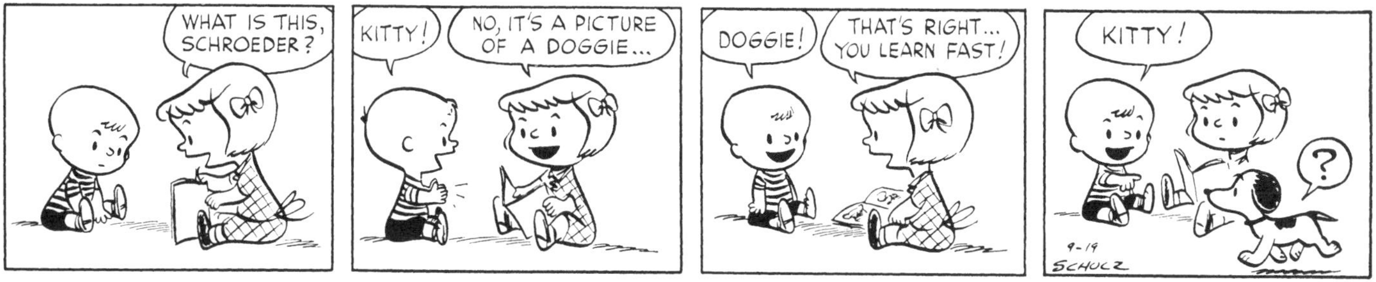

WHAT IS THIS, SCHROEDER?
KITTY!
NO, IT'S A PICTURE OF A DOGGIE...
DOGGIE!
THAT'S RIGHT... YOU LEARN FAST!
KITTY!
?
9-19
SCHULZ

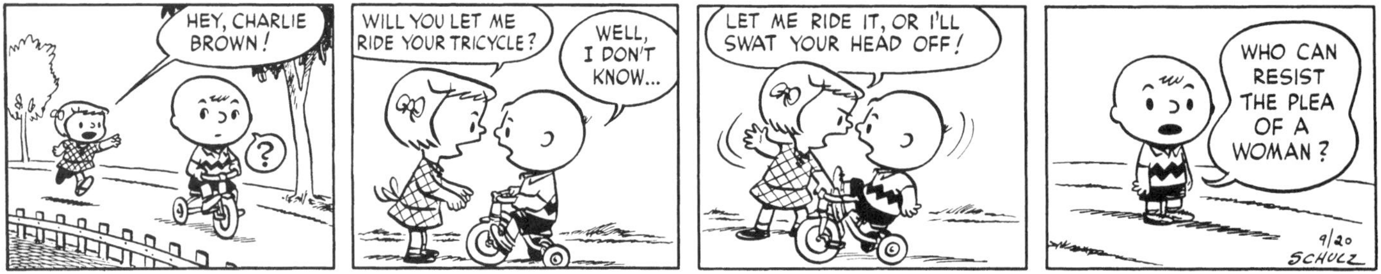
HEY, CHARLIE BROWN!
?
WILL YOU LET ME RIDE YOUR TRICYCLE?
WELL, I DON'T KNOW...
LET ME RIDE IT, OR I'LL SWAT YOUR HEAD OFF!
WHO CAN RESIST THE PLEA OF A WOMAN?
9/20
SCHULZ

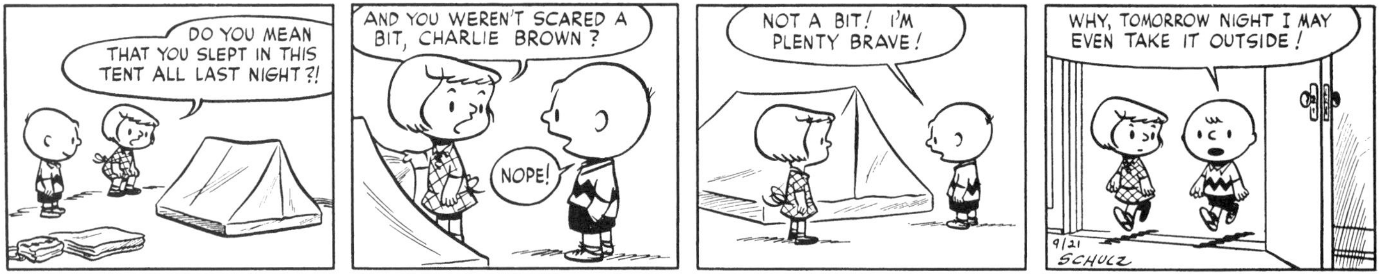
DO YOU MEAN THAT YOU SLEPT IN THIS TENT ALL LAST NIGHT?!
AND YOU WEREN'T SCARED A BIT, CHARLIE BROWN?
NOPE!
NOT A BIT! I'M PLENTY BRAVE!
WHY, TOMORROW NIGHT I MAY EVEN TAKE IT OUTSIDE!
9/21
SCHULZ

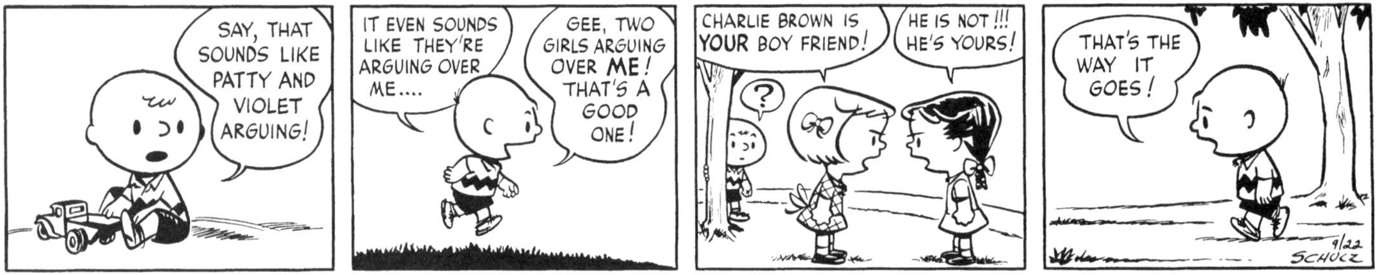
SAY, THAT SOUNDS LIKE PATTY AND VIOLET ARGUING!
IT EVEN SOUNDS LIKE THEY'RE ARGUING OVER ME....
GEE, TWO GIRLS ARGUING OVER ME! THAT'S A GOOD ONE!
CHARLIE BROWN IS YOUR BOY FRIEND!
HE IS NOT!!! HE'S YOURS!
?
THAT'S THE WAY IT GOES!
9/22
SCHULZ

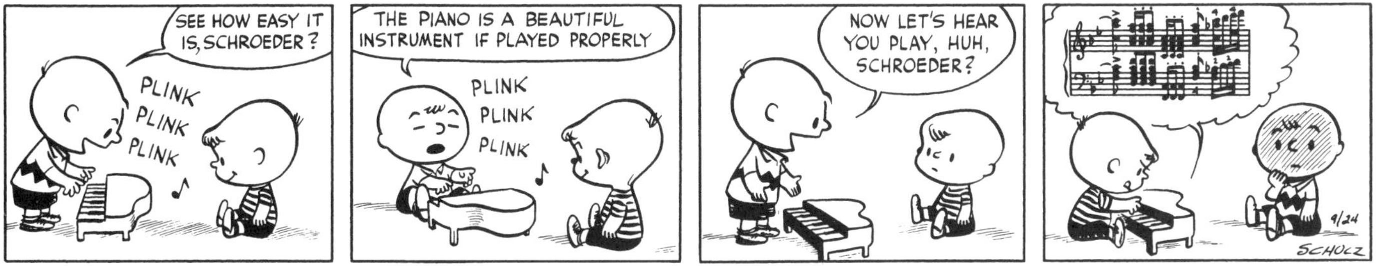
SEE HOW EASY IT IS, SCHROEDER?
PLINK
PLINK
PLINK
THE PIANO IS A BEAUTIFUL INSTRUMENT IF PLAYED PROPERLY
PLINK
PLINK
PLINK
NOW LET'S HEAR YOU PLAY, HUH, SCHROEDER?
9/24
SCHULZ

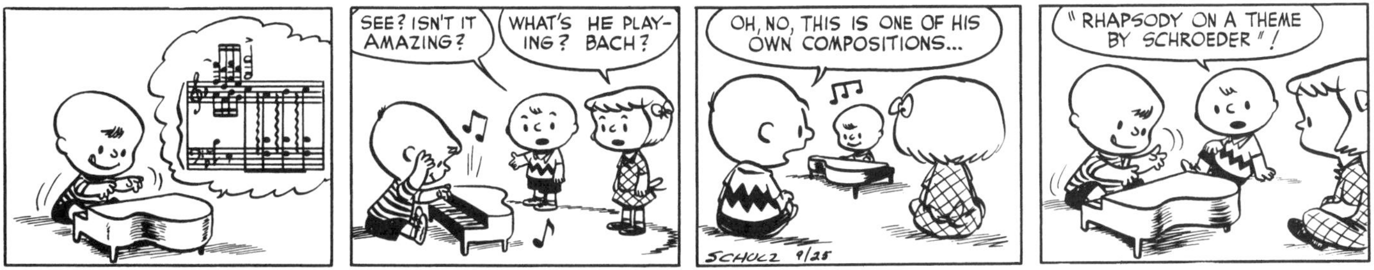
SEE? ISN'T IT AMAZING?
WHAT'S HE PLAYING? BACH?
OH, NO, THIS IS ONE OF HIS OWN COMPOSITIONS...
SCHULZ 9/25
"RHAPSODY ON A THEME BY SCHROEDER"!

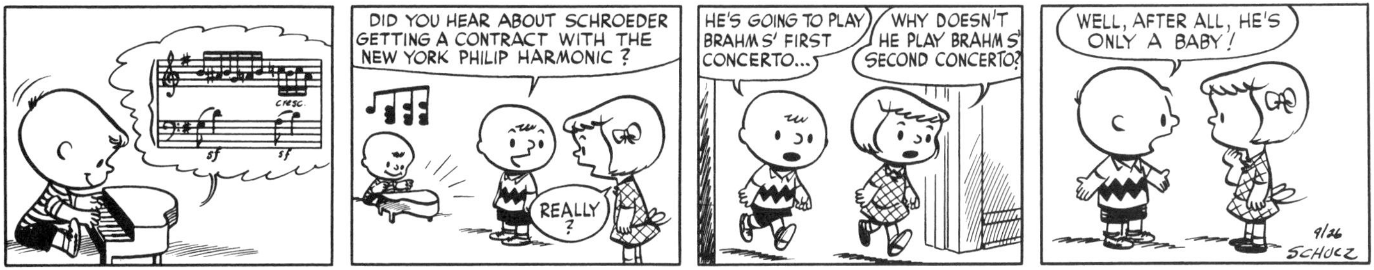
cresc.
sf
sf
DID YOU HEAR ABOUT SCHROEDER GETTING A CONTRACT WITH THE NEW YORK PHILIP HARMONIC?
REALLY?
HE'S GOING TO PLAY BRAHMS' FIRST CONCERTO...
WHY DOESN'T HE PLAY BRAHMS' SECOND CONCERTO?
WELL, AFTER ALL, HE'S ONLY A BABY!
9/26
SCHULZ

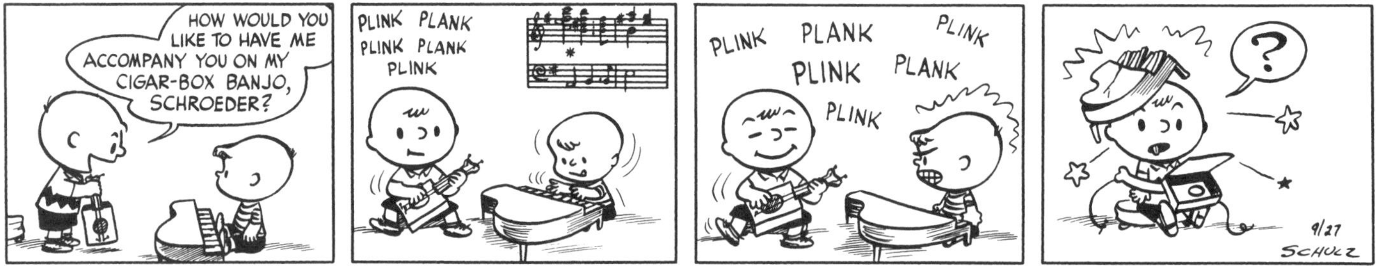
HOW WOULD YOU LIKE TO HAVE ME ACCOMPANY YOU ON MY CIGAR-BOX BANJO, SCHROEDER?
PLINK PLANK PLINK PLANK PLINK
PLINK PLANK PLINK PLINK PLANK PLINK
?
9/27
SCHULZ

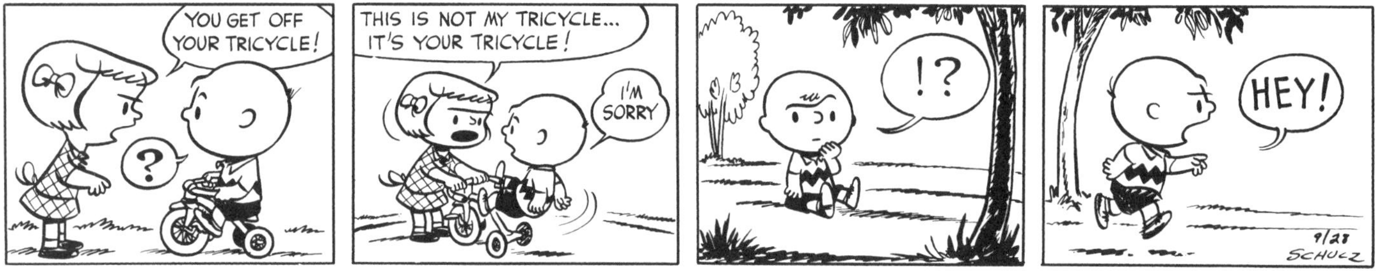
YOU GET OFF YOUR TRICYCLE!
?
THIS IS NOT MY TRICYCLE... IT'S YOUR TRICYCLE!
I'M SORRY
!?
HEY!
9/28
SCHULZ

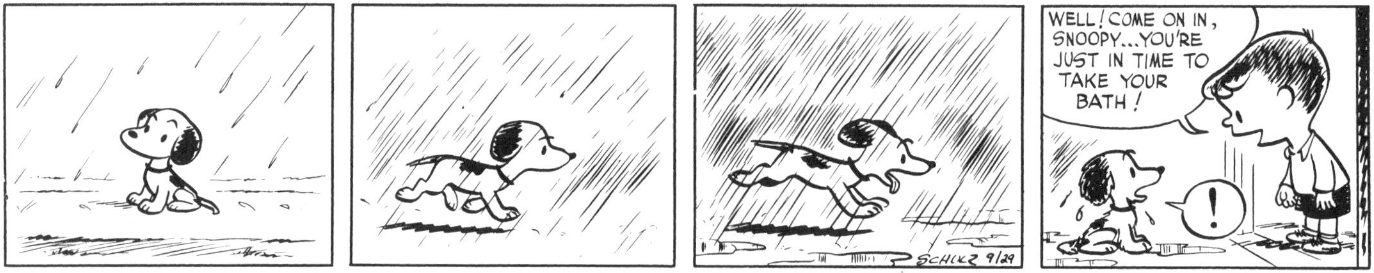
SCHULZ 9/29
WELL! COME ON IN, SNOOPY...YOU'RE JUST IN TIME TO TAKE YOUR BATH!
!

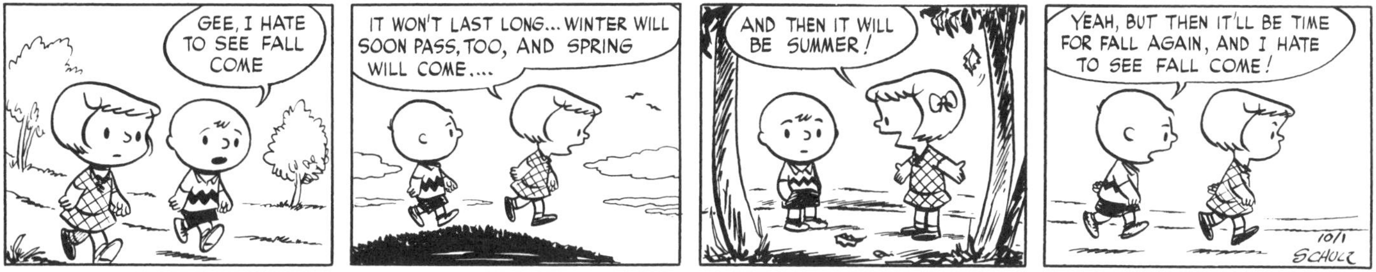
GEE, I HATE TO SEE FALL COME
IT WON'T LAST LONG... WINTER WILL SOON PASS, TOO, AND SPRING WILL COME....
AND THEN IT WILL BE SUMMER!
YEAH, BUT THEN IT'LL BE TIME FOR FALL AGAIN, AND I HATE TO SEE FALL COME!
10/1
SCHULZ

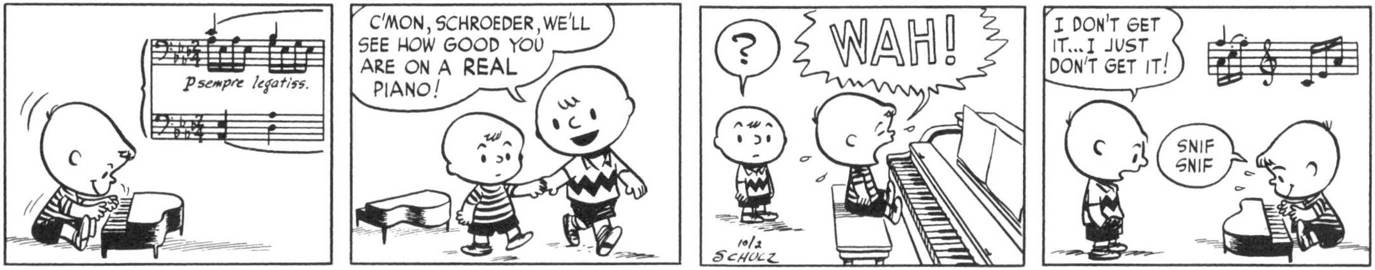
p sempre legatiss.
C'MON, SCHROEDER, WE'LL SEE HOW GOOD YOU ARE ON A REAL PIANO!
?
WAH!
10/2
SCHULZ
I DON'T GET IT... I JUST DON'T GET IT!
SNIF SNIF

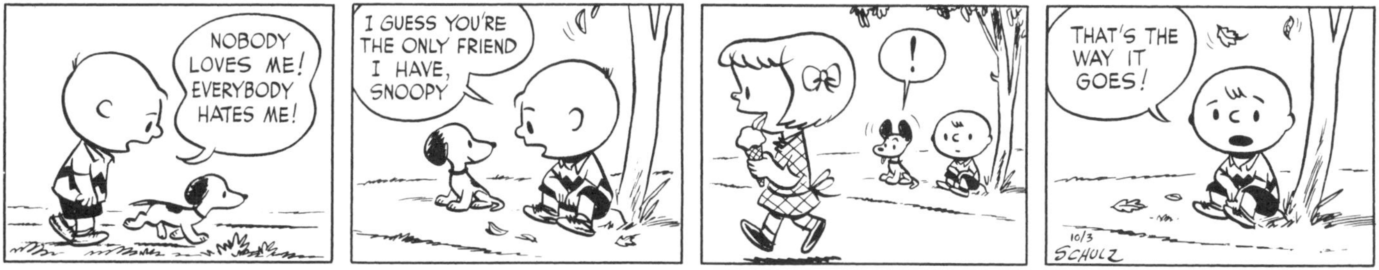
NOBODY LOVES ME! EVERYBODY HATES ME!
I GUESS YOU'RE THE ONLY FRIEND I HAVE, SNOOPY
!
THAT'S THE WAY IT GOES!
10/3
SCHULZ

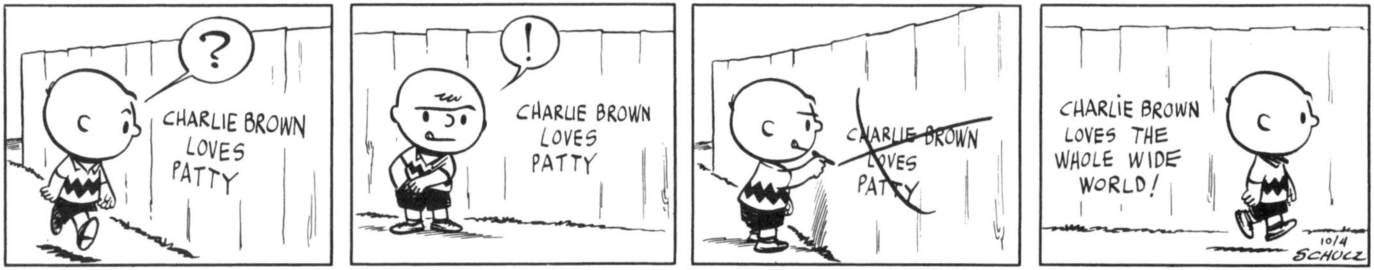
?
CHARLIE BROWN LOVES PATTY
!
CHARLIE BROWN LOVES PATTY
CHARLIE BROWN LOVES PATTY
CHARLIE BROWN LOVES THE WHOLE WIDE WORLD!
10/4
SCHULZ

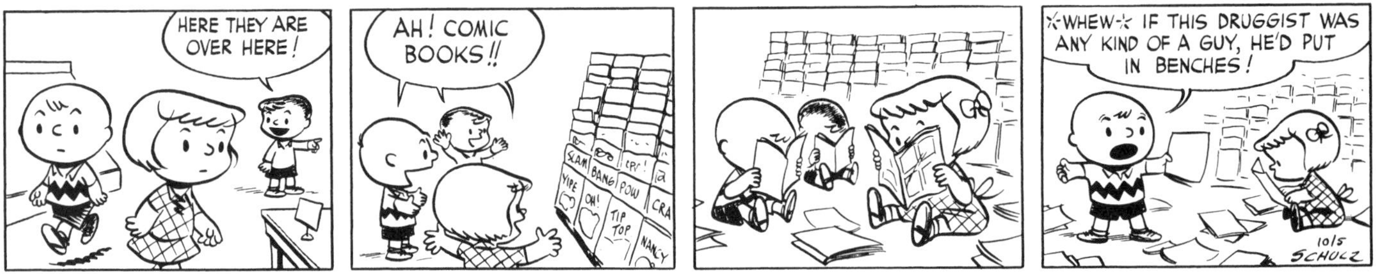
HERE THEY ARE OVER HERE!
AH! COMIC BOOKS!!
SLAM
BANG
POW
YIPE
OH!
TIP TOP
CRA
NANCY
WHEW IF THIS DRUGGIST WAS ANY KIND OF A GUY, HE'D PUT IN BENCHES!
10/5
SCHULZ

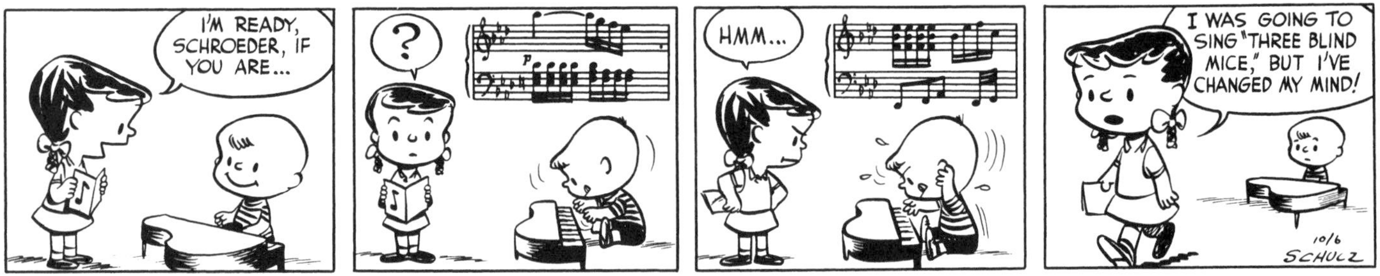
I'M READY, SCHROEDER, IF YOU ARE...
?
HMM...
I WAS GOING TO SING "THREE BLIND MICE," BUT I'VE CHANGED MY MIND!
10/6
SCHULZ

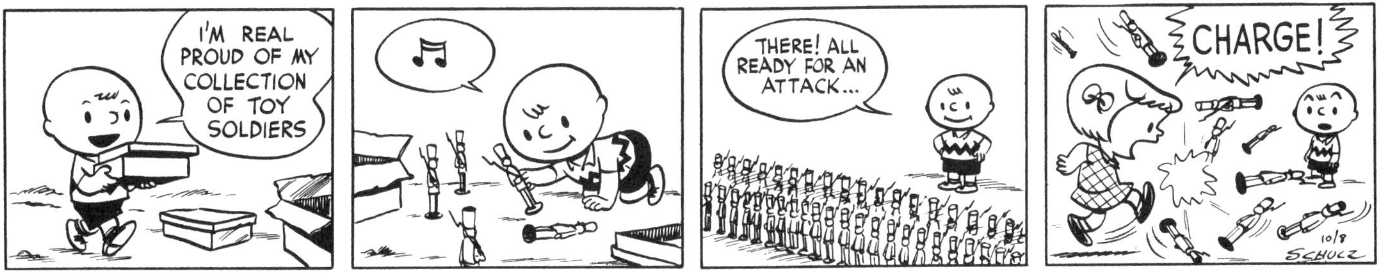
I'M REAL PROUD OF MY COLLECTION OF TOY SOLDIERS
THERE! ALL READY FOR AN ATTACK...
CHARGE!
10/8
SCHULZ

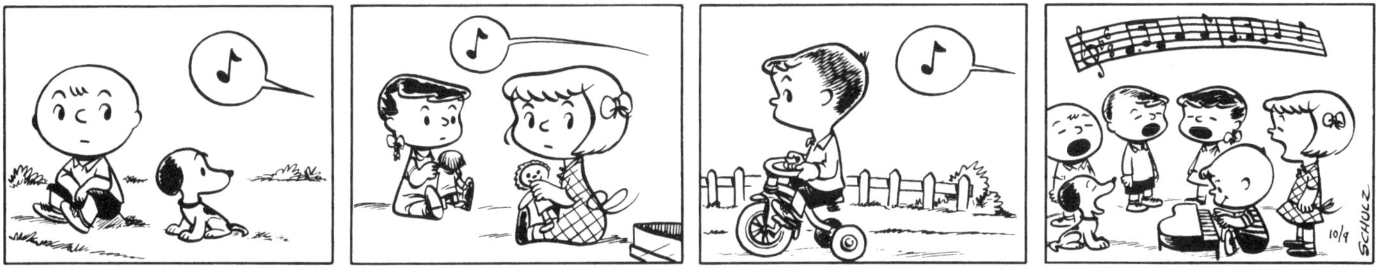
10/9
SCHULZ

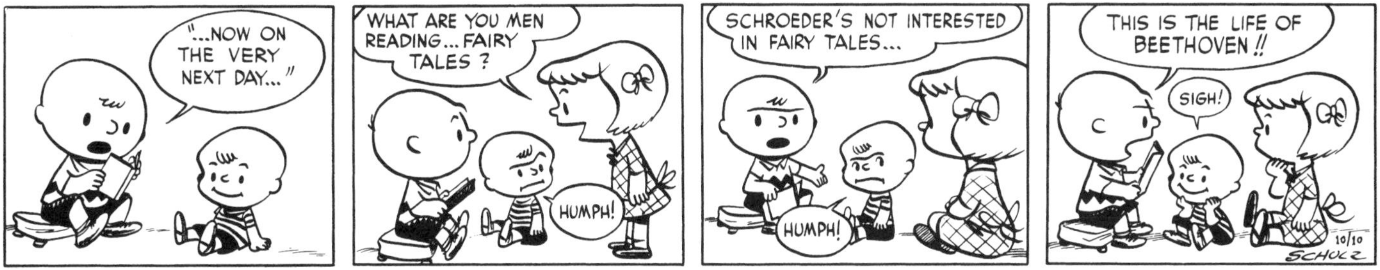
"...NOW ON THE VERY NEXT DAY..."
WHAT ARE YOU MEN READING... FAIRY TALES ?
HUMPH!
SCHROEDER'S NOT INTERESTED IN FAIRY TALES...
HUMPH!
THIS IS THE LIFE OF BEETHOVEN !!
SIGH!
10/10
SCHULZ

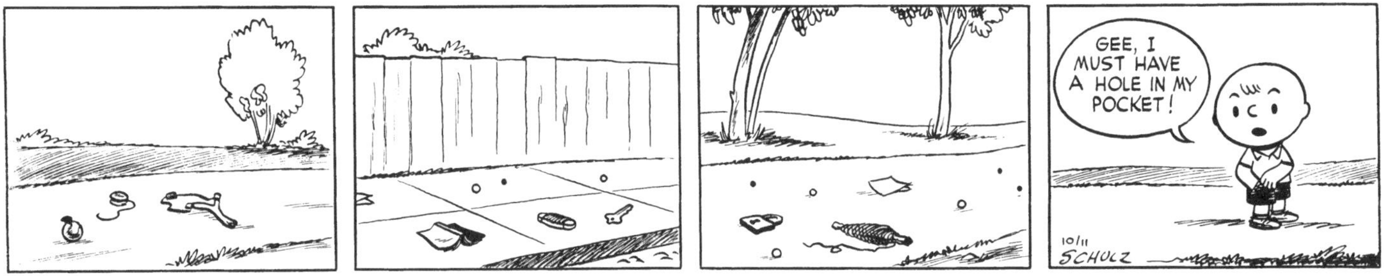
GEE, I MUST HAVE A HOLE IN MY POCKET!
10/11
SCHULZ

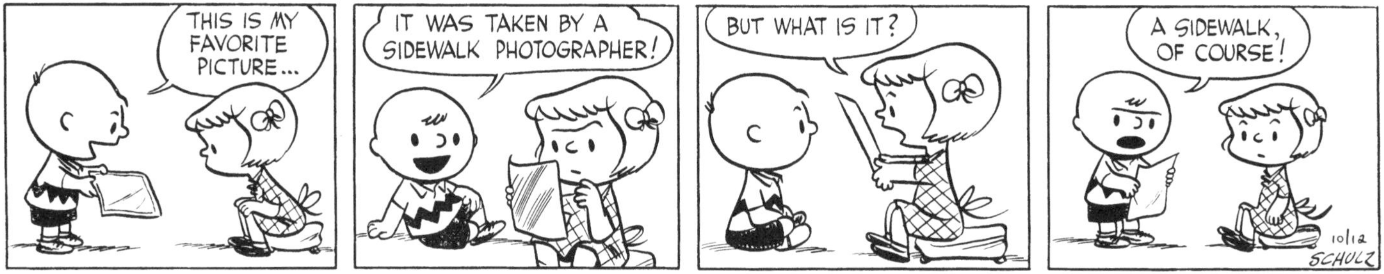
THIS IS MY FAVORITE PICTURE...
IT WAS TAKEN BY A SIDEWALK PHOTOGRAPHER!
BUT WHAT IS IT?
A SIDEWALK, OF COURSE!
10/12
SCHULZ

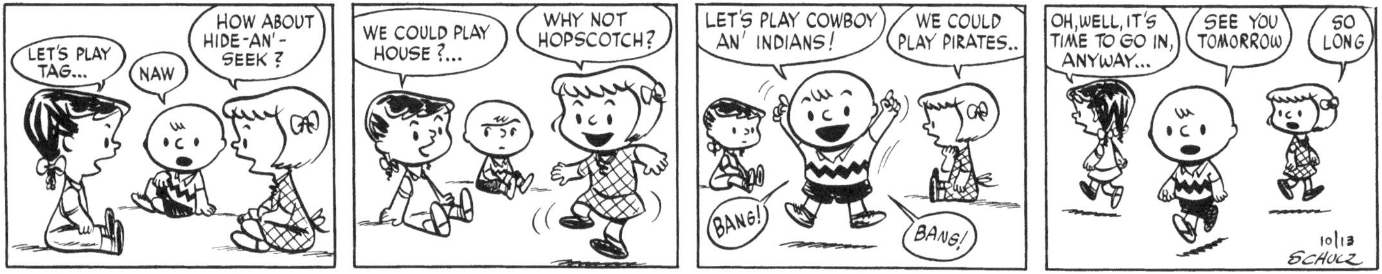
LET'S PLAY TAG...
NAW
HOW ABOUT HIDE-AN'-SEEK?
WE COULD PLAY HOUSE?...
WHY NOT HOPSCOTCH?
LET'S PLAY COWBOY AN' INDIANS!
WE COULD PLAY PIRATES..
BANG!
BANG!
OH, WELL, IT'S TIME TO GO IN, ANYWAY...
SEE YOU TOMORROW
SO LONG
10/13
SCHULZ

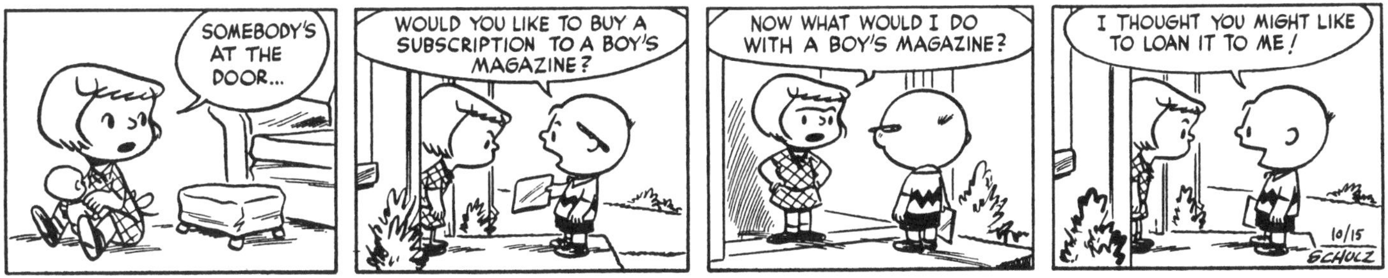
SOMEBODY'S AT THE DOOR...
WOULD YOU LIKE TO BUY A SUBSCRIPTION TO A BOY'S MAGAZINE?
NOW WHAT WOULD I DO WITH A BOY'S MAGAZINE?
I THOUGHT YOU MIGHT LIKE TO LOAN IT TO ME!
10/15
SCHULZ

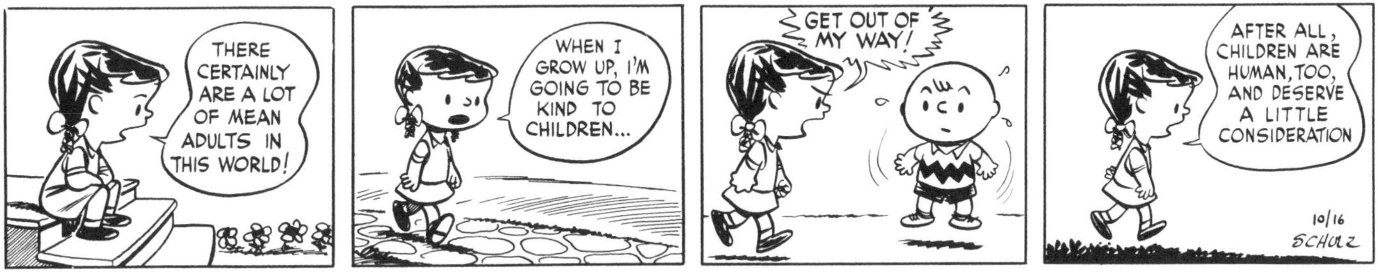
THERE CERTAINLY ARE A LOT OF MEAN ADULTS IN THIS WORLD!
WHEN I GROW UP, I'M GOING TO BE KIND TO CHILDREN...
GET OUT OF MY WAY!
AFTER ALL, CHILDREN ARE HUMAN, TOO, AND DESERVE A LITTLE CONSIDERATION
10/16
SCHULZ

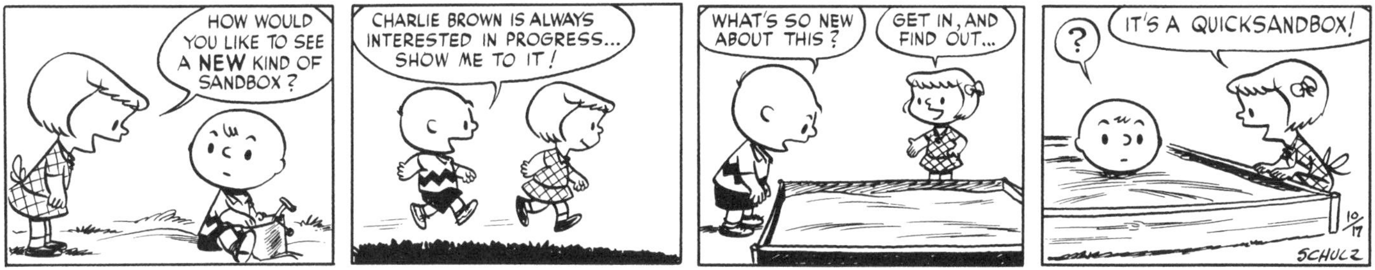
HOW WOULD YOU LIKE TO SEE A NEW KIND OF SANDBOX?
CHARLIE BROWN IS ALWAYS INTERESTED IN PROGRESS... SHOW ME TO IT!
WHAT'S SO NEW ABOUT THIS?
GET IN, AND FIND OUT...
?
IT'S A QUICKSANDBOX!
10/17
SCHULZ

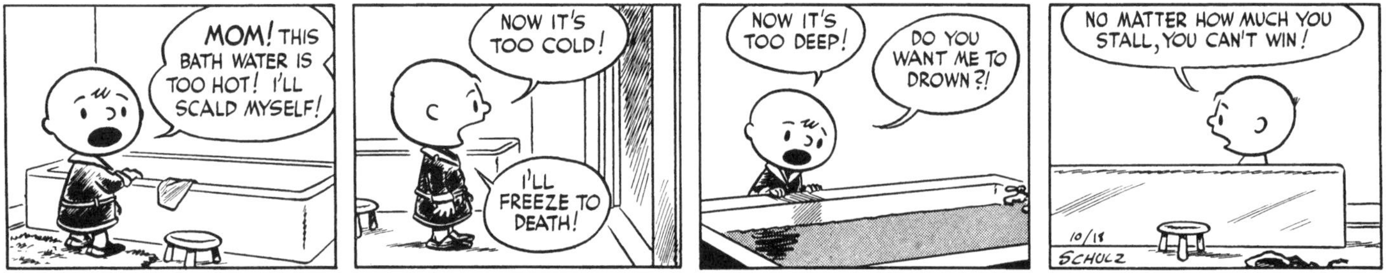
MOM! THIS BATH WATER IS TOO HOT! I'LL SCALD MYSELF!
NOW IT'S TOO COLD!
I'LL FREEZE TO DEATH!
NOW IT'S TOO DEEP!
DO YOU WANT ME TO DROWN?!
NO MATTER HOW MUCH YOU STALL, YOU CAN'T WIN!
10/18
SCHULZ

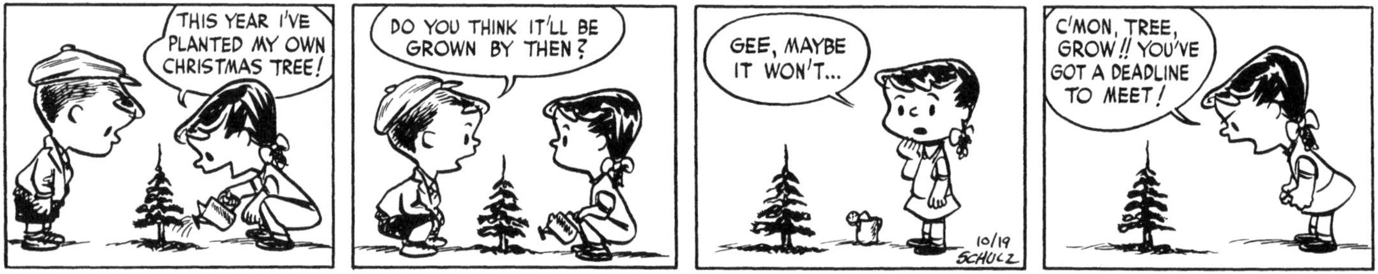
THIS YEAR I'VE PLANTED MY OWN CHRISTMAS TREE!
DO YOU THINK IT'LL BE GROWN BY THEN?
GEE, MAYBE IT WON'T...
10/19
SCHULZ
C'MON, TREE, GROW!! YOU'VE GOT A DEADLINE TO MEET!

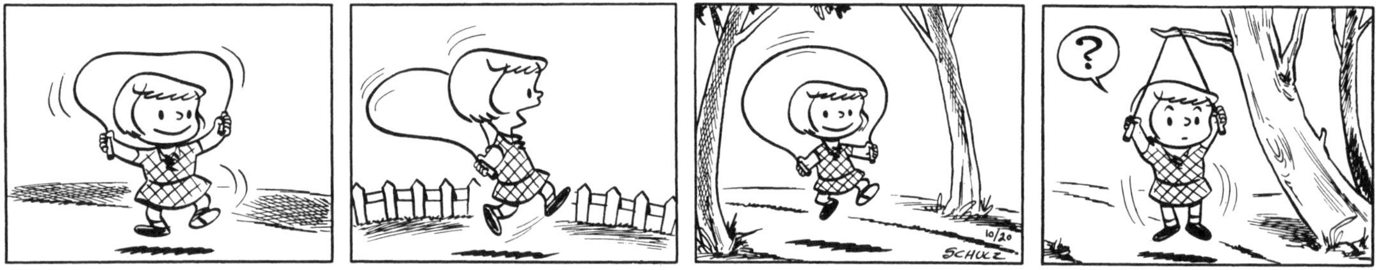
10/20
SCHULZ
?

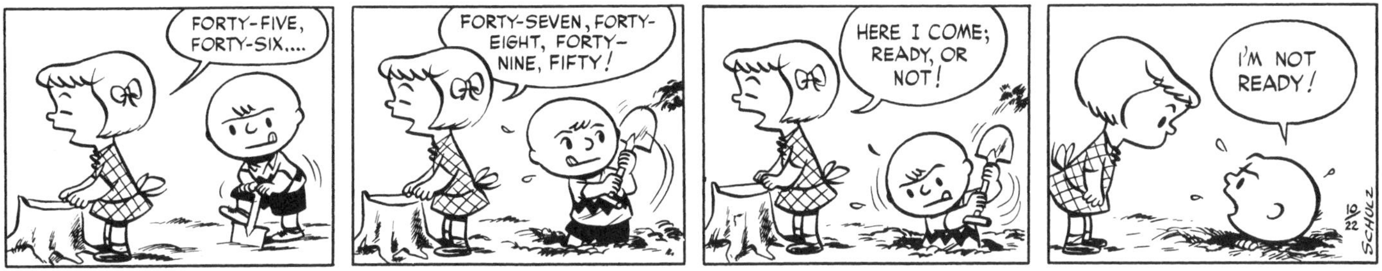
FORTY-FIVE, FORTY-SIX....
FORTY-SEVEN, FORTY-EIGHT, FORTY-NINE, FIFTY!
HERE I COME; READY, OR NOT!
I'M NOT READY!
10/22 SCHULZ

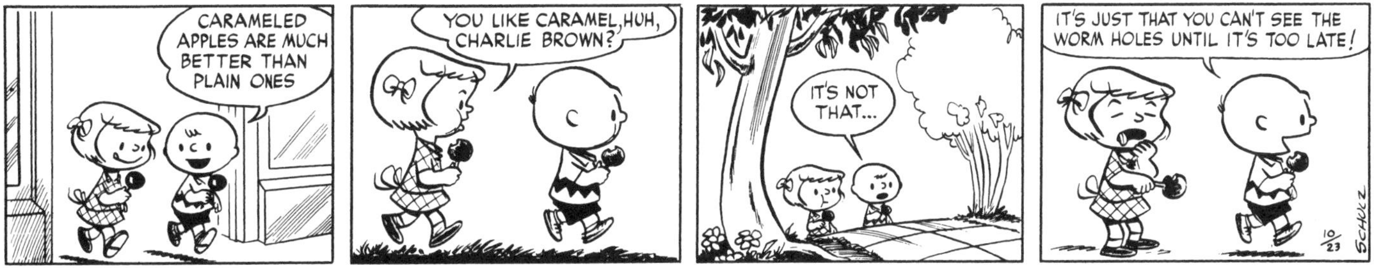
CARAMELED APPLES ARE MUCH BETTER THAN PLAIN ONES
YOU LIKE CARAMEL, HUH, CHARLIE BROWN?
IT'S NOT THAT...
IT'S JUST THAT YOU CAN'T SEE THE WORM HOLES UNTIL IT'S TOO LATE!
10/23 SCHULZ

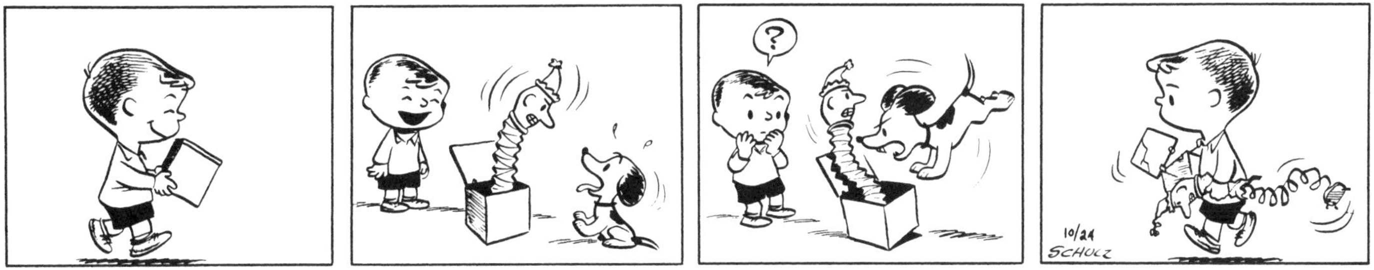
?
10/24 SCHULZ

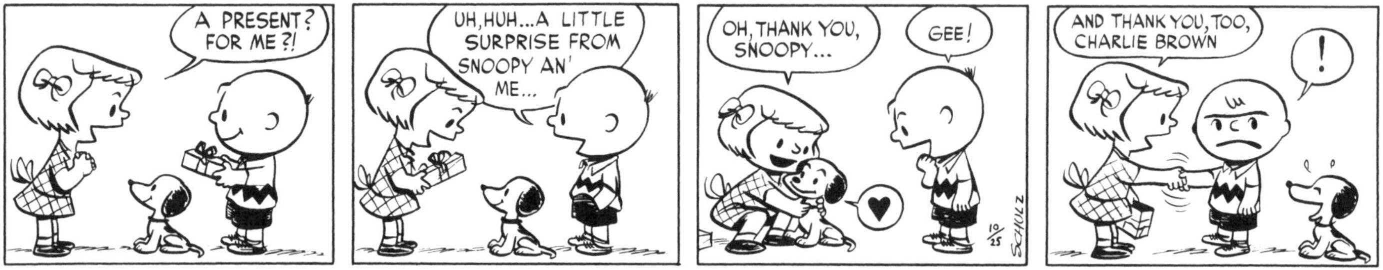
A PRESENT? FOR ME?!
UH, HUH...A LITTLE SURPRISE FROM SNOOPY AN' ME...
OH, THANK YOU, SNOOPY...
GEE!
10/25 SCHULZ
AND THANK YOU, TOO, CHARLIE BROWN
!

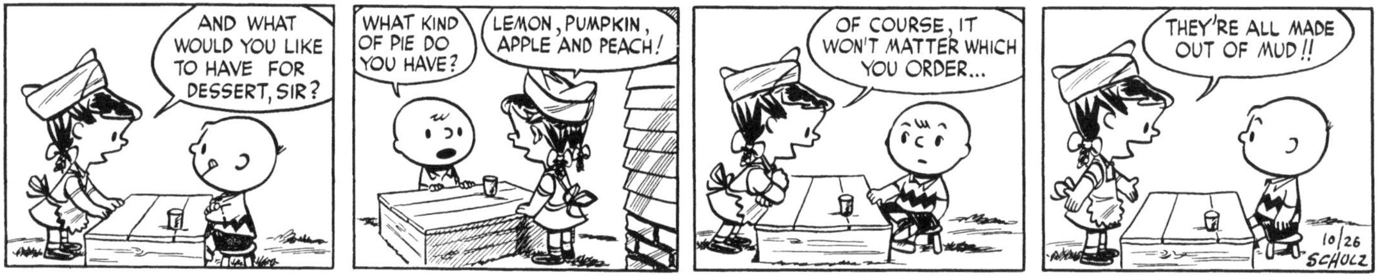
AND WHAT WOULD YOU LIKE TO HAVE FOR DESSERT, SIR?
WHAT KIND OF PIE DO YOU HAVE?
LEMON, PUMPKIN, APPLE AND PEACH!
OF COURSE, IT WON'T MATTER WHICH YOU ORDER...
THEY'RE ALL MADE OUT OF MUD!!
10/26 SCHULZ

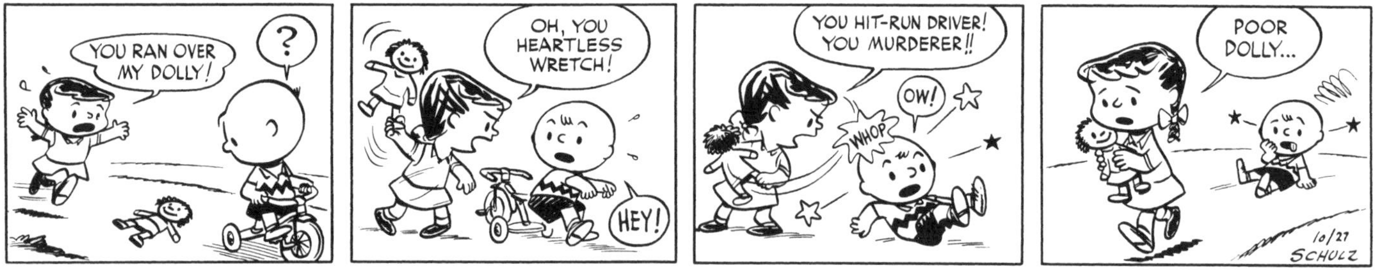
YOU RAN OVER MY DOLLY!
?
OH, YOU HEARTLESS WRETCH!
HEY!
YOU HIT-RUN DRIVER! YOU MURDERER!!
OW!
WHOP
POOR DOLLY...
10/27 SCHULZ

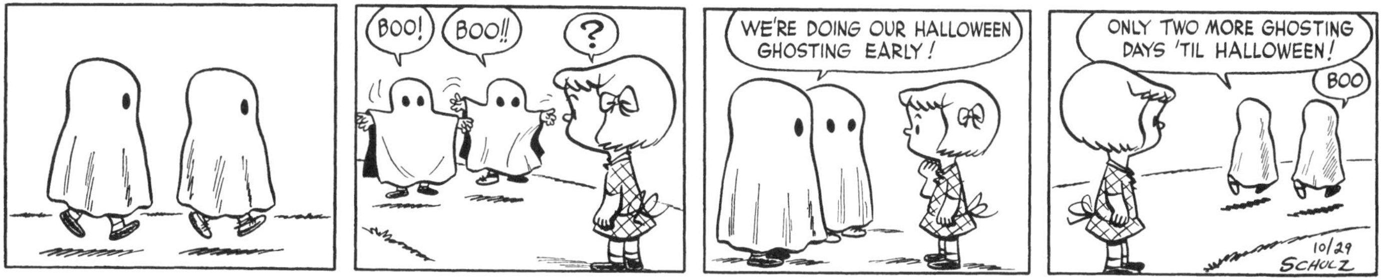
BOO!
BOO!!
?
WE'RE DOING OUR HALLOWEEN GHOSTING EARLY!
ONLY TWO MORE GHOSTING DAYS 'TIL HALLOWEEN!
BOO
10/29
SCHULZ

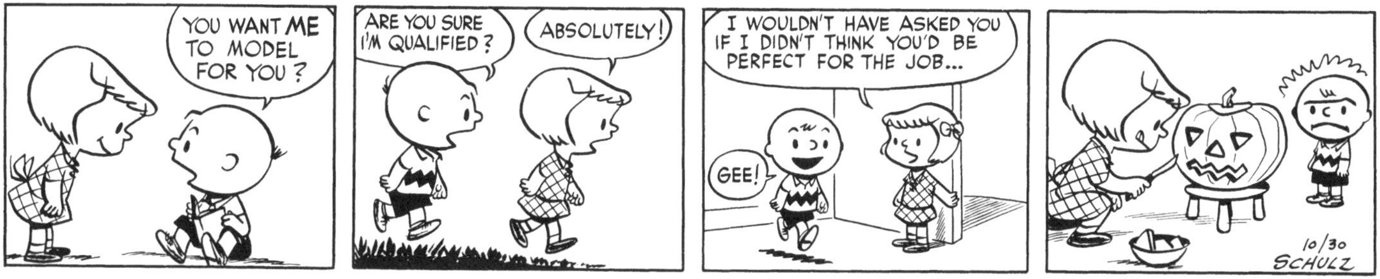
YOU WANT ME TO MODEL FOR YOU?
ARE YOU SURE I'M QUALIFIED?
ABSOLUTELY!
I WOULDN'T HAVE ASKED YOU IF I DIDN'T THINK YOU'D BE PERFECT FOR THE JOB...
GEE!
10/30
SCHULZ

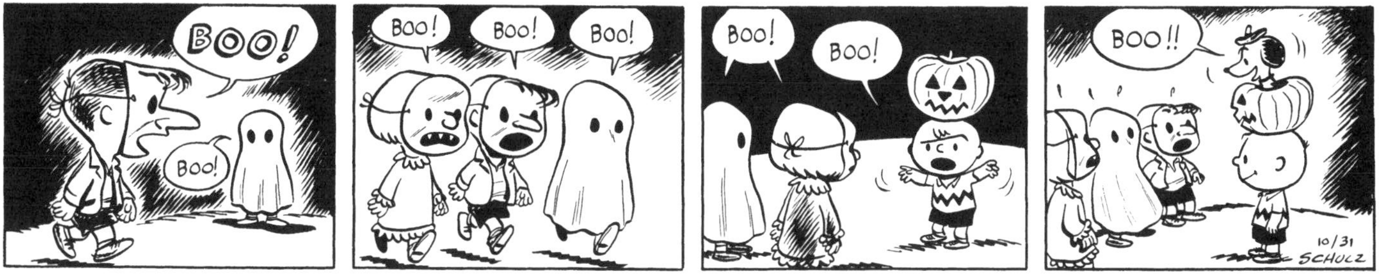
BOO!
BOO!
BOO!
BOO!
BOO!
BOO!
BOO!
BOO!!
10/31
SCHULZ

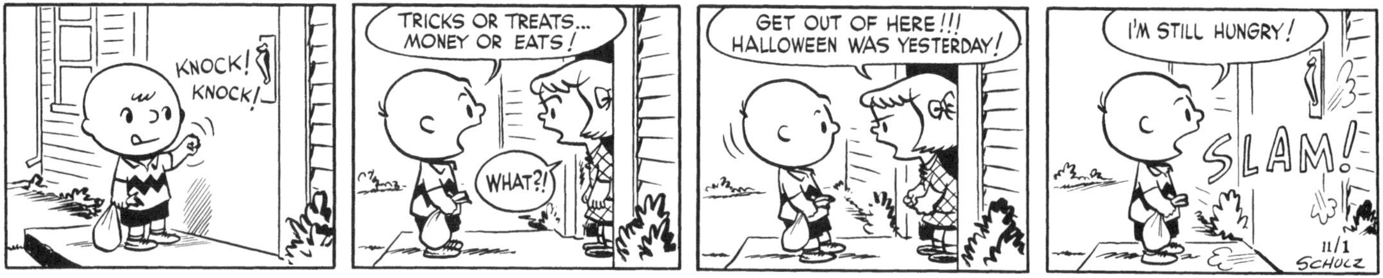
KNOCK! KNOCK!
TRICKS OR TREATS... MONEY OR EATS!
WHAT?!
GET OUT OF HERE!!! HALLOWEEN WAS YESTERDAY!
I'M STILL HUNGRY!
SLAM!
11/1 SCHULZ

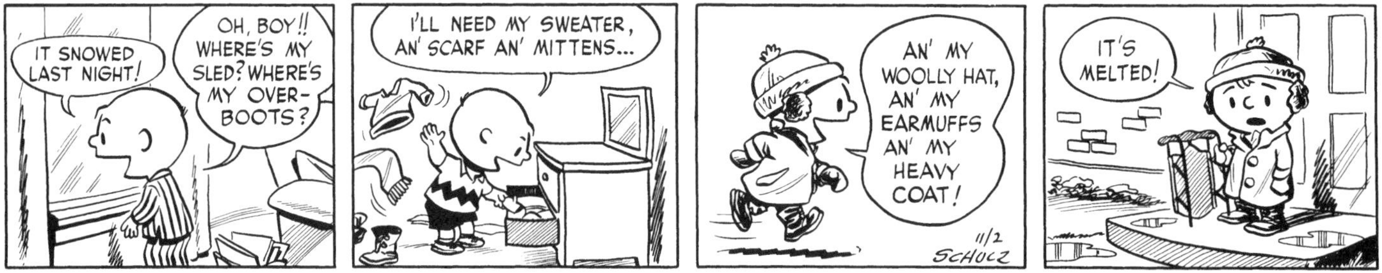
IT SNOWED LAST NIGHT!
OH, BOY!! WHERE'S MY SLED? WHERE'S MY OVER-BOOTS?
I'LL NEED MY SWEATER, AN' SCARF AN' MITTENS...
AN' MY WOOLLY HAT, AN' MY EARMUFFS AN' MY HEAVY COAT!
11/2 SCHULZ
IT'S MELTED!

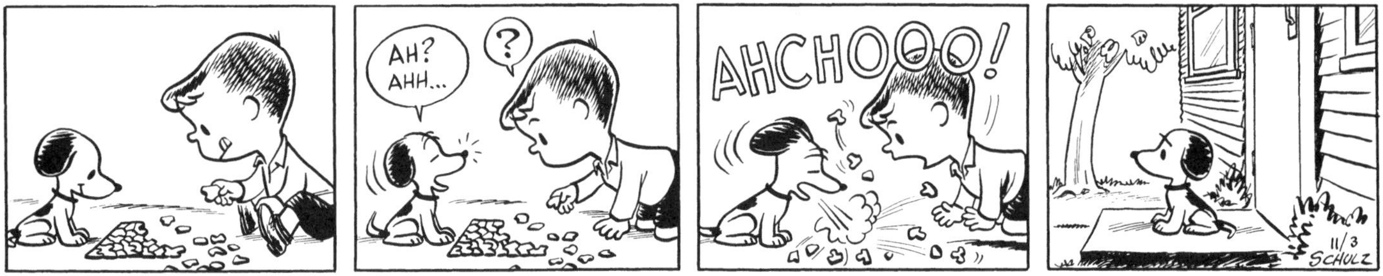
AH? AHH...
?
AHCHOOO!
11/3 SCHULZ

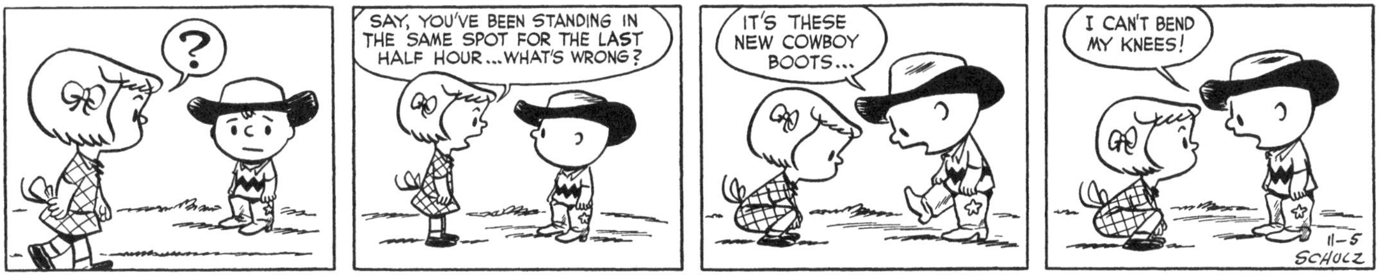
?
SAY, YOU'VE BEEN STANDING IN THE SAME SPOT FOR THE LAST HALF HOUR...WHAT'S WRONG?
IT'S THESE NEW COWBOY BOOTS...
I CAN'T BEND MY KNEES!
11-5
SCHULZ

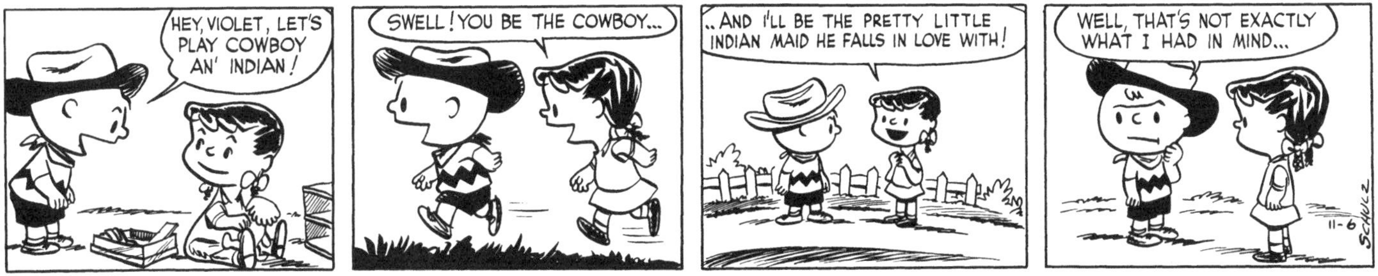
HEY, VIOLET, LET'S PLAY COWBOY AN' INDIAN!
SWELL! YOU BE THE COWBOY...
..AND I'LL BE THE PRETTY LITTLE INDIAN MAID HE FALLS IN LOVE WITH!
WELL, THAT'S NOT EXACTLY WHAT I HAD IN MIND...
11-6
SCHULZ

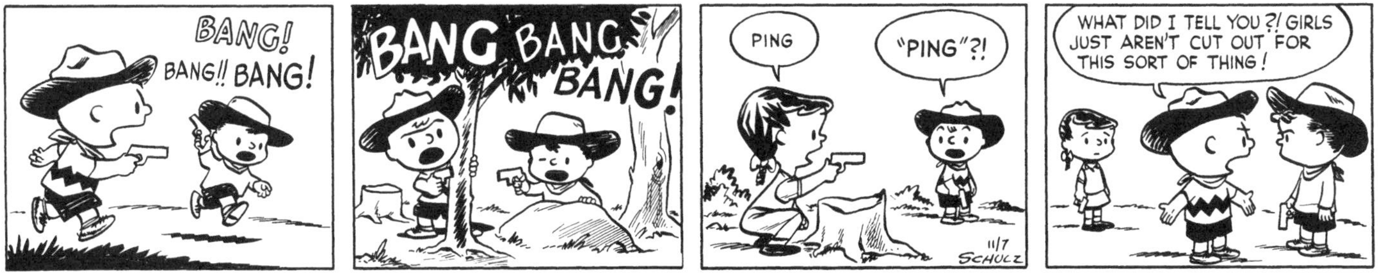
BANG!
BANG!! BANG!
BANG BANG
BANG!
PING
"PING"?!
11/7
SCHULZ
WHAT DID I TELL YOU?! GIRLS JUST AREN'T CUT OUT FOR THIS SORT OF THING!

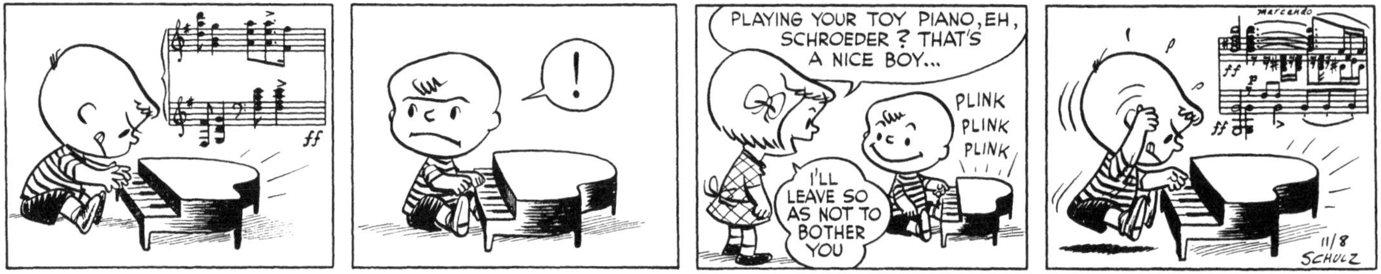
PLAYING YOUR TOY PIANO, EH, SCHROEDER? THAT'S A NICE BOY...
PLINK PLINK PLINK
I'LL LEAVE SO AS NOT TO BOTHER YOU
11/8
SCHULZ

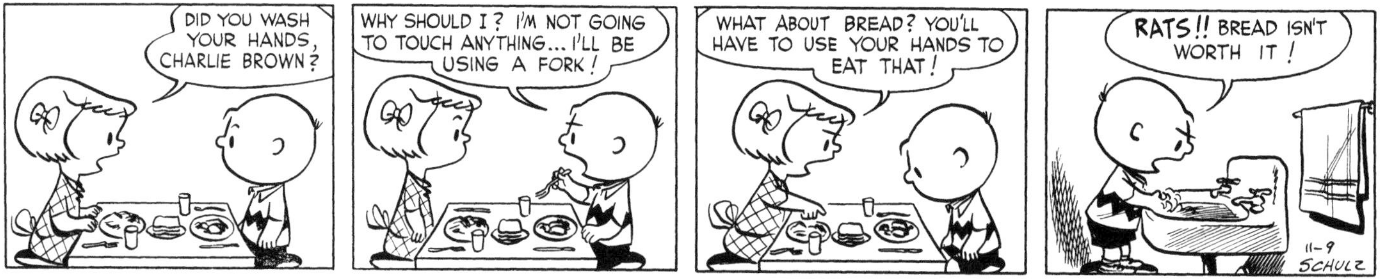
DID YOU WASH YOUR HANDS, CHARLIE BROWN?
WHY SHOULD I? I'M NOT GOING TO TOUCH ANYTHING... I'LL BE USING A FORK!
WHAT ABOUT BREAD? YOU'LL HAVE TO USE YOUR HANDS TO EAT THAT!
RATS!! BREAD ISN'T WORTH IT!
11-9
SCHULZ

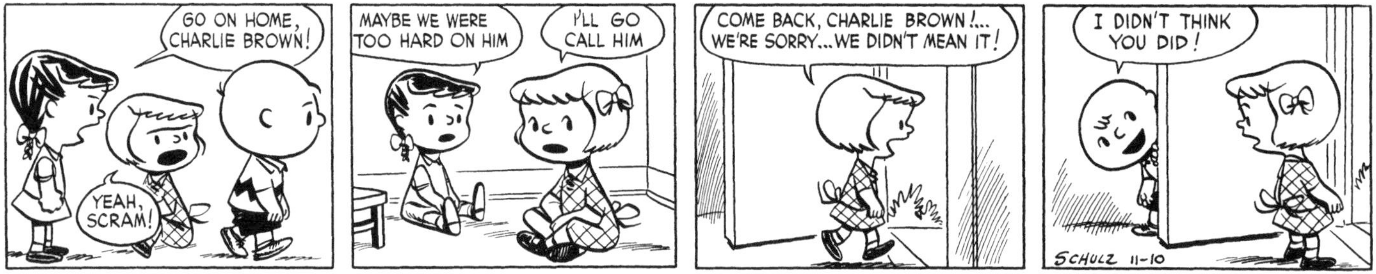
GO ON HOME, CHARLIE BROWN!
YEAH, SCRAM!
MAYBE WE WERE TOO HARD ON HIM
I'LL GO CALL HIM
COME BACK, CHARLIE BROWN!... WE'RE SORRY... WE DIDN'T MEAN IT!
I DIDN'T THINK YOU DID!
SCHULZ 11-10

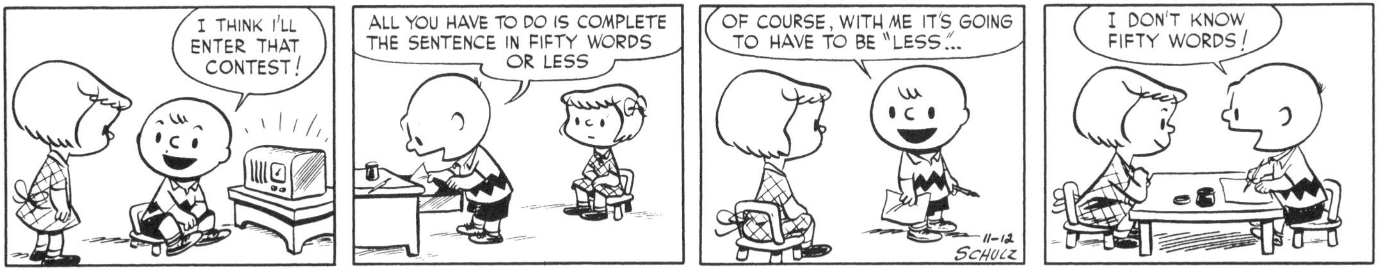
I THINK I'LL ENTER THAT CONTEST!
ALL YOU HAVE TO DO IS COMPLETE THE SENTENCE IN FIFTY WORDS OR LESS
OF COURSE, WITH ME IT'S GOING TO HAVE TO BE "LESS"...
11-12
SCHULZ
I DON'T KNOW FIFTY WORDS!

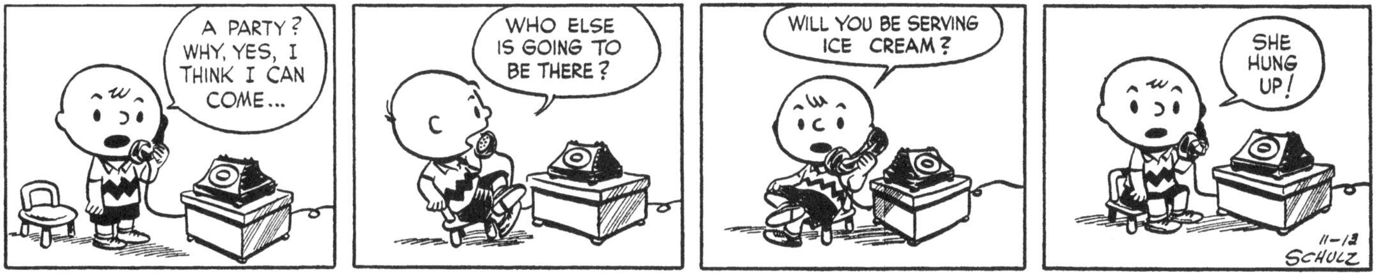
A PARTY? WHY, YES, I THINK I CAN COME...
WHO ELSE IS GOING TO BE THERE?
WILL YOU BE SERVING ICE CREAM?
SHE HUNG UP!
11-13
SCHULZ

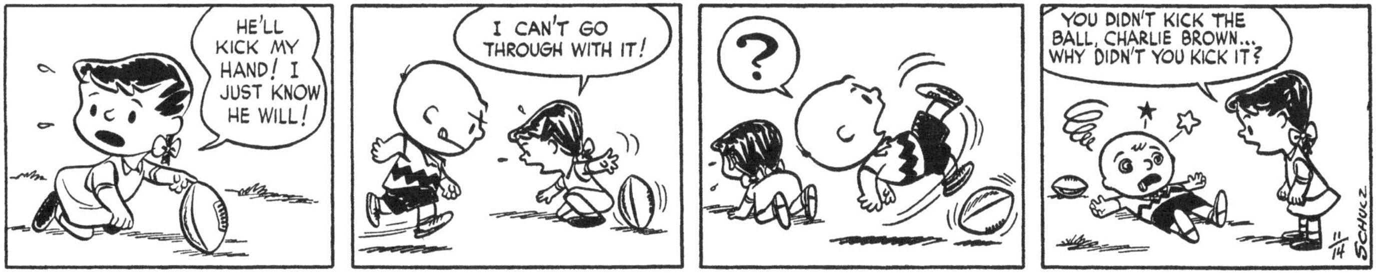
HE'LL KICK MY HAND! I JUST KNOW HE WILL!
I CAN'T GO THROUGH WITH IT!
?
YOU DIDN'T KICK THE BALL, CHARLIE BROWN... WHY DIDN'T YOU KICK IT?
11/14
SCHULZ

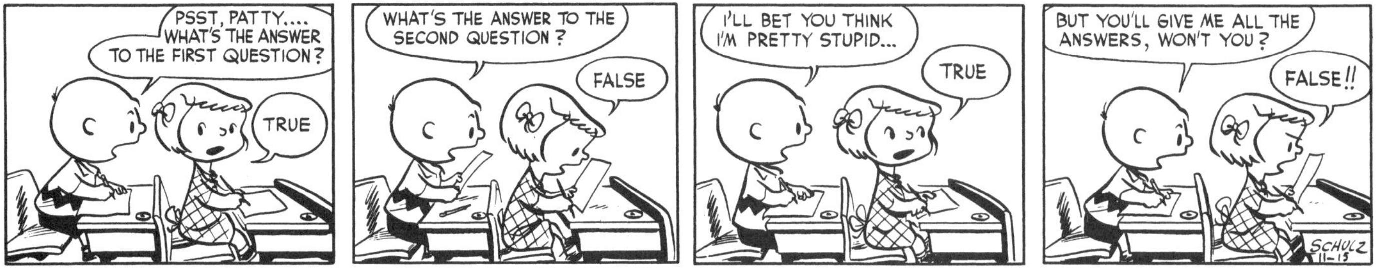
PSST, PATTY.... WHAT'S THE ANSWER TO THE FIRST QUESTION?
TRUE
WHAT'S THE ANSWER TO THE SECOND QUESTION?
FALSE
I'LL BET YOU THINK I'M PRETTY STUPID...
TRUE
BUT YOU'LL GIVE ME ALL THE ANSWERS, WON'T YOU?
FALSE!!
SCHULZ 11-15

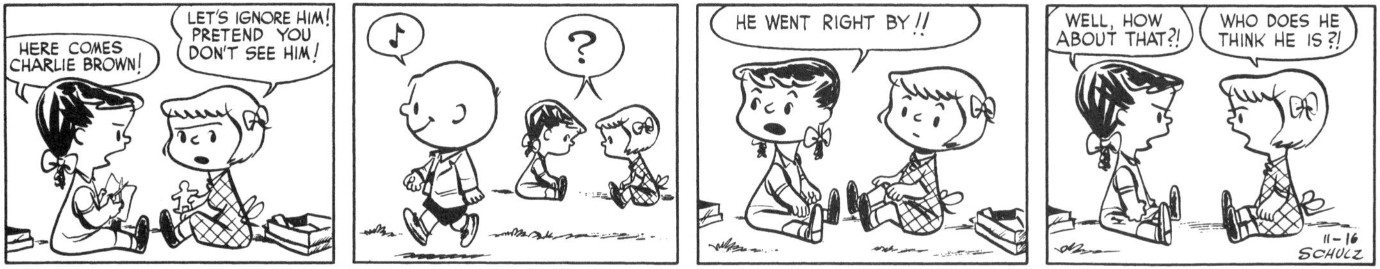
HERE COMES CHARLIE BROWN!
LET'S IGNORE HIM! PRETEND YOU DON'T SEE HIM!
♪
?
HE WENT RIGHT BY!!
WELL, HOW ABOUT THAT?!
WHO DOES HE THINK HE IS?!
11-16 SCHULZ

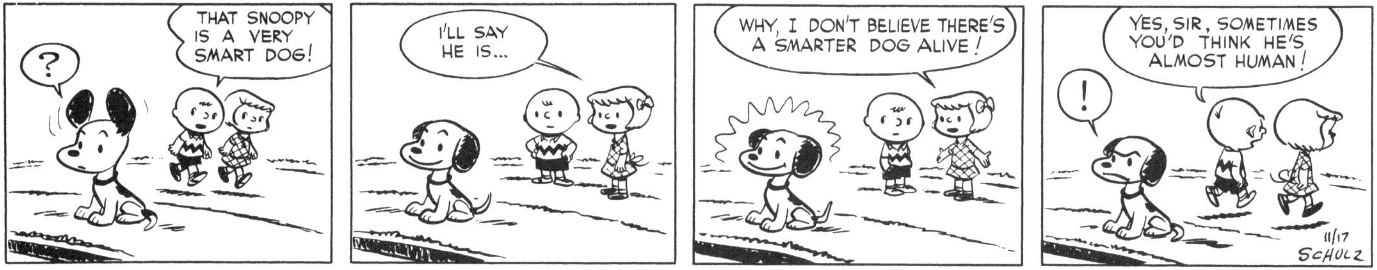
?
THAT SNOOPY IS A VERY SMART DOG!
I'LL SAY HE IS...
WHY, I DON'T BELIEVE THERE'S A SMARTER DOG ALIVE!
!
YES, SIR, SOMETIMES YOU'D THINK HE'S ALMOST HUMAN!
11/17 SCHULZ

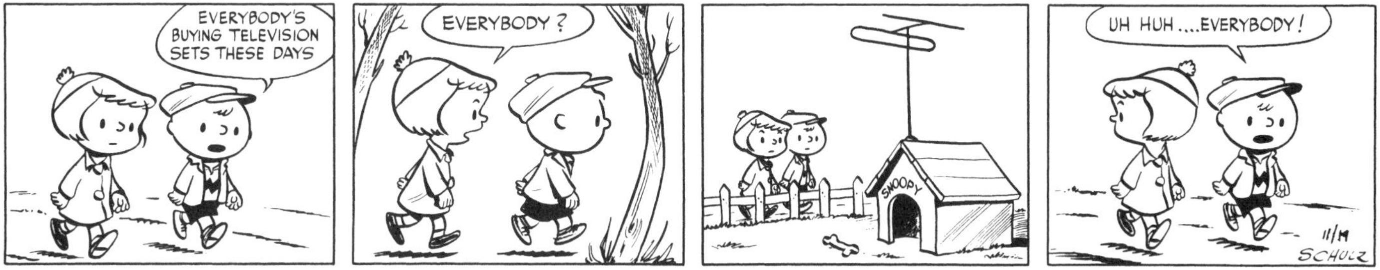
EVERYBODY'S BUYING TELEVISION SETS THESE DAYS
EVERYBODY ?
SNOOPY
UH HUH ....EVERYBODY !
11/19
SCHULZ

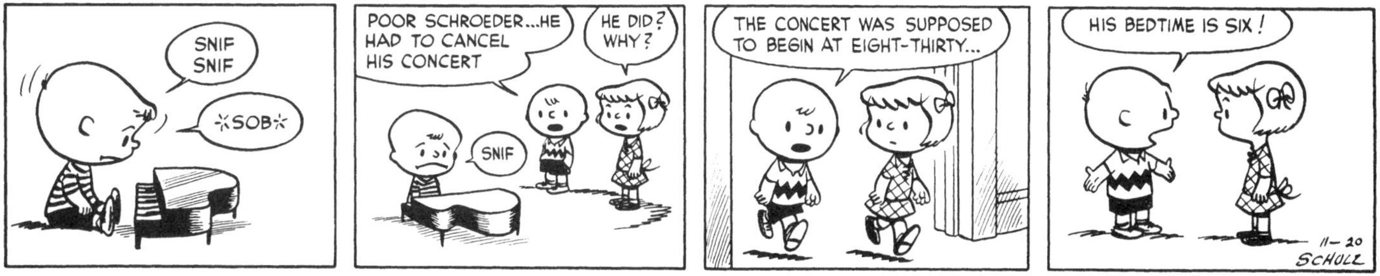
SNIF SNIF
SOB
POOR SCHROEDER...HE HAD TO CANCEL HIS CONCERT
SNIF
HE DID? WHY?
THE CONCERT WAS SUPPOSED TO BEGIN AT EIGHT-THIRTY...
HIS BEDTIME IS SIX !
11-20
SCHULZ

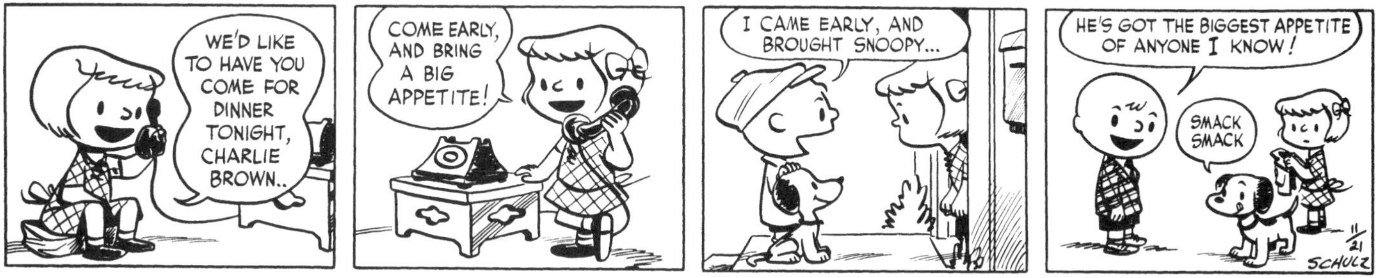
WE'D LIKE TO HAVE YOU COME FOR DINNER TONIGHT, CHARLIE BROWN..
COME EARLY, AND BRING A BIG APPETITE!
I CAME EARLY, AND BROUGHT SNOOPY...
HE'S GOT THE BIGGEST APPETITE OF ANYONE I KNOW!
SMACK SMACK
11/21
SCHULZ

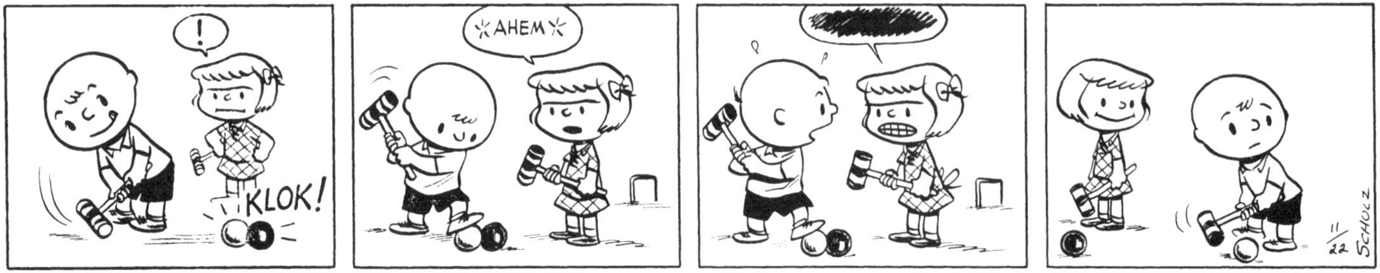
!
KLOK!
AHEM
11/22
SCHULZ

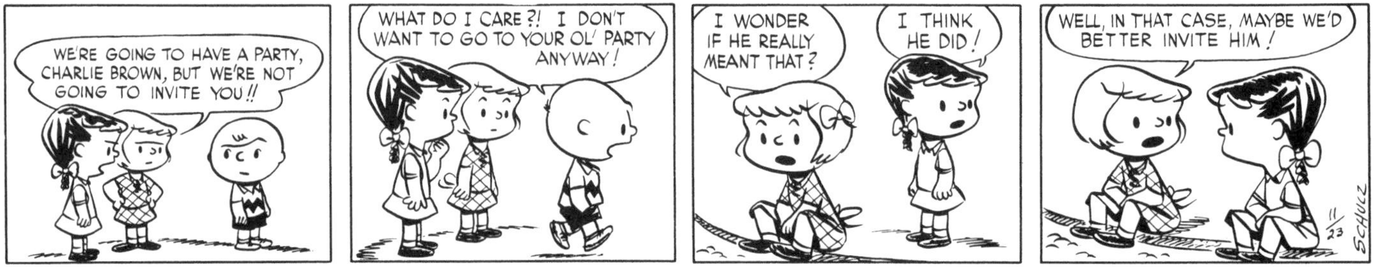
WE'RE GOING TO HAVE A PARTY, CHARLIE BROWN, BUT WE'RE NOT GOING TO INVITE YOU!!
WHAT DO I CARE?! I DON'T WANT TO GO TO YOUR OL' PARTY ANYWAY!
I WONDER IF HE REALLY MEANT THAT?
I THINK HE DID!
WELL, IN THAT CASE, MAYBE WE'D BETTER INVITE HIM!
11/23
SCHULZ

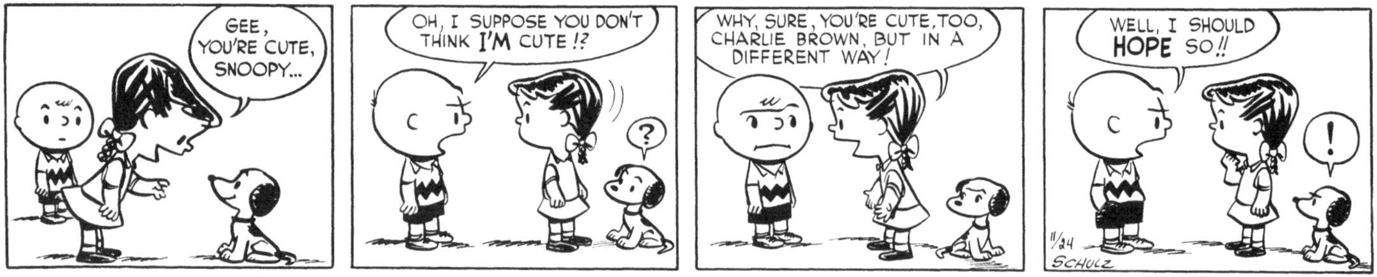
GEE, YOU'RE CUTE, SNOOPY...
OH, I SUPPOSE YOU DON'T THINK I'M CUTE!?
?
WHY, SURE, YOU'RE CUTE, TOO, CHARLIE BROWN, BUT IN A DIFFERENT WAY!
WELL, I SHOULD HOPE SO!!
!
11/24
SCHULZ

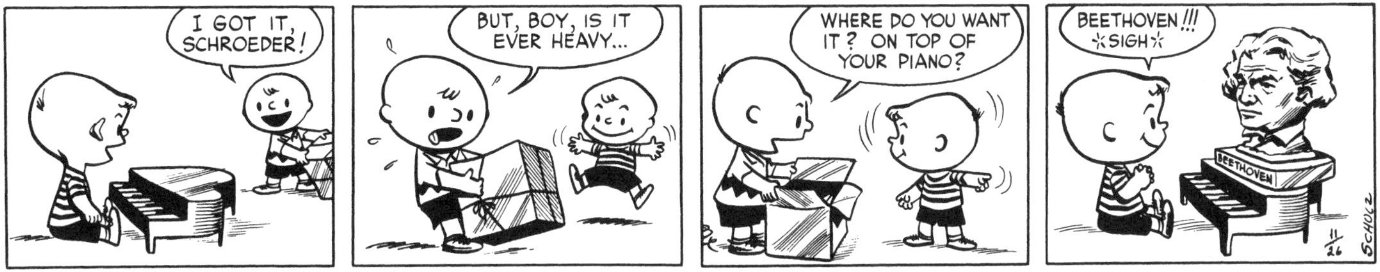
I GOT IT, SCHROEDER!
BUT, BOY, IS IT EVER HEAVY...
WHERE DO YOU WANT IT? ON TOP OF YOUR PIANO?
BEETHOVEN!!! *SIGH*
BEETHOVEN
11/26
SCHULZ

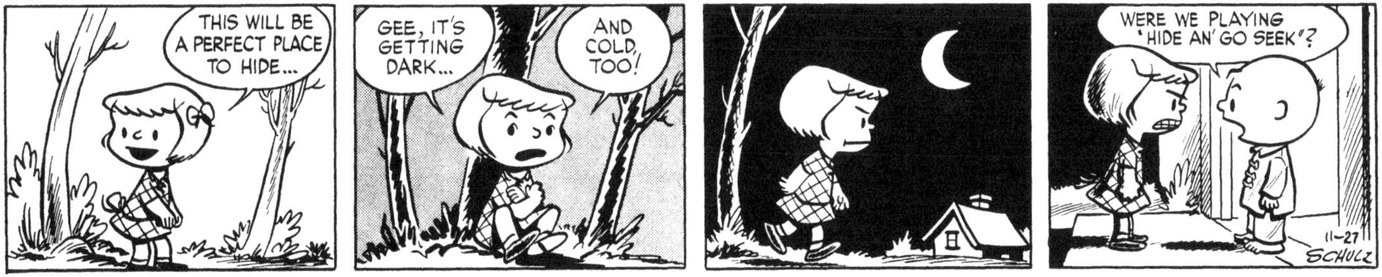
THIS WILL BE A PERFECT PLACE TO HIDE...
GEE, IT'S GETTING DARK...
AND COLD, TOO!
WERE WE PLAYING 'HIDE AN' GO SEEK'?
11-27
SCHULZ

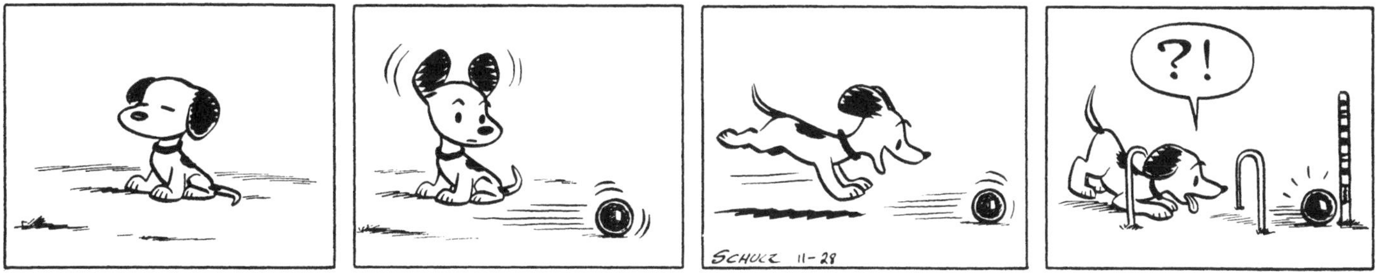
SCHULZ 11-28
?!

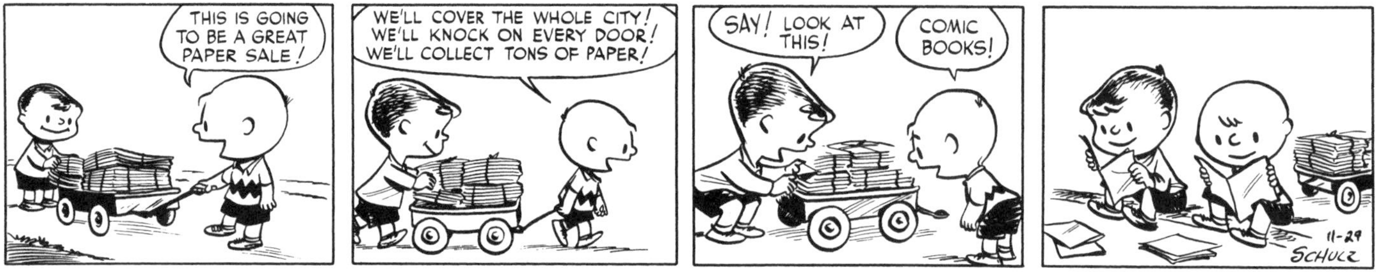
THIS IS GOING TO BE A GREAT PAPER SALE!
WE'LL COVER THE WHOLE CITY! WE'LL KNOCK ON EVERY DOOR! WE'LL COLLECT TONS OF PAPER!
SAY! LOOK AT THIS!
COMIC BOOKS!
11-29
SCHULZ

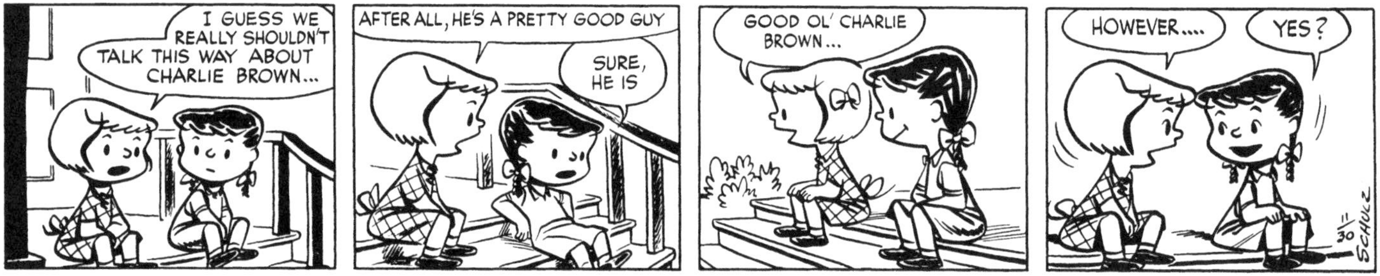
I GUESS WE REALLY SHOULDN'T TALK THIS WAY ABOUT CHARLIE BROWN...
AFTER ALL, HE'S A PRETTY GOOD GUY
SURE, HE IS
GOOD OL' CHARLIE BROWN...
HOWEVER....
YES?
11/30
SCHULZ

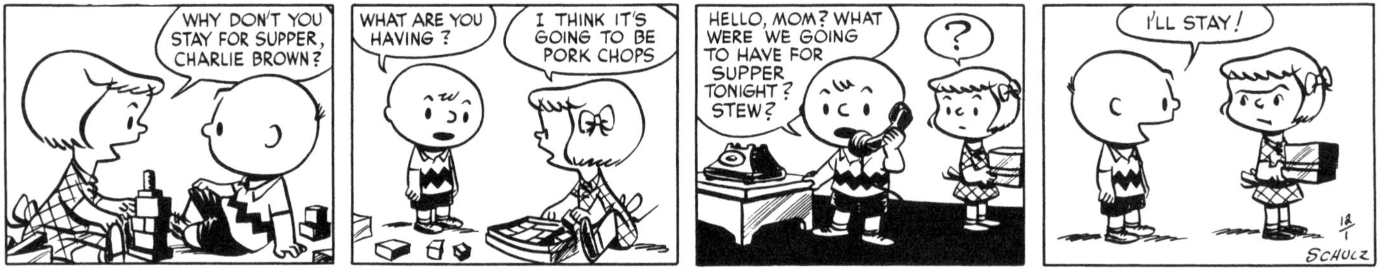
WHY DON'T YOU STAY FOR SUPPER, CHARLIE BROWN?
WHAT ARE YOU HAVING?
I THINK IT'S GOING TO BE PORK CHOPS
HELLO, MOM? WHAT WERE WE GOING TO HAVE FOR SUPPER TONIGHT? STEW?
?
I'LL STAY!
12/1
SCHULZ

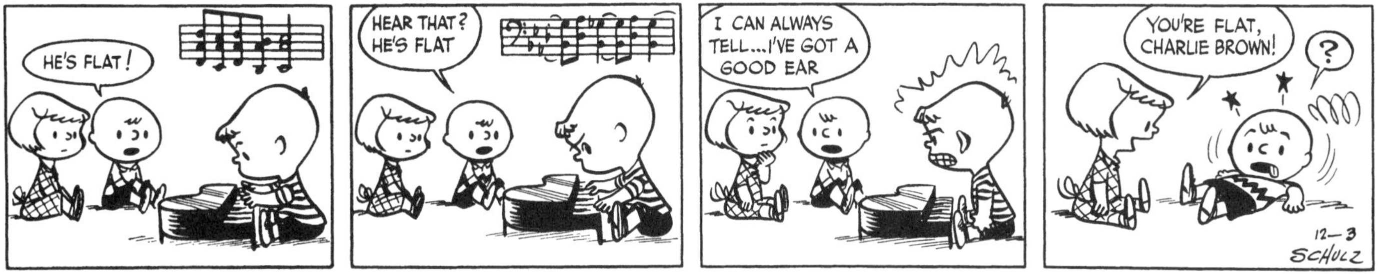
HE'S FLAT!
HEAR THAT? HE'S FLAT
I CAN ALWAYS TELL...I'VE GOT A GOOD EAR
YOU'RE FLAT, CHARLIE BROWN!
?
12-3
SCHULZ

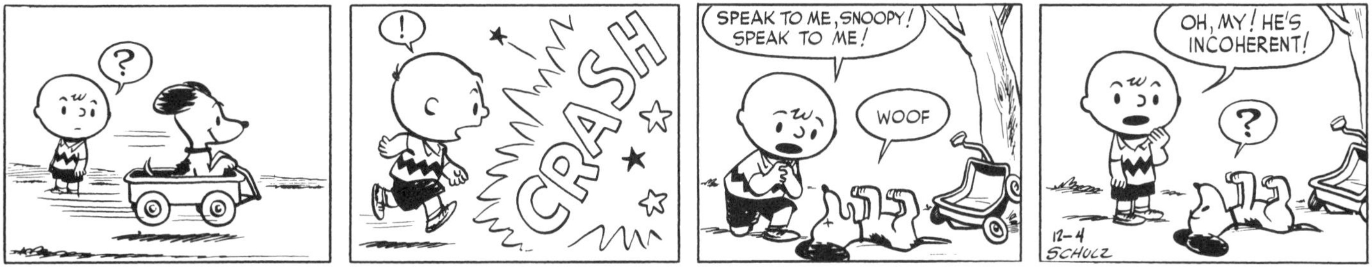
?
!
CRASH
SPEAK TO ME, SNOOPY! SPEAK TO ME!
WOOF
OH, MY! HE'S INCOHERENT!
?
12-4
SCHULZ

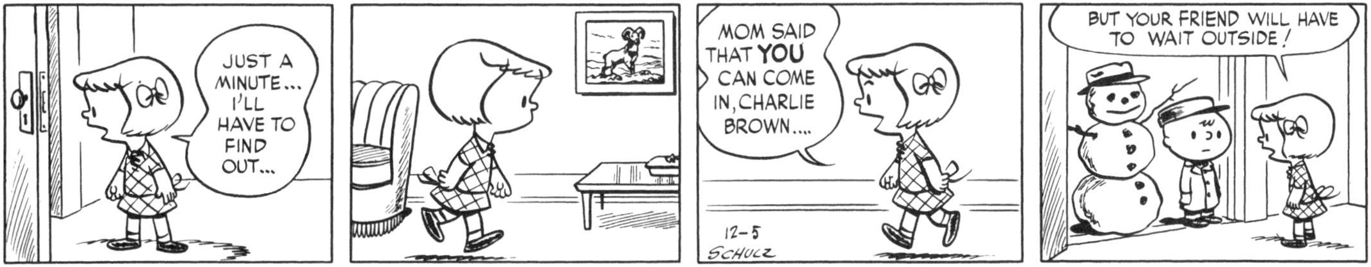
JUST A MINUTE... I'LL HAVE TO FIND OUT...
MOM SAID THAT **YOU** CAN COME IN, CHARLIE BROWN....
12-5
SCHULZ
BUT YOUR FRIEND WILL HAVE TO WAIT OUTSIDE!

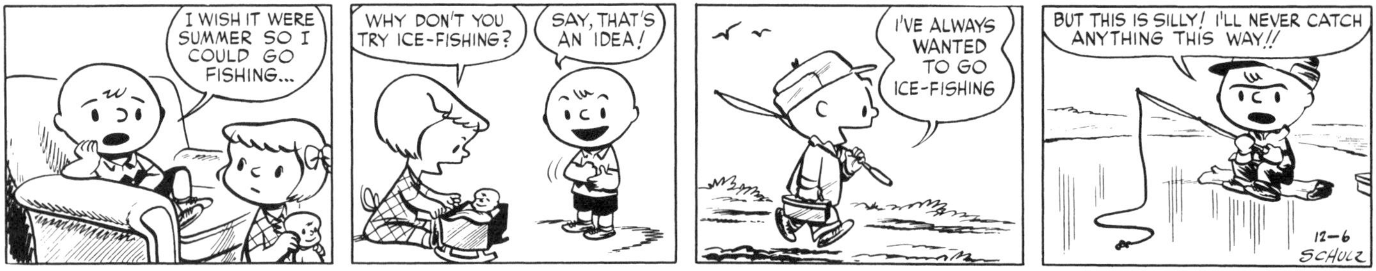
I WISH IT WERE SUMMER SO I COULD GO FISHING...
WHY DON'T YOU TRY ICE-FISHING?
SAY, THAT'S AN IDEA!
I'VE ALWAYS WANTED TO GO ICE-FISHING
BUT THIS IS SILLY! I'LL NEVER CATCH ANYTHING THIS WAY!!
12-6
SCHULZ

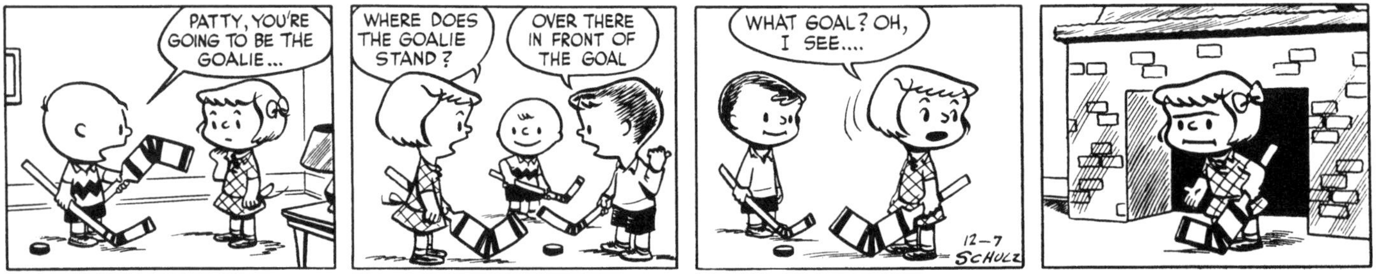
PATTY, YOU'RE GOING TO BE THE GOALIE...
WHERE DOES THE GOALIE STAND?
OVER THERE IN FRONT OF THE GOAL
WHAT GOAL? OH, I SEE....
12-7
SCHULZ

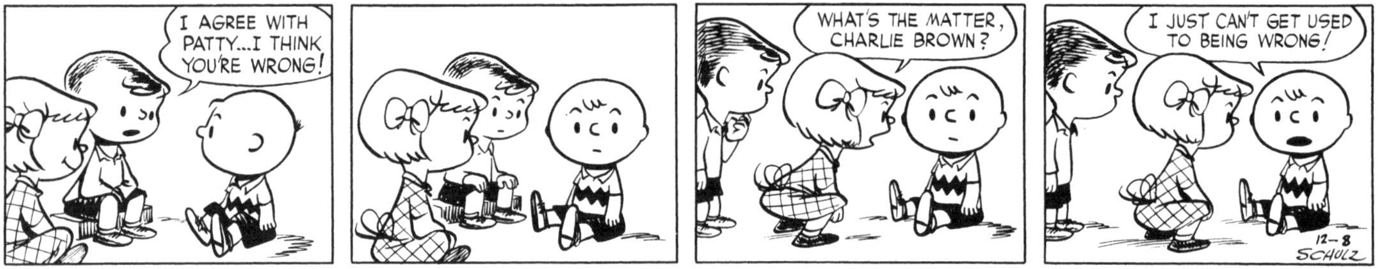
I AGREE WITH PATTY...I THINK YOU'RE WRONG!
WHAT'S THE MATTER, CHARLIE BROWN?
I JUST CAN'T GET USED TO BEING WRONG!
12-8
SCHULZ

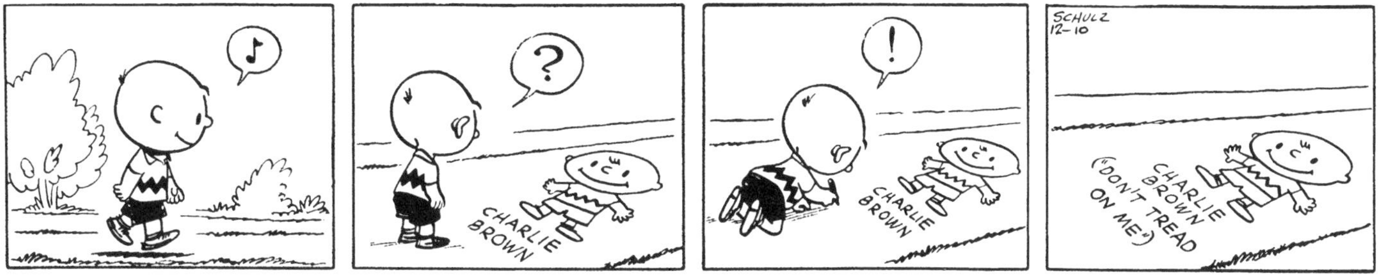
♪
?
CHARLIE BROWN
!
CHARLIE BROWN
SCHULZ 12-10
CHARLIE BROWN ("DON'T TREAD ON ME")

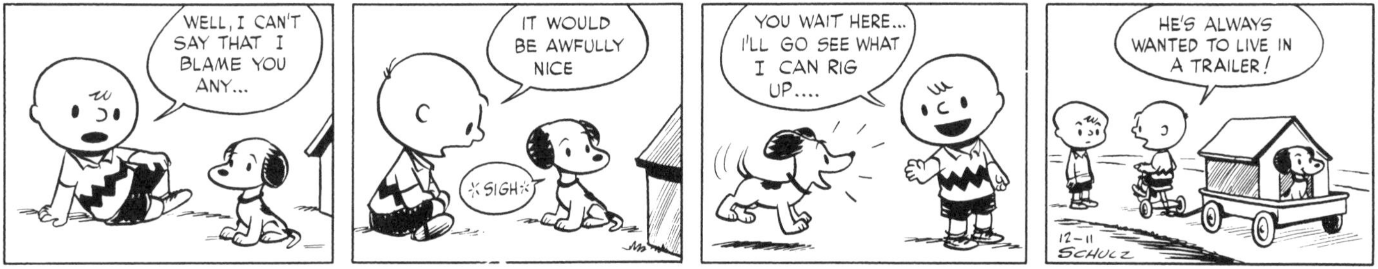
WELL, I CAN'T SAY THAT I BLAME YOU ANY...
IT WOULD BE AWFULLY NICE
SIGH
YOU WAIT HERE... I'LL GO SEE WHAT I CAN RIG UP....
HE'S ALWAYS WANTED TO LIVE IN A TRAILER!
12-11 SCHULZ

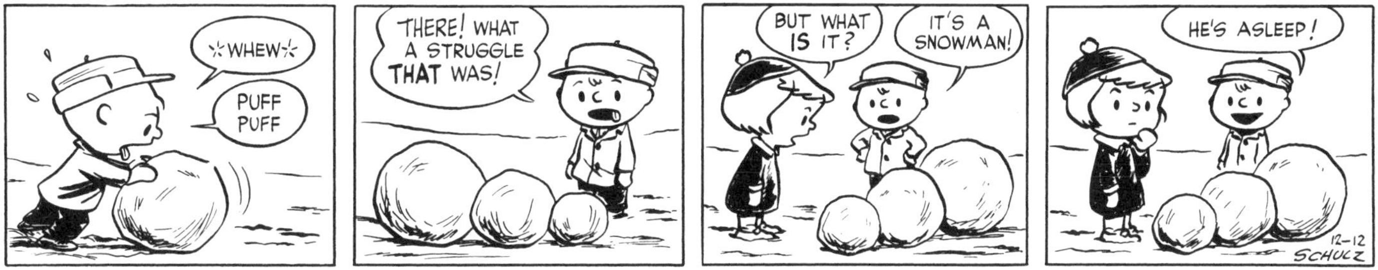
WHEW
PUFF PUFF
THERE! WHAT A STRUGGLE **THAT** WAS!
BUT WHAT **IS** IT?
IT'S A SNOWMAN!
HE'S ASLEEP!
12-12 SCHULZ

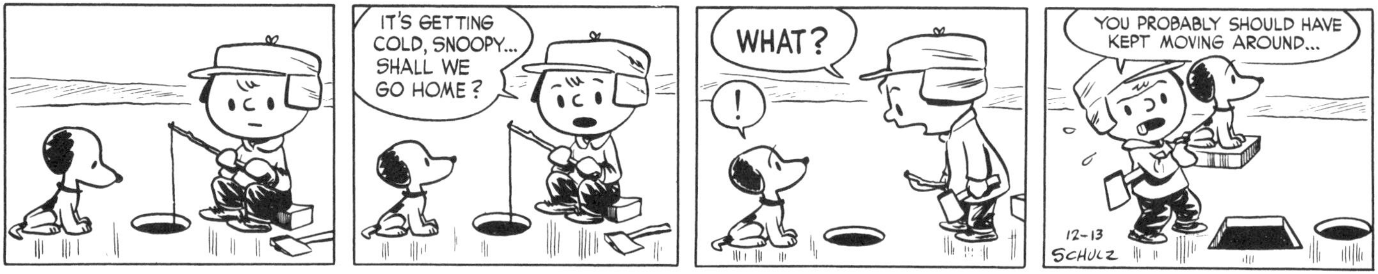
IT'S GETTING COLD, SNOOPY... SHALL WE GO HOME?
WHAT?
!
YOU PROBABLY SHOULD HAVE KEPT MOVING AROUND...
12-13
SCHULZ

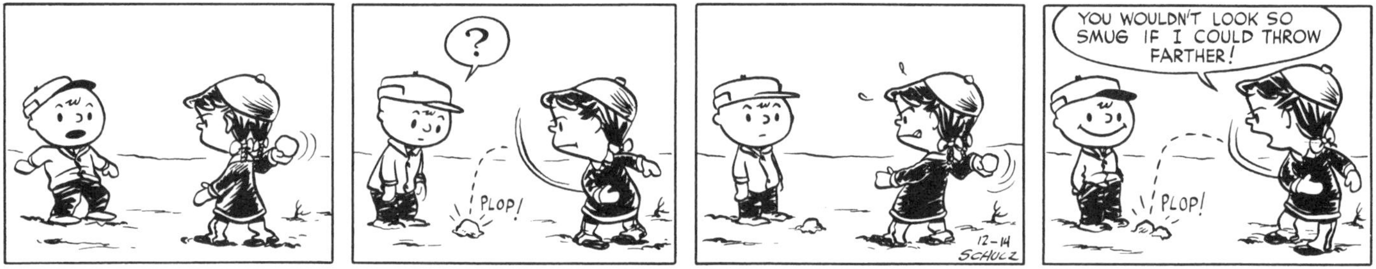
?
PLOP!
12-14
SCHULZ
YOU WOULDN'T LOOK SO SMUG IF I COULD THROW FARTHER!
PLOP!

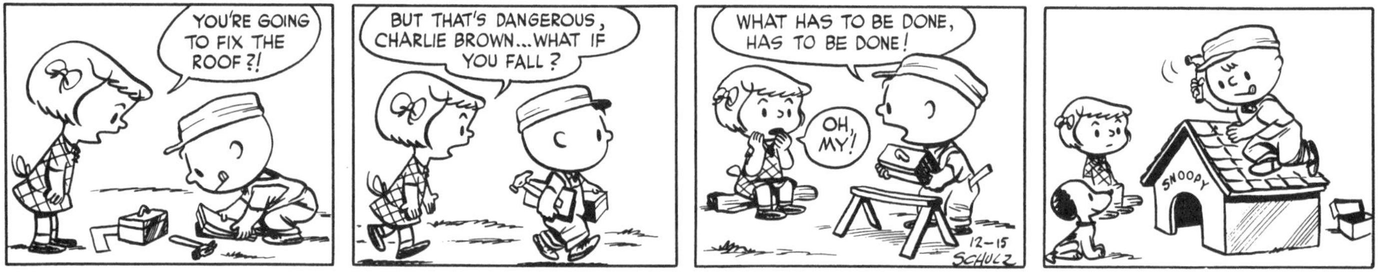
YOU'RE GOING TO FIX THE ROOF?!
BUT THAT'S DANGEROUS, CHARLIE BROWN...WHAT IF YOU FALL?
WHAT HAS TO BE DONE, HAS TO BE DONE!
OH, MY!
12-15
SCHULZ
SNOOPY

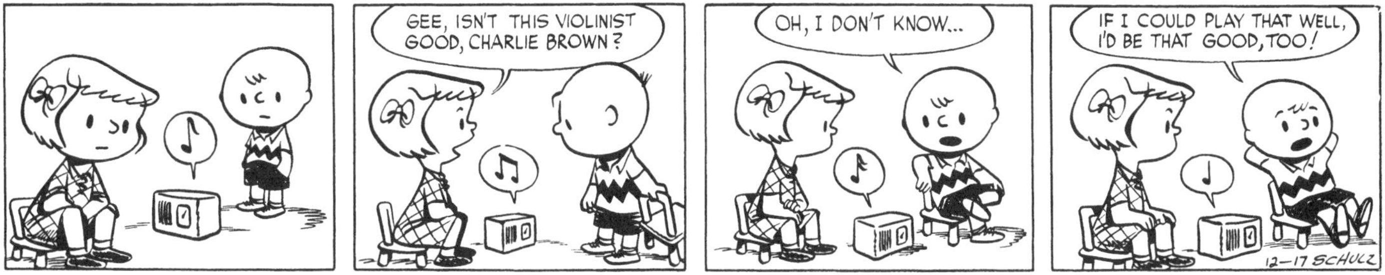
GEE, ISN'T THIS VIOLINIST GOOD, CHARLIE BROWN ?
OH, I DON'T KNOW...
IF I COULD PLAY THAT WELL, I'D BE THAT GOOD, TOO!
12-17 SCHULZ

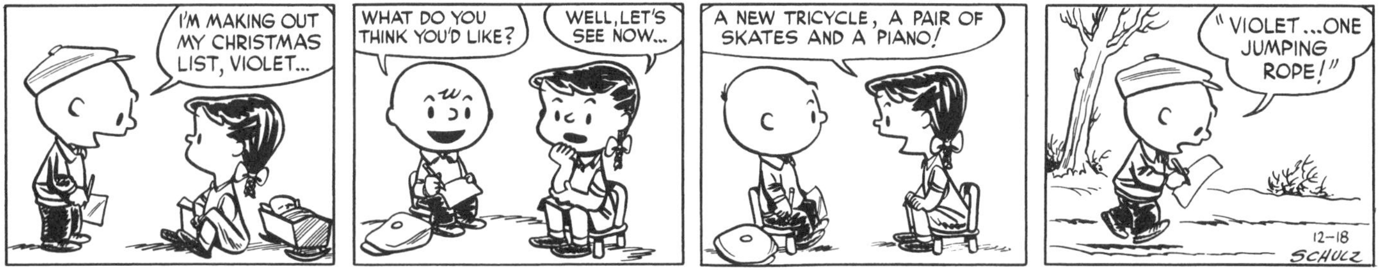
I'M MAKING OUT MY CHRISTMAS LIST, VIOLET...
WHAT DO YOU THINK YOU'D LIKE?
WELL, LET'S SEE NOW...
A NEW TRICYCLE, A PAIR OF SKATES AND A PIANO!
"VIOLET...ONE JUMPING ROPE!"
12-18
SCHULZ

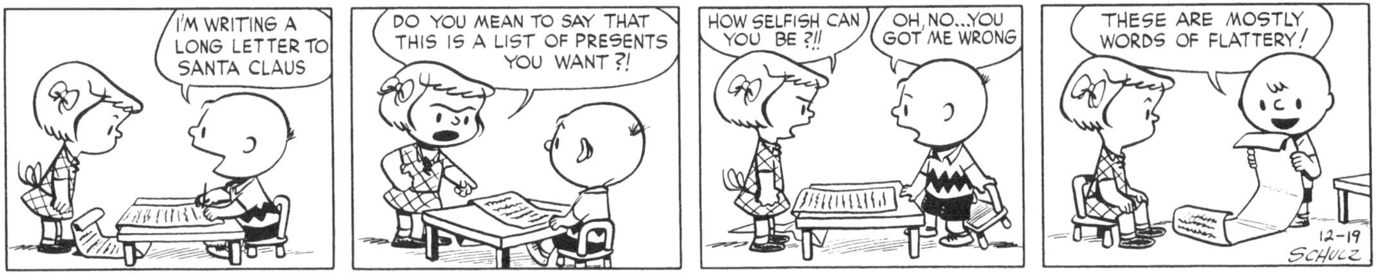
I'M WRITING A LONG LETTER TO SANTA CLAUS
DO YOU MEAN TO SAY THAT THIS IS A LIST OF PRESENTS YOU WANT ?!
HOW SELFISH CAN YOU BE ?!!
OH, NO...YOU GOT ME WRONG
THESE ARE MOSTLY WORDS OF FLATTERY!
12-19
SCHULZ

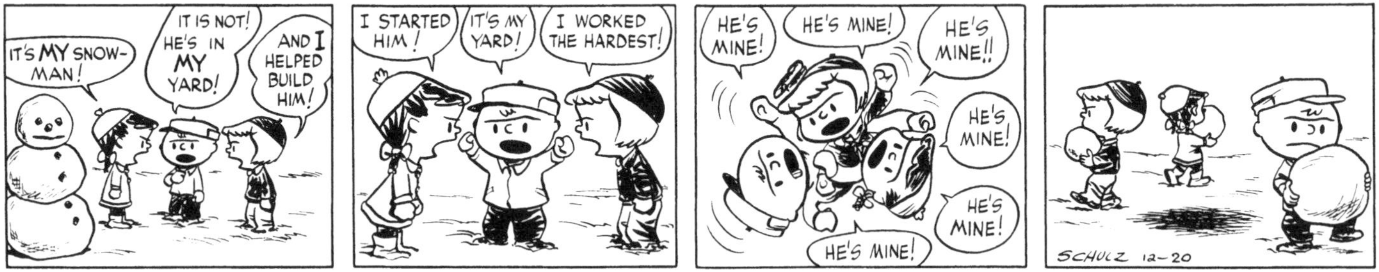
IT'S MY SNOW-MAN!
IT IS NOT! HE'S IN MY YARD!
AND I HELPED BUILD HIM!
I STARTED HIM!
IT'S MY YARD!
I WORKED THE HARDEST!
HE'S MINE!
HE'S MINE!
HE'S MINE!!
HE'S MINE!
HE'S MINE!
HE'S MINE!
SCHULZ 12-20

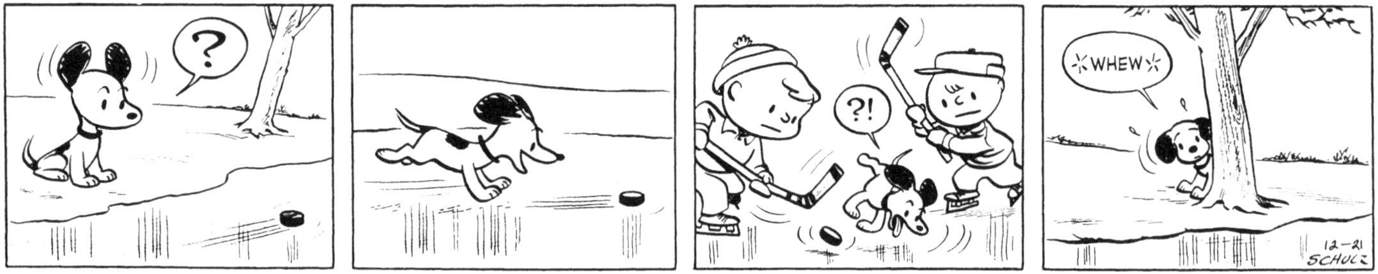
?
?!
WHEW
12-21 SCHULZ

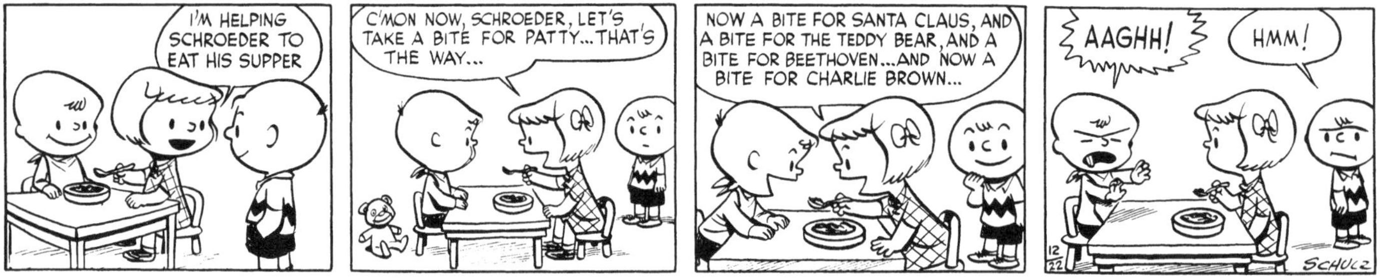
I'M HELPING SCHROEDER TO EAT HIS SUPPER
C'MON NOW, SCHROEDER, LET'S TAKE A BITE FOR PATTY...THAT'S THE WAY...
NOW A BITE FOR SANTA CLAUS, AND A BITE FOR THE TEDDY BEAR, AND A BITE FOR BEETHOVEN...AND NOW A BITE FOR CHARLIE BROWN...
AAGHH!
HMM!
12 22
SCHULZ

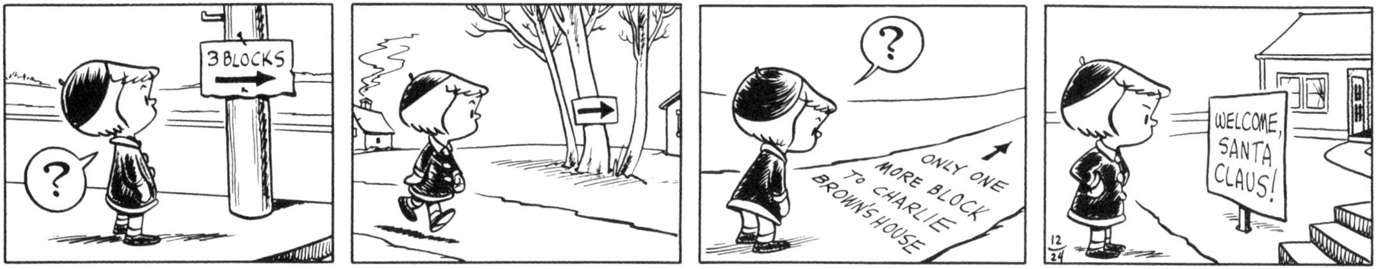
?
3 BLOCKS
?
ONLY ONE MORE BLOCK TO CHARLIE BROWN'S HOUSE
WELCOME, SANTA CLAUS!
12 24

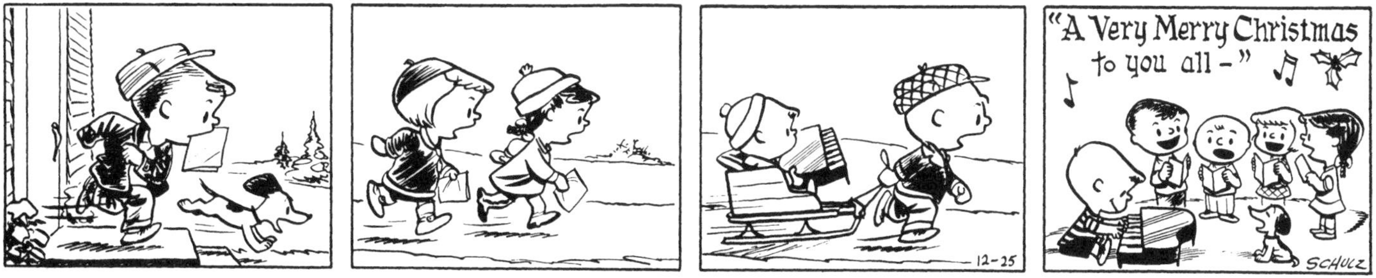
12-25
"A Very Merry Christmas to you all -"
SCHULZ

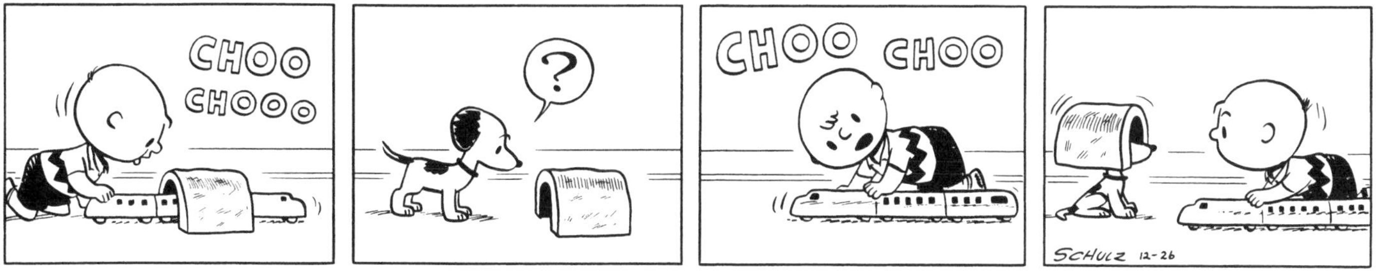
CHOO CHOOOO
?
CHOO CHOO
SCHULZ 12-26

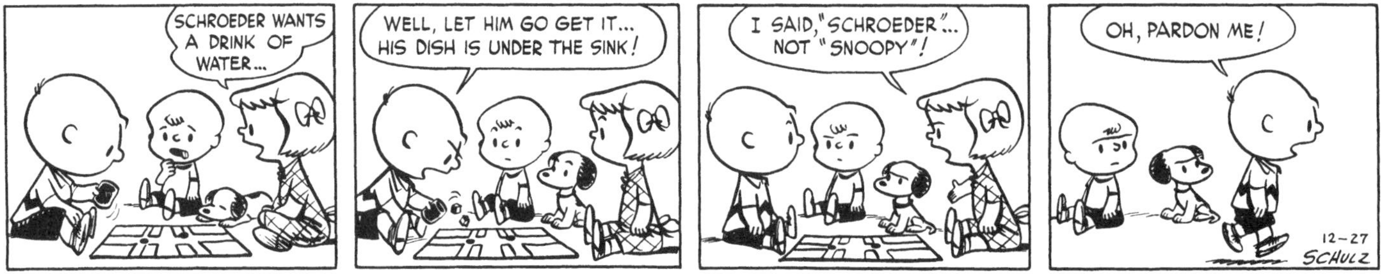
SCHROEDER WANTS A DRINK OF WATER...
WELL, LET HIM GO GET IT... HIS DISH IS UNDER THE SINK!
I SAID, "SCHROEDER"... NOT "SNOOPY"!
OH, PARDON ME!
12-27
SCHULZ

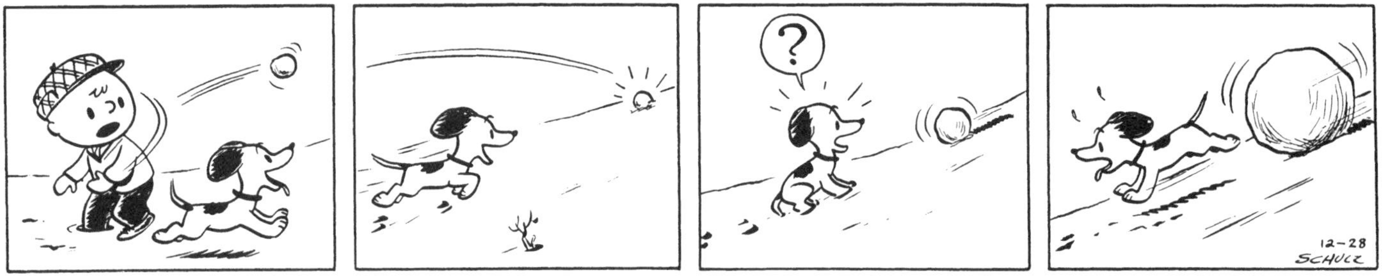
?
12-28
SCHULZ

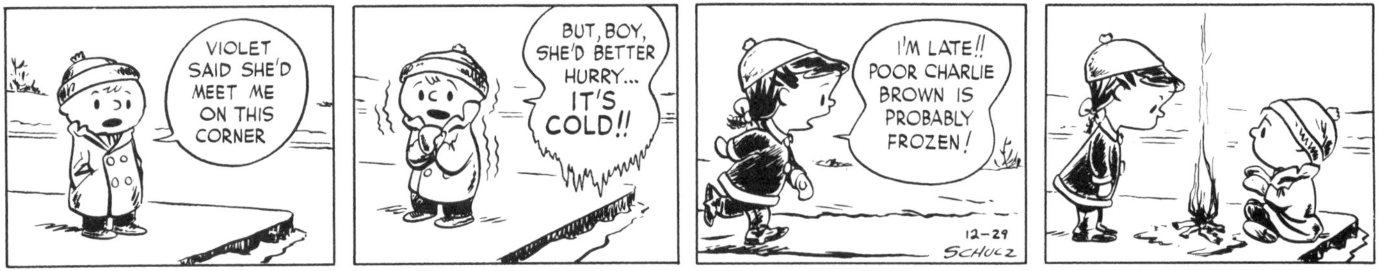
VIOLET SAID SHE'D MEET ME ON THIS CORNER
BUT, BOY, SHE'D BETTER HURRY... IT'S COLD!!
I'M LATE!! POOR CHARLIE BROWN IS PROBABLY FROZEN!
12-29
SCHULZ

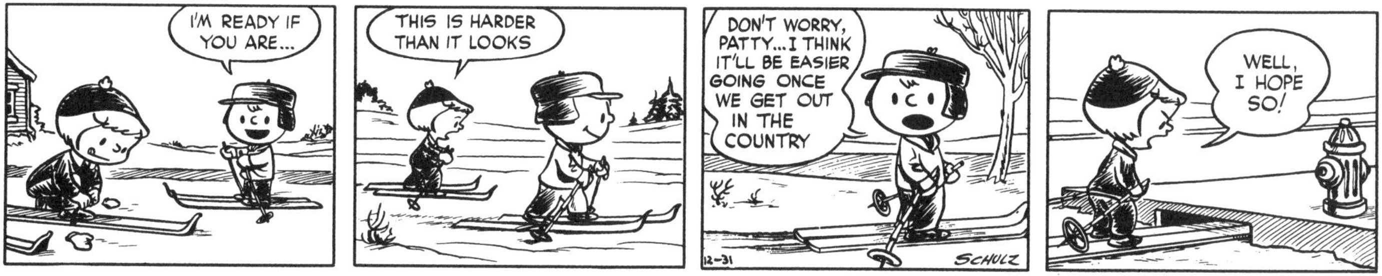
I'M READY IF YOU ARE...
THIS IS HARDER THAN IT LOOKS
DON'T WORRY, PATTY...I THINK IT'LL BE EASIER GOING ONCE WE GET OUT IN THE COUNTRY
12-31
SCHULZ
WELL, I HOPE SO!

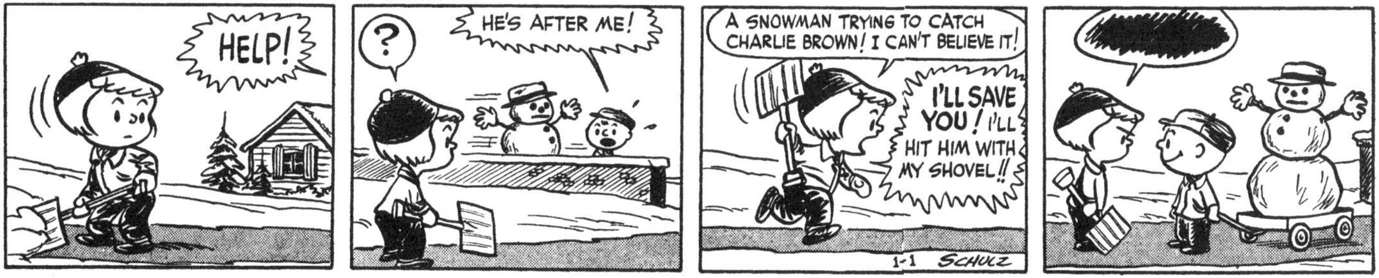
HELP!
?
HE'S AFTER ME!
A SNOWMAN TRYING TO CATCH CHARLIE BROWN! I CAN'T BELIEVE IT!
I'LL SAVE YOU! I'LL HIT HIM WITH MY SHOVEL!!
1-1
SCHULZ

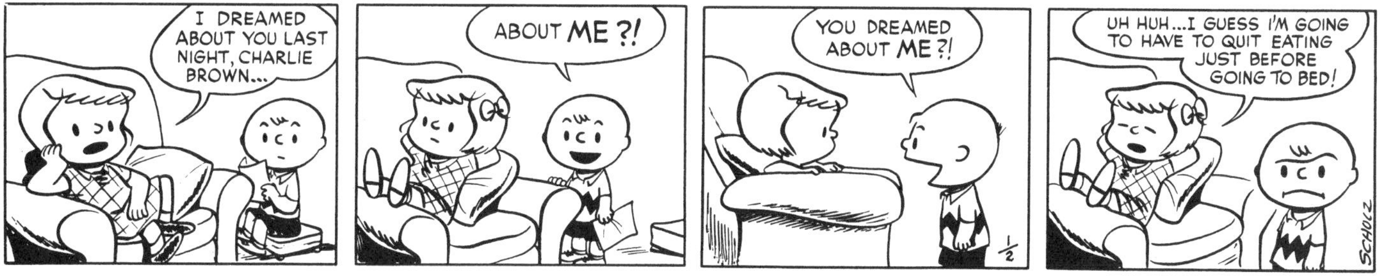
I DREAMED ABOUT YOU LAST NIGHT, CHARLIE BROWN...
ABOUT ME?!
YOU DREAMED ABOUT ME?!
1/2
UH HUH...I GUESS I'M GOING TO HAVE TO QUIT EATING JUST BEFORE GOING TO BED!
SCHULZ

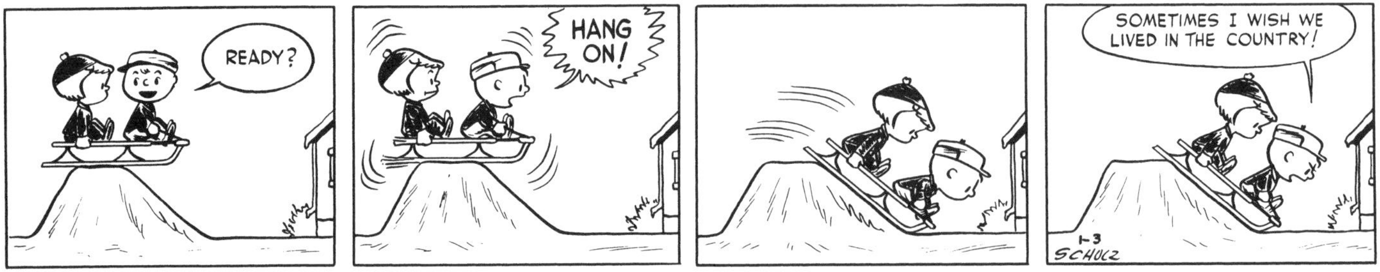
READY?
HANG ON!
SOMETIMES I WISH WE LIVED IN THE COUNTRY!
1-3
SCHULZ

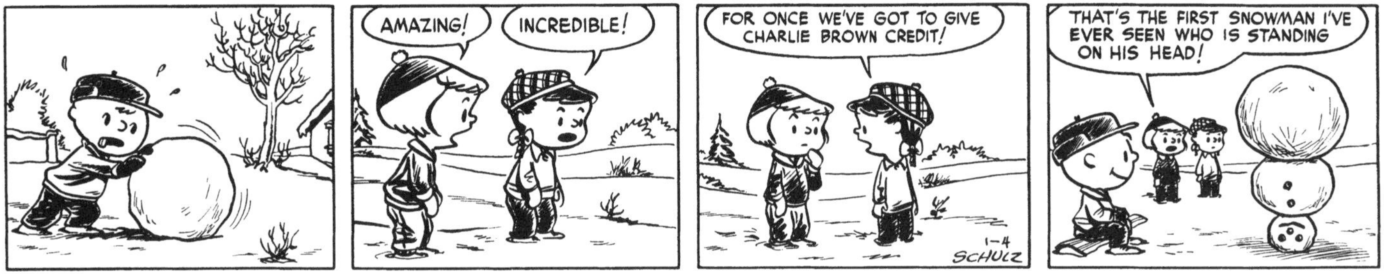
AMAZING!
INCREDIBLE!
FOR ONCE WE'VE GOT TO GIVE CHARLIE BROWN CREDIT!
1-4
SCHULZ
THAT'S THE FIRST SNOWMAN I'VE EVER SEEN WHO IS STANDING ON HIS HEAD!

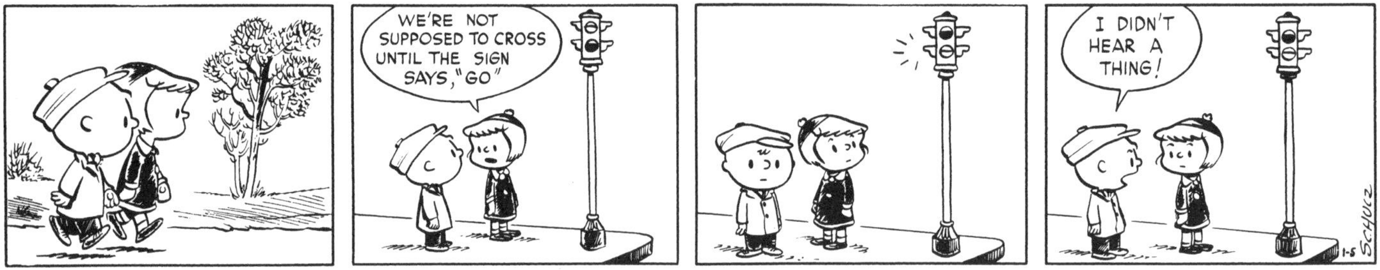
WE'RE NOT SUPPOSED TO CROSS UNTIL THE SIGN SAYS, "GO"
I DIDN'T HEAR A THING!
1-5
SCHULZ

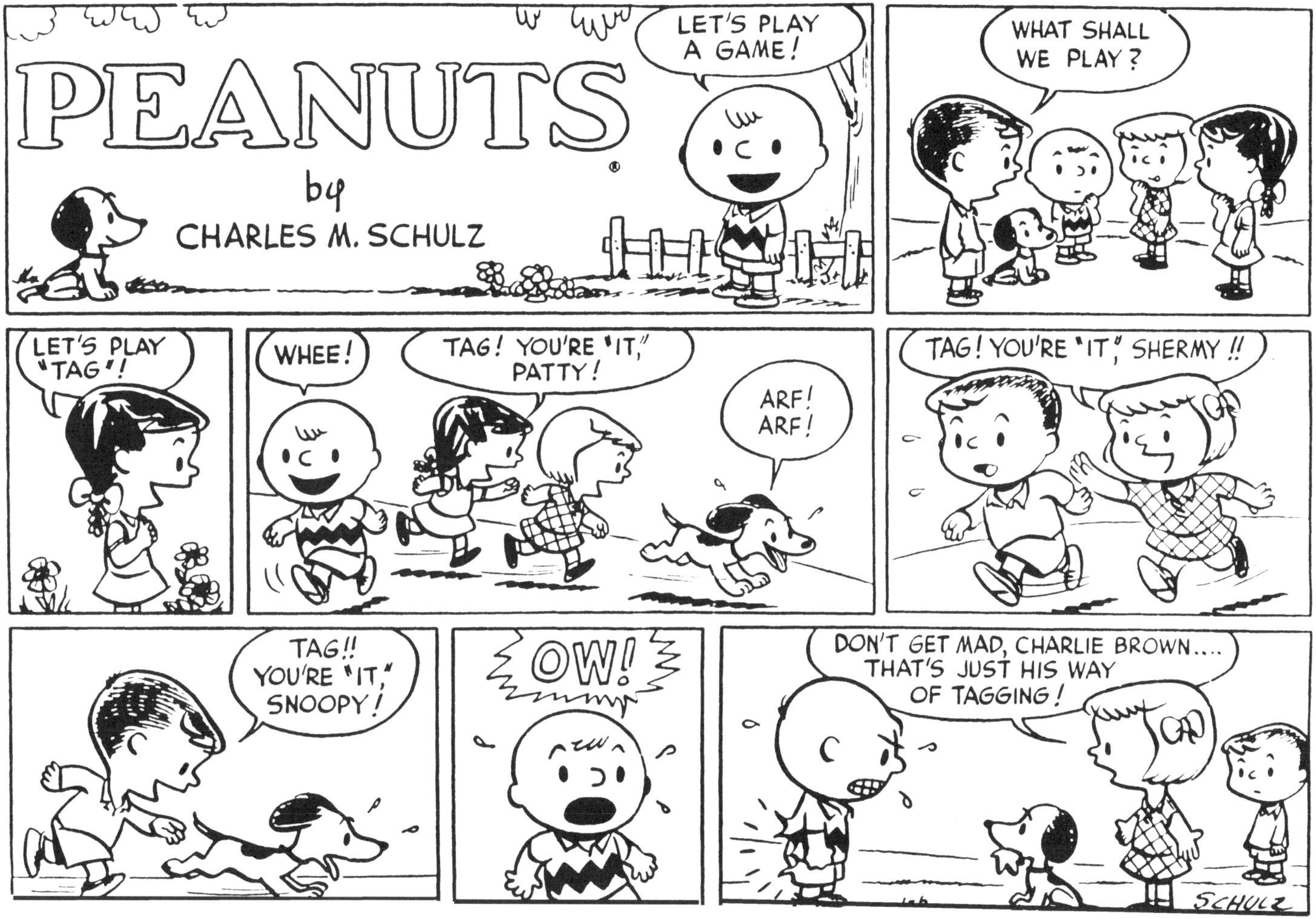
PEANUTS
by
CHARLES M. SCHULZ
LET'S PLAY A GAME!
WHAT SHALL WE PLAY?
LET'S PLAY "TAG"!
WHEE!
TAG! YOU'RE "IT," PATTY!
ARF! ARF!
TAG! YOU'RE "IT," SHERMY!!
TAG!! YOU'RE "IT," SNOOPY!
OW!
DON'T GET MAD, CHARLIE BROWN.... THAT'S JUST HIS WAY OF TAGGING!
SCHULZ

HIC
BANG!
I GOT YOU, CHARLIE BROWN!
SCHULZ 1-7
YOU WOULDN'T HAVE IF I HADN'T HICCUPED!

DO YOU MEAN TO SAY YOU'RE CRYING BECAUSE YOU CAN'T MAKE A SNOWBALL?
SOB
HERE, SCHROEDER, I'LL MAKE ONE FOR YOU... REGULATION MAJOR LEAGUE SIZE AND WEIGHT, TOO!
SNIF
A GOOD DEED NEVER GOES UNREWARDED...
POW!
SCHULZ 1-8

MUSH! MUSH!!
Y'KNOW, VIOLET, I THINK YOU'RE THE PRETTIEST GIRL IN THE WHOLE WORLD!
REALLY?
MUSH! MUSH!
!
?
WHAT DID I DO ?!
?
SCHULZ 1-9

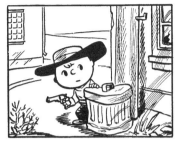

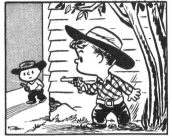

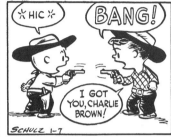

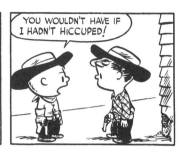

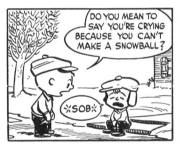

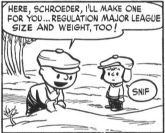

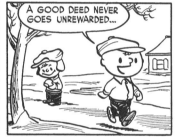

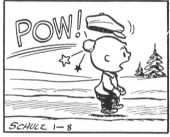

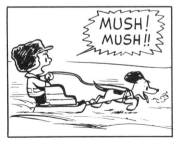

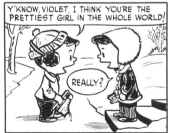

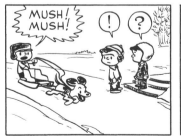

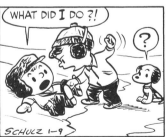

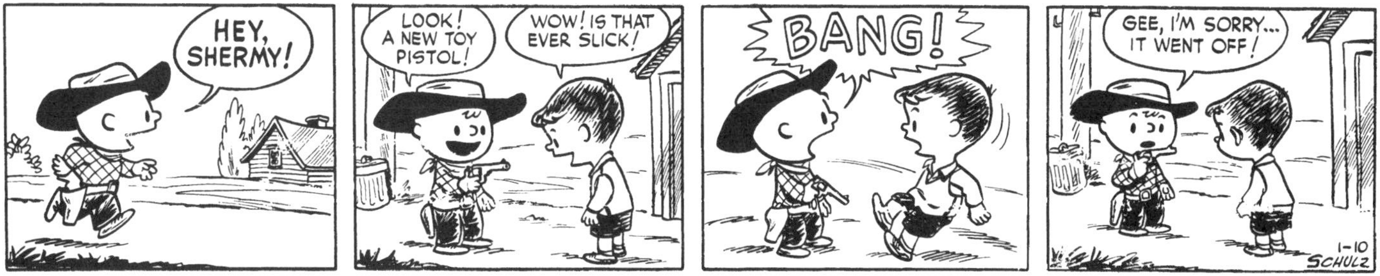
HEY, SHERMY!
LOOK! A NEW TOY PISTOL!
WOW! IS THAT EVER SLICK!
BANG!
GEE, I'M SORRY... IT WENT OFF!
1-10
SCHULZ

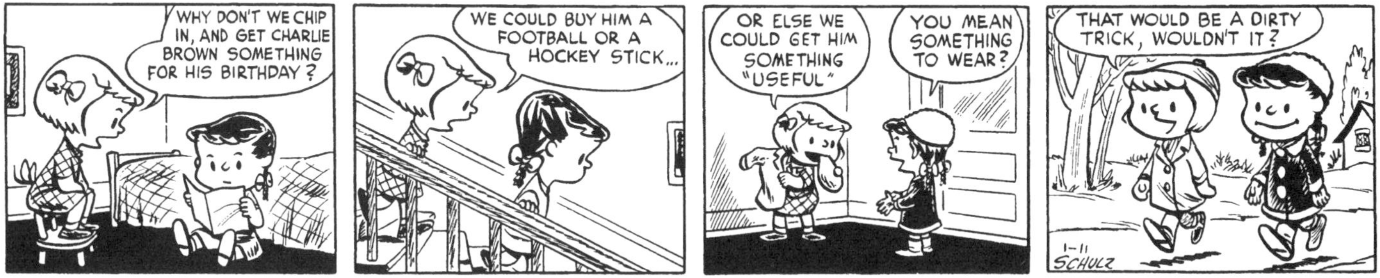
WHY DON'T WE CHIP IN, AND GET CHARLIE BROWN SOMETHING FOR HIS BIRTHDAY?
WE COULD BUY HIM A FOOTBALL OR A HOCKEY STICK...
OR ELSE WE COULD GET HIM SOMETHING "USEFUL"
YOU MEAN SOMETHING TO WEAR?
THAT WOULD BE A DIRTY TRICK, WOULDN'T IT?
1-11
SCHULZ

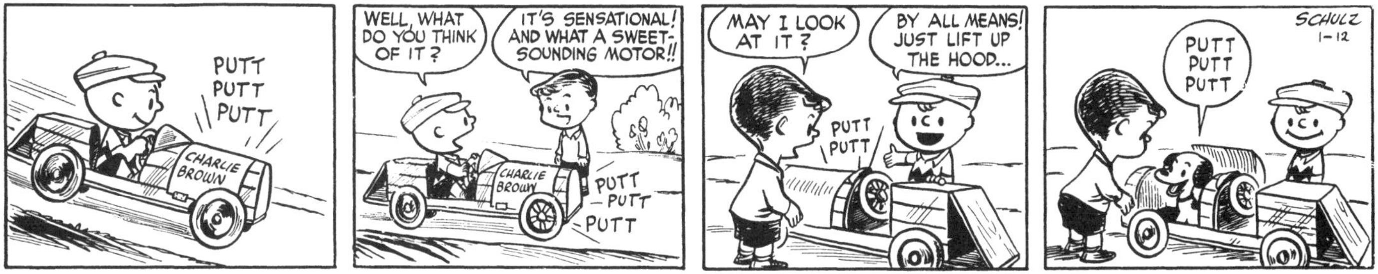
PUTT PUTT PUTT
CHARLIE BROWN
WELL, WHAT DO YOU THINK OF IT?
IT'S SENSATIONAL! AND WHAT A SWEET-SOUNDING MOTOR!!
CHARLIE BROWN
PUTT PUTT PUTT
MAY I LOOK AT IT?
BY ALL MEANS! JUST LIFT UP THE HOOD...
PUTT PUTT
SCHULZ
1-12
PUTT PUTT PUTT

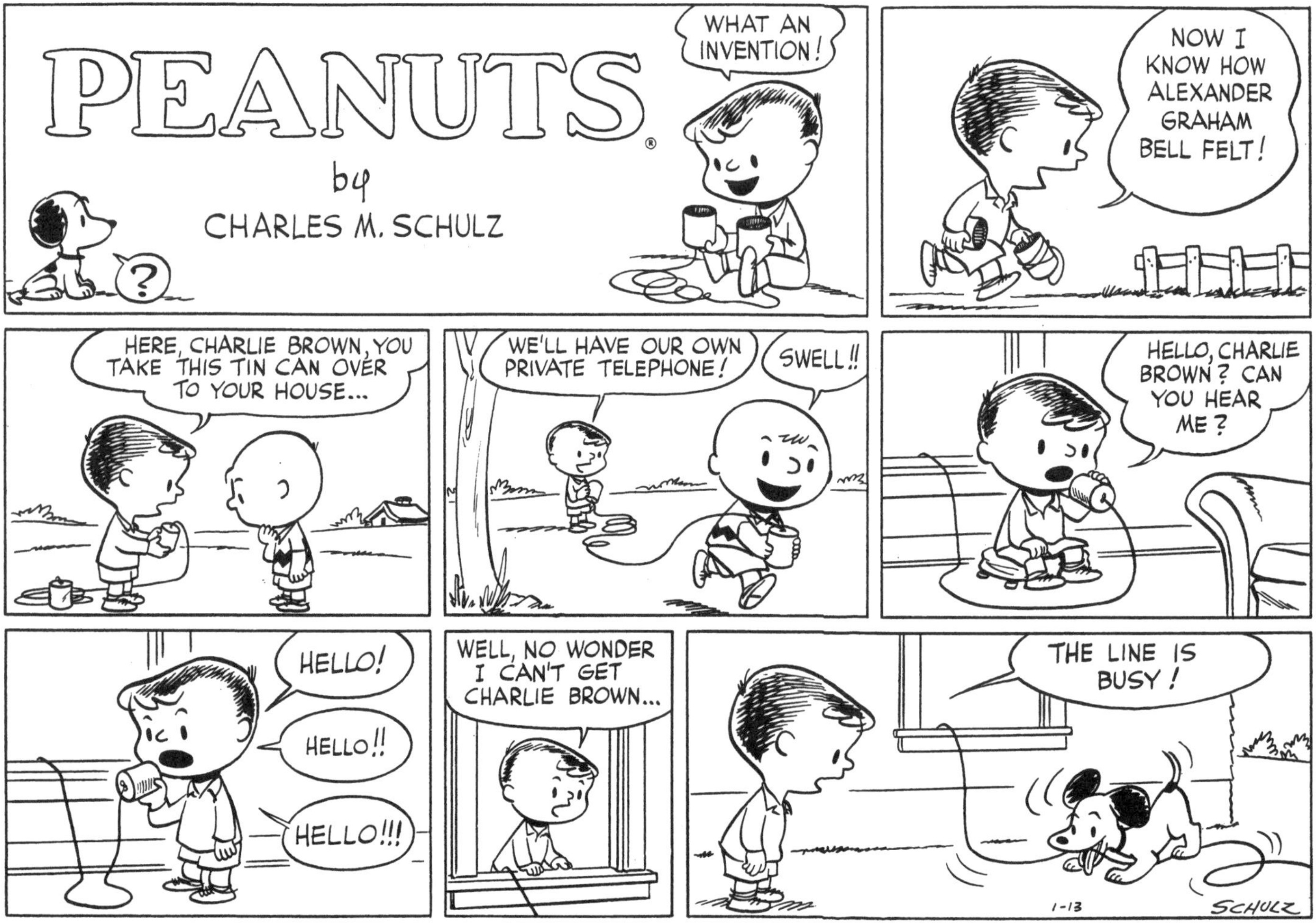
PEANUTS®
by
CHARLES M. SCHULZ
?
WHAT AN INVENTION!
NOW I KNOW HOW ALEXANDER GRAHAM BELL FELT!
HERE, CHARLIE BROWN, YOU TAKE THIS TIN CAN OVER TO YOUR HOUSE...
WE'LL HAVE OUR OWN PRIVATE TELEPHONE!
SWELL!!
HELLO, CHARLIE BROWN? CAN YOU HEAR ME?
HELLO!
HELLO!!
HELLO!!!
WELL, NO WONDER I CAN'T GET CHARLIE BROWN...
THE LINE IS BUSY!
1-13
SCHULZ

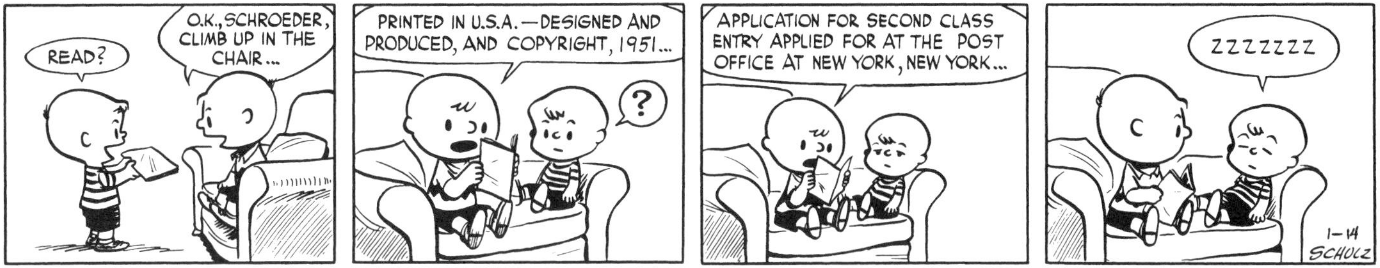
READ?
O.K., SCHROEDER, CLIMB UP IN THE CHAIR...
PRINTED IN U.S.A.—DESIGNED AND PRODUCED, AND COPYRIGHT, 1951...
?
APPLICATION FOR SECOND CLASS ENTRY APPLIED FOR AT THE POST OFFICE AT NEW YORK, NEW YORK...
ZZZZZZZ
1-14
SCHULZ

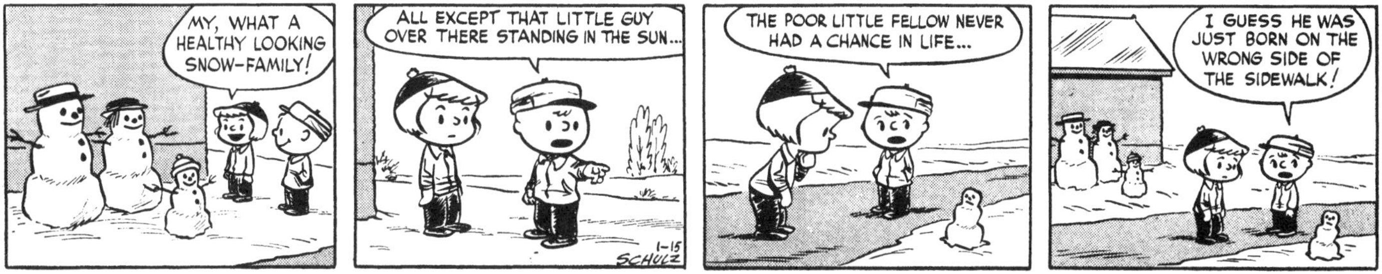
MY, WHAT A HEALTHY LOOKING SNOW-FAMILY!
ALL EXCEPT THAT LITTLE GUY OVER THERE STANDING IN THE SUN...
1-15
SCHULZ
THE POOR LITTLE FELLOW NEVER HAD A CHANCE IN LIFE...
I GUESS HE WAS JUST BORN ON THE WRONG SIDE OF THE SIDEWALK!

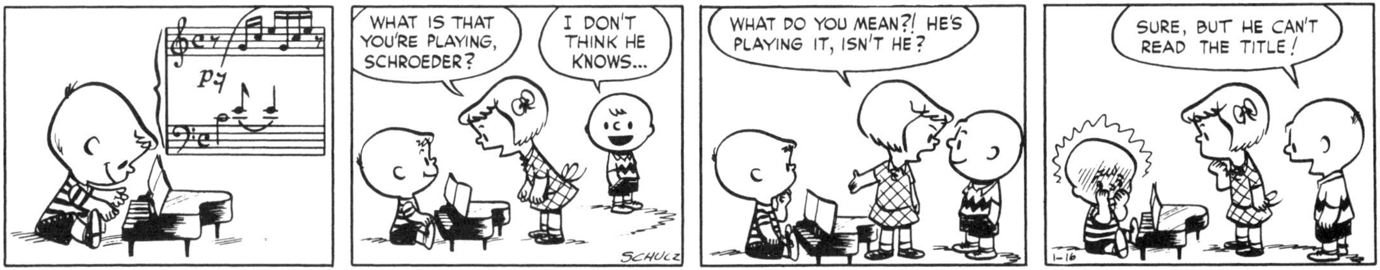
WHAT IS THAT YOU'RE PLAYING, SCHROEDER?
I DON'T THINK HE KNOWS...
SCHULZ
WHAT DO YOU MEAN?! HE'S PLAYING IT, ISN'T HE?
SURE, BUT HE CAN'T READ THE TITLE!
1-16

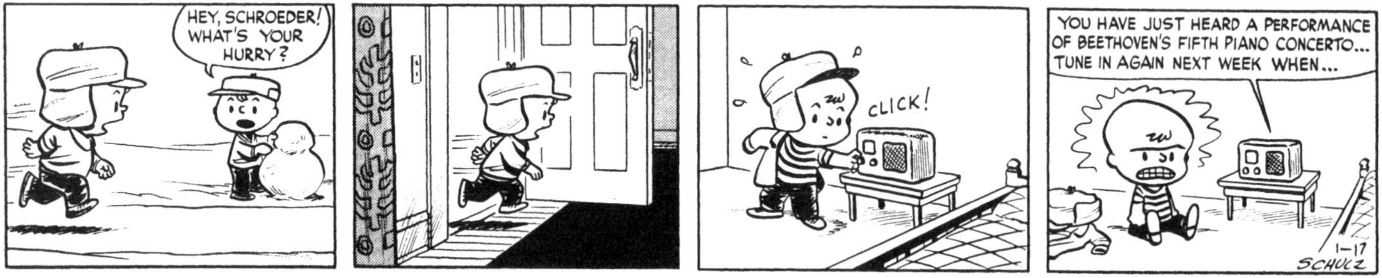
HEY, SCHROEDER! WHAT'S YOUR HURRY?
CLICK!
YOU HAVE JUST HEARD A PERFORMANCE OF BEETHOVEN'S FIFTH PIANO CONCERTO... TUNE IN AGAIN NEXT WEEK WHEN...
1-17
SCHULZ

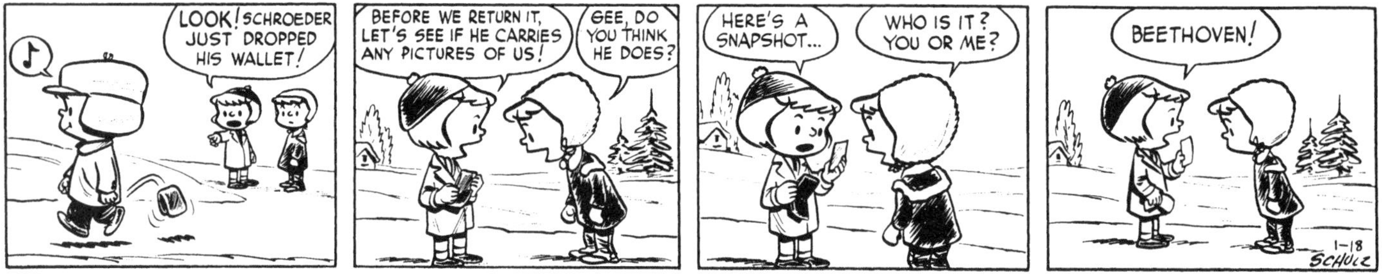
LOOK! SCHROEDER JUST DROPPED HIS WALLET!
BEFORE WE RETURN IT, LET'S SEE IF HE CARRIES ANY PICTURES OF US!
GEE, DO YOU THINK HE DOES?
HERE'S A SNAPSHOT...
WHO IS IT? YOU OR ME?
BEETHOVEN!
1-18
SCHULZ

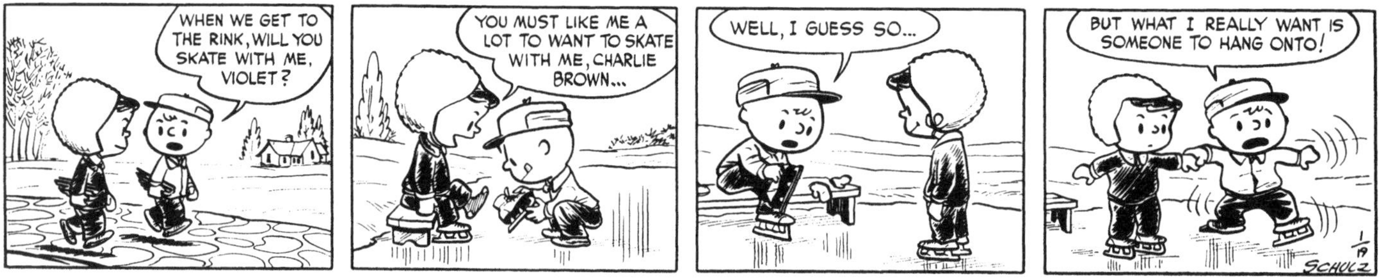
WHEN WE GET TO THE RINK, WILL YOU SKATE WITH ME, VIOLET?
YOU MUST LIKE ME A LOT TO WANT TO SKATE WITH ME, CHARLIE BROWN...
WELL, I GUESS SO...
BUT WHAT I REALLY WANT IS SOMEONE TO HANG ONTO!
1/19
SCHULZ

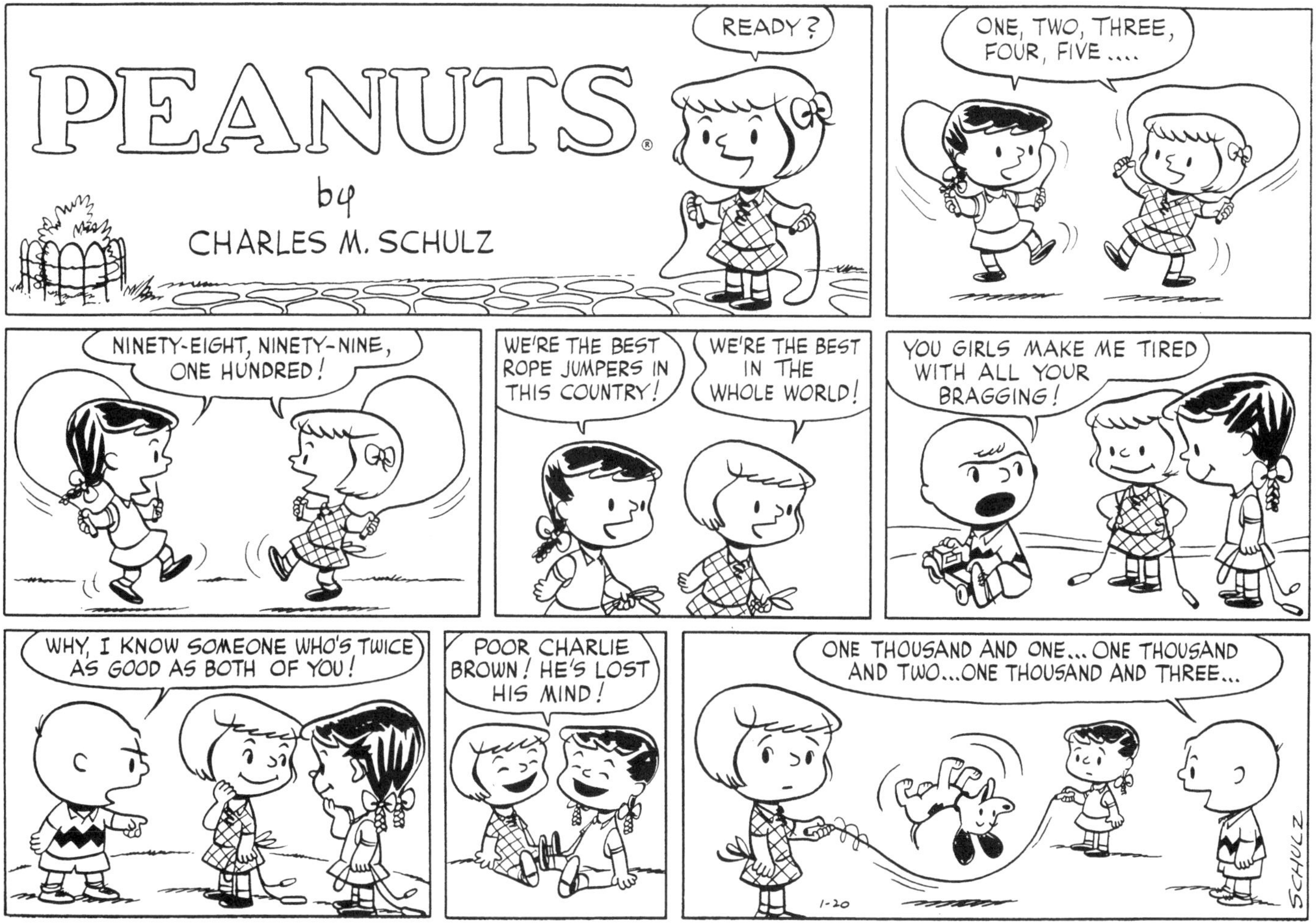
PEANUTS
by CHARLES M. SCHULZ
READY?
ONE, TWO, THREE, FOUR, FIVE....
NINETY-EIGHT, NINETY-NINE, ONE HUNDRED!
WE'RE THE BEST ROPE JUMPERS IN THIS COUNTRY!
WE'RE THE BEST IN THE WHOLE WORLD!
YOU GIRLS MAKE ME TIRED WITH ALL YOUR BRAGGING!
WHY, I KNOW SOMEONE WHO'S TWICE AS GOOD AS BOTH OF YOU!
POOR CHARLIE BROWN! HE'S LOST HIS MIND!
ONE THOUSAND AND ONE... ONE THOUSAND AND TWO...ONE THOUSAND AND THREE...
1-20
SCHULZ

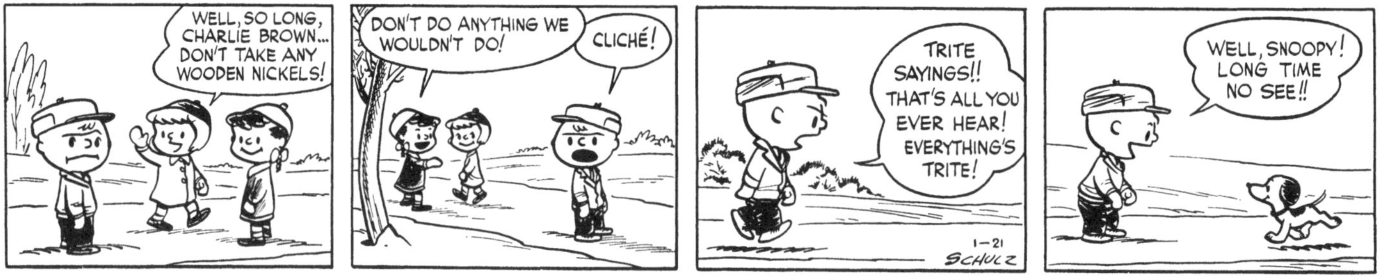
WELL, SO LONG, CHARLIE BROWN... DON'T TAKE ANY WOODEN NICKELS!
DON'T DO ANYTHING WE WOULDN'T DO!
CLICHÉ!
TRITE SAYINGS!! THAT'S ALL YOU EVER HEAR! EVERYTHING'S TRITE!
1-21
SCHULZ
WELL, SNOOPY! LONG TIME NO SEE!!

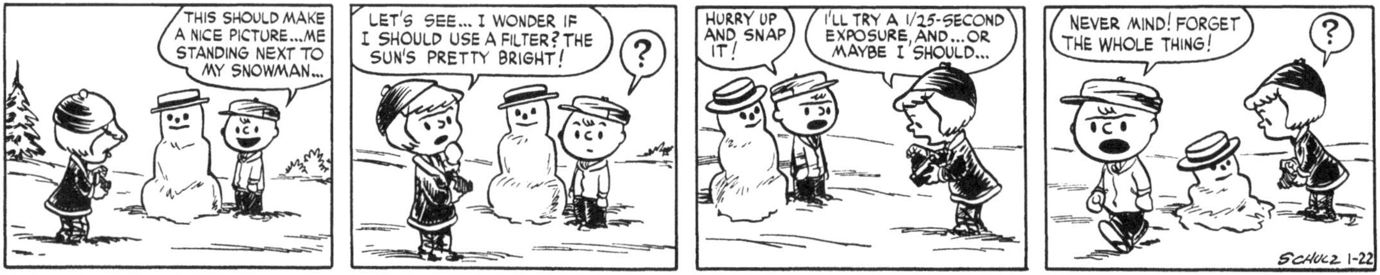
THIS SHOULD MAKE A NICE PICTURE...ME STANDING NEXT TO MY SNOWMAN...
LET'S SEE... I WONDER IF I SHOULD USE A FILTER? THE SUN'S PRETTY BRIGHT!
?
HURRY UP AND SNAP IT!
I'LL TRY A 1/25-SECOND EXPOSURE, AND...OR MAYBE I SHOULD...
NEVER MIND! FORGET THE WHOLE THING!
?
SCHULZ 1-22

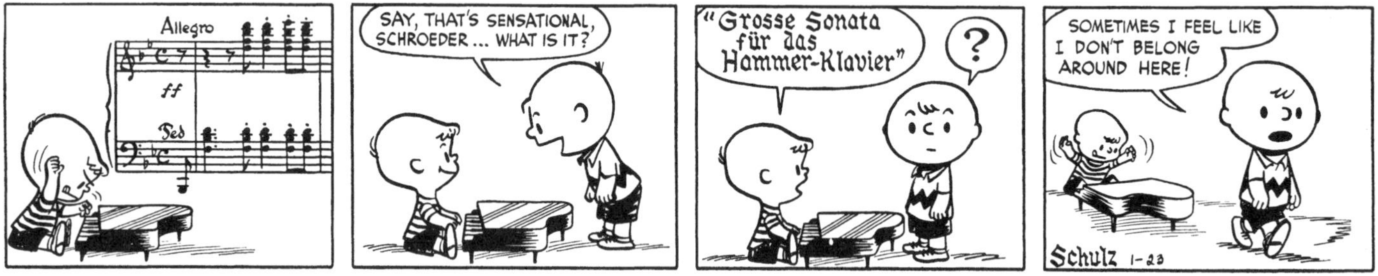
Allegro
ff
Ped
SAY, THAT'S SENSATIONAL, SCHROEDER ... WHAT IS IT?
"Grosse Sonata für das Hammer-Klavier"
?
SOMETIMES I FEEL LIKE I DON'T BELONG AROUND HERE!
Schulz 1-23

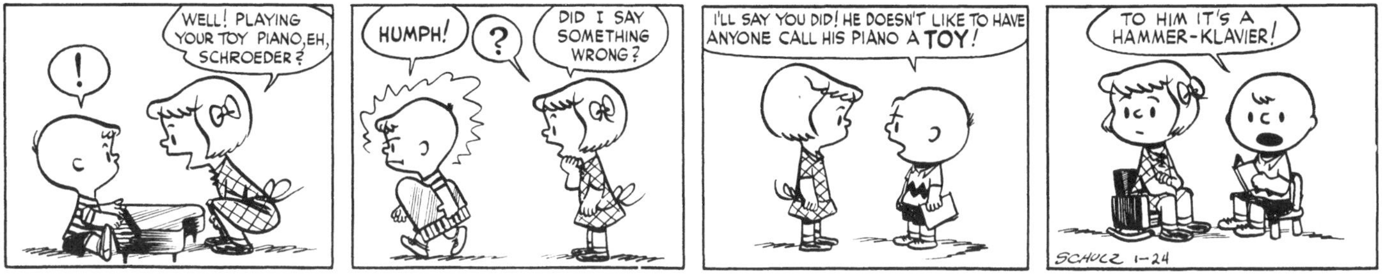
!
WELL! PLAYING YOUR TOY PIANO, EH, SCHROEDER?
HUMPH!
?
DID I SAY SOMETHING WRONG?
I'LL SAY YOU DID! HE DOESN'T LIKE TO HAVE ANYONE CALL HIS PIANO A TOY!
TO HIM IT'S A HAMMER-KLAVIER!
SCHULZ 1-24

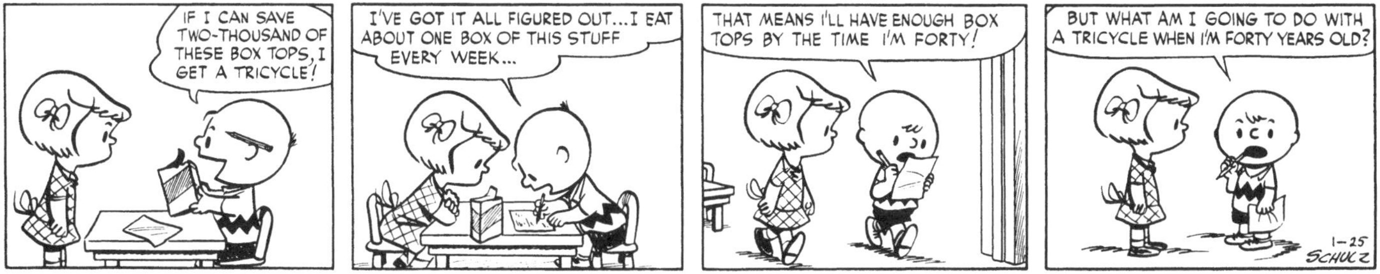
IF I CAN SAVE TWO-THOUSAND OF THESE BOX TOPS, I GET A TRICYCLE!
I'VE GOT IT ALL FIGURED OUT...I EAT ABOUT ONE BOX OF THIS STUFF EVERY WEEK...
THAT MEANS I'LL HAVE ENOUGH BOX TOPS BY THE TIME I'M FORTY!
BUT WHAT AM I GOING TO DO WITH A TRICYCLE WHEN I'M FORTY YEARS OLD?
1-25 SCHULZ

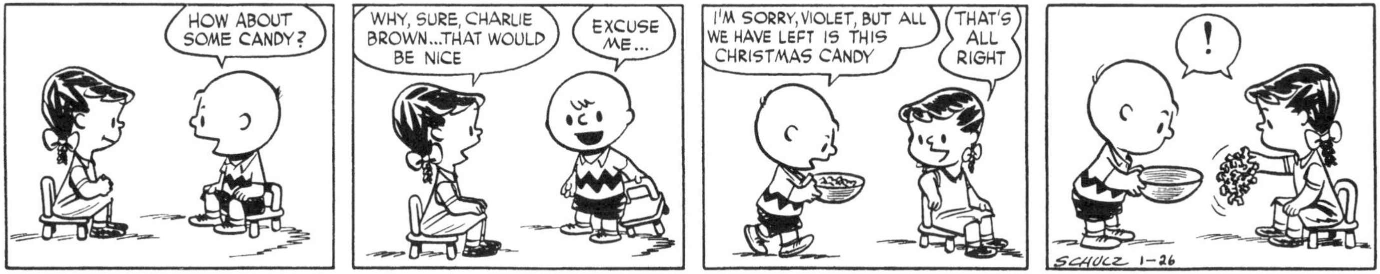
HOW ABOUT SOME CANDY?
WHY, SURE, CHARLIE BROWN...THAT WOULD BE NICE
EXCUSE ME...
I'M SORRY, VIOLET, BUT ALL WE HAVE LEFT IS THIS CHRISTMAS CANDY
THAT'S ALL RIGHT
!
SCHULZ 1-26

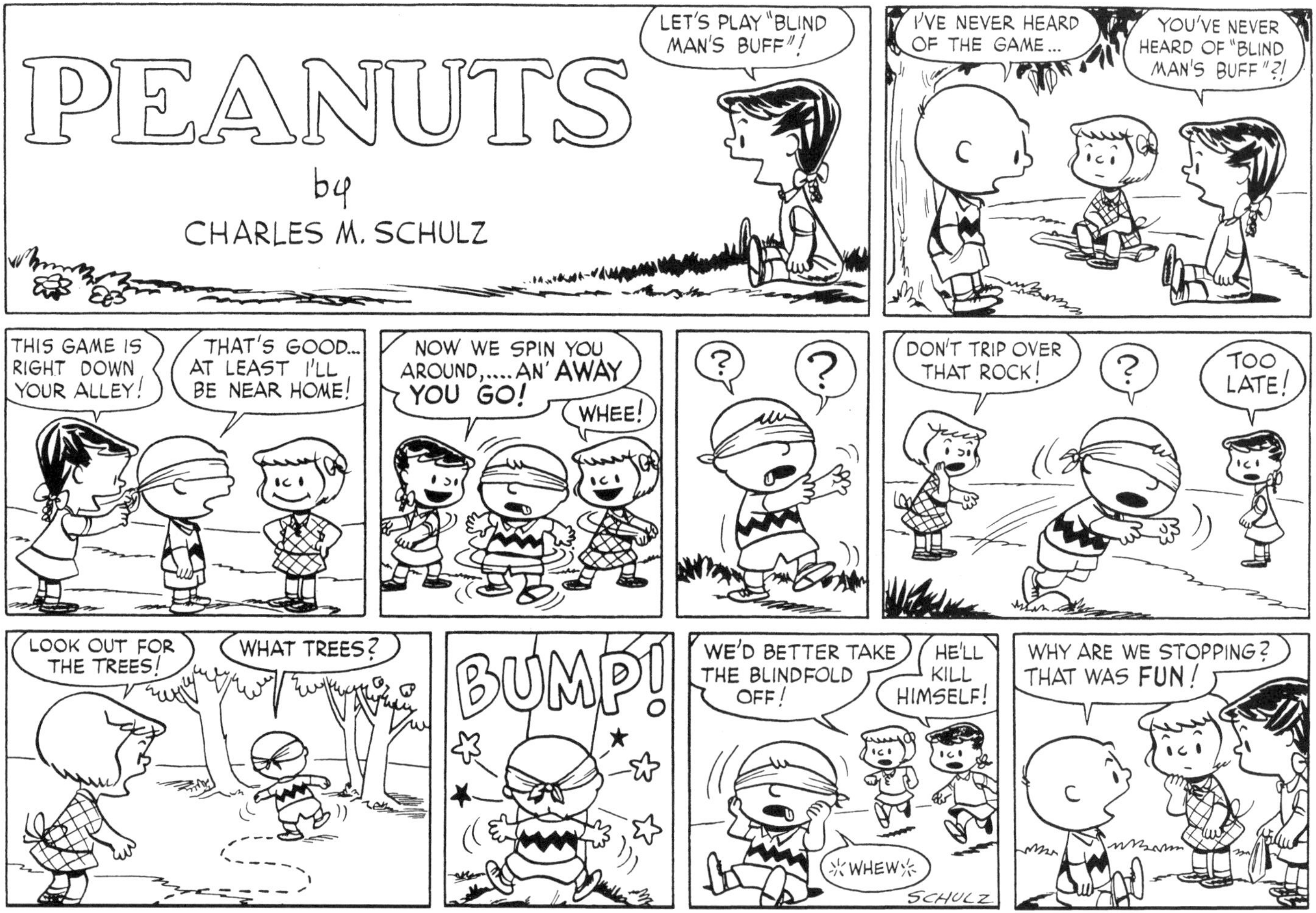
PEANUTS
by
CHARLES M. SCHULZ
LET'S PLAY "BLIND MAN'S BUFF"!
I'VE NEVER HEARD OF THE GAME...
YOU'VE NEVER HEARD OF "BLIND MAN'S BUFF"?!
THIS GAME IS RIGHT DOWN YOUR ALLEY!
THAT'S GOOD... AT LEAST I'LL BE NEAR HOME!
NOW WE SPIN YOU AROUND,....AN' AWAY YOU GO!
WHEE!
?
?
DON'T TRIP OVER THAT ROCK!
?
TOO LATE!
LOOK OUT FOR THE TREES!
WHAT TREES?
BUMP!
WE'D BETTER TAKE THE BLINDFOLD OFF!
HE'LL KILL HIMSELF!
WHEW
SCHULZ
WHY ARE WE STOPPING? THAT WAS FUN!

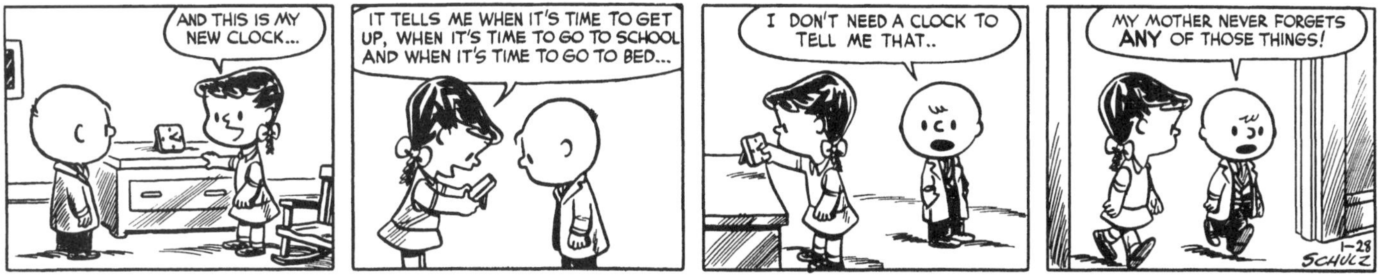
AND THIS IS MY NEW CLOCK...
IT TELLS ME WHEN IT'S TIME TO GET UP, WHEN IT'S TIME TO GO TO SCHOOL AND WHEN IT'S TIME TO GO TO BED...
I DON'T NEED A CLOCK TO TELL ME THAT..
MY MOTHER NEVER FORGETS ANY OF THOSE THINGS!
1-28
SCHULZ

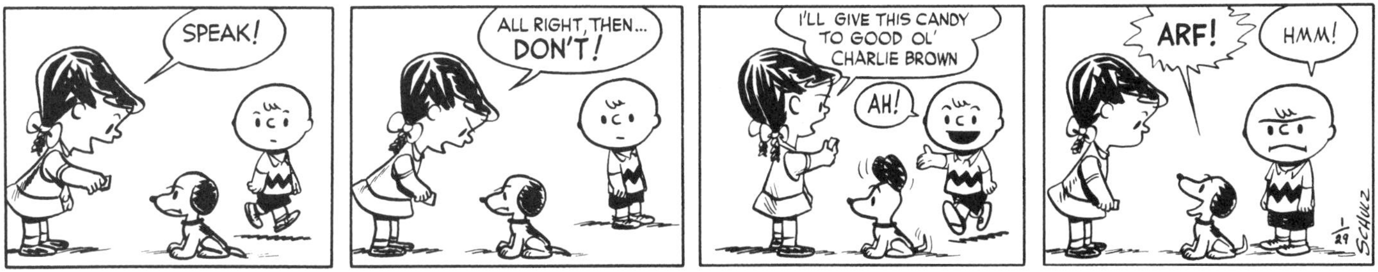
SPEAK!
ALL RIGHT, THEN... DON'T!
I'LL GIVE THIS CANDY TO GOOD OL' CHARLIE BROWN
AH!
ARF!
HMM!
1/29
SCHULZ

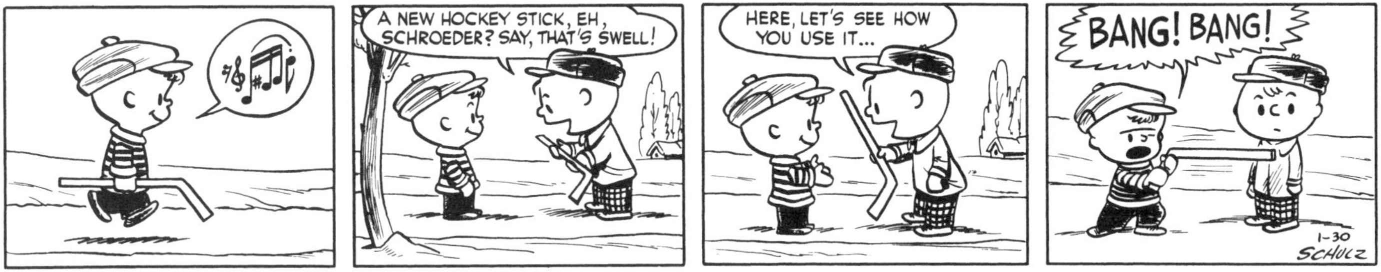
A NEW HOCKEY STICK, EH, SCHROEDER? SAY, THAT'S SWELL!
HERE, LET'S SEE HOW YOU USE IT...
BANG! BANG!
1-30
SCHULZ

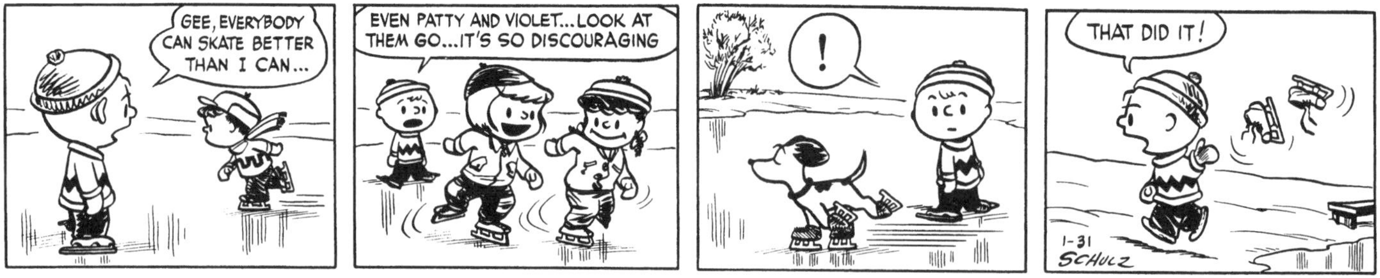
GEE, EVERYBODY CAN SKATE BETTER THAN I CAN...
EVEN PATTY AND VIOLET...LOOK AT THEM GO...IT'S SO DISCOURAGING
!
THAT DID IT!
1-31
SCHULZ

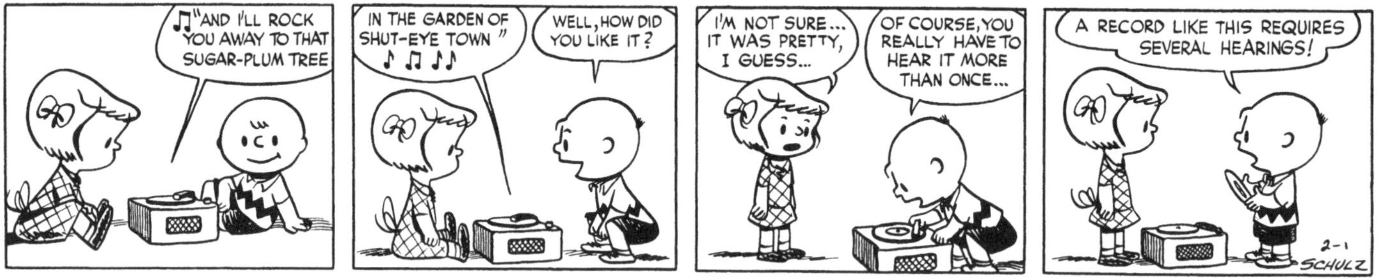
"AND I'LL ROCK YOU AWAY TO THAT SUGAR-PLUM TREE
IN THE GARDEN OF SHUT-EYE TOWN"
WELL, HOW DID YOU LIKE IT?
I'M NOT SURE... IT WAS PRETTY, I GUESS...
OF COURSE, YOU REALLY HAVE TO HEAR IT MORE THAN ONCE...
A RECORD LIKE THIS REQUIRES SEVERAL HEARINGS!
2-1
SCHULZ

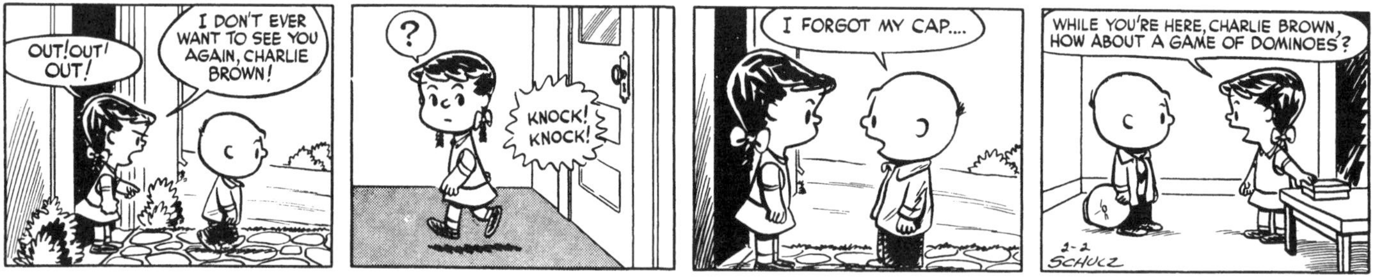
OUT! OUT! OUT!
I DON'T EVER WANT TO SEE YOU AGAIN, CHARLIE BROWN!
?
KNOCK! KNOCK!
I FORGOT MY CAP....
WHILE YOU'RE HERE, CHARLIE BROWN, HOW ABOUT A GAME OF DOMINOES?
2-2
SCHULZ

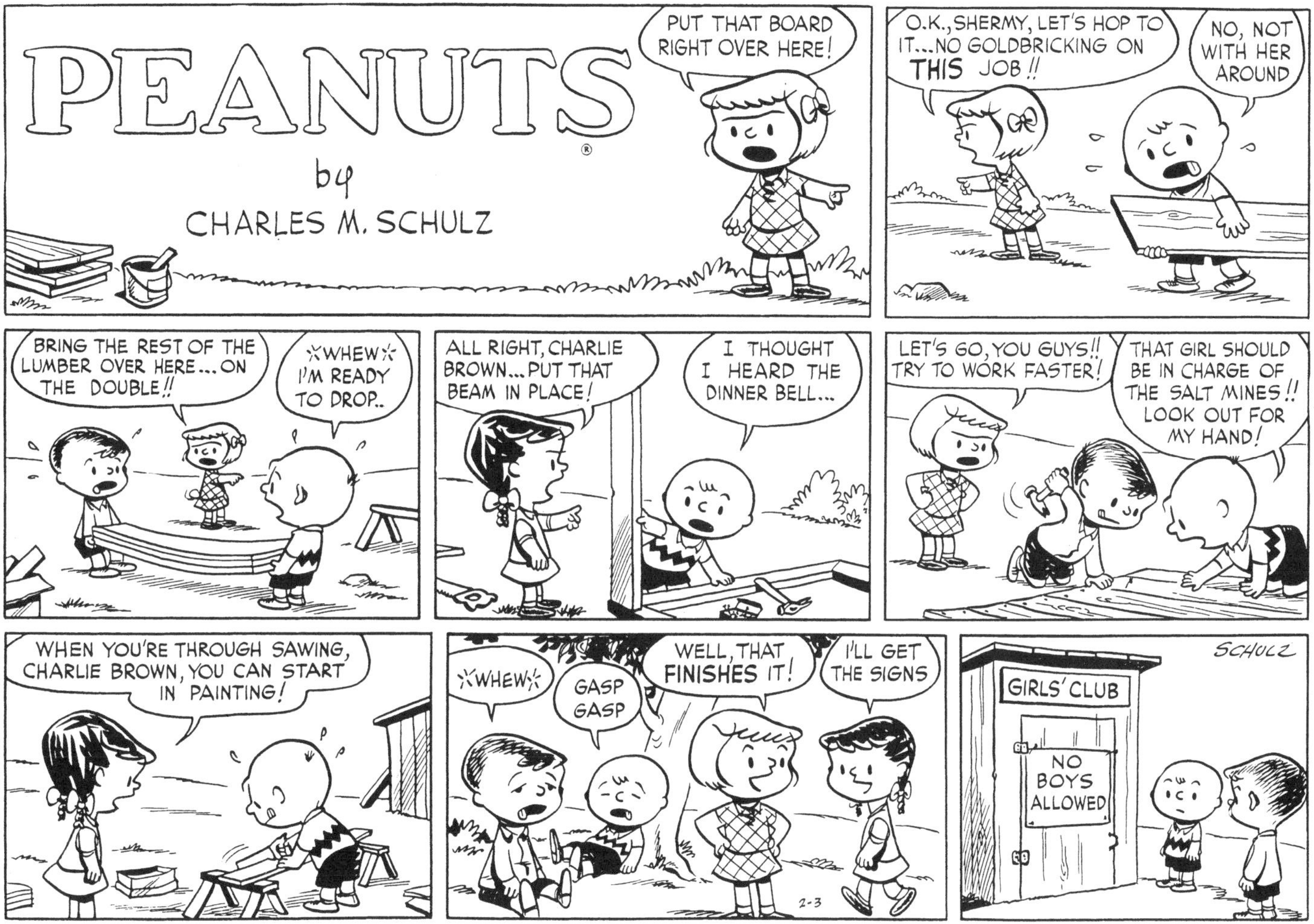
PEANUTS
by CHARLES M. SCHULZ
PUT THAT BOARD RIGHT OVER HERE!
O.K., SHERMY, LET'S HOP TO IT...NO GOLDBRICKING ON THIS JOB!!
NO, NOT WITH HER AROUND
BRING THE REST OF THE LUMBER OVER HERE...ON THE DOUBLE!!
WHEW I'M READY TO DROP..
ALL RIGHT, CHARLIE BROWN...PUT THAT BEAM IN PLACE!
I THOUGHT I HEARD THE DINNER BELL...
LET'S GO, YOU GUYS!! TRY TO WORK FASTER!
THAT GIRL SHOULD BE IN CHARGE OF THE SALT MINES!! LOOK OUT FOR MY HAND!
WHEN YOU'RE THROUGH SAWING, CHARLIE BROWN, YOU CAN START IN PAINTING!
WHEW
GASP GASP
WELL, THAT FINISHES IT!
I'LL GET THE SIGNS
2-3
SCHULZ
GIRLS' CLUB
NO BOYS ALLOWED

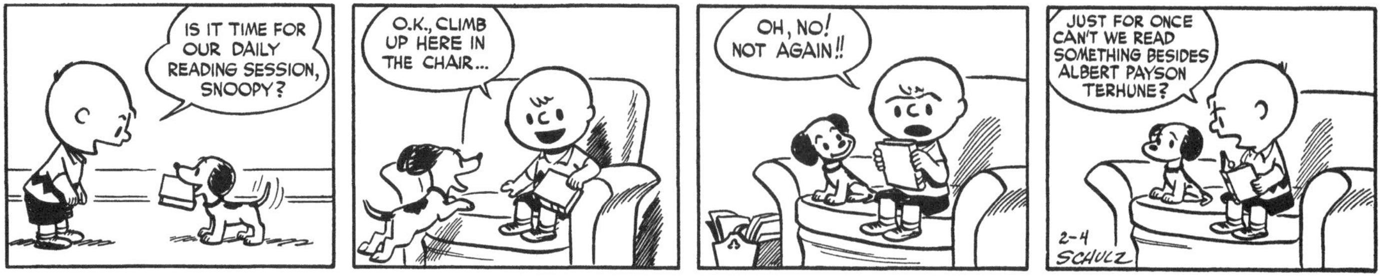
IS IT TIME FOR OUR DAILY READING SESSION, SNOOPY?
O.K., CLIMB UP HERE IN THE CHAIR...
OH, NO! NOT AGAIN!!
JUST FOR ONCE CAN'T WE READ SOMETHING BESIDES ALBERT PAYSON TERHUNE?
2-4
SCHULZ

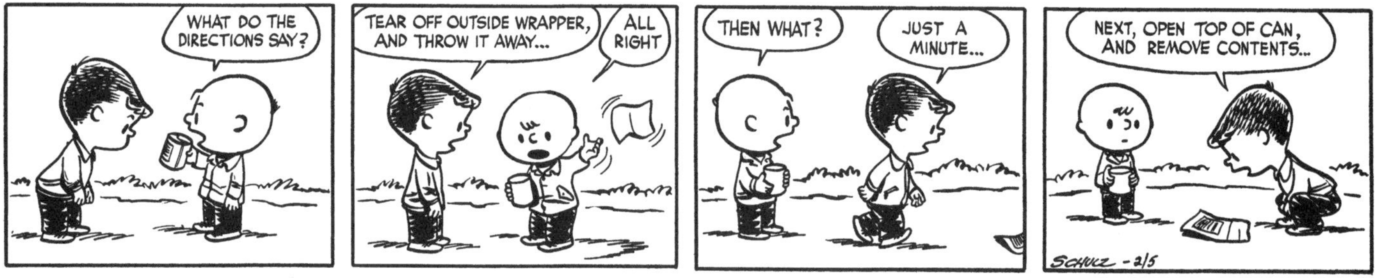
WHAT DO THE DIRECTIONS SAY?
TEAR OFF OUTSIDE WRAPPER, AND THROW IT AWAY...
ALL RIGHT
THEN WHAT?
JUST A MINUTE...
NEXT, OPEN TOP OF CAN, AND REMOVE CONTENTS...
SCHULZ - 2/5

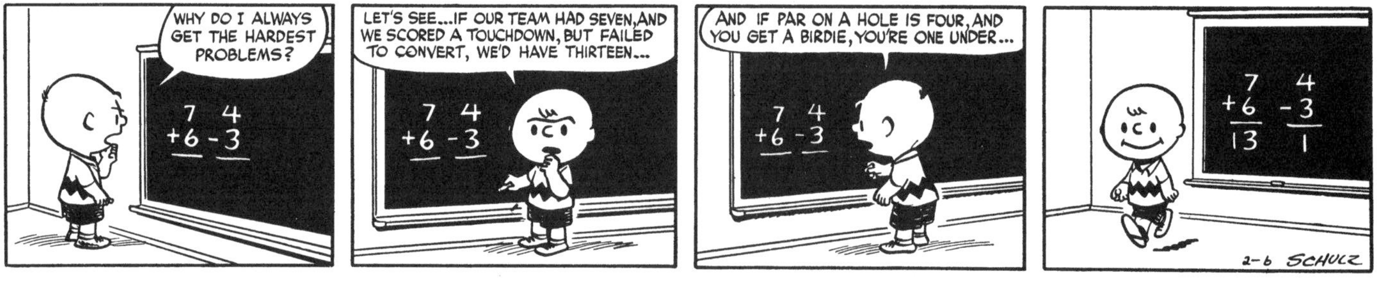
WHY DO I ALWAYS GET THE HARDEST PROBLEMS?
7 4
+6 -3
LET'S SEE...IF OUR TEAM HAD SEVEN, AND WE SCORED A TOUCHDOWN, BUT FAILED TO CONVERT, WE'D HAVE THIRTEEN...
7 4
+6 -3
AND IF PAR ON A HOLE IS FOUR, AND YOU GET A BIRDIE, YOU'RE ONE UNDER...
7 4
+6 -3
7 4
+6 -3
13 1
2-6 SCHULZ

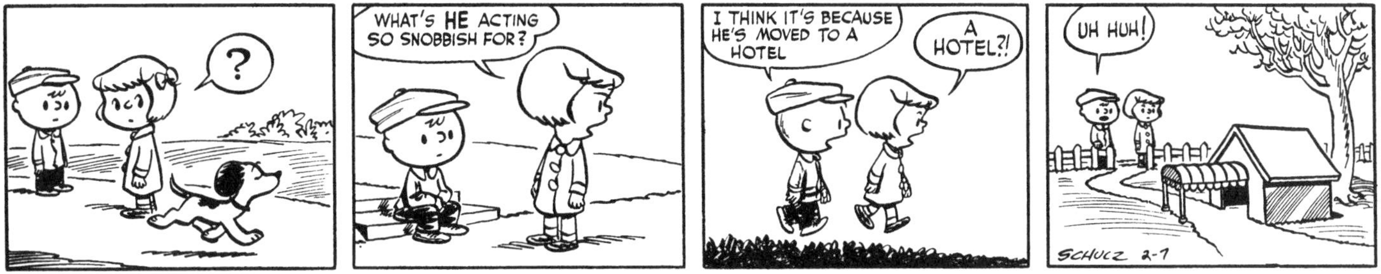
?
WHAT'S HE ACTING SO SNOBBISH FOR?
I THINK IT'S BECAUSE HE'S MOVED TO A HOTEL
A HOTEL?!
UH HUH!
SCHULZ 2-7

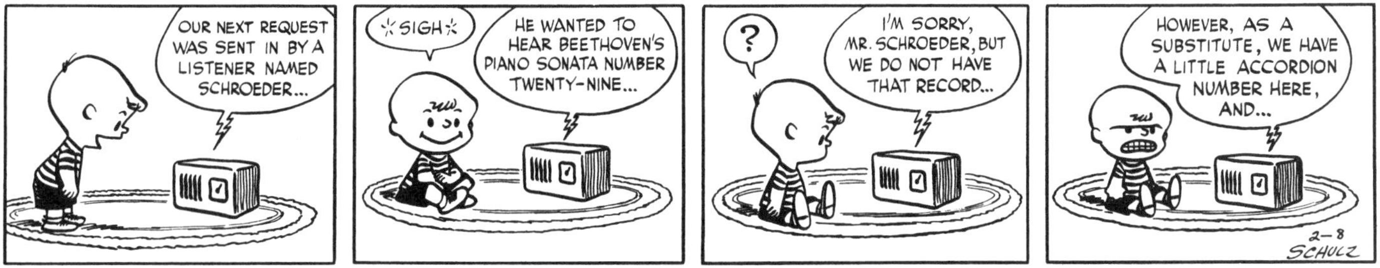
OUR NEXT REQUEST WAS SENT IN BY A LISTENER NAMED SCHROEDER...
SIGH
HE WANTED TO HEAR BEETHOVEN'S PIANO SONATA NUMBER TWENTY-NINE...
?
I'M SORRY, MR. SCHROEDER, BUT WE DO NOT HAVE THAT RECORD...
HOWEVER, AS A SUBSTITUTE, WE HAVE A LITTLE ACCORDION NUMBER HERE, AND...
2-8 SCHULZ

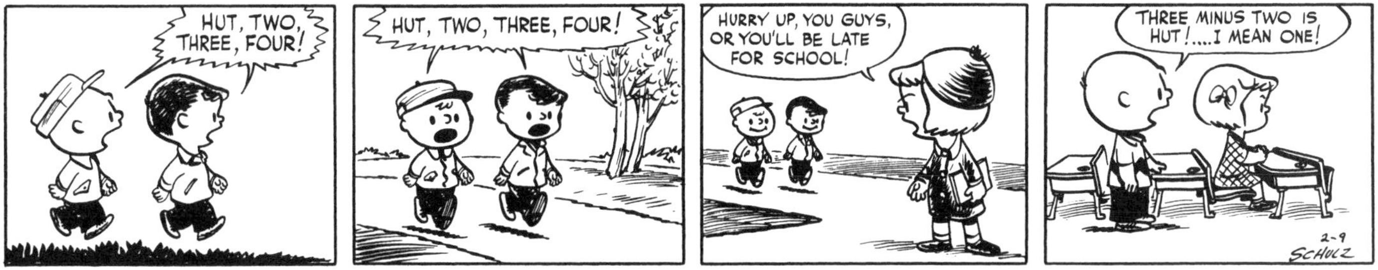
HUT, TWO, THREE, FOUR!
HUT, TWO, THREE, FOUR!
HURRY UP, YOU GUYS, OR YOU'LL BE LATE FOR SCHOOL!
THREE MINUS TWO IS HUT!....I MEAN ONE!
2-9 SCHULZ

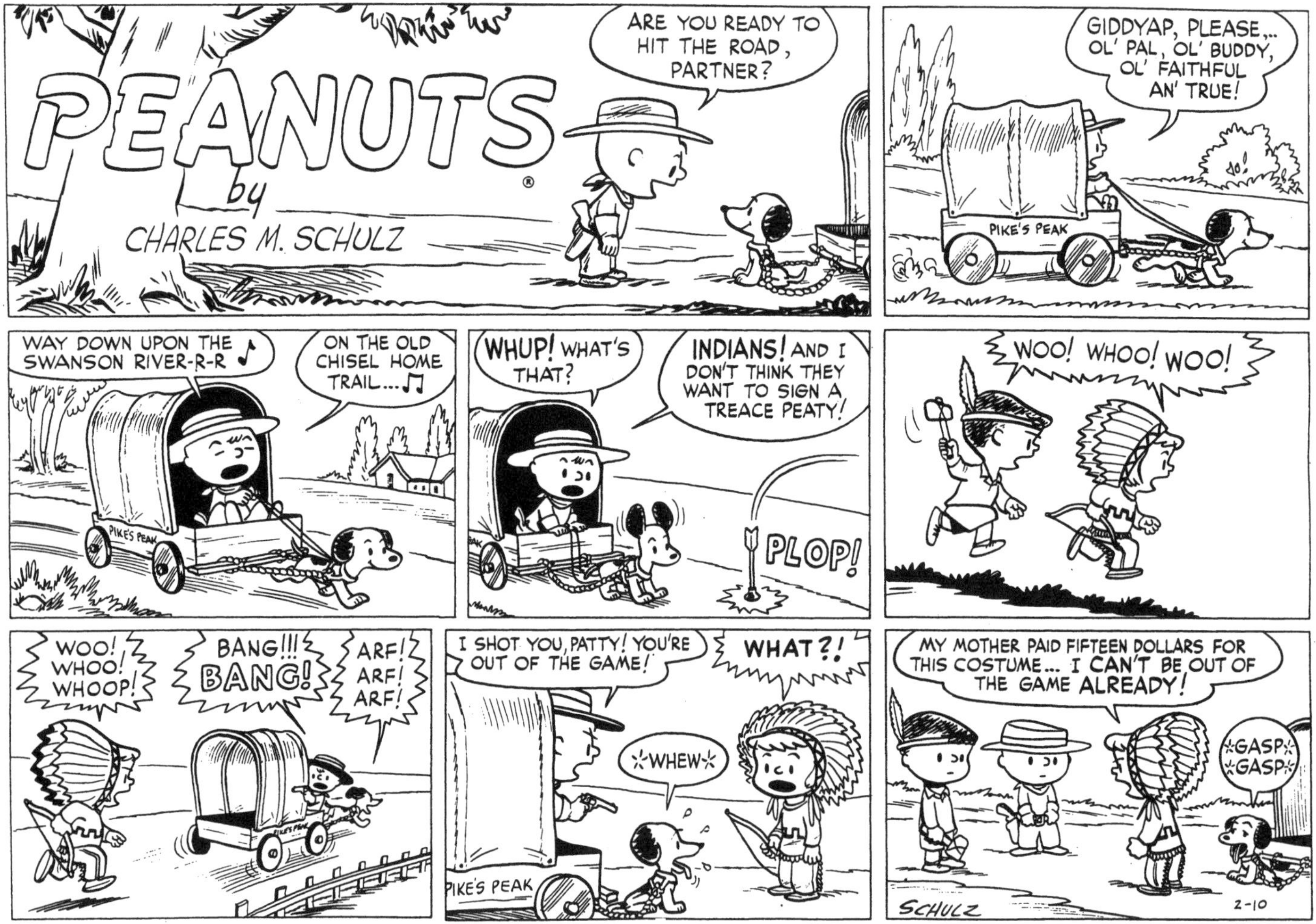
PEANUTS
by
CHARLES M. SCHULZ
ARE YOU READY TO HIT THE ROAD, PARTNER?
GIDDYAP, PLEASE,... OL' PAL, OL' BUDDY, OL' FAITHFUL AN' TRUE!
PIKE'S PEAK
WAY DOWN UPON THE SWANSON RIVER-R-R ♪
ON THE OLD CHISEL HOME TRAIL...♫
PIKE'S PEAK
WHUP! WHAT'S THAT?
INDIANS! AND I DON'T THINK THEY WANT TO SIGN A TREACE PEATY!
PLOP!
WOO! WHOO! WOO!
WOO! WHOO! WHOOP!
BANG!!! BANG!
ARF! ARF! ARF!
I SHOT YOU, PATTY! YOU'RE OUT OF THE GAME!
WHAT?!
WHEW
PIKE'S PEAK
MY MOTHER PAID FIFTEEN DOLLARS FOR THIS COSTUME... I CAN'T BE OUT OF THE GAME ALREADY!
GASP GASP
SCHULZ
2-10

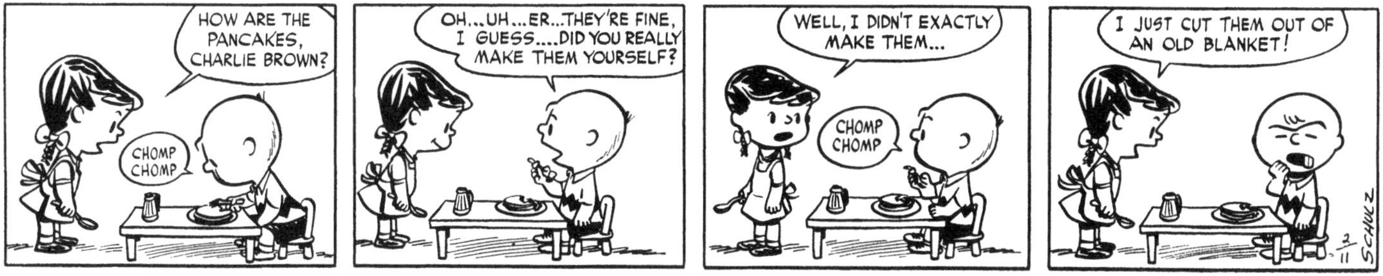
HOW ARE THE PANCAKES, CHARLIE BROWN?
CHOMP CHOMP
OH...UH...ER...THEY'RE FINE, I GUESS....DID YOU REALLY MAKE THEM YOURSELF?
WELL, I DIDN'T EXACTLY MAKE THEM...
CHOMP CHOMP
I JUST CUT THEM OUT OF AN OLD BLANKET!
2/11 SCHULZ

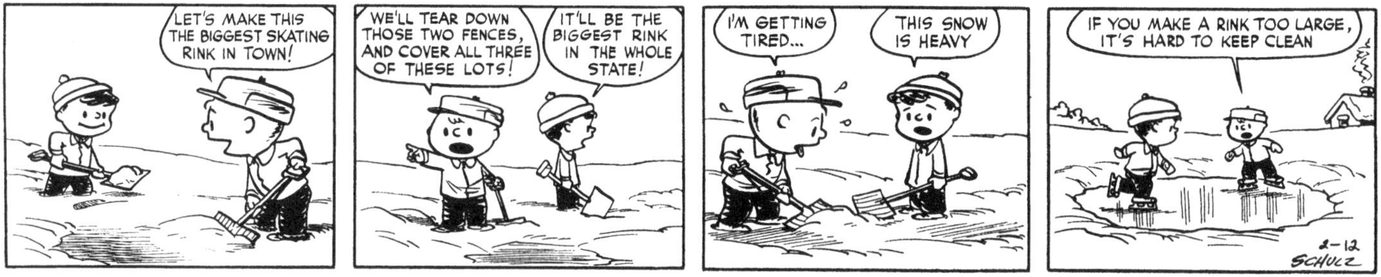
LET'S MAKE THIS THE BIGGEST SKATING RINK IN TOWN!
WE'LL TEAR DOWN THOSE TWO FENCES, AND COVER ALL THREE OF THESE LOTS!
IT'LL BE THE BIGGEST RINK IN THE WHOLE STATE!
I'M GETTING TIRED...
THIS SNOW IS HEAVY
IF YOU MAKE A RINK TOO LARGE, IT'S HARD TO KEEP CLEAN
2-12 SCHULZ

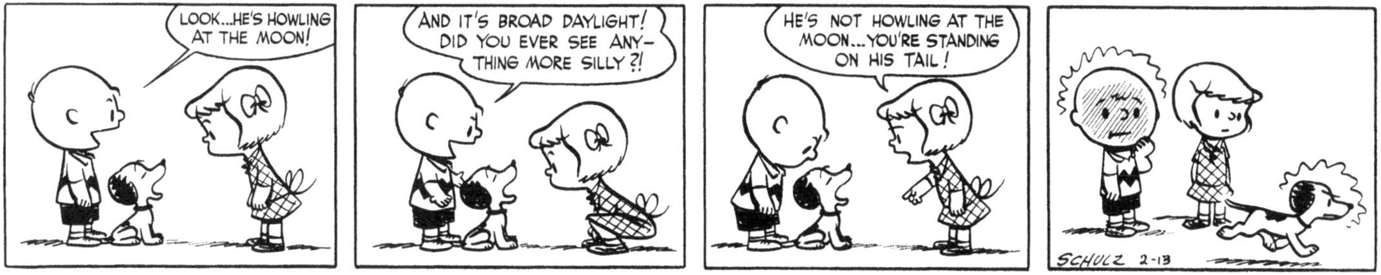
LOOK...HE'S HOWLING AT THE MOON!
AND IT'S BROAD DAYLIGHT! DID YOU EVER SEE ANY-THING MORE SILLY?!
HE'S NOT HOWLING AT THE MOON...YOU'RE STANDING ON HIS TAIL!
SCHULZ 2-13

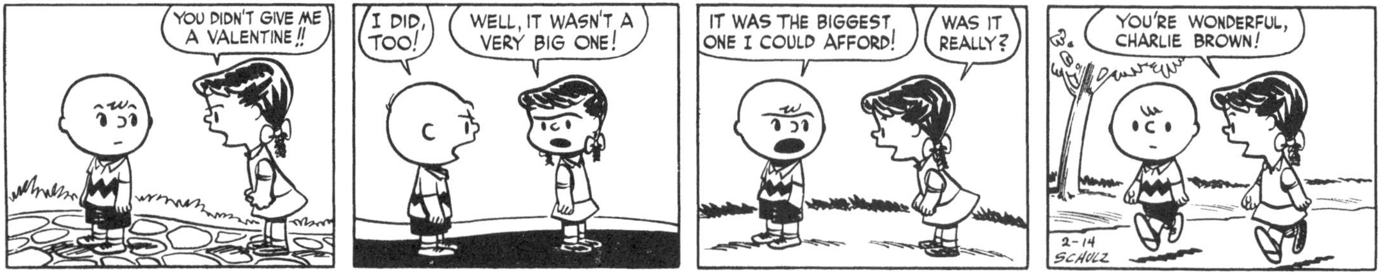
YOU DIDN'T GIVE ME A VALENTINE!!
I DID, TOO!
WELL, IT WASN'T A VERY BIG ONE!
IT WAS THE BIGGEST ONE I COULD AFFORD!
WAS IT REALLY?
YOU'RE WONDERFUL, CHARLIE BROWN!
2-14
SCHULZ

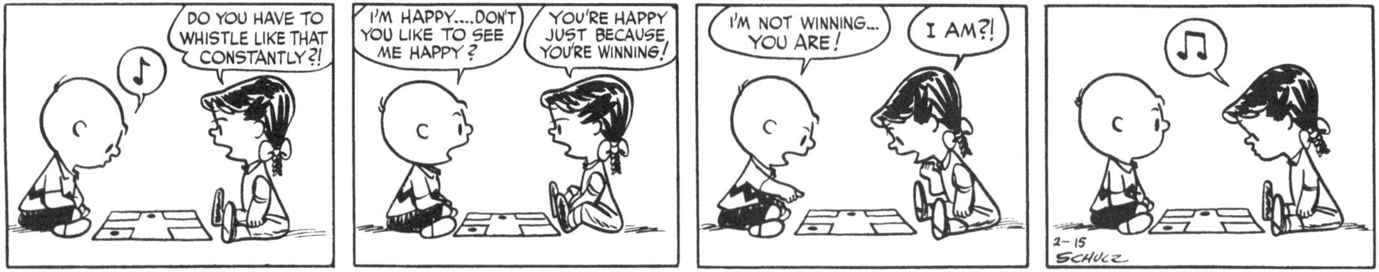
DO YOU HAVE TO WHISTLE LIKE THAT CONSTANTLY?!
I'M HAPPY....DON'T YOU LIKE TO SEE ME HAPPY?
YOU'RE HAPPY JUST BECAUSE YOU'RE WINNING!
I'M NOT WINNING... YOU ARE!
I AM?!
2-15
SCHULZ

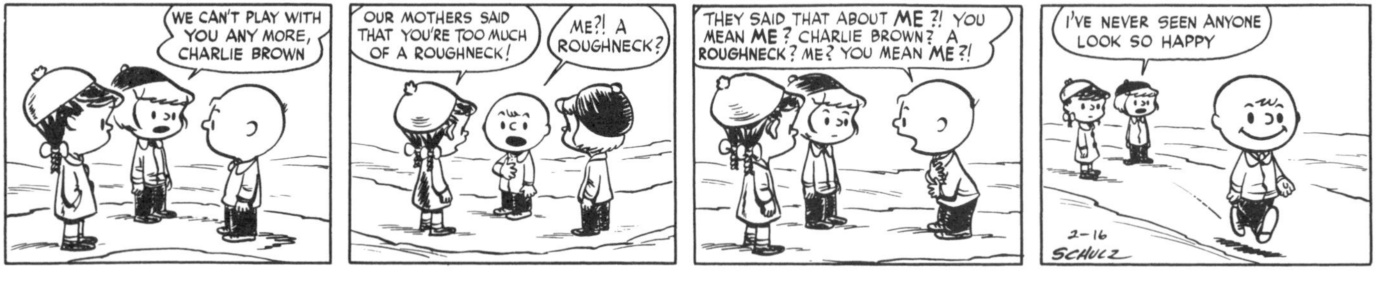
WE CAN'T PLAY WITH YOU ANY MORE, CHARLIE BROWN
OUR MOTHERS SAID THAT YOU'RE TOO MUCH OF A ROUGHNECK!
ME?! A ROUGHNECK?
THEY SAID THAT ABOUT ME?! YOU MEAN ME? CHARLIE BROWN? A ROUGHNECK? ME? YOU MEAN ME?!
I'VE NEVER SEEN ANYONE LOOK SO HAPPY
2-16
SCHULZ

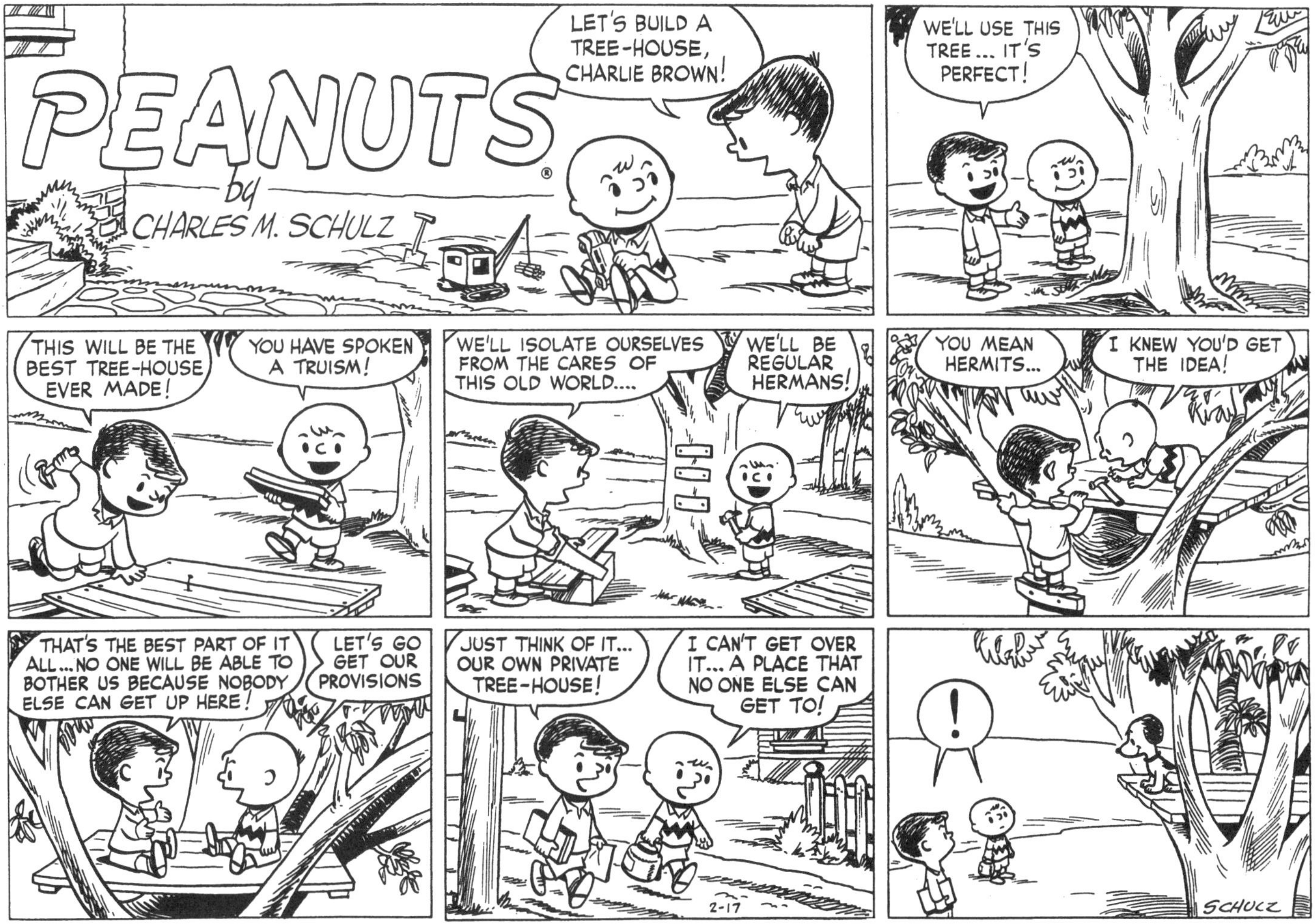
PEANUTS
by CHARLES M. SCHULZ
LET'S BUILD A TREE-HOUSE, CHARLIE BROWN!
WE'LL USE THIS TREE... IT'S PERFECT!
THIS WILL BE THE BEST TREE-HOUSE EVER MADE!
YOU HAVE SPOKEN A TRUISM!
WE'LL ISOLATE OURSELVES FROM THE CARES OF THIS OLD WORLD....
WE'LL BE REGULAR HERMANS!
YOU MEAN HERMITS...
I KNEW YOU'D GET THE IDEA!
THAT'S THE BEST PART OF IT ALL...NO ONE WILL BE ABLE TO BOTHER US BECAUSE NOBODY ELSE CAN GET UP HERE!
LET'S GO GET OUR PROVISIONS
JUST THINK OF IT... OUR OWN PRIVATE TREE-HOUSE!
I CAN'T GET OVER IT... A PLACE THAT NO ONE ELSE CAN GET TO!
2-17
!
SCHULZ

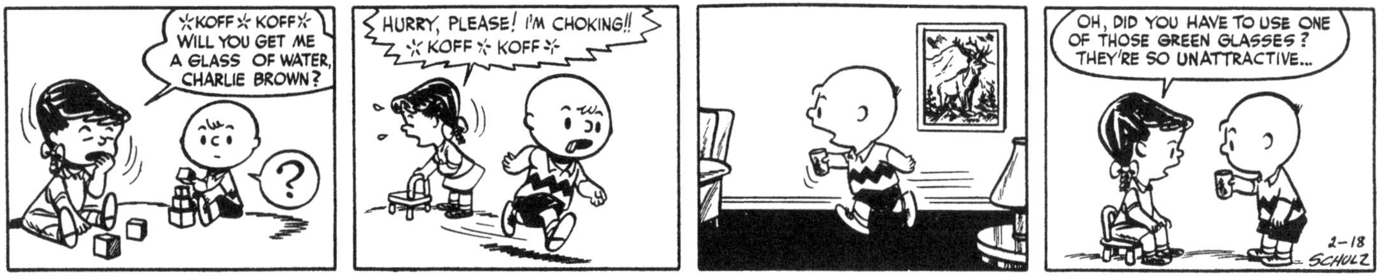
KOFF KOFF* WILL YOU GET ME A GLASS OF WATER, CHARLIE BROWN?
?
HURRY, PLEASE! I'M CHOKING!! *KOFF* KOFF*
OH, DID YOU HAVE TO USE ONE OF THOSE GREEN GLASSES? THEY'RE SO UNATTRACTIVE...
2-18
SCHULZ

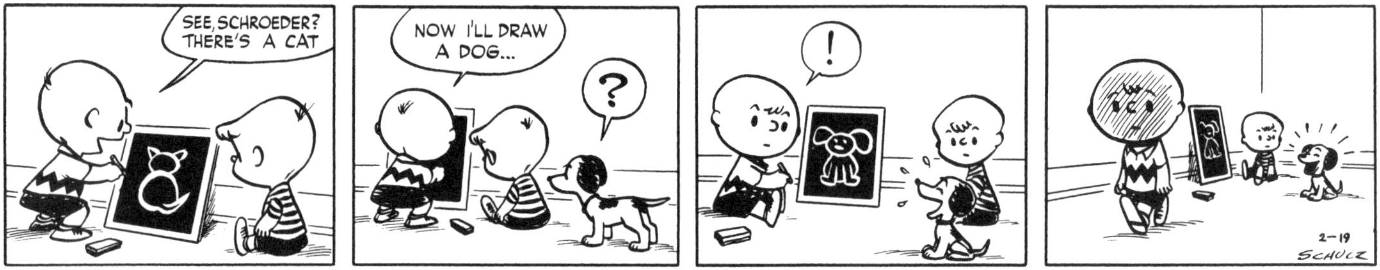
SEE, SCHROEDER? THERE'S A CAT
NOW I'LL DRAW A DOG...
?
!
2-19
SCHULZ

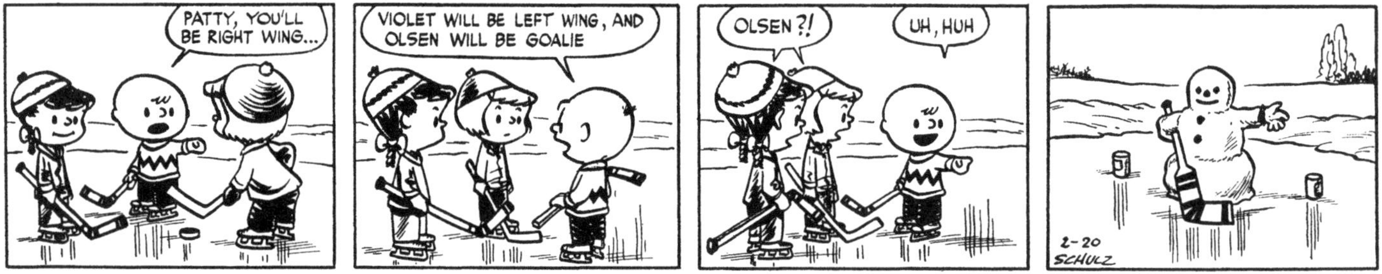
PATTY, YOU'LL BE RIGHT WING...
VIOLET WILL BE LEFT WING, AND OLSEN WILL BE GOALIE
OLSEN?!
UH, HUH
2-20
SCHULZ

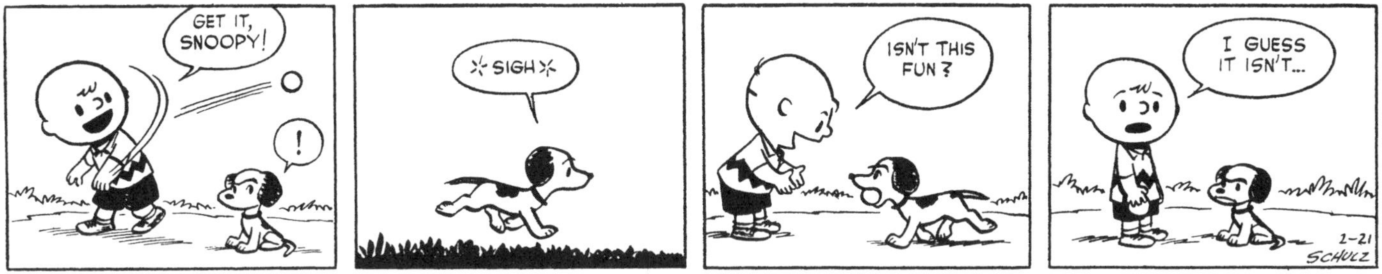
GET IT, SNOOPY!
!
SIGH
ISN'T THIS FUN?
I GUESS IT ISN'T...
2-21
SCHULZ

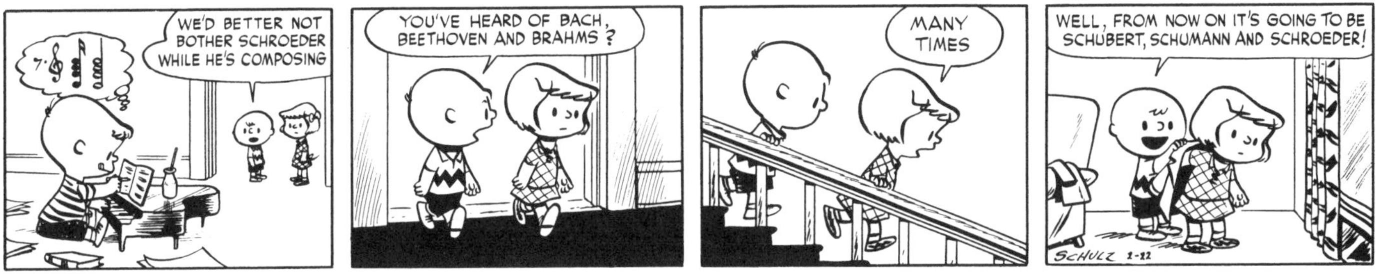
WE'D BETTER NOT BOTHER SCHROEDER WHILE HE'S COMPOSING
YOU'VE HEARD OF BACH, BEETHOVEN AND BRAHMS?
MANY TIMES
WELL, FROM NOW ON IT'S GOING TO BE SCHUBERT, SCHUMANN AND SCHROEDER!
SCHULZ 2-22

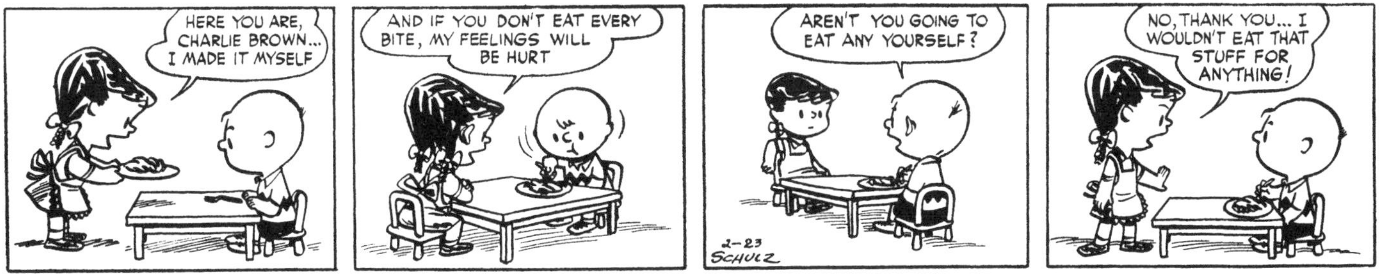
HERE YOU ARE, CHARLIE BROWN... I MADE IT MYSELF
AND IF YOU DON'T EAT EVERY BITE, MY FEELINGS WILL BE HURT
AREN'T YOU GOING TO EAT ANY YOURSELF?
2-23
SCHULZ
NO, THANK YOU... I WOULDN'T EAT THAT STUFF FOR ANYTHING!

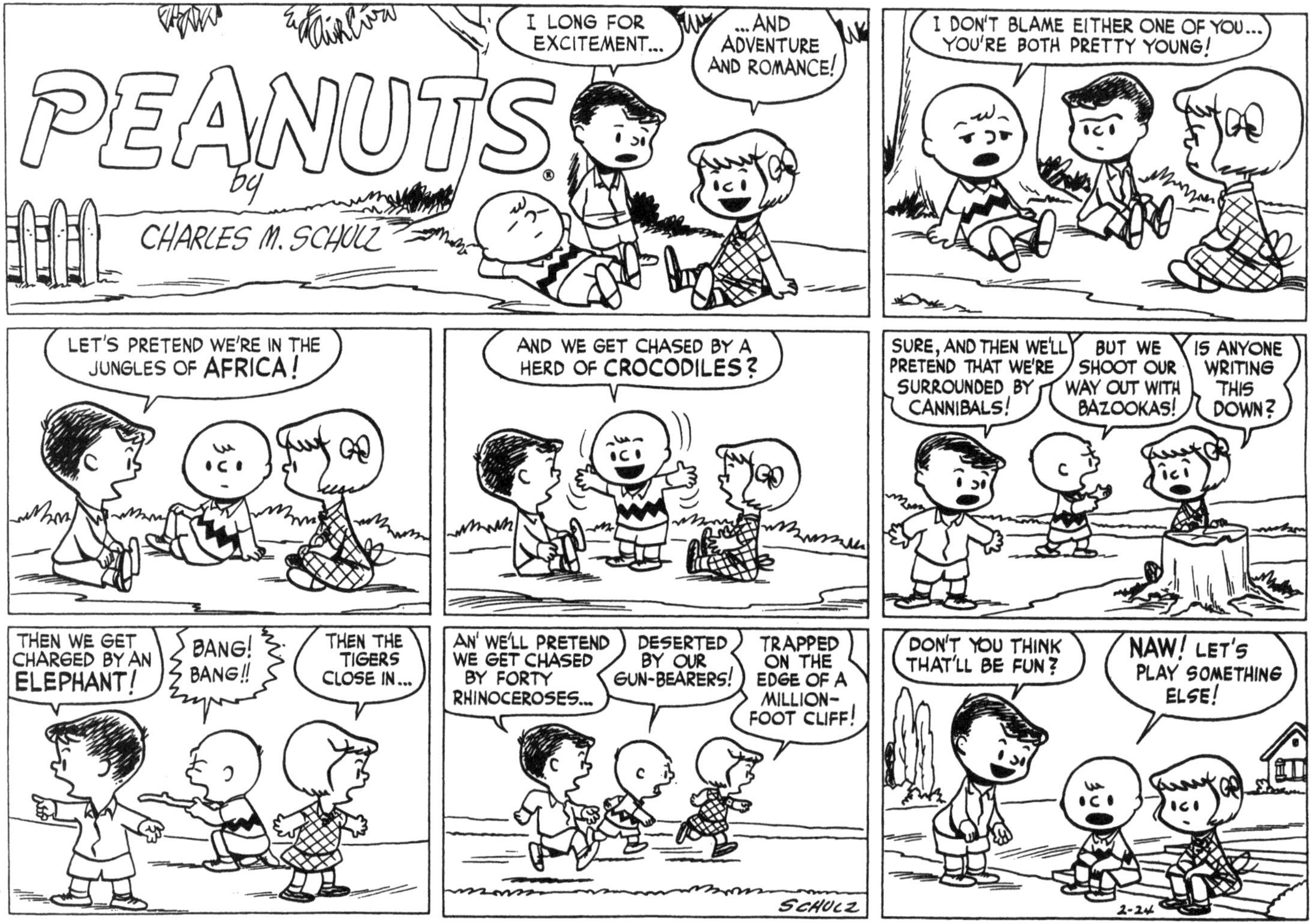
PEANUTS
by
CHARLES M. SCHULZ
I LONG FOR EXCITEMENT...
...AND ADVENTURE AND ROMANCE!
I DON'T BLAME EITHER ONE OF YOU... YOU'RE BOTH PRETTY YOUNG!
LET'S PRETEND WE'RE IN THE JUNGLES OF AFRICA!
AND WE GET CHASED BY A HERD OF CROCODILES?
SURE, AND THEN WE'LL PRETEND THAT WE'RE SURROUNDED BY CANNIBALS!
BUT WE SHOOT OUR WAY OUT WITH BAZOOKAS!
IS ANYONE WRITING THIS DOWN?
THEN WE GET CHARGED BY AN ELEPHANT!
BANG! BANG!!
THEN THE TIGERS CLOSE IN...
AN' WE'LL PRETEND WE GET CHASED BY FORTY RHINOCEROSES...
DESERTED BY OUR GUN-BEARERS!
TRAPPED ON THE EDGE OF A MILLION-FOOT CLIFF!
SCHULZ
DON'T YOU THINK THAT'LL BE FUN?
NAW! LET'S PLAY SOMETHING ELSE!
2-24

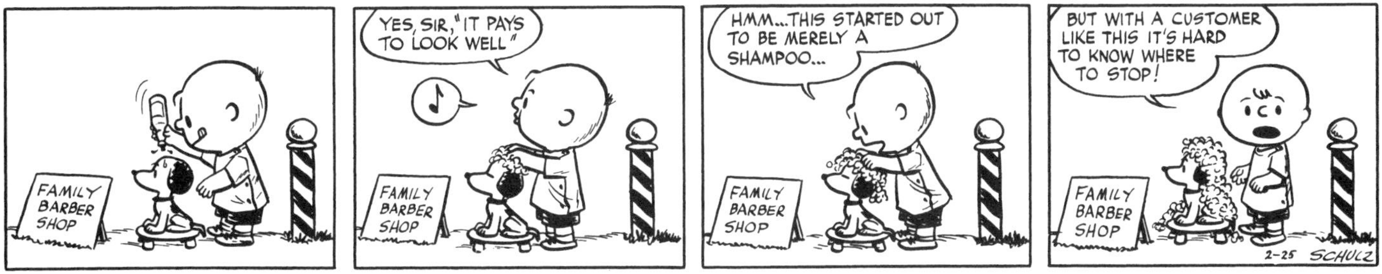
FAMILY BARBER SHOP
YES, SIR, "IT PAYS TO LOOK WELL"
♪
HMM...THIS STARTED OUT TO BE MERELY A SHAMPOO...
BUT WITH A CUSTOMER LIKE THIS IT'S HARD TO KNOW WHERE TO STOP!
2-25 SCHULZ

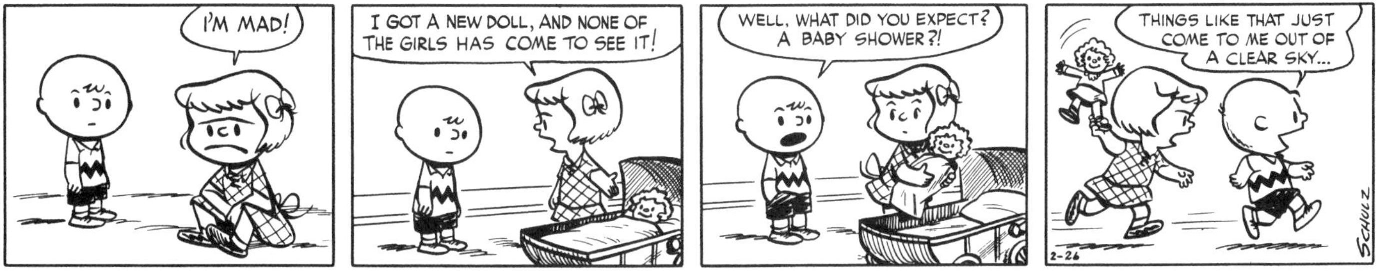
I'M MAD!
I GOT A NEW DOLL, AND NONE OF THE GIRLS HAS COME TO SEE IT!
WELL, WHAT DID YOU EXPECT? A BABY SHOWER?!
THINGS LIKE THAT JUST COME TO ME OUT OF A CLEAR SKY...
2-26
SCHULZ

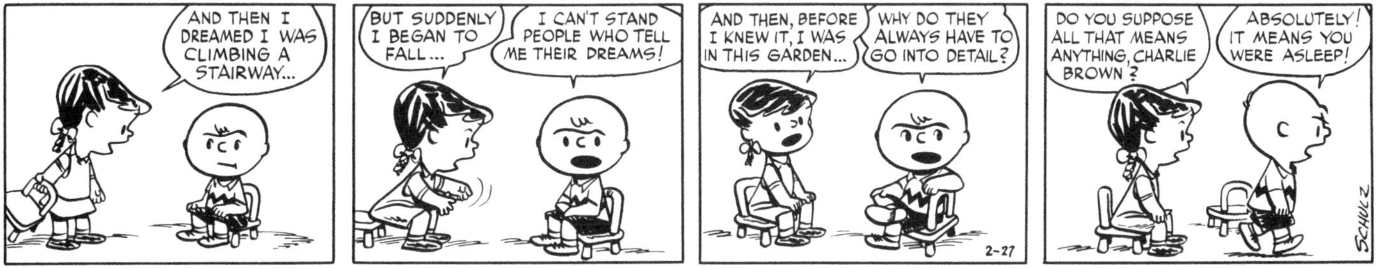
AND THEN I DREAMED I WAS CLIMBING A STAIRWAY...
BUT SUDDENLY I BEGAN TO FALL...
I CAN'T STAND PEOPLE WHO TELL ME THEIR DREAMS!
AND THEN, BEFORE I KNEW IT, I WAS IN THIS GARDEN...
WHY DO THEY ALWAYS HAVE TO GO INTO DETAIL?
2-27
DO YOU SUPPOSE ALL THAT MEANS ANYTHING, CHARLIE BROWN?
ABSOLUTELY! IT MEANS YOU WERE ASLEEP!
SCHULZ

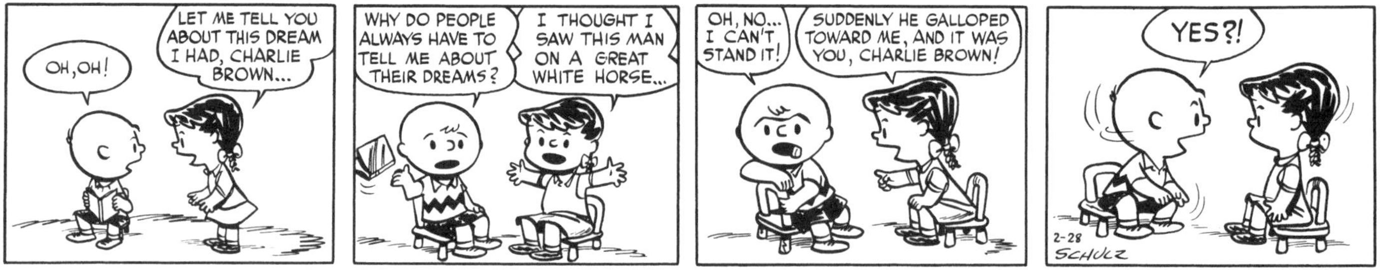
OH, OH!
LET ME TELL YOU ABOUT THIS DREAM I HAD, CHARLIE BROWN...
WHY DO PEOPLE ALWAYS HAVE TO TELL ME ABOUT THEIR DREAMS?
I THOUGHT I SAW THIS MAN ON A GREAT WHITE HORSE...
OH, NO... I CAN'T STAND IT!
SUDDENLY HE GALLOPED TOWARD ME, AND IT WAS YOU, CHARLIE BROWN!
YES?!
2-28
SCHULZ

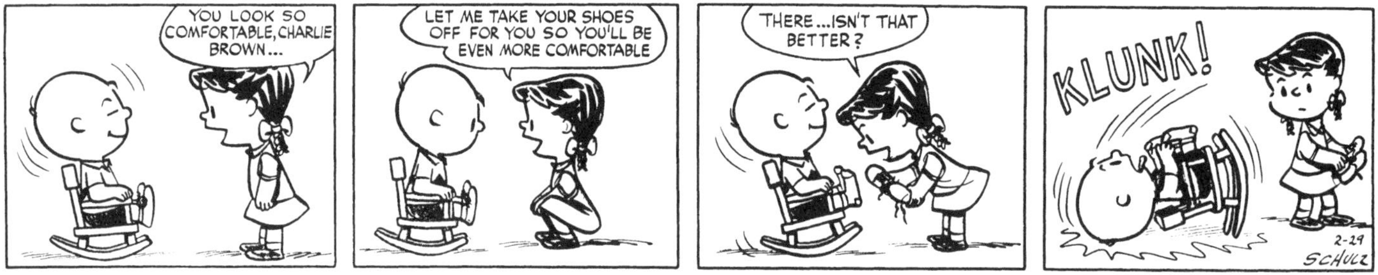
YOU LOOK SO COMFORTABLE, CHARLIE BROWN...
LET ME TAKE YOUR SHOES OFF FOR YOU SO YOU'LL BE EVEN MORE COMFORTABLE
THERE...ISN'T THAT BETTER?
KLUNK!
2-29
SCHULZ

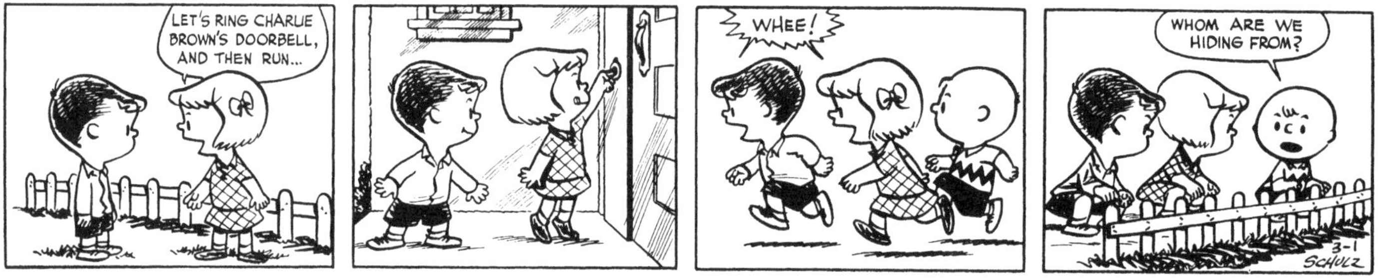
LET'S RING CHARLIE BROWN'S DOORBELL, AND THEN RUN...
WHEE!
WHOM ARE WE HIDING FROM?
3-1
SCHULZ

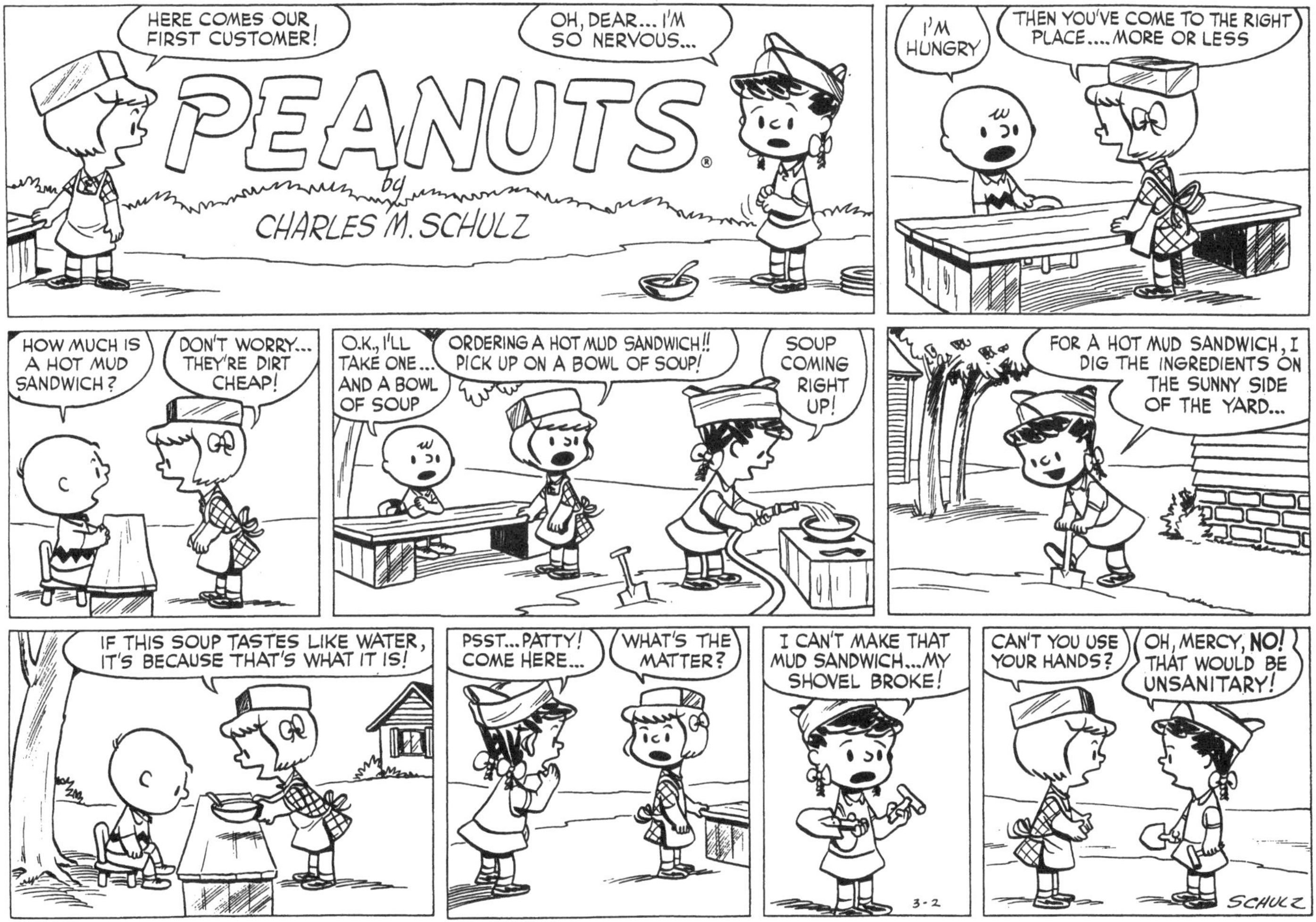
HERE COMES OUR FIRST CUSTOMER!
OH, DEAR... I'M SO NERVOUS...
PEANUTS®
by CHARLES M. SCHULZ
I'M HUNGRY
THEN YOU'VE COME TO THE RIGHT PLACE.... MORE OR LESS
HOW MUCH IS A HOT MUD SANDWICH?
DON'T WORRY... THEY'RE DIRT CHEAP!
O.K., I'LL TAKE ONE... AND A BOWL OF SOUP
ORDERING A HOT MUD SANDWICH!! PICK UP ON A BOWL OF SOUP!
SOUP COMING RIGHT UP!
FOR A HOT MUD SANDWICH, I DIG THE INGREDIENTS ON THE SUNNY SIDE OF THE YARD...
IF THIS SOUP TASTES LIKE WATER, IT'S BECAUSE THAT'S WHAT IT IS!
PSST... PATTY! COME HERE...
WHAT'S THE MATTER?
I CAN'T MAKE THAT MUD SANDWICH... MY SHOVEL BROKE!
3-2
CAN'T YOU USE YOUR HANDS?
OH, MERCY, NO! THAT WOULD BE UNSANITARY!
SCHULZ

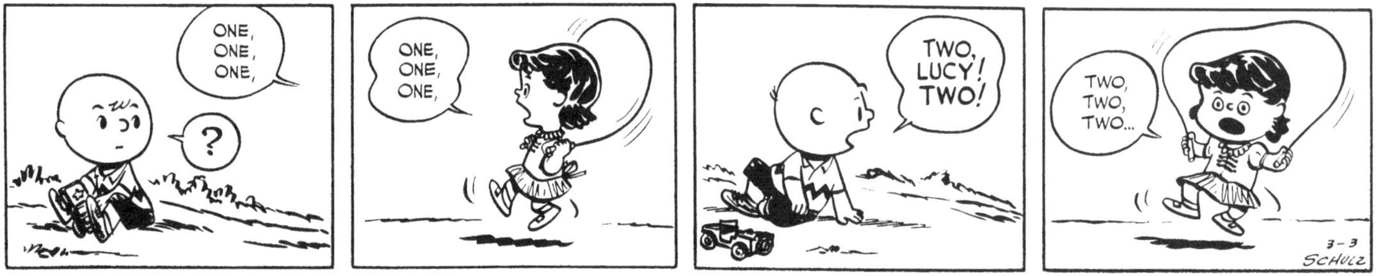
ONE, ONE, ONE,
?
ONE, ONE, ONE,
TWO, LUCY! TWO!
TWO, TWO, TWO...
3-3
SCHULZ

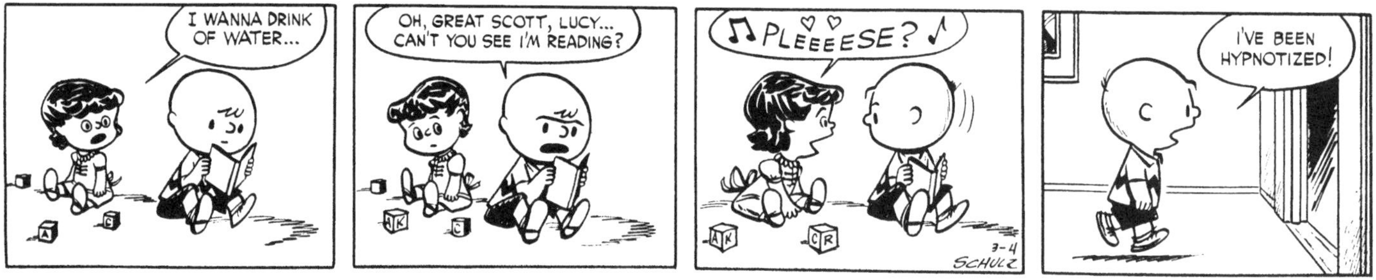
I WANNA DRINK OF WATER...
OH, GREAT SCOTT, LUCY... CAN'T YOU SEE I'M READING?
PLEEEEESE?
3-4
SCHULZ
I'VE BEEN HYPNOTIZED!

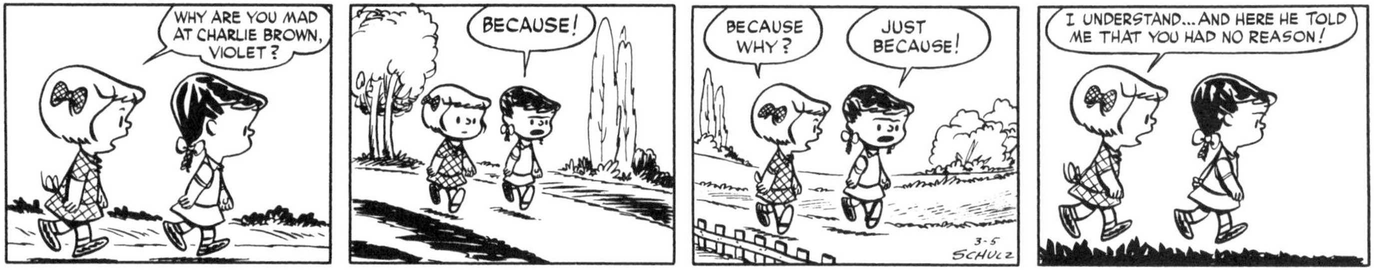
WHY ARE YOU MAD AT CHARLIE BROWN, VIOLET?
BECAUSE!
BECAUSE WHY?
JUST BECAUSE!
3-5
SCHULZ
I UNDERSTAND...AND HERE HE TOLD ME THAT YOU HAD NO REASON!

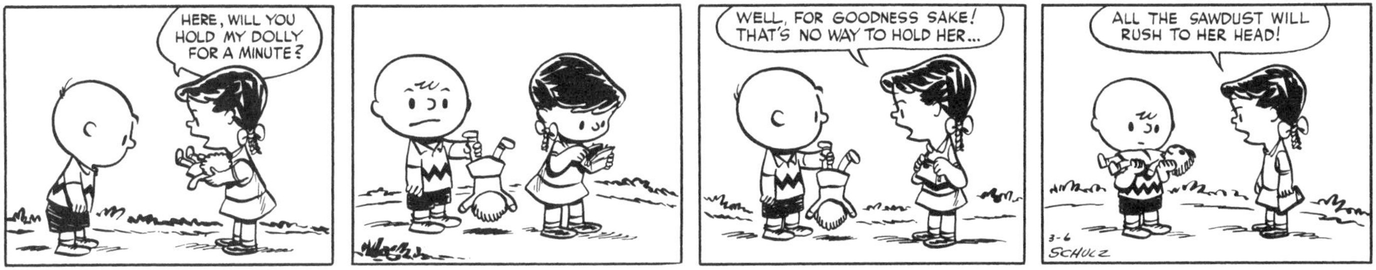
HERE, WILL YOU HOLD MY DOLLY FOR A MINUTE?
WELL, FOR GOODNESS SAKE! THAT'S NO WAY TO HOLD HER...
ALL THE SAWDUST WILL RUSH TO HER HEAD!
3-6
SCHULZ

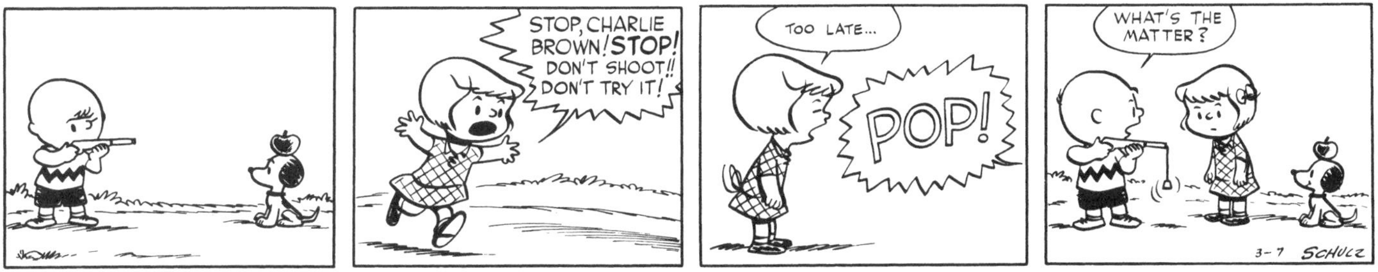
STOP, CHARLIE BROWN! STOP! DON'T SHOOT!! DON'T TRY IT!
TOO LATE...
POP!
WHAT'S THE MATTER?
3-7 SCHULZ

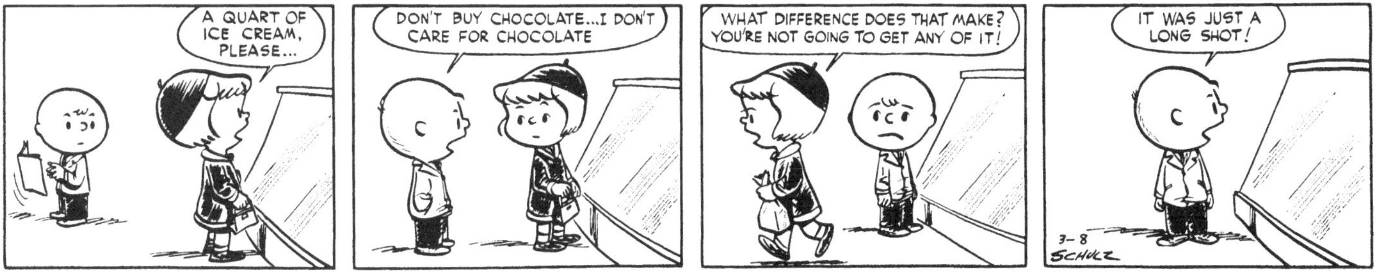
A QUART OF ICE CREAM, PLEASE...
DON'T BUY CHOCOLATE...I DON'T CARE FOR CHOCOLATE
WHAT DIFFERENCE DOES THAT MAKE? YOU'RE NOT GOING TO GET ANY OF IT!
IT WAS JUST A LONG SHOT!
3-8
SCHULZ

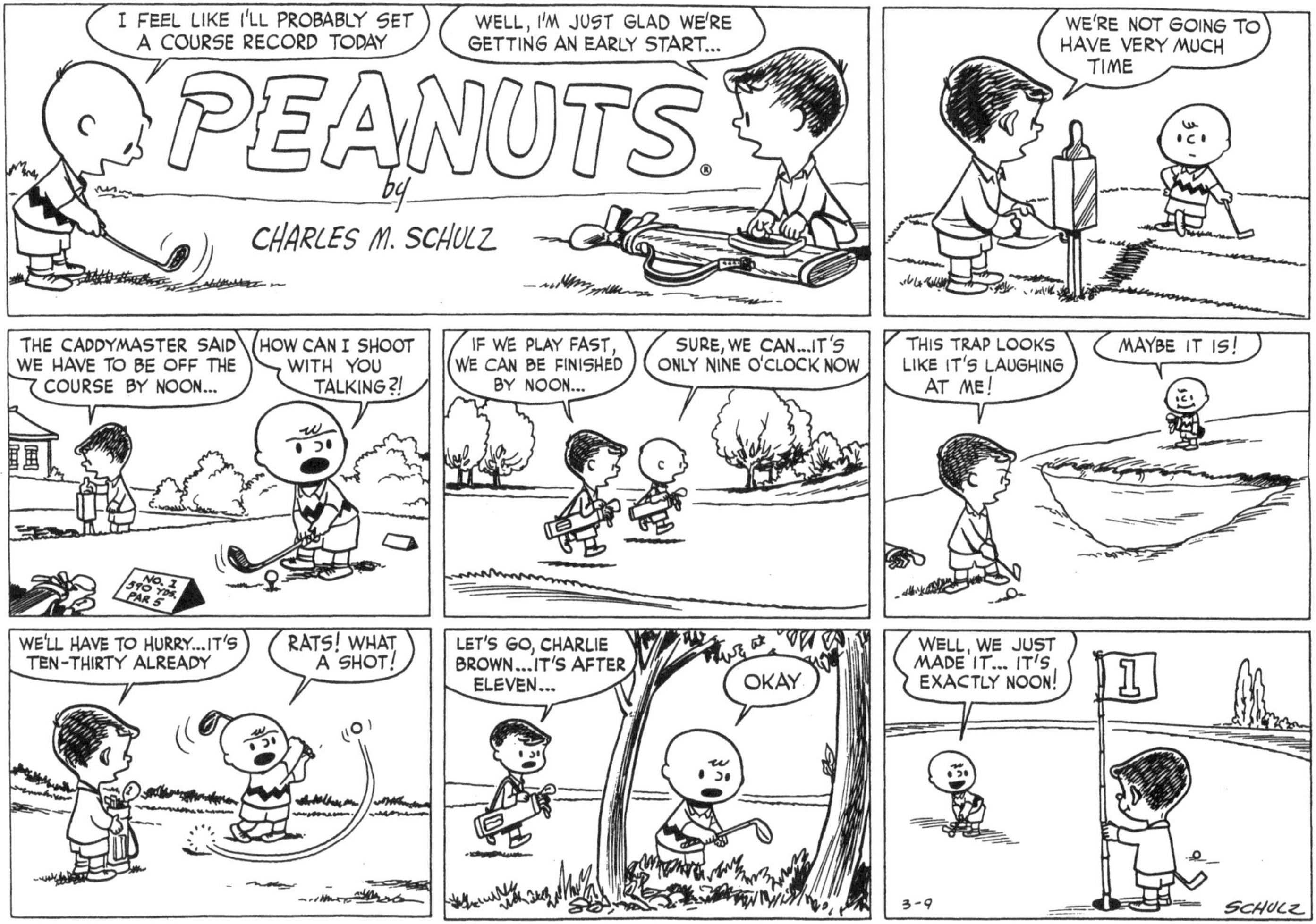
I FEEL LIKE I'LL PROBABLY SET A COURSE RECORD TODAY
WELL, I'M JUST GLAD WE'RE GETTING AN EARLY START...
PEANUTS®
by
CHARLES M. SCHULZ
WE'RE NOT GOING TO HAVE VERY MUCH TIME
THE CADDYMASTER SAID WE HAVE TO BE OFF THE COURSE BY NOON...
HOW CAN I SHOOT WITH YOU TALKING?!
NO. 1 590 YDS. PAR 5
IF WE PLAY FAST, WE CAN BE FINISHED BY NOON...
SURE, WE CAN...IT'S ONLY NINE O'CLOCK NOW
THIS TRAP LOOKS LIKE IT'S LAUGHING AT ME!
MAYBE IT IS!
WE'LL HAVE TO HURRY...IT'S TEN-THIRTY ALREADY
RATS! WHAT A SHOT!
LET'S GO, CHARLIE BROWN...IT'S AFTER ELEVEN...
OKAY
WELL, WE JUST MADE IT... IT'S EXACTLY NOON!
1
3-9
SCHULZ

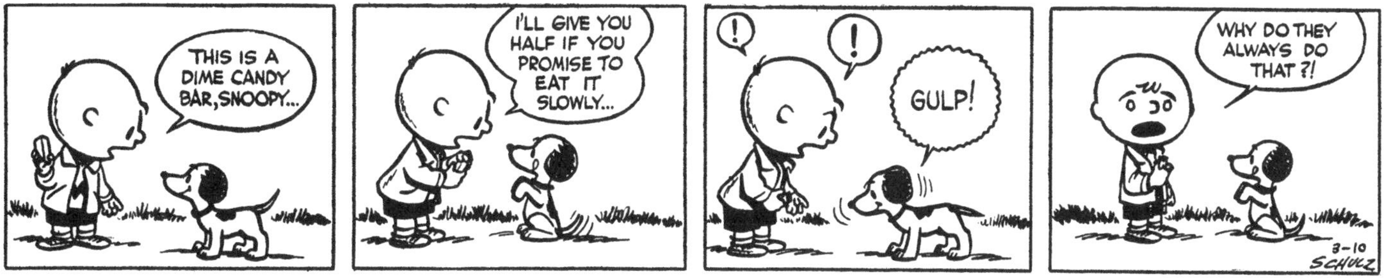
THIS IS A DIME CANDY BAR, SNOOPY...
I'LL GIVE YOU HALF IF YOU PROMISE TO EAT IT SLOWLY...
!
!
GULP!
WHY DO THEY ALWAYS DO THAT ?!
3-10
SCHULZ

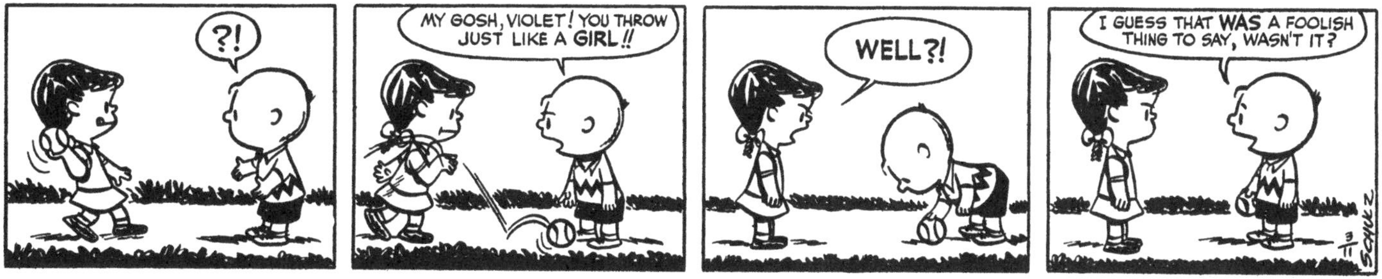
?!
MY GOSH, VIOLET! YOU THROW JUST LIKE A GIRL!!
WELL?!
I GUESS THAT WAS A FOOLISH THING TO SAY, WASN'T IT?
3 11
SCHULZ

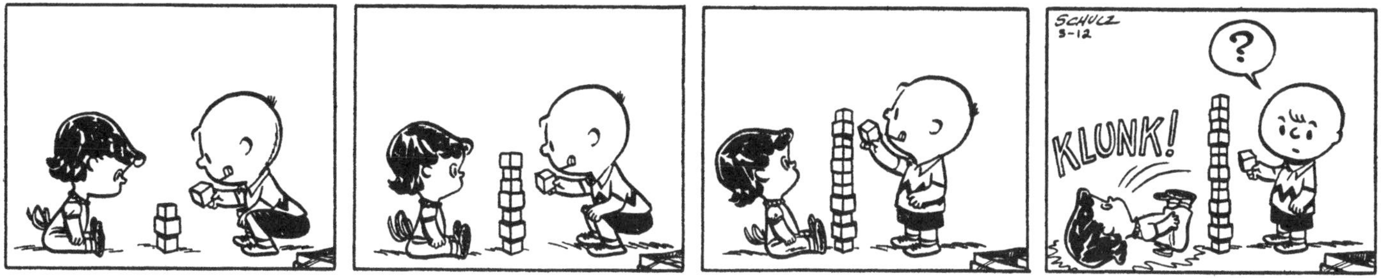
SCHULZ
3-12
KLUNK!
?

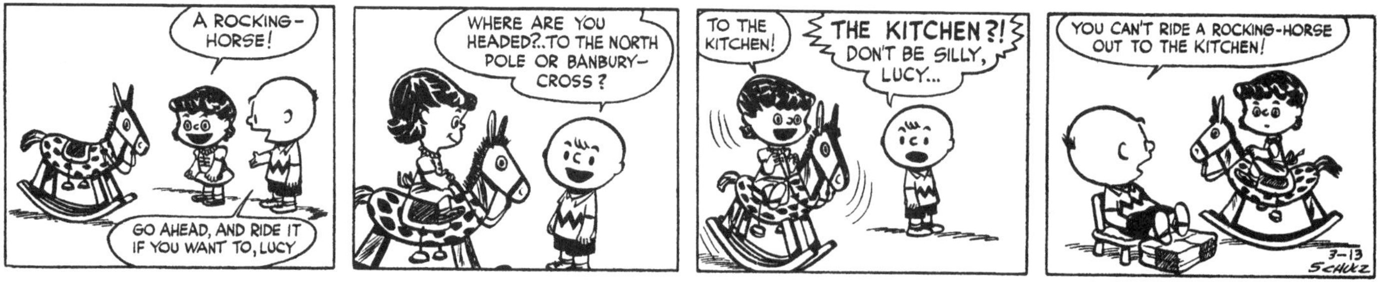
A ROCKING-HORSE!
GO AHEAD, AND RIDE IT IF YOU WANT TO, LUCY
WHERE ARE YOU HEADED?..TO THE NORTH POLE OR BANBURY-CROSS?
TO THE KITCHEN!
THE KITCHEN?! DON'T BE SILLY, LUCY...
YOU CAN'T RIDE A ROCKING-HORSE OUT TO THE KITCHEN!
3-13
SCHULZ

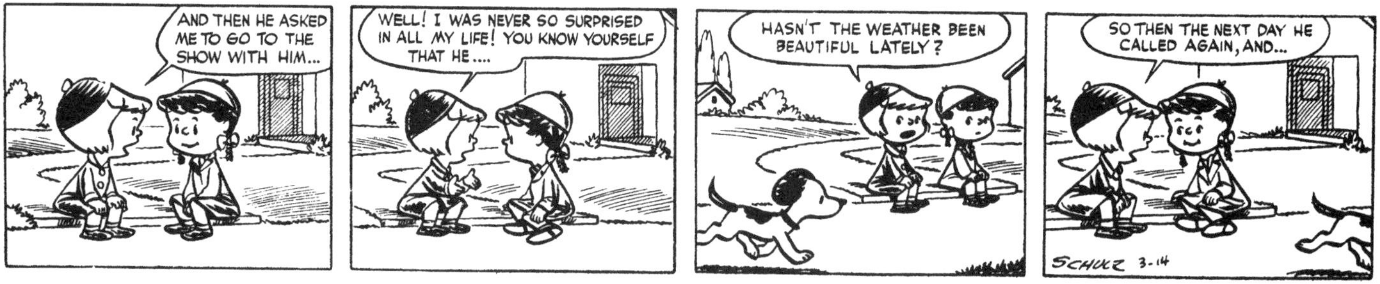
AND THEN HE ASKED ME TO GO TO THE SHOW WITH HIM...
WELL! I WAS NEVER SO SURPRISED IN ALL MY LIFE! YOU KNOW YOURSELF THAT HE....
HASN'T THE WEATHER BEEN BEAUTIFUL LATELY?
SO THEN THE NEXT DAY HE CALLED AGAIN, AND...
SCHULZ 3-14

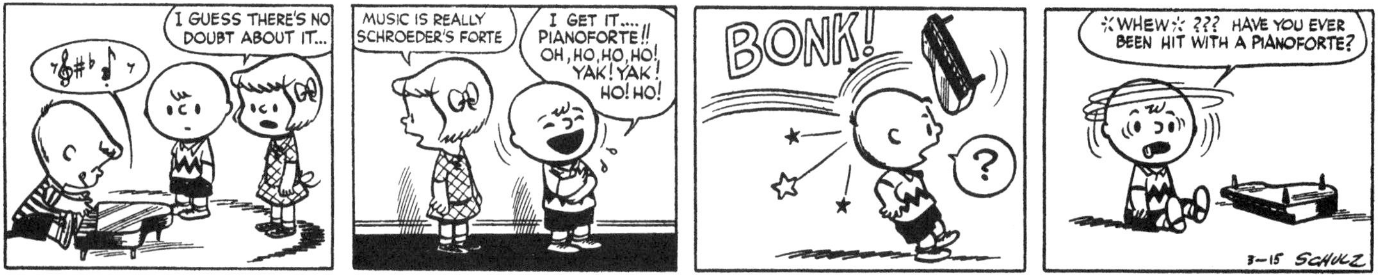
I GUESS THERE'S NO DOUBT ABOUT IT...
MUSIC IS REALLY SCHROEDER'S FORTE
I GET IT.... PIANOFORTE!! OH, HO, HO, HO! YAK! YAK! HO! HO!
BONK!
?
WHEW ??? HAVE YOU EVER BEEN HIT WITH A PIANOFORTE?
3-15 SCHULZ

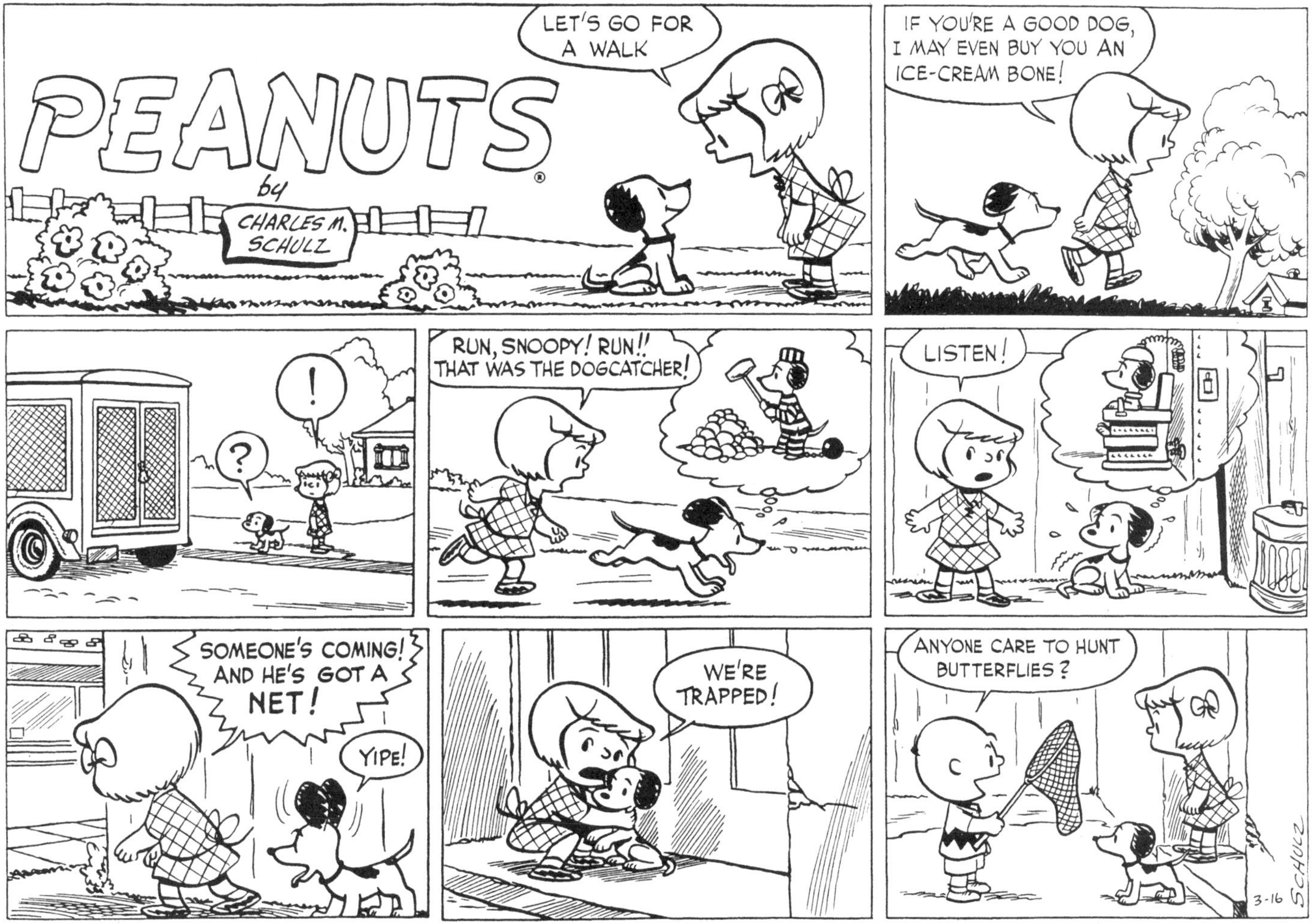
PEANUTS
by CHARLES M. SCHULZ
LET'S GO FOR A WALK
IF YOU'RE A GOOD DOG, I MAY EVEN BUY YOU AN ICE-CREAM BONE!
?
!
RUN, SNOOPY! RUN!! THAT WAS THE DOGCATCHER!
LISTEN!
SOMEONE'S COMING! AND HE'S GOT A NET!
YIPE!
WE'RE TRAPPED!
ANYONE CARE TO HUNT BUTTERFLIES?
3-16 SCHULZ

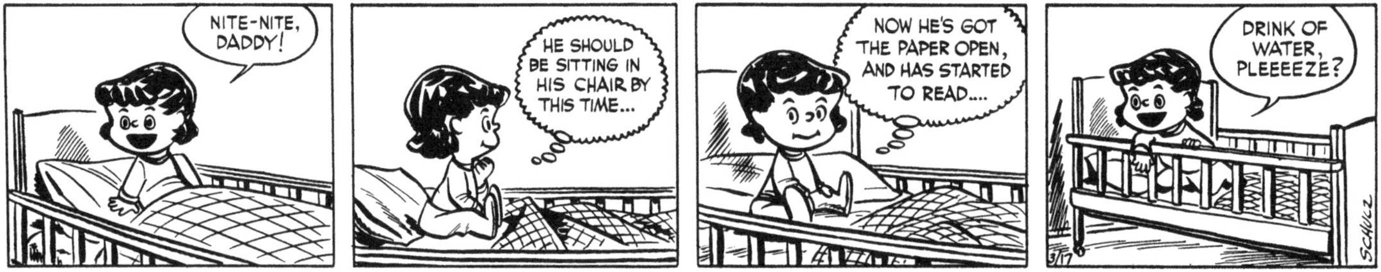
NITE-NITE, DADDY!
HE SHOULD BE SITTING IN HIS CHAIR BY THIS TIME...
NOW HE'S GOT THE PAPER OPEN, AND HAS STARTED TO READ....
DRINK OF WATER, PLEEEEZE?
SCHULZ

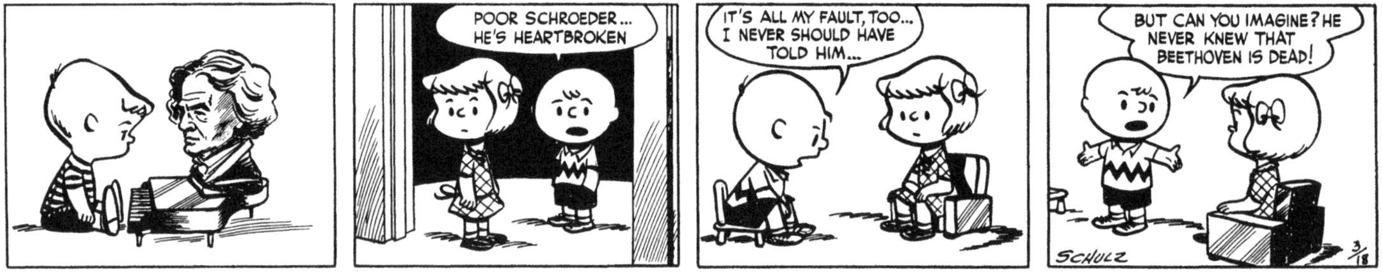
POOR SCHROEDER... HE'S HEARTBROKEN
IT'S ALL MY FAULT, TOO... I NEVER SHOULD HAVE TOLD HIM...
BUT CAN YOU IMAGINE? HE NEVER KNEW THAT BEETHOVEN IS DEAD!
SCHULZ

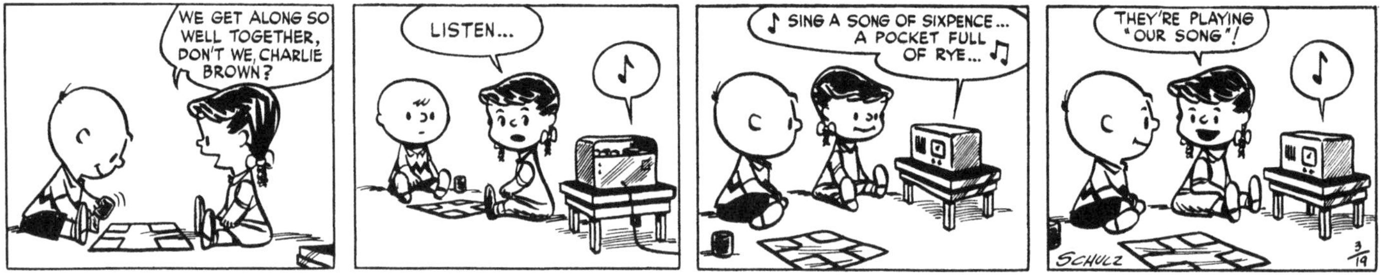
WE GET ALONG SO WELL TOGETHER, DON'T WE, CHARLIE BROWN?
LISTEN...
♪ SING A SONG OF SIXPENCE... A POCKET FULL OF RYE... ♫
THEY'RE PLAYING "OUR SONG"!
SCHULZ

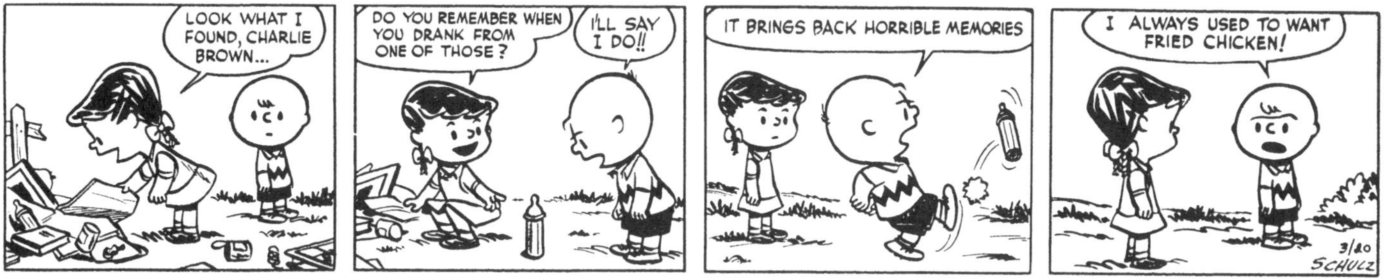
LOOK WHAT I FOUND, CHARLIE BROWN...
DO YOU REMEMBER WHEN YOU DRANK FROM ONE OF THOSE?
I'LL SAY I DO!!
IT BRINGS BACK HORRIBLE MEMORIES
I ALWAYS USED TO WANT FRIED CHICKEN!
3/20
SCHULZ

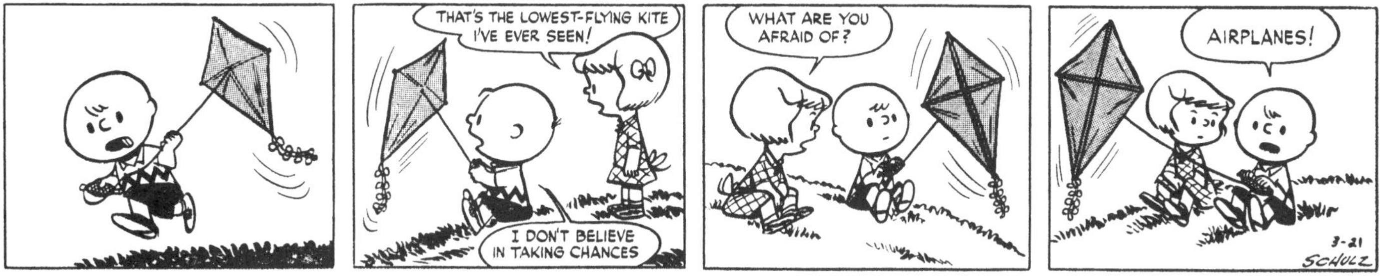
THAT'S THE LOWEST-FLYING KITE I'VE EVER SEEN!
I DON'T BELIEVE IN TAKING CHANCES
WHAT ARE YOU AFRAID OF?
AIRPLANES!
3-21
SCHULZ

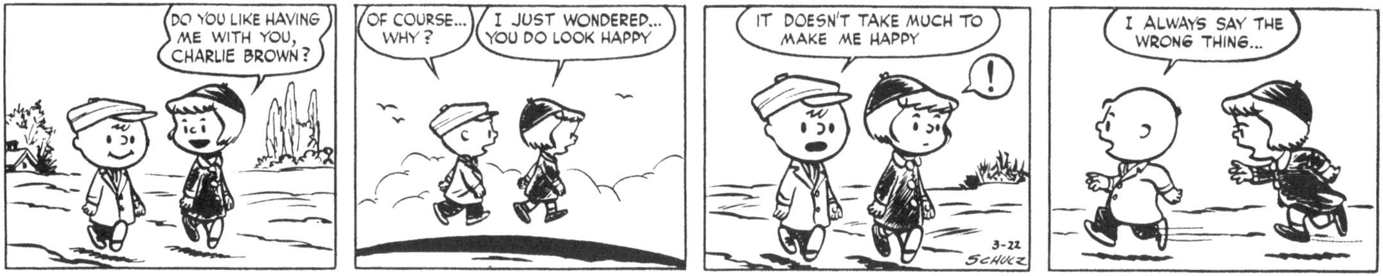
DO YOU LIKE HAVING ME WITH YOU, CHARLIE BROWN?
OF COURSE... WHY?
I JUST WONDERED... YOU DO LOOK HAPPY
IT DOESN'T TAKE MUCH TO MAKE ME HAPPY
!
3-22
SCHULZ
I ALWAYS SAY THE WRONG THING...

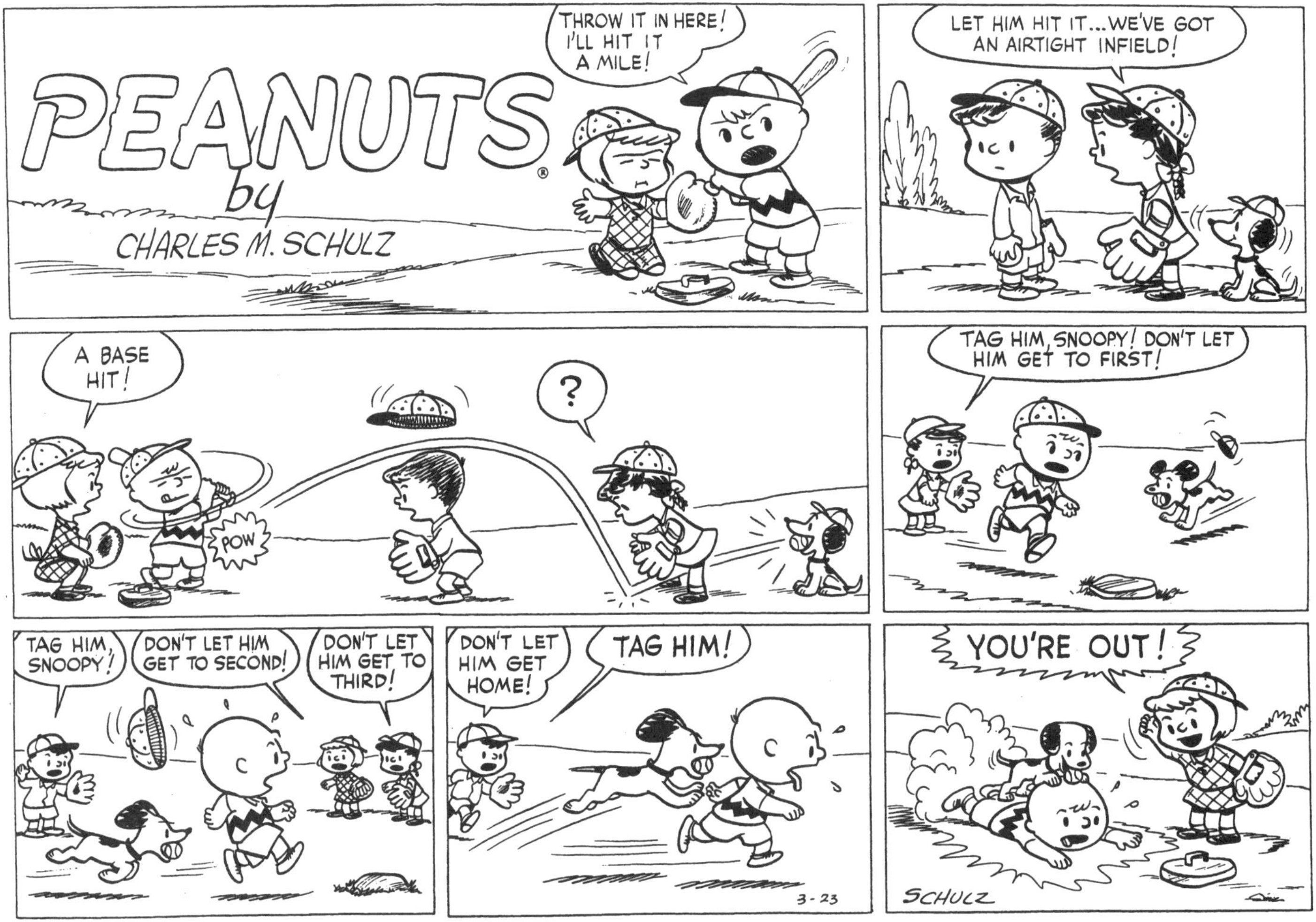
PEANUTS
by
CHARLES M. SCHULZ
THROW IT IN HERE! I'LL HIT IT A MILE!
LET HIM HIT IT...WE'VE GOT AN AIRTIGHT INFIELD!
A BASE HIT!
POW
?
TAG HIM, SNOOPY! DON'T LET HIM GET TO FIRST!
TAG HIM, SNOOPY!
DON'T LET HIM GET TO SECOND!
DON'T LET HIM GET TO THIRD!
DON'T LET HIM GET HOME!
TAG HIM!
3-23
YOU'RE OUT!
SCHULZ

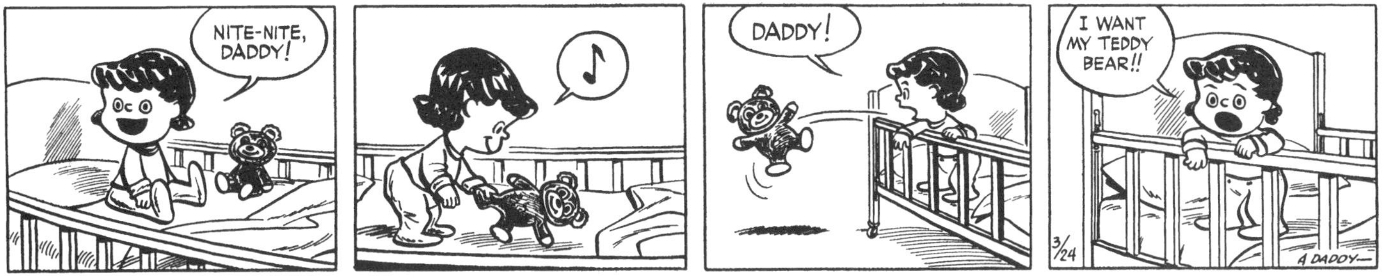
NITE-NITE, DADDY!
DADDY!
I WANT MY TEDDY BEAR!!
3/24
A DADDY—

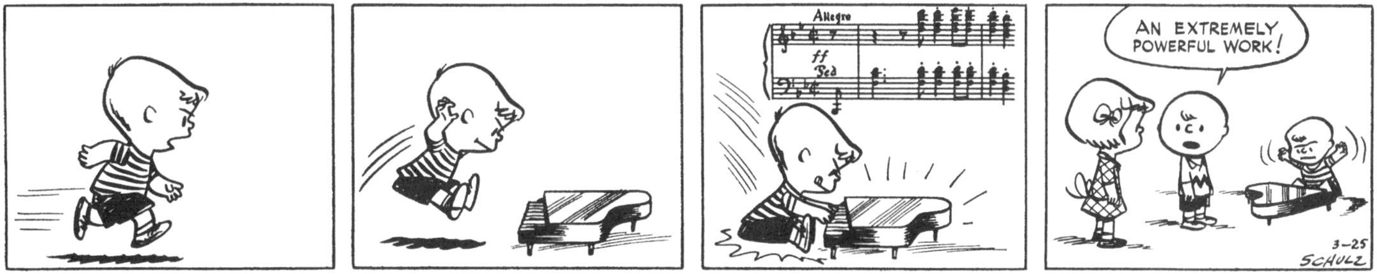
Allegro
ff
Ped
AN EXTREMELY POWERFUL WORK!
3-25
SCHULZ

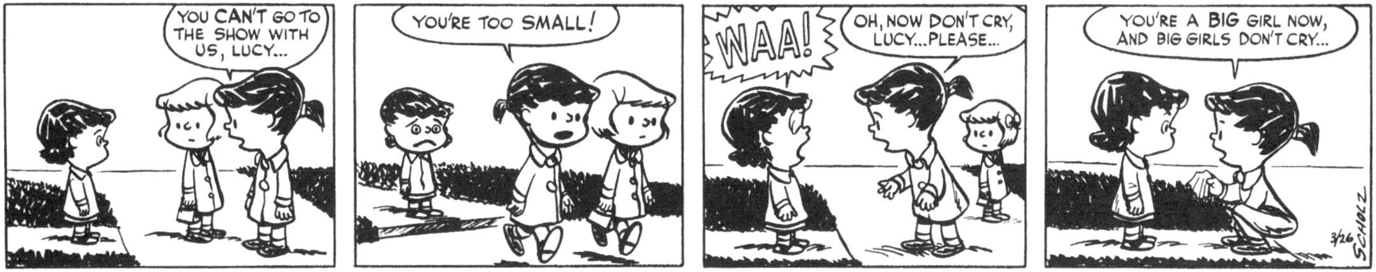
YOU CAN'T GO TO THE SHOW WITH US, LUCY...
YOU'RE TOO SMALL!
WAA!
OH, NOW DON'T CRY, LUCY...PLEASE...
YOU'RE A BIG GIRL NOW, AND BIG GIRLS DON'T CRY...
3/26
SCHULZ

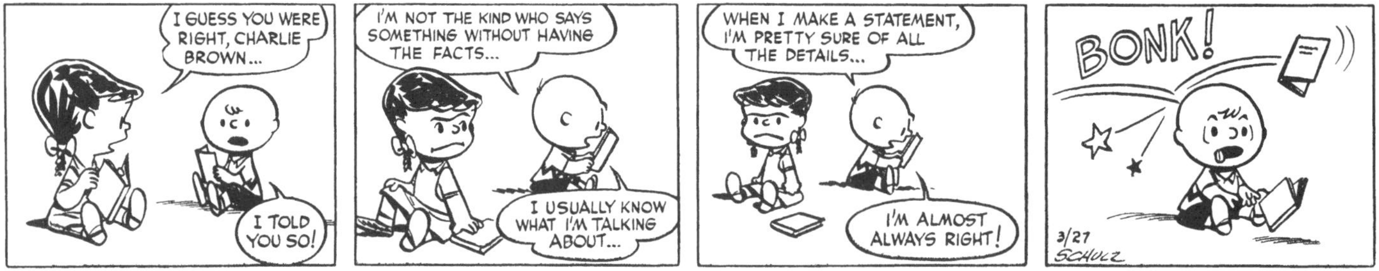
I GUESS YOU WERE RIGHT, CHARLIE BROWN...
I TOLD YOU SO!
I'M NOT THE KIND WHO SAYS SOMETHING WITHOUT HAVING THE FACTS...
I USUALLY KNOW WHAT I'M TALKING ABOUT...
WHEN I MAKE A STATEMENT, I'M PRETTY SURE OF ALL THE DETAILS...
I'M ALMOST ALWAYS RIGHT!
BONK!
3/27
SCHULZ

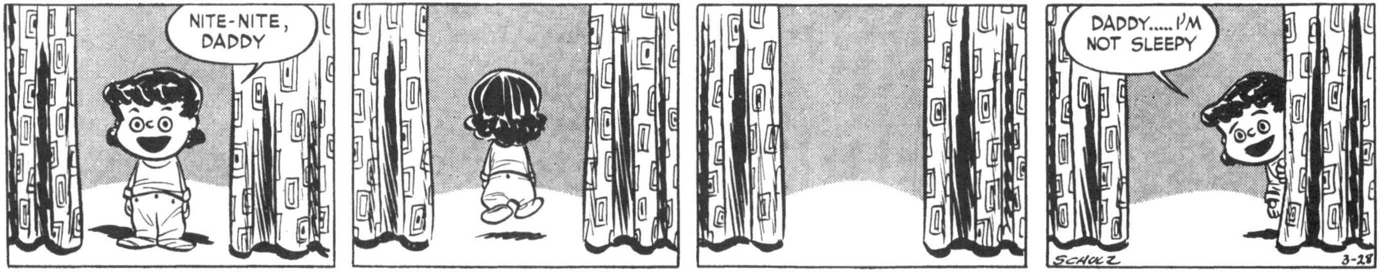
NITE-NITE, DADDY
DADDY..... I'M NOT SLEEPY
SCHULZ
3-28

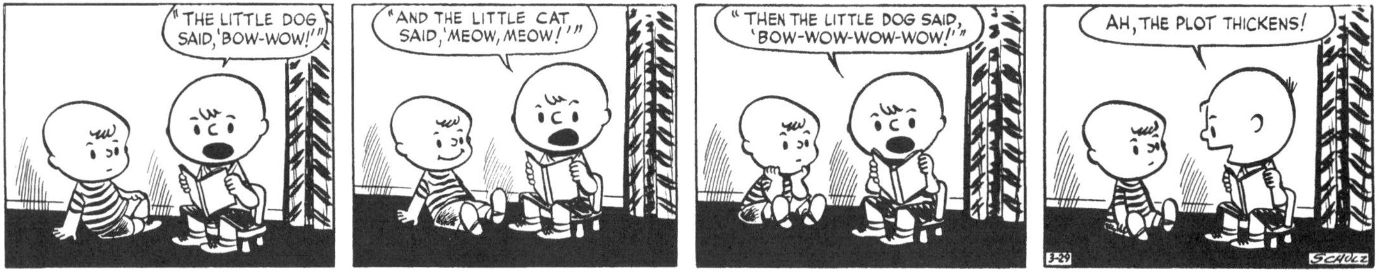
"THE LITTLE DOG SAID, 'BOW-WOW!'"
"AND THE LITTLE CAT SAID, 'MEOW, MEOW!'"
"THEN THE LITTLE DOG SAID, 'BOW-WOW-WOW-WOW!'"
AH, THE PLOT THICKENS!
3-29
SCHULZ

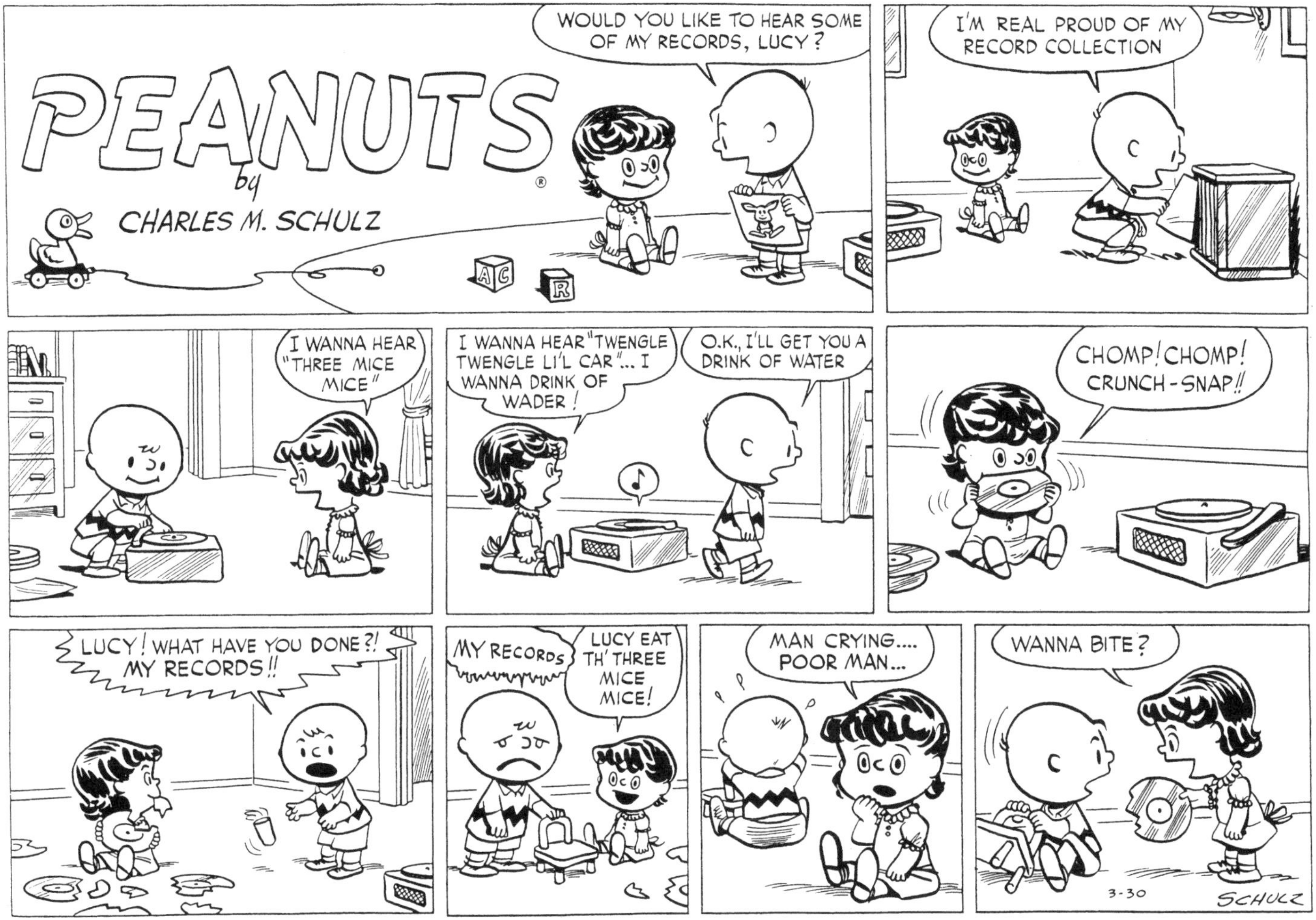
PEANUTS
by CHARLES M. SCHULZ
WOULD YOU LIKE TO HEAR SOME OF MY RECORDS, LUCY?
I'M REAL PROUD OF MY RECORD COLLECTION
I WANNA HEAR "THREE MICE MICE"
I WANNA HEAR "TWENGLE TWENGLE LI'L CAR"... I WANNA DRINK OF WADER!
O.K., I'LL GET YOU A DRINK OF WATER
CHOMP! CHOMP! CRUNCH-SNAP!!
LUCY! WHAT HAVE YOU DONE?! MY RECORDS!!
MY RECORDS
LUCY EAT TH' THREE MICE MICE!
MAN CRYING.... POOR MAN...
WANNA BITE?
3-30
SCHULZ

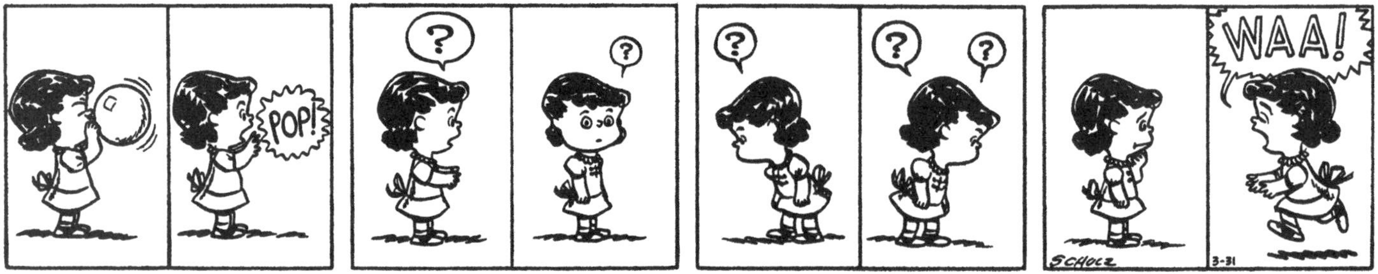
POP!
?
?
?
?
?
WAA!
SCHULZ
3-31

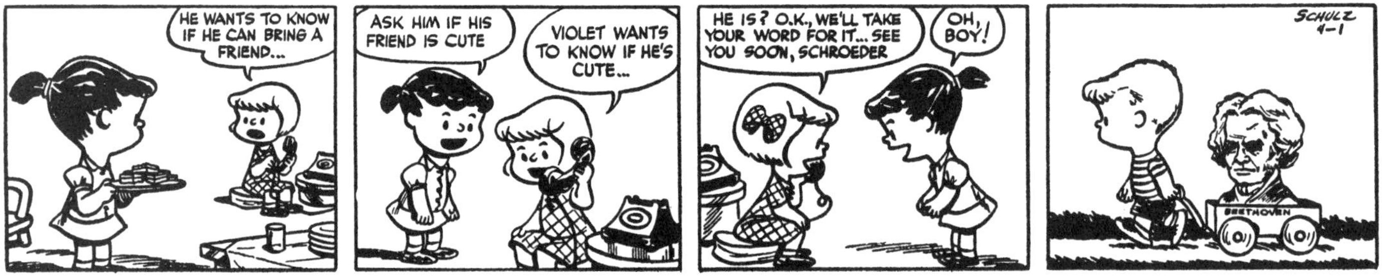
HE WANTS TO KNOW IF HE CAN BRING A FRIEND...
ASK HIM IF HIS FRIEND IS CUTE
VIOLET WANTS TO KNOW IF HE'S CUTE...
HE IS? O.K., WE'LL TAKE YOUR WORD FOR IT... SEE YOU SOON, SCHROEDER
OH, BOY!
SCHULZ
4-1
BEETHOVEN

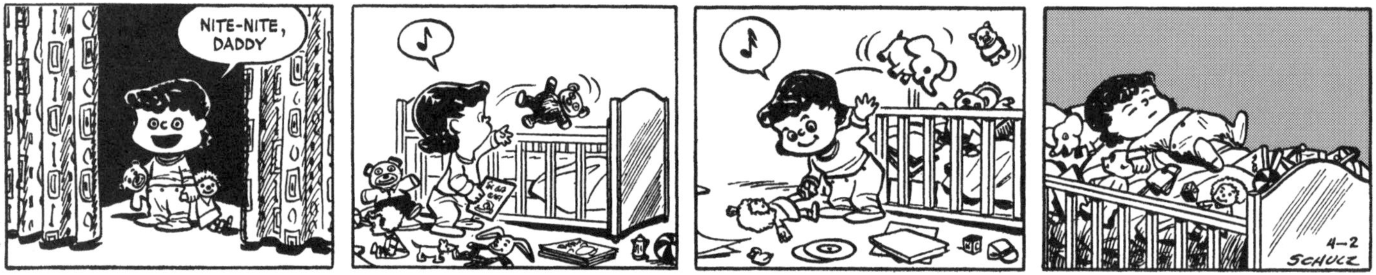
NITE-NITE, DADDY
4-2
SCHULZ

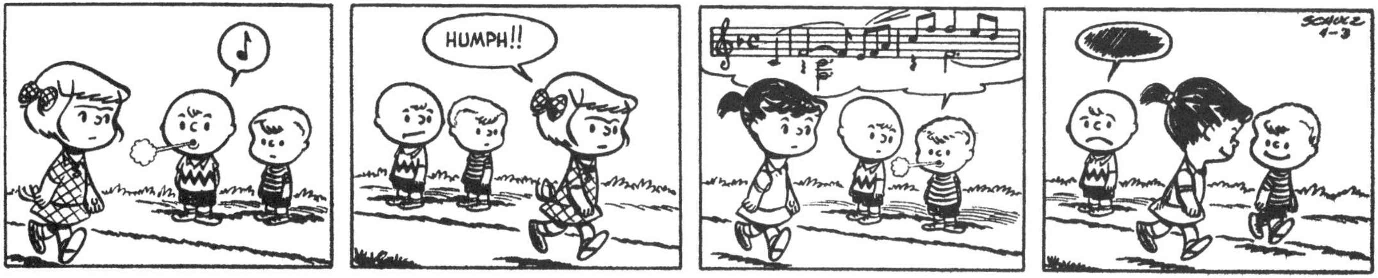
HUMPH!!
SCHULZ 4-3

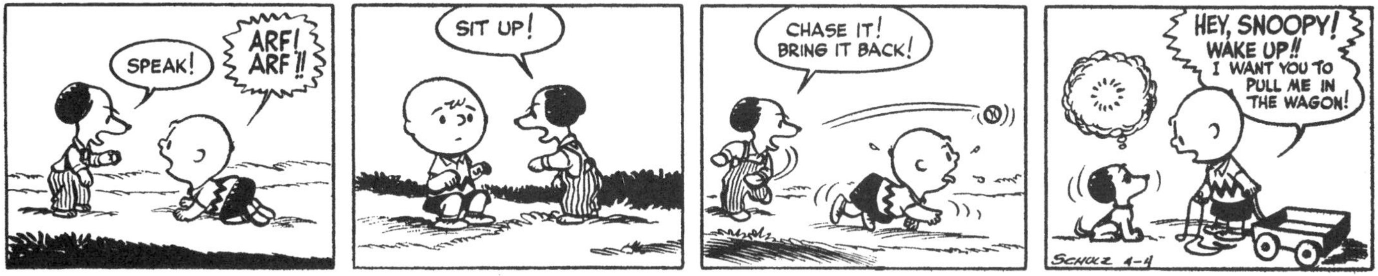
SPEAK!
ARF! ARF!!
SIT UP!
CHASE IT! BRING IT BACK!
HEY, SNOOPY! WAKE UP!! I WANT YOU TO PULL ME IN THE WAGON!
SCHULZ 4-4

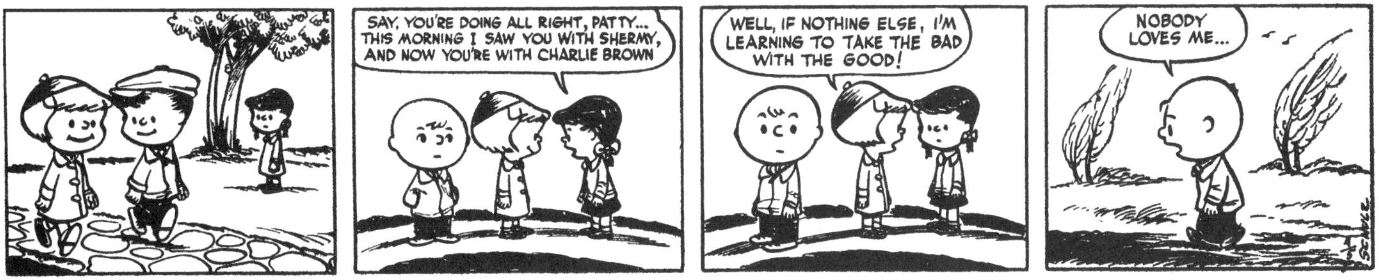
SAY, YOU'RE DOING ALL RIGHT, PATTY... THIS MORNING I SAW YOU WITH SHERMY, AND NOW YOU'RE WITH CHARLIE BROWN
WELL, IF NOTHING ELSE, I'M LEARNING TO TAKE THE BAD WITH THE GOOD!
NOBODY LOVES ME...
SCHULZ

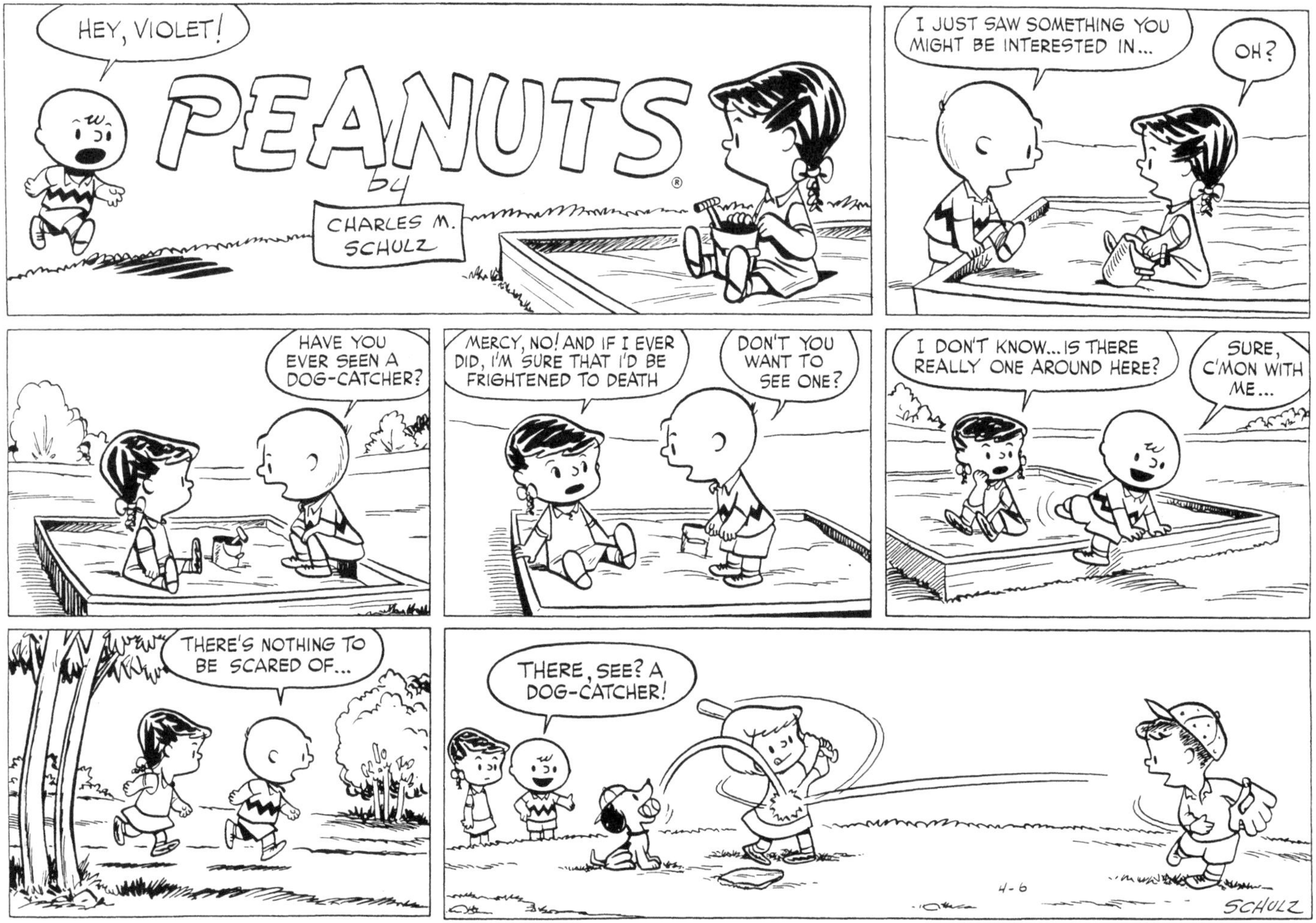
HEY, VIOLET!
PEANUTS
by
CHARLES M. SCHULZ
I JUST SAW SOMETHING YOU MIGHT BE INTERESTED IN...
OH?
HAVE YOU EVER SEEN A DOG-CATCHER?
MERCY, NO! AND IF I EVER DID, I'M SURE THAT I'D BE FRIGHTENED TO DEATH
DON'T YOU WANT TO SEE ONE?
I DON'T KNOW... IS THERE REALLY ONE AROUND HERE?
SURE, C'MON WITH ME...
THERE'S NOTHING TO BE SCARED OF...
THERE, SEE? A DOG-CATCHER!
4-6
SCHULZ

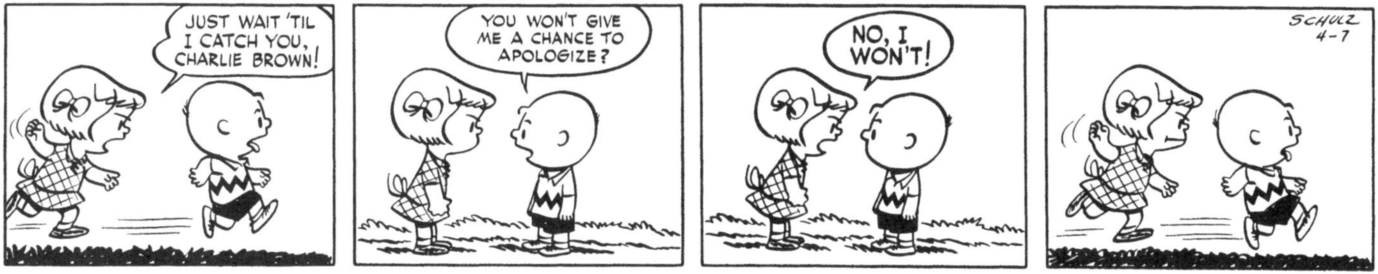
JUST WAIT 'TIL I CATCH YOU, CHARLIE BROWN!
YOU WON'T GIVE ME A CHANCE TO APOLOGIZE?
NO, I WON'T!
SCHULZ 4-7

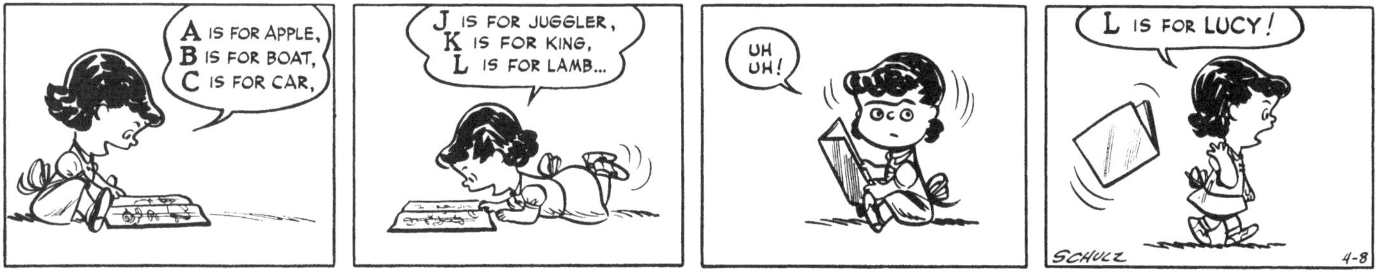
A IS FOR APPLE, B IS FOR BOAT, C IS FOR CAR,
J IS FOR JUGGLER, K IS FOR KING, L IS FOR LAMB...
UH UH!
L IS FOR LUCY!
SCHULZ
4-8

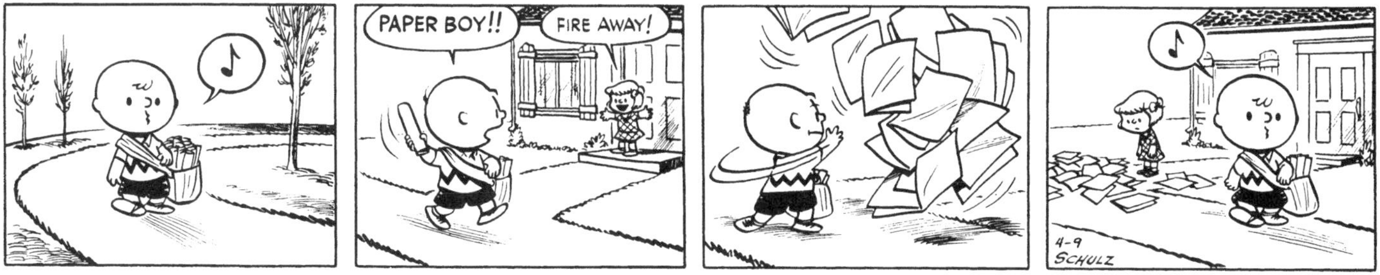
PAPER BOY!!
FIRE AWAY!
4-9 SCHULZ

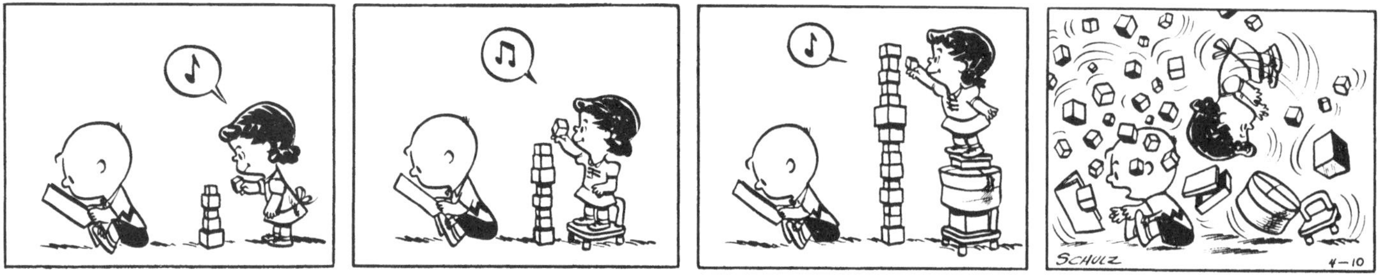
SCHULZ
4—10

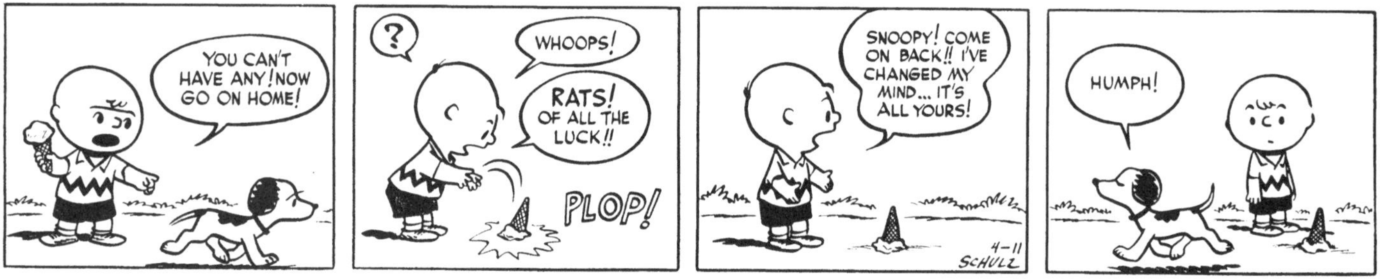
YOU CAN'T HAVE ANY! NOW GO ON HOME!
?
WHOOPS!
RATS! OF ALL THE LUCK!!
PLOP!
SNOOPY! COME ON BACK!! I'VE CHANGED MY MIND... IT'S ALL YOURS!
4—11
SCHULZ
HUMPH!

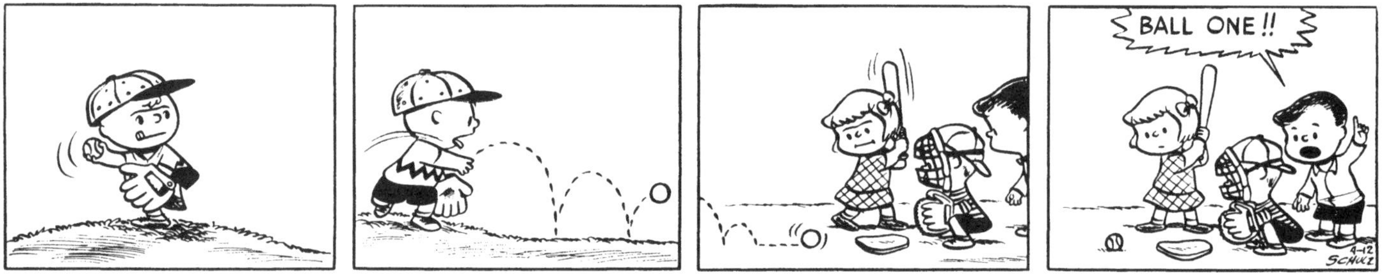
BALL ONE!!
4-12
SCHULZ

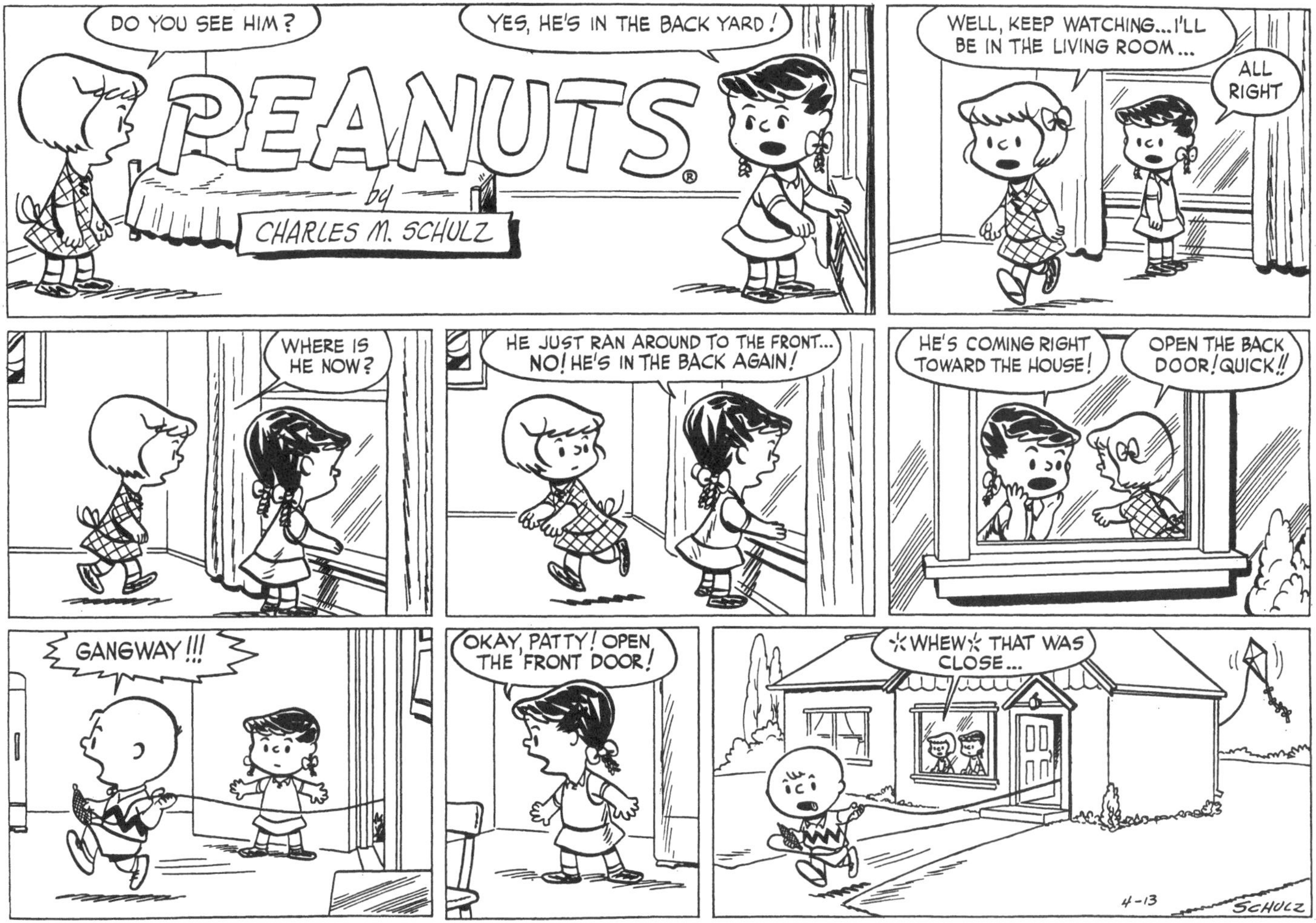
DO YOU SEE HIM?
YES, HE'S IN THE BACK YARD!
PEANUTS®
by
CHARLES M. SCHULZ
WELL, KEEP WATCHING... I'LL BE IN THE LIVING ROOM...
ALL RIGHT
WHERE IS HE NOW?
HE JUST RAN AROUND TO THE FRONT... NO! HE'S IN THE BACK AGAIN!
HE'S COMING RIGHT TOWARD THE HOUSE!
OPEN THE BACK DOOR! QUICK!!
GANGWAY!!!
OKAY, PATTY! OPEN THE FRONT DOOR!
WHEW THAT WAS CLOSE...
4-13
SCHULZ

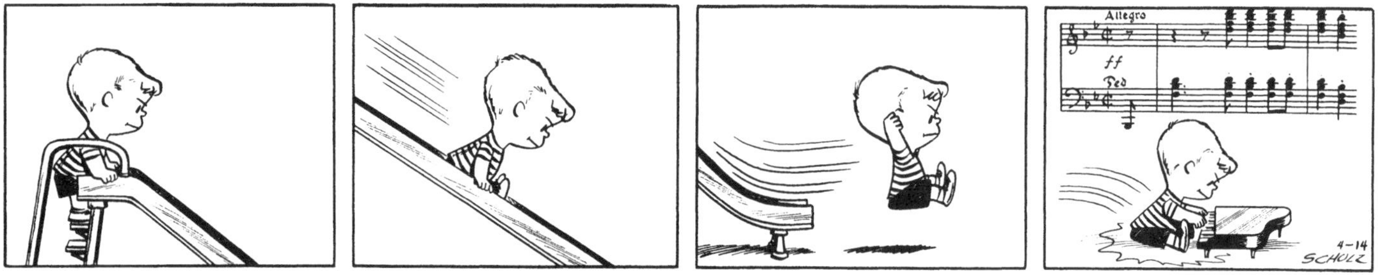
Allegro
ff
Ped
4-14
SCHULZ

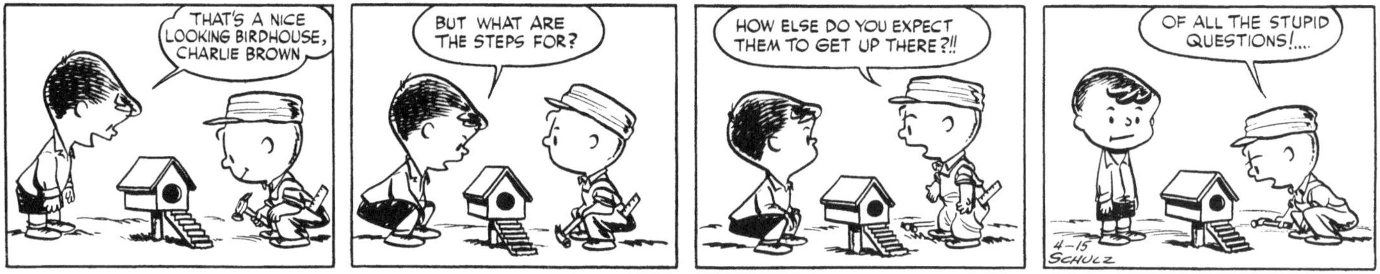
THAT'S A NICE LOOKING BIRDHOUSE, CHARLIE BROWN
BUT WHAT ARE THE STEPS FOR?
HOW ELSE DO YOU EXPECT THEM TO GET UP THERE?!!
OF ALL THE STUPID QUESTIONS!....
4-15
SCHULZ

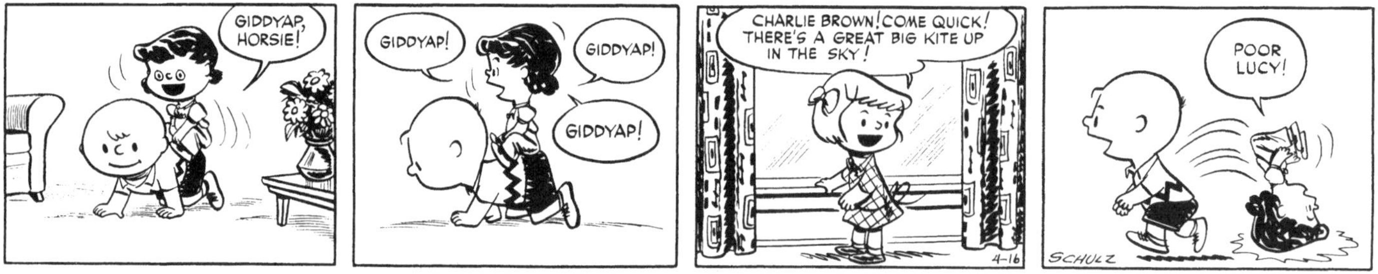
GIDDYAP, HORSIE!
GIDDYAP!
GIDDYAP!
GIDDYAP!
CHARLIE BROWN! COME QUICK! THERE'S A GREAT BIG KITE UP IN THE SKY!
4-16
POOR LUCY!
SCHULZ

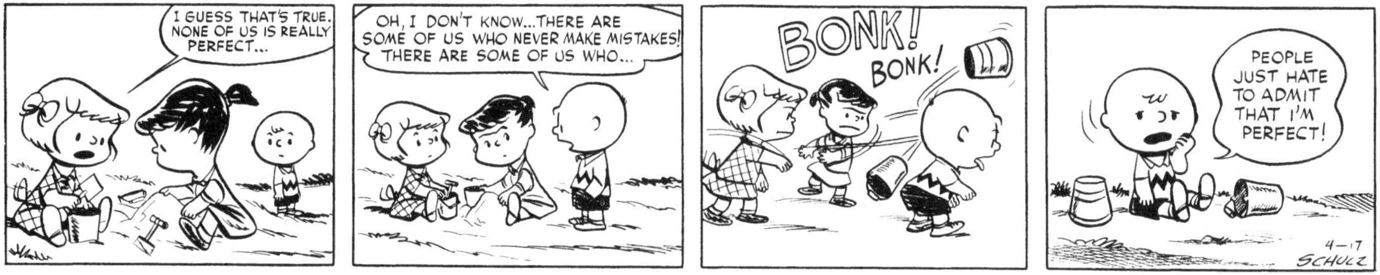
I GUESS THAT'S TRUE. NONE OF US IS REALLY PERFECT...
OH, I DON'T KNOW...THERE ARE SOME OF US WHO NEVER MAKE MISTAKES! THERE ARE SOME OF US WHO...
BONK!
BONK!
PEOPLE JUST HATE TO ADMIT THAT I'M PERFECT!
4-17
SCHULZ

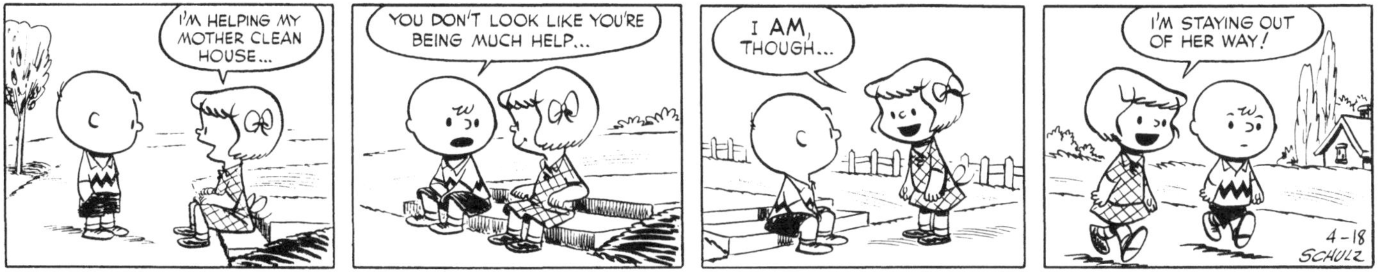
I'M HELPING MY MOTHER CLEAN HOUSE...
YOU DON'T LOOK LIKE YOU'RE BEING MUCH HELP...
I AM, THOUGH...
I'M STAYING OUT OF HER WAY!
4-18
SCHULZ

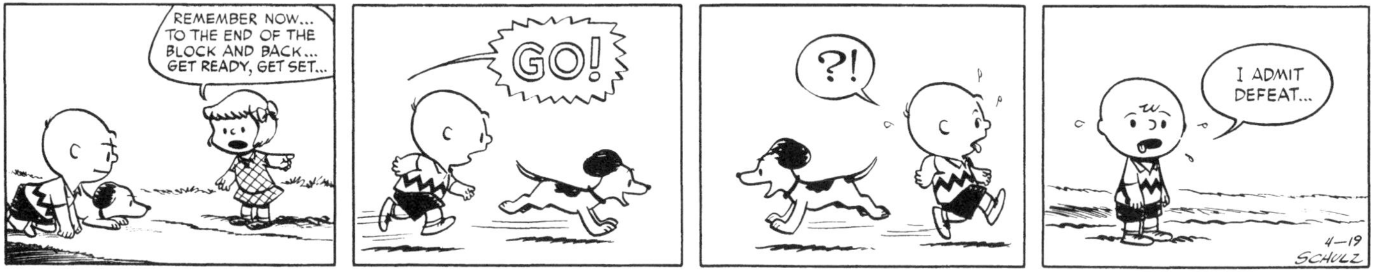
REMEMBER NOW... TO THE END OF THE BLOCK AND BACK... GET READY, GET SET...
GO!
?!
I ADMIT DEFEAT...
4-19
SCHULZ

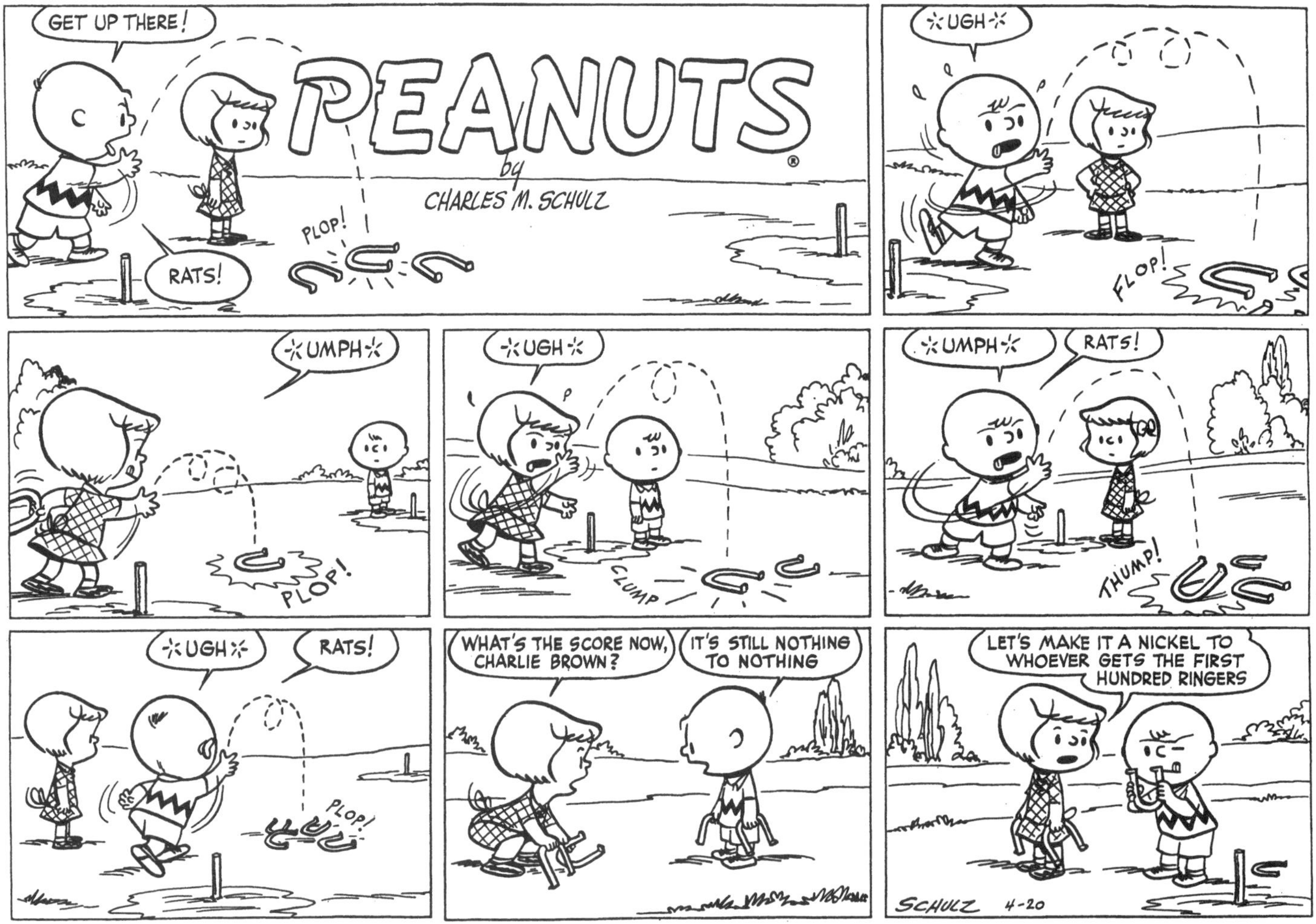
GET UP THERE!
PEANUTS
by CHARLES M. SCHULZ
PLOP!
RATS!
UGH
FLOP!
UMPH
PLOP!
UGH
CLUMP
UMPH
RATS!
THUMP!
UGH
RATS!
PLOP!
WHAT'S THE SCORE NOW, CHARLIE BROWN?
IT'S STILL NOTHING TO NOTHING
LET'S MAKE IT A NICKEL TO WHOEVER GETS THE FIRST HUNDRED RINGERS
SCHULZ 4-20

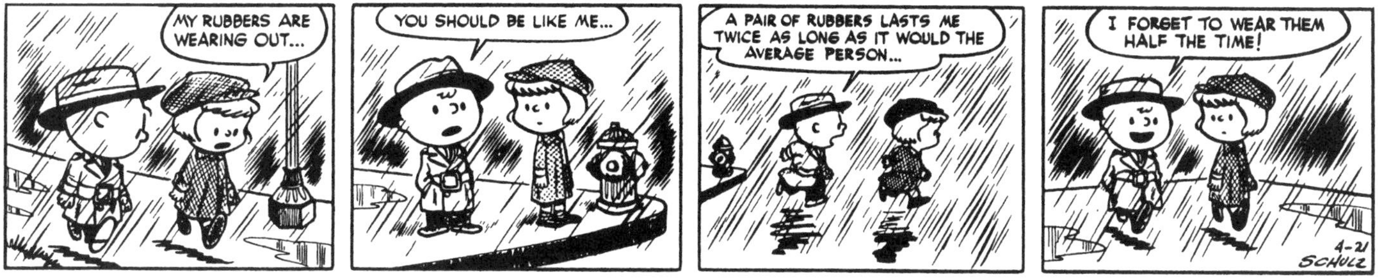
MY RUBBERS ARE WEARING OUT...
YOU SHOULD BE LIKE ME...
A PAIR OF RUBBERS LASTS ME TWICE AS LONG AS IT WOULD THE AVERAGE PERSON...
I FORGET TO WEAR THEM HALF THE TIME!
4-21
SCHULZ

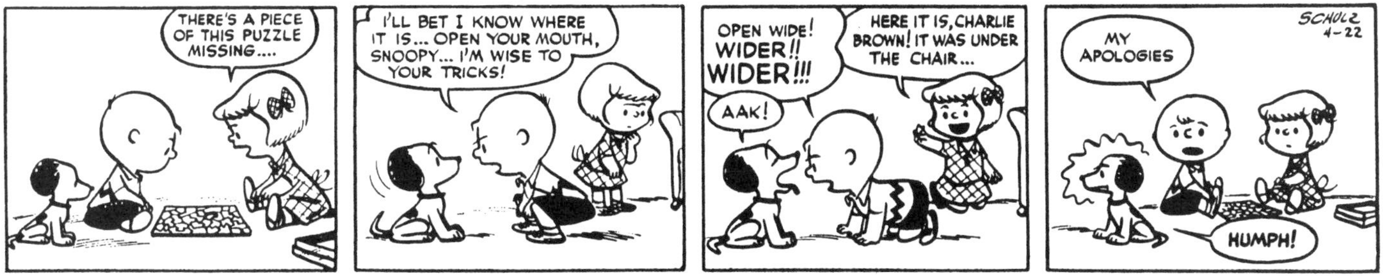
THERE'S A PIECE OF THIS PUZZLE MISSING....
I'LL BET I KNOW WHERE IT IS... OPEN YOUR MOUTH, SNOOPY... I'M WISE TO YOUR TRICKS!
OPEN WIDE! WIDER!! WIDER!!!
AAK!
HERE IT IS, CHARLIE BROWN! IT WAS UNDER THE CHAIR...
SCHULZ
4-22
MY APOLOGIES
HUMPH!

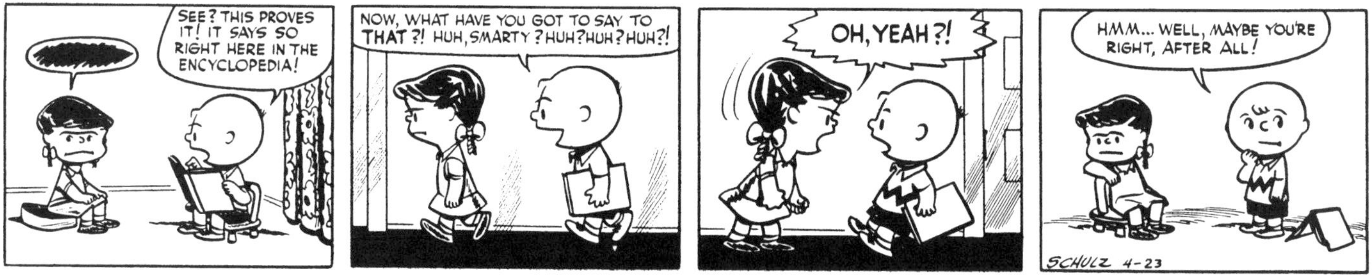
SEE? THIS PROVES IT! IT SAYS SO RIGHT HERE IN THE ENCYCLOPEDIA!
NOW, WHAT HAVE YOU GOT TO SAY TO THAT?! HUH, SMARTY? HUH? HUH? HUH?!
OH, YEAH?!
HMM... WELL, MAYBE YOU'RE RIGHT, AFTER ALL!
SCHULZ 4-23

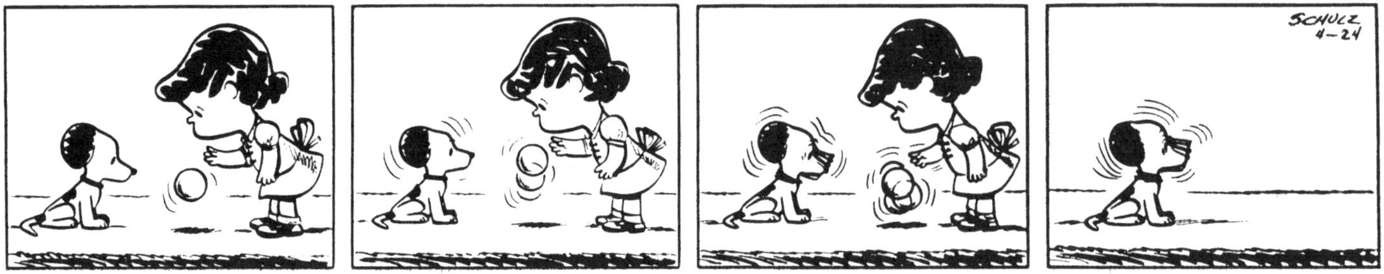
SCHULZ
4-24

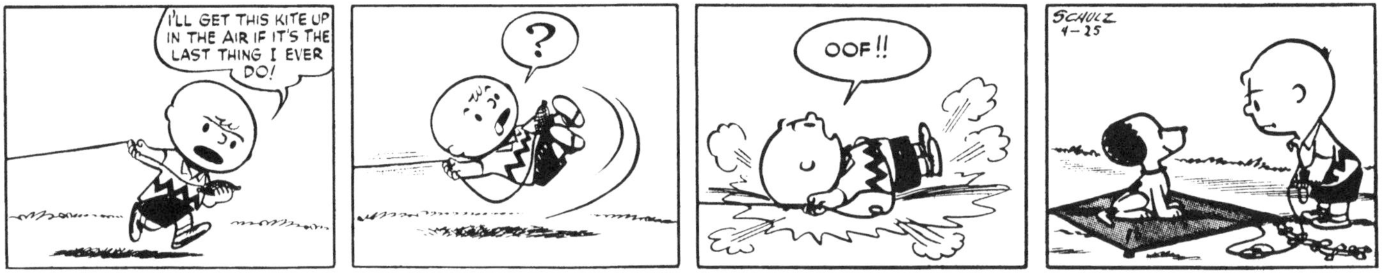
I'LL GET THIS KITE UP IN THE AIR IF IT'S THE LAST THING I EVER DO!
?
OOF!!
SCHULZ
4-25

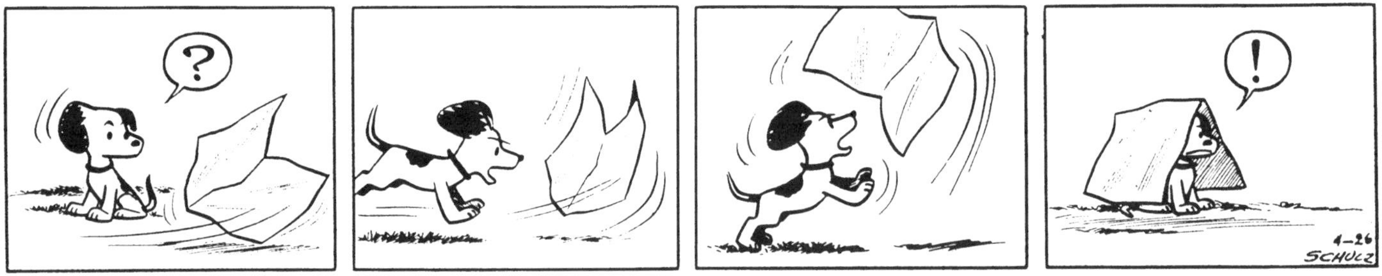
?
!
4-26
SCHULZ

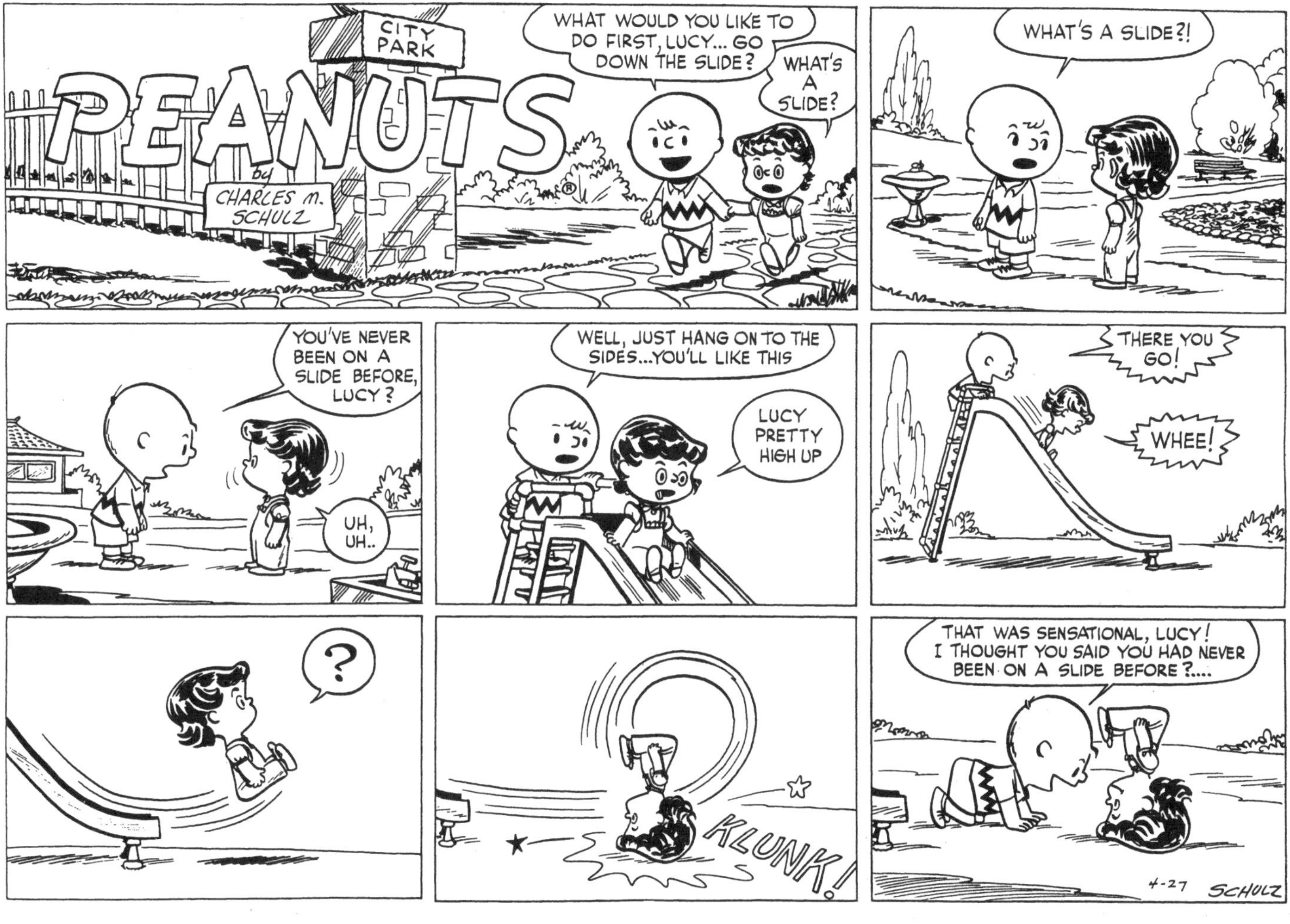
CITY PARK
PEANUTS
by CHARLES M. SCHULZ
WHAT WOULD YOU LIKE TO DO FIRST, LUCY... GO DOWN THE SLIDE?
WHAT'S A SLIDE?
WHAT'S A SLIDE?!
YOU'VE NEVER BEEN ON A SLIDE BEFORE, LUCY?
UH, UH..
WELL, JUST HANG ON TO THE SIDES...YOU'LL LIKE THIS
LUCY PRETTY HIGH UP
THERE YOU GO!
WHEE!
?
KLUNK!
THAT WAS SENSATIONAL, LUCY! I THOUGHT YOU SAID YOU HAD NEVER BEEN ON A SLIDE BEFORE?....
4-27 SCHULZ

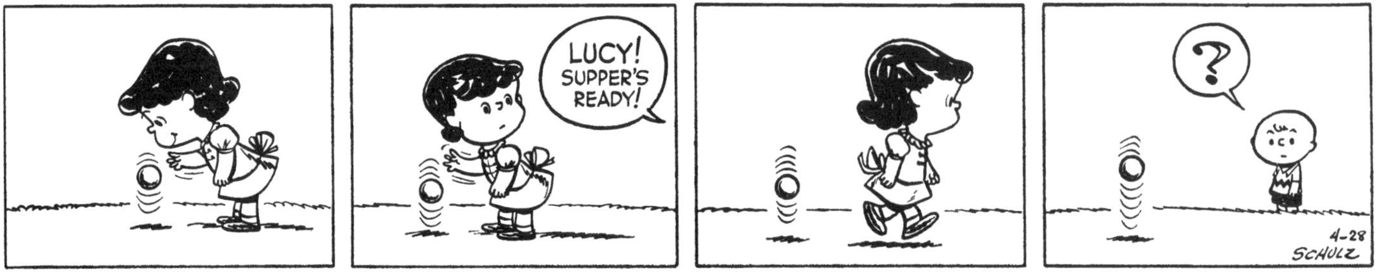
LUCY! SUPPER'S READY!
?
4-28
SCHULZ

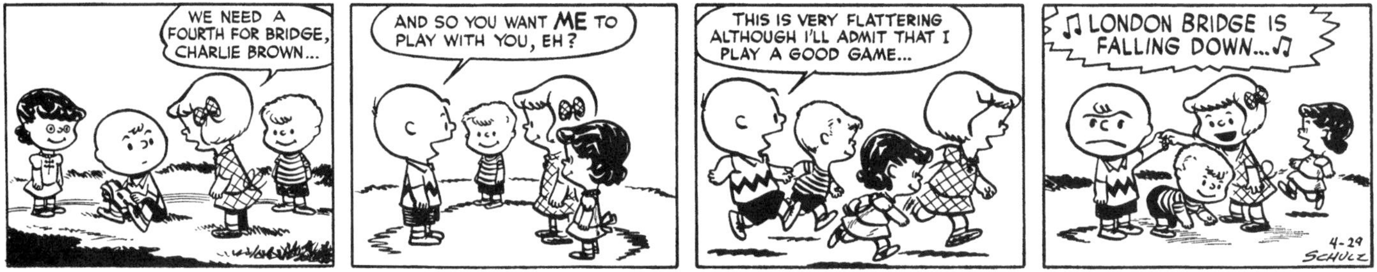
WE NEED A FOURTH FOR BRIDGE, CHARLIE BROWN...
AND SO YOU WANT ME TO PLAY WITH YOU, EH?
THIS IS VERY FLATTERING ALTHOUGH I'LL ADMIT THAT I PLAY A GOOD GAME...
♫ LONDON BRIDGE IS FALLING DOWN...♫
4-29
SCHULZ

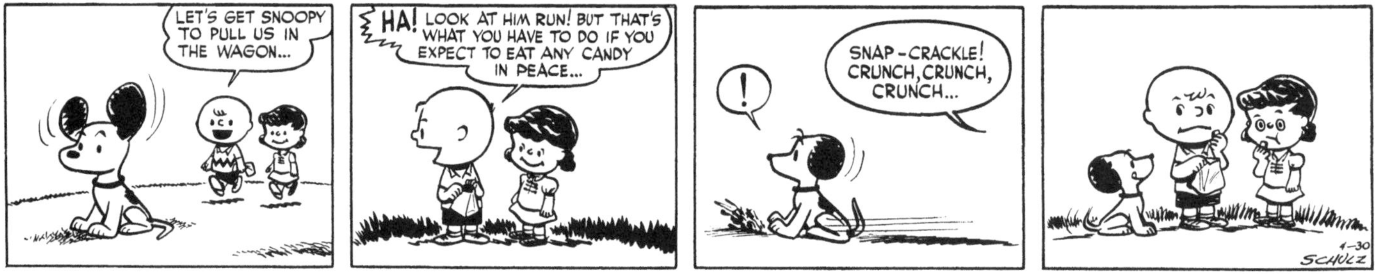
LET'S GET SNOOPY TO PULL US IN THE WAGON...
HA! LOOK AT HIM RUN! BUT THAT'S WHAT YOU HAVE TO DO IF YOU EXPECT TO EAT ANY CANDY IN PEACE...
!
SNAP-CRACKLE! CRUNCH, CRUNCH, CRUNCH...
4-30
SCHULZ

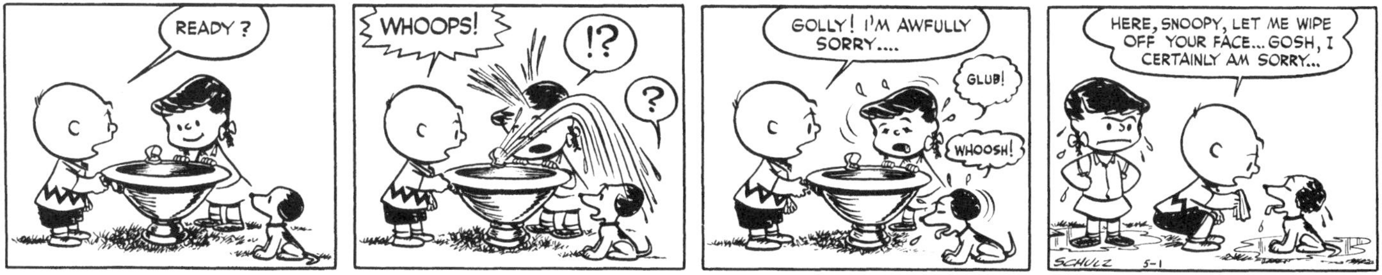
READY ?
WHOOPS!
!?
?
GOLLY! I'M AWFULLY SORRY....
GLUB!
WHOOSH!
HERE, SNOOPY, LET ME WIPE OFF YOUR FACE... GOSH, I CERTAINLY AM SORRY...
SCHULZ 5-1

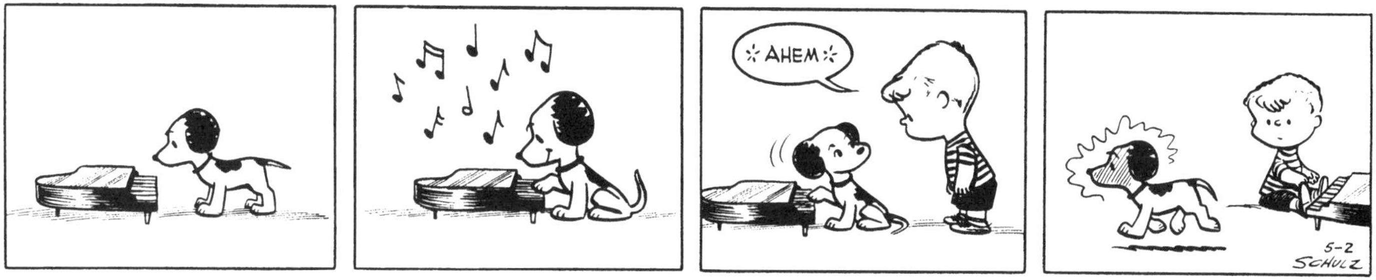
AHEM
5-2
SCHULZ

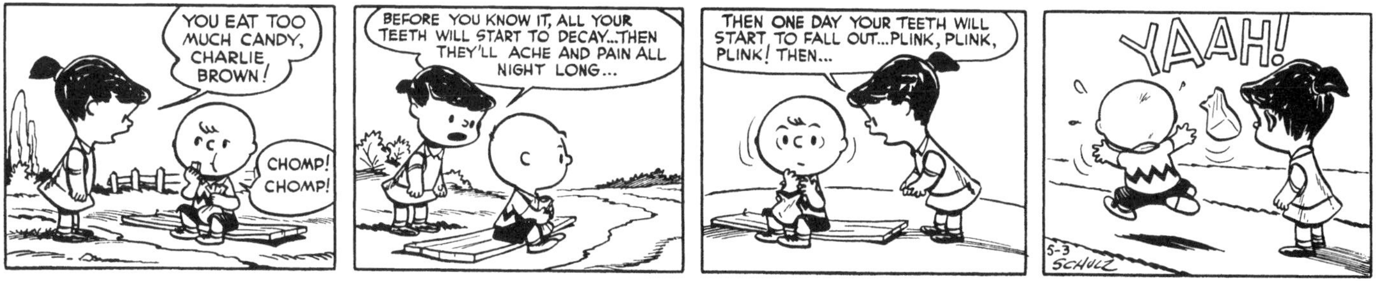
YOU EAT TOO MUCH CANDY, CHARLIE BROWN!
CHOMP! CHOMP!
BEFORE YOU KNOW IT, ALL YOUR TEETH WILL START TO DECAY...THEN THEY'LL ACHE AND PAIN ALL NIGHT LONG...
THEN ONE DAY YOUR TEETH WILL START TO FALL OUT...PLINK, PLINK, PLINK! THEN...
YAAH!
5-3
SCHULZ

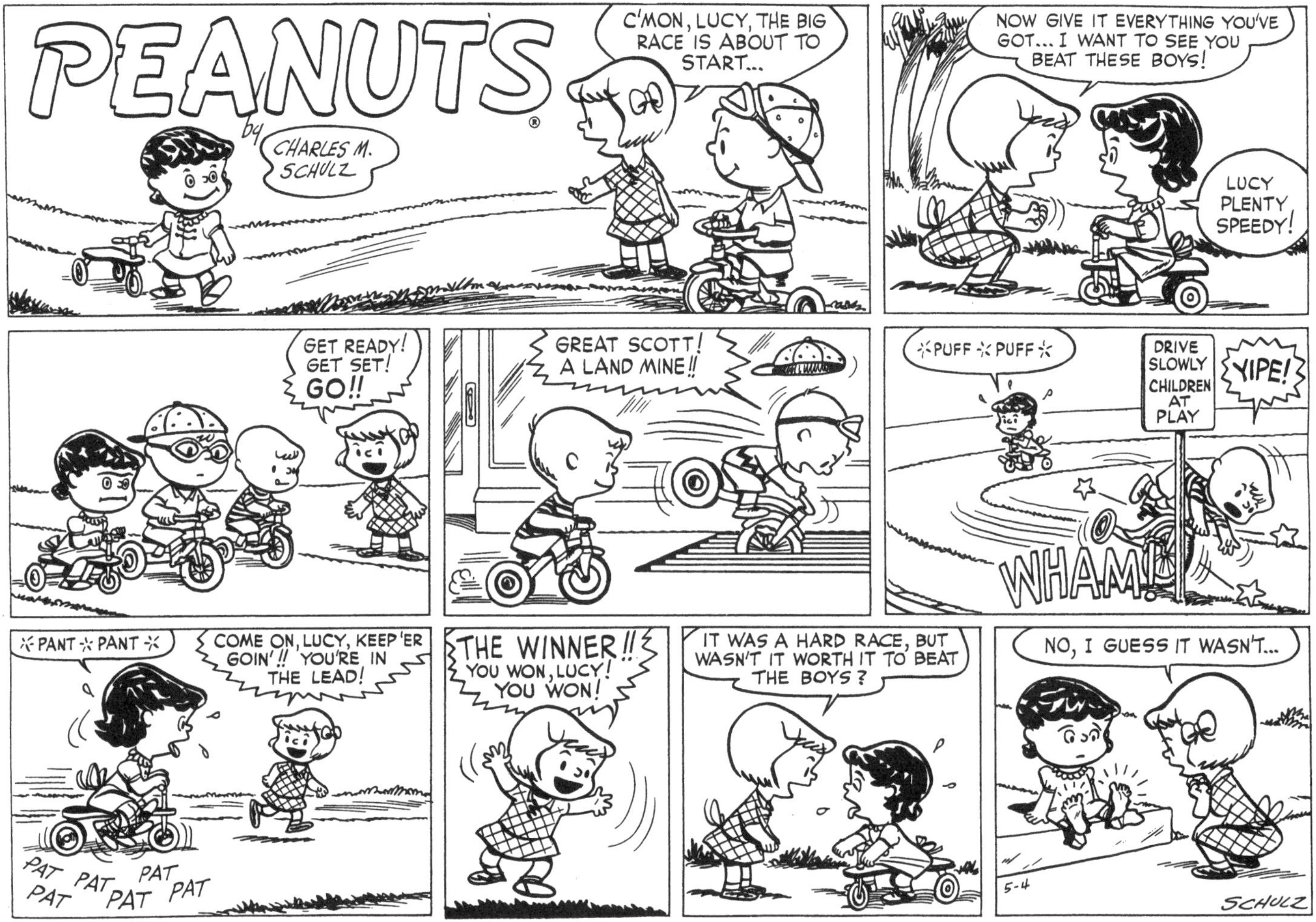
PEANUTS
by CHARLES M. SCHULZ
C'MON, LUCY, THE BIG RACE IS ABOUT TO START...
NOW GIVE IT EVERYTHING YOU'VE GOT... I WANT TO SEE YOU BEAT THESE BOYS!
LUCY PLENTY SPEEDY!
GET READY! GET SET! GO!!
GREAT SCOTT! A LAND MINE!!
PUFF PUFF
DRIVE SLOWLY CHILDREN AT PLAY
YIPE!
WHAM!
PANT PANT
COME ON, LUCY, KEEP 'ER GOIN'!! YOU'RE IN THE LEAD!
PAT PAT PAT PAT PAT PAT
THE WINNER!! YOU WON, LUCY! YOU WON!
IT WAS A HARD RACE, BUT WASN'T IT WORTH IT TO BEAT THE BOYS?
NO, I GUESS IT WASN'T...
5-4
SCHULZ

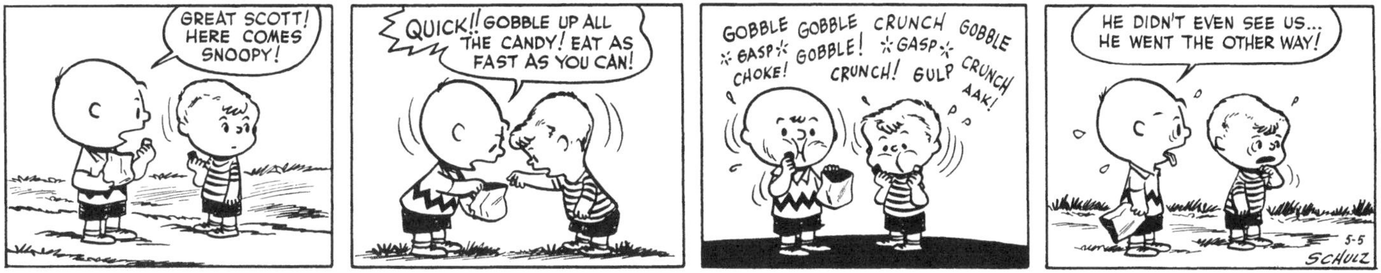
GREAT SCOTT! HERE COMES SNOOPY!
QUICK!! GOBBLE UP ALL THE CANDY! EAT AS FAST AS YOU CAN!
GOBBLE GOBBLE CRUNCH GOBBLE
GASP GOBBLE! GASP
CHOKE! CRUNCH! GULP CRUNCH
AAK!
HE DIDN'T EVEN SEE US... HE WENT THE OTHER WAY!
5-5
SCHULZ

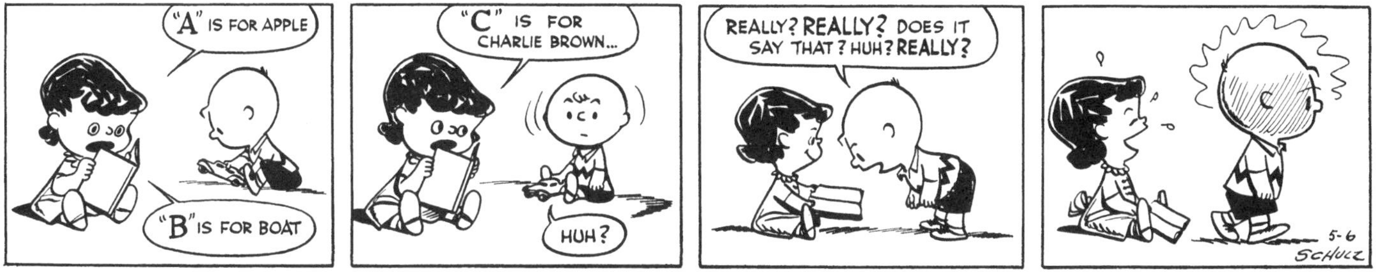
"A" IS FOR APPLE
"B" IS FOR BOAT
"C" IS FOR CHARLIE BROWN...
HUH?
REALLY? REALLY? DOES IT SAY THAT? HUH? REALLY?
5-6
SCHULZ

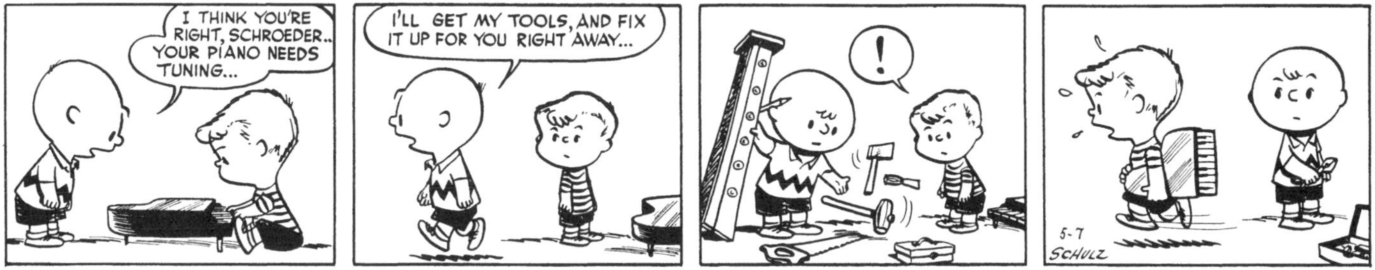
I THINK YOU'RE RIGHT, SCHROEDER.. YOUR PIANO NEEDS TUNING...
I'LL GET MY TOOLS, AND FIX IT UP FOR YOU RIGHT AWAY...
!
5-7
SCHULZ

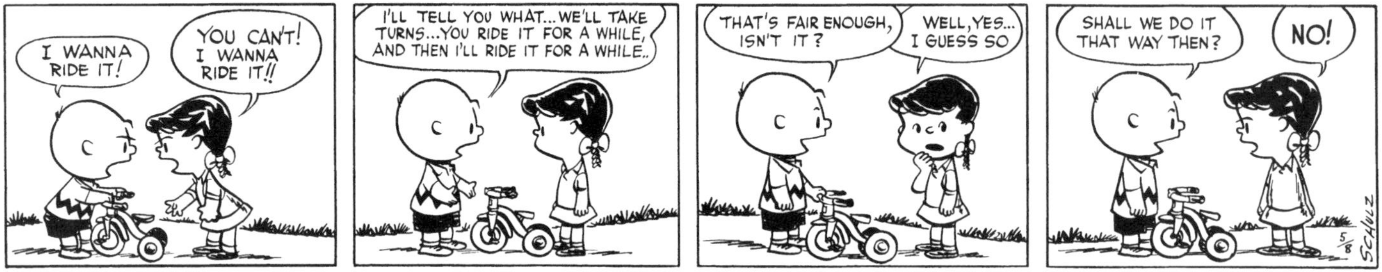
I WANNA RIDE IT!
YOU CAN'T! I WANNA RIDE IT!!
I'LL TELL YOU WHAT... WE'LL TAKE TURNS... YOU RIDE IT FOR A WHILE, AND THEN I'LL RIDE IT FOR A WHILE..
THAT'S FAIR ENOUGH, ISN'T IT?
WELL, YES... I GUESS SO
SHALL WE DO IT THAT WAY THEN?
NO!
5/8
SCHULZ

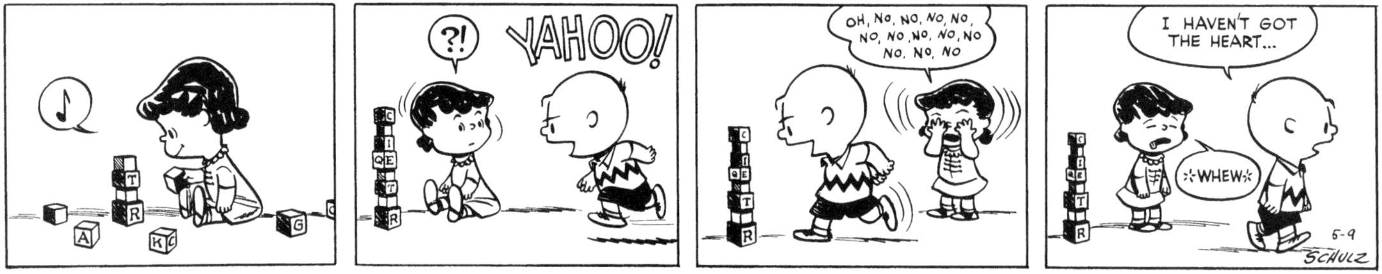
?!
YAHOO!
OH, NO, NO, NO, NO, NO, NO, NO, NO, NO, NO. NO. NO
I HAVEN'T GOT THE HEART...
WHEW
5-9
SCHULZ

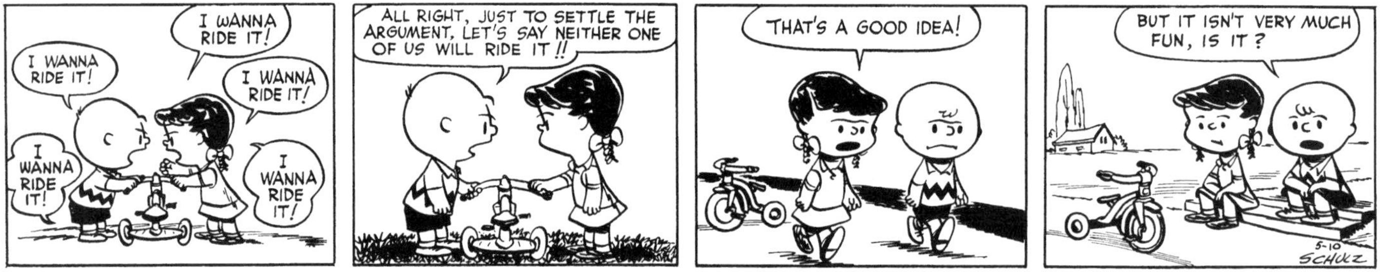
I WANNA RIDE IT!
I WANNA RIDE IT!
I WANNA RIDE IT!
I WANNA RIDE IT!
I WANNA RIDE IT!
ALL RIGHT, JUST TO SETTLE THE ARGUMENT, LET'S SAY NEITHER ONE OF US WILL RIDE IT!!
THAT'S A GOOD IDEA!
BUT IT ISN'T VERY MUCH FUN, IS IT?
5-10
SCHULZ

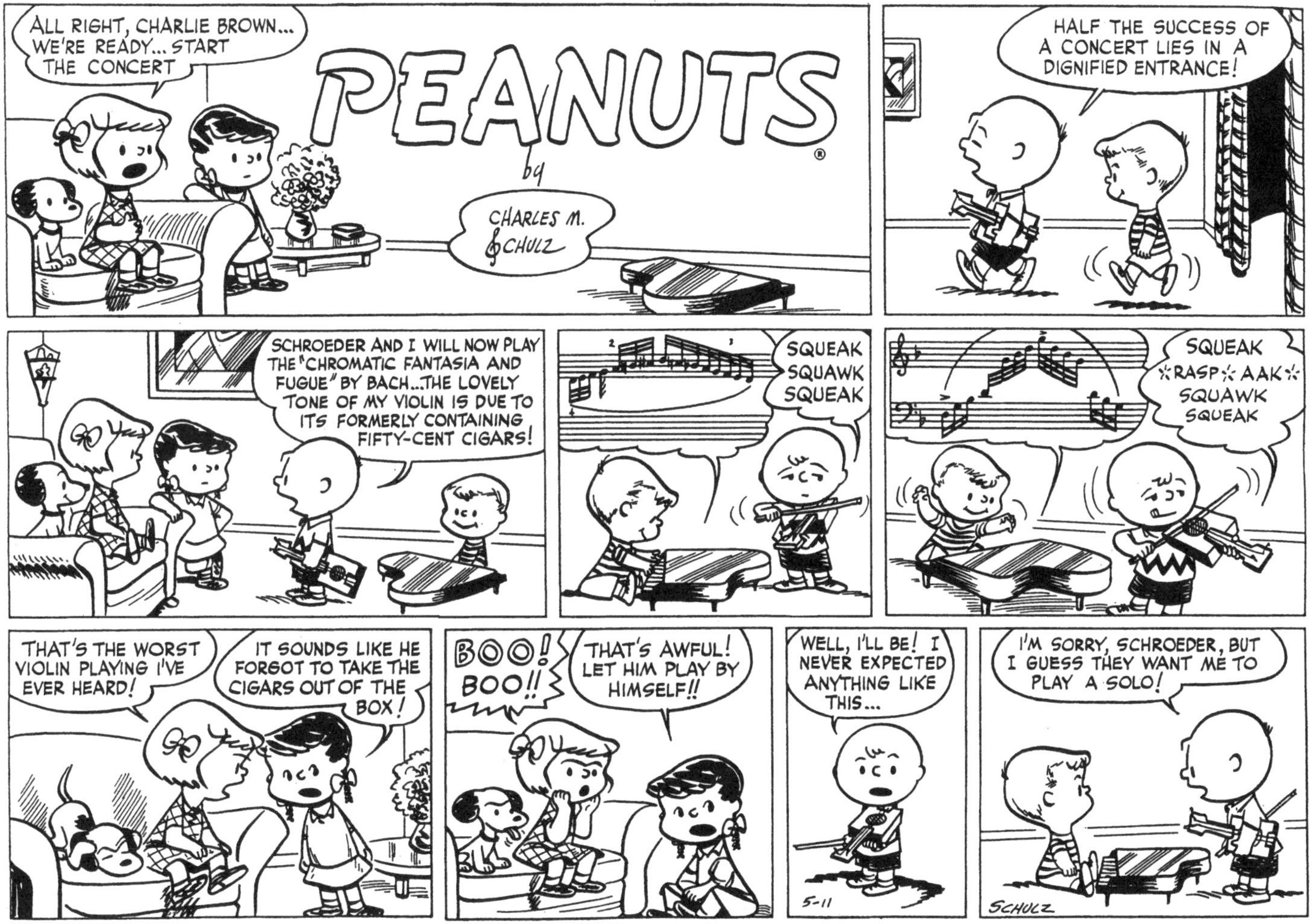
ALL RIGHT, CHARLIE BROWN... WE'RE READY... START THE CONCERT
PEANUTS
by
CHARLES M. SCHULZ
HALF THE SUCCESS OF A CONCERT LIES IN A DIGNIFIED ENTRANCE!
SCHROEDER AND I WILL NOW PLAY THE "CHROMATIC FANTASIA AND FUGUE" BY BACH...THE LOVELY TONE OF MY VIOLIN IS DUE TO ITS FORMERLY CONTAINING FIFTY-CENT CIGARS!
SQUEAK SQUAWK SQUEAK
SQUEAK RASP AAK SQUAWK SQUEAK
THAT'S THE WORST VIOLIN PLAYING I'VE EVER HEARD!
IT SOUNDS LIKE HE FORGOT TO TAKE THE CIGARS OUT OF THE BOX!
BOO! BOO!!
THAT'S AWFUL! LET HIM PLAY BY HIMSELF!!
WELL, I'LL BE! I NEVER EXPECTED ANYTHING LIKE THIS...
5-11
I'M SORRY, SCHROEDER, BUT I GUESS THEY WANT ME TO PLAY A SOLO!
SCHULZ

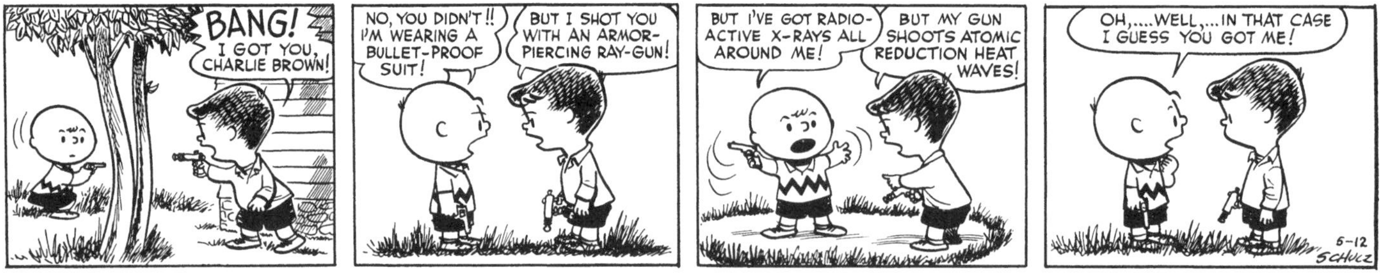
BANG! I GOT YOU, CHARLIE BROWN!
NO, YOU DIDN'T!! I'M WEARING A BULLET-PROOF SUIT!
BUT I SHOT YOU WITH AN ARMOR-PIERCING RAY-GUN!
BUT I'VE GOT RADIO-ACTIVE X-RAYS ALL AROUND ME!
BUT MY GUN SHOOTS ATOMIC REDUCTION HEAT WAVES!
OH,....WELL,...IN THAT CASE I GUESS YOU GOT ME!
5-12
SCHULZ

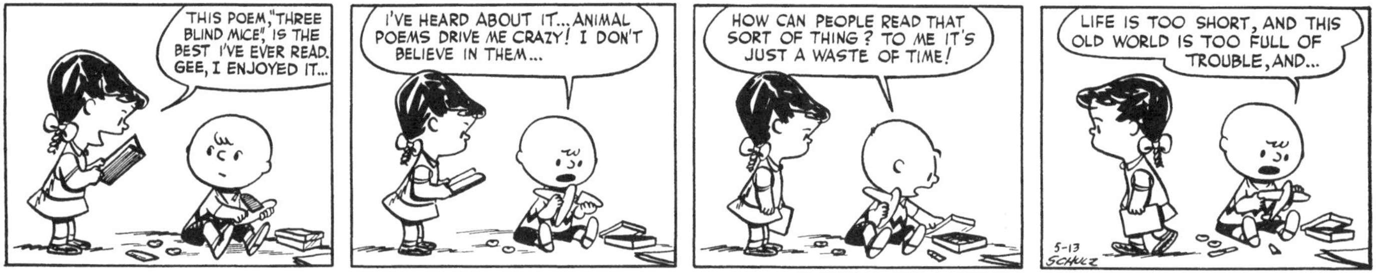
THIS POEM, "THREE BLIND MICE," IS THE BEST I'VE EVER READ. GEE, I ENJOYED IT...
I'VE HEARD ABOUT IT... ANIMAL POEMS DRIVE ME CRAZY! I DON'T BELIEVE IN THEM...
HOW CAN PEOPLE READ THAT SORT OF THING? TO ME IT'S JUST A WASTE OF TIME!
LIFE IS TOO SHORT, AND THIS OLD WORLD IS TOO FULL OF TROUBLE, AND...
5-13
SCHULZ

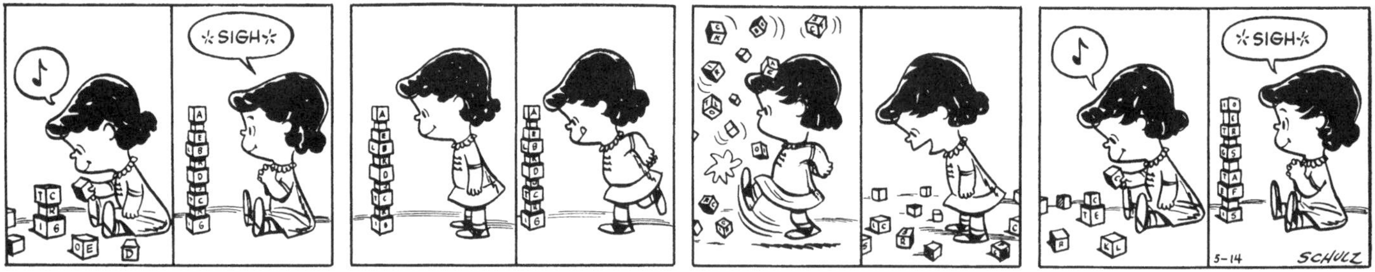
♪
SIGH
♪
SIGH
5-14
SCHULZ

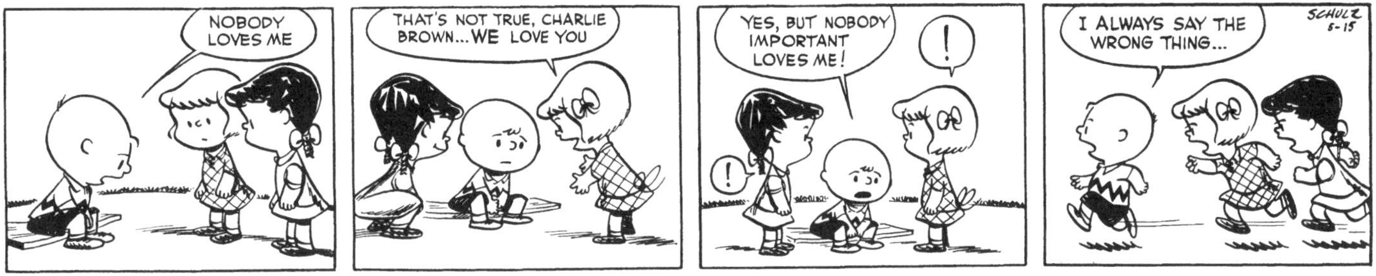
NOBODY LOVES ME
THAT'S NOT TRUE, CHARLIE BROWN...WE LOVE YOU
YES, BUT NOBODY IMPORTANT LOVES ME!
!
!
SCHULZ 5-15
I ALWAYS SAY THE WRONG THING...

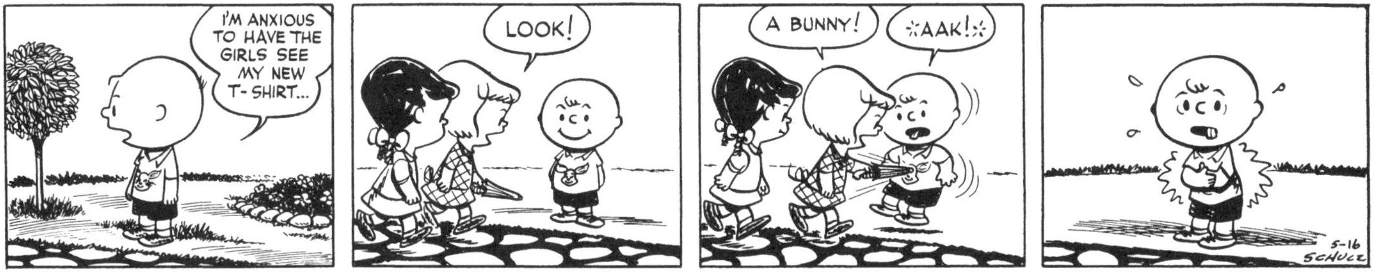
I'M ANXIOUS TO HAVE THE GIRLS SEE MY NEW T-SHIRT...
LOOK!
A BUNNY!
AAK!
5-16 SCHULZ

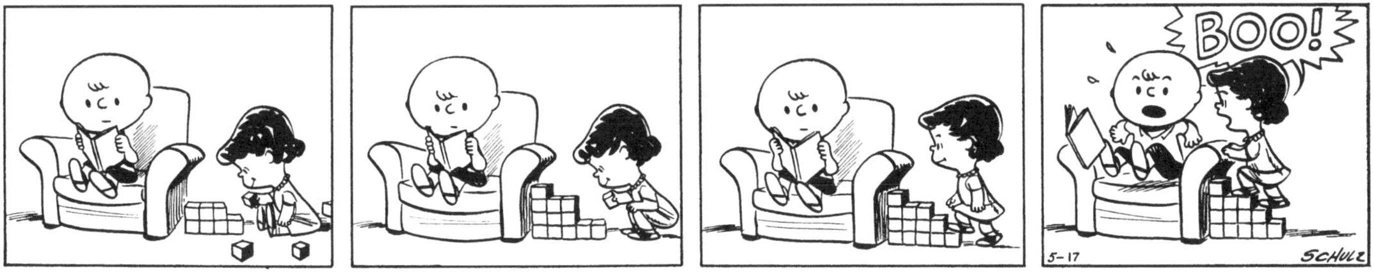
BOO!
5-17
SCHULZ

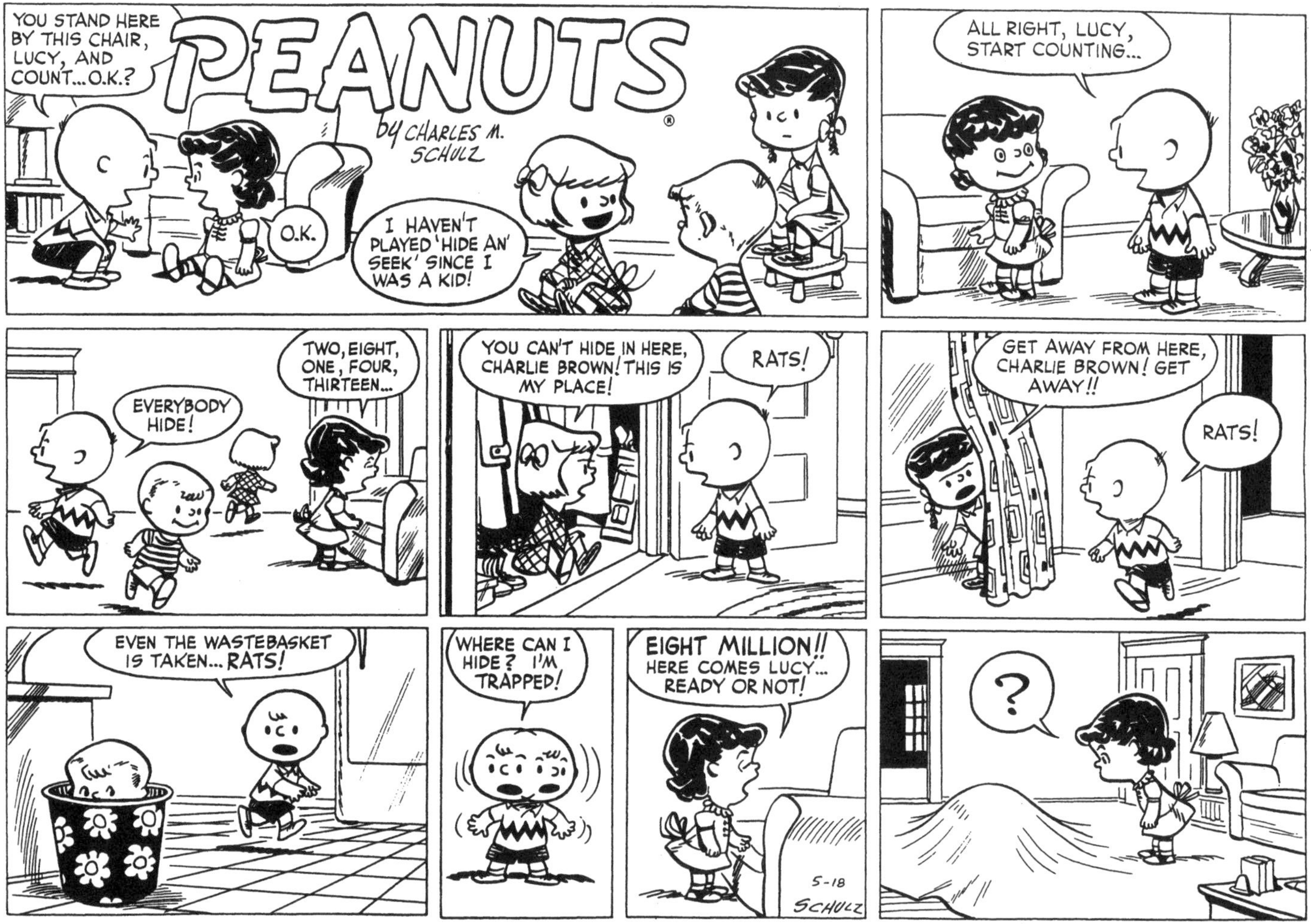
PEANUTS
by CHARLES M. SCHULZ
YOU STAND HERE BY THIS CHAIR, LUCY, AND COUNT...O.K.?
O.K.
I HAVEN'T PLAYED 'HIDE AN' SEEK' SINCE I WAS A KID!
ALL RIGHT, LUCY, START COUNTING...
EVERYBODY HIDE!
TWO, EIGHT, ONE, FOUR, THIRTEEN...
YOU CAN'T HIDE IN HERE, CHARLIE BROWN! THIS IS MY PLACE!
RATS!
GET AWAY FROM HERE, CHARLIE BROWN! GET AWAY!!
RATS!
EVEN THE WASTEBASKET IS TAKEN... RATS!
WHERE CAN I HIDE? I'M TRAPPED!
EIGHT MILLION!! HERE COMES LUCY... READY OR NOT!
5-18
SCHULZ
?

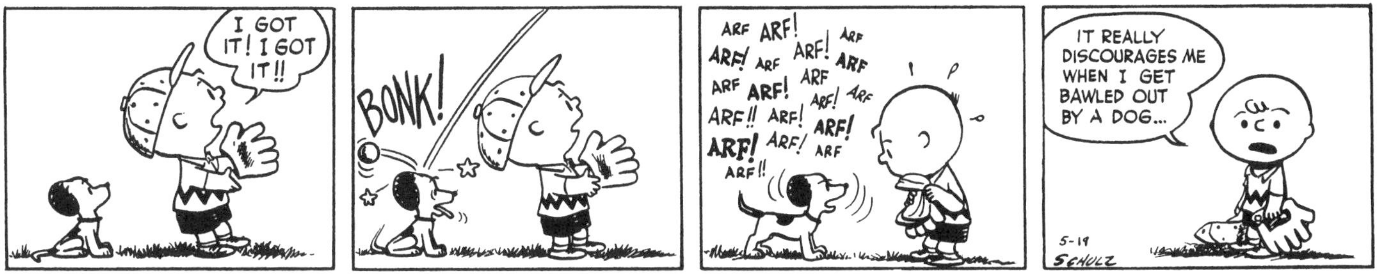
I GOT IT! I GOT IT!!
BONK!
ARF ARF! ARF
ARF! ARF ARF! ARF
ARF ARF! ARF ARF! ARF
ARF!! ARF! ARF!
ARF! ARF! ARF
ARF!!
IT REALLY DISCOURAGES ME WHEN I GET BAWLED OUT BY A DOG...
5-19
SCHULZ

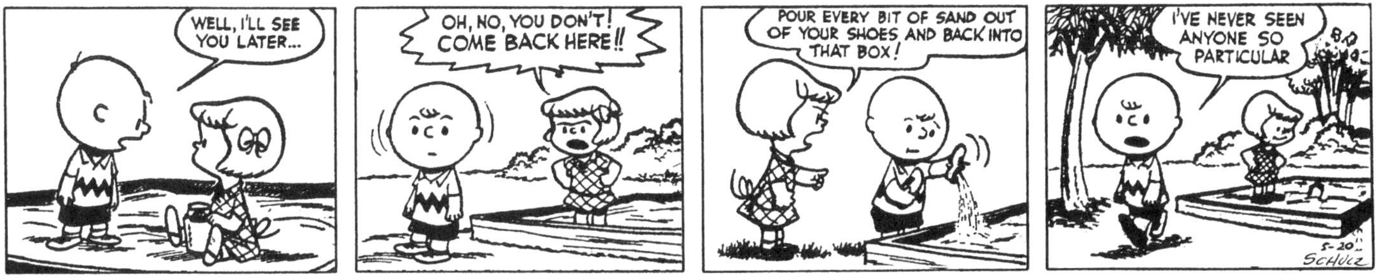
WELL, I'LL SEE YOU LATER...
OH, NO, YOU DON'T! COME BACK HERE!!
POUR EVERY BIT OF SAND OUT OF YOUR SHOES AND BACK INTO THAT BOX!
I'VE NEVER SEEN ANYONE SO PARTICULAR
5-20
SCHULZ

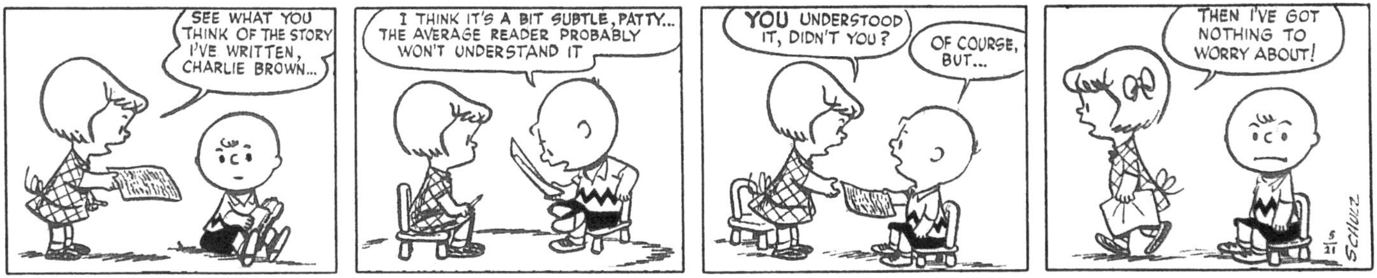
SEE WHAT YOU THINK OF THE STORY I'VE WRITTEN, CHARLIE BROWN...
I THINK IT'S A BIT SUBTLE, PATTY... THE AVERAGE READER PROBABLY WON'T UNDERSTAND IT
YOU UNDERSTOOD IT, DIDN'T YOU?
OF COURSE, BUT...
THEN I'VE GOT NOTHING TO WORRY ABOUT!
5 21
SCHULZ

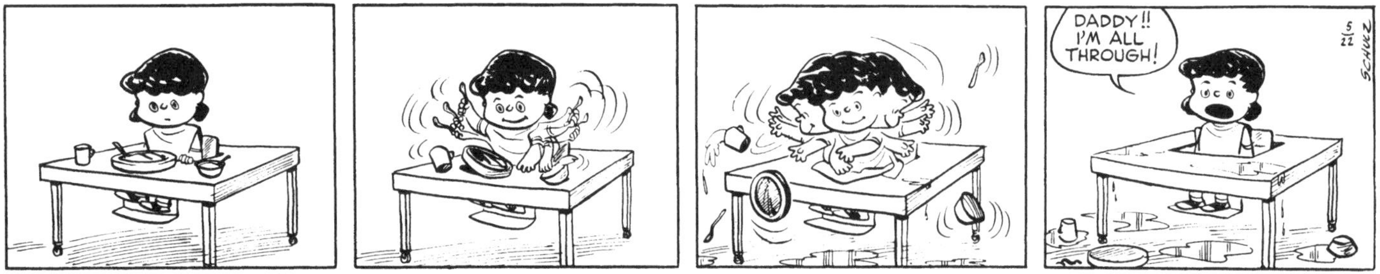
DADDY!! I'M ALL THROUGH!
5/22 SCHULZ

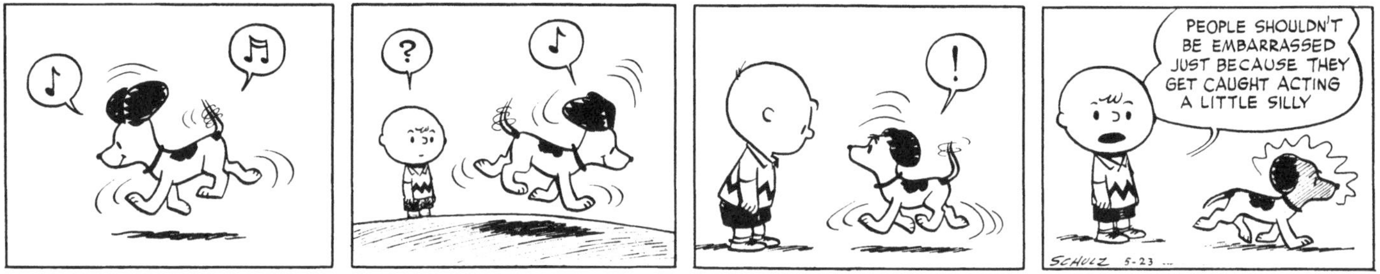
?
!
PEOPLE SHOULDN'T BE EMBARRASSED JUST BECAUSE THEY GET CAUGHT ACTING A LITTLE SILLY
SCHULZ 5-23

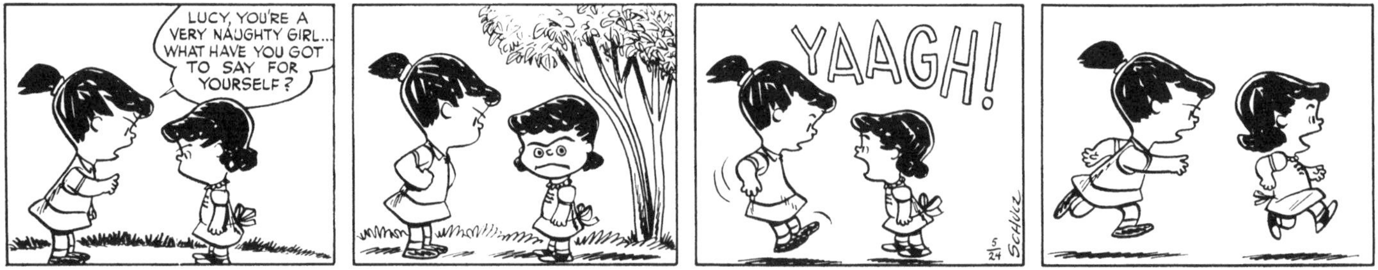
LUCY, YOU'RE A VERY NAUGHTY GIRL... WHAT HAVE YOU GOT TO SAY FOR YOURSELF?
YAAGH!
5/24 SCHULZ

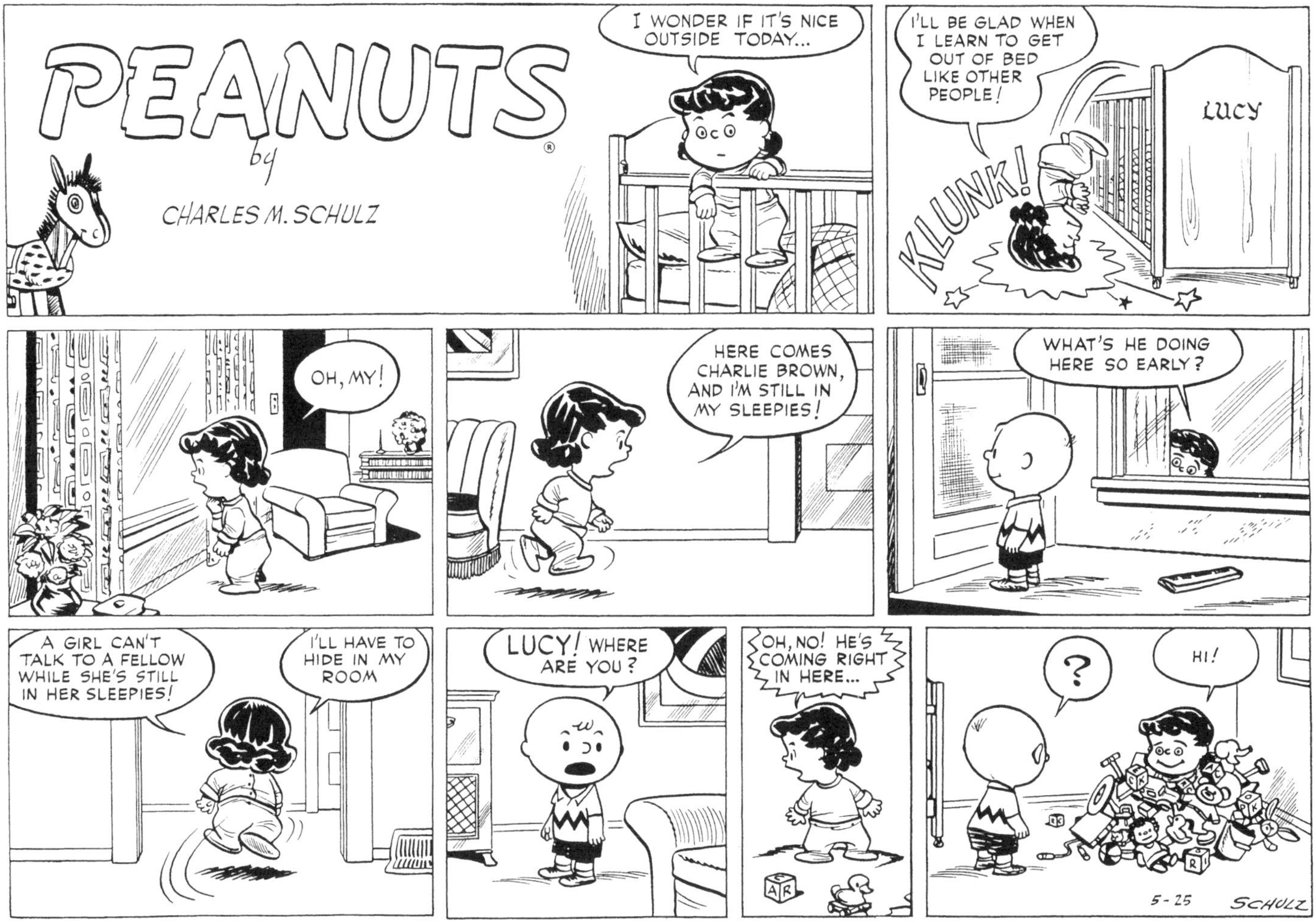
PEANUTS
by
CHARLES M. SCHULZ
I WONDER IF IT'S NICE OUTSIDE TODAY...
I'LL BE GLAD WHEN I LEARN TO GET OUT OF BED LIKE OTHER PEOPLE!
LUCY
KLUNK!
OH, MY!
HERE COMES CHARLIE BROWN, AND I'M STILL IN MY SLEEPIES!
WHAT'S HE DOING HERE SO EARLY?
A GIRL CAN'T TALK TO A FELLOW WHILE SHE'S STILL IN HER SLEEPIES!
I'LL HAVE TO HIDE IN MY ROOM
LUCY! WHERE ARE YOU?
OH, NO! HE'S COMING RIGHT IN HERE...
?
HI!
5-25
SCHULZ

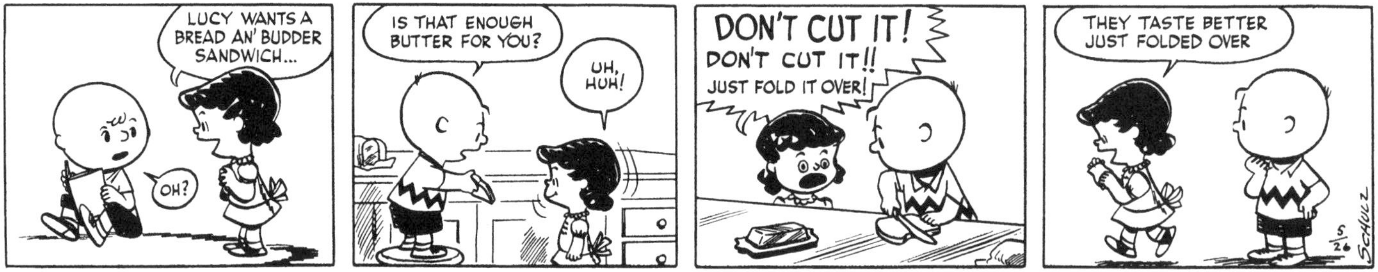
LUCY WANTS A BREAD AN' BUDDER SANDWICH...
OH?
IS THAT ENOUGH BUTTER FOR YOU?
UH, HUH!
DON'T CUT IT! DON'T CUT IT!! JUST FOLD IT OVER!
THEY TASTE BETTER JUST FOLDED OVER
5/26
SCHULZ

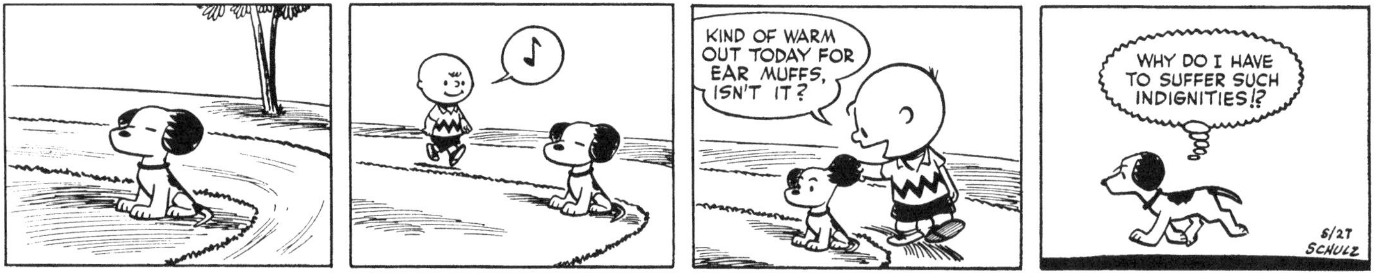
♪
KIND OF WARM OUT TODAY FOR EAR MUFFS, ISN'T IT?
WHY DO I HAVE TO SUFFER SUCH INDIGNITIES!?
5/27
SCHULZ

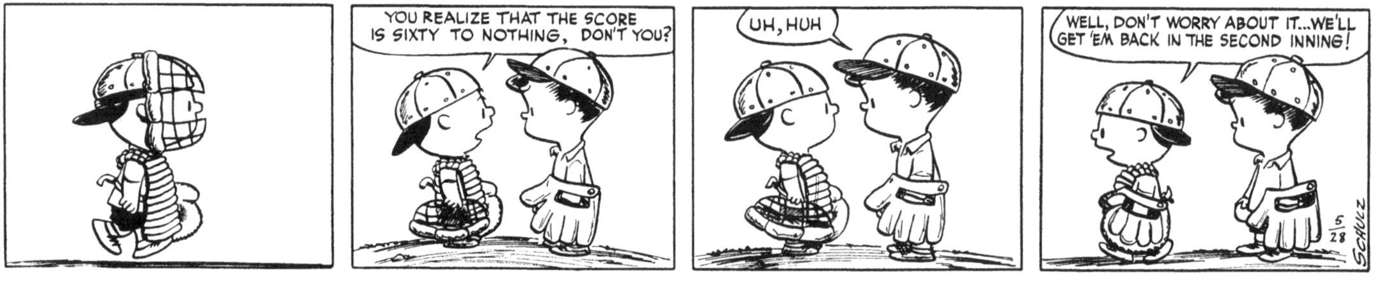
YOU REALIZE THAT THE SCORE IS SIXTY TO NOTHING, DON'T YOU?
UH, HUH
WELL, DON'T WORRY ABOUT IT...WE'LL GET 'EM BACK IN THE SECOND INNING!
5/28
SCHULZ

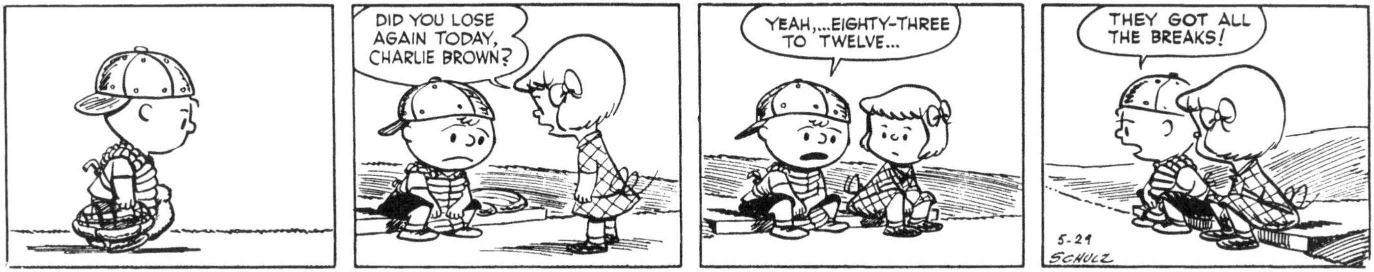
DID YOU LOSE AGAIN TODAY, CHARLIE BROWN?
YEAH,...EIGHTY-THREE TO TWELVE...
THEY GOT ALL THE BREAKS!
5-29
SCHULZ

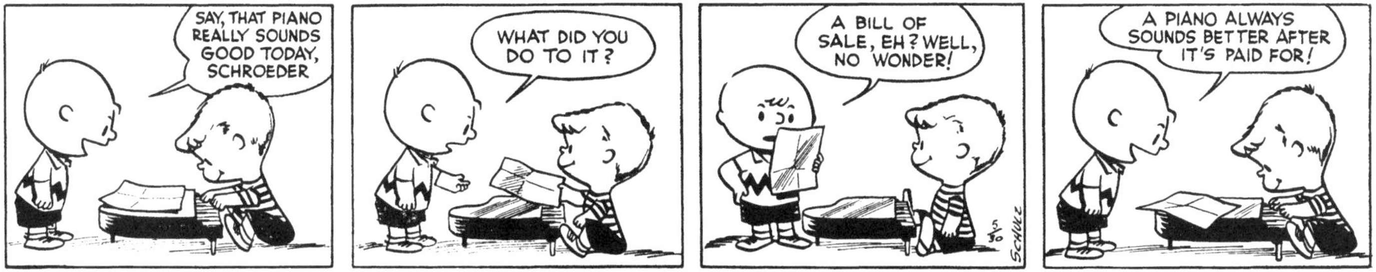
SAY, THAT PIANO REALLY SOUNDS GOOD TODAY, SCHROEDER
WHAT DID YOU DO TO IT?
A BILL OF SALE, EH? WELL, NO WONDER!
5/30
SCHULZ
A PIANO ALWAYS SOUNDS BETTER AFTER IT'S PAID FOR!

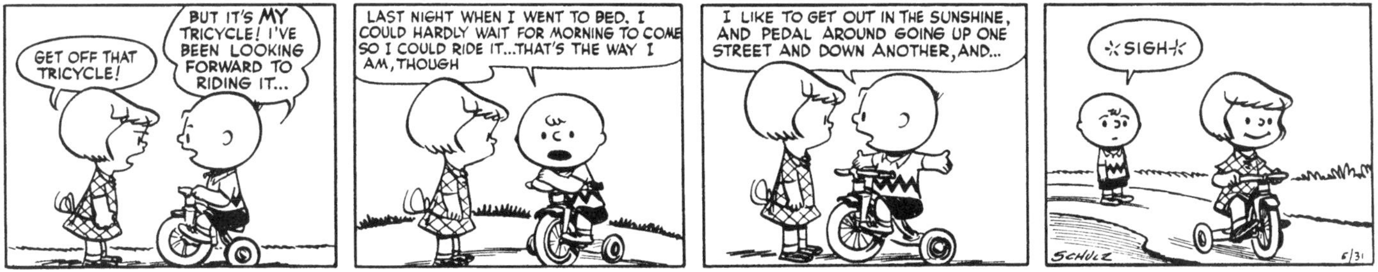
GET OFF THAT TRICYCLE!
BUT IT'S MY TRICYCLE! I'VE BEEN LOOKING FORWARD TO RIDING IT...
LAST NIGHT WHEN I WENT TO BED, I COULD HARDLY WAIT FOR MORNING TO COME SO I COULD RIDE IT...THAT'S THE WAY I AM, THOUGH
I LIKE TO GET OUT IN THE SUNSHINE, AND PEDAL AROUND GOING UP ONE STREET AND DOWN ANOTHER, AND...
SIGH
SCHULZ
5/31

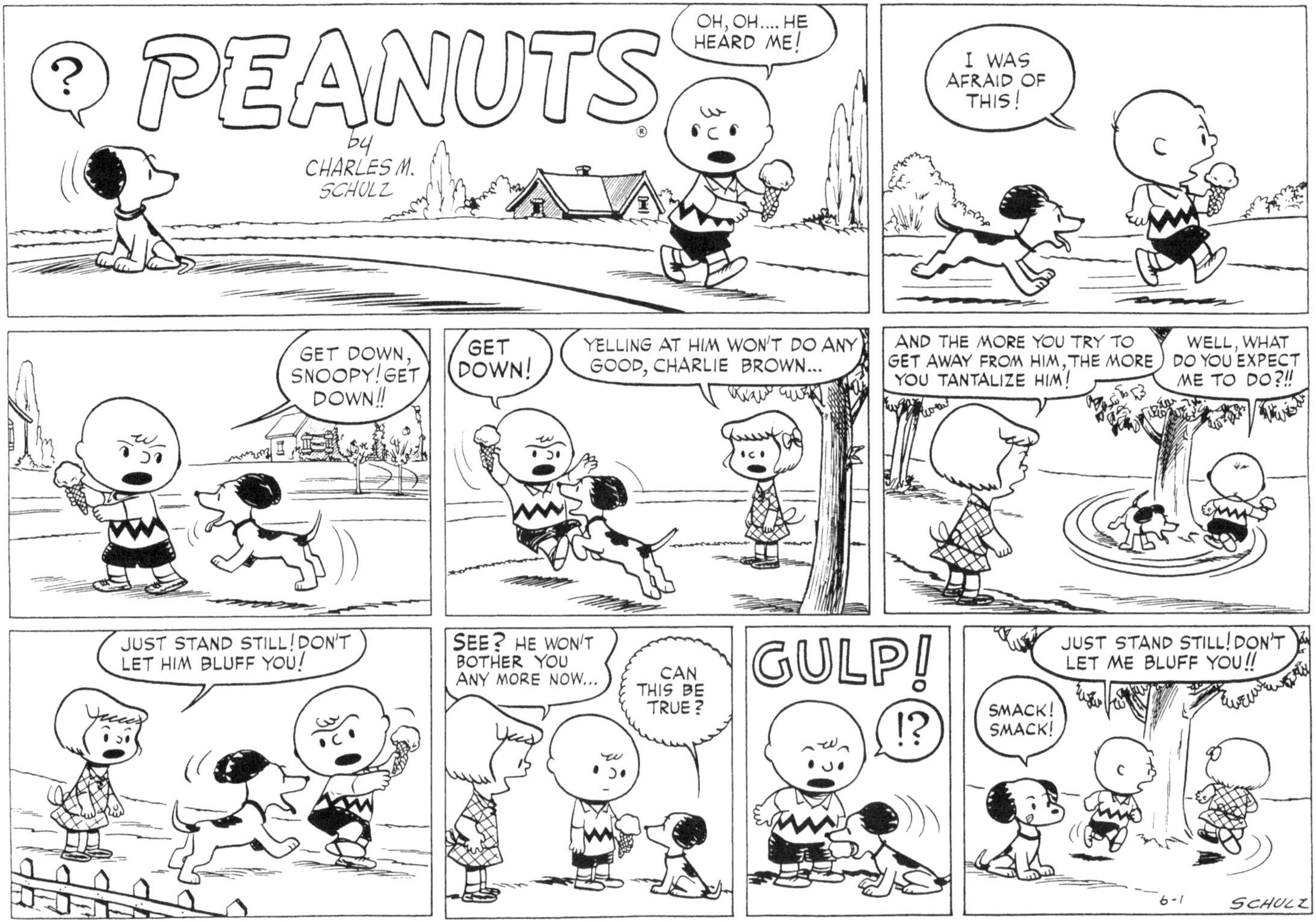
?
PEANUTS
by CHARLES M. SCHULZ
OH, OH.... HE HEARD ME!
I WAS AFRAID OF THIS!
GET DOWN, SNOOPY! GET DOWN!!
GET DOWN!
YELLING AT HIM WON'T DO ANY GOOD, CHARLIE BROWN...
AND THE MORE YOU TRY TO GET AWAY FROM HIM, THE MORE YOU TANTALIZE HIM!
WELL, WHAT DO YOU EXPECT ME TO DO?!!
JUST STAND STILL! DON'T LET HIM BLUFF YOU!
SEE? HE WON'T BOTHER YOU ANY MORE NOW...
CAN THIS BE TRUE?
GULP!
!?
SMACK! SMACK!
JUST STAND STILL! DON'T LET ME BLUFF YOU!!
6-1
SCHULZ

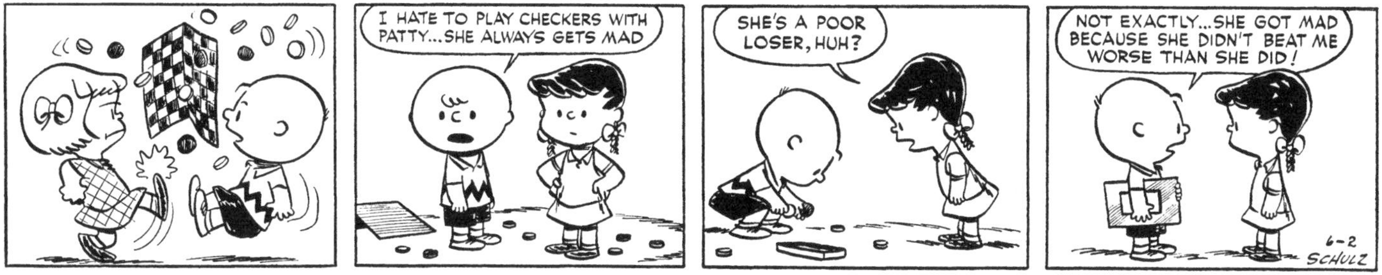
I HATE TO PLAY CHECKERS WITH PATTY...SHE ALWAYS GETS MAD
SHE'S A POOR LOSER, HUH?
NOT EXACTLY...SHE GOT MAD BECAUSE SHE DIDN'T BEAT ME WORSE THAN SHE DID!
6-2
SCHULZ

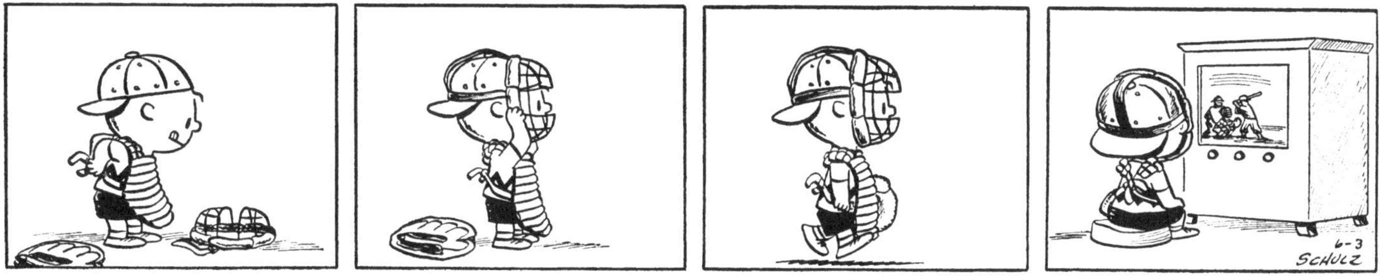
6-3
SCHULZ

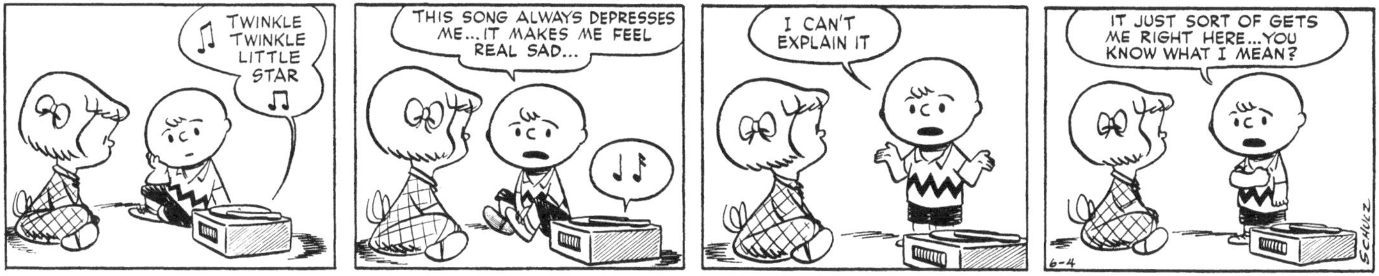
TWINKLE TWINKLE LITTLE STAR
THIS SONG ALWAYS DEPRESSES ME...IT MAKES ME FEEL REAL SAD...
I CAN'T EXPLAIN IT
IT JUST SORT OF GETS ME RIGHT HERE...YOU KNOW WHAT I MEAN?
6-4
SCHULZ

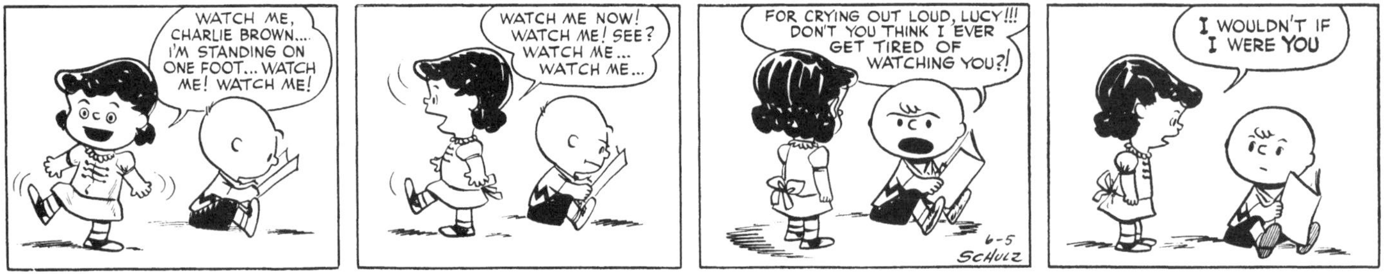
WATCH ME, CHARLIE BROWN.... I'M STANDING ON ONE FOOT... WATCH ME! WATCH ME!
WATCH ME NOW! WATCH ME! SEE? WATCH ME... WATCH ME...
FOR CRYING OUT LOUD, LUCY!!! DON'T YOU THINK I EVER GET TIRED OF WATCHING YOU?!
6-5
SCHULZ
I WOULDN'T IF I WERE YOU

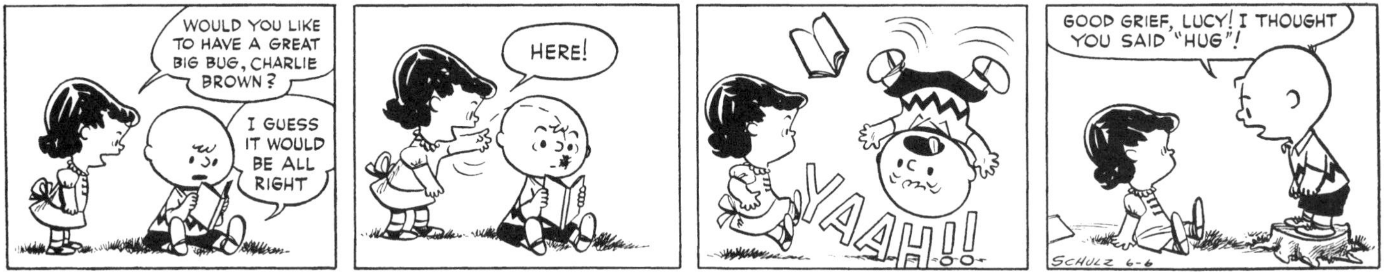
WOULD YOU LIKE TO HAVE A GREAT BIG BUG, CHARLIE BROWN?
I GUESS IT WOULD BE ALL RIGHT
HERE!
YAAH!!
GOOD GRIEF, LUCY! I THOUGHT YOU SAID "HUG"!
SCHULZ 6-6

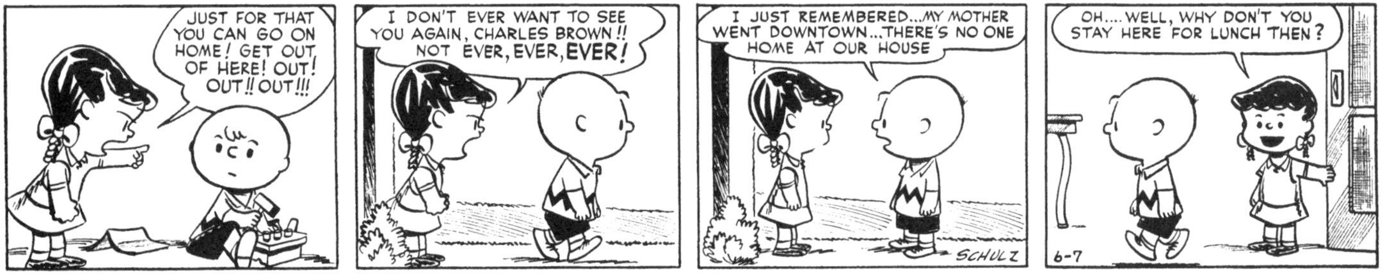
JUST FOR THAT YOU CAN GO ON HOME! GET OUT OF HERE! OUT! OUT!! OUT!!!
I DON'T EVER WANT TO SEE YOU AGAIN, CHARLES BROWN!! NOT EVER, EVER, EVER!
I JUST REMEMBERED...MY MOTHER WENT DOWNTOWN...THERE'S NO ONE HOME AT OUR HOUSE
SCHULZ
6-7
OH.... WELL, WHY DON'T YOU STAY HERE FOR LUNCH THEN?

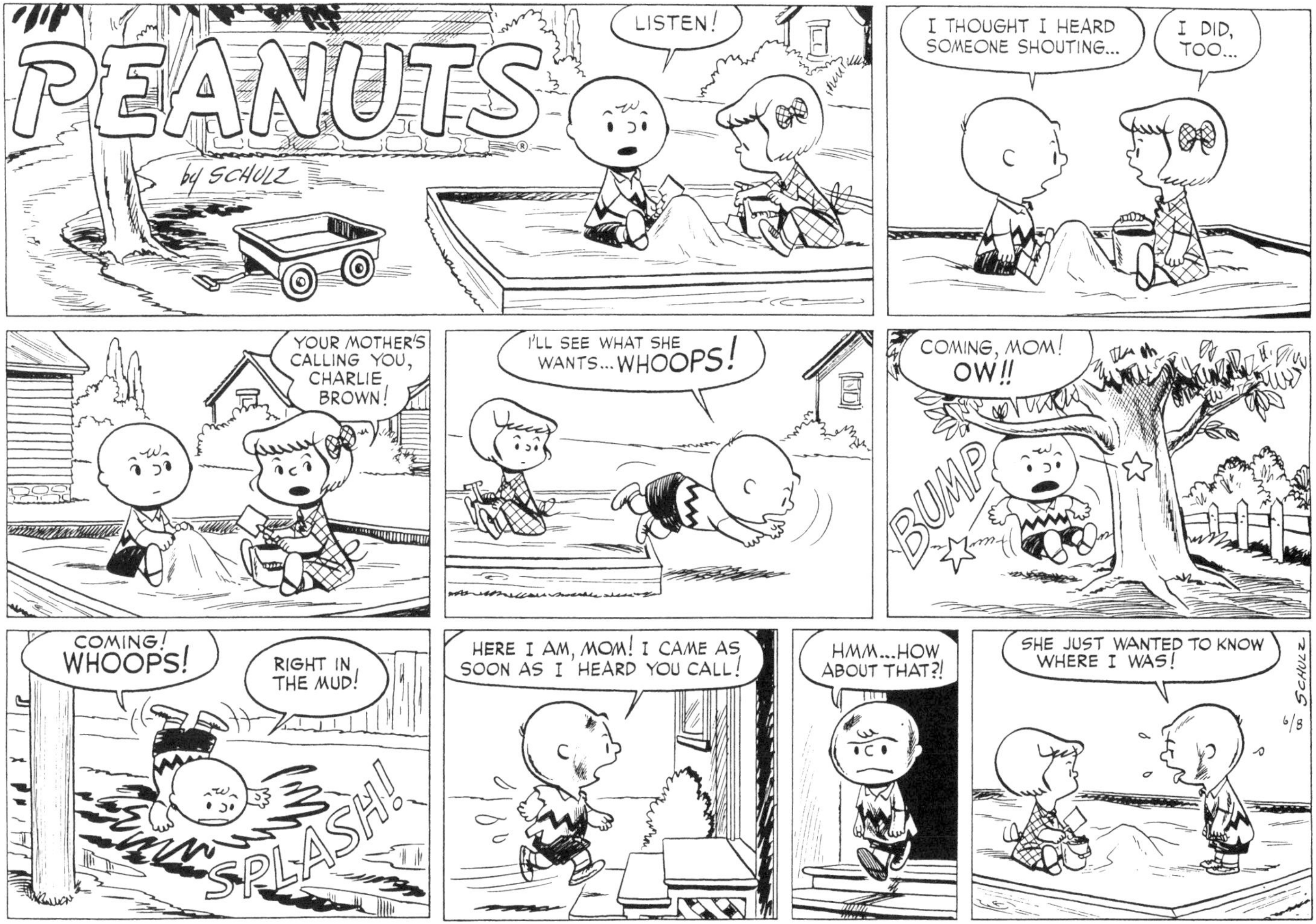
PEANUTS
by SCHULZ
LISTEN!
I THOUGHT I HEARD SOMEONE SHOUTING...
I DID, TOO...
YOUR MOTHER'S CALLING YOU, CHARLIE BROWN!
I'LL SEE WHAT SHE WANTS... WHOOPS!
COMING, MOM! OW!!
BUMP
COMING! WHOOPS!
RIGHT IN THE MUD!
SPLASH!
HERE I AM, MOM! I CAME AS SOON AS I HEARD YOU CALL!
HMM...HOW ABOUT THAT?!
SHE JUST WANTED TO KNOW WHERE I WAS!
SCHULZ
6/8

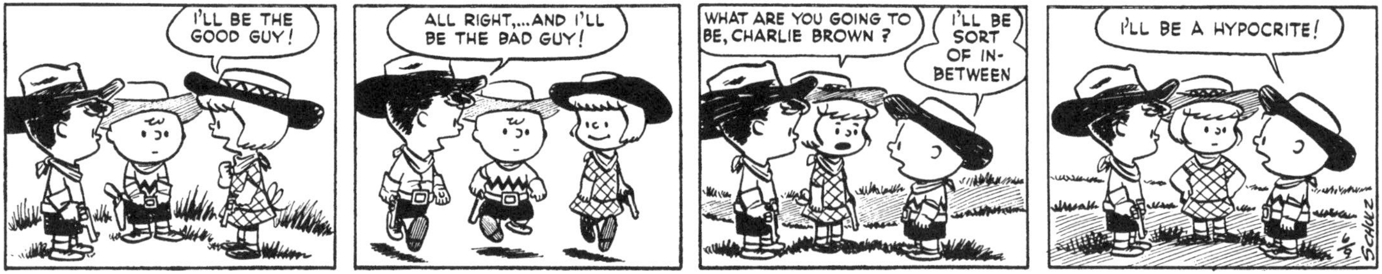
I'LL BE THE GOOD GUY!
ALL RIGHT,...AND I'LL BE THE BAD GUY!
WHAT ARE YOU GOING TO BE, CHARLIE BROWN ?
I'LL BE SORT OF IN-BETWEEN
I'LL BE A HYPOCRITE!
SCHULZ
6/9

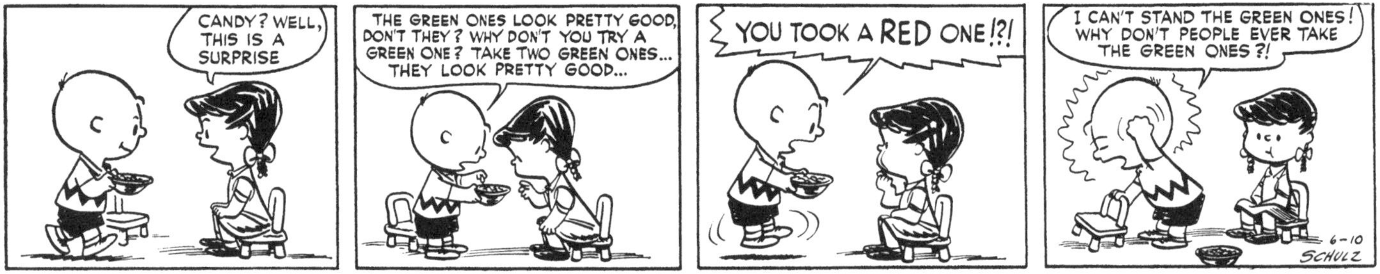
CANDY? WELL, THIS IS A SURPRISE
THE GREEN ONES LOOK PRETTY GOOD, DON'T THEY? WHY DON'T YOU TRY A GREEN ONE? TAKE TWO GREEN ONES... THEY LOOK PRETTY GOOD...
YOU TOOK A RED ONE!?!
I CAN'T STAND THE GREEN ONES! WHY DON'T PEOPLE EVER TAKE THE GREEN ONES?!
6-10
SCHULZ

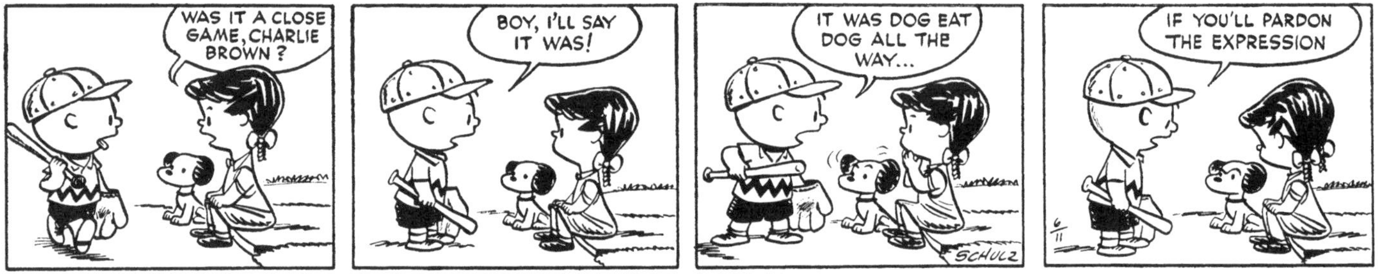
WAS IT A CLOSE GAME, CHARLIE BROWN ?
BOY, I'LL SAY IT WAS!
IT WAS DOG EAT DOG ALL THE WAY...
SCHULZ
IF YOU'LL PARDON THE EXPRESSION
6/11

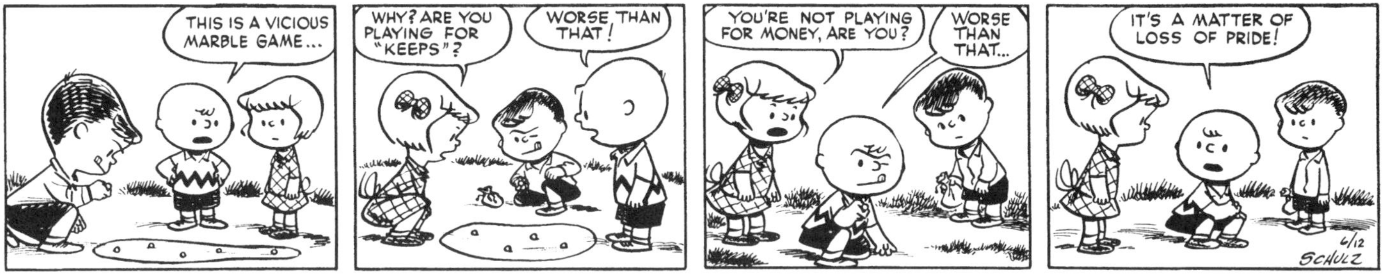
THIS IS A VICIOUS MARBLE GAME...
WHY? ARE YOU PLAYING FOR "KEEPS"?
WORSE THAN THAT!
YOU'RE NOT PLAYING FOR MONEY, ARE YOU?
WORSE THAN THAT...
IT'S A MATTER OF LOSS OF PRIDE!
6/12
SCHULZ

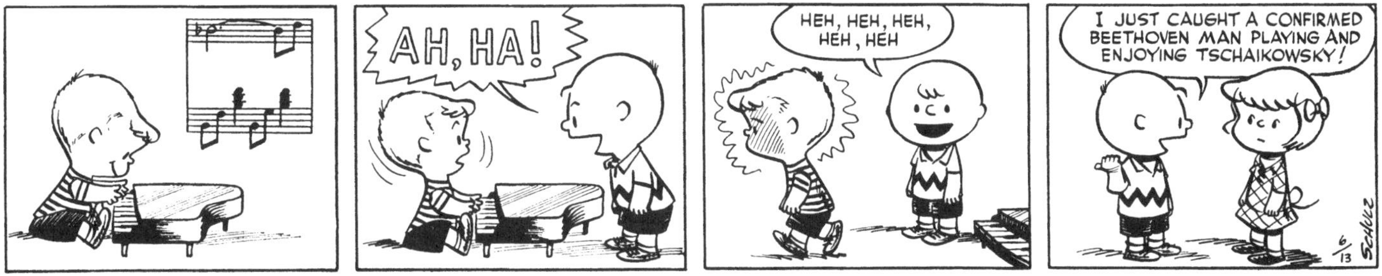
AH, HA!
HEH, HEH, HEH, HEH, HEH
I JUST CAUGHT A CONFIRMED BEETHOVEN MAN PLAYING AND ENJOYING TSCHAIKOWSKY!
6/13
SCHULZ

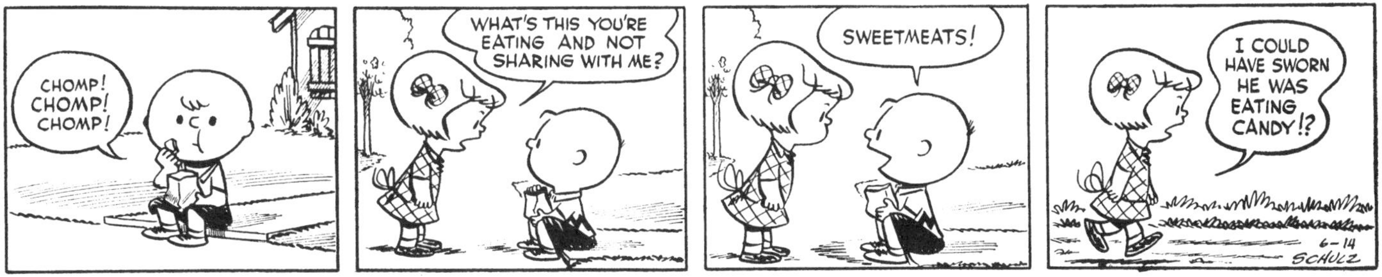
CHOMP! CHOMP! CHOMP!
WHAT'S THIS YOU'RE EATING AND NOT SHARING WITH ME?
SWEETMEATS!
I COULD HAVE SWORN HE WAS EATING CANDY!?
6-14
SCHULZ

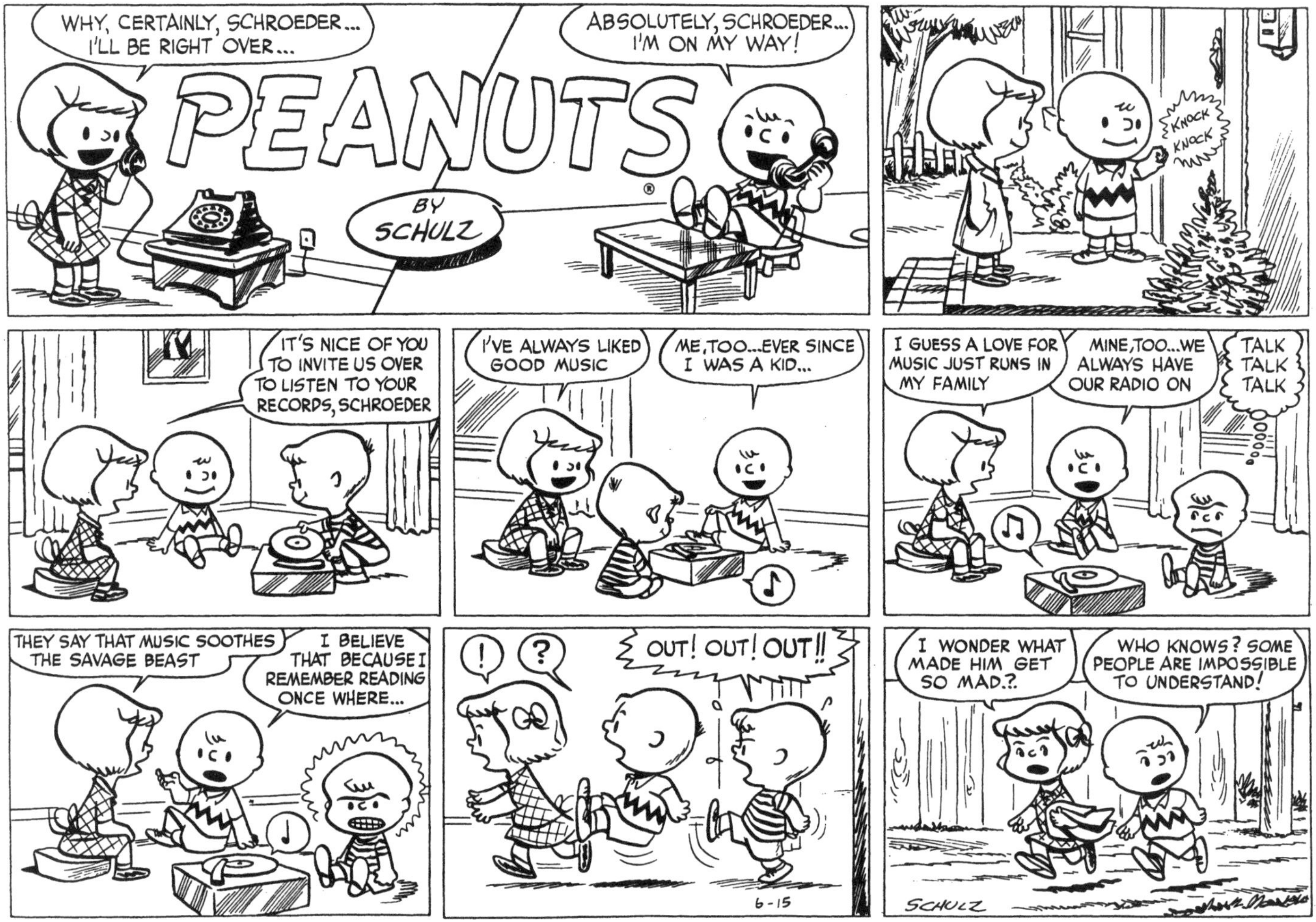
WHY, CERTAINLY, SCHROEDER... I'LL BE RIGHT OVER...
PEANUTS
BY SCHULZ
ABSOLUTELY, SCHROEDER... I'M ON MY WAY!
KNOCK KNOCK
IT'S NICE OF YOU TO INVITE US OVER TO LISTEN TO YOUR RECORDS, SCHROEDER
I'VE ALWAYS LIKED GOOD MUSIC
ME, TOO...EVER SINCE I WAS A KID...
I GUESS A LOVE FOR MUSIC JUST RUNS IN MY FAMILY
MINE, TOO...WE ALWAYS HAVE OUR RADIO ON
TALK TALK TALK
THEY SAY THAT MUSIC SOOTHES THE SAVAGE BEAST
I BELIEVE THAT BECAUSE I REMEMBER READING ONCE WHERE...
!
?
OUT! OUT! OUT!!
6-15
I WONDER WHAT MADE HIM GET SO MAD.?.
WHO KNOWS? SOME PEOPLE ARE IMPOSSIBLE TO UNDERSTAND!
SCHULZ

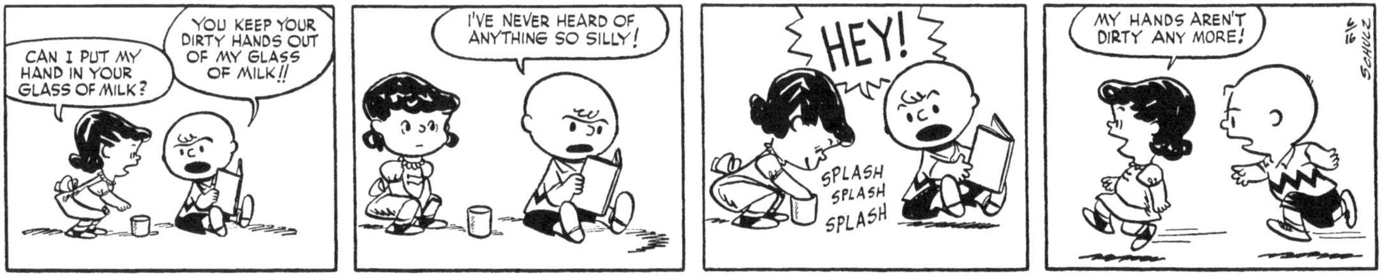
CAN I PUT MY HAND IN YOUR GLASS OF MILK?
YOU KEEP YOUR DIRTY HANDS OUT OF MY GLASS OF MILK!!
I'VE NEVER HEARD OF ANYTHING SO SILLY!
HEY!
SPLASH SPLASH SPLASH
MY HANDS AREN'T DIRTY ANY MORE!
6/16 SCHULZ

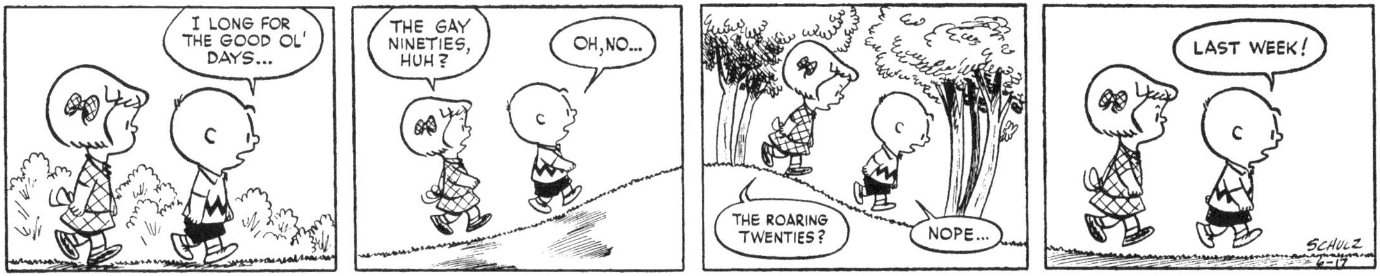
I LONG FOR THE GOOD OL' DAYS...
THE GAY NINETIES, HUH?
OH, NO...
THE ROARING TWENTIES?
NOPE...
LAST WEEK!
SCHULZ 6-17

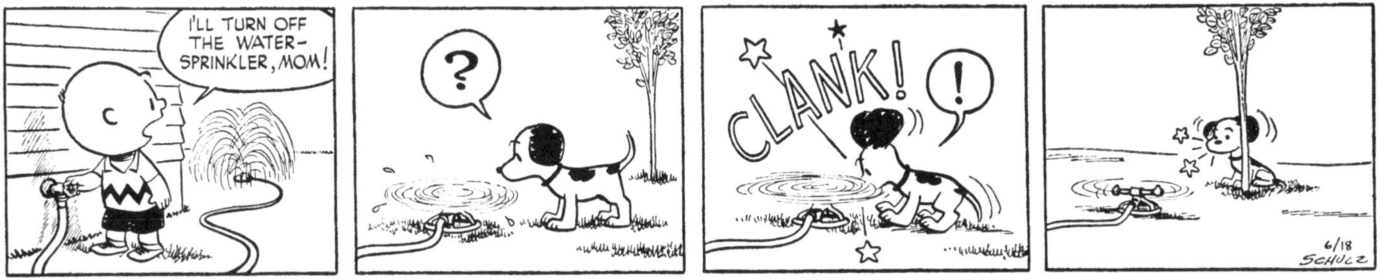
I'LL TURN OFF THE WATER-SPRINKLER, MOM!
?
CLANK!
!
6/18 SCHULZ

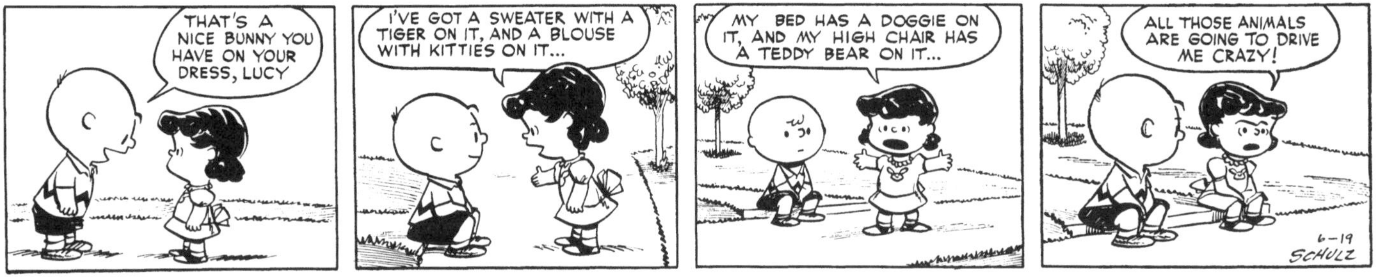
THAT'S A NICE BUNNY YOU HAVE ON YOUR DRESS, LUCY
I'VE GOT A SWEATER WITH A TIGER ON IT, AND A BLOUSE WITH KITTIES ON IT...
MY BED HAS A DOGGIE ON IT, AND MY HIGH CHAIR HAS A TEDDY BEAR ON IT...
ALL THOSE ANIMALS ARE GOING TO DRIVE ME CRAZY!
6-19
SCHULZ

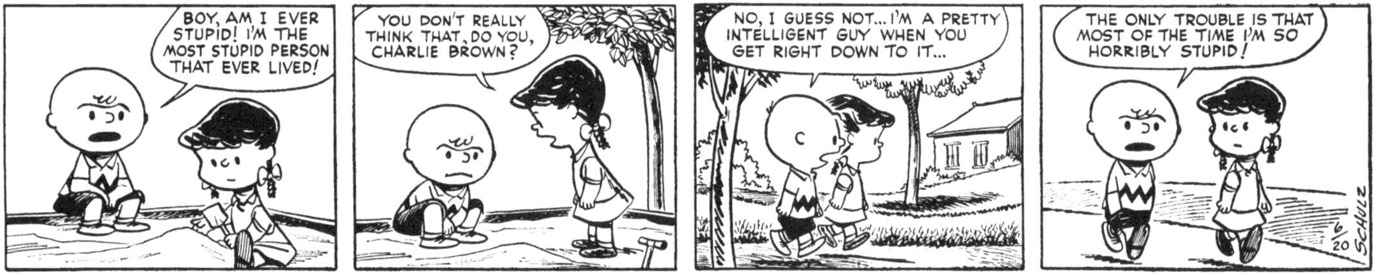
BOY, AM I EVER STUPID! I'M THE MOST STUPID PERSON THAT EVER LIVED!
YOU DON'T REALLY THINK THAT, DO YOU, CHARLIE BROWN?
NO, I GUESS NOT... I'M A PRETTY INTELLIGENT GUY WHEN YOU GET RIGHT DOWN TO IT...
THE ONLY TROUBLE IS THAT MOST OF THE TIME I'M SO HORRIBLY STUPID!
6/20
SCHULZ

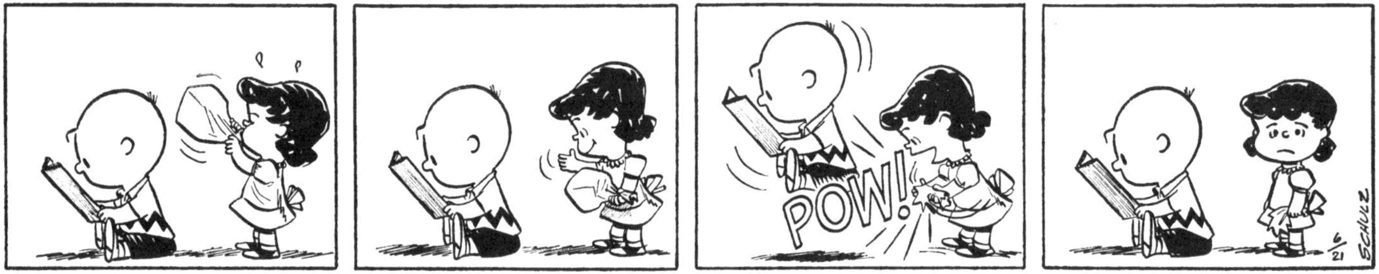
POW!
6/21
SCHULZ

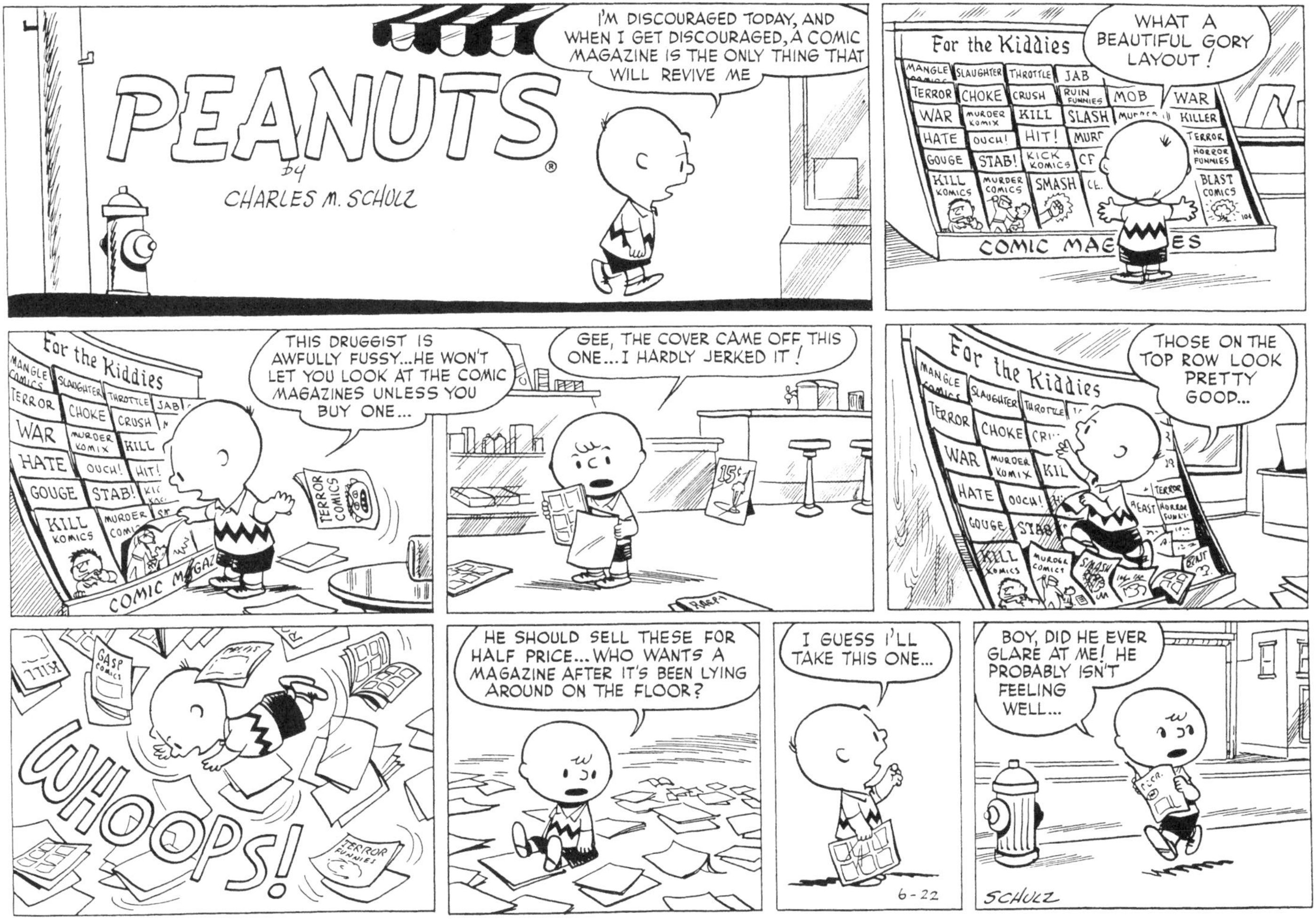
PEANUTS
by CHARLES M. SCHULZ
I'M DISCOURAGED TODAY, AND WHEN I GET DISCOURAGED, A COMIC MAGAZINE IS THE ONLY THING THAT WILL REVIVE ME
For the Kiddies
WHAT A BEAUTIFUL GORY LAYOUT!
COMIC MAG ES
THIS DRUGGIST IS AWFULLY FUSSY...HE WON'T LET YOU LOOK AT THE COMIC MAGAZINES UNLESS YOU BUY ONE...
GEE, THE COVER CAME OFF THIS ONE...I HARDLY JERKED IT!
THOSE ON THE TOP ROW LOOK PRETTY GOOD...
WHOOPS!
HE SHOULD SELL THESE FOR HALF PRICE...WHO WANTS A MAGAZINE AFTER IT'S BEEN LYING AROUND ON THE FLOOR?
I GUESS I'LL TAKE THIS ONE...
6-22
BOY, DID HE EVER GLARE AT ME! HE PROBABLY ISN'T FEELING WELL...
SCHULZ

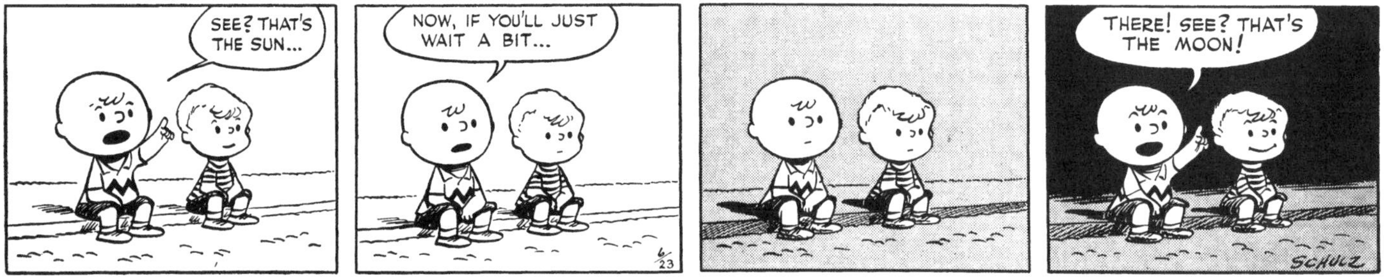
SEE? THAT'S THE SUN...
NOW, IF YOU'LL JUST WAIT A BIT...
6/23
THERE! SEE? THAT'S THE MOON!
SCHULZ

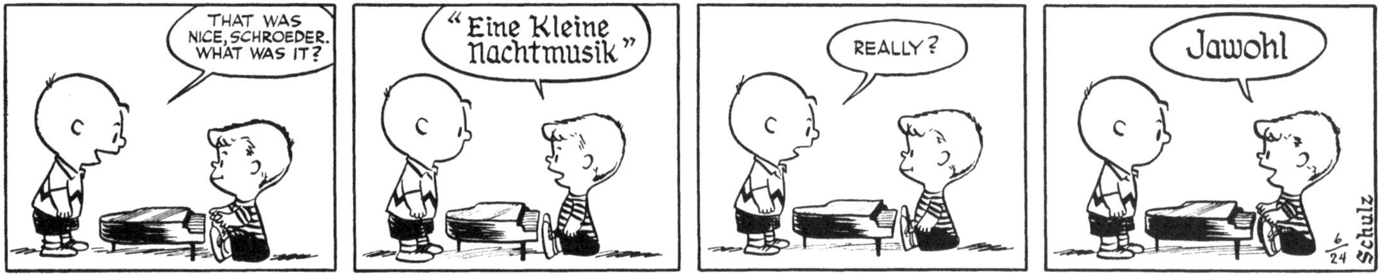
THAT WAS NICE, SCHROEDER. WHAT WAS IT?
"Eine Kleine Nachtmusik"
REALLY?
Jawohl
6/24
Schulz

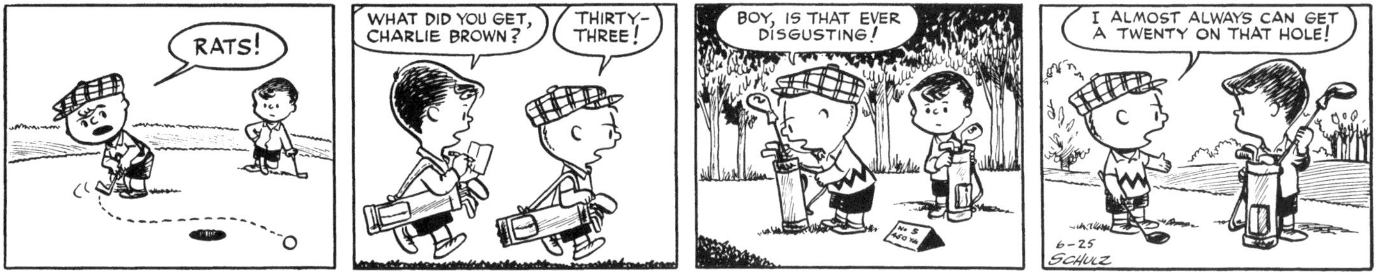
RATS!
WHAT DID YOU GET, CHARLIE BROWN?
THIRTY-THREE!
BOY, IS THAT EVER DISGUSTING!
I ALMOST ALWAYS CAN GET A TWENTY ON THAT HOLE!
6-25
SCHULZ

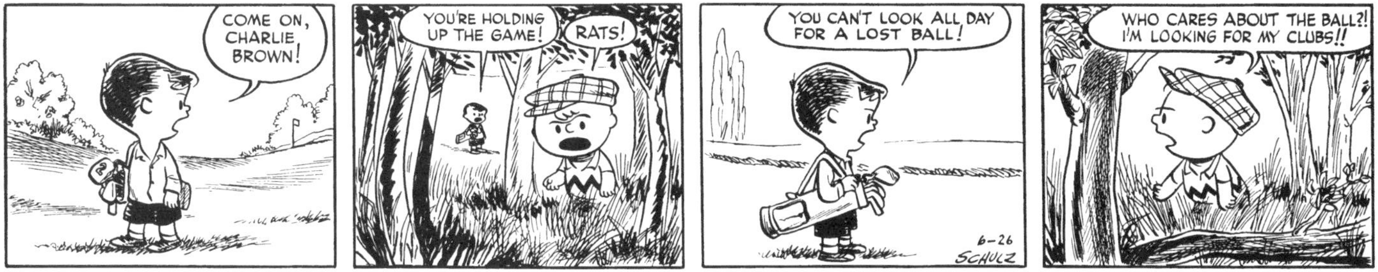
COME ON, CHARLIE BROWN!
YOU'RE HOLDING UP THE GAME!
RATS!
YOU CAN'T LOOK ALL DAY FOR A LOST BALL!
6-26
SCHULZ
WHO CARES ABOUT THE BALL?! I'M LOOKING FOR MY CLUBS!!

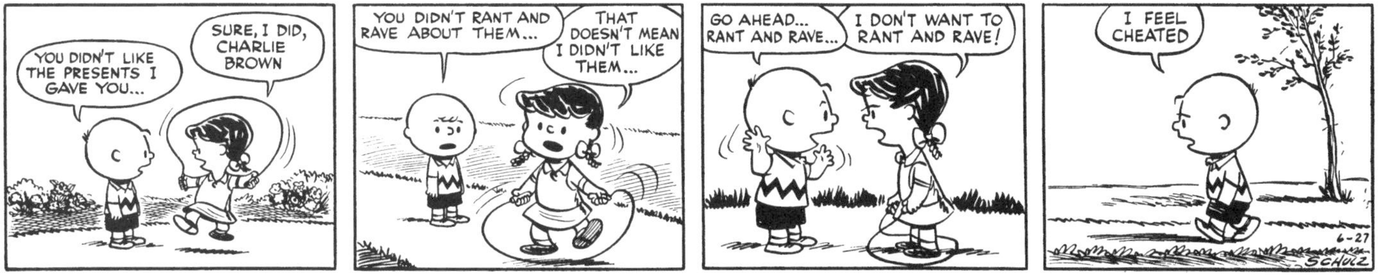
YOU DIDN'T LIKE THE PRESENTS I GAVE YOU...
SURE, I DID, CHARLIE BROWN
YOU DIDN'T RANT AND RAVE ABOUT THEM...
THAT DOESN'T MEAN I DIDN'T LIKE THEM...
GO AHEAD... RANT AND RAVE...
I DON'T WANT TO RANT AND RAVE!
I FEEL CHEATED
6-27
SCHULZ

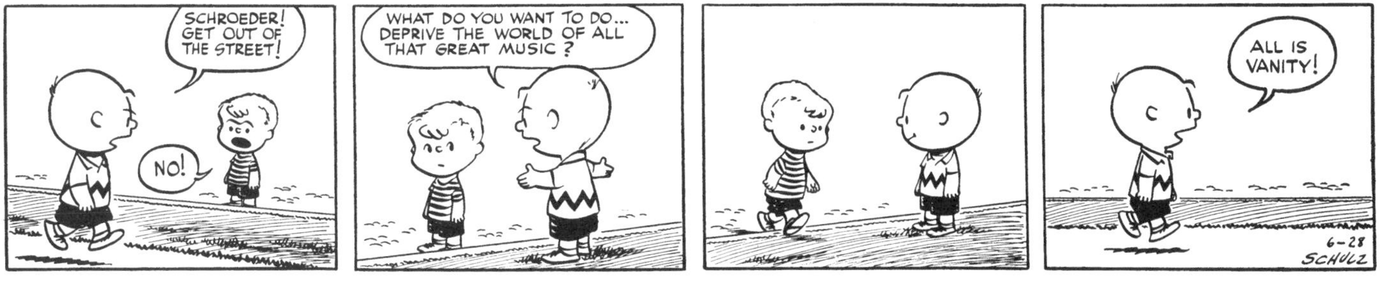
SCHROEDER! GET OUT OF THE STREET!
NO!
WHAT DO YOU WANT TO DO... DEPRIVE THE WORLD OF ALL THAT GREAT MUSIC ?
ALL IS VANITY!
6-28
SCHULZ

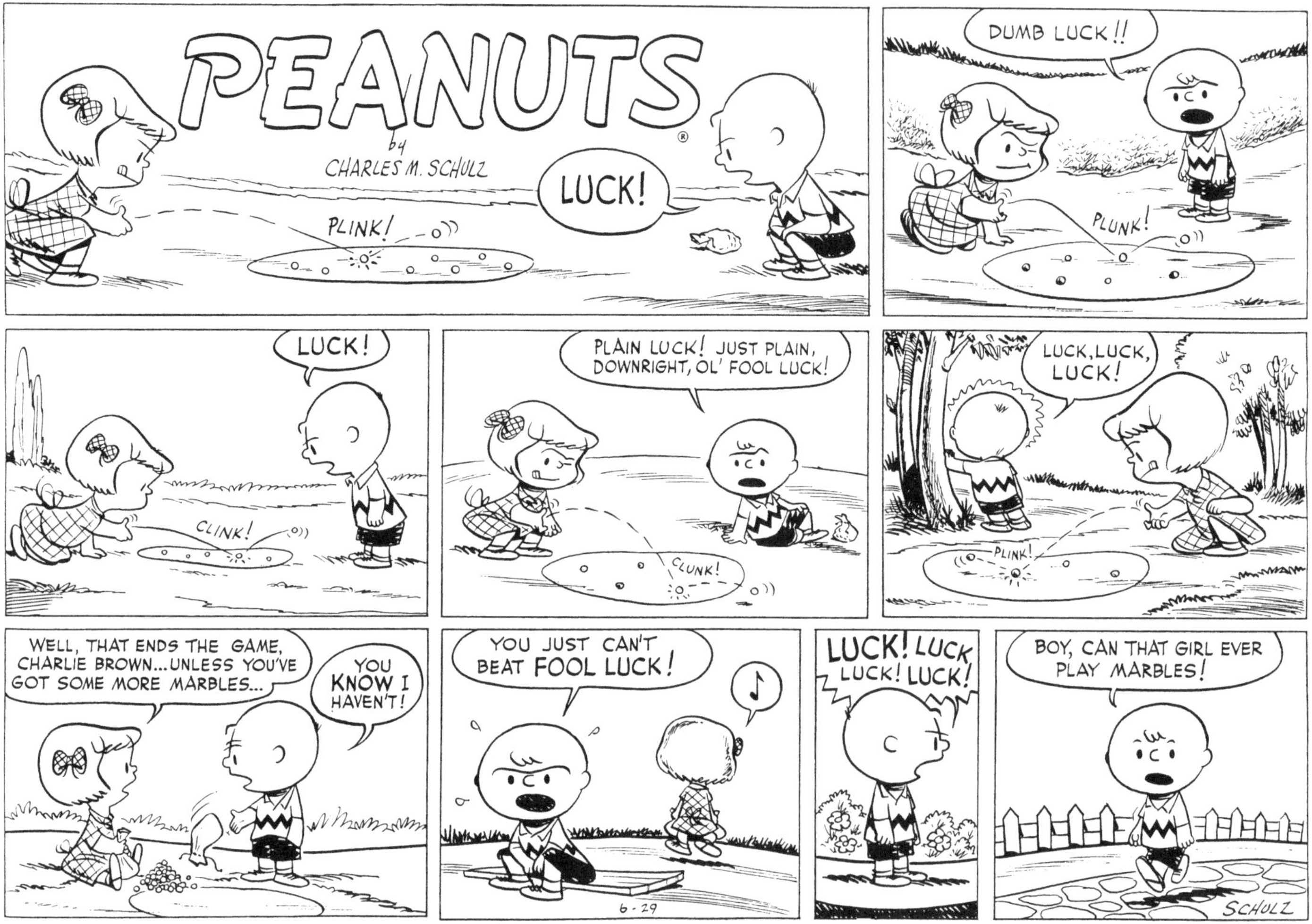
PEANUTS
by
CHARLES M. SCHULZ
LUCK!
PLINK!
DUMB LUCK!!
PLUNK!
LUCK!
CLINK!
PLAIN LUCK! JUST PLAIN, DOWNRIGHT, OL' FOOL LUCK!
CLUNK!
LUCK, LUCK, LUCK!
PLINK!
WELL, THAT ENDS THE GAME, CHARLIE BROWN...UNLESS YOU'VE GOT SOME MORE MARBLES...
YOU KNOW I HAVEN'T!
YOU JUST CAN'T BEAT FOOL LUCK!
♪
6-29
LUCK! LUCK LUCK! LUCK!
BOY, CAN THAT GIRL EVER PLAY MARBLES!
SCHULZ

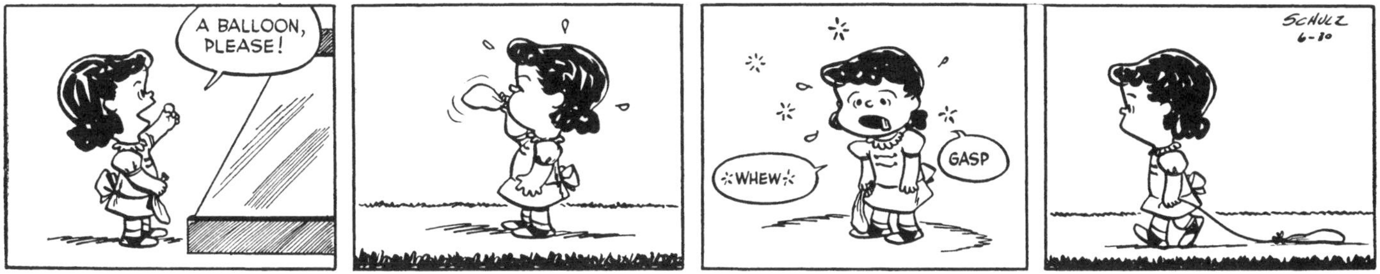
A BALLOON, PLEASE!
WHEW
GASP
SCHULZ 6-30

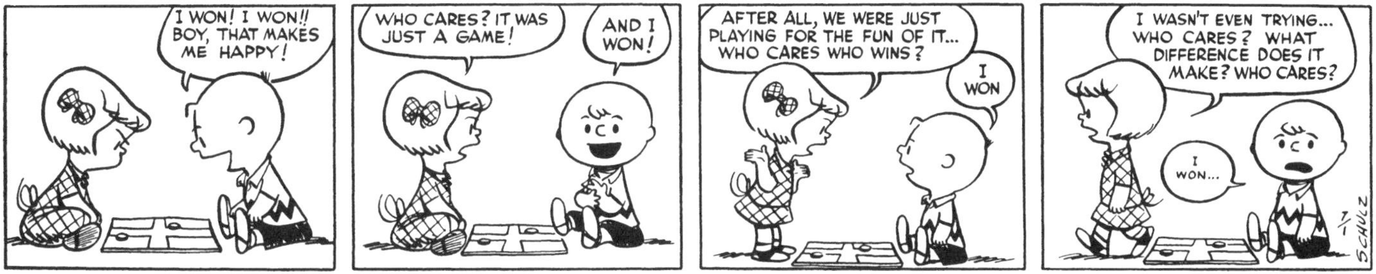
I WON! I WON!! BOY, THAT MAKES ME HAPPY!
WHO CARES? IT WAS JUST A GAME!
AND I WON!
AFTER ALL, WE WERE JUST PLAYING FOR THE FUN OF IT... WHO CARES WHO WINS?
I WON
I WASN'T EVEN TRYING... WHO CARES? WHAT DIFFERENCE DOES IT MAKE? WHO CARES?
I WON...
7-1 SCHULZ

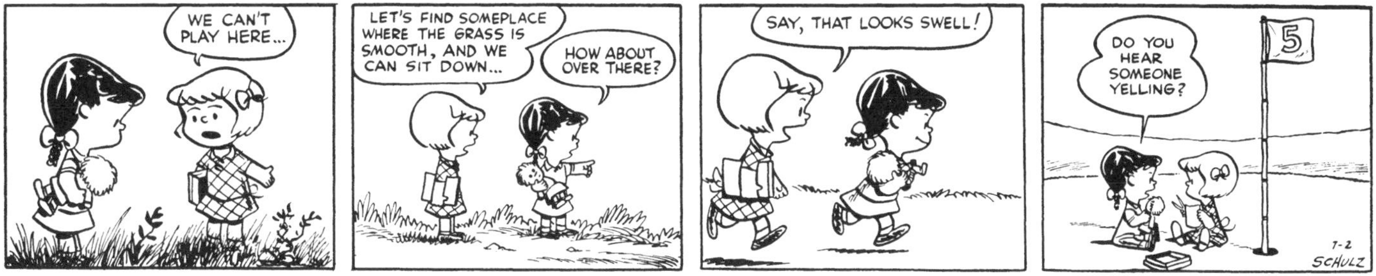
WE CAN'T PLAY HERE...
LET'S FIND SOMEPLACE WHERE THE GRASS IS SMOOTH, AND WE CAN SIT DOWN...
HOW ABOUT OVER THERE?
SAY, THAT LOOKS SWELL!
DO YOU HEAR SOMEONE YELLING?
5
7-2 SCHULZ

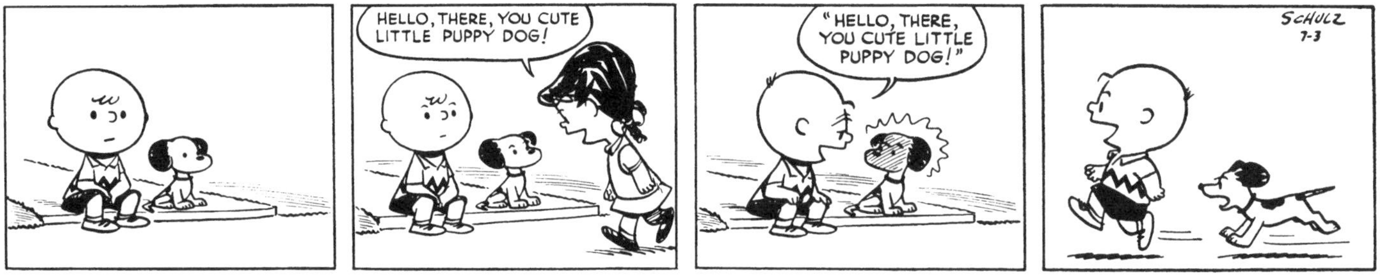
HELLO, THERE, YOU CUTE LITTLE PUPPY DOG!
"HELLO, THERE, YOU CUTE LITTLE PUPPY DOG!"
SCHULZ 7-3

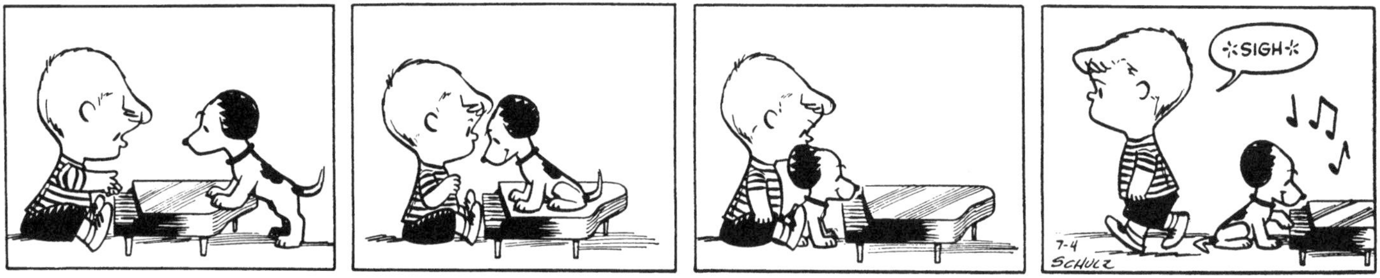
SIGH
7-4 SCHULZ

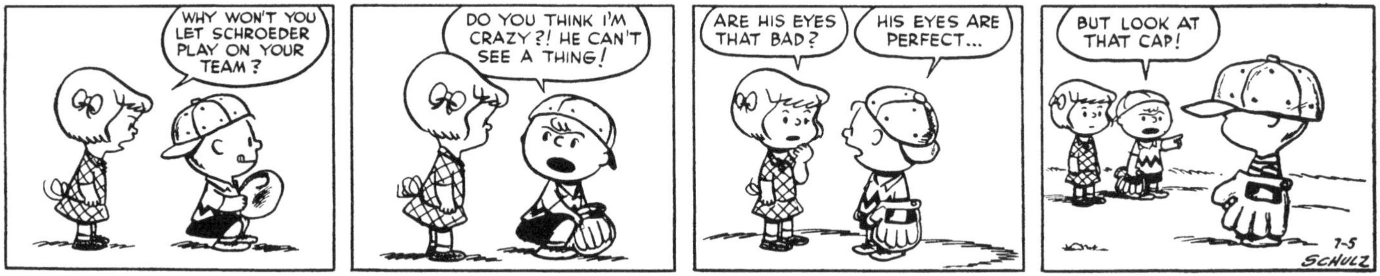
WHY WON'T YOU LET SCHROEDER PLAY ON YOUR TEAM?
DO YOU THINK I'M CRAZY?! HE CAN'T SEE A THING!
ARE HIS EYES THAT BAD?
HIS EYES ARE PERFECT...
BUT LOOK AT THAT CAP!
7-5 SCHULZ

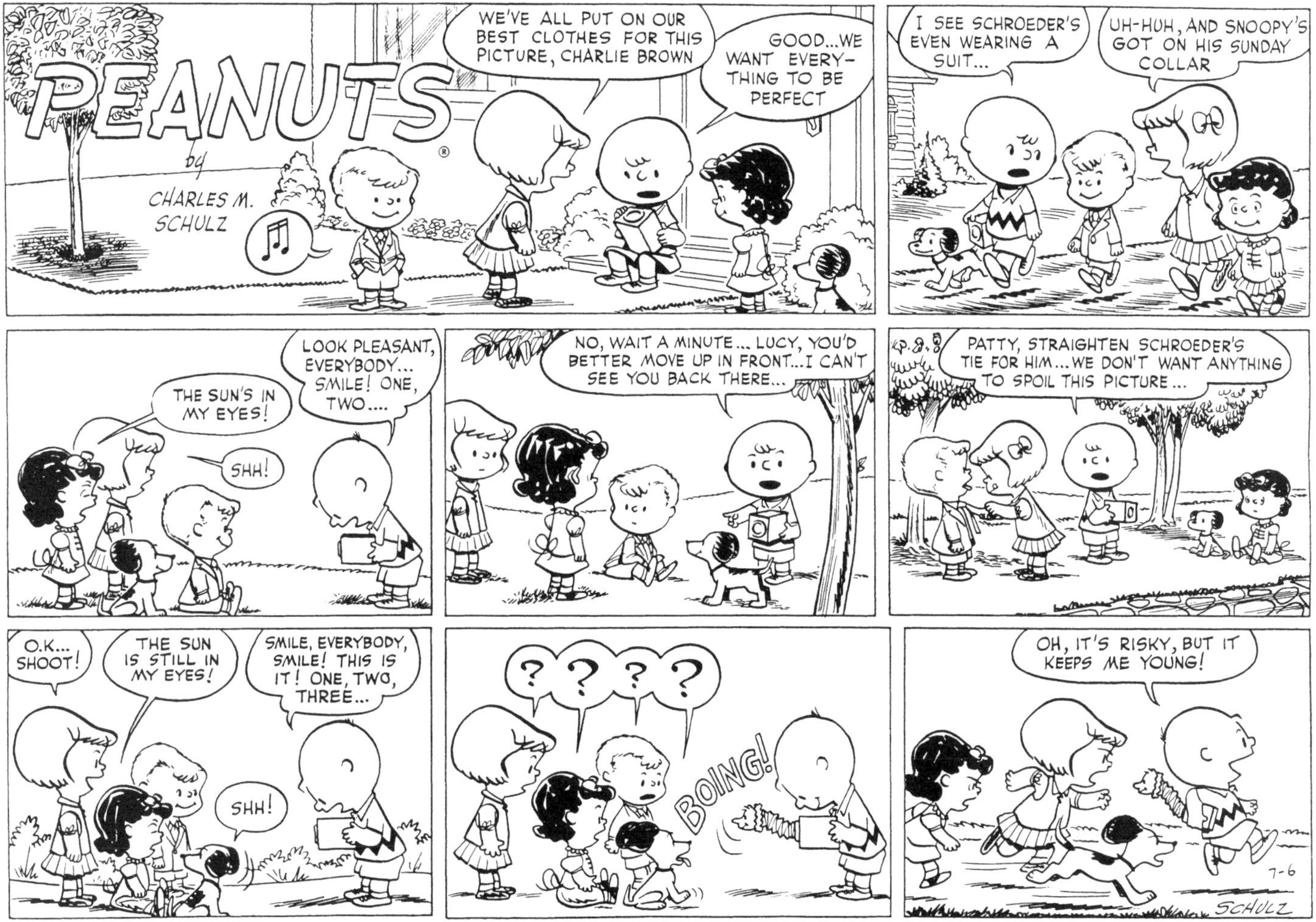
PEANUTS
by CHARLES M. SCHULZ
WE'VE ALL PUT ON OUR BEST CLOTHES FOR THIS PICTURE, CHARLIE BROWN
GOOD...WE WANT EVERYTHING TO BE PERFECT
I SEE SCHROEDER'S EVEN WEARING A SUIT...
UH-HUH, AND SNOOPY'S GOT ON HIS SUNDAY COLLAR
LOOK PLEASANT, EVERYBODY... SMILE! ONE, TWO....
THE SUN'S IN MY EYES!
SHH!
NO, WAIT A MINUTE... LUCY, YOU'D BETTER MOVE UP IN FRONT...I CAN'T SEE YOU BACK THERE...
PATTY, STRAIGHTEN SCHROEDER'S TIE FOR HIM...WE DON'T WANT ANYTHING TO SPOIL THIS PICTURE...
O.K... SHOOT!
THE SUN IS STILL IN MY EYES!
SMILE, EVERYBODY, SMILE! THIS IS IT! ONE, TWO, THREE...
SHH!
? ? ? ?
BOING!
OH, IT'S RISKY, BUT IT KEEPS ME YOUNG!
7-6
SCHULZ

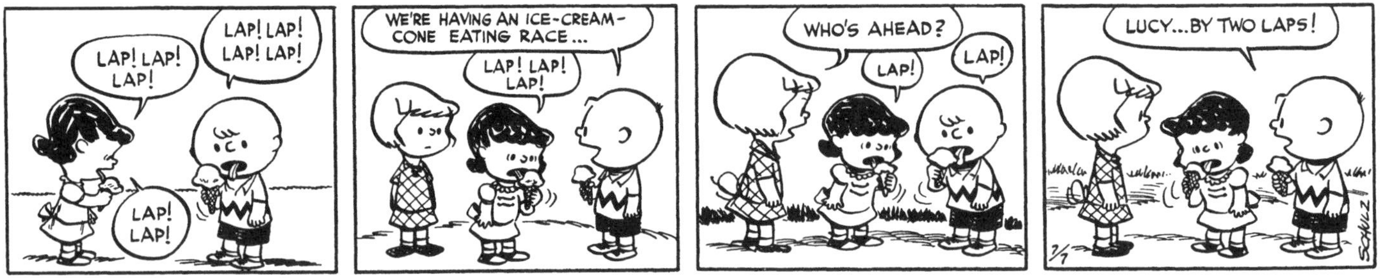
LAP! LAP! LAP!
LAP! LAP! LAP! LAP!
LAP! LAP!
WE'RE HAVING AN ICE-CREAM-CONE EATING RACE...
LAP! LAP! LAP!
WHO'S AHEAD?
LAP!
LAP!
LUCY...BY TWO LAPS!
7/7
SCHULZ

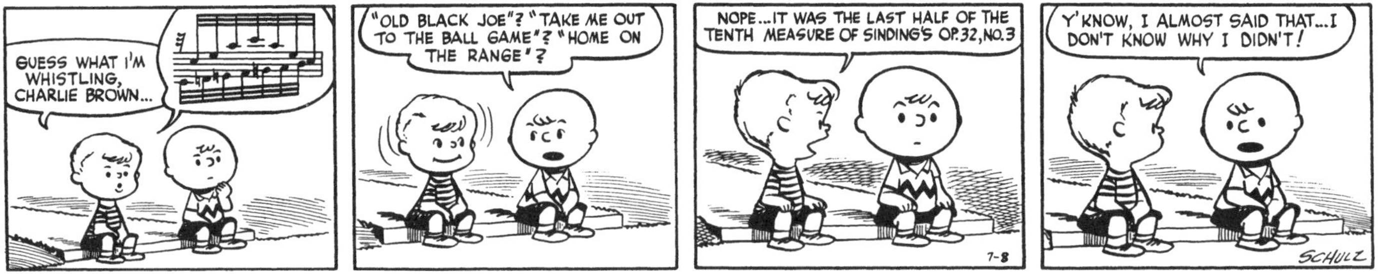
GUESS WHAT I'M WHISTLING, CHARLIE BROWN...
"OLD BLACK JOE"? "TAKE ME OUT TO THE BALL GAME"? "HOME ON THE RANGE"?
NOPE...IT WAS THE LAST HALF OF THE TENTH MEASURE OF SINDING'S OP.32, NO.3
7-8
Y'KNOW, I ALMOST SAID THAT...I DON'T KNOW WHY I DIDN'T!
SCHULZ

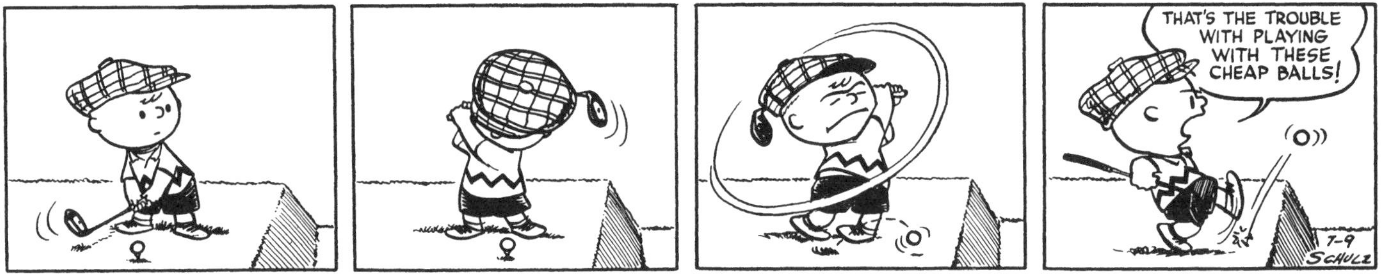
THAT'S THE TROUBLE WITH PLAYING WITH THESE CHEAP BALLS!
7-9
SCHULZ

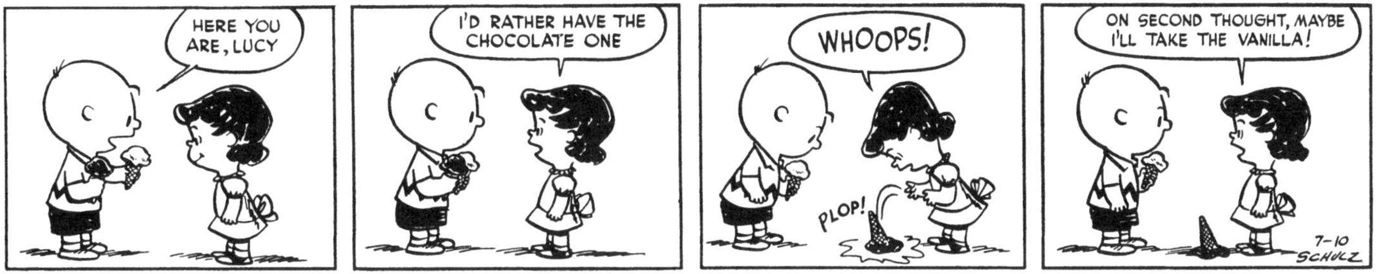
HERE YOU ARE, LUCY
I'D RATHER HAVE THE CHOCOLATE ONE
WHOOPS!
PLOP!
ON SECOND THOUGHT, MAYBE I'LL TAKE THE VANILLA!
7-10
SCHULZ

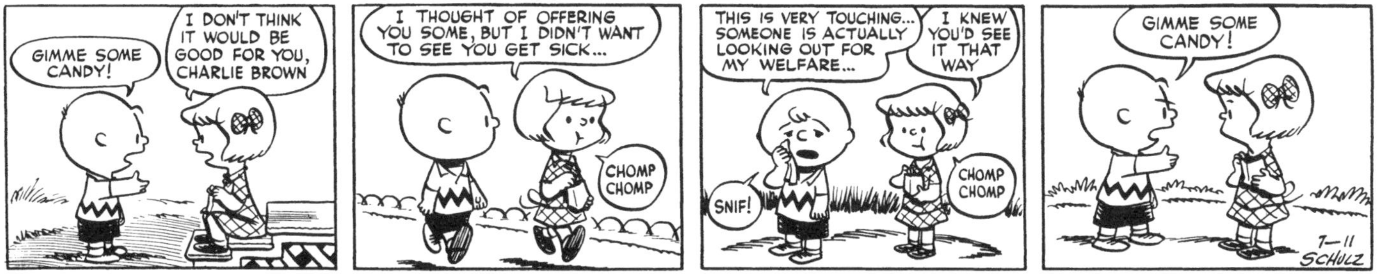
GIMME SOME CANDY!
I DON'T THINK IT WOULD BE GOOD FOR YOU, CHARLIE BROWN
I THOUGHT OF OFFERING YOU SOME, BUT I DIDN'T WANT TO SEE YOU GET SICK...
CHOMP CHOMP
THIS IS VERY TOUCHING... SOMEONE IS ACTUALLY LOOKING OUT FOR MY WELFARE...
I KNEW YOU'D SEE IT THAT WAY
SNIF!
CHOMP CHOMP
GIMME SOME CANDY!
7-11
SCHULZ

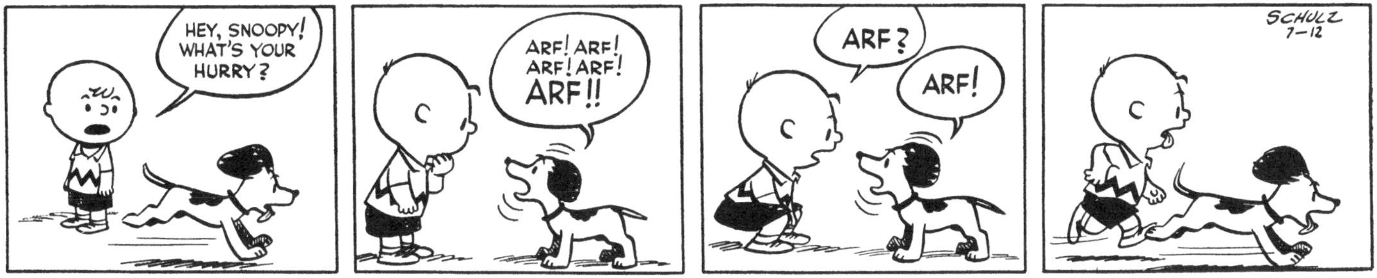
HEY, SNOOPY! WHAT'S YOUR HURRY?
ARF! ARF! ARF! ARF! ARF!!
ARF?
ARF!
SCHULZ
7-12

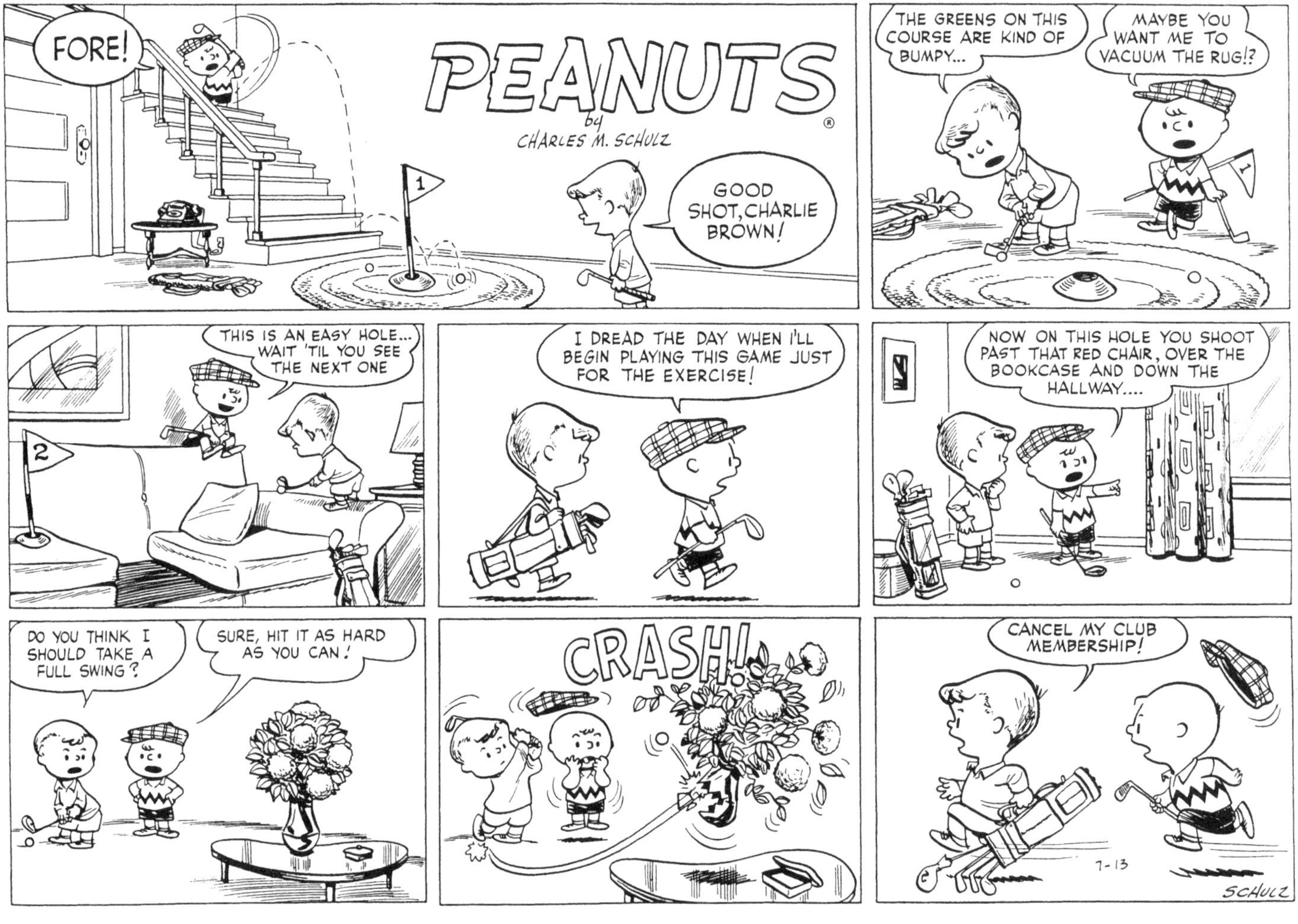
FORE!
PEANUTS
by CHARLES M. SCHULZ
GOOD SHOT, CHARLIE BROWN!
THE GREENS ON THIS COURSE ARE KIND OF BUMPY...
MAYBE YOU WANT ME TO VACUUM THE RUG!?
THIS IS AN EASY HOLE... WAIT 'TIL YOU SEE THE NEXT ONE
I DREAD THE DAY WHEN I'LL BEGIN PLAYING THIS GAME JUST FOR THE EXERCISE!
NOW ON THIS HOLE YOU SHOOT PAST THAT RED CHAIR, OVER THE BOOKCASE AND DOWN THE HALLWAY....
DO YOU THINK I SHOULD TAKE A FULL SWING?
SURE, HIT IT AS HARD AS YOU CAN!
CRASH!
CANCEL MY CLUB MEMBERSHIP!
7-13
SCHULZ

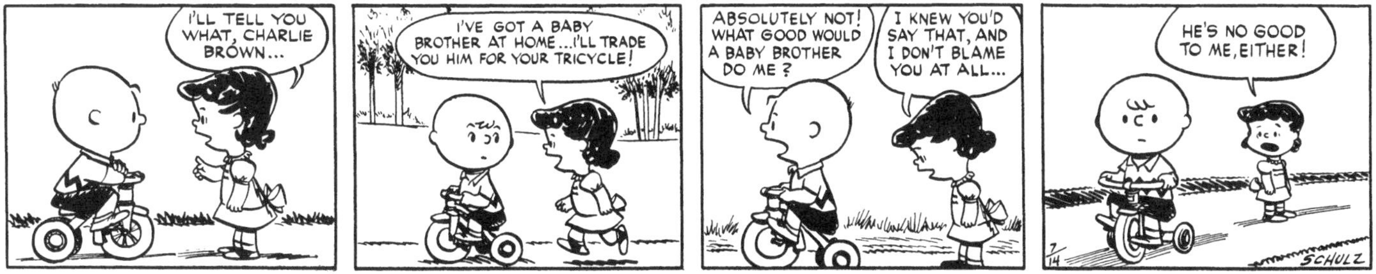
I'LL TELL YOU WHAT, CHARLIE BROWN...
I'VE GOT A BABY BROTHER AT HOME...I'LL TRADE YOU HIM FOR YOUR TRICYCLE!
ABSOLUTELY NOT! WHAT GOOD WOULD A BABY BROTHER DO ME?
I KNEW YOU'D SAY THAT, AND I DON'T BLAME YOU AT ALL...
HE'S NO GOOD TO ME, EITHER!
7/14
SCHULZ

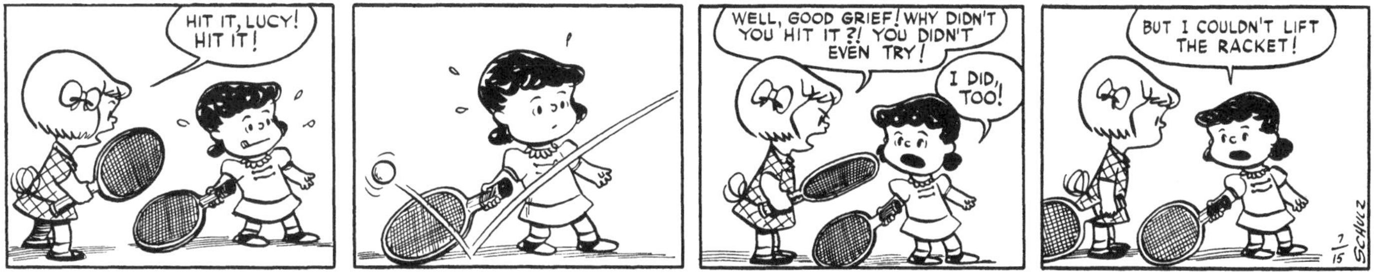
HIT IT, LUCY! HIT IT!
WELL, GOOD GRIEF! WHY DIDN'T YOU HIT IT?! YOU DIDN'T EVEN TRY!
I DID, TOO!
BUT I COULDN'T LIFT THE RACKET!
7/15
SCHULZ

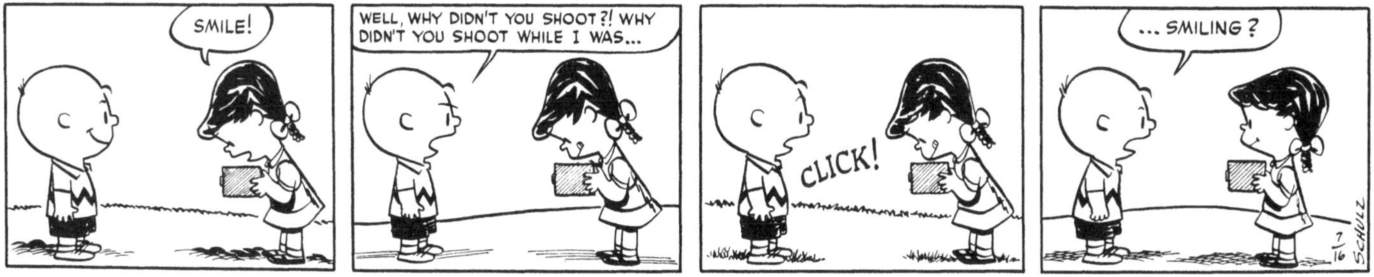
SMILE!
WELL, WHY DIDN'T YOU SHOOT?! WHY DIDN'T YOU SHOOT WHILE I WAS...
CLICK!
...SMILING?
7/16
SCHULZ

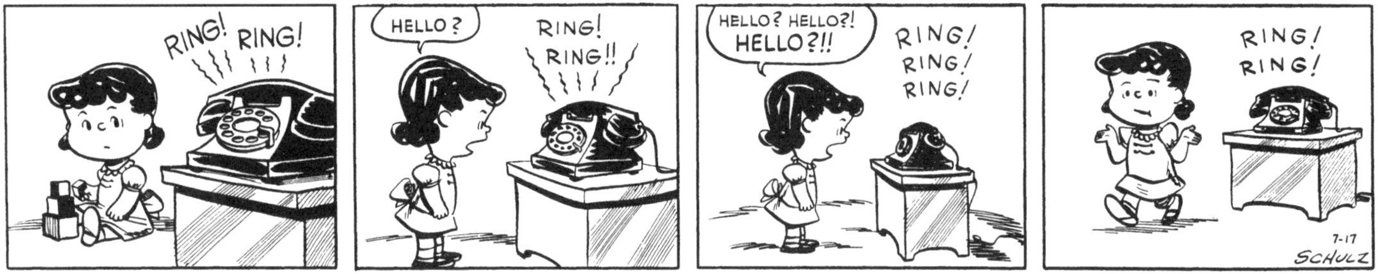
RING! RING!
HELLO?
RING! RING!!
HELLO? HELLO?! HELLO?!!
RING! RING! RING!
RING! RING!
7-17
SCHULZ

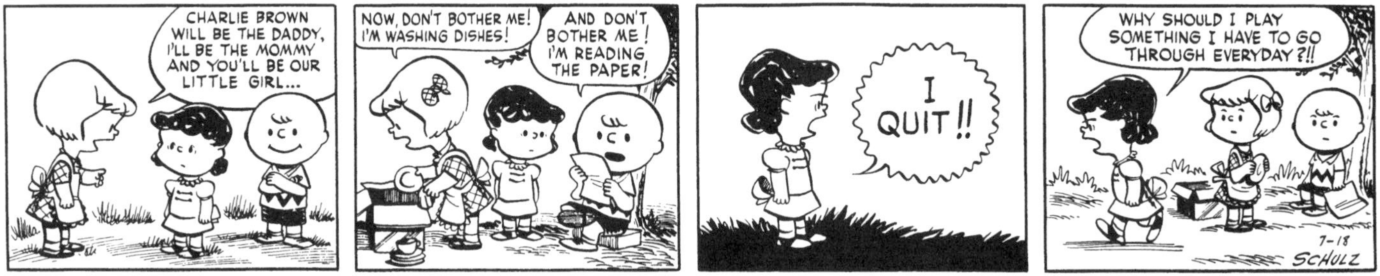
CHARLIE BROWN WILL BE THE DADDY, I'LL BE THE MOMMY AND YOU'LL BE OUR LITTLE GIRL...
NOW, DON'T BOTHER ME! I'M WASHING DISHES!
AND DON'T BOTHER ME! I'M READING THE PAPER!
I QUIT!!
WHY SHOULD I PLAY SOMETHING I HAVE TO GO THROUGH EVERYDAY?!!
7-18
SCHULZ

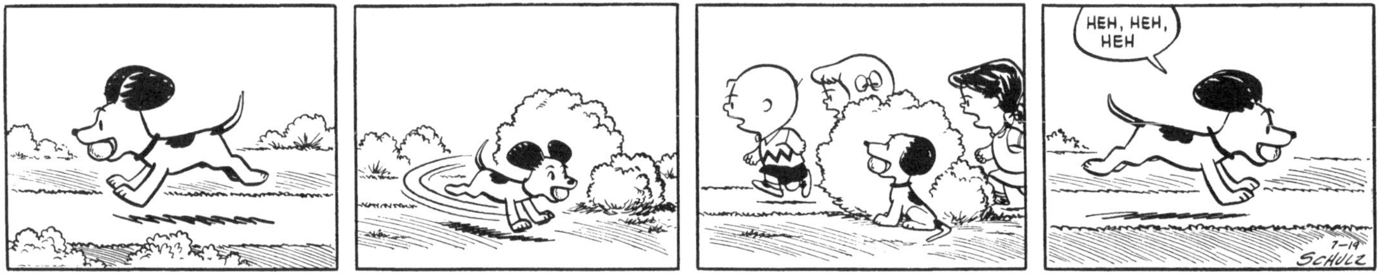
HEH, HEH, HEH
7-19
SCHULZ

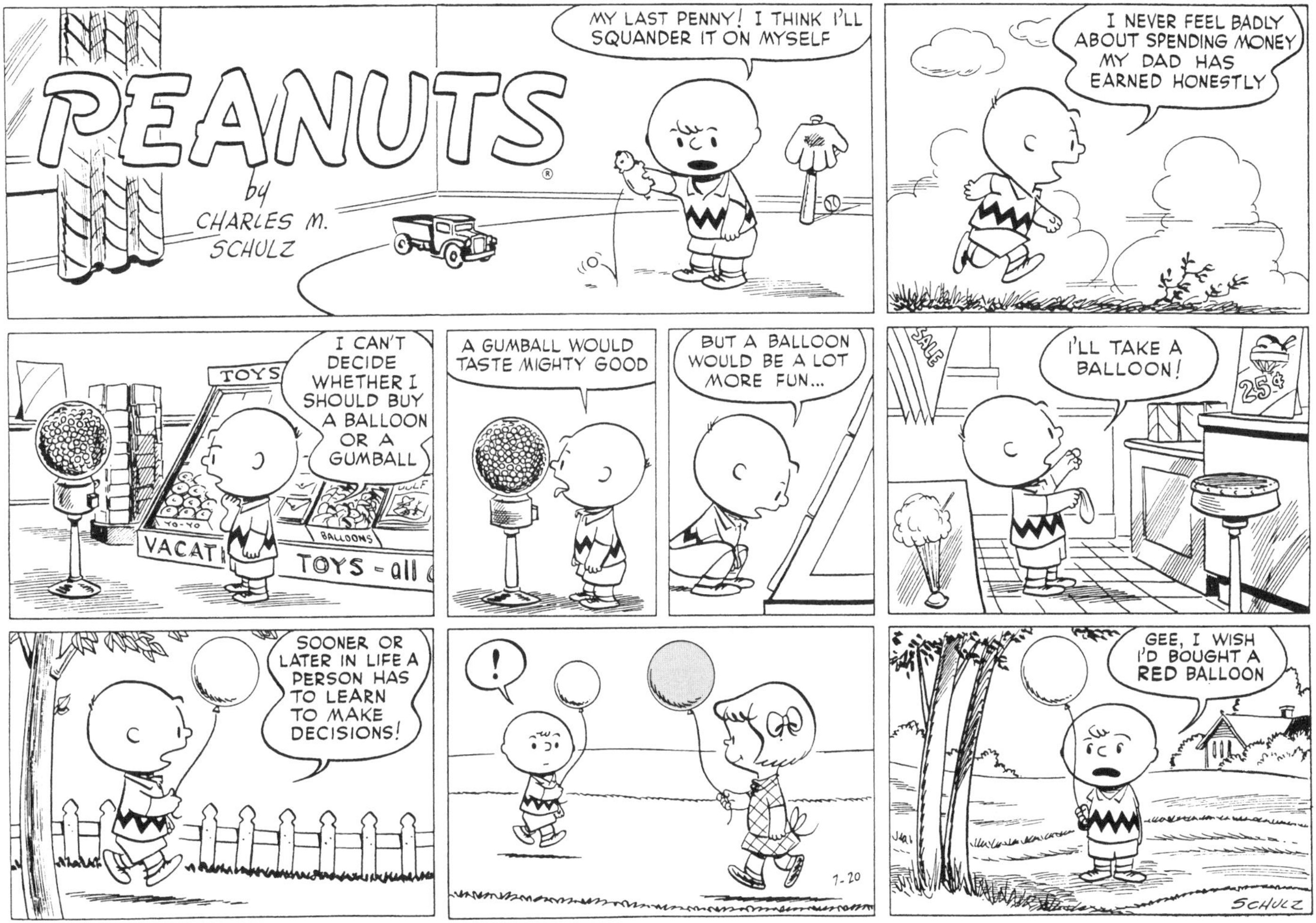

PEANUTS
by CHARLES M. SCHULZ
MY LAST PENNY! I THINK I'LL SQUANDER IT ON MYSELF
I NEVER FEEL BADLY ABOUT SPENDING MONEY MY DAD HAS EARNED HONESTLY
I CAN'T DECIDE WHETHER I SHOULD BUY A BALLOON OR A GUMBALL
TOYS
YO-YO
BALLOONS
VACAT
TOYS - all
A GUMBALL WOULD TASTE MIGHTY GOOD
BUT A BALLOON WOULD BE A LOT MORE FUN...
SALE
I'LL TAKE A BALLOON!
25¢
SOONER OR LATER IN LIFE A PERSON HAS TO LEARN TO MAKE DECISIONS!
!
7-20
GEE, I WISH I'D BOUGHT A RED BALLOON
SCHULZ

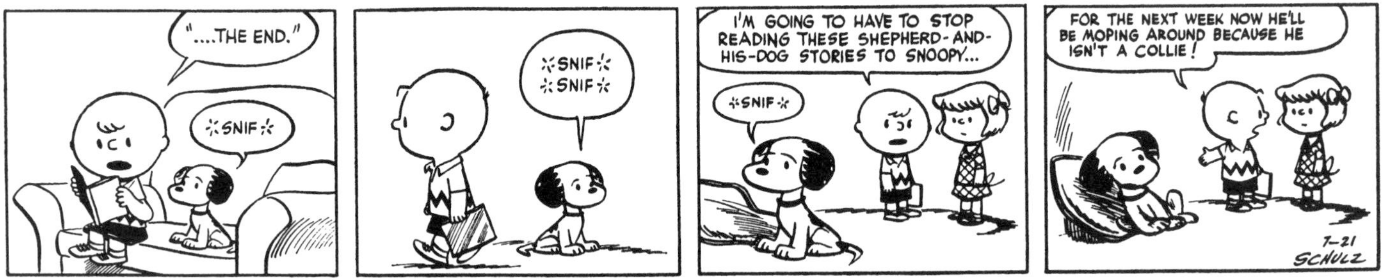
"....THE END."
SNIF
SNIF
SNIF
I'M GOING TO HAVE TO STOP READING THESE SHEPHERD-AND-HIS-DOG STORIES TO SNOOPY...
SNIF
FOR THE NEXT WEEK NOW HE'LL BE MOPING AROUND BECAUSE HE ISN'T A COLLIE!
7-21
SCHULZ

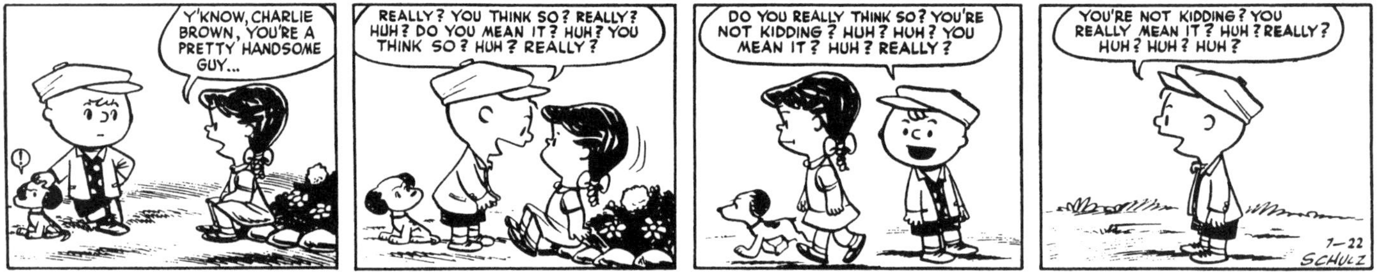
Y'KNOW, CHARLIE BROWN, YOU'RE A PRETTY HANDSOME GUY...
!
REALLY? YOU THINK SO? REALLY? HUH? DO YOU MEAN IT? HUH? YOU THINK SO? HUH? REALLY?
DO YOU REALLY THINK SO? YOU'RE NOT KIDDING? HUH? HUH? YOU MEAN IT? HUH? REALLY?
YOU'RE NOT KIDDING? YOU REALLY MEAN IT? HUH? REALLY? HUH? HUH? HUH?
7-22
SCHULZ

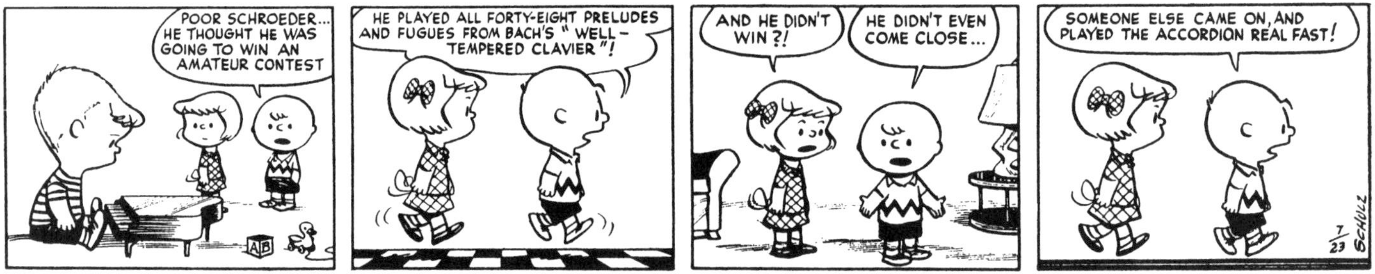
POOR SCHROEDER... HE THOUGHT HE WAS GOING TO WIN AN AMATEUR CONTEST
AB
HE PLAYED ALL FORTY-EIGHT PRELUDES AND FUGUES FROM BACH'S "WELL-TEMPERED CLAVIER"!
AND HE DIDN'T WIN?!
HE DIDN'T EVEN COME CLOSE...
SOMEONE ELSE CAME ON, AND PLAYED THE ACCORDION REAL FAST!
7/23
SCHULZ

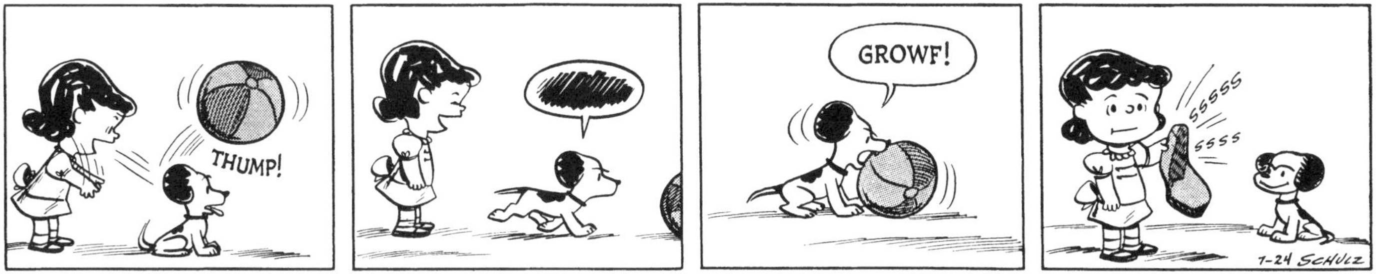
THUMP!
GROWF!
SSSSS
SSSS
7-24 SCHULZ

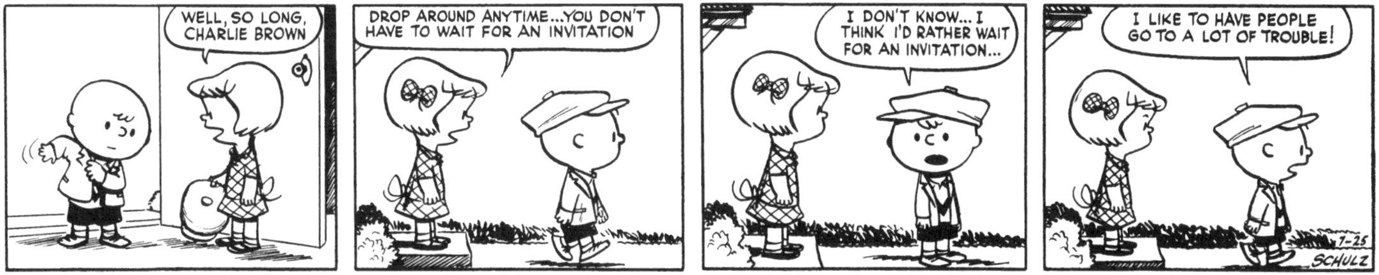
WELL, SO LONG, CHARLIE BROWN
DROP AROUND ANYTIME...YOU DON'T HAVE TO WAIT FOR AN INVITATION
I DON'T KNOW... I THINK I'D RATHER WAIT FOR AN INVITATION...
I LIKE TO HAVE PEOPLE GO TO A LOT OF TROUBLE!
7-25 SCHULZ

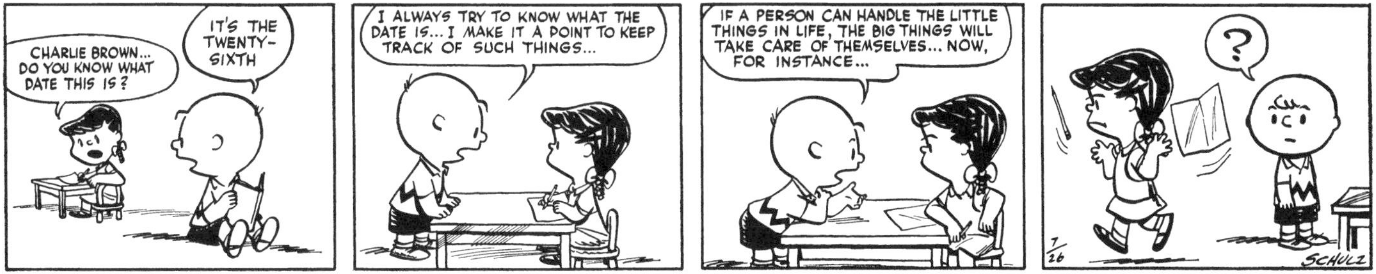
CHARLIE BROWN... DO YOU KNOW WHAT DATE THIS IS?
IT'S THE TWENTY-SIXTH
I ALWAYS TRY TO KNOW WHAT THE DATE IS... I MAKE IT A POINT TO KEEP TRACK OF SUCH THINGS...
IF A PERSON CAN HANDLE THE LITTLE THINGS IN LIFE, THE BIG THINGS WILL TAKE CARE OF THEMSELVES... NOW, FOR INSTANCE...
?
7/26
SCHULZ

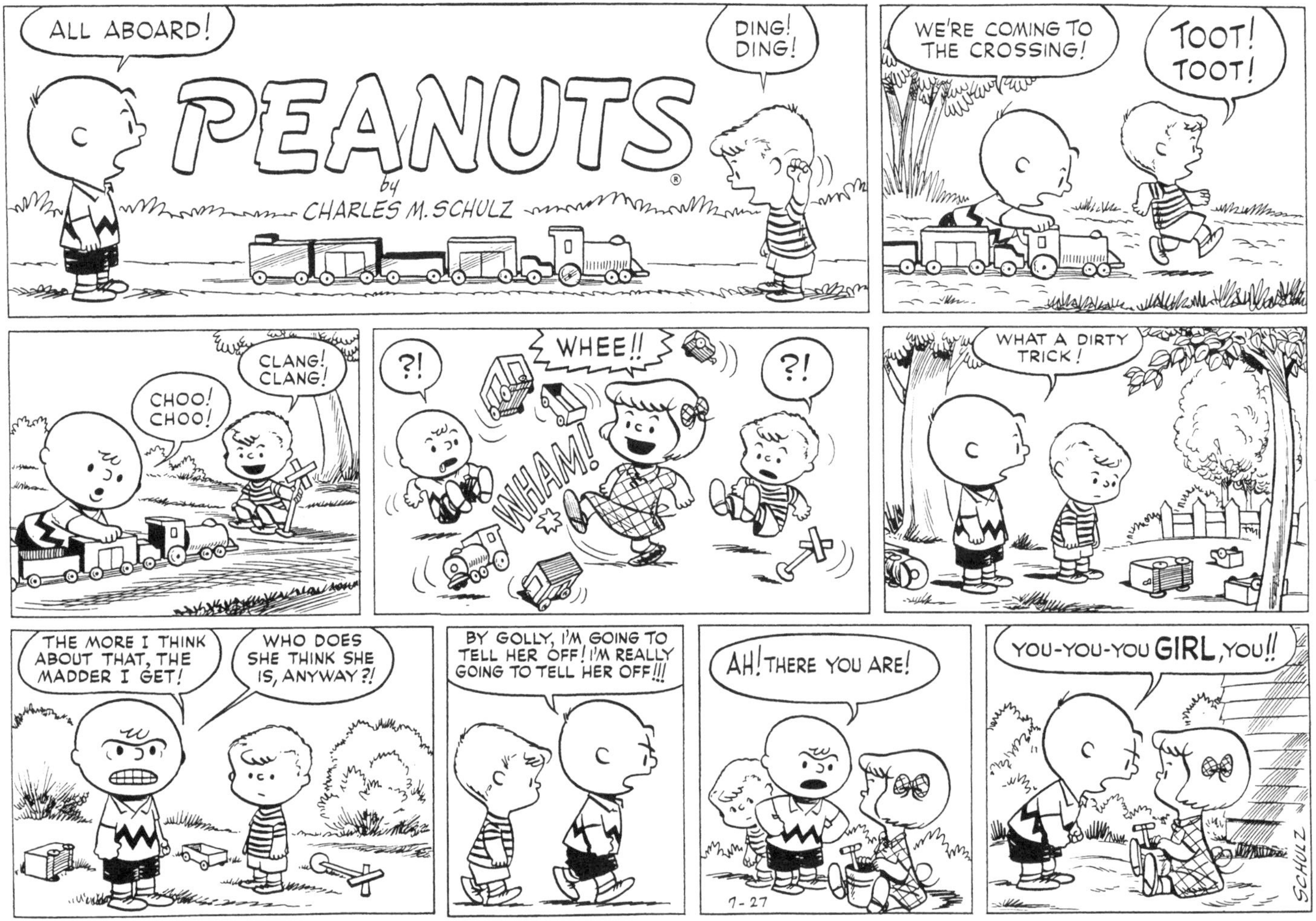
ALL ABOARD!
PEANUTS
by CHARLES M. SCHULZ
DING! DING!
WE'RE COMING TO THE CROSSING!
TOOT! TOOT!
CHOO! CHOO!
CLANG! CLANG!
?!
WHEE!!
?!
WHAM!
WHAT A DIRTY TRICK!
THE MORE I THINK ABOUT THAT, THE MADDER I GET!
WHO DOES SHE THINK SHE IS, ANYWAY?!
BY GOLLY, I'M GOING TO TELL HER OFF! I'M REALLY GOING TO TELL HER OFF!!!
AH! THERE YOU ARE!
7-27
YOU-YOU-YOU GIRL, YOU!!
SCHULZ

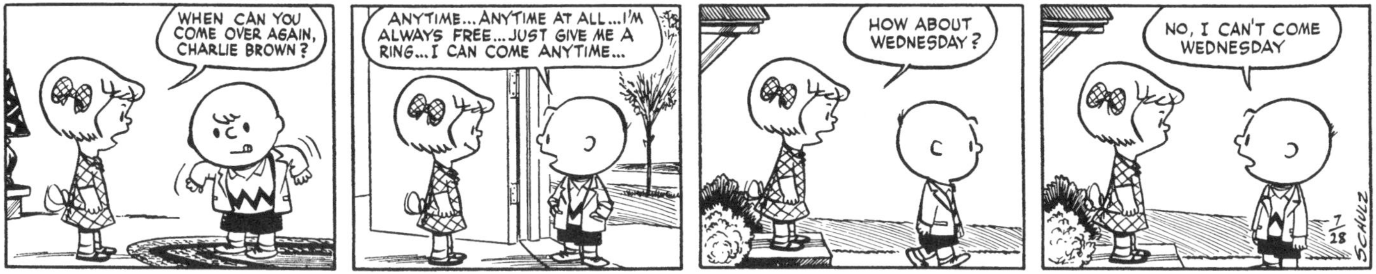

WHEN CAN YOU COME OVER AGAIN, CHARLIE BROWN?
ANYTIME... ANYTIME AT ALL... I'M ALWAYS FREE... JUST GIVE ME A RING... I CAN COME ANYTIME...
HOW ABOUT WEDNESDAY?
NO, I CAN'T COME WEDNESDAY
7/28
SCHULZ

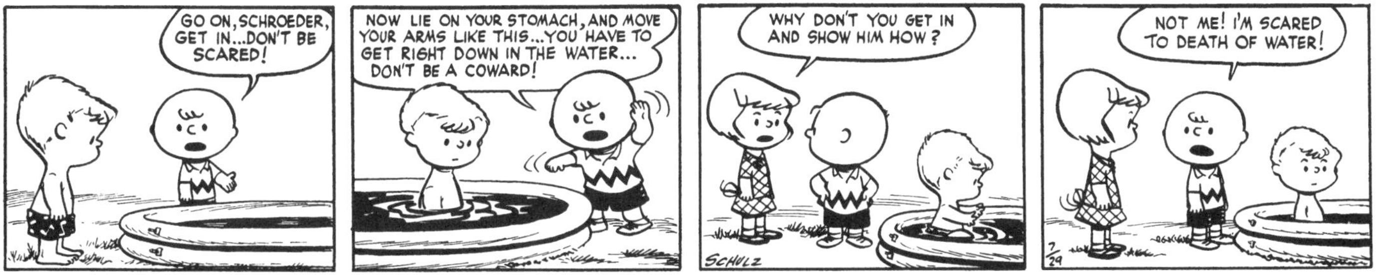

GO ON, SCHROEDER, GET IN... DON'T BE SCARED!
NOW LIE ON YOUR STOMACH, AND MOVE YOUR ARMS LIKE THIS... YOU HAVE TO GET RIGHT DOWN IN THE WATER... DON'T BE A COWARD!
WHY DON'T YOU GET IN AND SHOW HIM HOW?
SCHULZ
NOT ME! I'M SCARED TO DEATH OF WATER!
7/29

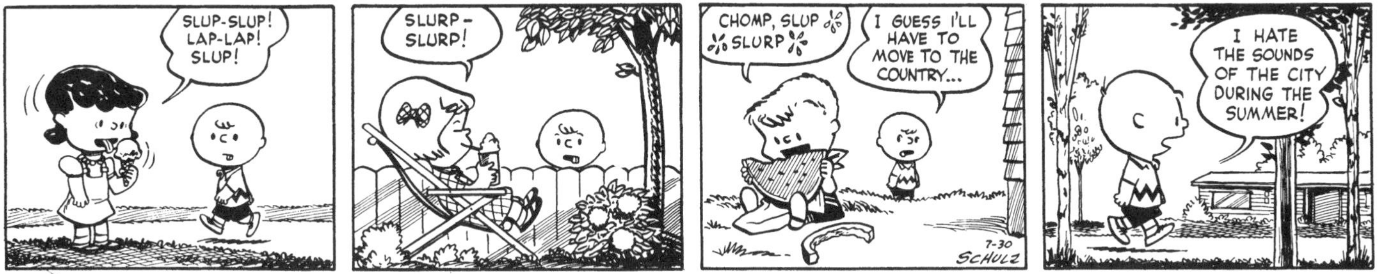

SLUP-SLUP! LAP-LAP! SLUP!
SLURP-SLURP!
CHOMP, SLUP SLURP
I GUESS I'LL HAVE TO MOVE TO THE COUNTRY...
7-30
SCHULZ
I HATE THE SOUNDS OF THE CITY DURING THE SUMMER!

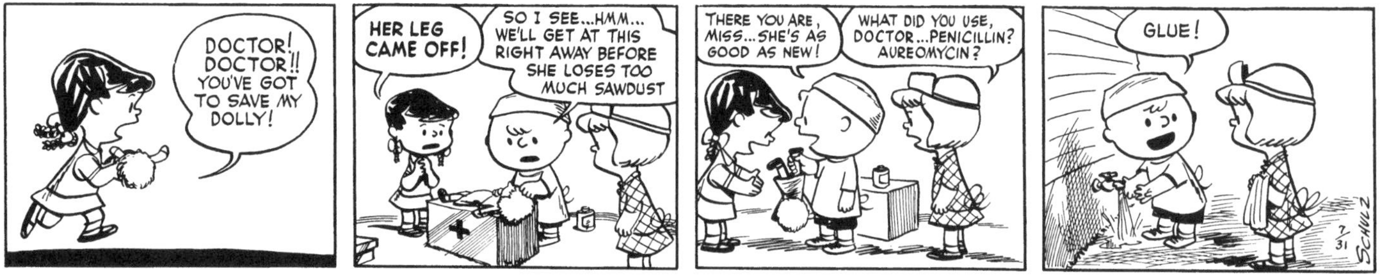
DOCTOR! DOCTOR!! YOU'VE GOT TO SAVE MY DOLLY!
HER LEG CAME OFF!
SO I SEE...HMM... WE'LL GET AT THIS RIGHT AWAY BEFORE SHE LOSES TOO MUCH SAWDUST
THERE YOU ARE, MISS...SHE'S AS GOOD AS NEW!
WHAT DID YOU USE, DOCTOR...PENICILLIN? AUREOMYCIN?
GLUE!
7/31
SCHULZ

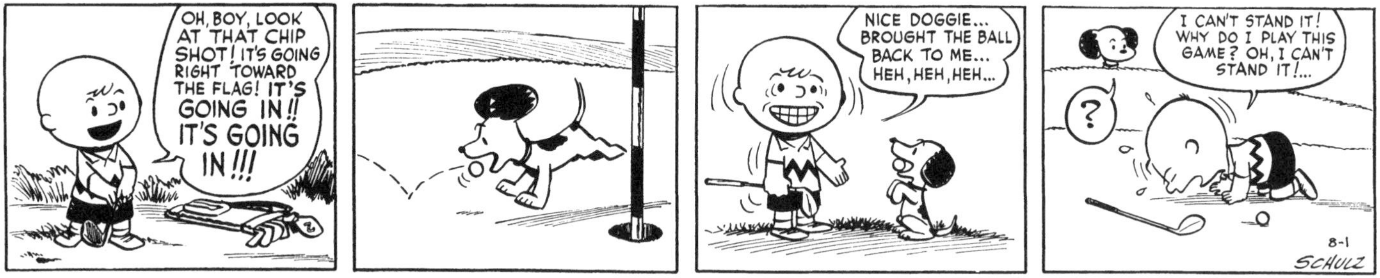
OH, BOY, LOOK AT THAT CHIP SHOT! IT'S GOING RIGHT TOWARD THE FLAG! IT'S GOING IN!! IT'S GOING IN!!!
NICE DOGGIE... BROUGHT THE BALL BACK TO ME... HEH, HEH, HEH...
?
I CAN'T STAND IT! WHY DO I PLAY THIS GAME? OH, I CAN'T STAND IT!...
8-1
SCHULZ

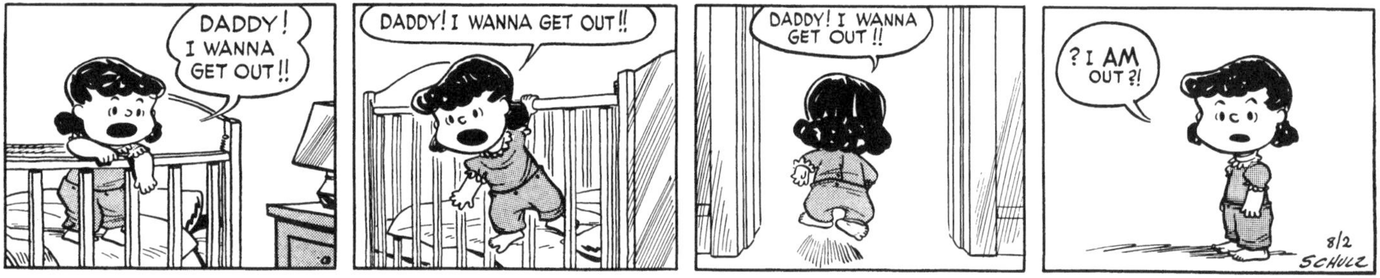
DADDY! I WANNA GET OUT!!
DADDY! I WANNA GET OUT!!
DADDY! I WANNA GET OUT!!
? I AM OUT ?!
8/2
SCHULZ

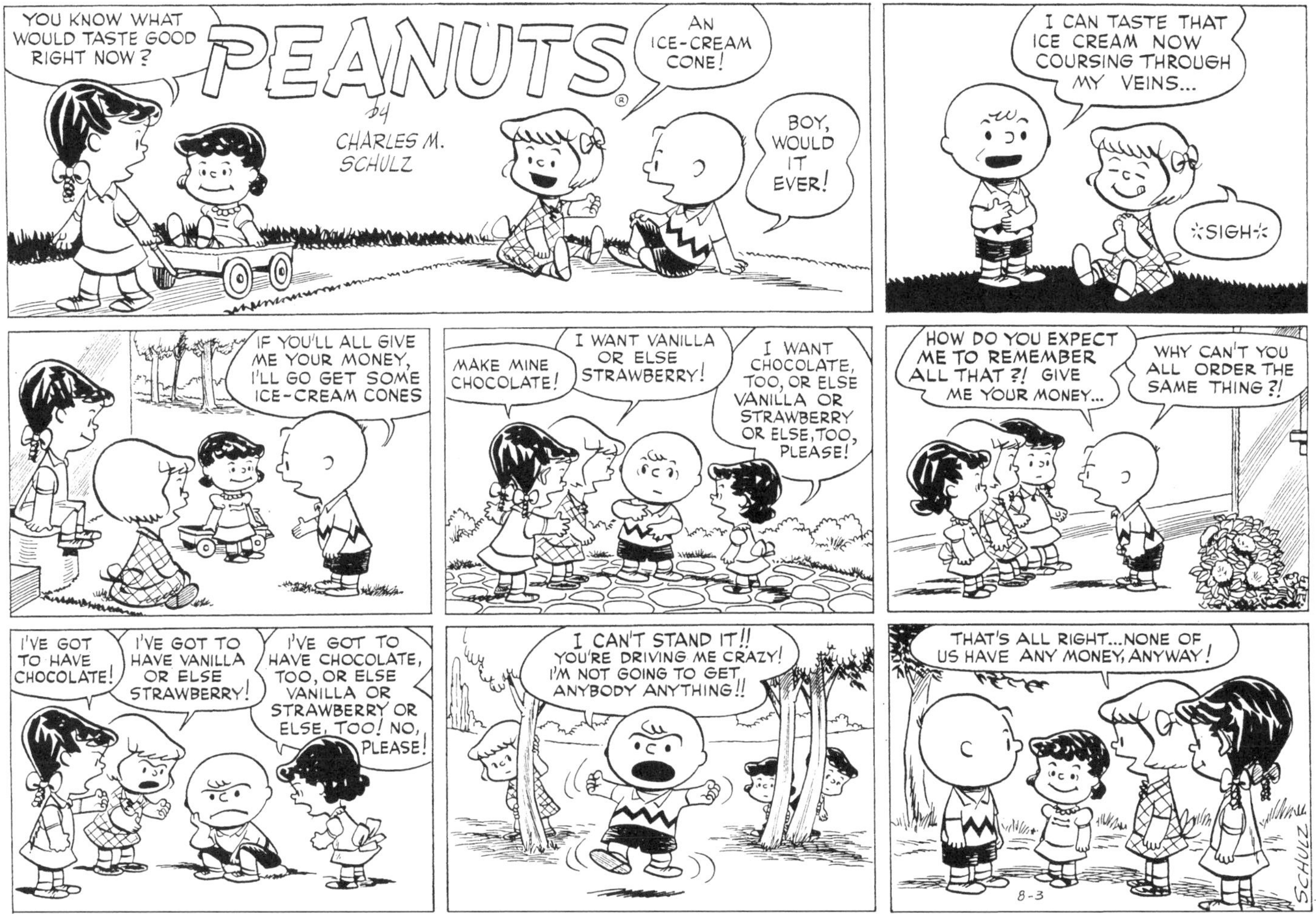
YOU KNOW WHAT WOULD TASTE GOOD RIGHT NOW?
PEANUTS
by CHARLES M. SCHULZ
AN ICE-CREAM CONE!
BOY, WOULD IT EVER!
I CAN TASTE THAT ICE CREAM NOW COURSING THROUGH MY VEINS...
SIGH
IF YOU'LL ALL GIVE ME YOUR MONEY, I'LL GO GET SOME ICE-CREAM CONES
MAKE MINE CHOCOLATE!
I WANT VANILLA OR ELSE STRAWBERRY!
I WANT CHOCOLATE, TOO, OR ELSE VANILLA OR STRAWBERRY OR ELSE, TOO, PLEASE!
HOW DO YOU EXPECT ME TO REMEMBER ALL THAT?! GIVE ME YOUR MONEY...
WHY CAN'T YOU ALL ORDER THE SAME THING?!
I'VE GOT TO HAVE CHOCOLATE!
I'VE GOT TO HAVE VANILLA OR ELSE STRAWBERRY!
I'VE GOT TO HAVE CHOCOLATE, TOO, OR ELSE VANILLA OR STRAWBERRY OR ELSE, TOO! NO, PLEASE!
I CAN'T STAND IT!! YOU'RE DRIVING ME CRAZY! I'M NOT GOING TO GET ANYBODY ANYTHING!!
THAT'S ALL RIGHT...NONE OF US HAVE ANY MONEY, ANYWAY!
8-3
SCHULZ

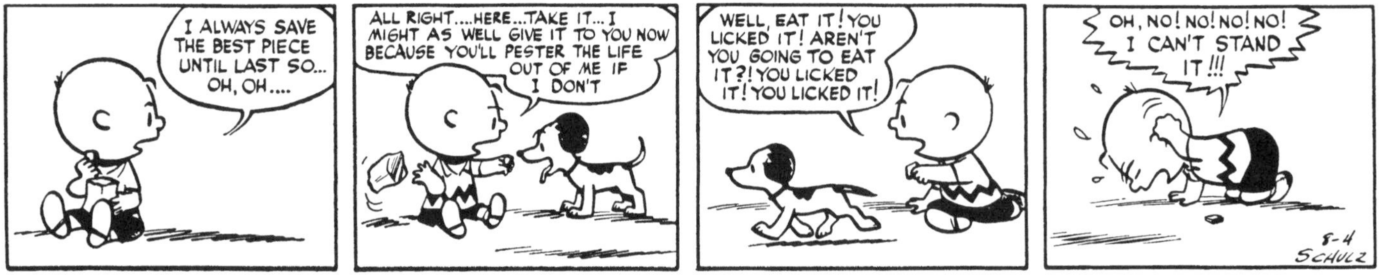
I ALWAYS SAVE THE BEST PIECE UNTIL LAST SO... OH, OH....
ALL RIGHT....HERE...TAKE IT... I MIGHT AS WELL GIVE IT TO YOU NOW BECAUSE YOU'LL PESTER THE LIFE OUT OF ME IF I DON'T
WELL, EAT IT! YOU LICKED IT! AREN'T YOU GOING TO EAT IT?! YOU LICKED IT! YOU LICKED IT!
OH, NO! NO! NO! NO! I CAN'T STAND IT!!!
8-4
SCHULZ

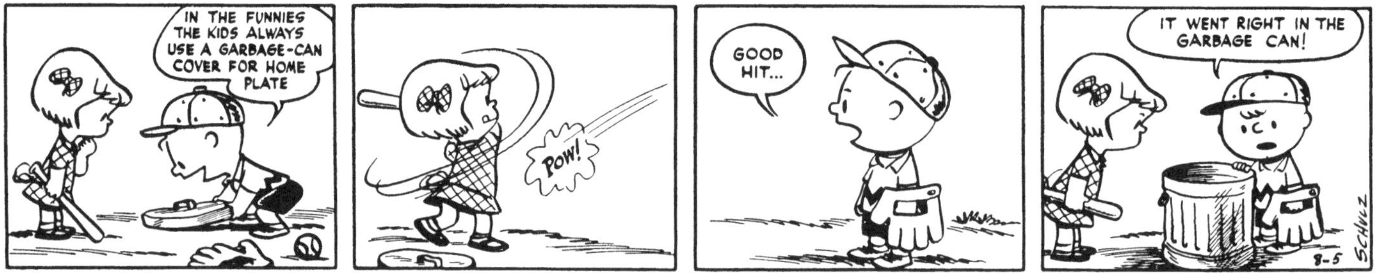
IN THE FUNNIES THE KIDS ALWAYS USE A GARBAGE-CAN COVER FOR HOME PLATE
POW!
GOOD HIT...
IT WENT RIGHT IN THE GARBAGE CAN!
8-5
SCHULZ

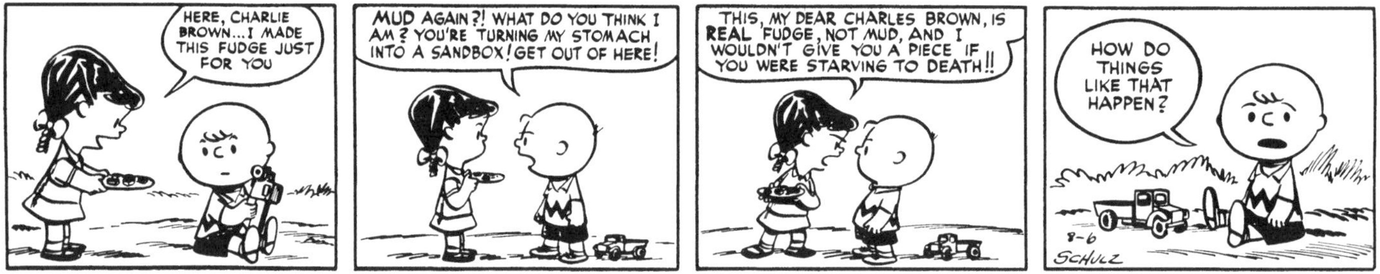
HERE, CHARLIE BROWN...I MADE THIS FUDGE JUST FOR YOU
MUD AGAIN?! WHAT DO YOU THINK I AM? YOU'RE TURNING MY STOMACH INTO A SANDBOX! GET OUT OF HERE!
THIS, MY DEAR CHARLES BROWN, IS REAL FUDGE, NOT MUD, AND I WOULDN'T GIVE YOU A PIECE IF YOU WERE STARVING TO DEATH!!
HOW DO THINGS LIKE THAT HAPPEN?
8-6
SCHULZ

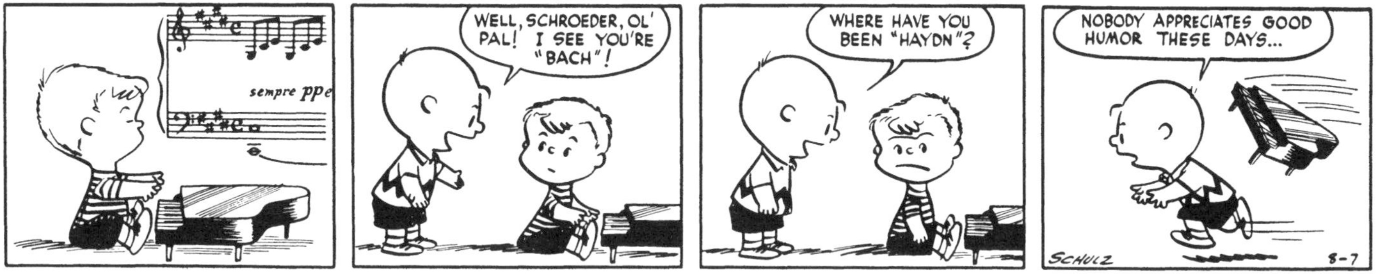
sempre pp
WELL, SCHROEDER, OL' PAL! I SEE YOU'RE "BACH"!
WHERE HAVE YOU BEEN "HAYDN"?
NOBODY APPRECIATES GOOD HUMOR THESE DAYS...
SCHULZ
8-7

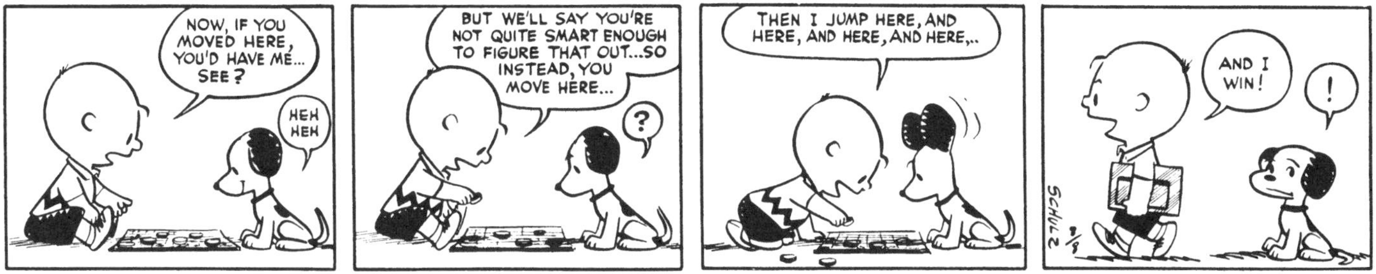
NOW, IF YOU MOVED HERE, YOU'D HAVE ME... SEE?
HEH HEH
BUT WE'LL SAY YOU'RE NOT QUITE SMART ENOUGH TO FIGURE THAT OUT...SO INSTEAD, YOU MOVE HERE...
?
THEN I JUMP HERE, AND HERE, AND HERE, AND HERE,..
AND I WIN!
!
SCHULZ
8/8

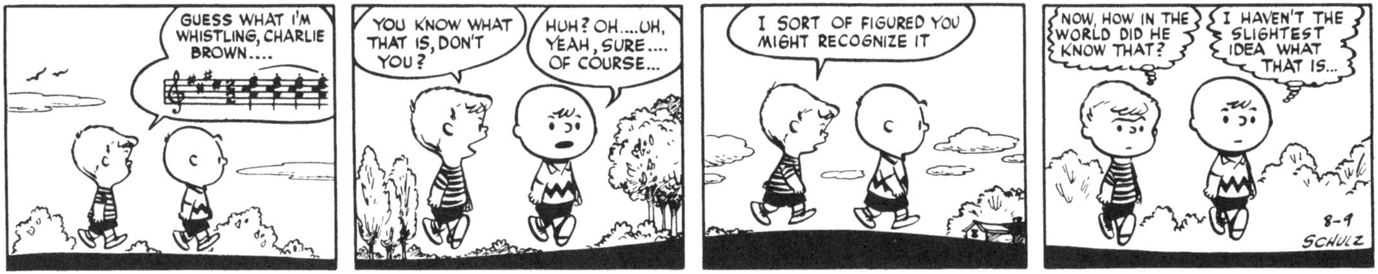
GUESS WHAT I'M WHISTLING, CHARLIE BROWN....
YOU KNOW WHAT THAT IS, DON'T YOU?
HUH? OH....UH, YEAH, SURE.... OF COURSE...
I SORT OF FIGURED YOU MIGHT RECOGNIZE IT
NOW, HOW IN THE WORLD DID HE KNOW THAT?
I HAVEN'T THE SLIGHTEST IDEA WHAT THAT IS...
8-9
SCHULZ

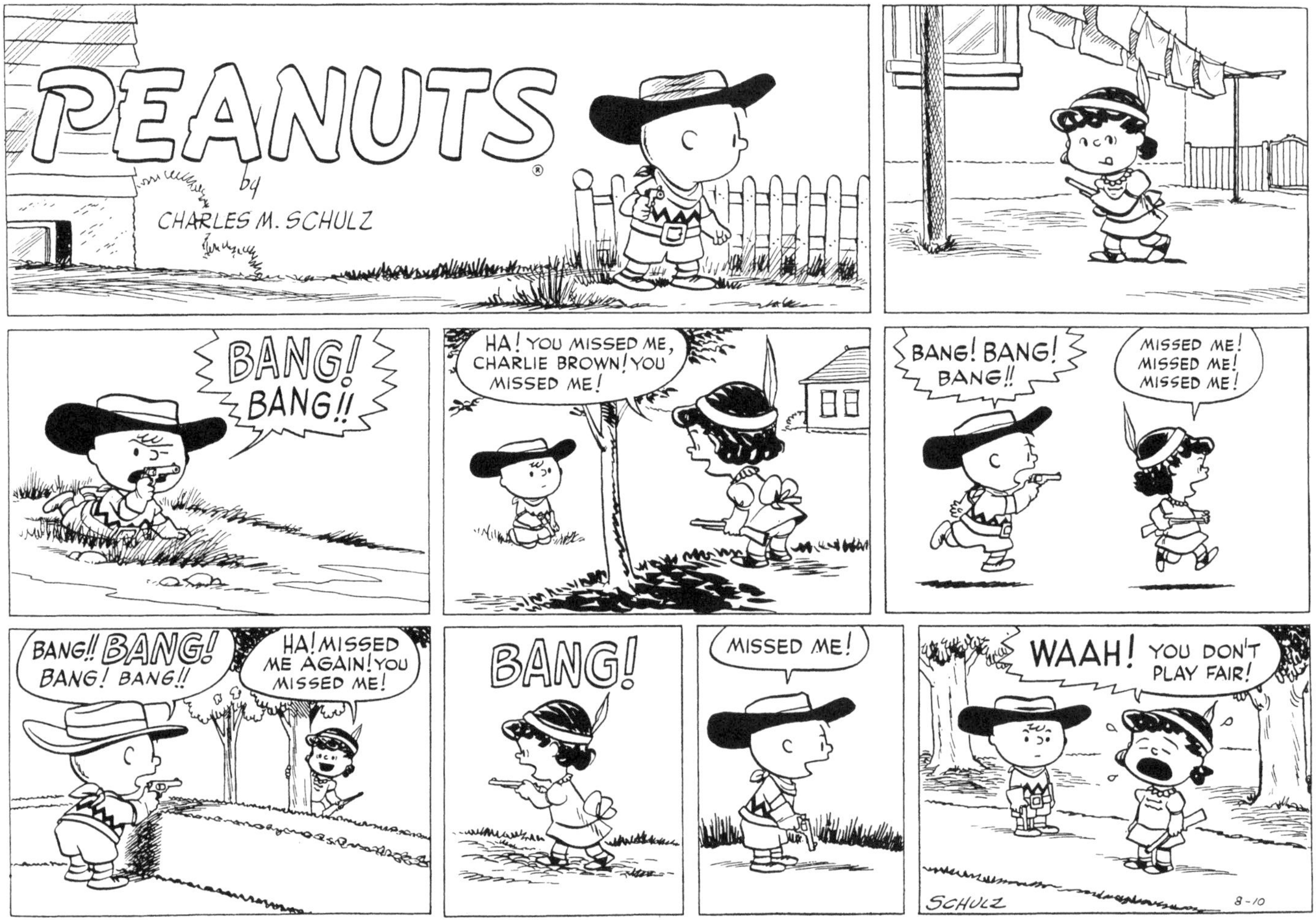
PEANUTS
by
CHARLES M. SCHULZ
BANG! BANG!!
HA! YOU MISSED ME, CHARLIE BROWN! YOU MISSED ME!
BANG! BANG! BANG!!
MISSED ME! MISSED ME! MISSED ME!
BANG!! BANG! BANG! BANG!!
HA! MISSED ME AGAIN! YOU MISSED ME!
BANG!
MISSED ME!
WAAH! YOU DON'T PLAY FAIR!
SCHULZ
8-10

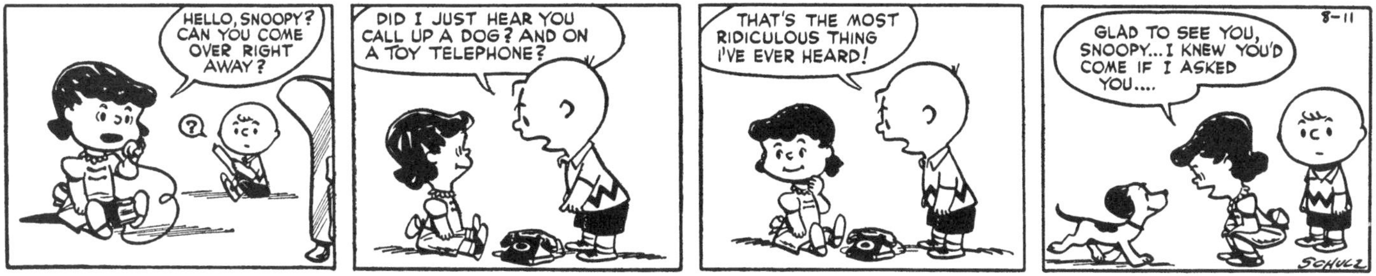
HELLO, SNOOPY? CAN YOU COME OVER RIGHT AWAY?
?
DID I JUST HEAR YOU CALL UP A DOG? AND ON A TOY TELEPHONE?
THAT'S THE MOST RIDICULOUS THING I'VE EVER HEARD!
8-11
GLAD TO SEE YOU, SNOOPY... I KNEW YOU'D COME IF I ASKED YOU....
SCHULZ

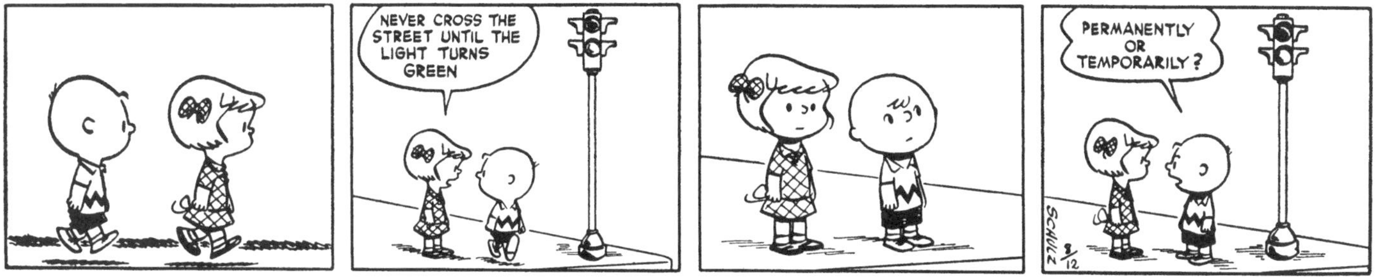
NEVER CROSS THE STREET UNTIL THE LIGHT TURNS GREEN
SCHULZ 8/12
PERMANENTLY OR TEMPORARILY?

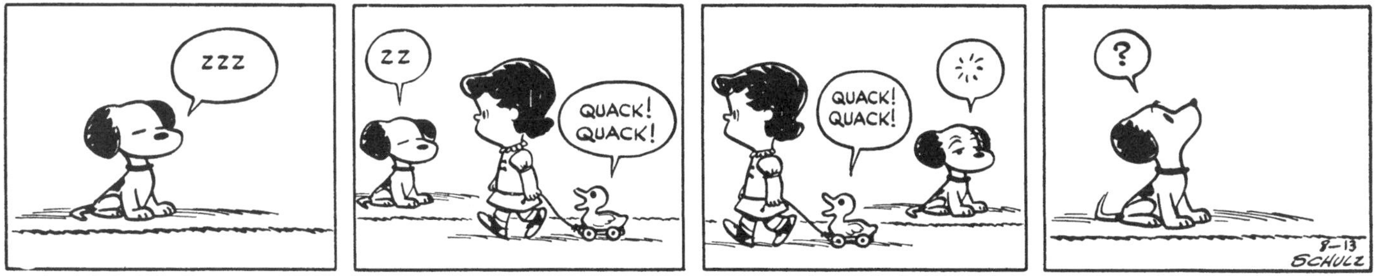
ZZZ
ZZ
QUACK! QUACK!
QUACK! QUACK!
?
8-13
SCHULZ

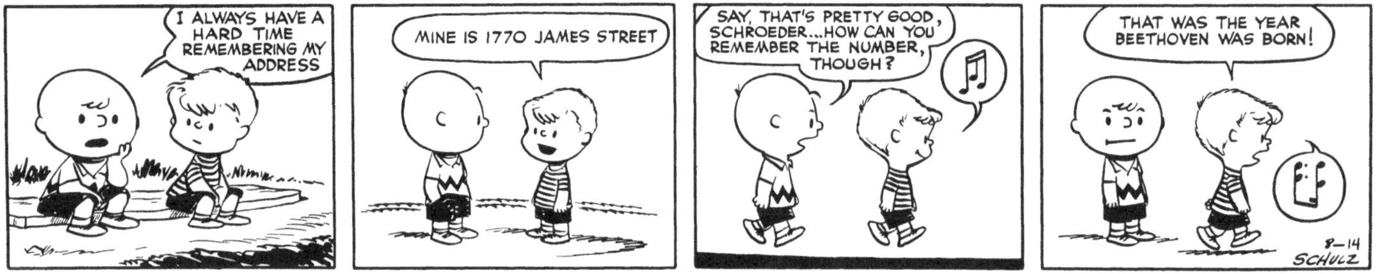
I ALWAYS HAVE A HARD TIME REMEMBERING MY ADDRESS
MINE IS 1770 JAMES STREET
SAY, THAT'S PRETTY GOOD, SCHROEDER...HOW CAN YOU REMEMBER THE NUMBER, THOUGH?
THAT WAS THE YEAR BEETHOVEN WAS BORN!
8-14
SCHULZ

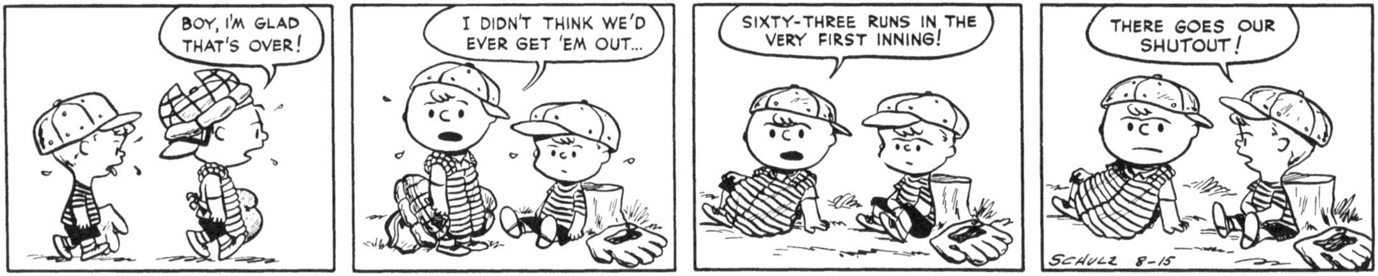
BOY, I'M GLAD THAT'S OVER!
I DIDN'T THINK WE'D EVER GET 'EM OUT...
SIXTY-THREE RUNS IN THE VERY FIRST INNING!
THERE GOES OUR SHUTOUT!
SCHULZ 8-15

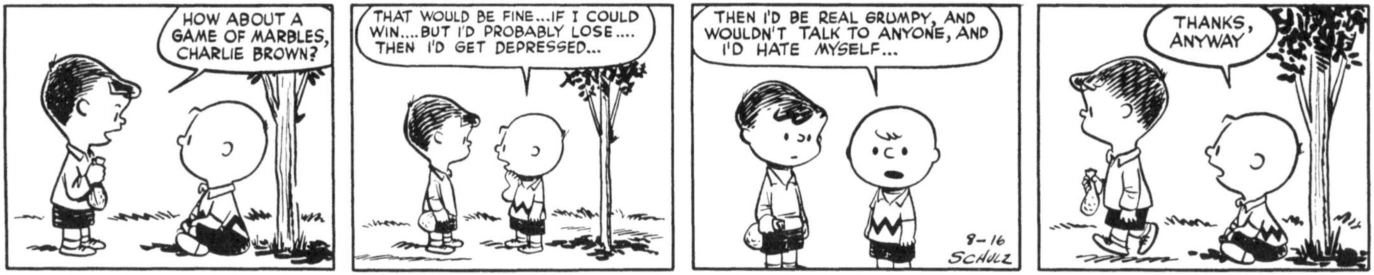
HOW ABOUT A GAME OF MARBLES, CHARLIE BROWN?
THAT WOULD BE FINE...IF I COULD WIN....BUT I'D PROBABLY LOSE.... THEN I'D GET DEPRESSED...
THEN I'D BE REAL GRUMPY, AND WOULDN'T TALK TO ANYONE, AND I'D HATE MYSELF...
8-16
SCHULZ
THANKS, ANYWAY

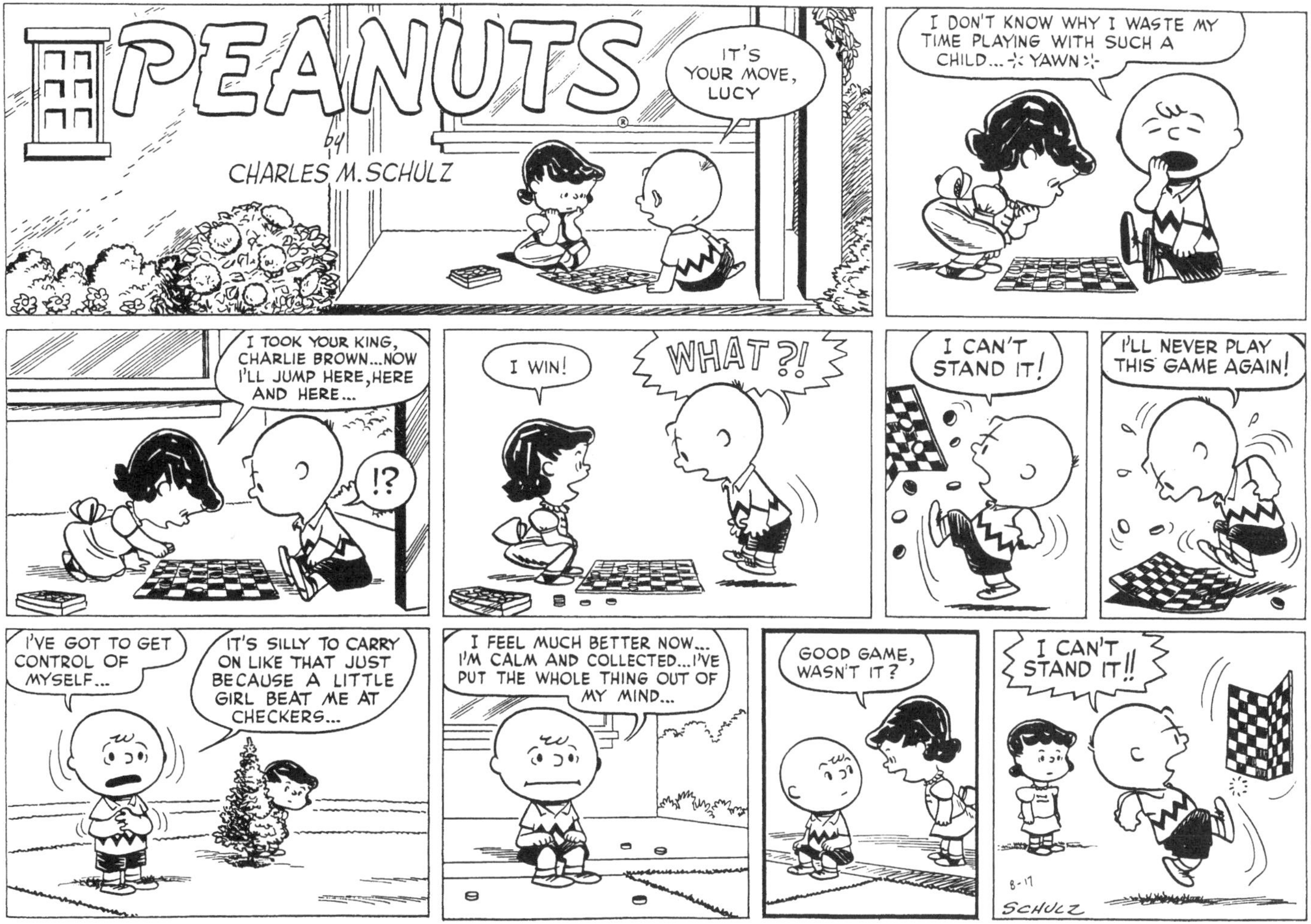
PEANUTS
by CHARLES M. SCHULZ
IT'S YOUR MOVE, LUCY
I DON'T KNOW WHY I WASTE MY TIME PLAYING WITH SUCH A CHILD... YAWN
I TOOK YOUR KING, CHARLIE BROWN...NOW I'LL JUMP HERE, HERE AND HERE...
!?
I WIN!
WHAT ?!
I CAN'T STAND IT!
I'LL NEVER PLAY THIS GAME AGAIN!
I'VE GOT TO GET CONTROL OF MYSELF...
IT'S SILLY TO CARRY ON LIKE THAT JUST BECAUSE A LITTLE GIRL BEAT ME AT CHECKERS...
I FEEL MUCH BETTER NOW... I'M CALM AND COLLECTED...I'VE PUT THE WHOLE THING OUT OF MY MIND...
GOOD GAME, WASN'T IT?
I CAN'T STAND IT!!
8-17
SCHULZ

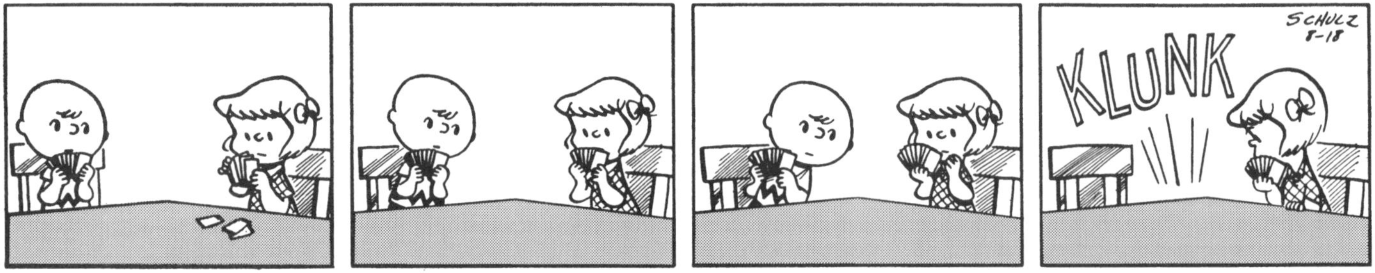
SCHULZ 8-18
KLUNK

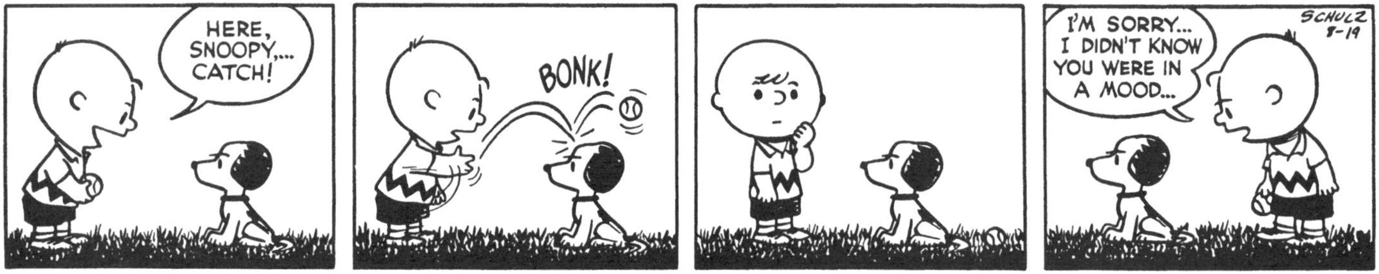
HERE, SNOOPY,... CATCH!
BONK!
I'M SORRY... I DIDN'T KNOW YOU WERE IN A MOOD...
SCHULZ 8-19

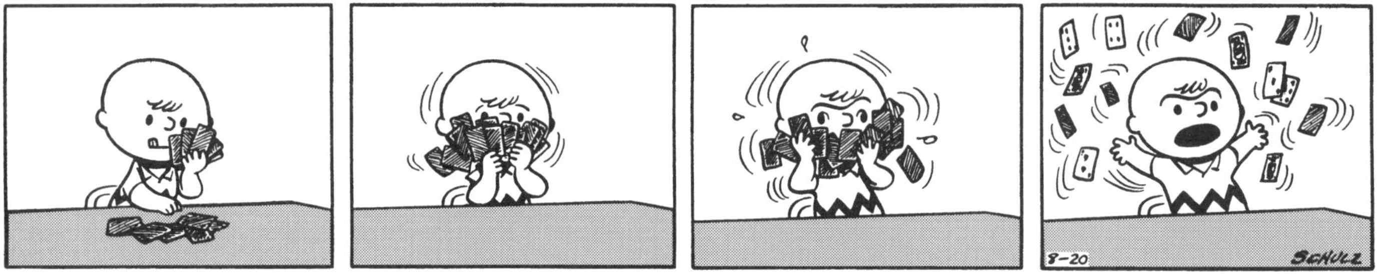
8-20
SCHULZ

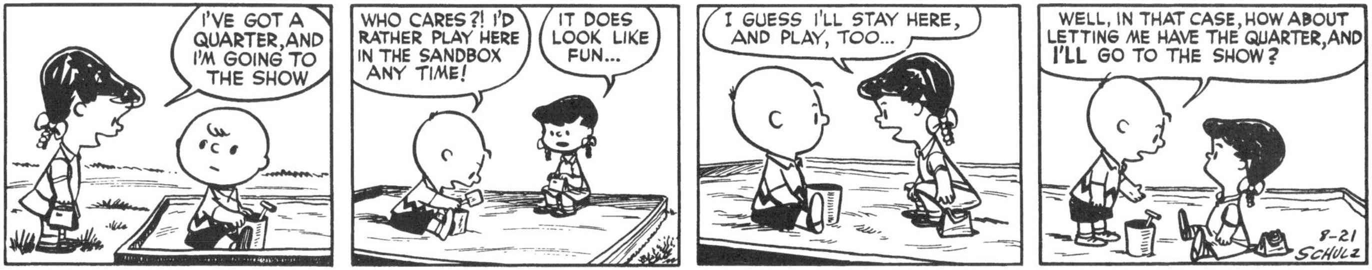
I'VE GOT A QUARTER, AND I'M GOING TO THE SHOW
WHO CARES?! I'D RATHER PLAY HERE IN THE SANDBOX ANY TIME!
IT DOES LOOK LIKE FUN...
I GUESS I'LL STAY HERE, AND PLAY, TOO...
WELL, IN THAT CASE, HOW ABOUT LETTING ME HAVE THE QUARTER, AND I'LL GO TO THE SHOW?
8-21
SCHULZ

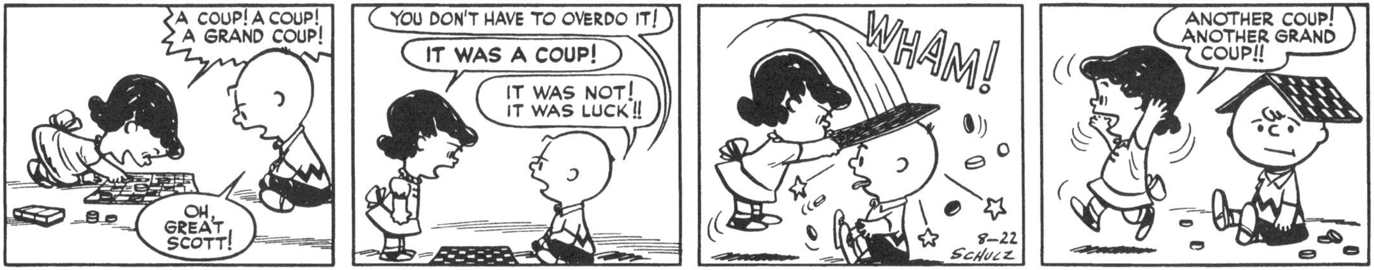
A COUP! A COUP! A GRAND COUP!
OH, GREAT SCOTT!
YOU DON'T HAVE TO OVERDO IT!
IT WAS A COUP!
IT WAS NOT! IT WAS LUCK!!
WHAM!
8-22
SCHULZ
ANOTHER COUP! ANOTHER GRAND COUP!!

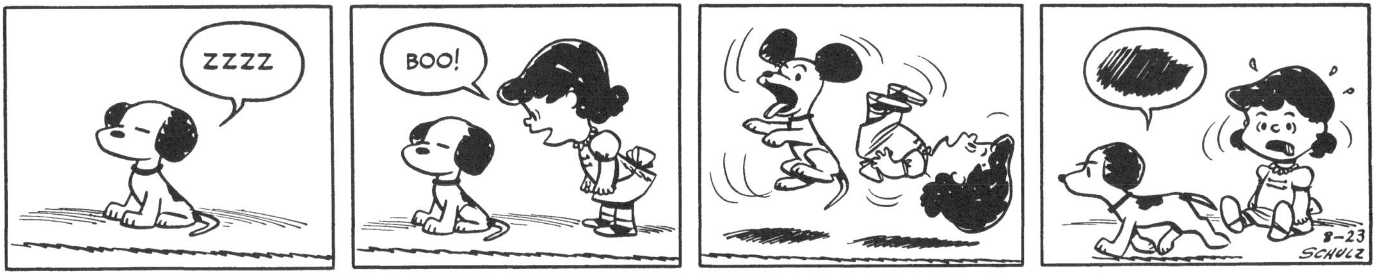
ZZZZ
BOO!
8-23
SCHULZ

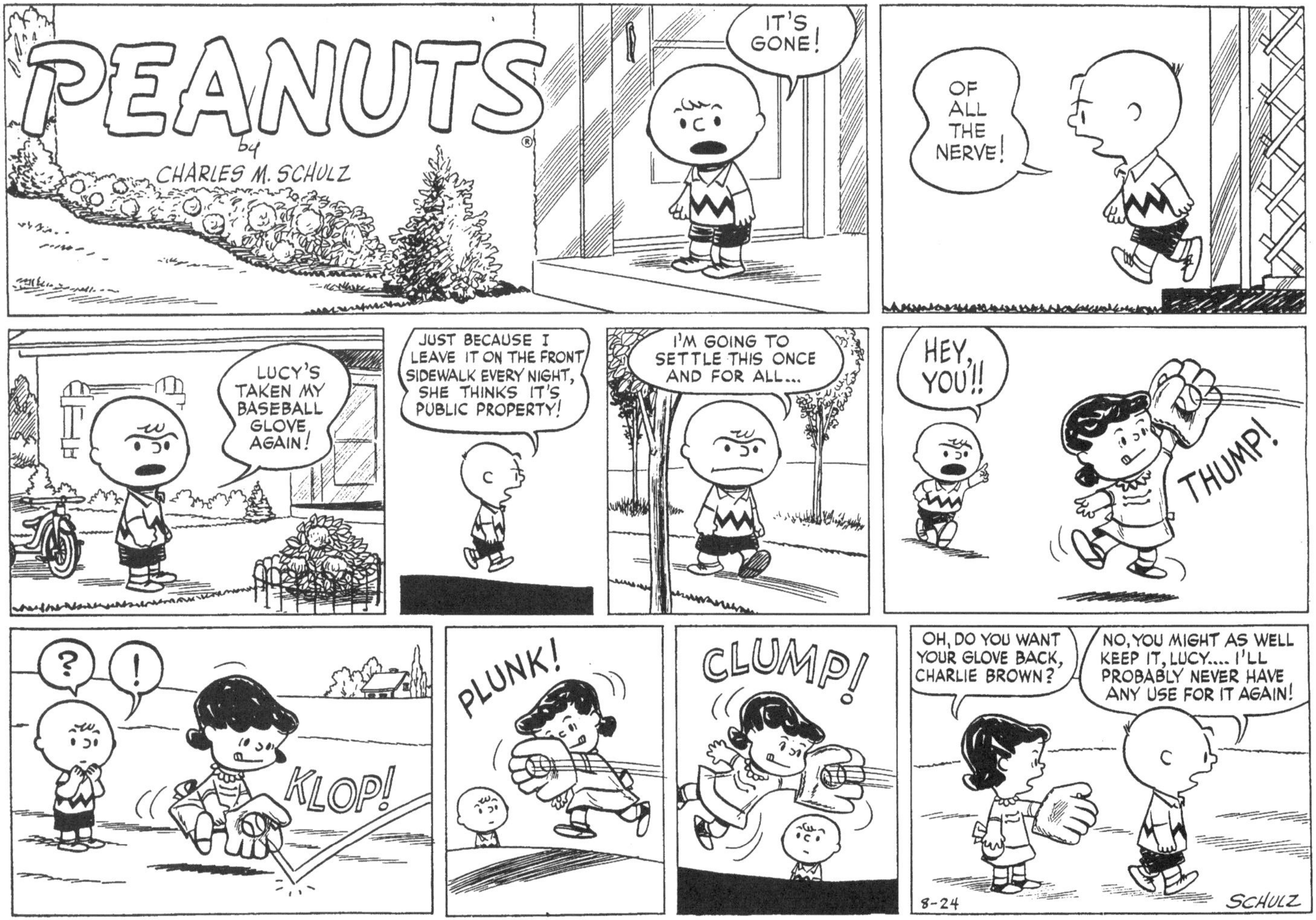
PEANUTS
by CHARLES M. SCHULZ
IT'S GONE!
OF ALL THE NERVE!
LUCY'S TAKEN MY BASEBALL GLOVE AGAIN!
JUST BECAUSE I LEAVE IT ON THE FRONT SIDEWALK EVERY NIGHT, SHE THINKS IT'S PUBLIC PROPERTY!
I'M GOING TO SETTLE THIS ONCE AND FOR ALL...
HEY, YOU!!
THUMP!
?
!
KLOP!
PLUNK!
CLUMP!
OH, DO YOU WANT YOUR GLOVE BACK, CHARLIE BROWN?
NO, YOU MIGHT AS WELL KEEP IT, LUCY.... I'LL PROBABLY NEVER HAVE ANY USE FOR IT AGAIN!
8-24
SCHULZ

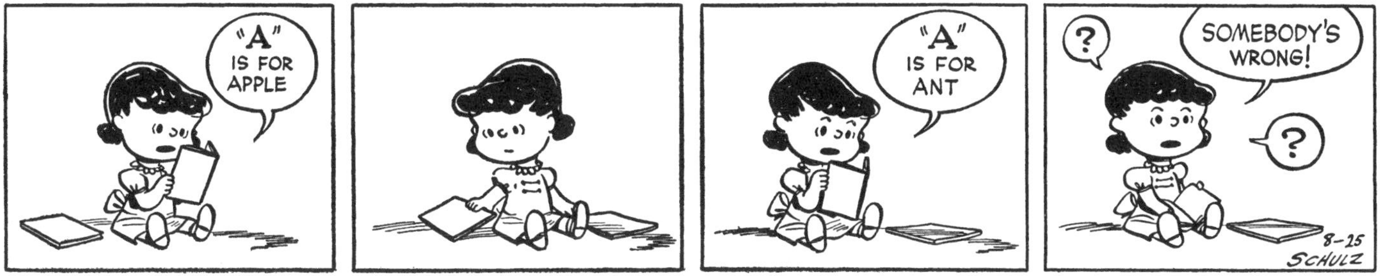
"A" IS FOR APPLE
"A" IS FOR ANT
?
SOMEBODY'S WRONG!
?
8-25
SCHULZ

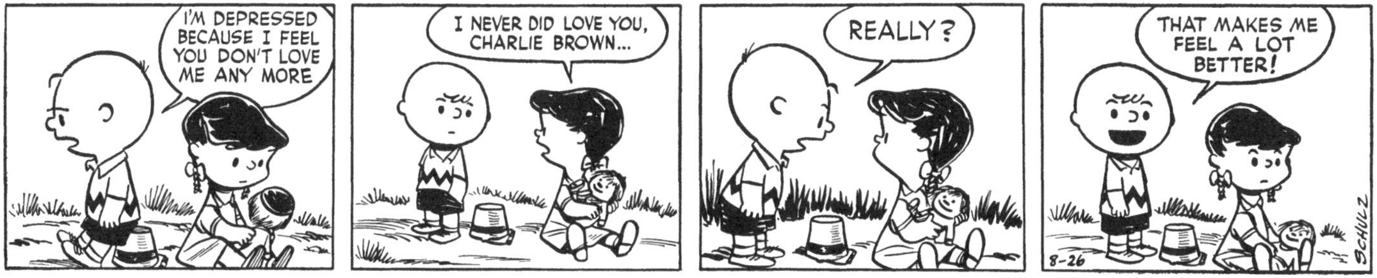
I'M DEPRESSED BECAUSE I FEEL YOU DON'T LOVE ME ANY MORE
I NEVER DID LOVE YOU, CHARLIE BROWN...
REALLY?
THAT MAKES ME FEEL A LOT BETTER!
8-26
SCHULZ

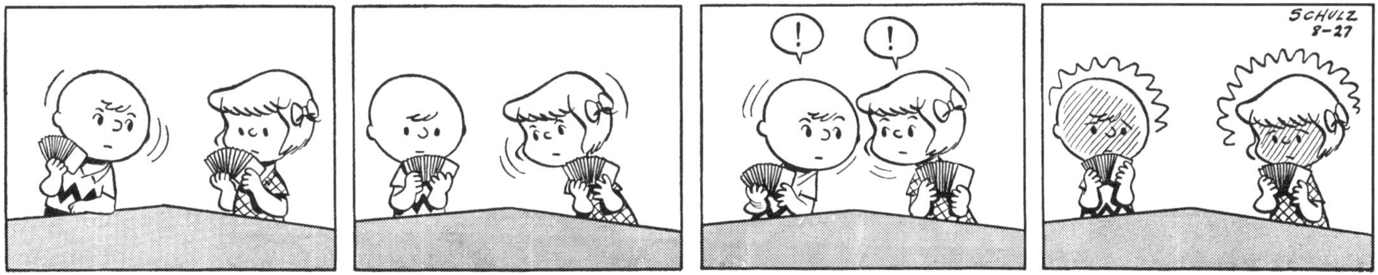
!
!
SCHULZ
8-27

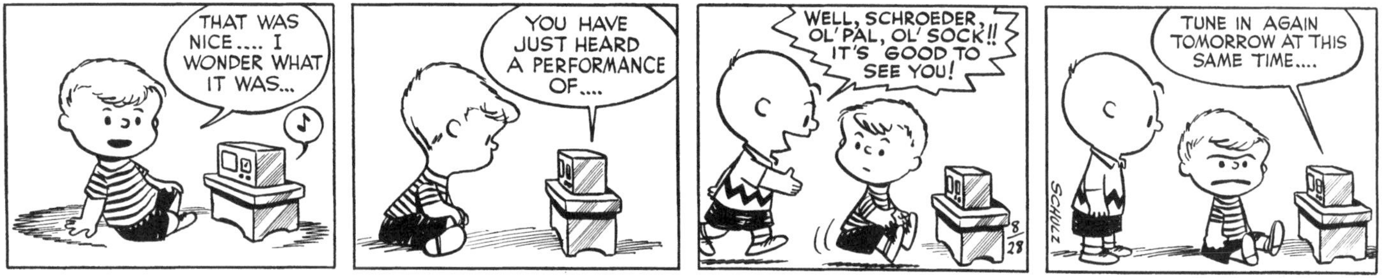
THAT WAS NICE.... I WONDER WHAT IT WAS...
YOU HAVE JUST HEARD A PERFORMANCE OF....
WELL, SCHROEDER, OL' PAL, OL' SOCK!! IT'S GOOD TO SEE YOU!
8/28
SCHULZ
TUNE IN AGAIN TOMORROW AT THIS SAME TIME....

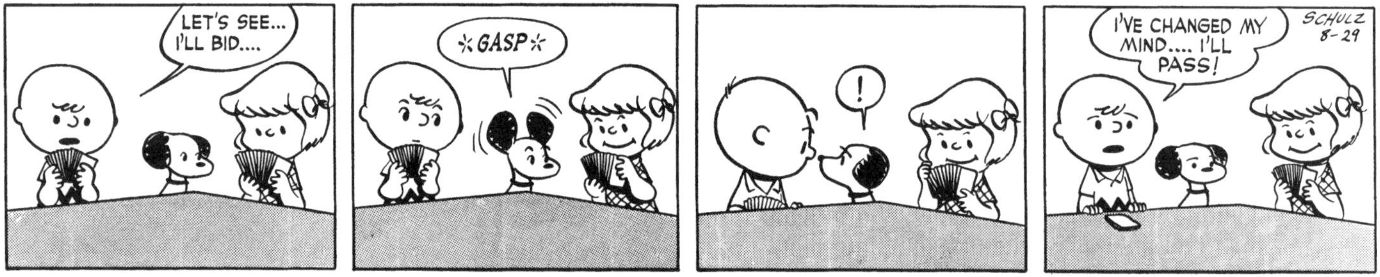
LET'S SEE... I'LL BID....
GASP
!
SCHULZ 8-29
I'VE CHANGED MY MIND.... I'LL PASS!

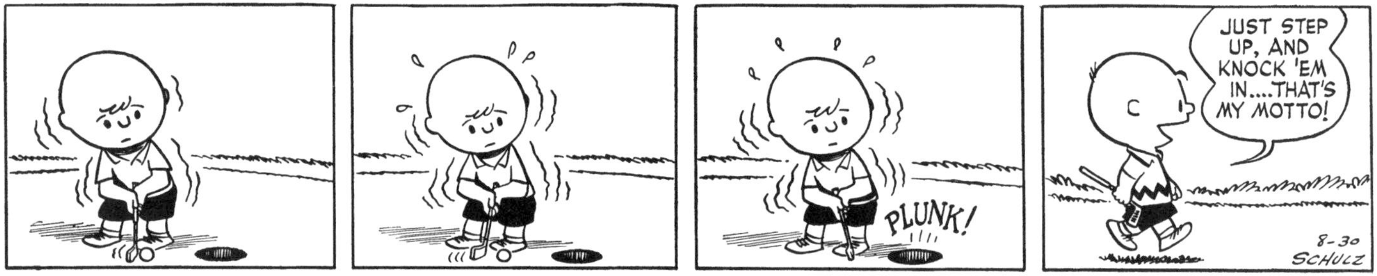
PLUNK!
JUST STEP UP, AND KNOCK 'EM IN....THAT'S MY MOTTO!
8-30 SCHULZ

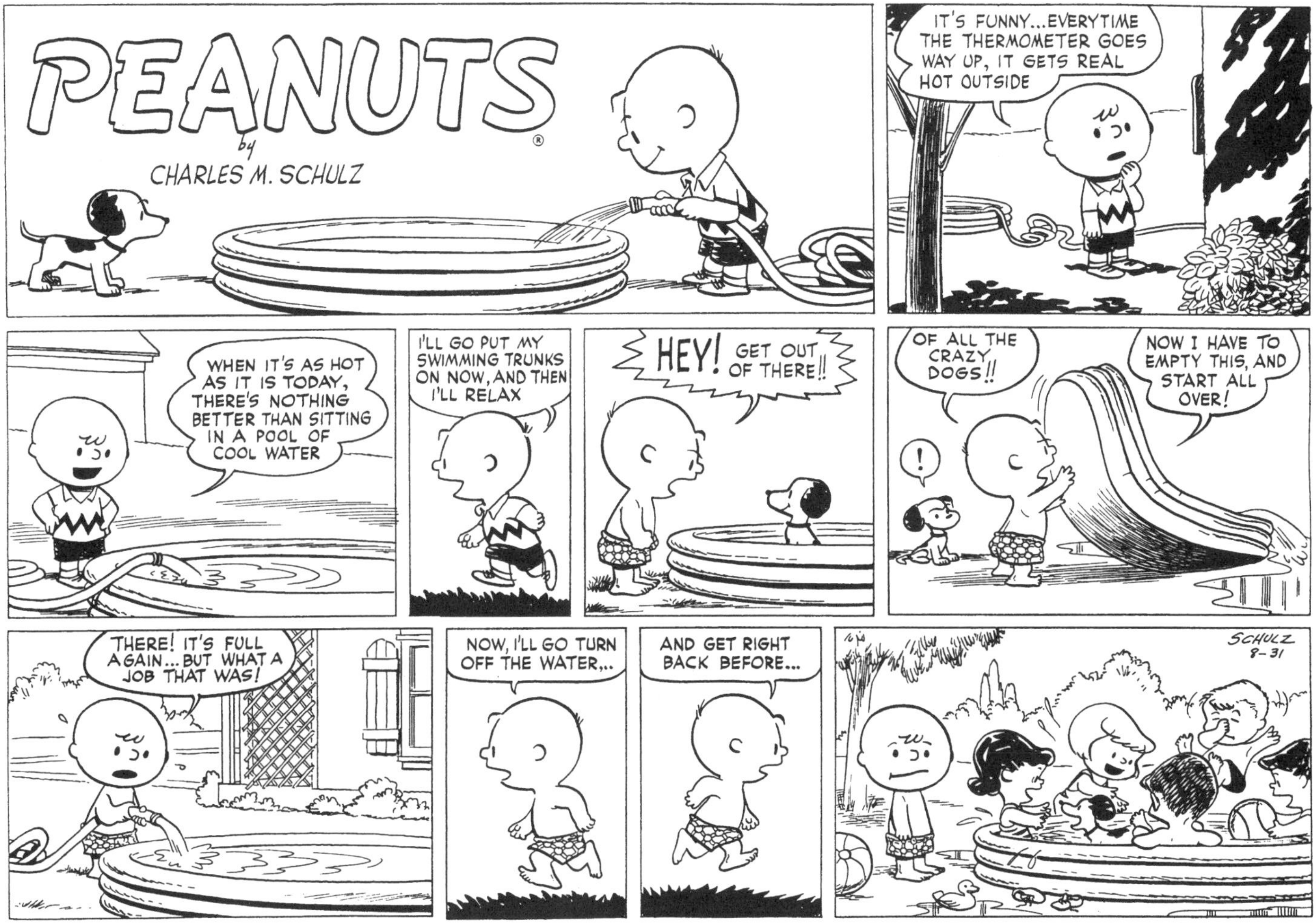
PEANUTS
by
CHARLES M. SCHULZ
IT'S FUNNY...EVERYTIME THE THERMOMETER GOES WAY UP, IT GETS REAL HOT OUTSIDE
WHEN IT'S AS HOT AS IT IS TODAY, THERE'S NOTHING BETTER THAN SITTING IN A POOL OF COOL WATER
I'LL GO PUT MY SWIMMING TRUNKS ON NOW, AND THEN I'LL RELAX
HEY! GET OUT OF THERE!!
OF ALL THE CRAZY DOGS!!
!
NOW I HAVE TO EMPTY THIS, AND START ALL OVER!
THERE! IT'S FULL AGAIN... BUT WHAT A JOB THAT WAS!
NOW, I'LL GO TURN OFF THE WATER,..
AND GET RIGHT BACK BEFORE...
SCHULZ 8-31

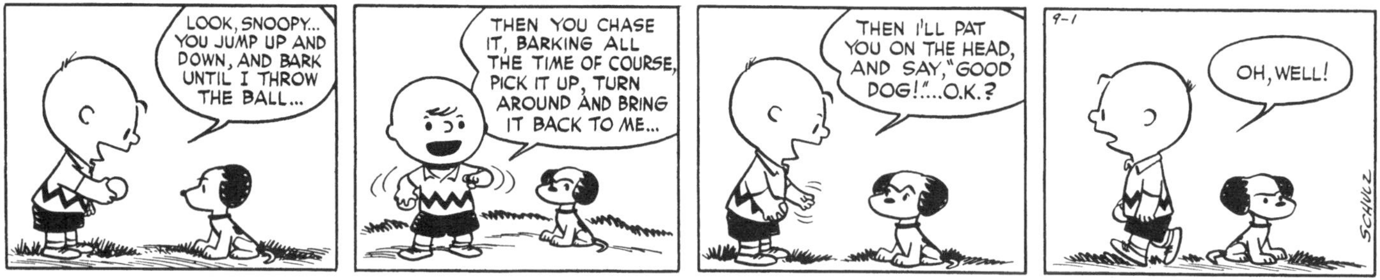
LOOK, SNOOPY... YOU JUMP UP AND DOWN, AND BARK UNTIL I THROW THE BALL...
THEN YOU CHASE IT, BARKING ALL THE TIME OF COURSE, PICK IT UP, TURN AROUND AND BRING IT BACK TO ME...
THEN I'LL PAT YOU ON THE HEAD, AND SAY, "GOOD DOG!"...O.K.?
9-1
OH, WELL!
SCHULZ

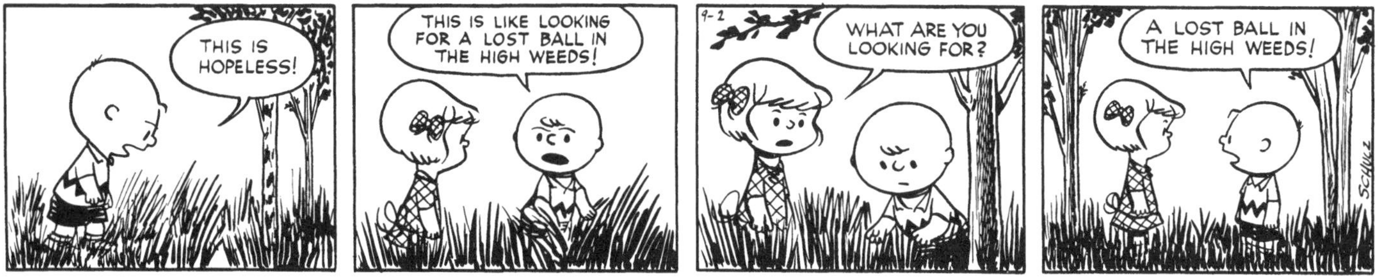
THIS IS HOPELESS!
THIS IS LIKE LOOKING FOR A LOST BALL IN THE HIGH WEEDS!
9-2
WHAT ARE YOU LOOKING FOR?
A LOST BALL IN THE HIGH WEEDS!
SCHULZ

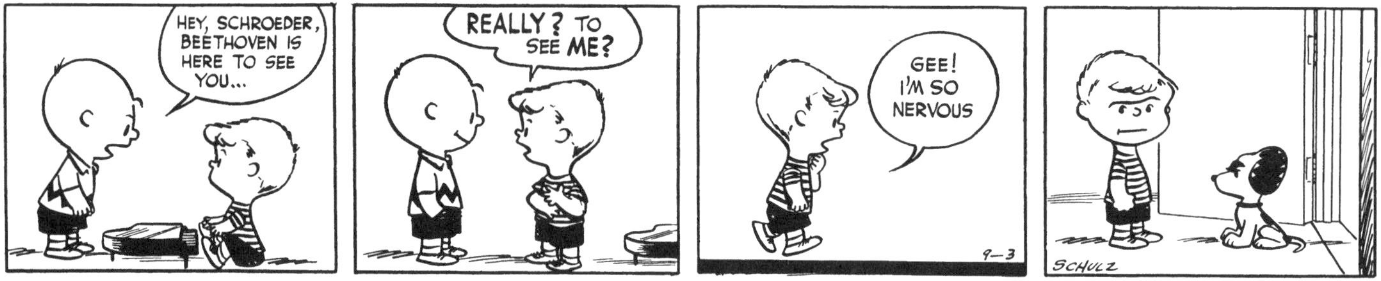
HEY, SCHROEDER, BEETHOVEN IS HERE TO SEE YOU...
REALLY? TO SEE ME?
GEE! I'M SO NERVOUS
9-3
SCHULZ

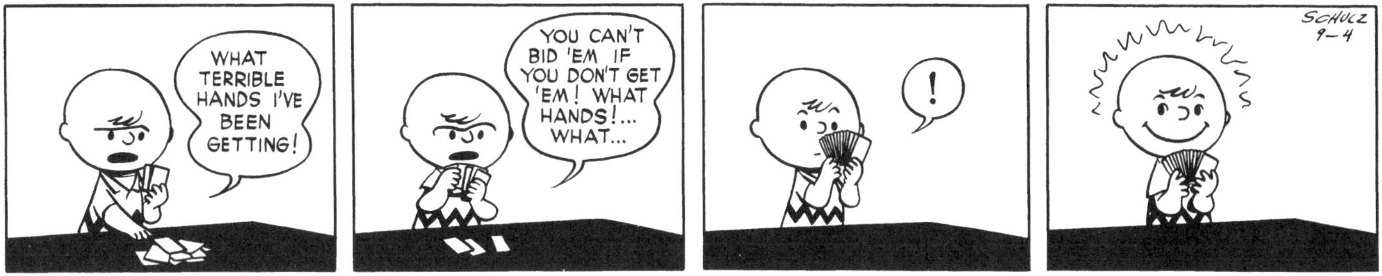
WHAT TERRIBLE HANDS I'VE BEEN GETTING!
YOU CAN'T BID 'EM IF YOU DON'T GET 'EM! WHAT HANDS!... WHAT...
!
SCHULZ 9-4

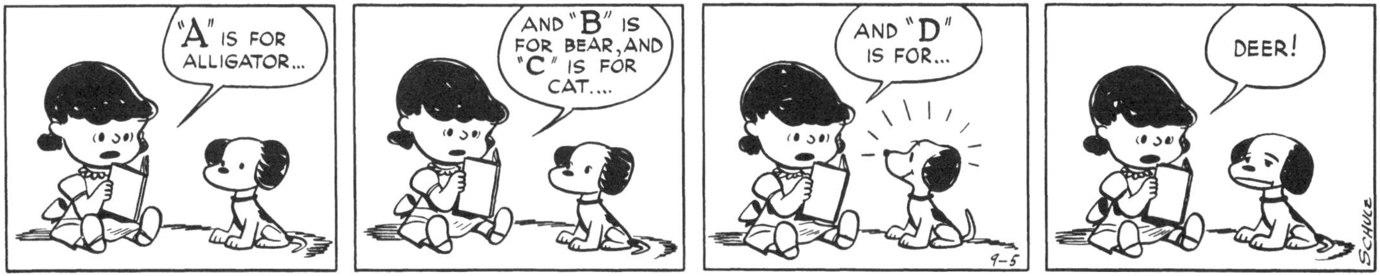
"A" IS FOR ALLIGATOR...
AND "B" IS FOR BEAR, AND "C" IS FOR CAT....
AND "D" IS FOR...
9-5
DEER!
SCHULZ

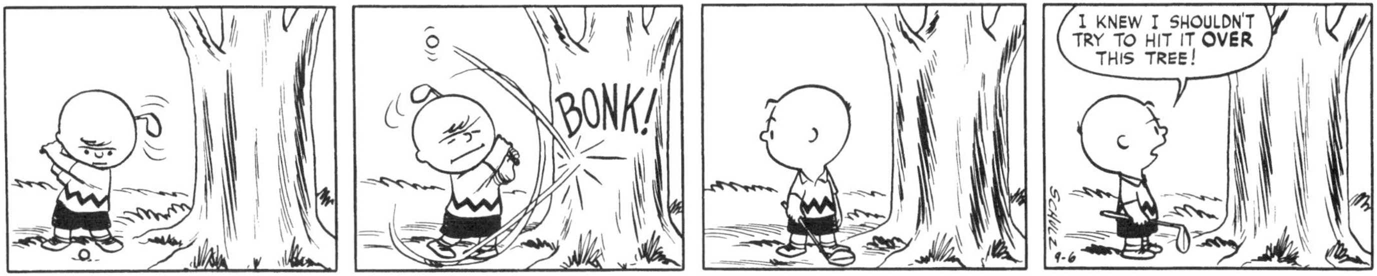
BONK!
SCHULZ 9-6
I KNEW I SHOULDN'T TRY TO HIT IT OVER THIS TREE!

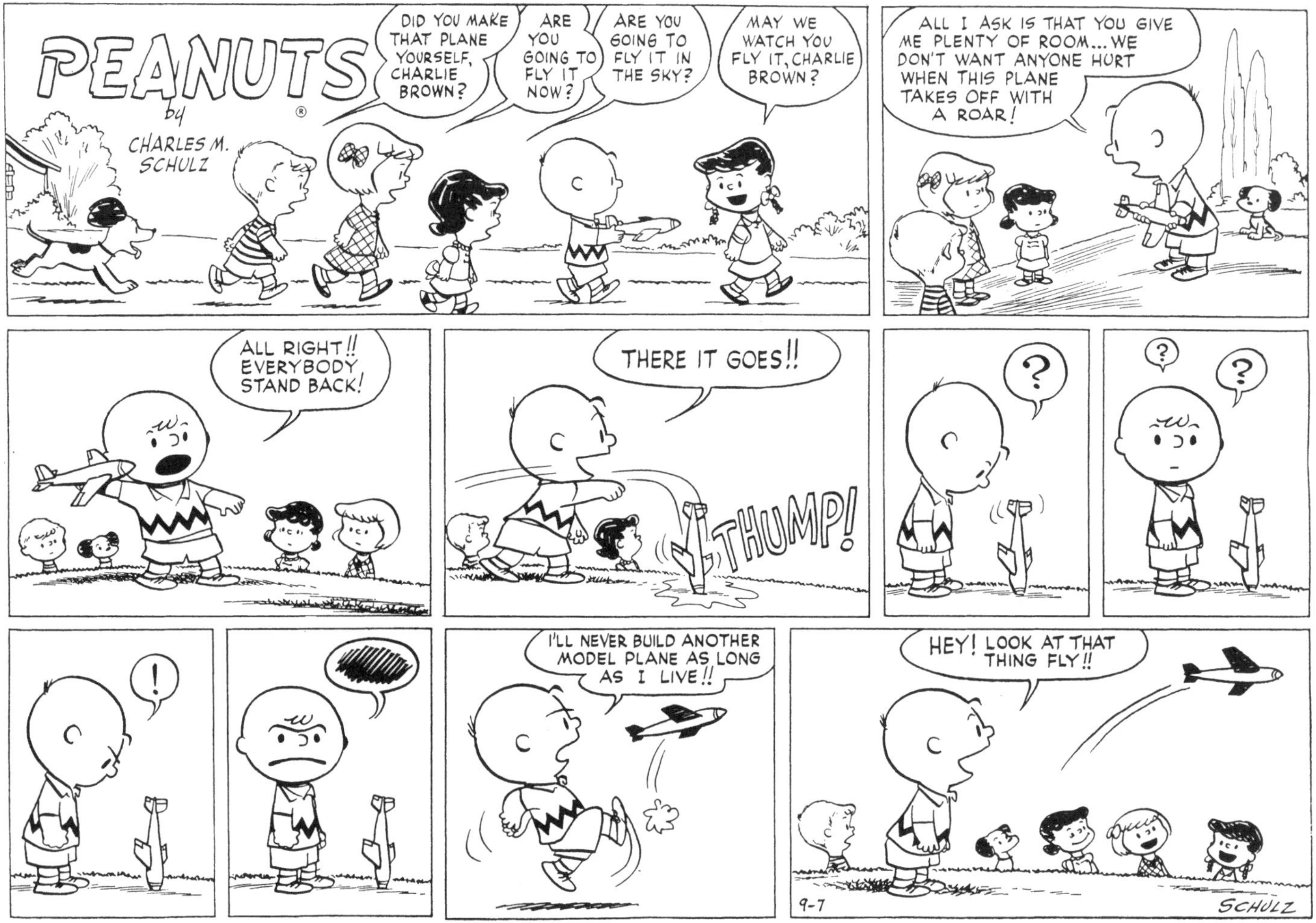
PEANUTS
by
CHARLES M. SCHULZ
DID YOU MAKE THAT PLANE YOURSELF, CHARLIE BROWN?
ARE YOU GOING TO FLY IT NOW?
ARE YOU GOING TO FLY IT IN THE SKY?
MAY WE WATCH YOU FLY IT, CHARLIE BROWN?
ALL I ASK IS THAT YOU GIVE ME PLENTY OF ROOM... WE DON'T WANT ANYONE HURT WHEN THIS PLANE TAKES OFF WITH A ROAR!
ALL RIGHT!! EVERYBODY STAND BACK!
THERE IT GOES!!
THUMP!
?
? ?
!
I'LL NEVER BUILD ANOTHER MODEL PLANE AS LONG AS I LIVE!!
HEY! LOOK AT THAT THING FLY!!
9-7
SCHULZ

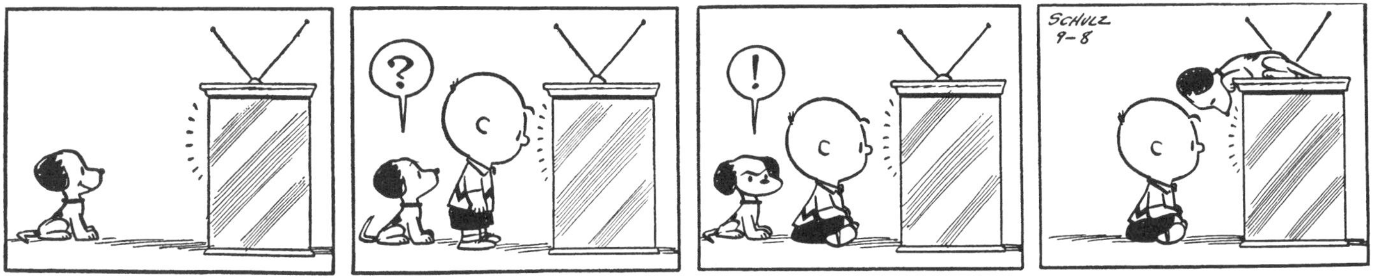
?
!
SCHULZ 9-8

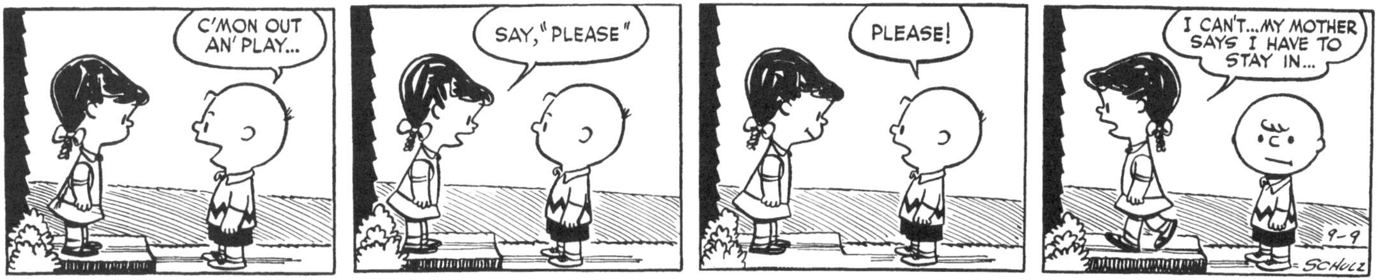
C'MON OUT AN' PLAY...
SAY, "PLEASE"
PLEASE!
I CAN'T...MY MOTHER SAYS I HAVE TO STAY IN...
9-9 SCHULZ

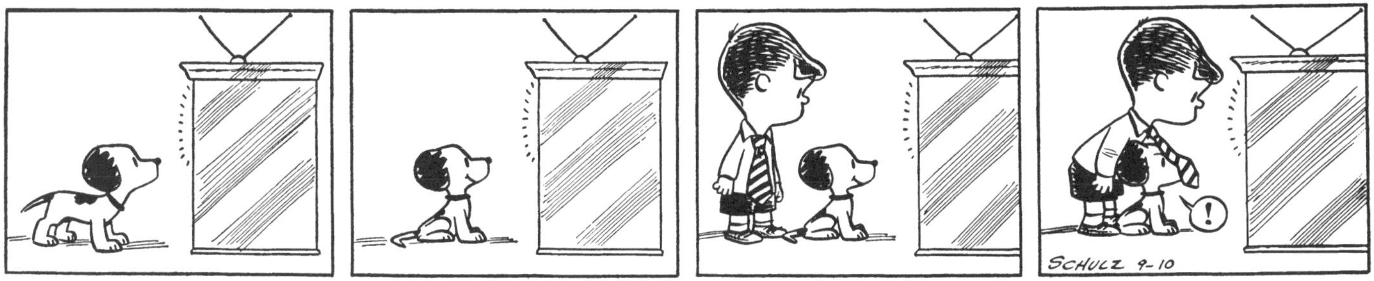
!
SCHULZ 9-10

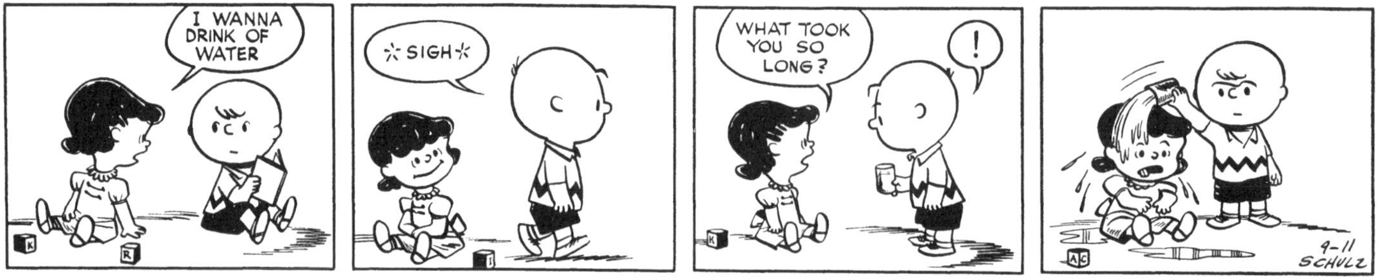
I WANNA DRINK OF WATER
SIGH
WHAT TOOK YOU SO LONG?
!
9-11
SCHULZ

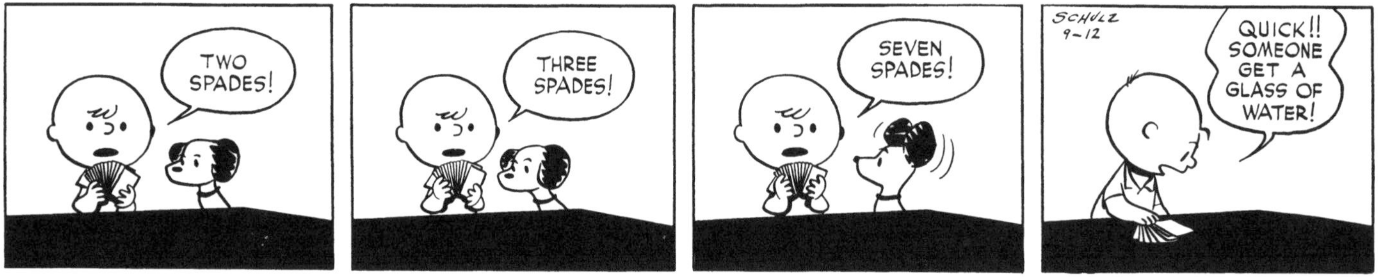
TWO SPADES!
THREE SPADES!
SEVEN SPADES!
SCHULZ
9-12
QUICK!! SOMEONE GET A GLASS OF WATER!

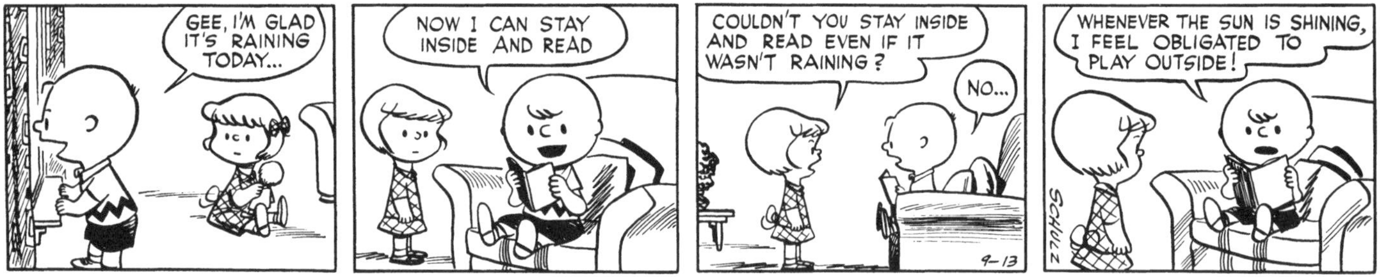
GEE, I'M GLAD IT'S RAINING TODAY...
NOW I CAN STAY INSIDE AND READ
COULDN'T YOU STAY INSIDE AND READ EVEN IF IT WASN'T RAINING?
NO...
9-13
SCHULZ
WHENEVER THE SUN IS SHINING, I FEEL OBLIGATED TO PLAY OUTSIDE!

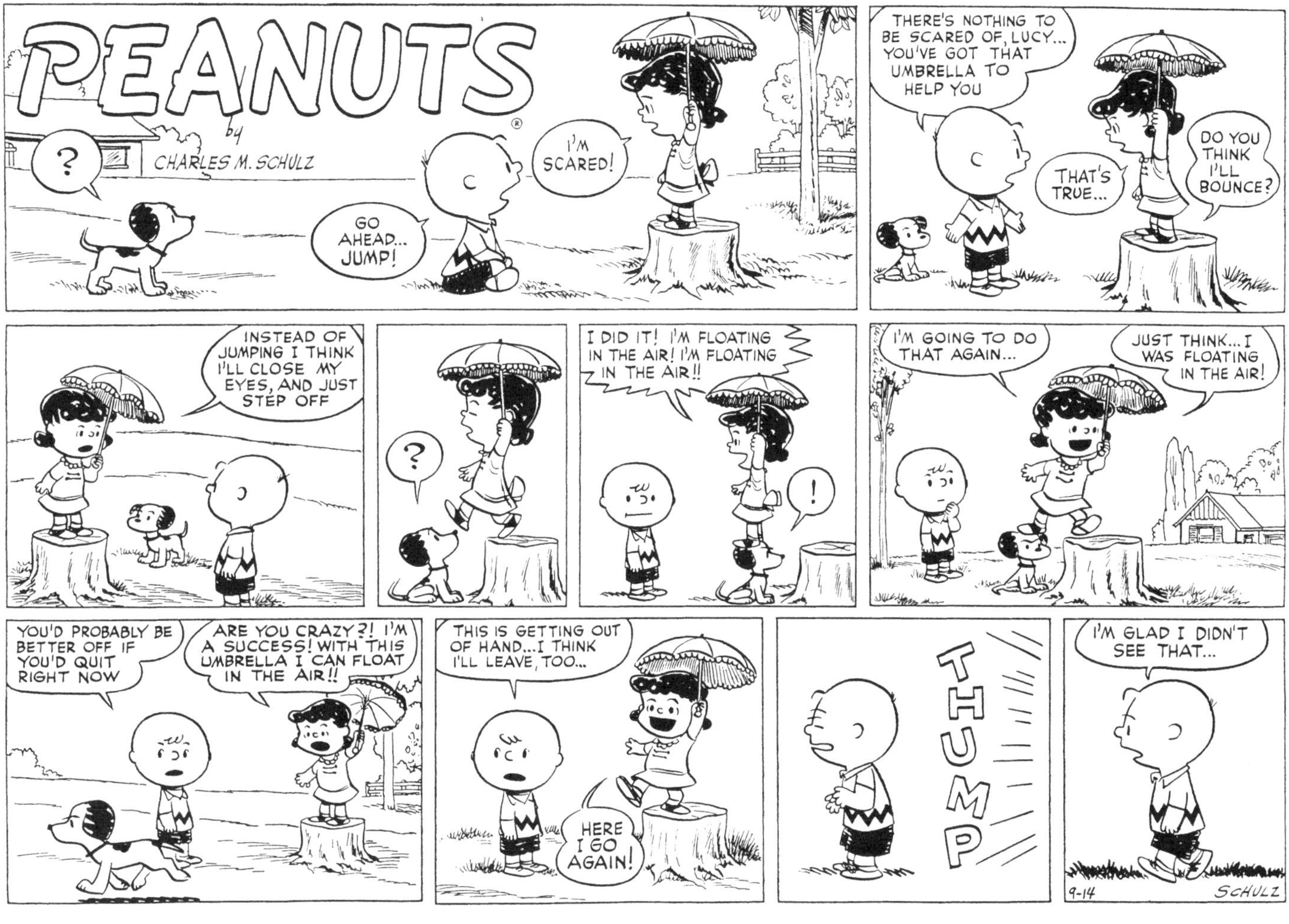
PEANUTS
by CHARLES M. SCHULZ
?
GO AHEAD... JUMP!
I'M SCARED!
THERE'S NOTHING TO BE SCARED OF, LUCY... YOU'VE GOT THAT UMBRELLA TO HELP YOU
THAT'S TRUE...
DO YOU THINK I'LL BOUNCE?
INSTEAD OF JUMPING I THINK I'LL CLOSE MY EYES, AND JUST STEP OFF
?
I DID IT! I'M FLOATING IN THE AIR! I'M FLOATING IN THE AIR!!
!
I'M GOING TO DO THAT AGAIN...
JUST THINK... I WAS FLOATING IN THE AIR!
YOU'D PROBABLY BE BETTER OFF IF YOU'D QUIT RIGHT NOW
ARE YOU CRAZY?! I'M A SUCCESS! WITH THIS UMBRELLA I CAN FLOAT IN THE AIR!!
THIS IS GETTING OUT OF HAND... I THINK I'LL LEAVE, TOO...
HERE I GO AGAIN!
THUMP
I'M GLAD I DIDN'T SEE THAT...
9-14
SCHULZ

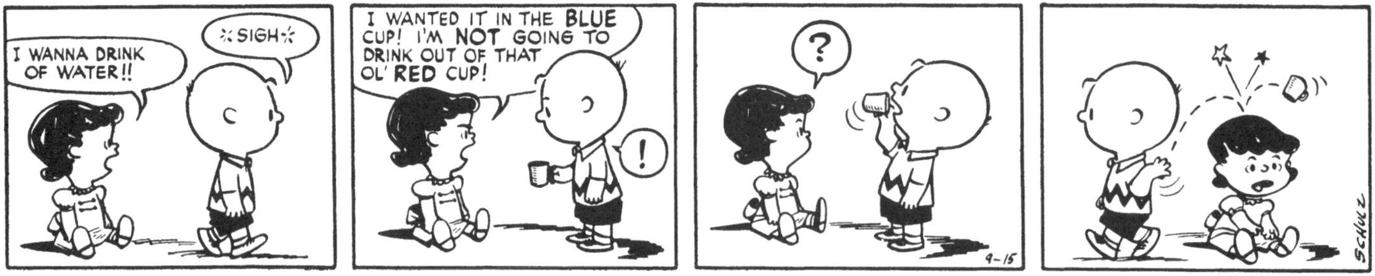
I WANNA DRINK OF WATER!!
⁘SIGH⁘
I WANTED IT IN THE BLUE CUP! I'M NOT GOING TO DRINK OUT OF THAT OL' RED CUP!
!
?
9-15
SCHULZ

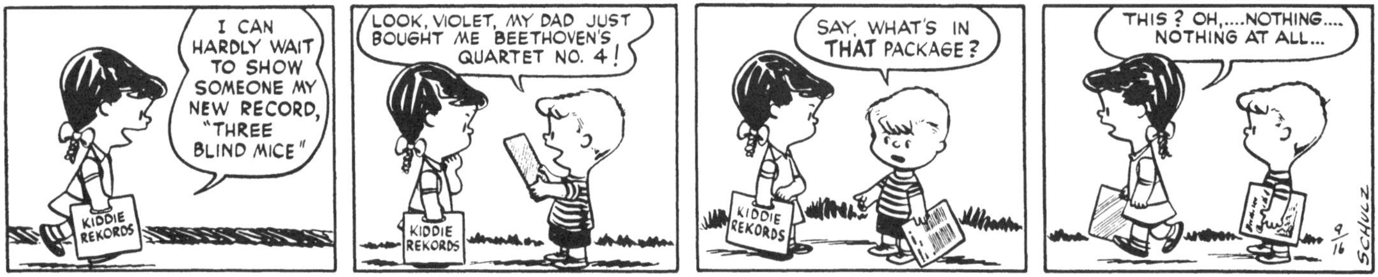
I CAN HARDLY WAIT TO SHOW SOMEONE MY NEW RECORD, "THREE BLIND MICE"
KIDDIE REKORDS
LOOK, VIOLET, MY DAD JUST BOUGHT ME BEETHOVEN'S QUARTET NO. 4!
KIDDIE REKORDS
SAY, WHAT'S IN THAT PACKAGE?
KIDDIE REKORDS
THIS? OH,....NOTHING.... NOTHING AT ALL...
9/16
SCHULZ

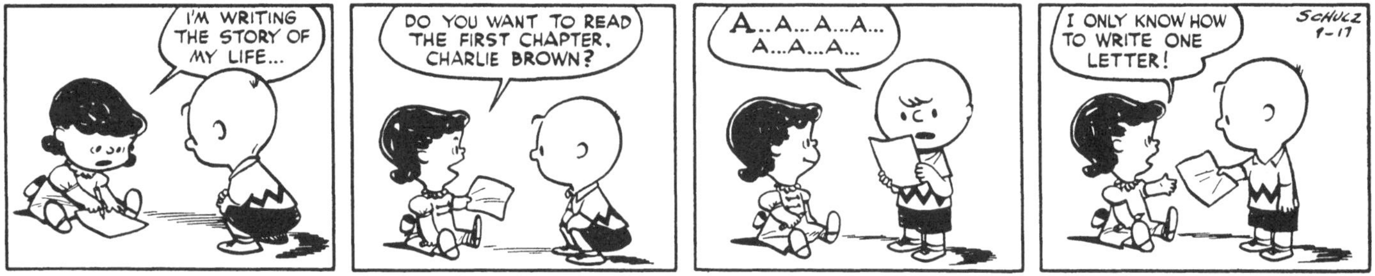
I'M WRITING THE STORY OF MY LIFE...
DO YOU WANT TO READ THE FIRST CHAPTER, CHARLIE BROWN?
A..A...A...A... A...A...A...
I ONLY KNOW HOW TO WRITE ONE LETTER!
SCHULZ 9-17

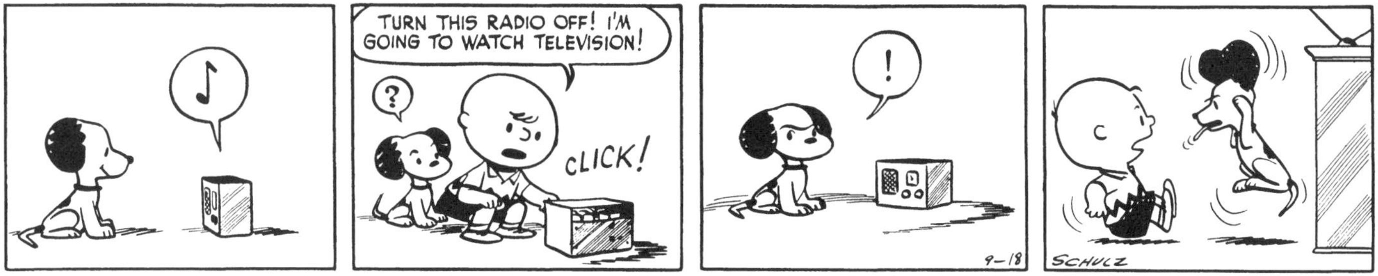
TURN THIS RADIO OFF! I'M GOING TO WATCH TELEVISION!
?
CLICK!
!
9-18
SCHULZ

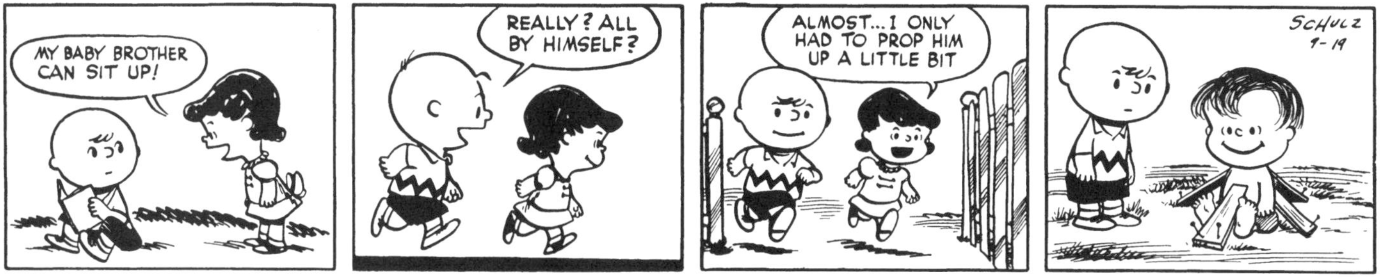
MY BABY BROTHER CAN SIT UP!
REALLY? ALL BY HIMSELF?
ALMOST...I ONLY HAD TO PROP HIM UP A LITTLE BIT
SCHULZ 9-19

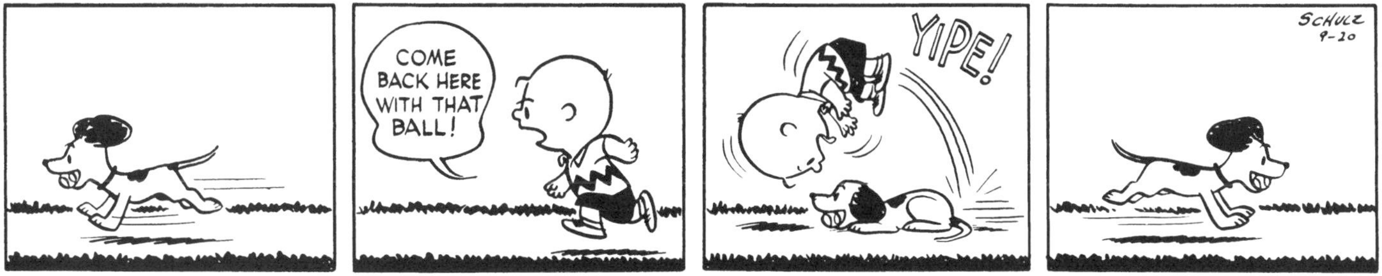
COME BACK HERE WITH THAT BALL!
YIPE!
SCHULZ 9-20

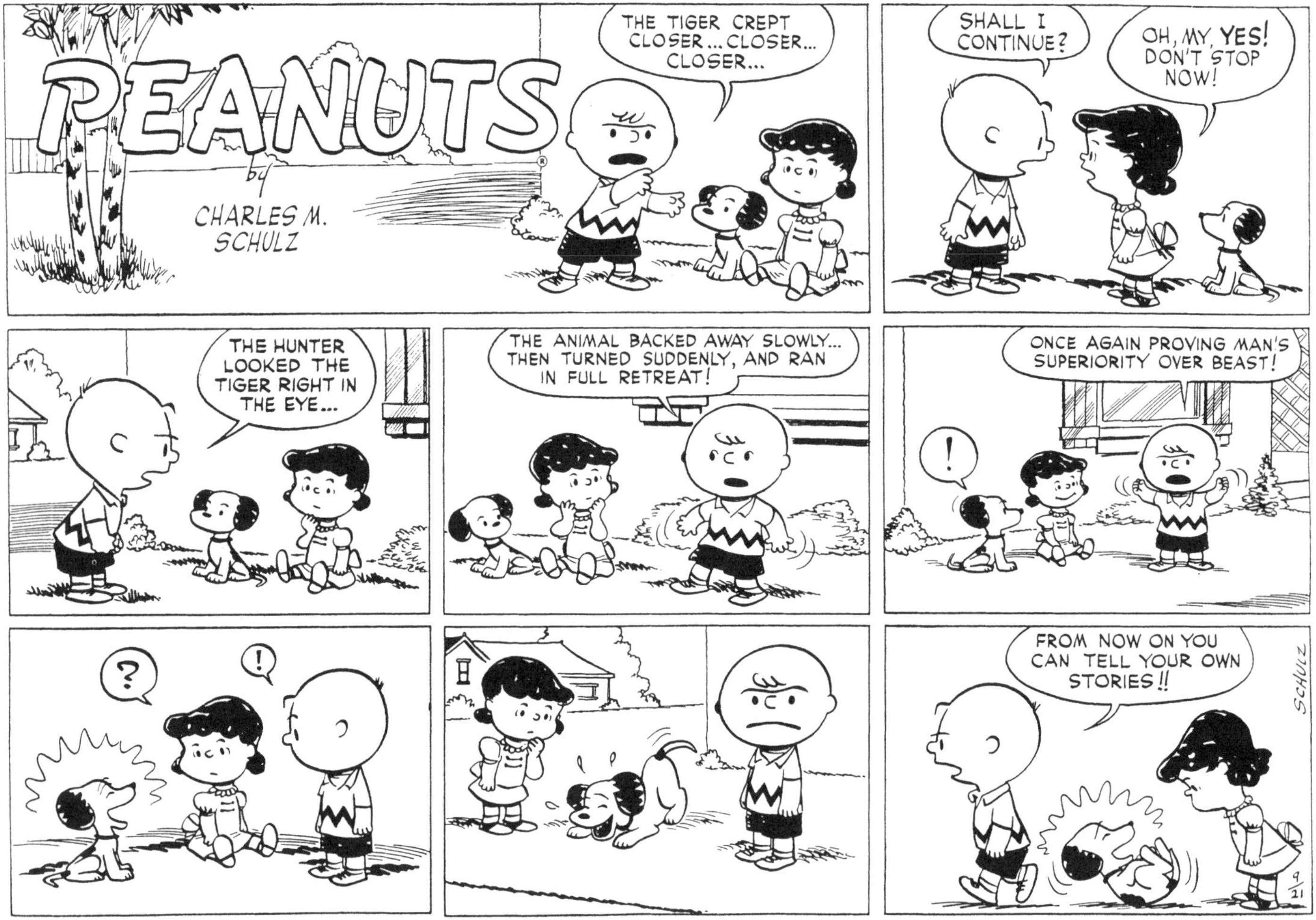
PEANUTS
by
CHARLES M. SCHULZ
THE TIGER CREPT CLOSER...CLOSER... CLOSER...
SHALL I CONTINUE?
OH, MY, YES! DON'T STOP NOW!
THE HUNTER LOOKED THE TIGER RIGHT IN THE EYE...
THE ANIMAL BACKED AWAY SLOWLY... THEN TURNED SUDDENLY, AND RAN IN FULL RETREAT!
ONCE AGAIN PROVING MAN'S SUPERIORITY OVER BEAST!
!
?
!
FROM NOW ON YOU CAN TELL YOUR OWN STORIES!!
SCHULZ
9/21

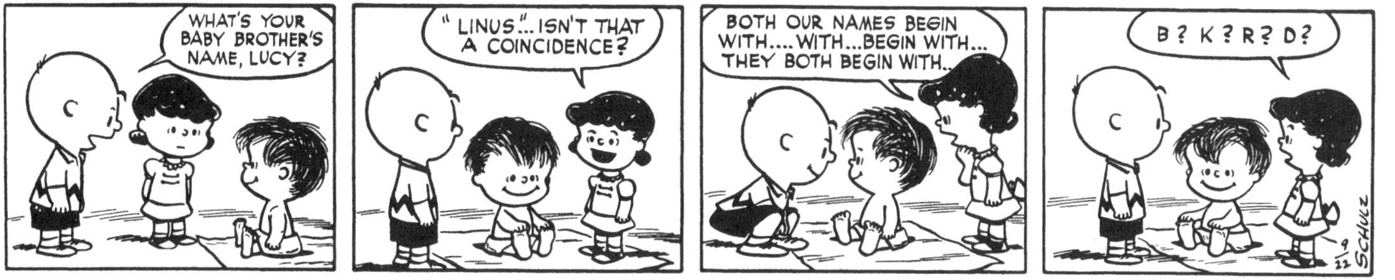
WHAT'S YOUR BABY BROTHER'S NAME, LUCY?
"LINUS"... ISN'T THAT A COINCIDENCE?
BOTH OUR NAMES BEGIN WITH.... WITH...BEGIN WITH... THEY BOTH BEGIN WITH...
B? K? R? D?
SCHULZ 9/22

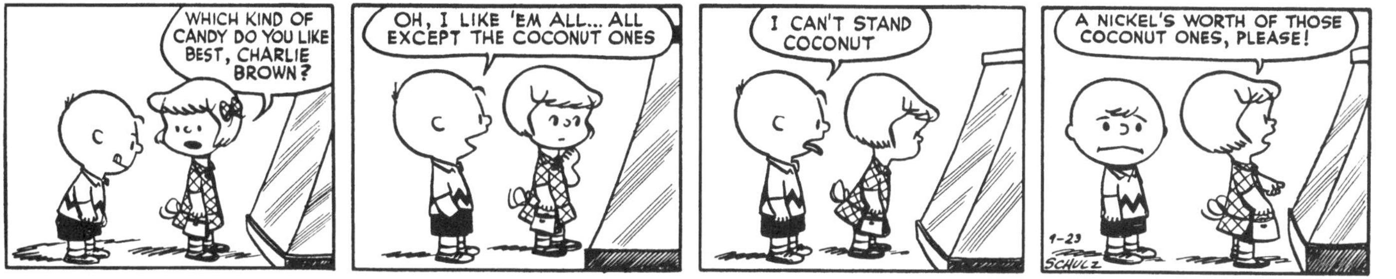
WHICH KIND OF CANDY DO YOU LIKE BEST, CHARLIE BROWN?
OH, I LIKE 'EM ALL... ALL EXCEPT THE COCONUT ONES
I CAN'T STAND COCONUT
A NICKEL'S WORTH OF THOSE COCONUT ONES, PLEASE!
9-23
SCHULZ

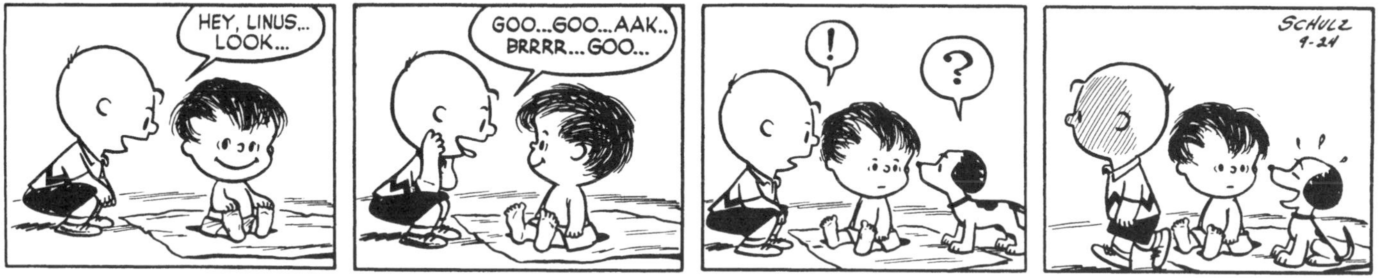
HEY, LINUS... LOOK...
GOO...GOO...AAK.. BRRRR...GOO...
!
?
SCHULZ 9-24

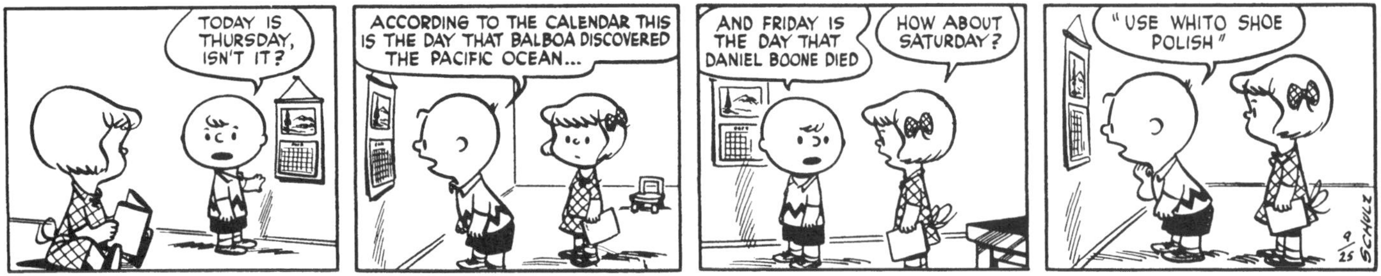
TODAY IS THURSDAY, ISN'T IT?
ACCORDING TO THE CALENDAR THIS IS THE DAY THAT BALBOA DISCOVERED THE PACIFIC OCEAN...
AND FRIDAY IS THE DAY THAT DANIEL BOONE DIED
HOW ABOUT SATURDAY?
"USE WHITO SHOE POLISH"
9/25
SCHULZ

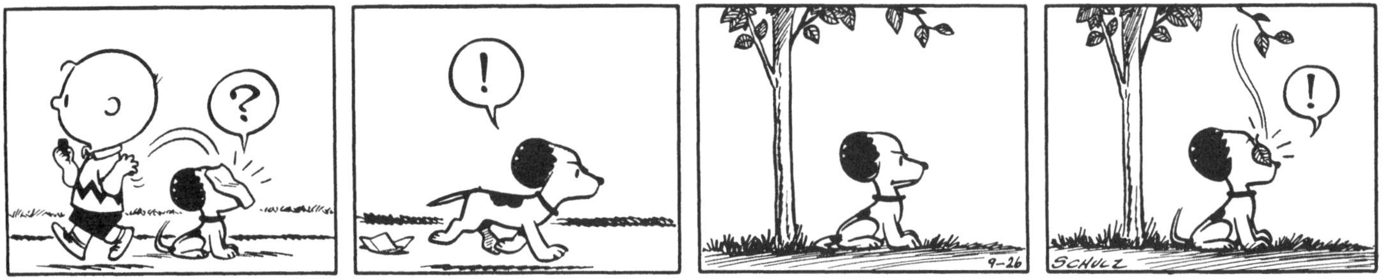
?
!
9-26
!
SCHULZ

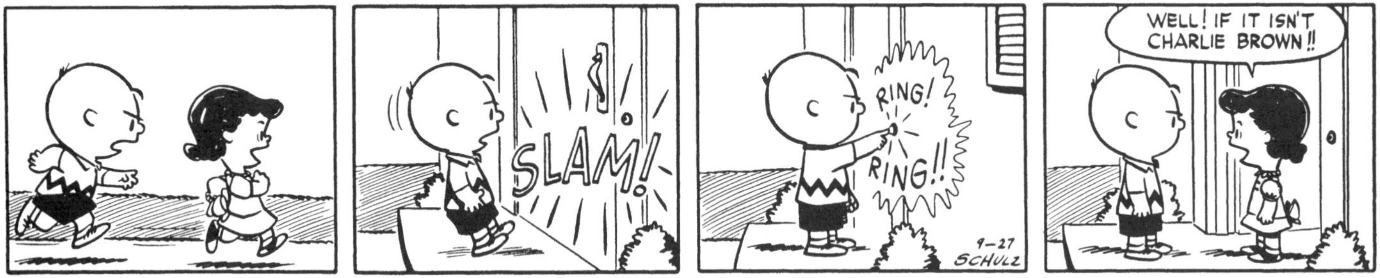
SLAM!
RING!
RING!!
9-27
SCHULZ
WELL! IF IT ISN'T CHARLIE BROWN!!

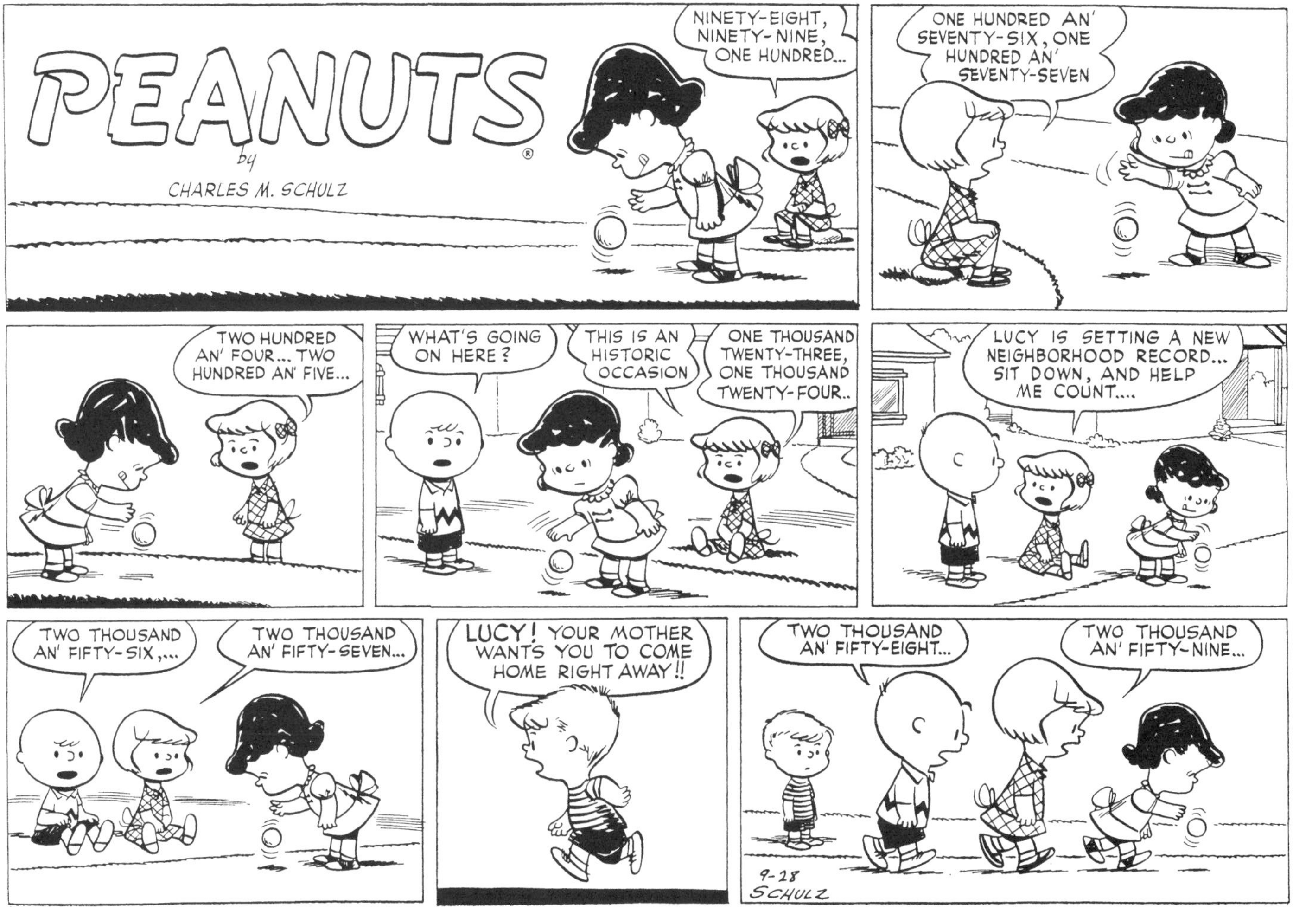
PEANUTS
by
CHARLES M. SCHULZ
NINETY-EIGHT, NINETY-NINE, ONE HUNDRED...
ONE HUNDRED AN' SEVENTY-SIX, ONE HUNDRED AN' SEVENTY-SEVEN
TWO HUNDRED AN' FOUR... TWO HUNDRED AN' FIVE...
WHAT'S GOING ON HERE?
THIS IS AN HISTORIC OCCASION
ONE THOUSAND TWENTY-THREE, ONE THOUSAND TWENTY-FOUR..
LUCY IS SETTING A NEW NEIGHBORHOOD RECORD... SIT DOWN, AND HELP ME COUNT....
TWO THOUSAND AN' FIFTY-SIX,...
TWO THOUSAND AN' FIFTY-SEVEN...
LUCY! YOUR MOTHER WANTS YOU TO COME HOME RIGHT AWAY!!
TWO THOUSAND AN' FIFTY-EIGHT...
TWO THOUSAND AN' FIFTY-NINE...
9-28
SCHULZ

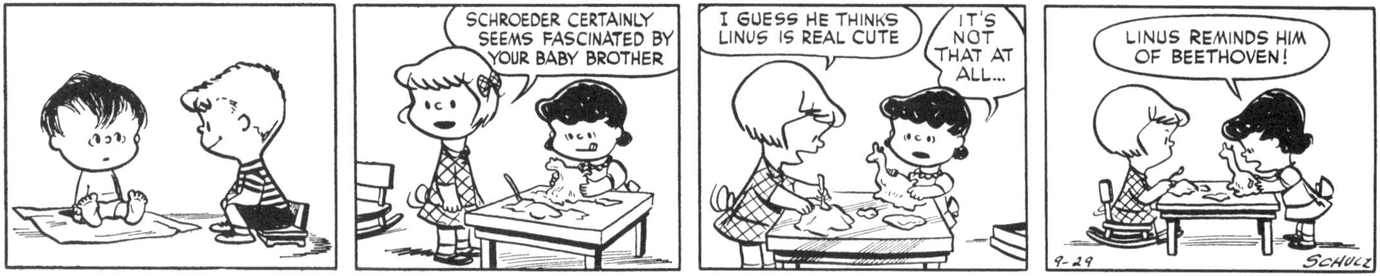
SCHROEDER CERTAINLY SEEMS FASCINATED BY YOUR BABY BROTHER
I GUESS HE THINKS LINUS IS REAL CUTE
IT'S NOT THAT AT ALL...
LINUS REMINDS HIM OF BEETHOVEN!
9-29
SCHULZ

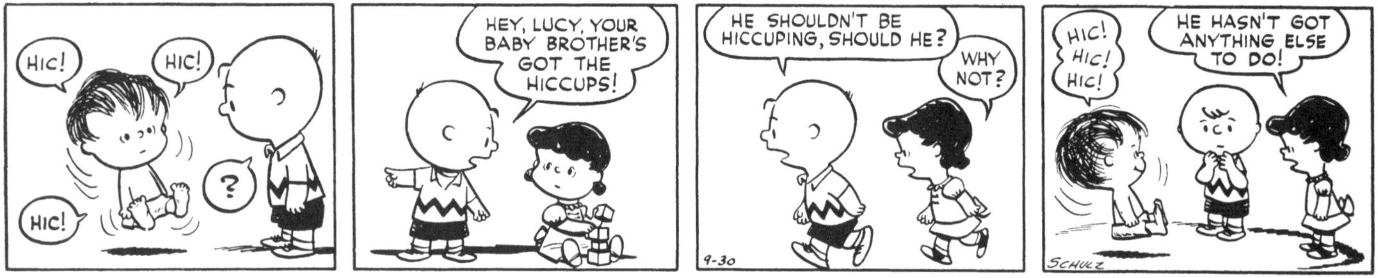
HIC!
HIC!
HIC!
?
HEY, LUCY, YOUR BABY BROTHER'S GOT THE HICCUPS!
HE SHOULDN'T BE HICCUPING, SHOULD HE?
WHY NOT?
9-30
HIC! HIC! HIC!
HE HASN'T GOT ANYTHING ELSE TO DO!
SCHULZ

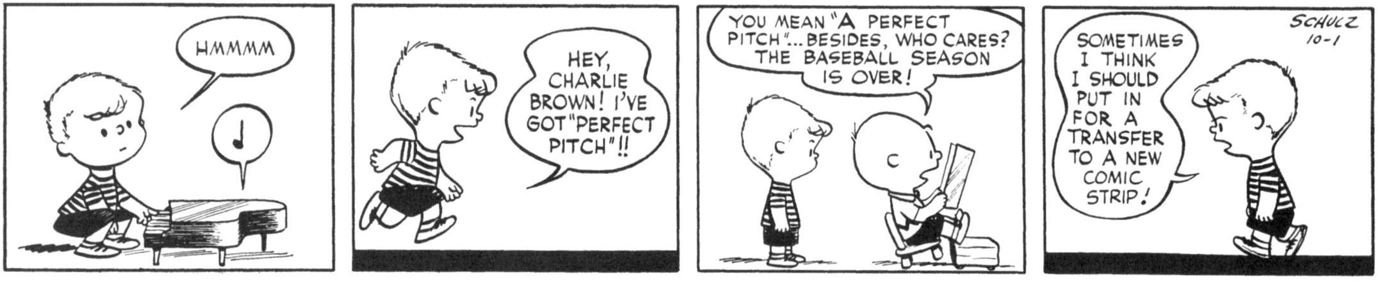
HMMMM
HEY, CHARLIE BROWN! I'VE GOT "PERFECT PITCH"!!
YOU MEAN "A PERFECT PITCH"... BESIDES, WHO CARES? THE BASEBALL SEASON IS OVER!
SCHULZ
10-1
SOMETIMES I THINK I SHOULD PUT IN FOR A TRANSFER TO A NEW COMIC STRIP!

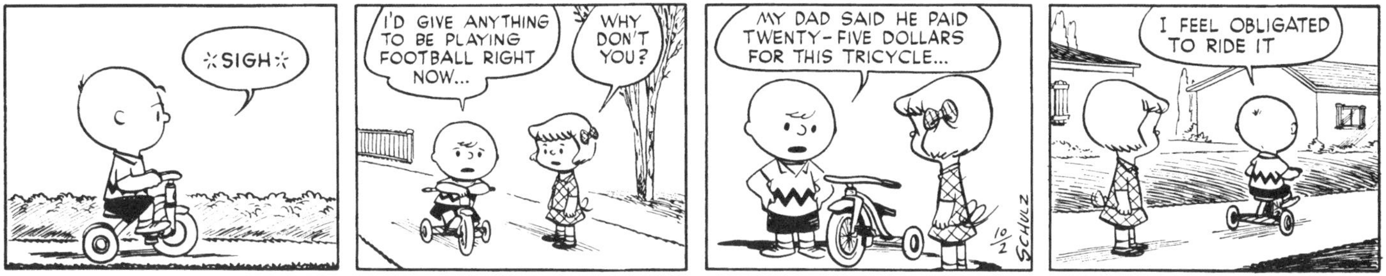
⁘SIGH⁘
I'D GIVE ANYTHING TO BE PLAYING FOOTBALL RIGHT NOW...
WHY DON'T YOU?
MY DAD SAID HE PAID TWENTY-FIVE DOLLARS FOR THIS TRICYCLE...
10/2 SCHULZ
I FEEL OBLIGATED TO RIDE IT

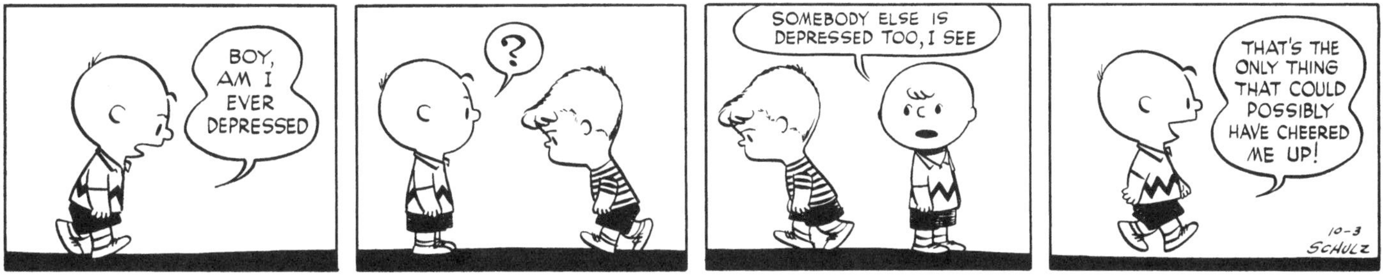
BOY, AM I EVER DEPRESSED
?
SOMEBODY ELSE IS DEPRESSED TOO, I SEE
THAT'S THE ONLY THING THAT COULD POSSIBLY HAVE CHEERED ME UP!
10-3 SCHULZ

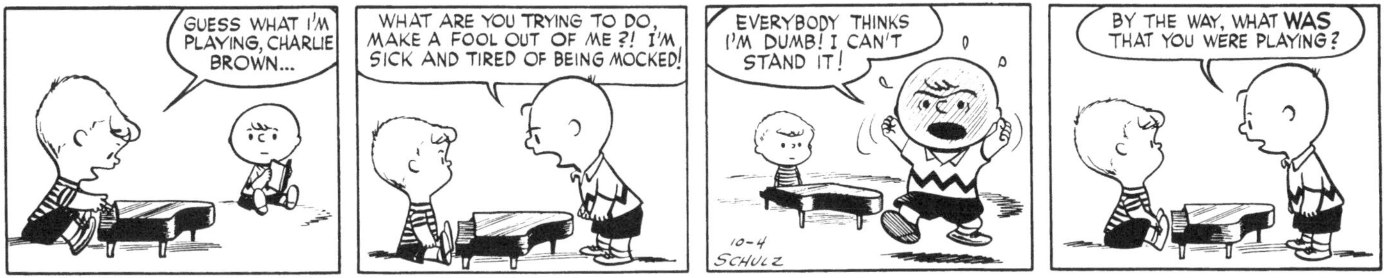
GUESS WHAT I'M PLAYING, CHARLIE BROWN...
WHAT ARE YOU TRYING TO DO, MAKE A FOOL OUT OF ME?! I'M SICK AND TIRED OF BEING MOCKED!
EVERYBODY THINKS I'M DUMB! I CAN'T STAND IT!
10-4 SCHULZ
BY THE WAY, WHAT WAS THAT YOU WERE PLAYING?

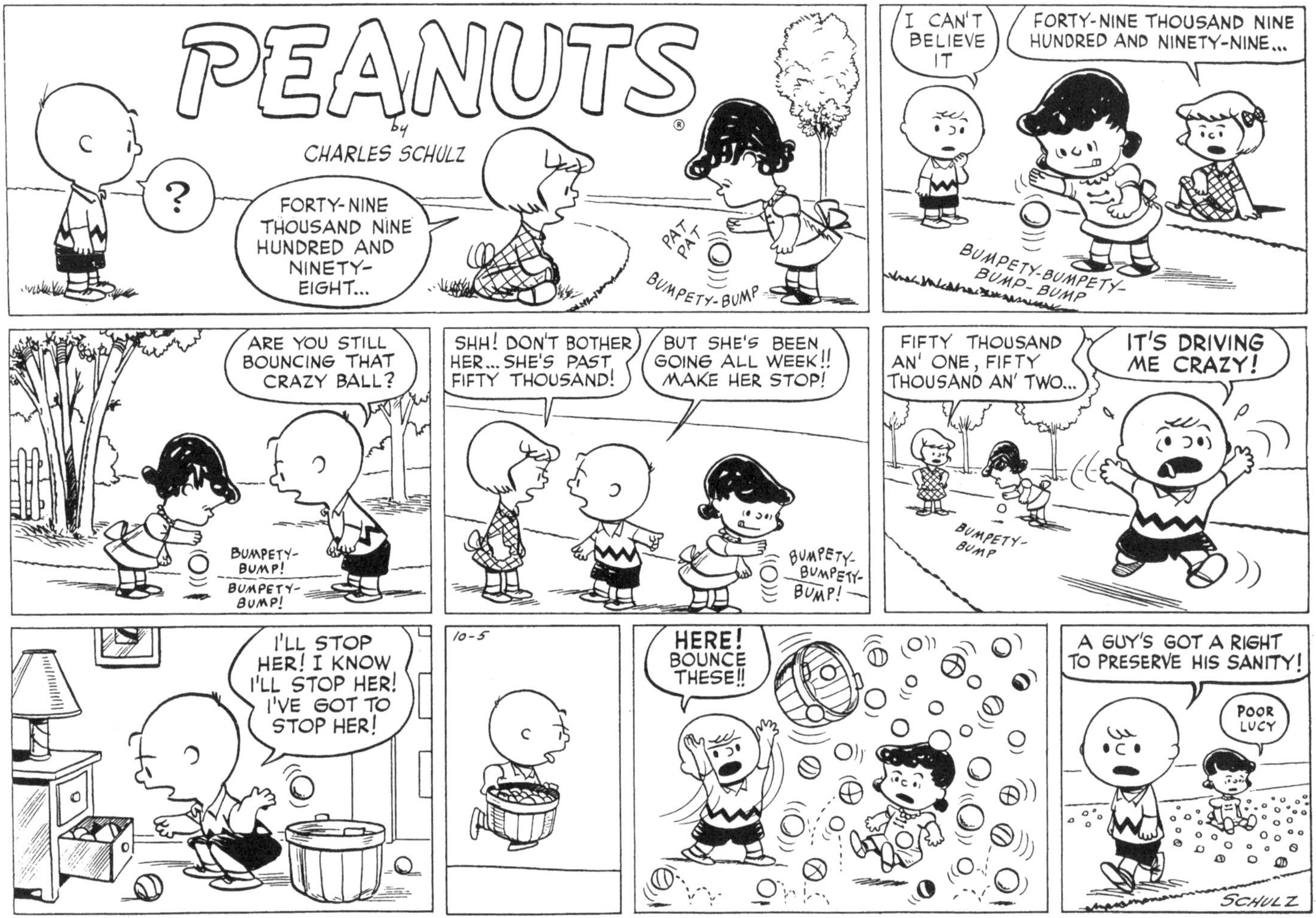
PEANUTS
by CHARLES SCHULZ
?
FORTY-NINE THOUSAND NINE HUNDRED AND NINETY-EIGHT...
PAT PAT
BUMPETY-BUMP
I CAN'T BELIEVE IT
FORTY-NINE THOUSAND NINE HUNDRED AND NINETY-NINE...
BUMPETY-BUMPETY-BUMP-BUMP
ARE YOU STILL BOUNCING THAT CRAZY BALL?
BUMPETY-BUMP!
BUMPETY-BUMP!
SHH! DON'T BOTHER HER... SHE'S PAST FIFTY THOUSAND!
BUT SHE'S BEEN GOING ALL WEEK!! MAKE HER STOP!
BUMPETY-BUMPETY-BUMP!
FIFTY THOUSAND AN' ONE, FIFTY THOUSAND AN' TWO...
IT'S DRIVING ME CRAZY!
BUMPETY-BUMP
I'LL STOP HER! I KNOW I'LL STOP HER! I'VE GOT TO STOP HER!
10-5
HERE! BOUNCE THESE!!
A GUY'S GOT A RIGHT TO PRESERVE HIS SANITY!
POOR LUCY
SCHULZ

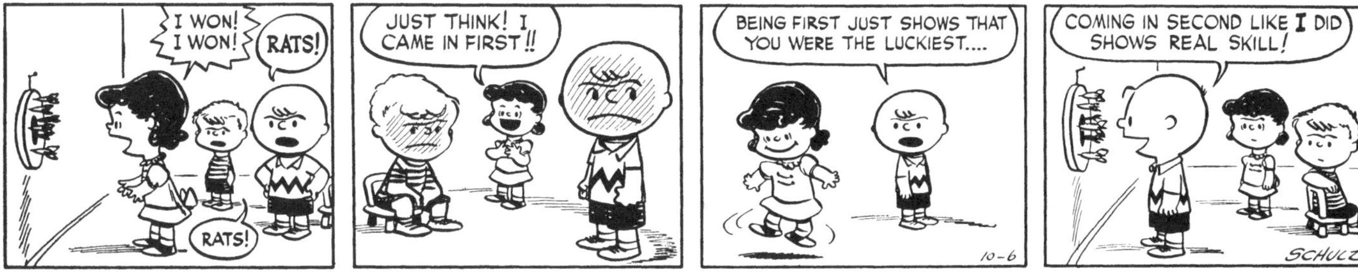
I WON! I WON!
RATS!
RATS!
JUST THINK! I CAME IN FIRST!!
BEING FIRST JUST SHOWS THAT YOU WERE THE LUCKIEST....
10-6
COMING IN SECOND LIKE I DID SHOWS REAL SKILL!
SCHULZ

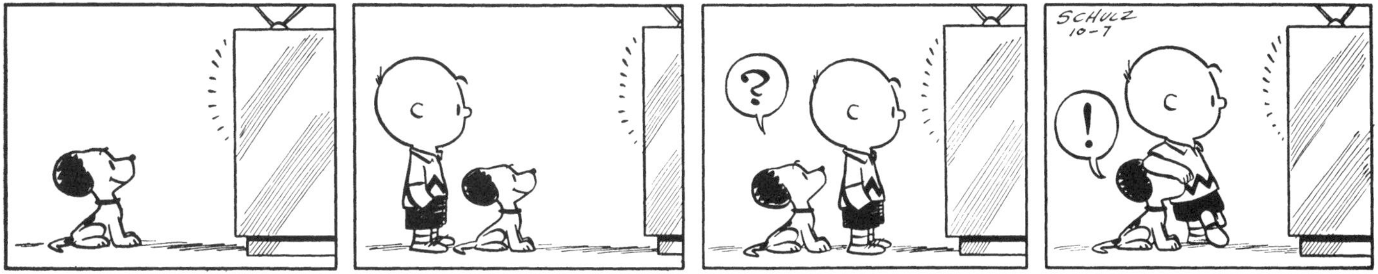
?
SCHULZ 10-7
!

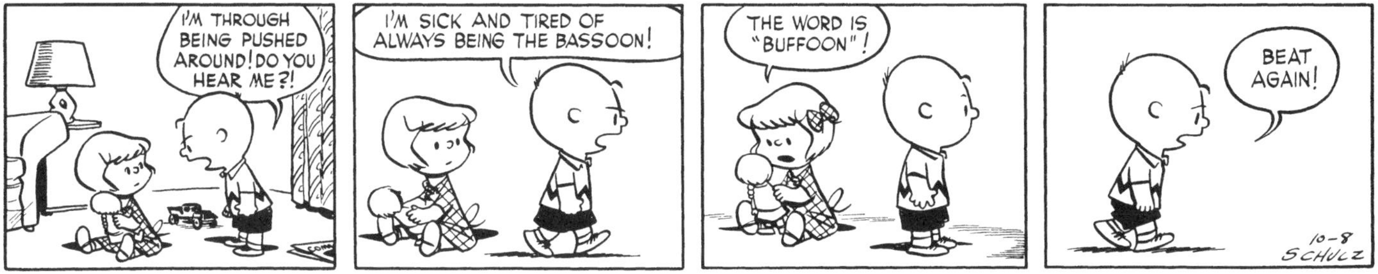
I'M THROUGH BEING PUSHED AROUND! DO YOU HEAR ME?!
I'M SICK AND TIRED OF ALWAYS BEING THE BASSOON!
THE WORD IS "BUFFOON"!
BEAT AGAIN!
10-8 SCHULZ

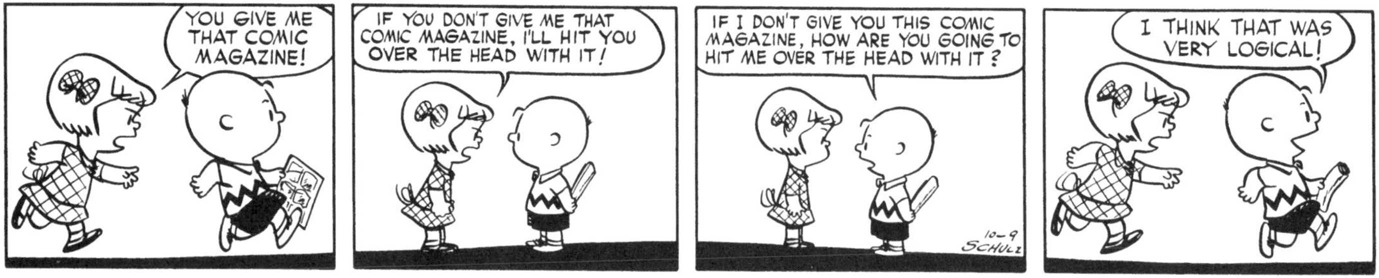
YOU GIVE ME THAT COMIC MAGAZINE!
IF YOU DON'T GIVE ME THAT COMIC MAGAZINE, I'LL HIT YOU OVER THE HEAD WITH IT!
IF I DON'T GIVE YOU THIS COMIC MAGAZINE, HOW ARE YOU GOING TO HIT ME OVER THE HEAD WITH IT?
10-9 SCHULZ
I THINK THAT WAS VERY LOGICAL!

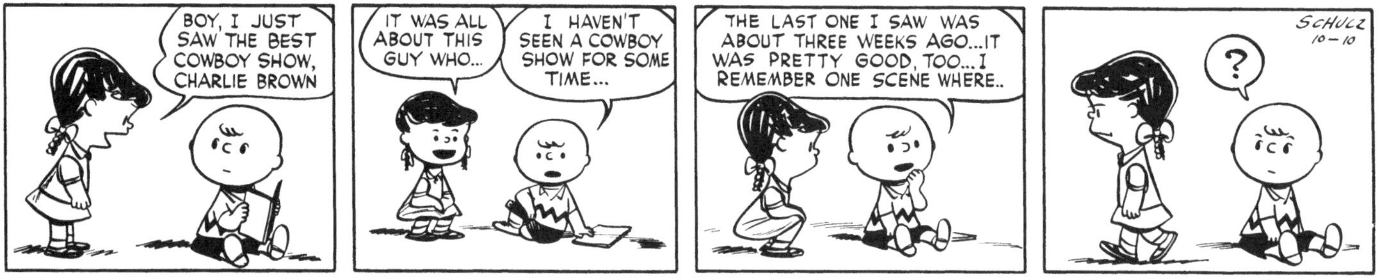
BOY, I JUST SAW THE BEST COWBOY SHOW, CHARLIE BROWN
IT WAS ALL ABOUT THIS GUY WHO...
I HAVEN'T SEEN A COWBOY SHOW FOR SOME TIME...
THE LAST ONE I SAW WAS ABOUT THREE WEEKS AGO...IT WAS PRETTY GOOD, TOO...I REMEMBER ONE SCENE WHERE..
SCHULZ 10-10
?

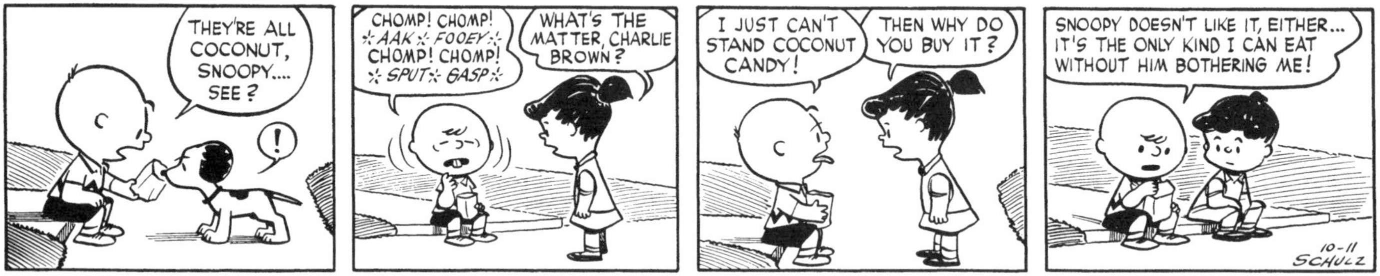
THEY'RE ALL COCONUT, SNOOPY.... SEE?
!
CHOMP! CHOMP! AAK FOOEY CHOMP! CHOMP! SPUT GASP
WHAT'S THE MATTER, CHARLIE BROWN?
I JUST CAN'T STAND COCONUT CANDY!
THEN WHY DO YOU BUY IT?
SNOOPY DOESN'T LIKE IT, EITHER... IT'S THE ONLY KIND I CAN EAT WITHOUT HIM BOTHERING ME!
10-11 SCHULZ

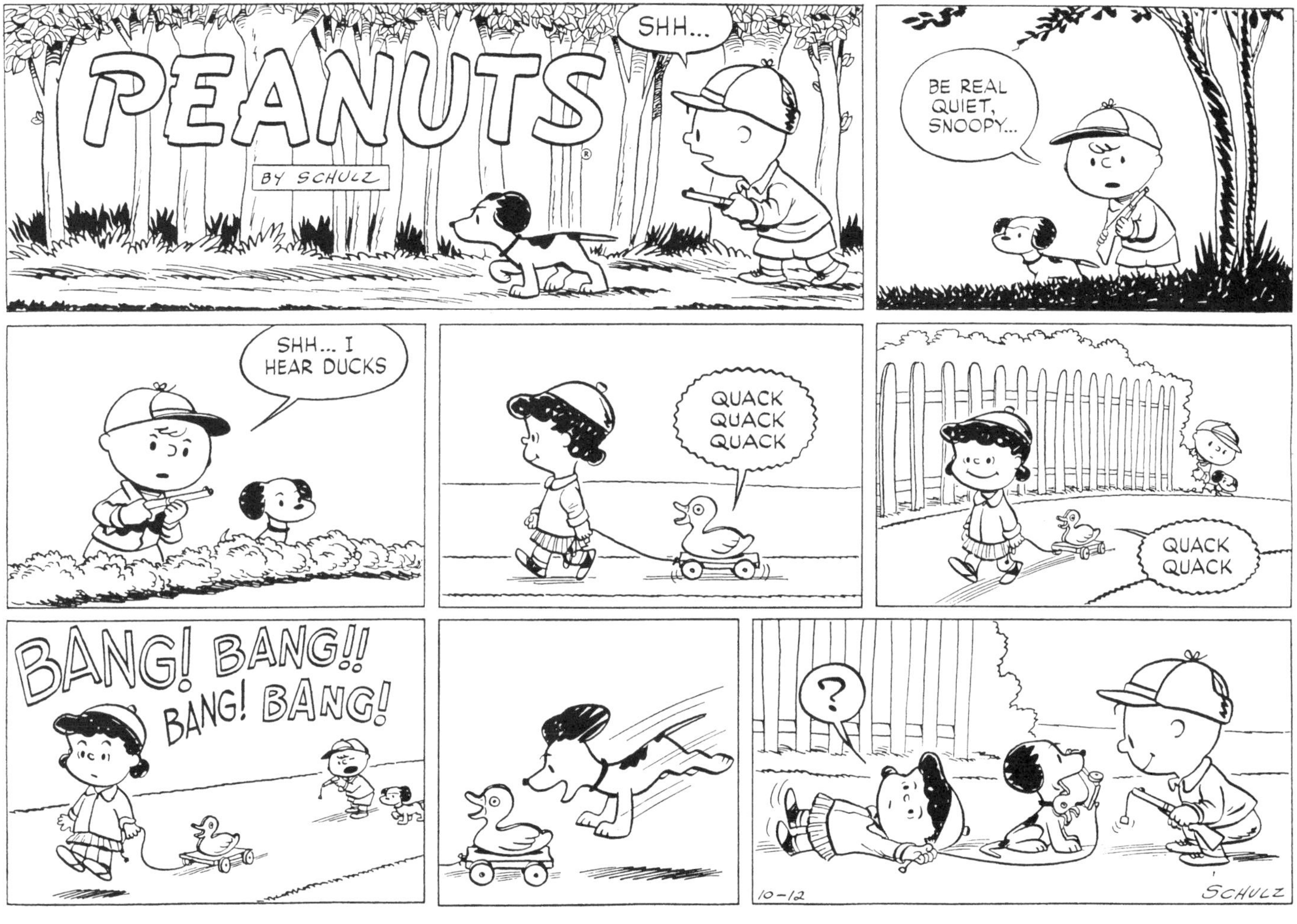
PEANUTS
BY SCHULZ
SHH...
BE REAL QUIET, SNOOPY...
SHH... I HEAR DUCKS
QUACK QUACK QUACK
QUACK QUACK
BANG! BANG!! BANG! BANG!
?
10-12
SCHULZ

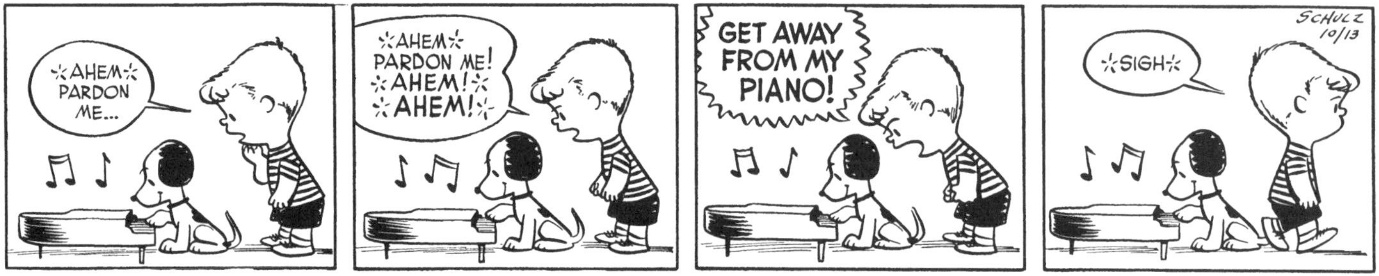
AHEM PARDON ME...
AHEM PARDON ME! AHEM! AHEM!
GET AWAY FROM MY PIANO!
SCHULZ 10/13
SIGH

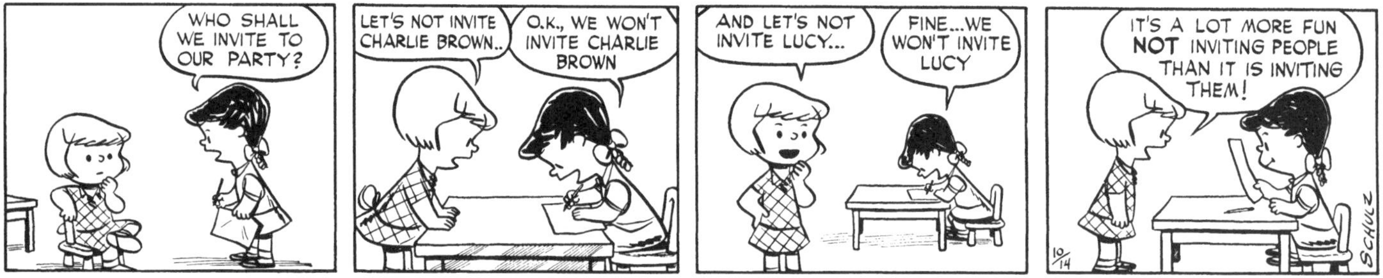
WHO SHALL WE INVITE TO OUR PARTY?
LET'S NOT INVITE CHARLIE BROWN..
O.K., WE WON'T INVITE CHARLIE BROWN
AND LET'S NOT INVITE LUCY...
FINE...WE WON'T INVITE LUCY
IT'S A LOT MORE FUN **NOT** INVITING PEOPLE THAN IT IS INVITING THEM!
10/14
SCHULZ

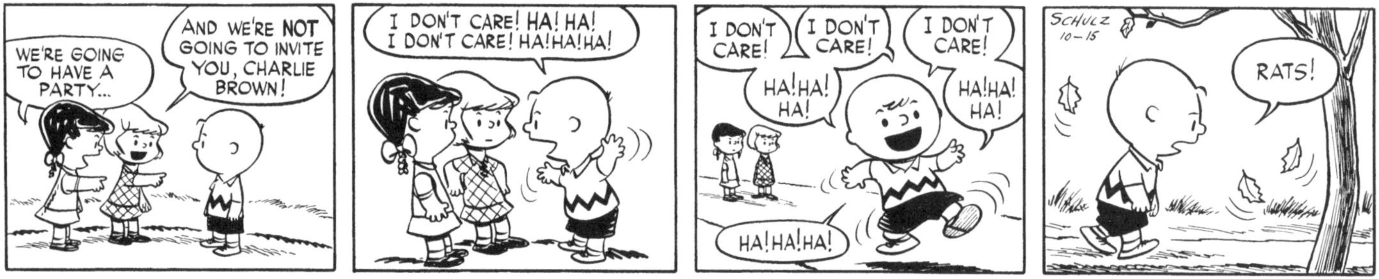
WE'RE GOING TO HAVE A PARTY...
AND WE'RE **NOT** GOING TO INVITE YOU, CHARLIE BROWN!
I DON'T CARE! HA! HA! I DON'T CARE! HA!HA!HA!
I DON'T CARE!
HA!HA! HA!
I DON'T CARE!
I DON'T CARE!
HA!HA! HA!
HA!HA!HA!
SCHULZ 10-15
RATS!

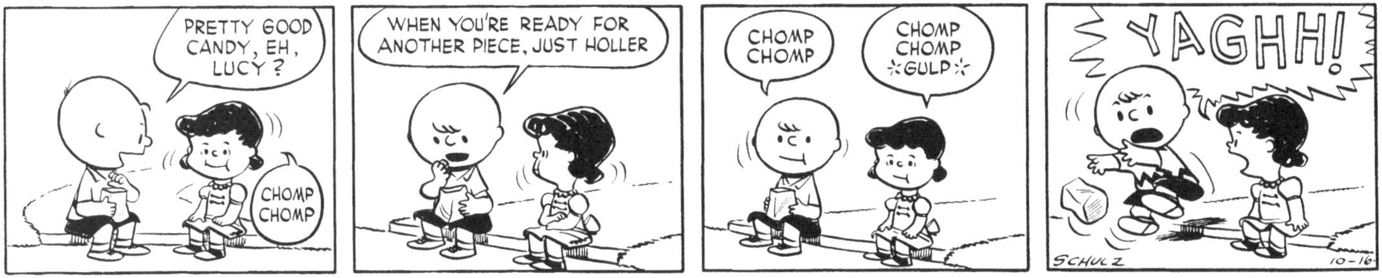
PRETTY GOOD CANDY, EH, LUCY?
CHOMP CHOMP
WHEN YOU'RE READY FOR ANOTHER PIECE, JUST HOLLER
CHOMP CHOMP
CHOMP CHOMP *GULP*
YAGHH!
SCHULZ
10-16

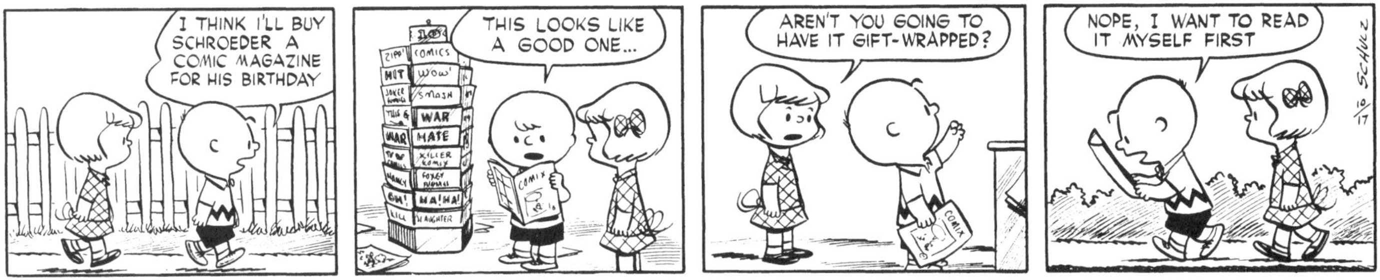
I THINK I'LL BUY SCHROEDER A COMIC MAGAZINE FOR HIS BIRTHDAY
THIS LOOKS LIKE A GOOD ONE...
COMIX
AREN'T YOU GOING TO HAVE IT GIFT-WRAPPED?
NOPE, I WANT TO READ IT MYSELF FIRST
SCHULZ

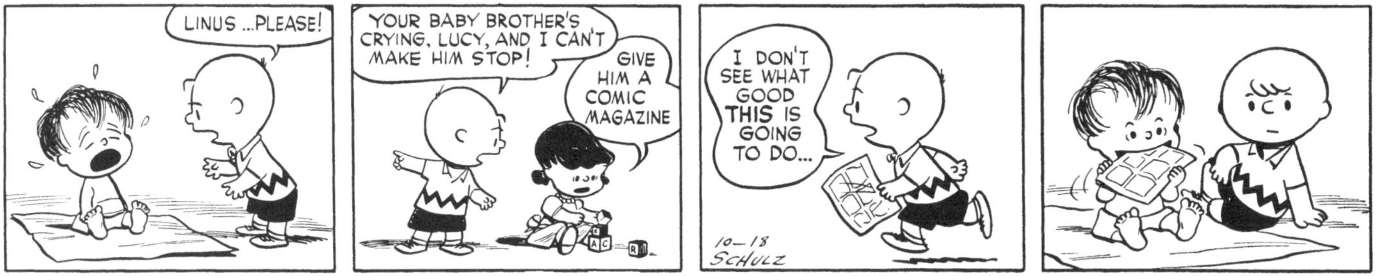
LINUS ...PLEASE!
YOUR BABY BROTHER'S CRYING, LUCY, AND I CAN'T MAKE HIM STOP!
GIVE HIM A COMIC MAGAZINE
I DON'T SEE WHAT GOOD THIS IS GOING TO DO...
10-18
SCHULZ

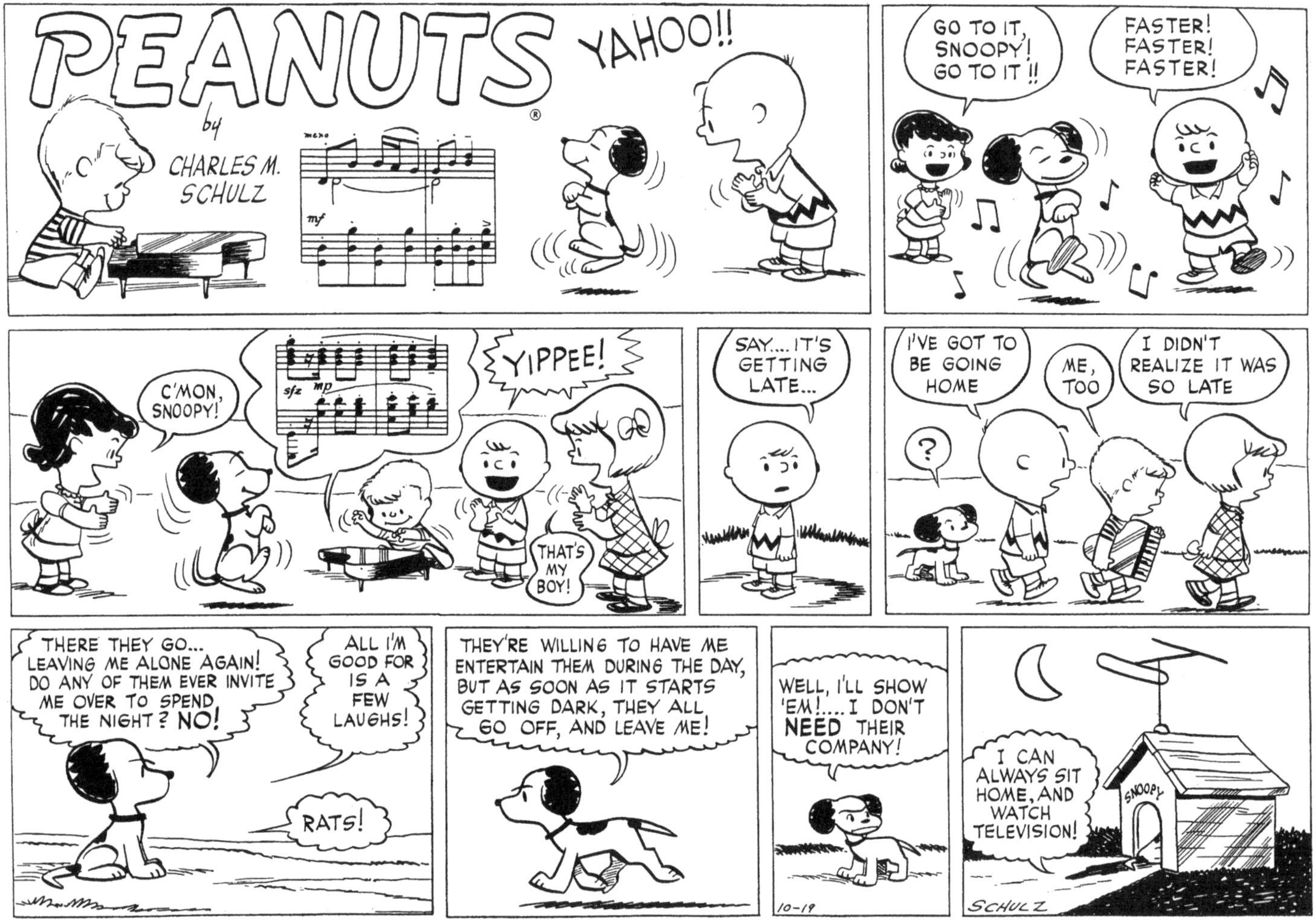
PEANUTS
by CHARLES M. SCHULZ
YAHOO!!
GO TO IT, SNOOPY! GO TO IT !!
FASTER! FASTER! FASTER!
C'MON, SNOOPY!
YIPPEE!
THAT'S MY BOY!
SAY.... IT'S GETTING LATE...
I'VE GOT TO BE GOING HOME
?
ME, TOO
I DIDN'T REALIZE IT WAS SO LATE
THERE THEY GO... LEAVING ME ALONE AGAIN! DO ANY OF THEM EVER INVITE ME OVER TO SPEND THE NIGHT? NO!
ALL I'M GOOD FOR IS A FEW LAUGHS!
RATS!
THEY'RE WILLING TO HAVE ME ENTERTAIN THEM DURING THE DAY, BUT AS SOON AS IT STARTS GETTING DARK, THEY ALL GO OFF, AND LEAVE ME!
WELL, I'LL SHOW 'EM!.... I DON'T NEED THEIR COMPANY!
10-19
I CAN ALWAYS SIT HOME, AND WATCH TELEVISION!
SNOOPY
SCHULZ

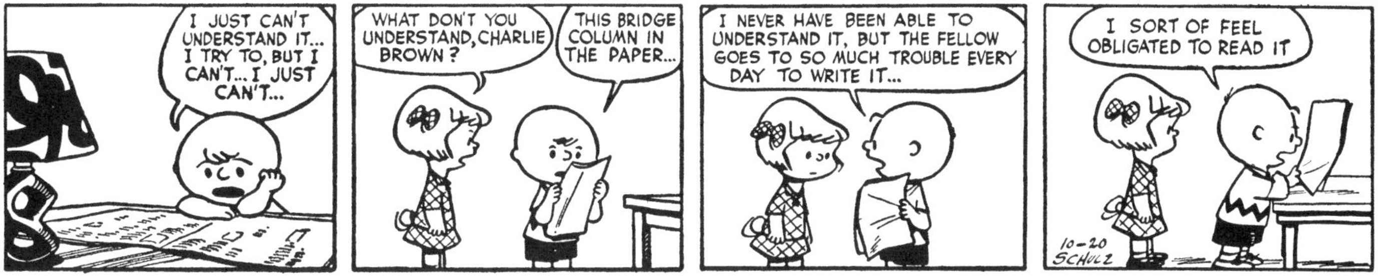
I JUST CAN'T UNDERSTAND IT... I TRY TO, BUT I CAN'T... I JUST CAN'T...
WHAT DON'T YOU UNDERSTAND, CHARLIE BROWN ?
THIS BRIDGE COLUMN IN THE PAPER...
I NEVER HAVE BEEN ABLE TO UNDERSTAND IT, BUT THE FELLOW GOES TO SO MUCH TROUBLE EVERY DAY TO WRITE IT...
I SORT OF FEEL OBLIGATED TO READ IT
10-20 SCHULZ

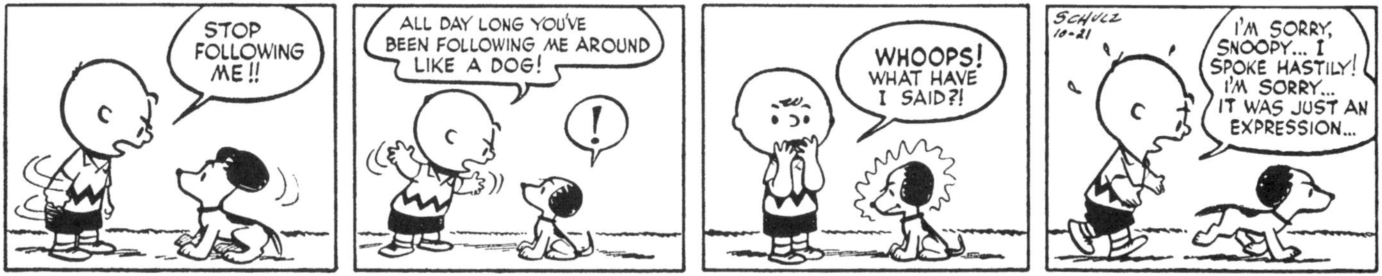
STOP FOLLOWING ME!!
ALL DAY LONG YOU'VE BEEN FOLLOWING ME AROUND LIKE A DOG!
!
WHOOPS! WHAT HAVE I SAID?!
SCHULZ 10-21
I'M SORRY, SNOOPY... I SPOKE HASTILY! I'M SORRY... IT WAS JUST AN EXPRESSION...

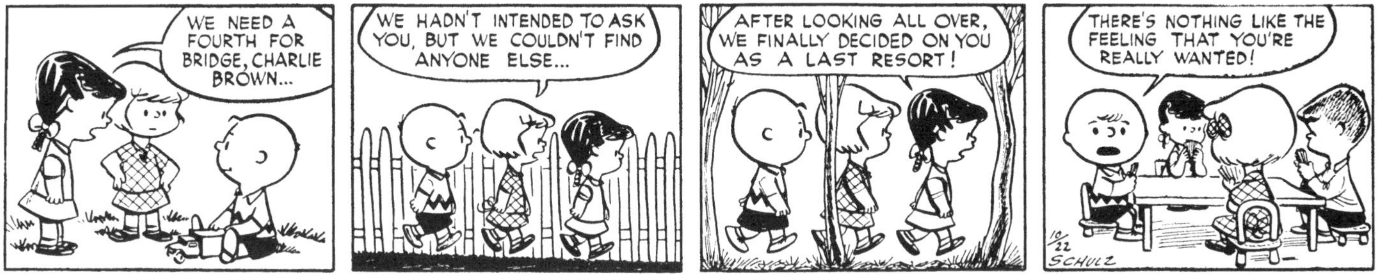
WE NEED A FOURTH FOR BRIDGE, CHARLIE BROWN...
WE HADN'T INTENDED TO ASK YOU, BUT WE COULDN'T FIND ANYONE ELSE...
AFTER LOOKING ALL OVER, WE FINALLY DECIDED ON YOU AS A LAST RESORT!
THERE'S NOTHING LIKE THE FEELING THAT YOU'RE REALLY WANTED!
10/22 SCHULZ

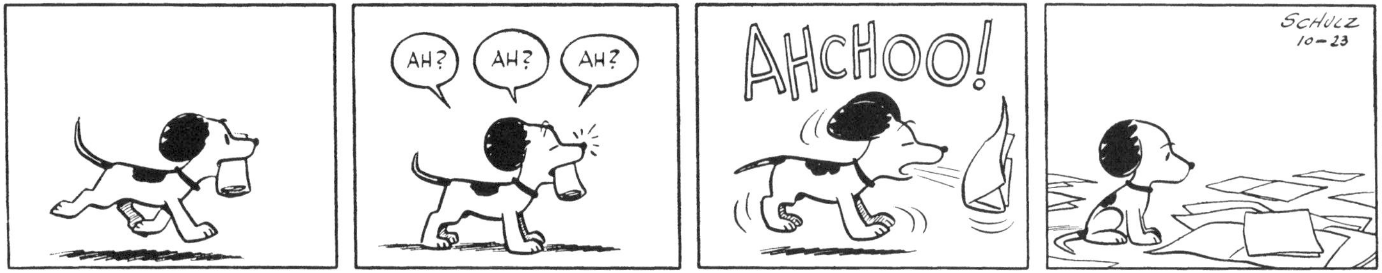
SCHULZ
10-23
AH?
AH?
AH?
AHCHOO!

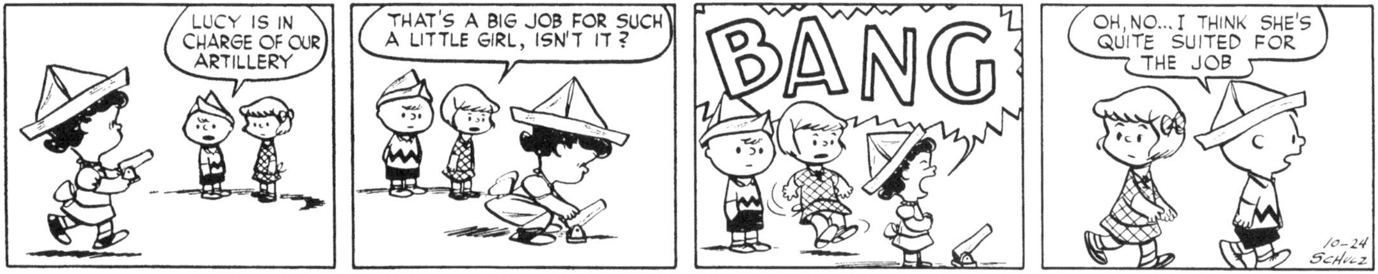
LUCY IS IN CHARGE OF OUR ARTILLERY
THAT'S A BIG JOB FOR SUCH A LITTLE GIRL, ISN'T IT?
BANG
OH, NO... I THINK SHE'S QUITE SUITED FOR THE JOB
10-24
SCHULZ

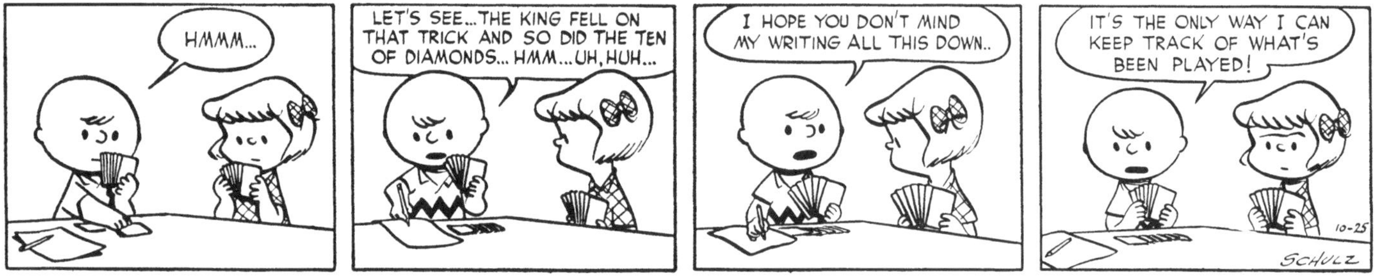
HMMM...
LET'S SEE... THE KING FELL ON THAT TRICK AND SO DID THE TEN OF DIAMONDS... HMM... UH, HUH...
I HOPE YOU DON'T MIND MY WRITING ALL THIS DOWN..
IT'S THE ONLY WAY I CAN KEEP TRACK OF WHAT'S BEEN PLAYED!
10-25
SCHULZ

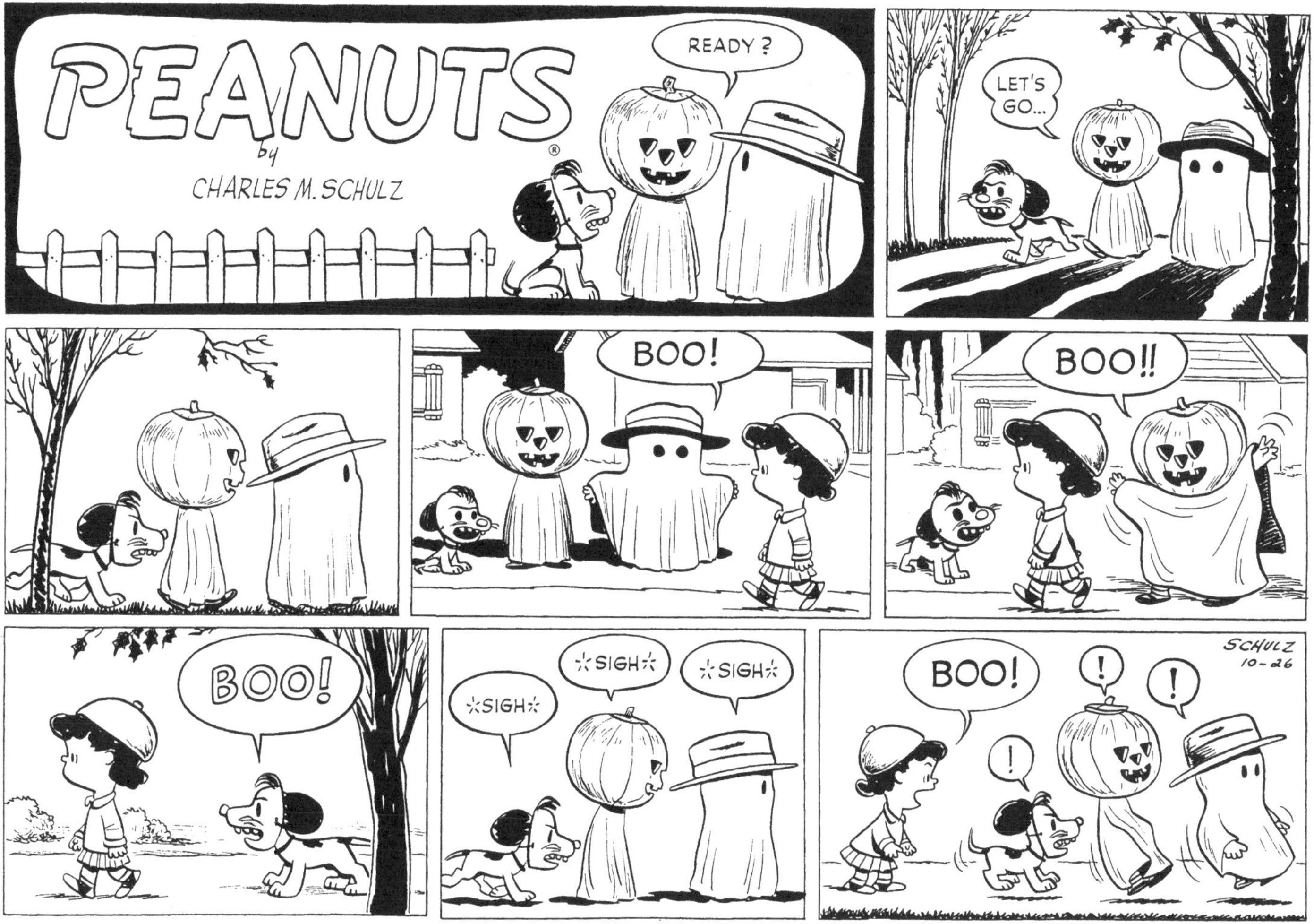
PEANUTS
by
CHARLES M. SCHULZ
READY ?
LET'S GO...
BOO!
BOO!!
BOO!
SIGH
SIGH
SIGH
SCHULZ
10-26
BOO!
!
!
!

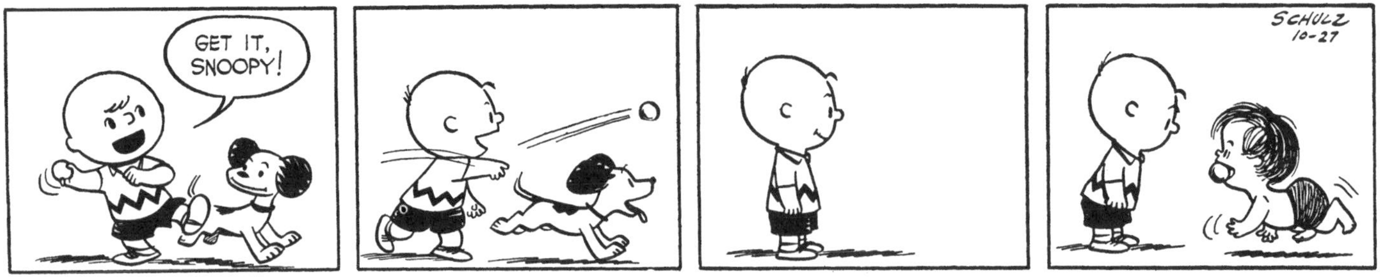
GET IT, SNOOPY!
SCHULZ 10-27

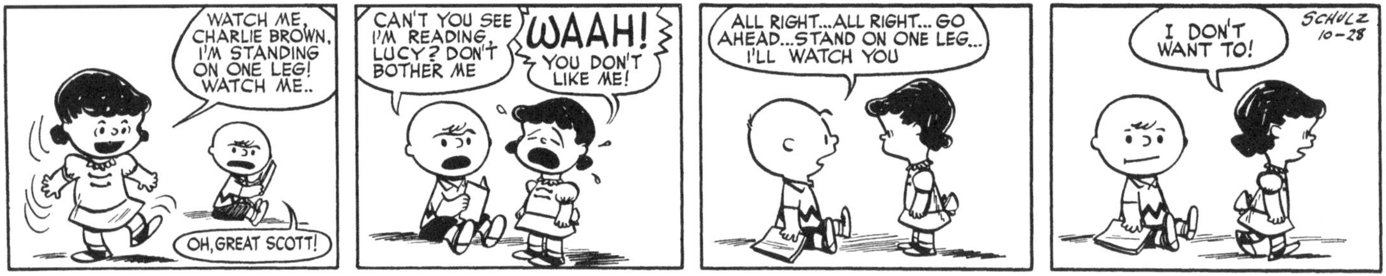
WATCH ME, CHARLIE BROWN, I'M STANDING ON ONE LEG! WATCH ME..
OH, GREAT SCOTT!
CAN'T YOU SEE I'M READING, LUCY? DON'T BOTHER ME
WAAH! YOU DON'T LIKE ME!
ALL RIGHT...ALL RIGHT... GO AHEAD...STAND ON ONE LEG... I'LL WATCH YOU
I DON'T WANT TO!
SCHULZ 10-28

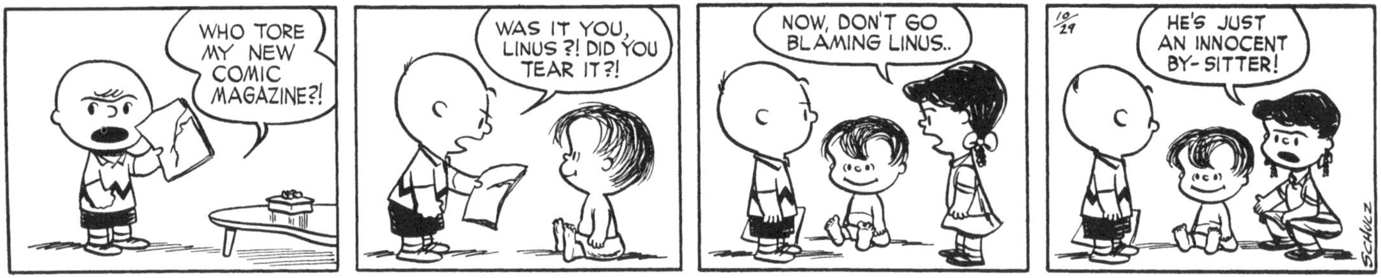
WHO TORE MY NEW COMIC MAGAZINE?!
WAS IT YOU, LINUS?! DID YOU TEAR IT?!
NOW, DON'T GO BLAMING LINUS..
10/29
HE'S JUST AN INNOCENT BY-SITTER!
SCHULZ

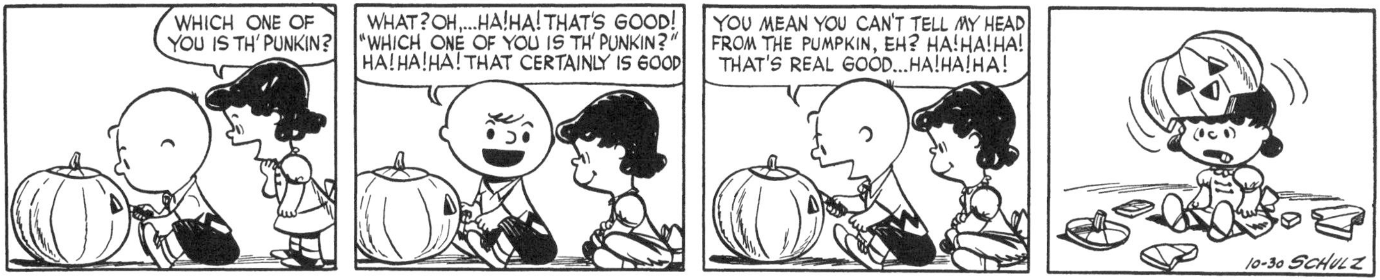
WHICH ONE OF YOU IS TH' PUNKIN?
WHAT? OH,...HA!HA! THAT'S GOOD! "WHICH ONE OF YOU IS TH' PUNKIN?" HA!HA!HA! THAT CERTAINLY IS GOOD
YOU MEAN YOU CAN'T TELL MY HEAD FROM THE PUMPKIN, EH? HA!HA!HA! THAT'S REAL GOOD...HA!HA!HA!
10-30 SCHULZ

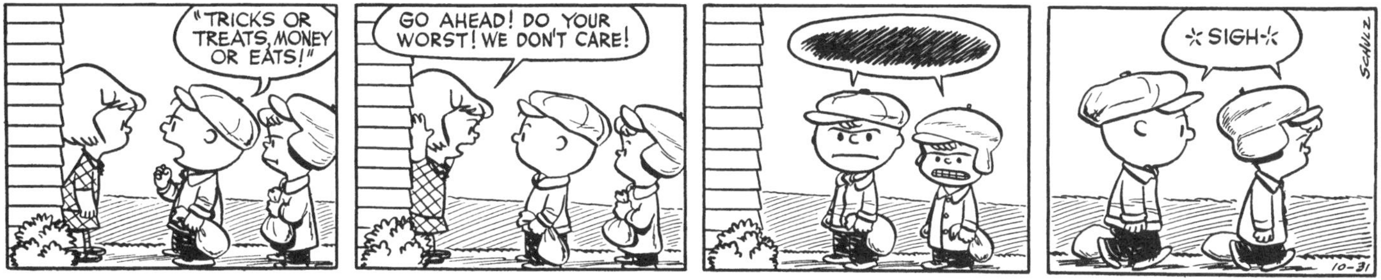
"TRICKS OR TREATS, MONEY OR EATS!"
GO AHEAD! DO YOUR WORST! WE DON'T CARE!
SCHULZ
SIGH
10-31

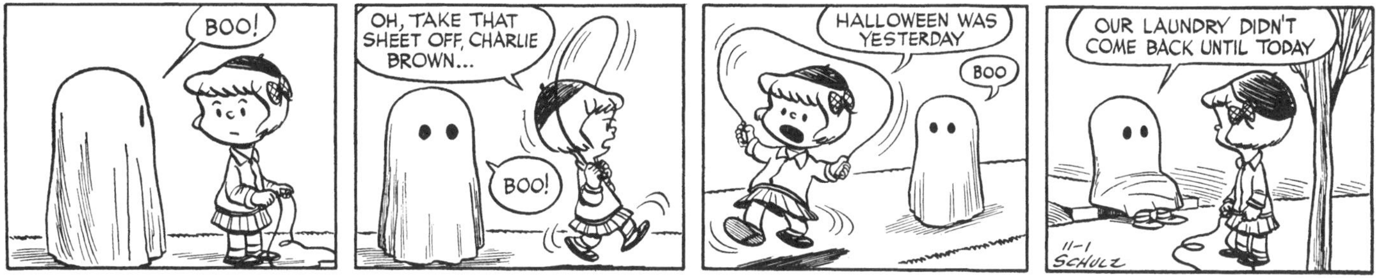
BOO!
OH, TAKE THAT SHEET OFF, CHARLIE BROWN...
BOO!
HALLOWEEN WAS YESTERDAY
BOO
OUR LAUNDRY DIDN'T COME BACK UNTIL TODAY
11-1 SCHULZ

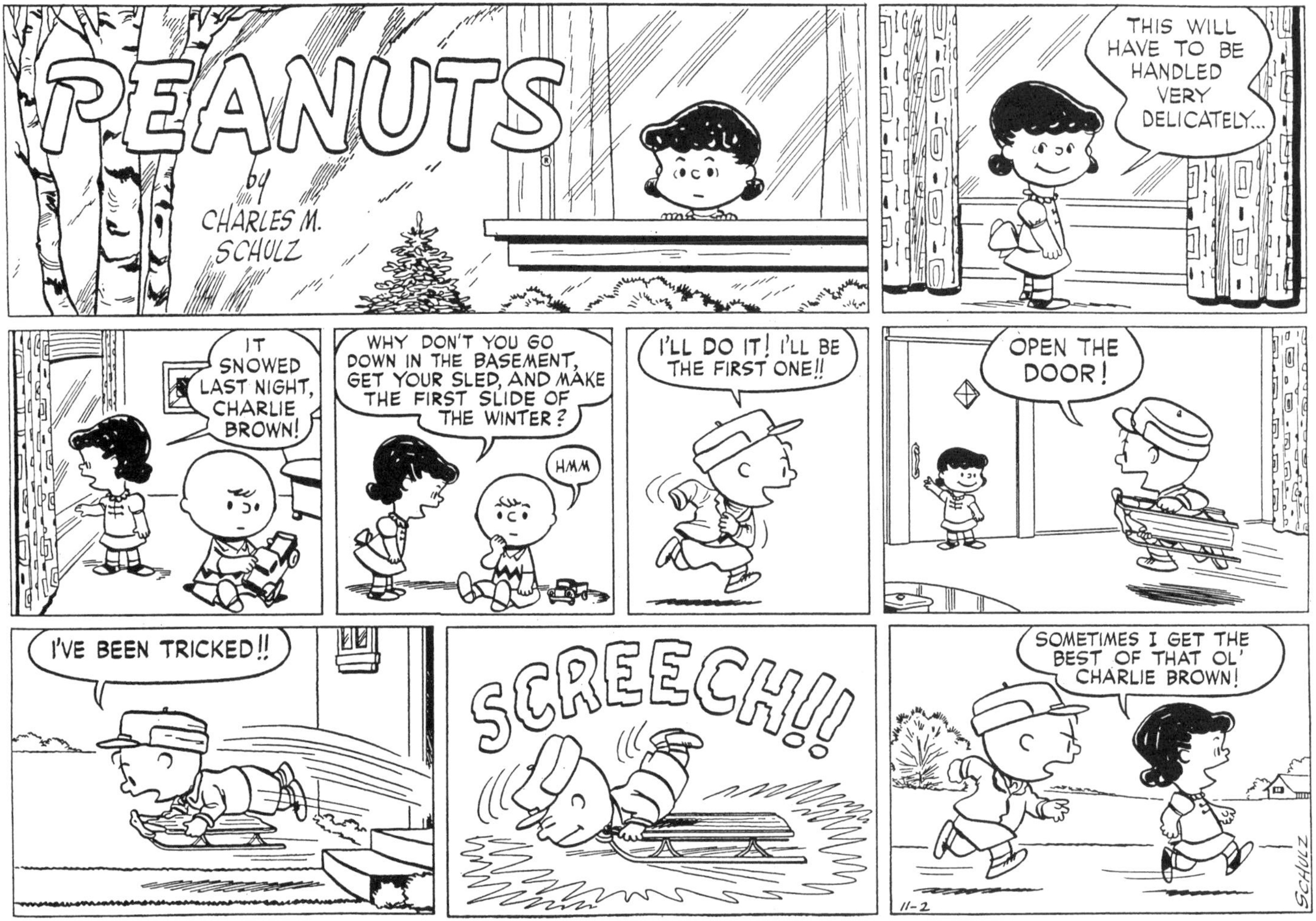
PEANUTS
by
CHARLES M.
SCHULZ
THIS WILL HAVE TO BE HANDLED VERY DELICATELY...
IT SNOWED LAST NIGHT, CHARLIE BROWN!
WHY DON'T YOU GO DOWN IN THE BASEMENT, GET YOUR SLED, AND MAKE THE FIRST SLIDE OF THE WINTER?
HMM
I'LL DO IT! I'LL BE THE FIRST ONE!!
OPEN THE DOOR!
I'VE BEEN TRICKED!!
SCREECH!!
SOMETIMES I GET THE BEST OF THAT OL' CHARLIE BROWN!
11-2
SCHULZ

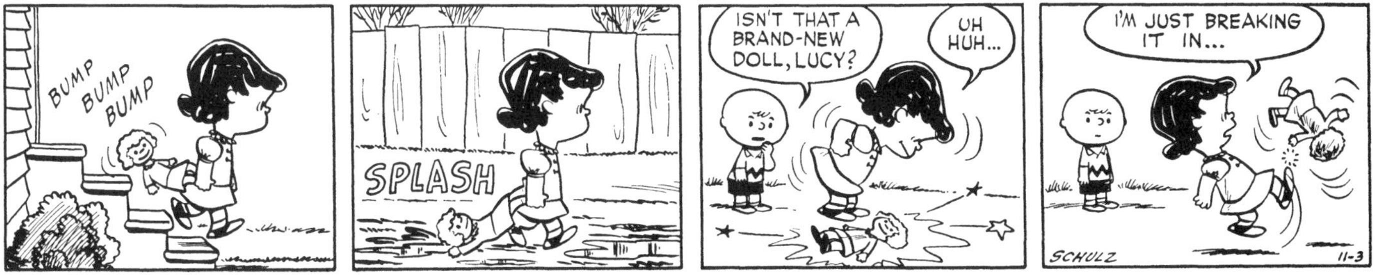
BUMP BUMP BUMP
SPLASH
ISN'T THAT A BRAND-NEW DOLL, LUCY?
UH HUH...
I'M JUST BREAKING IT IN...
SCHULZ 11-3

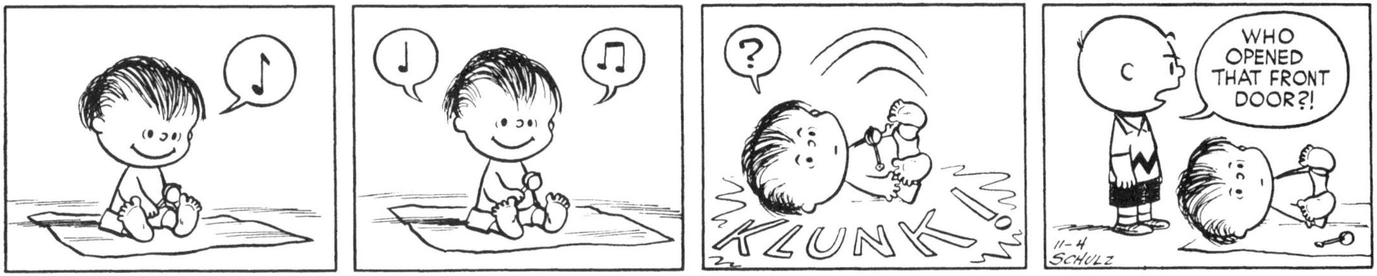
?
KLUNK!
WHO OPENED THAT FRONT DOOR?!
11-4 SCHULZ

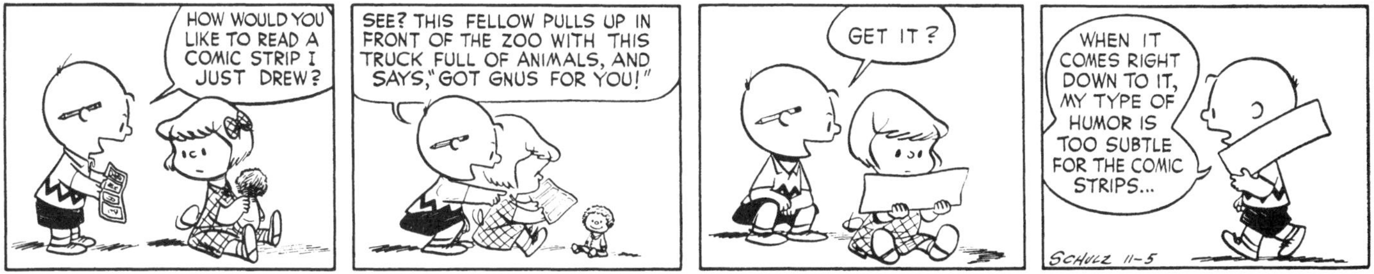
HOW WOULD YOU LIKE TO READ A COMIC STRIP I JUST DREW?
SEE? THIS FELLOW PULLS UP IN FRONT OF THE ZOO WITH THIS TRUCK FULL OF ANIMALS, AND SAYS, "GOT GNUS FOR YOU!"
GET IT?
WHEN IT COMES RIGHT DOWN TO IT, MY TYPE OF HUMOR IS TOO SUBTLE FOR THE COMIC STRIPS...
SCHULZ 11-5

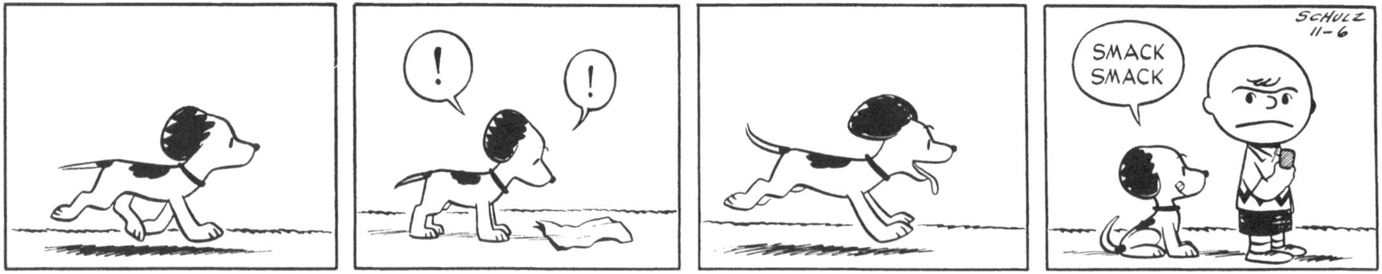
!
!
SMACK SMACK
SCHULZ 11-6

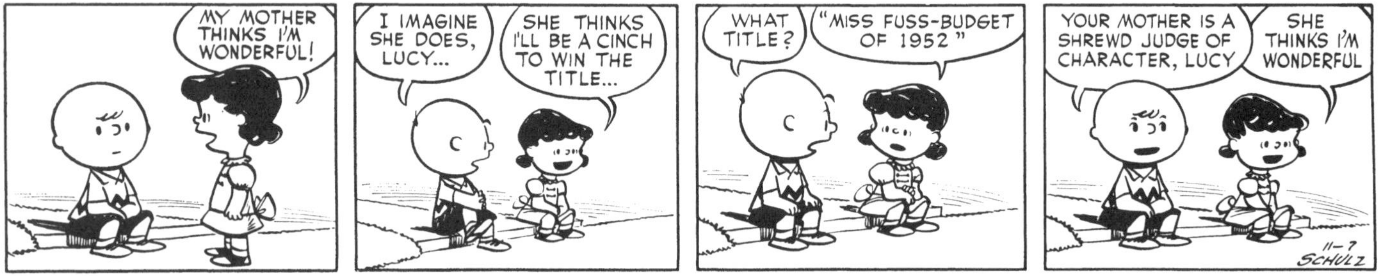
MY MOTHER THINKS I'M WONDERFUL!
I IMAGINE SHE DOES, LUCY...
SHE THINKS I'LL BE A CINCH TO WIN THE TITLE...
WHAT TITLE?
"MISS FUSS-BUDGET OF 1952"
YOUR MOTHER IS A SHREWD JUDGE OF CHARACTER, LUCY
SHE THINKS I'M WONDERFUL
11-7 SCHULZ

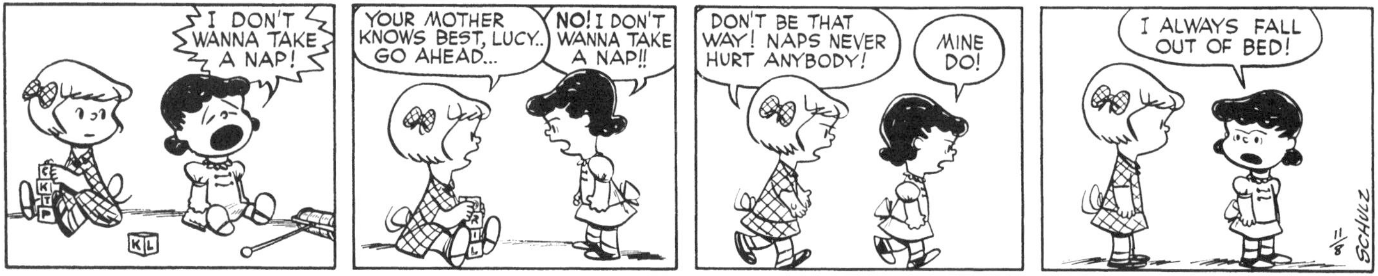
I DON'T WANNA TAKE A NAP!
YOUR MOTHER KNOWS BEST, LUCY.. GO AHEAD...
NO! I DON'T WANNA TAKE A NAP!!
DON'T BE THAT WAY! NAPS NEVER HURT ANYBODY!
MINE DO!
I ALWAYS FALL OUT OF BED!
11/8 SCHULZ

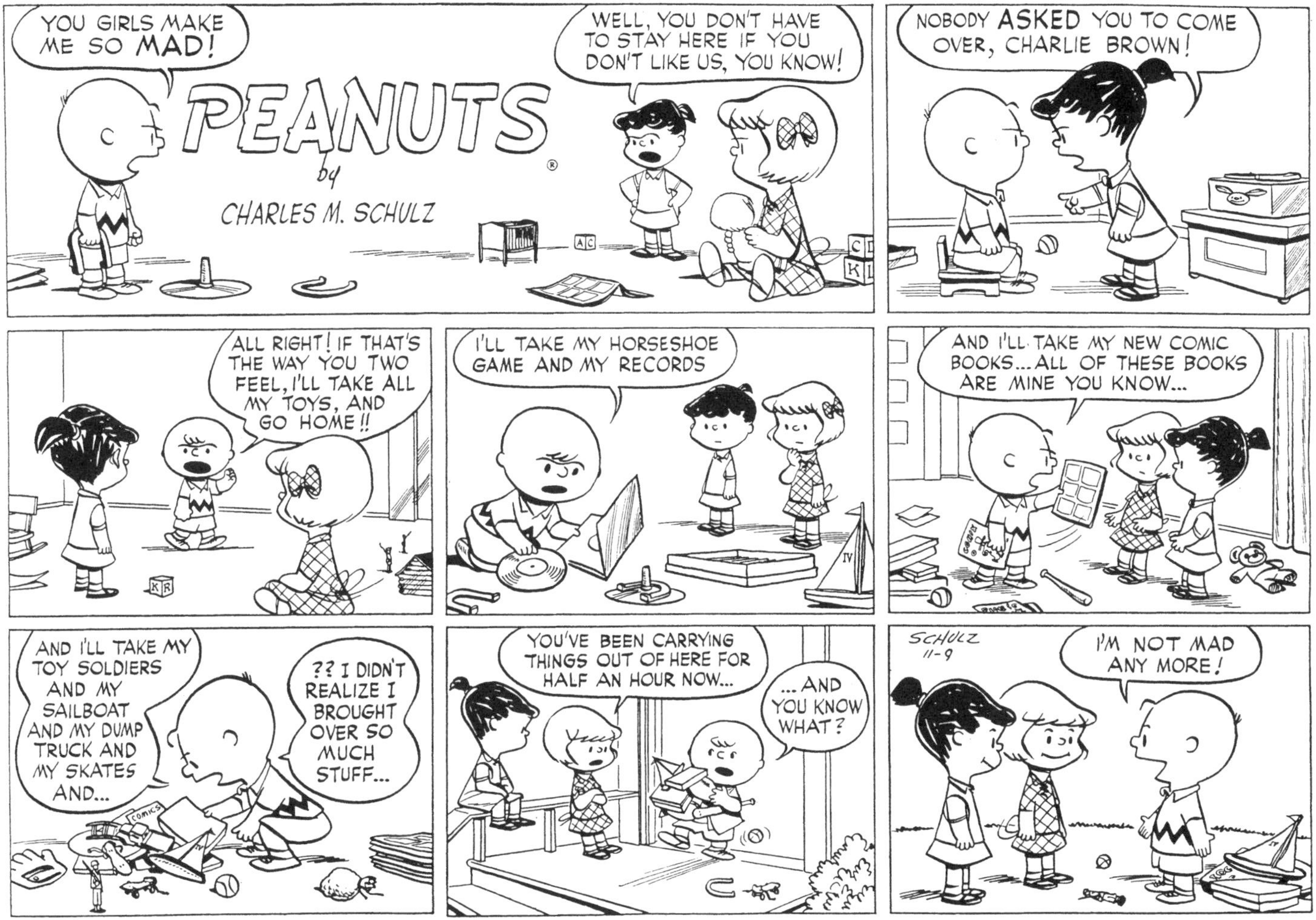
YOU GIRLS MAKE ME SO MAD!
PEANUTS
by
CHARLES M. SCHULZ
WELL, YOU DON'T HAVE TO STAY HERE IF YOU DON'T LIKE US, YOU KNOW!
NOBODY ASKED YOU TO COME OVER, CHARLIE BROWN!
ALL RIGHT! IF THAT'S THE WAY YOU TWO FEEL, I'LL TAKE ALL MY TOYS, AND GO HOME!!
I'LL TAKE MY HORSESHOE GAME AND MY RECORDS
AND I'LL TAKE MY NEW COMIC BOOKS... ALL OF THESE BOOKS ARE MINE YOU KNOW...
AND I'LL TAKE MY TOY SOLDIERS AND MY SAILBOAT AND MY DUMP TRUCK AND MY SKATES AND...
?? I DIDN'T REALIZE I BROUGHT OVER SO MUCH STUFF...
COMICS
YOU'VE BEEN CARRYING THINGS OUT OF HERE FOR HALF AN HOUR NOW...
...AND YOU KNOW WHAT?
SCHULZ 11-9
I'M NOT MAD ANY MORE!

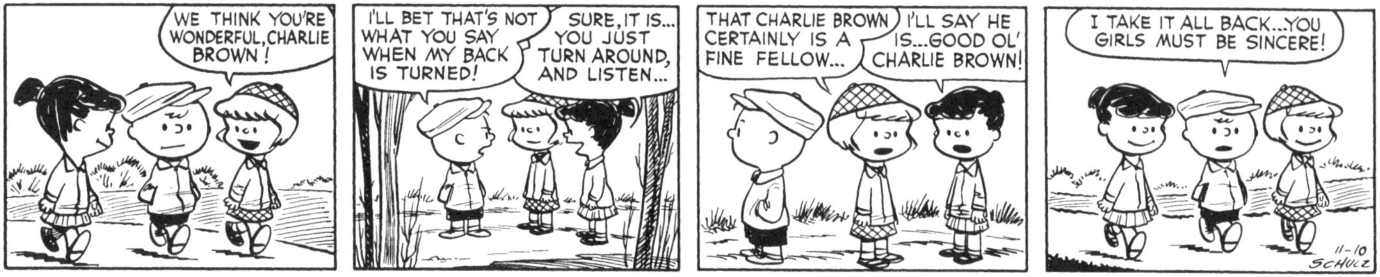
WE THINK YOU'RE WONDERFUL, CHARLIE BROWN!
I'LL BET THAT'S NOT WHAT YOU SAY WHEN MY BACK IS TURNED!
SURE, IT IS... YOU JUST TURN AROUND, AND LISTEN...
THAT CHARLIE BROWN CERTAINLY IS A FINE FELLOW...
I'LL SAY HE IS...GOOD OL' CHARLIE BROWN!
I TAKE IT ALL BACK...YOU GIRLS MUST BE SINCERE!
11-10
SCHULZ

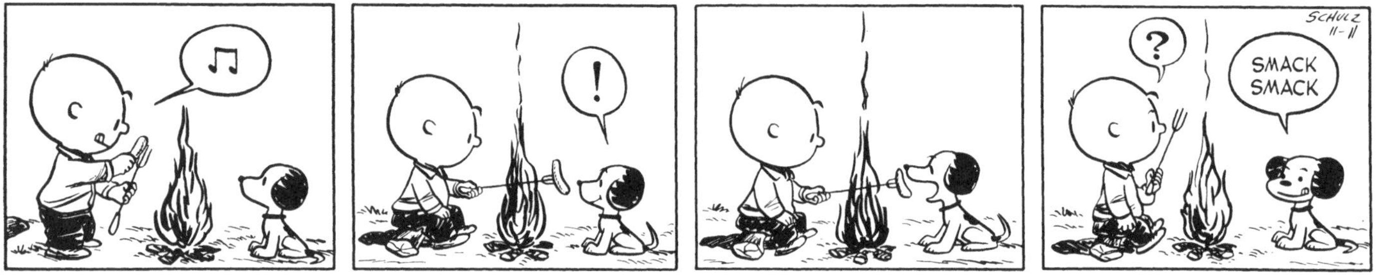
!
SCHULZ
11-11
?
SMACK SMACK

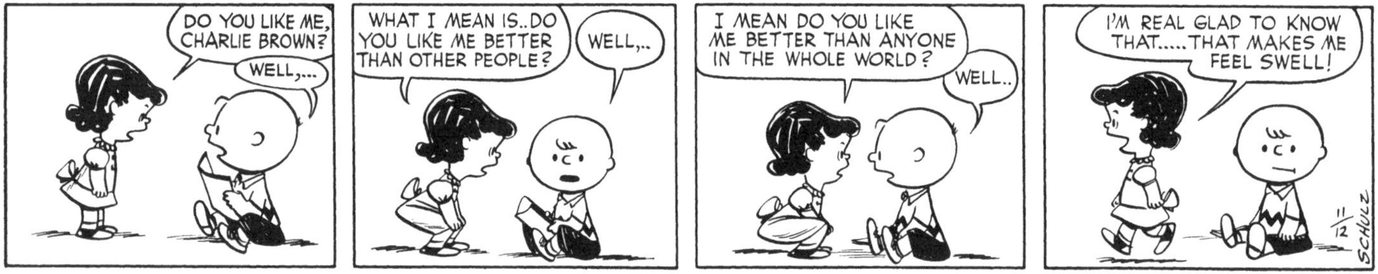
DO YOU LIKE ME, CHARLIE BROWN?
WELL,...
WHAT I MEAN IS..DO YOU LIKE ME BETTER THAN OTHER PEOPLE?
WELL,..
I MEAN DO YOU LIKE ME BETTER THAN ANYONE IN THE WHOLE WORLD?
WELL..
I'M REAL GLAD TO KNOW THAT.....THAT MAKES ME FEEL SWELL!
11/12
SCHULZ

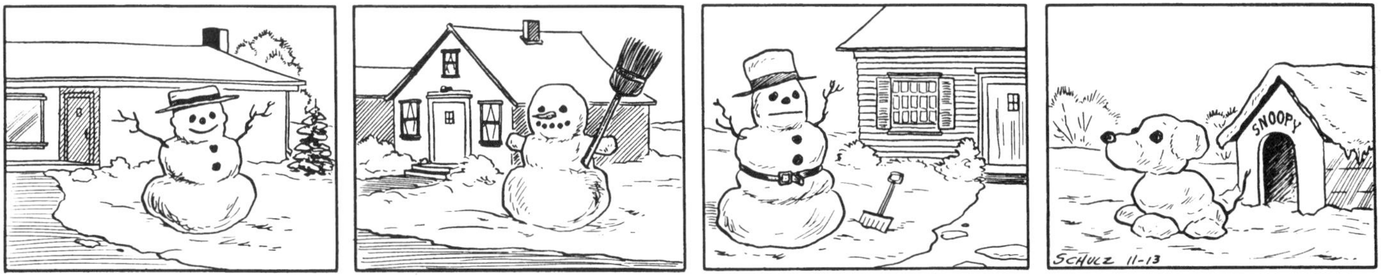
SNOOPY
SCHULZ 11-13

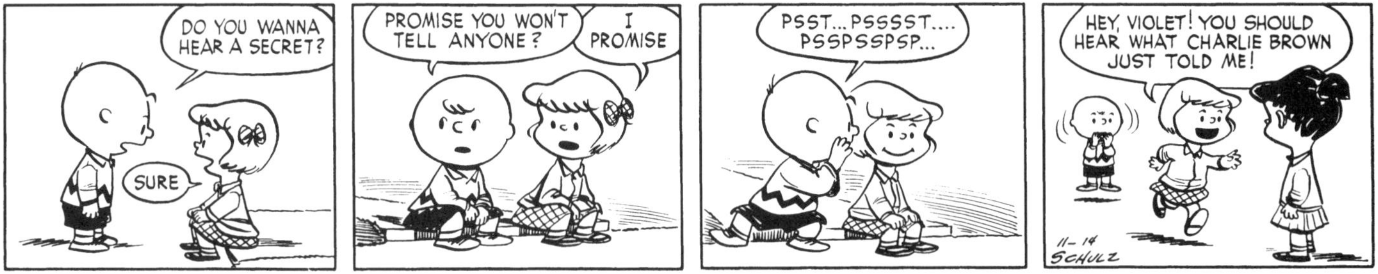
DO YOU WANNA HEAR A SECRET?
SURE
PROMISE YOU WON'T TELL ANYONE?
I PROMISE
PSST...PSSSST.... PSSPSSPSP...
HEY, VIOLET! YOU SHOULD HEAR WHAT CHARLIE BROWN JUST TOLD ME!
11-14 SCHULZ

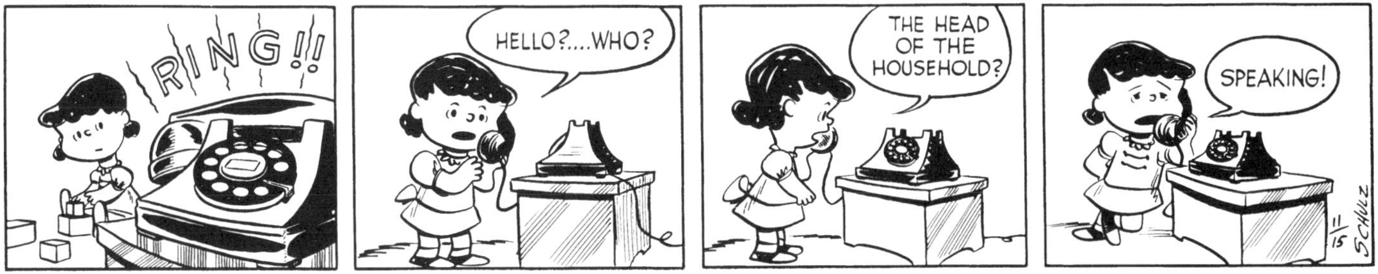
RING!!!
HELLO?....WHO?
THE HEAD OF THE HOUSEHOLD?
SPEAKING!
11/15 SCHULZ

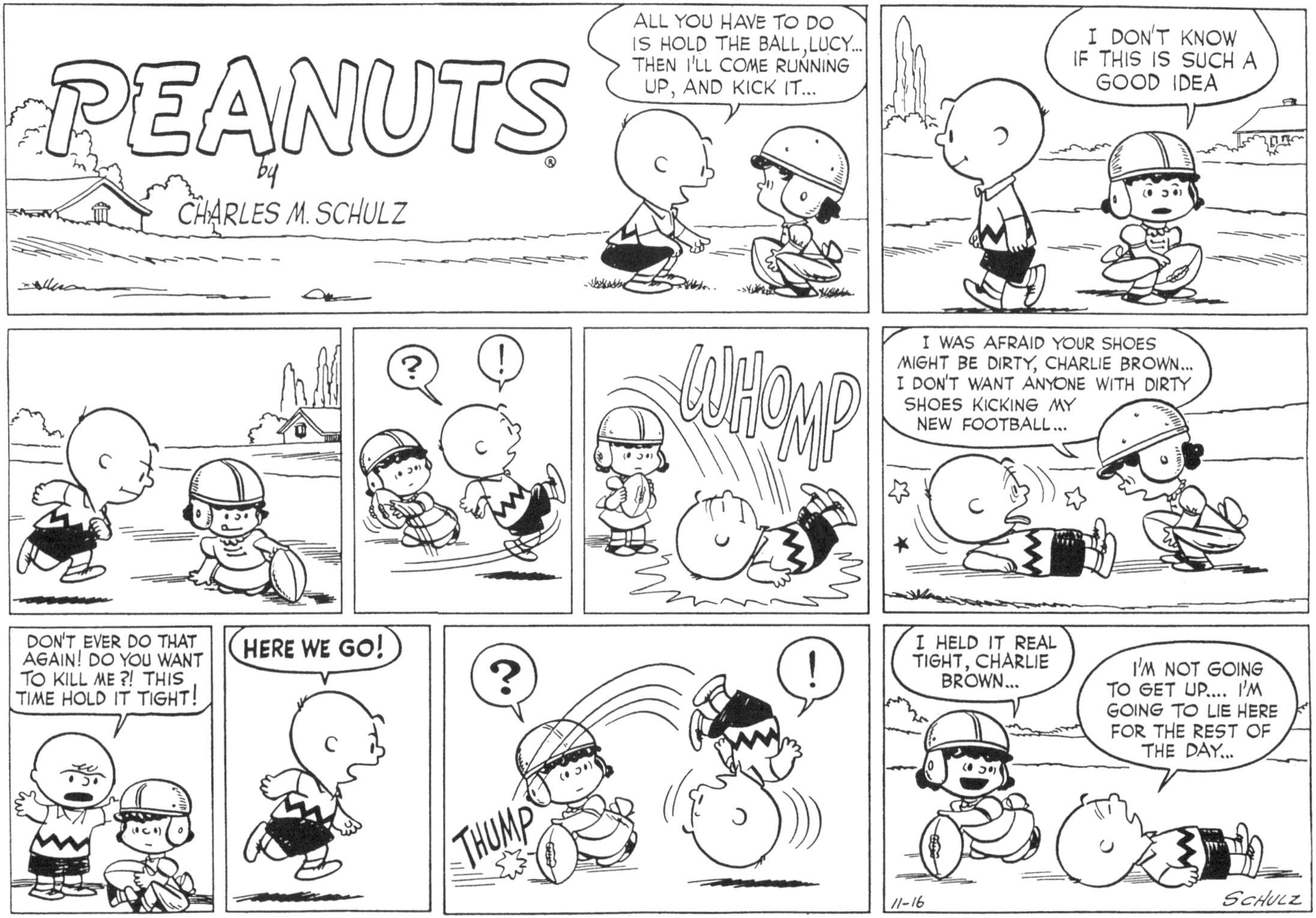
PEANUTS
by
CHARLES M. SCHULZ
ALL YOU HAVE TO DO IS HOLD THE BALL, LUCY... THEN I'LL COME RUNNING UP, AND KICK IT...
I DON'T KNOW IF THIS IS SUCH A GOOD IDEA
?
!
WHOMP
I WAS AFRAID YOUR SHOES MIGHT BE DIRTY, CHARLIE BROWN... I DON'T WANT ANYONE WITH DIRTY SHOES KICKING MY NEW FOOTBALL...
DON'T EVER DO THAT AGAIN! DO YOU WANT TO KILL ME?! THIS TIME HOLD IT TIGHT!
HERE WE GO!
?
!
THUMP
I HELD IT REAL TIGHT, CHARLIE BROWN...
I'M NOT GOING TO GET UP.... I'M GOING TO LIE HERE FOR THE REST OF THE DAY...
11-16
SCHULZ

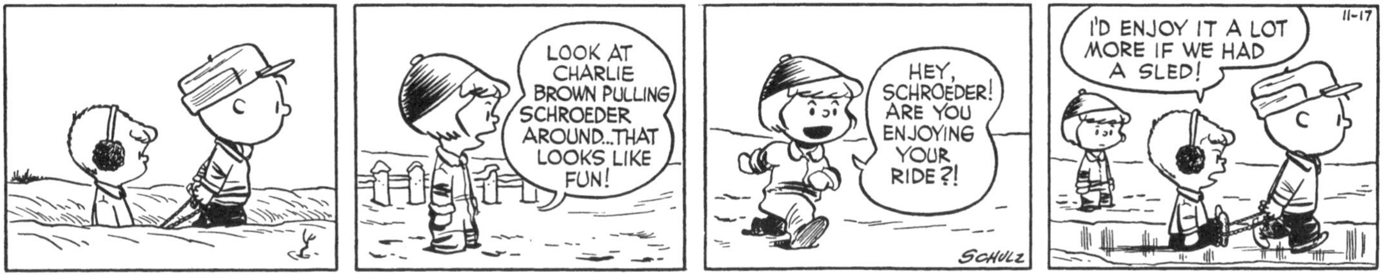
LOOK AT CHARLIE BROWN PULLING SCHROEDER AROUND...THAT LOOKS LIKE FUN!
HEY, SCHROEDER! ARE YOU ENJOYING YOUR RIDE?!
SCHULZ
I'D ENJOY IT A LOT MORE IF WE HAD A SLED!
11-17

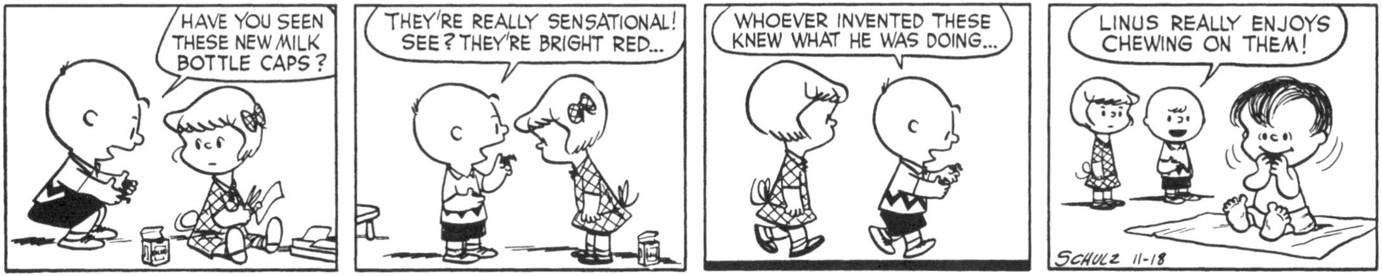
HAVE YOU SEEN THESE NEW MILK BOTTLE CAPS?
THEY'RE REALLY SENSATIONAL! SEE? THEY'RE BRIGHT RED...
WHOEVER INVENTED THESE KNEW WHAT HE WAS DOING...
LINUS REALLY ENJOYS CHEWING ON THEM!
SCHULZ 11-18

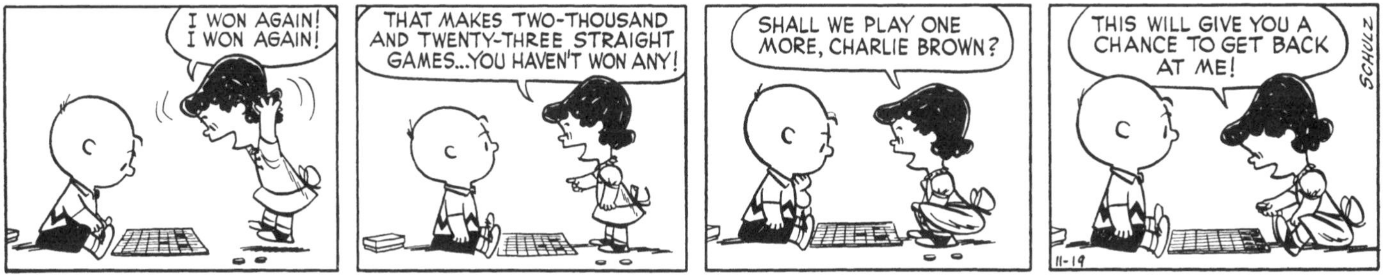
I WON AGAIN! I WON AGAIN!
THAT MAKES TWO-THOUSAND AND TWENTY-THREE STRAIGHT GAMES...YOU HAVEN'T WON ANY!
SHALL WE PLAY ONE MORE, CHARLIE BROWN?
THIS WILL GIVE YOU A CHANCE TO GET BACK AT ME!
SCHULZ
11-19

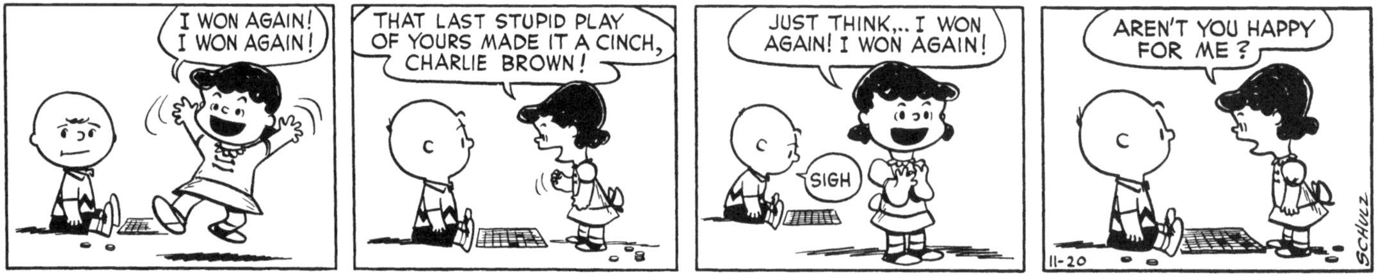
I WON AGAIN! I WON AGAIN!
THAT LAST STUPID PLAY OF YOURS MADE IT A CINCH, CHARLIE BROWN!
JUST THINK,.. I WON AGAIN! I WON AGAIN!
SIGH
AREN'T YOU HAPPY FOR ME?
11-20
SCHULZ

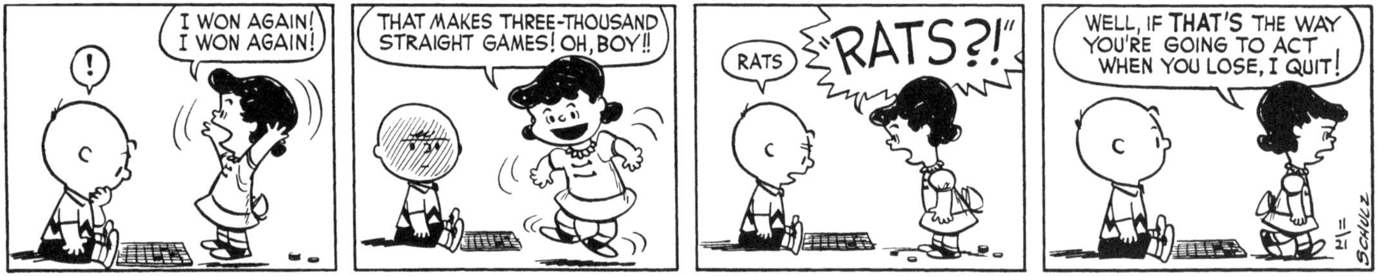
!
I WON AGAIN! I WON AGAIN!
THAT MAKES THREE-THOUSAND STRAIGHT GAMES! OH, BOY!!
RATS
"RATS?!"
WELL, IF THAT'S THE WAY YOU'RE GOING TO ACT WHEN YOU LOSE, I QUIT!
11/21
SCHULZ

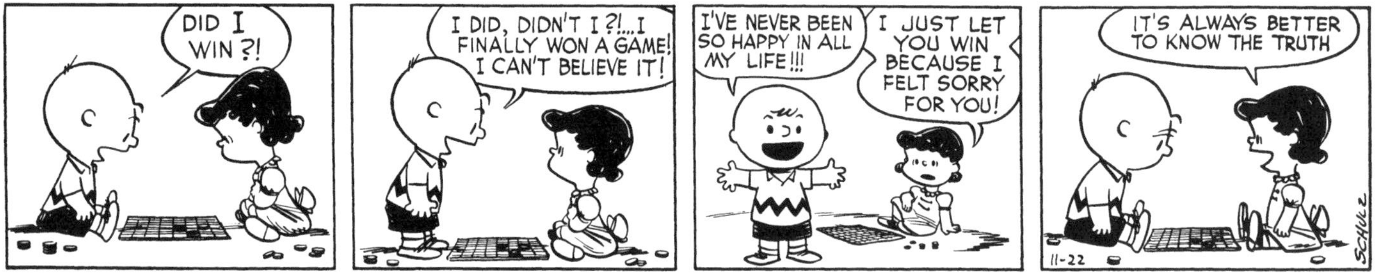
DID I WIN?!
I DID, DIDN'T I?!...I FINALLY WON A GAME! I CAN'T BELIEVE IT!
I'VE NEVER BEEN SO HAPPY IN ALL MY LIFE!!!
I JUST LET YOU WIN BECAUSE I FELT SORRY FOR YOU!
IT'S ALWAYS BETTER TO KNOW THE TRUTH
11-22
SCHULZ

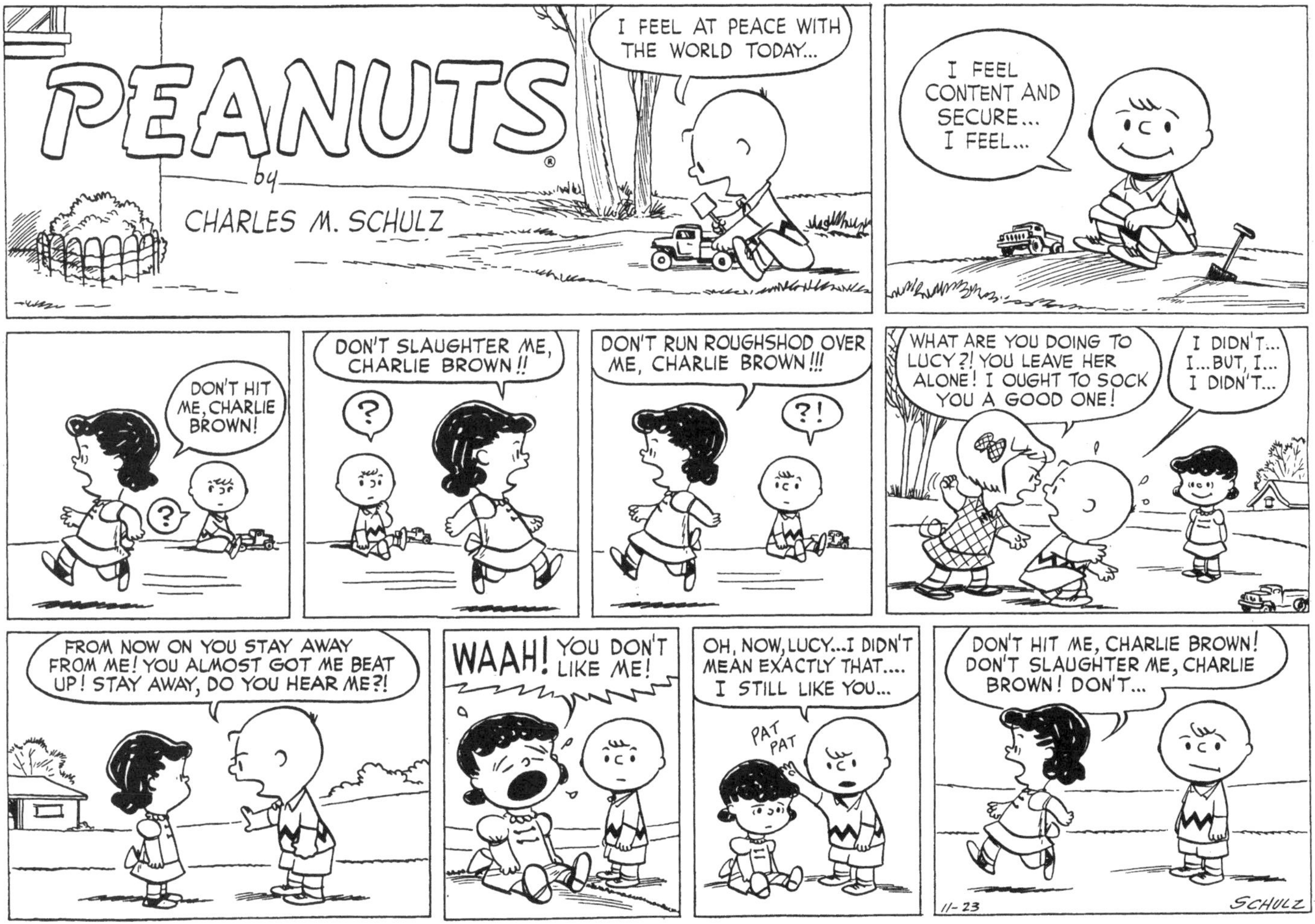
PEANUTS
by
CHARLES M. SCHULZ
I FEEL AT PEACE WITH THE WORLD TODAY...
I FEEL CONTENT AND SECURE... I FEEL...
DON'T HIT ME, CHARLIE BROWN!
?
DON'T SLAUGHTER ME, CHARLIE BROWN!!
?
DON'T RUN ROUGHSHOD OVER ME, CHARLIE BROWN!!!
?!
WHAT ARE YOU DOING TO LUCY?! YOU LEAVE HER ALONE! I OUGHT TO SOCK YOU A GOOD ONE!
I DIDN'T... I...BUT, I... I DIDN'T...
FROM NOW ON YOU STAY AWAY FROM ME! YOU ALMOST GOT ME BEAT UP! STAY AWAY, DO YOU HEAR ME?!
WAAH! YOU DON'T LIKE ME!
OH, NOW, LUCY...I DIDN'T MEAN EXACTLY THAT.... I STILL LIKE YOU...
PAT PAT
DON'T HIT ME, CHARLIE BROWN! DON'T SLAUGHTER ME, CHARLIE BROWN! DON'T...
11-23
SCHULZ

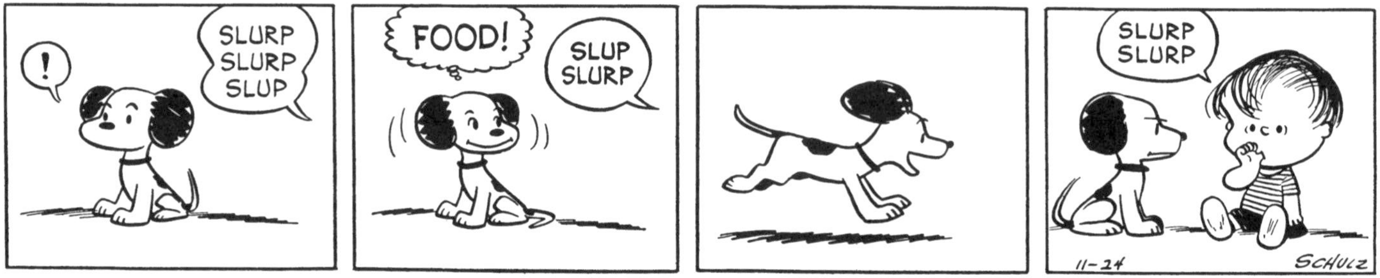
!
SLURP SLURP SLUP
FOOD!
SLUP SLURP
SLURP SLURP
11-24
SCHULZ

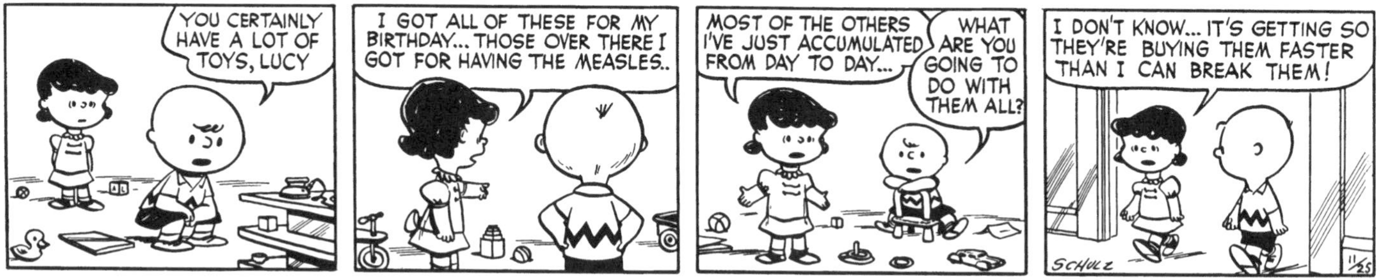
YOU CERTAINLY HAVE A LOT OF TOYS, LUCY
I GOT ALL OF THESE FOR MY BIRTHDAY... THOSE OVER THERE I GOT FOR HAVING THE MEASLES..
MOST OF THE OTHERS I'VE JUST ACCUMULATED FROM DAY TO DAY...
WHAT ARE YOU GOING TO DO WITH THEM ALL?
I DON'T KNOW... IT'S GETTING SO THEY'RE BUYING THEM FASTER THAN I CAN BREAK THEM!
SCHULZ
11/25

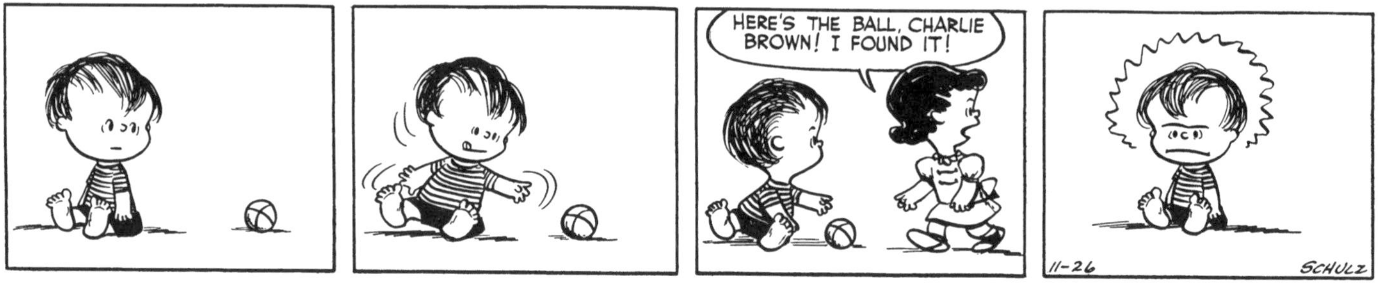
HERE'S THE BALL, CHARLIE BROWN! I FOUND IT!
11-26
SCHULZ

SNIF SNOOPY

?

Happy Thanksgiving, Snoopy, Ol' Pal!

!

GOOD OL' CHARLIE BROWN *SIGH*

HE DIDN'T THINK ANYONE CARED

11-27 SCHULZ

ISN'T YOUR FAVORITE RADIO PROGRAM ON AT SIX O'CLOCK?

YOU'RE RIGHT! IT IS!!

HEY! IT'S SIX-THIRTY ALREADY! I'VE MISSED IT!

I KNOW IT... I CAN'T STAND THAT PROGRAM!

11-28 SCHULZ

HERE, SNOOPY, CATCH THE BALL...

WELL, NOW... WHAT'S THE MATTER WITH YOU?

TODAY IS SATURDAY...

11-29

HE FEELS IT'S HIS DAY OFF

SCHULZ

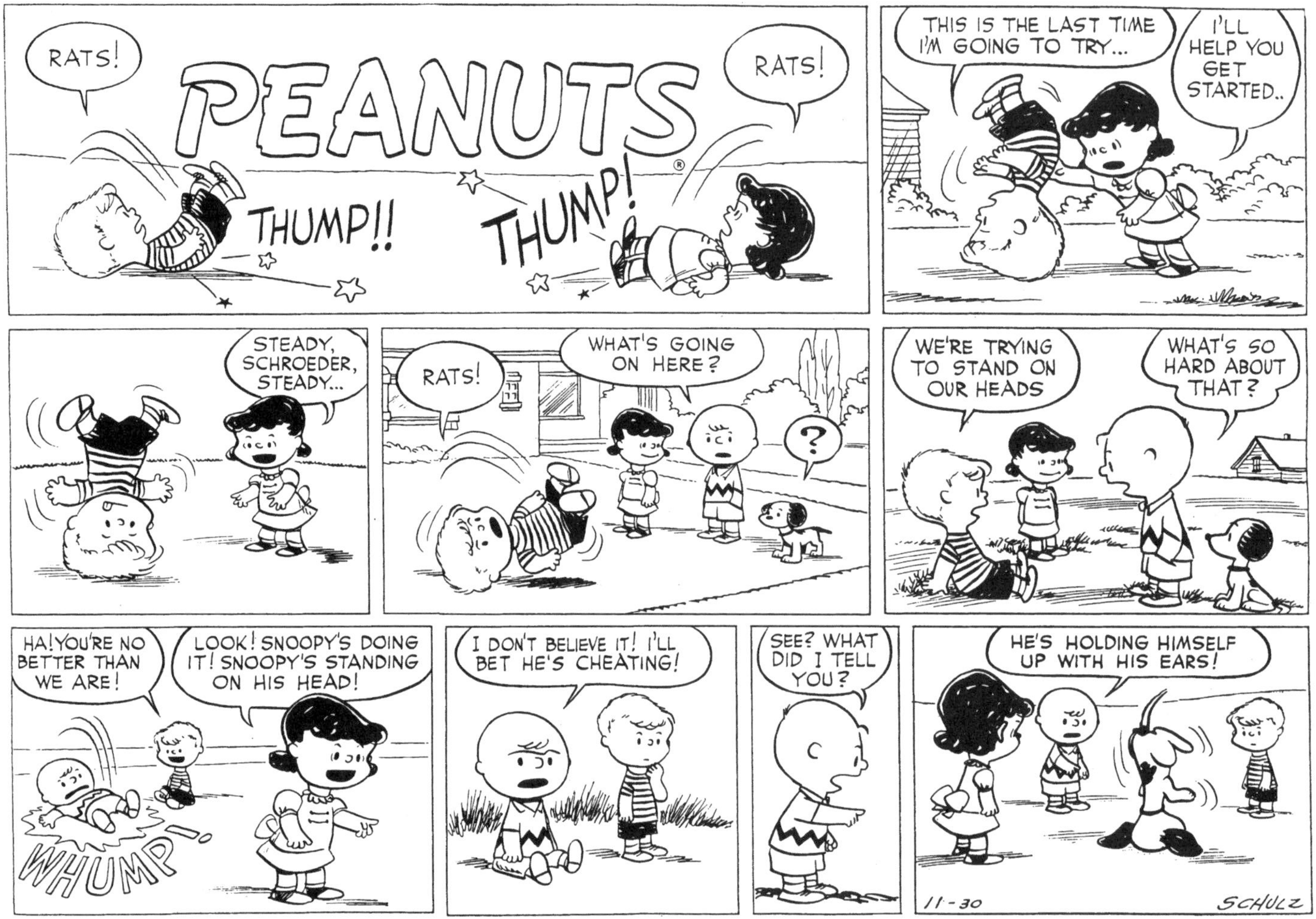
RATS!
PEANUTS
RATS!
THUMP!!
THUMP!
THIS IS THE LAST TIME I'M GOING TO TRY...
I'LL HELP YOU GET STARTED..
STEADY, SCHROEDER, STEADY...
RATS!
WHAT'S GOING ON HERE?
?
WE'RE TRYING TO STAND ON OUR HEADS
WHAT'S SO HARD ABOUT THAT?
HA! YOU'RE NO BETTER THAN WE ARE!
LOOK! SNOOPY'S DOING IT! SNOOPY'S STANDING ON HIS HEAD!
WHUMP!
I DON'T BELIEVE IT! I'LL BET HE'S CHEATING!
SEE? WHAT DID I TELL YOU?
HE'S HOLDING HIMSELF UP WITH HIS EARS!
11-30
SCHULZ

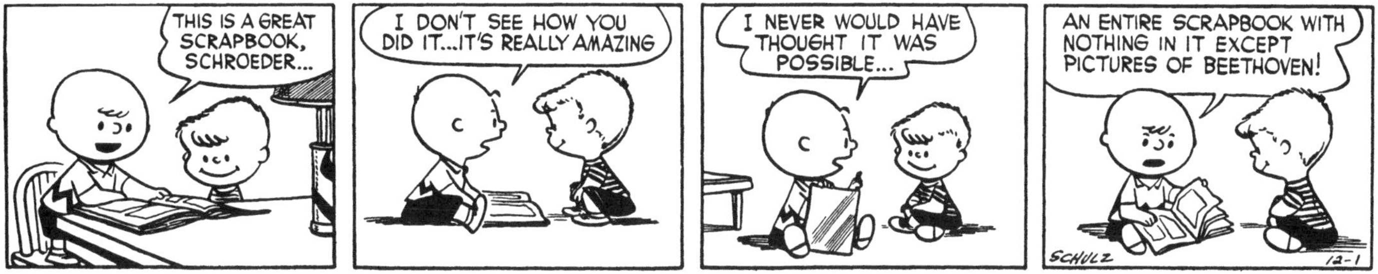
THIS IS A GREAT SCRAPBOOK, SCHROEDER...
I DON'T SEE HOW YOU DID IT...IT'S REALLY AMAZING
I NEVER WOULD HAVE THOUGHT IT WAS POSSIBLE...
AN ENTIRE SCRAPBOOK WITH NOTHING IN IT EXCEPT PICTURES OF BEETHOVEN!
SCHULZ
12-1

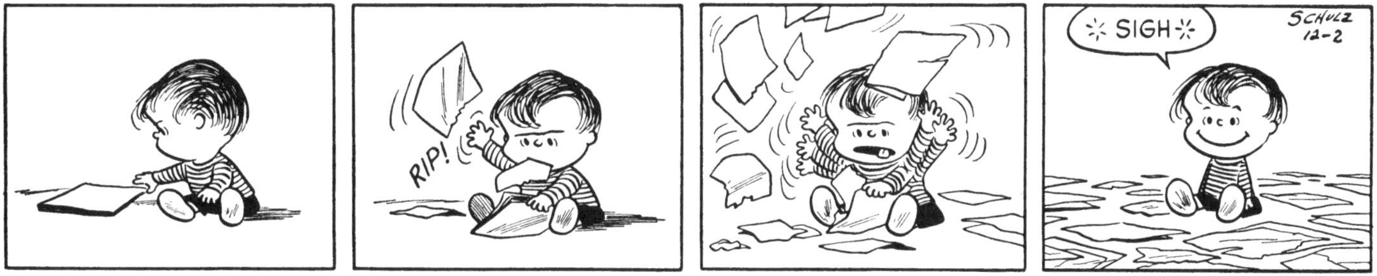
RIP!
SIGH
SCHULZ 12-2

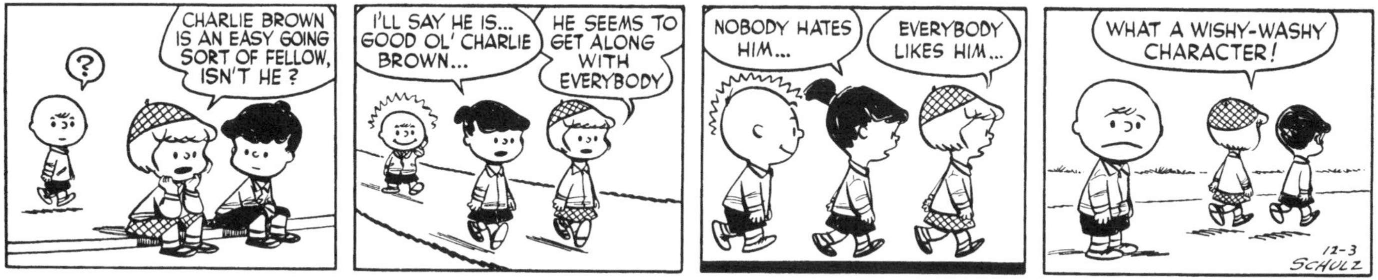
?
CHARLIE BROWN IS AN EASY GOING SORT OF FELLOW, ISN'T HE ?
I'LL SAY HE IS... GOOD OL' CHARLIE BROWN...
HE SEEMS TO GET ALONG WITH EVERYBODY
NOBODY HATES HIM...
EVERYBODY LIKES HIM...
WHAT A WISHY-WASHY CHARACTER!
12-3
SCHULZ

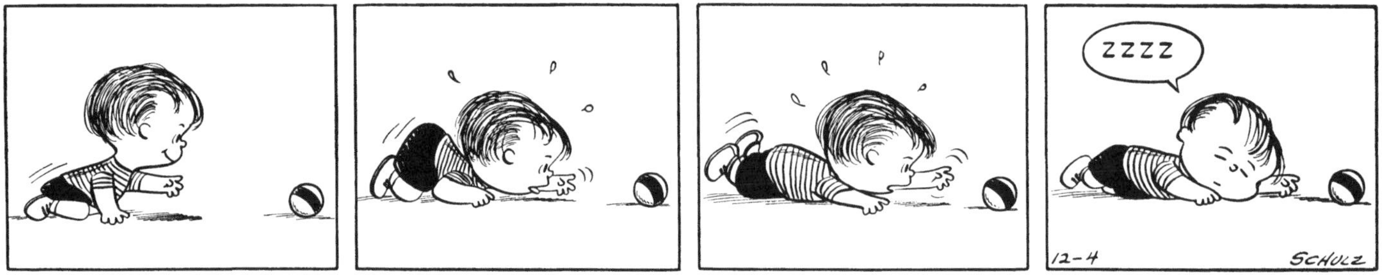
ZZZZ
12-4
SCHULZ

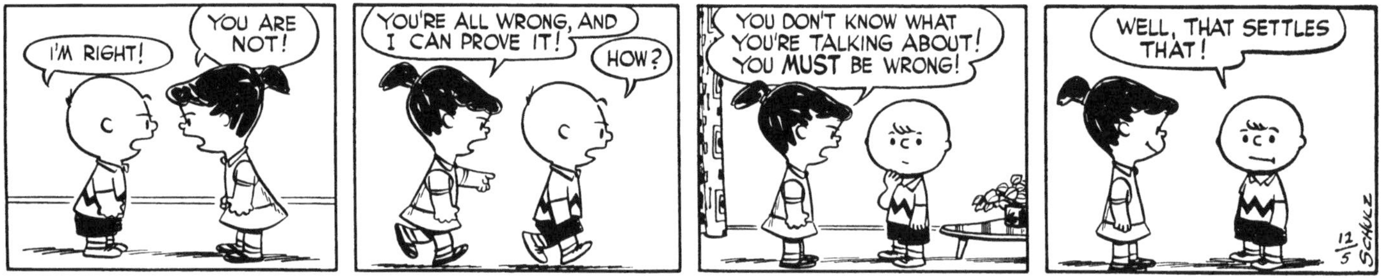
I'M RIGHT!
YOU ARE NOT!
YOU'RE ALL WRONG, AND I CAN PROVE IT!
HOW?
YOU DON'T KNOW WHAT YOU'RE TALKING ABOUT! YOU MUST BE WRONG!
WELL, THAT SETTLES THAT!
12/5
SCHULZ

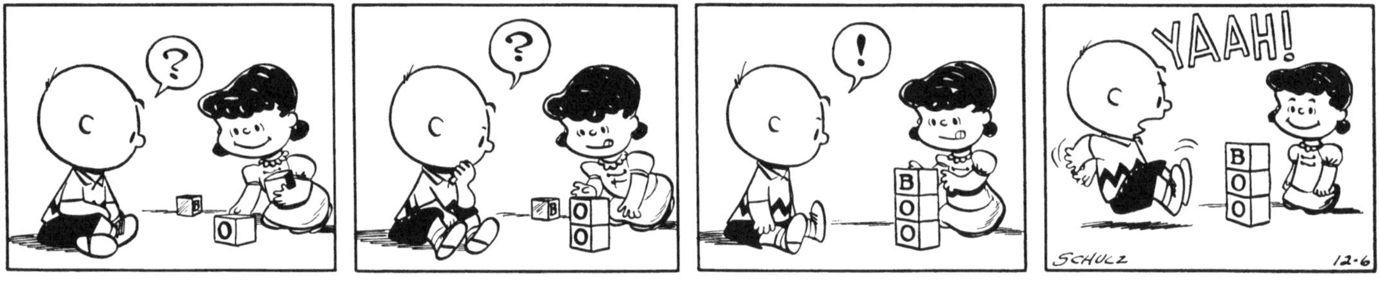
?
?
!
YAAH!
BOO
SCHULZ
12-6

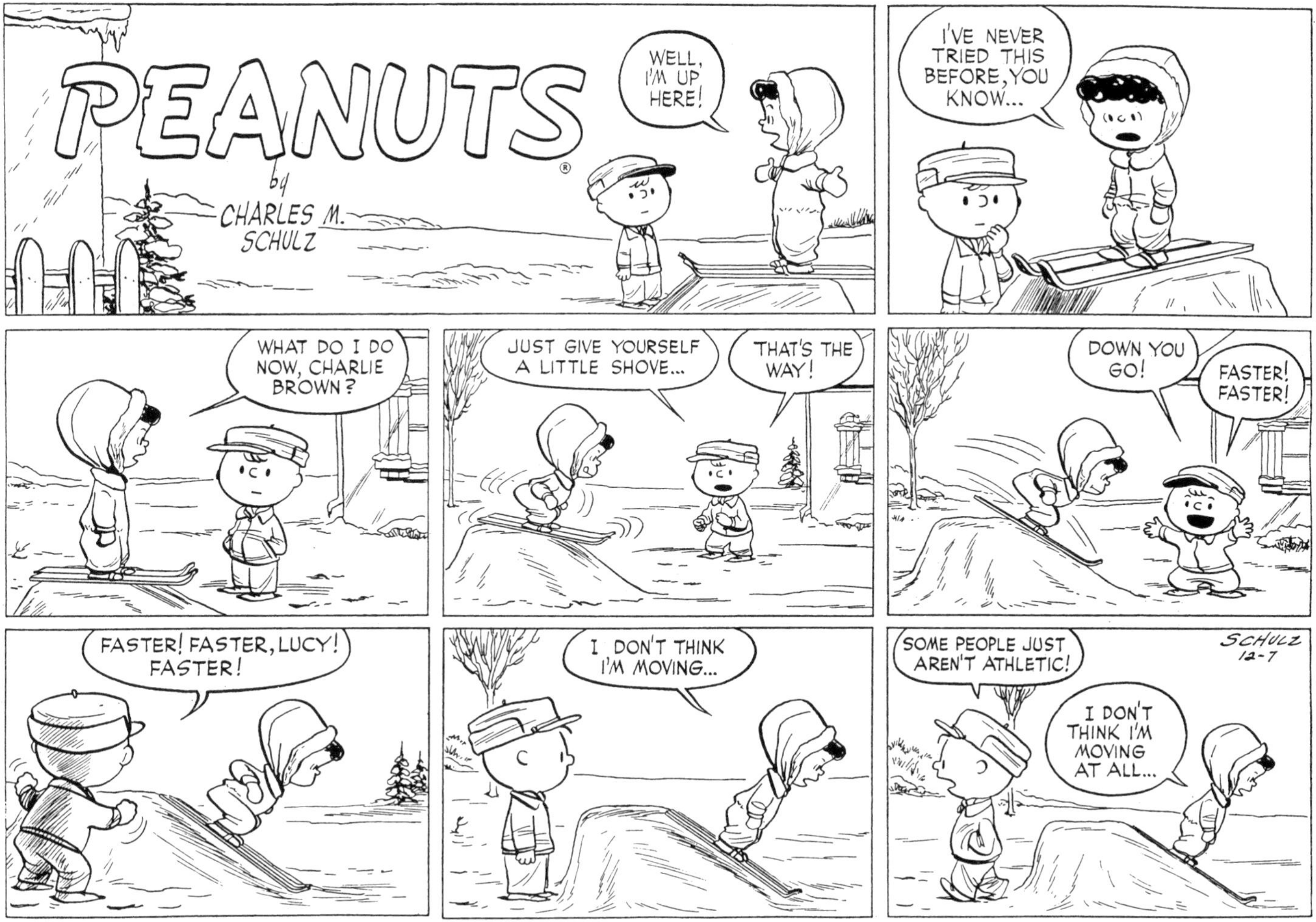
PEANUTS
by CHARLES M. SCHULZ
WELL, I'M UP HERE!
I'VE NEVER TRIED THIS BEFORE, YOU KNOW...
WHAT DO I DO NOW, CHARLIE BROWN?
JUST GIVE YOURSELF A LITTLE SHOVE...
THAT'S THE WAY!
DOWN YOU GO!
FASTER! FASTER!
FASTER! FASTER, LUCY! FASTER!
I DON'T THINK I'M MOVING...
SOME PEOPLE JUST AREN'T ATHLETIC!
I DON'T THINK I'M MOVING AT ALL...
SCHULZ 12-7

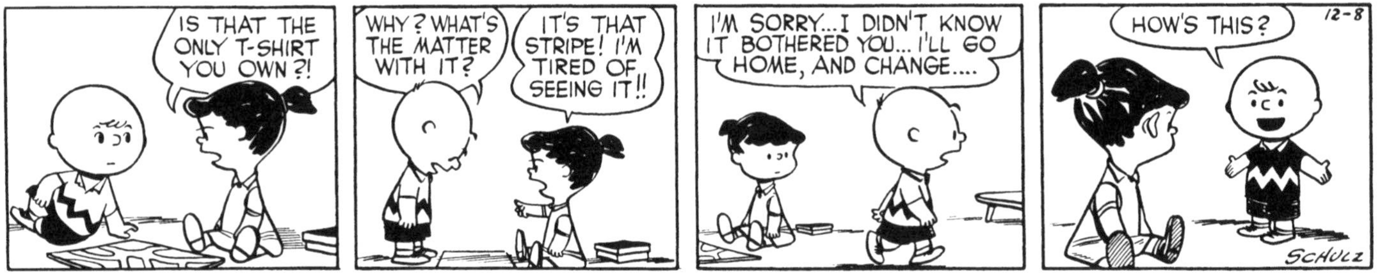
IS THAT THE ONLY T-SHIRT YOU OWN ?!
WHY ? WHAT'S THE MATTER WITH IT ?
IT'S THAT STRIPE! I'M TIRED OF SEEING IT!!
I'M SORRY... I DIDN'T KNOW IT BOTHERED YOU... I'LL GO HOME, AND CHANGE....
HOW'S THIS ?
12-8
SCHULZ

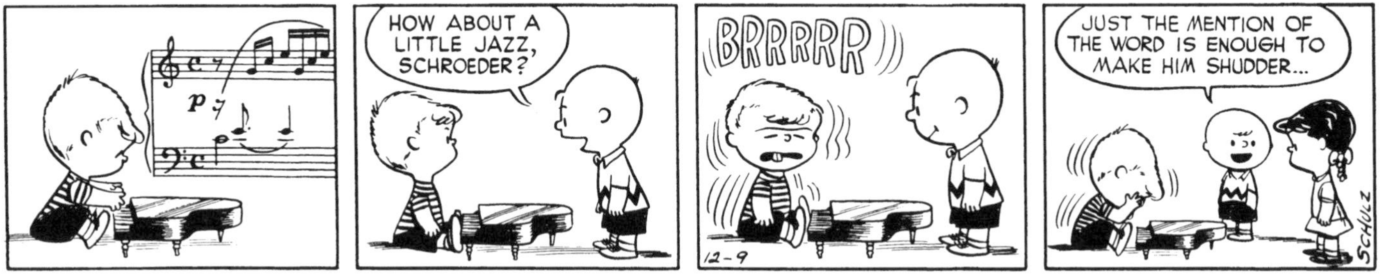
HOW ABOUT A LITTLE JAZZ, SCHROEDER ?
BRRRRR
12-9
JUST THE MENTION OF THE WORD IS ENOUGH TO MAKE HIM SHUDDER...
SCHULZ

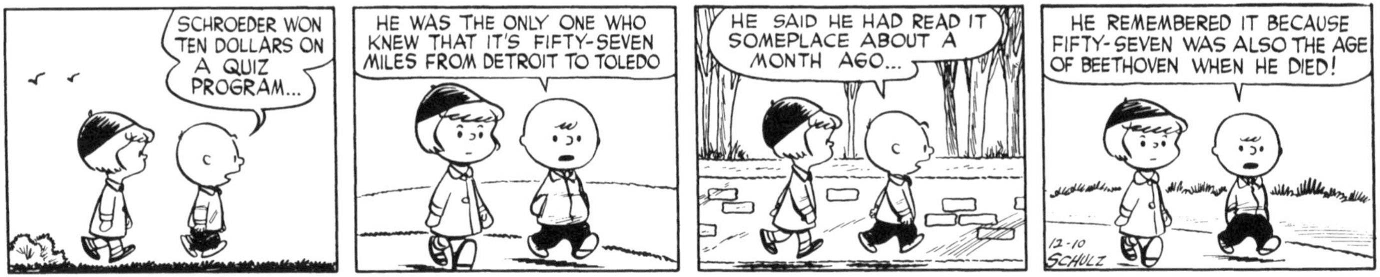
SCHROEDER WON TEN DOLLARS ON A QUIZ PROGRAM...
HE WAS THE ONLY ONE WHO KNEW THAT IT'S FIFTY-SEVEN MILES FROM DETROIT TO TOLEDO
HE SAID HE HAD READ IT SOMEPLACE ABOUT A MONTH AGO...
HE REMEMBERED IT BECAUSE FIFTY-SEVEN WAS ALSO THE AGE OF BEETHOVEN WHEN HE DIED!
12-10
SCHULZ

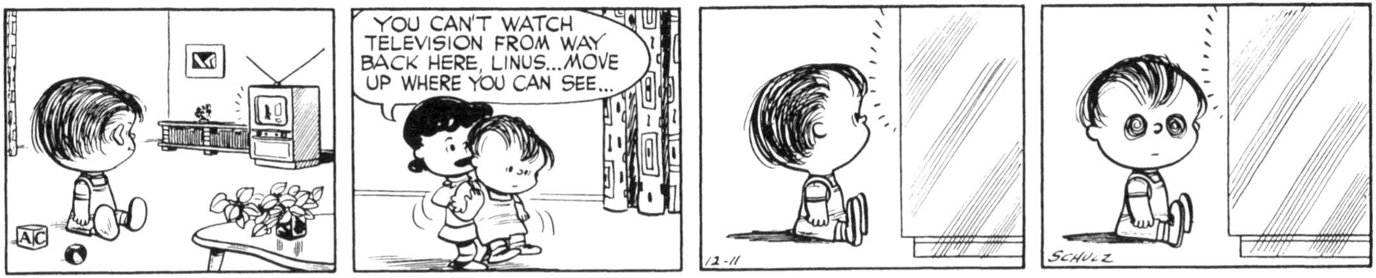
YOU CAN'T WATCH TELEVISION FROM WAY BACK HERE, LINUS...MOVE UP WHERE YOU CAN SEE...
12-11
SCHULZ

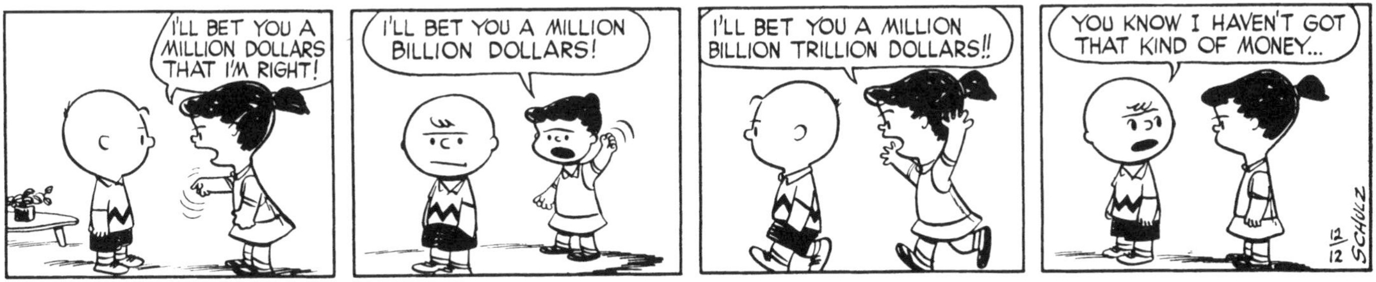
I'LL BET YOU A MILLION DOLLARS THAT I'M RIGHT!
I'LL BET YOU A MILLION BILLION DOLLARS!
I'LL BET YOU A MILLION BILLION TRILLION DOLLARS!!
YOU KNOW I HAVEN'T GOT THAT KIND OF MONEY...
12/12
SCHULZ

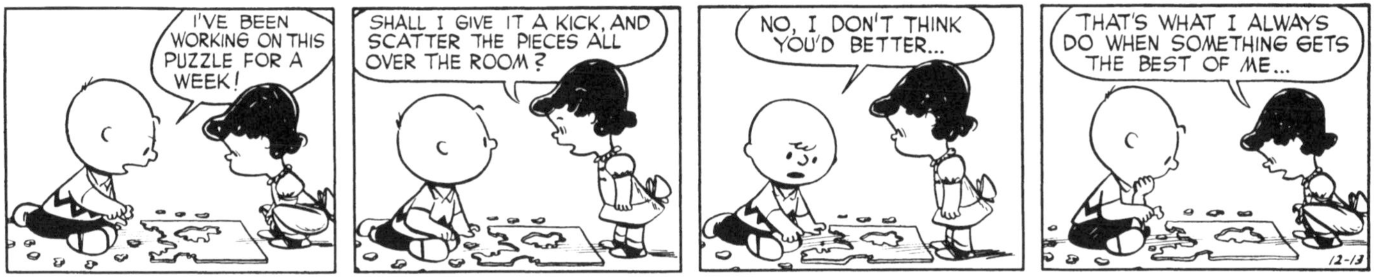
I'VE BEEN WORKING ON THIS PUZZLE FOR A WEEK!
SHALL I GIVE IT A KICK, AND SCATTER THE PIECES ALL OVER THE ROOM?
NO, I DON'T THINK YOU'D BETTER...
THAT'S WHAT I ALWAYS DO WHEN SOMETHING GETS THE BEST OF ME...
12-13

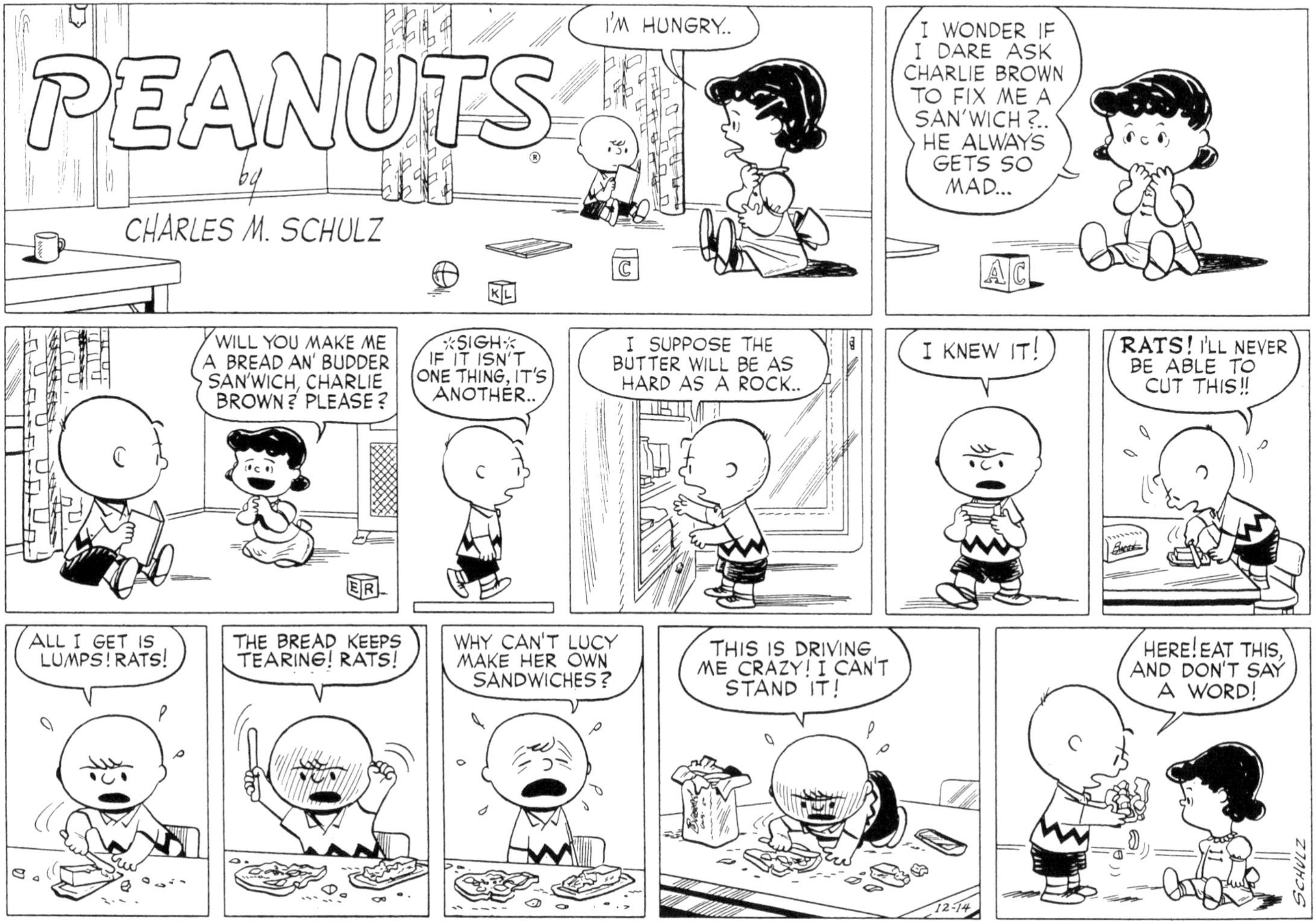
PEANUTS
by
CHARLES M. SCHULZ
I'M HUNGRY..
I WONDER IF I DARE ASK CHARLIE BROWN TO FIX ME A SAN'WICH ?.. HE ALWAYS GETS SO MAD...
WILL YOU MAKE ME A BREAD AN' BUDDER SAN'WICH, CHARLIE BROWN? PLEASE?
SIGH IF IT ISN'T ONE THING, IT'S ANOTHER..
I SUPPOSE THE BUTTER WILL BE AS HARD AS A ROCK..
I KNEW IT!
RATS! I'LL NEVER BE ABLE TO CUT THIS!!
ALL I GET IS LUMPS! RATS!
THE BREAD KEEPS TEARING! RATS!
WHY CAN'T LUCY MAKE HER OWN SANDWICHES?
THIS IS DRIVING ME CRAZY! I CAN'T STAND IT!
12-14
HERE! EAT THIS, AND DON'T SAY A WORD!
SCHULZ

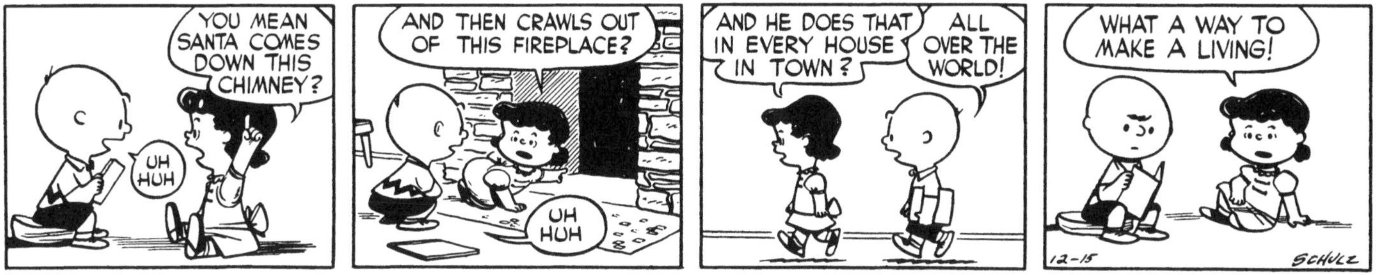
YOU MEAN SANTA COMES DOWN THIS CHIMNEY?
UH HUH
AND THEN CRAWLS OUT OF THIS FIREPLACE?
UH HUH
AND HE DOES THAT IN EVERY HOUSE IN TOWN?
ALL OVER THE WORLD!
WHAT A WAY TO MAKE A LIVING!
12-15
SCHULZ

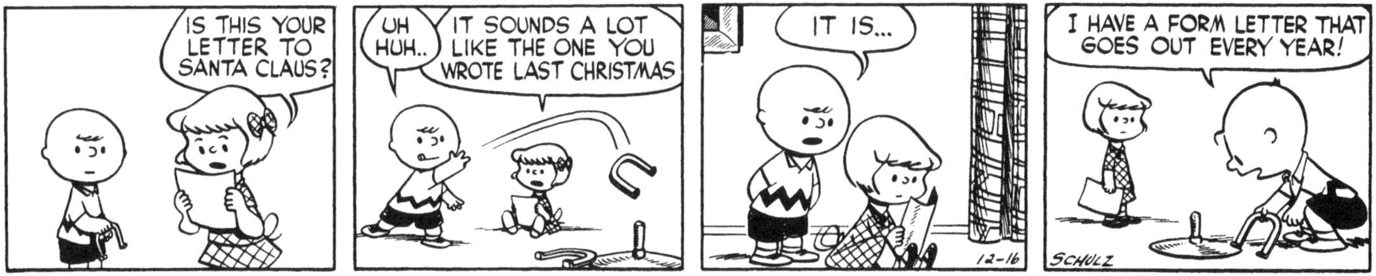
IS THIS YOUR LETTER TO SANTA CLAUS?
UH HUH..
IT SOUNDS A LOT LIKE THE ONE YOU WROTE LAST CHRISTMAS
IT IS...
12-16
I HAVE A FORM LETTER THAT GOES OUT EVERY YEAR!
SCHULZ

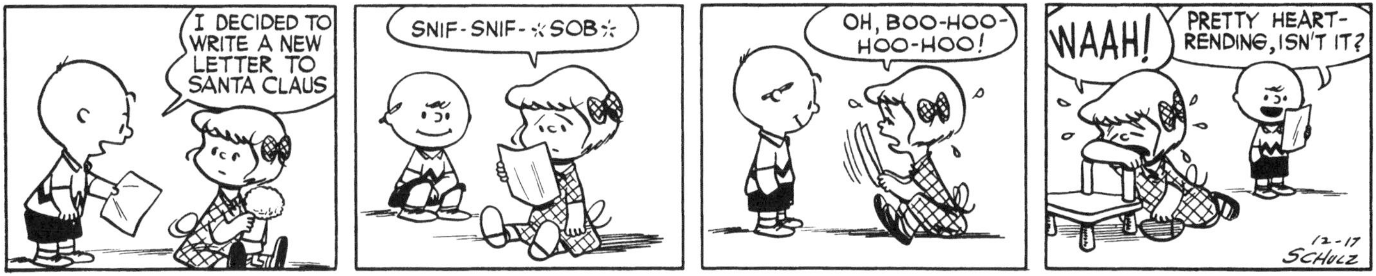
I DECIDED TO WRITE A NEW LETTER TO SANTA CLAUS
SNIF-SNIF-*SOB*
OH, BOO-HOO-HOO-HOO!
WAAH!
PRETTY HEART-RENDING, ISN'T IT?
12-17
SCHULZ

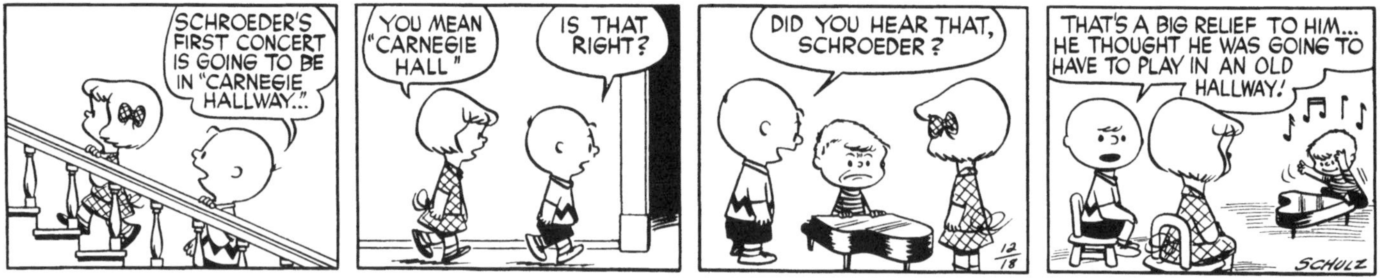
SCHROEDER'S FIRST CONCERT IS GOING TO BE IN "CARNEGIE HALLWAY..."
YOU MEAN "CARNEGIE HALL"
IS THAT RIGHT?
DID YOU HEAR THAT, SCHROEDER?
12/18
THAT'S A BIG RELIEF TO HIM... HE THOUGHT HE WAS GOING TO HAVE TO PLAY IN AN OLD HALLWAY!
SCHULZ

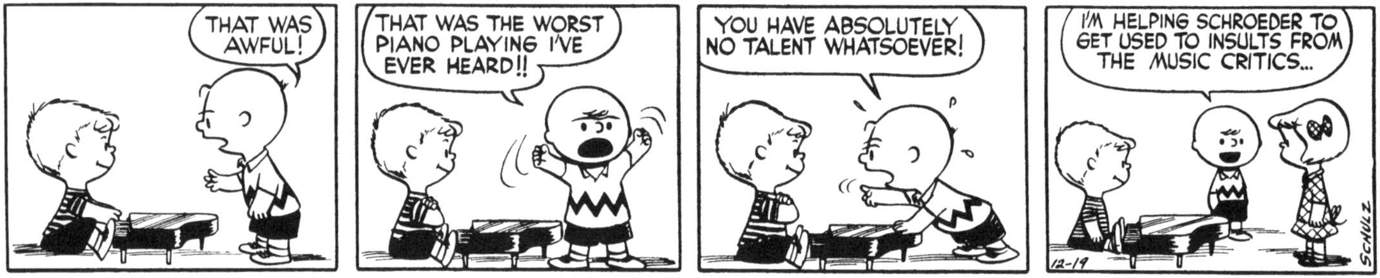
THAT WAS AWFUL!
THAT WAS THE WORST PIANO PLAYING I'VE EVER HEARD!!
YOU HAVE ABSOLUTELY NO TALENT WHATSOEVER!
I'M HELPING SCHROEDER TO GET USED TO INSULTS FROM THE MUSIC CRITICS...
12-19
SCHULZ

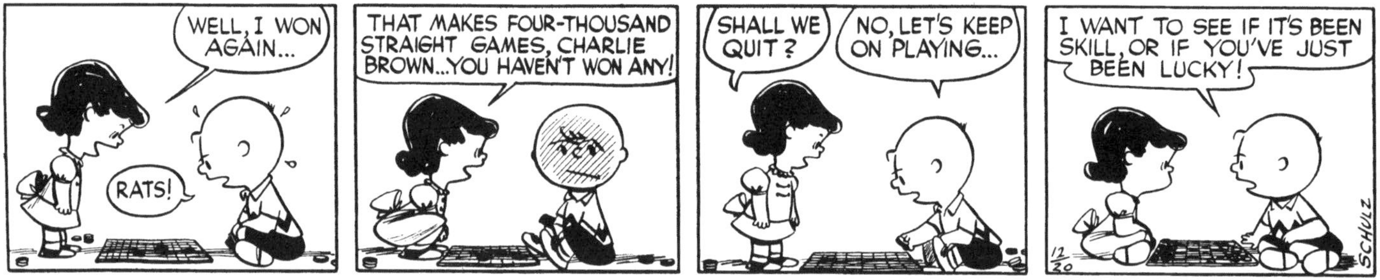
WELL, I WON AGAIN...
RATS!
THAT MAKES FOUR-THOUSAND STRAIGHT GAMES, CHARLIE BROWN...YOU HAVEN'T WON ANY!
SHALL WE QUIT?
NO, LET'S KEEP ON PLAYING...
I WANT TO SEE IF IT'S BEEN SKILL, OR IF YOU'VE JUST BEEN LUCKY!
12/20
SCHULZ

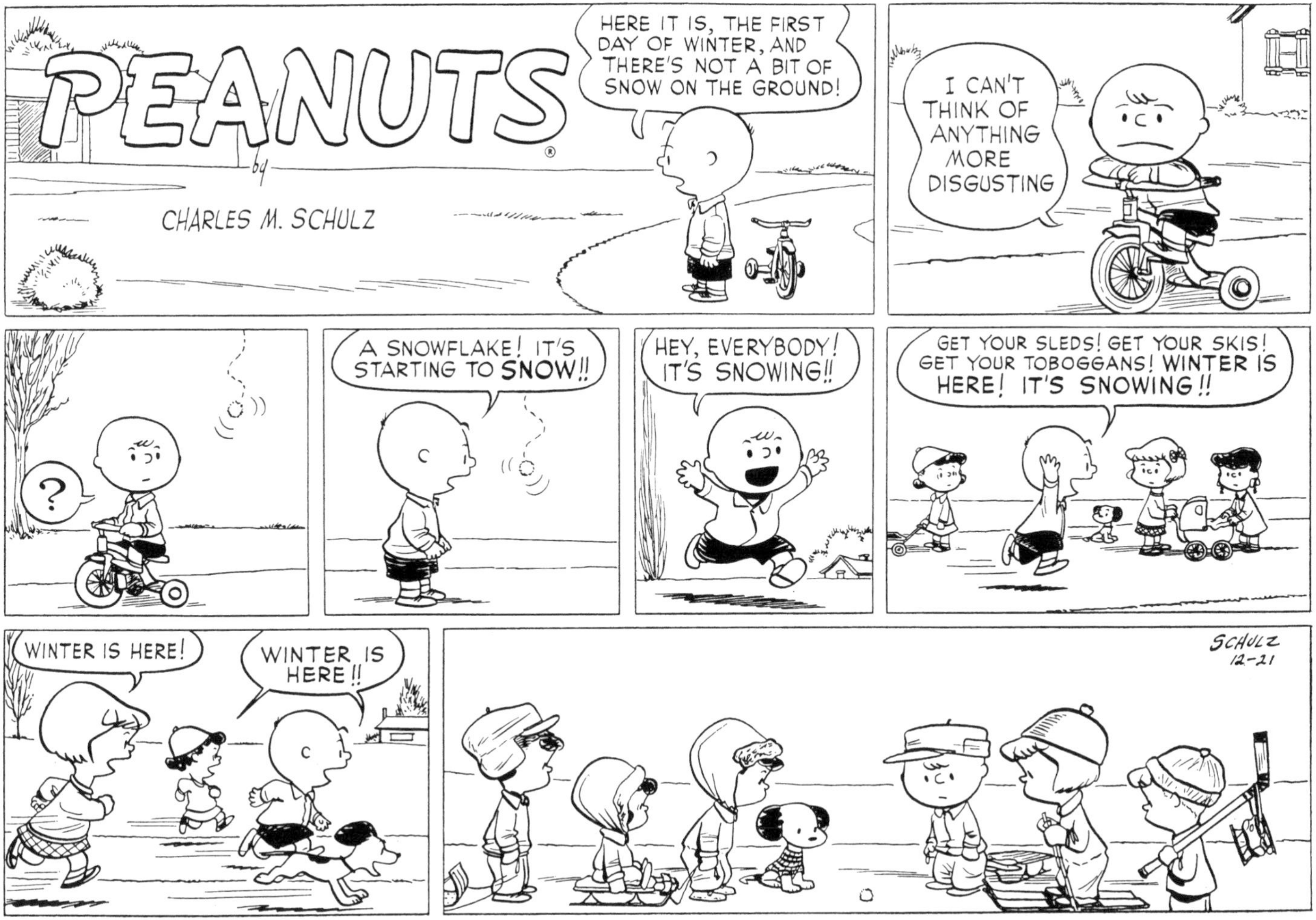
PEANUTS
by
CHARLES M. SCHULZ
HERE IT IS, THE FIRST DAY OF WINTER, AND THERE'S NOT A BIT OF SNOW ON THE GROUND!
I CAN'T THINK OF ANYTHING MORE DISGUSTING
?
A SNOWFLAKE! IT'S STARTING TO SNOW!!
HEY, EVERYBODY! IT'S SNOWING!!
GET YOUR SLEDS! GET YOUR SKIS! GET YOUR TOBOGGANS! WINTER IS HERE! IT'S SNOWING!!
WINTER IS HERE!
WINTER IS HERE!!
SCHULZ 12-21

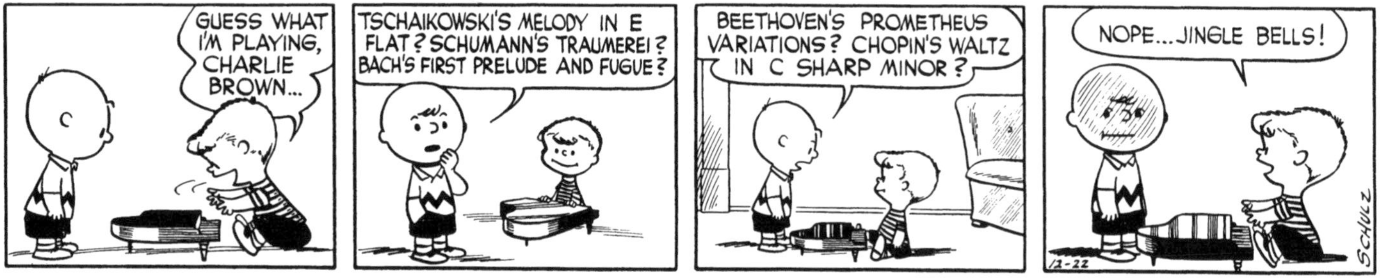
GUESS WHAT I'M PLAYING, CHARLIE BROWN...
TSCHAIKOWSKI'S MELODY IN E FLAT? SCHUMANN'S TRAUMEREI? BACH'S FIRST PRELUDE AND FUGUE?
BEETHOVEN'S PROMETHEUS VARIATIONS? CHOPIN'S WALTZ IN C SHARP MINOR?
NOPE... JINGLE BELLS!
12-22
SCHULZ

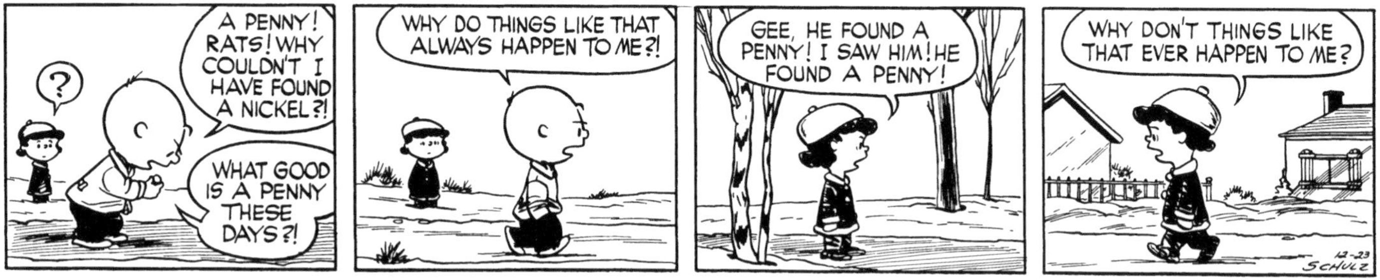
?
A PENNY! RATS! WHY COULDN'T I HAVE FOUND A NICKEL?!
WHAT GOOD IS A PENNY THESE DAYS?!
WHY DO THINGS LIKE THAT ALWAYS HAPPEN TO ME?!
GEE, HE FOUND A PENNY! I SAW HIM! HE FOUND A PENNY!
WHY DON'T THINGS LIKE THAT EVER HAPPEN TO ME?
12-23
SCHULZ

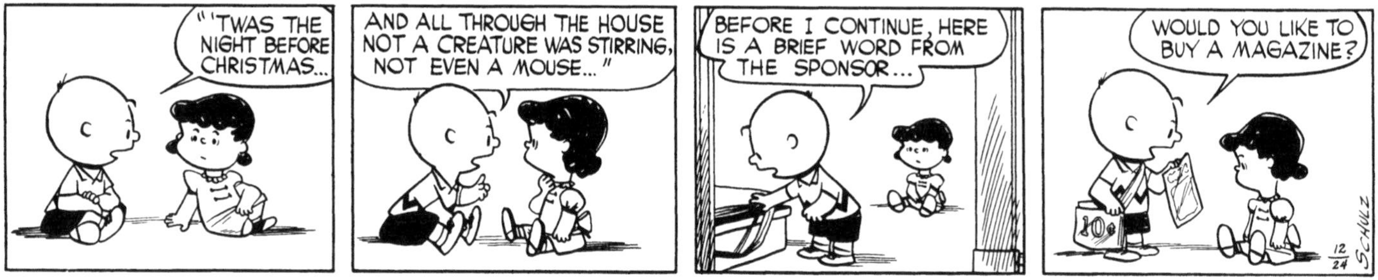
"'TWAS THE NIGHT BEFORE CHRISTMAS...
AND ALL THROUGH THE HOUSE NOT A CREATURE WAS STIRRING, NOT EVEN A MOUSE..."
BEFORE I CONTINUE, HERE IS A BRIEF WORD FROM THE SPONSOR...
WOULD YOU LIKE TO BUY A MAGAZINE?
10¢
12/24
SCHULZ

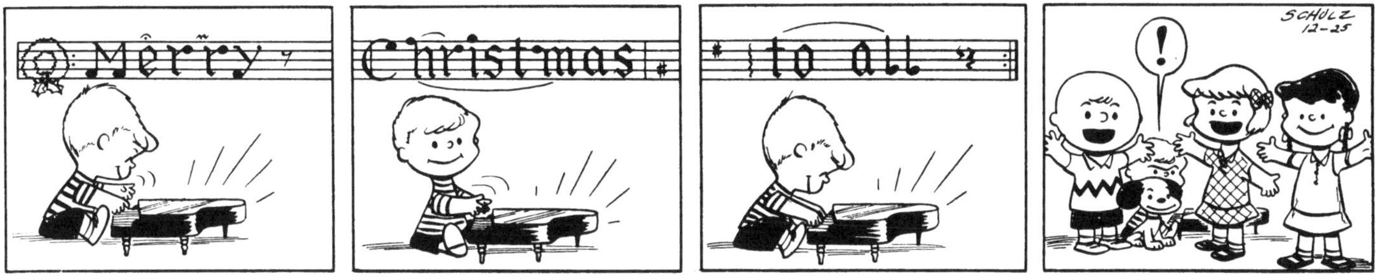
Merry
Christmas
to all
SCHULZ 12-25
!

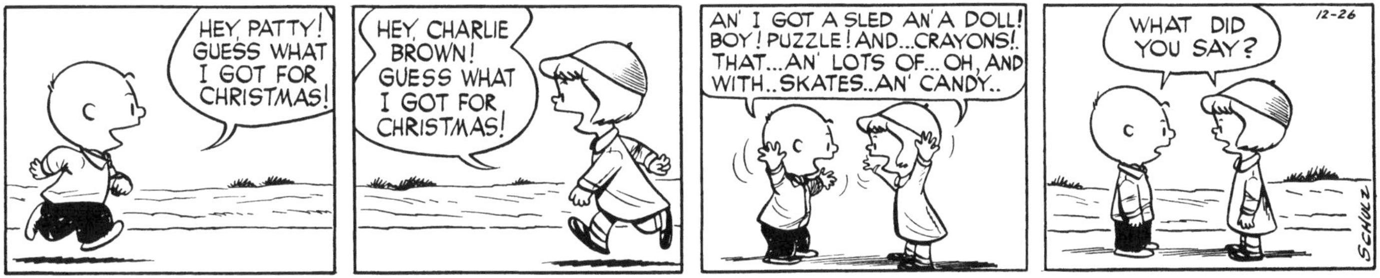
HEY, PATTY! GUESS WHAT I GOT FOR CHRISTMAS!
HEY, CHARLIE BROWN! GUESS WHAT I GOT FOR CHRISTMAS!
AN' I GOT A SLED AN' A DOLL! BOY! PUZZLE! AND...CRAYONS!. THAT...AN' LOTS OF...OH, AND WITH..SKATES..AN' CANDY..
12-26
WHAT DID YOU SAY?
SCHULZ

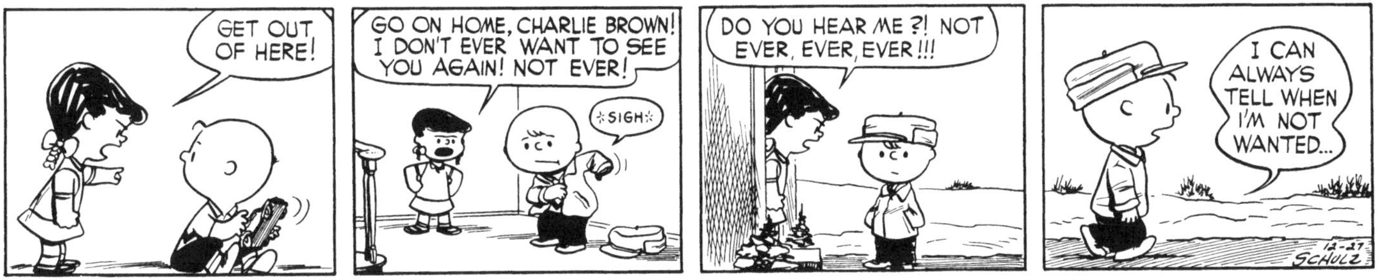
GET OUT OF HERE!
GO ON HOME, CHARLIE BROWN! I DON'T EVER WANT TO SEE YOU AGAIN! NOT EVER!
SIGH
DO YOU HEAR ME ?! NOT EVER, EVER, EVER!!!
I CAN ALWAYS TELL WHEN I'M NOT WANTED...
12-27 SCHULZ

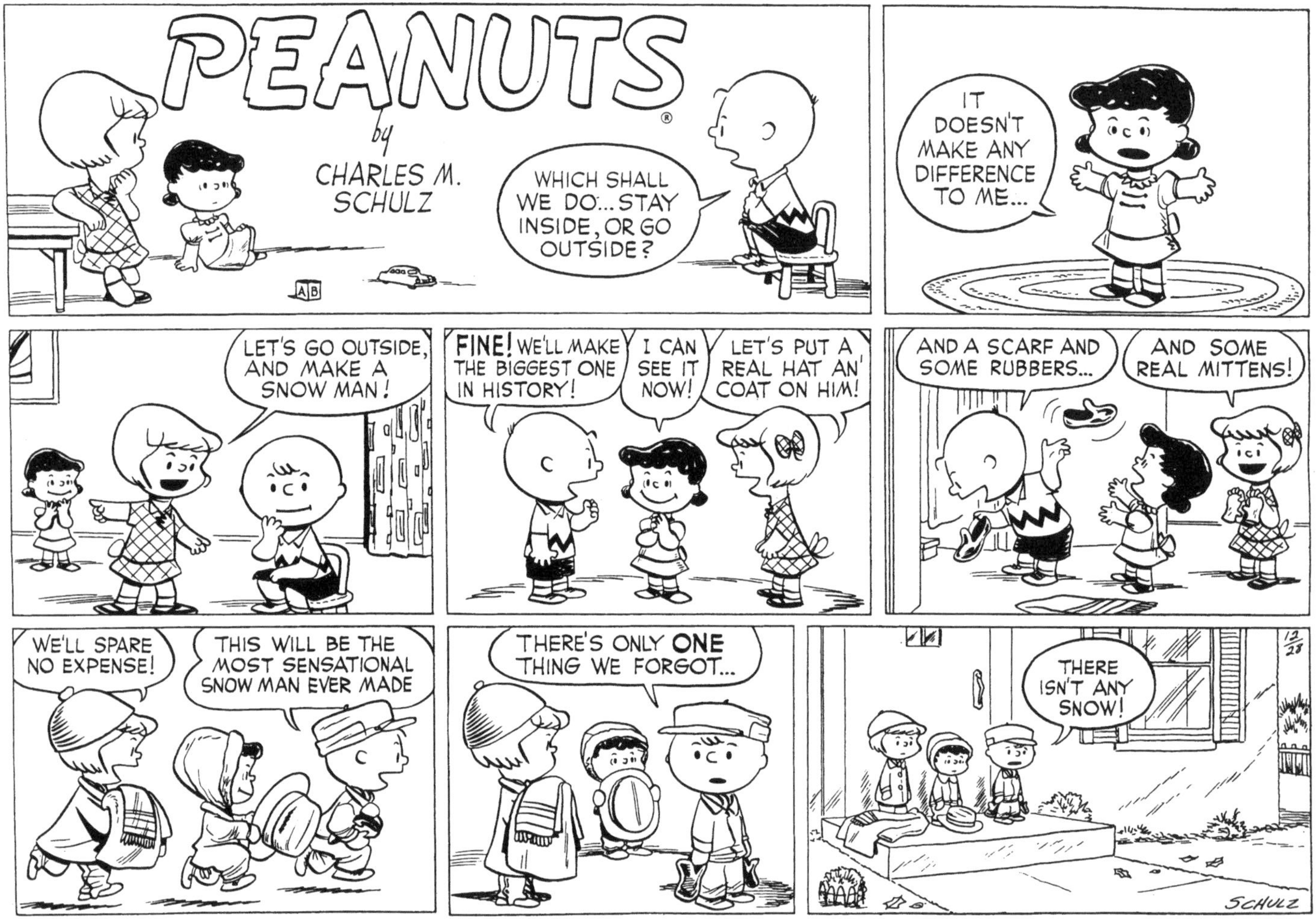
PEANUTS
by
CHARLES M. SCHULZ
WHICH SHALL WE DO... STAY INSIDE, OR GO OUTSIDE?
IT DOESN'T MAKE ANY DIFFERENCE TO ME...
LET'S GO OUTSIDE, AND MAKE A SNOW MAN!
FINE! WE'LL MAKE THE BIGGEST ONE IN HISTORY!
I CAN SEE IT NOW!
LET'S PUT A REAL HAT AN' COAT ON HIM!
AND A SCARF AND SOME RUBBERS...
AND SOME REAL MITTENS!
WE'LL SPARE NO EXPENSE!
THIS WILL BE THE MOST SENSATIONAL SNOW MAN EVER MADE
THERE'S ONLY ONE THING WE FORGOT...
12/28
THERE ISN'T ANY SNOW!
SCHULZ

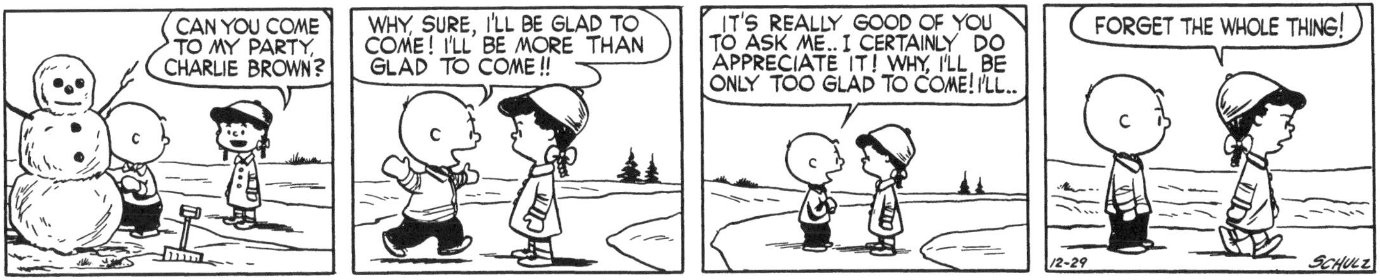
CAN YOU COME TO MY PARTY, CHARLIE BROWN?
WHY, SURE, I'LL BE GLAD TO COME! I'LL BE MORE THAN GLAD TO COME!!
IT'S REALLY GOOD OF YOU TO ASK ME.. I CERTAINLY DO APPRECIATE IT! WHY, I'LL BE ONLY TOO GLAD TO COME! I'LL..
FORGET THE WHOLE THING!
12-29
SCHULZ

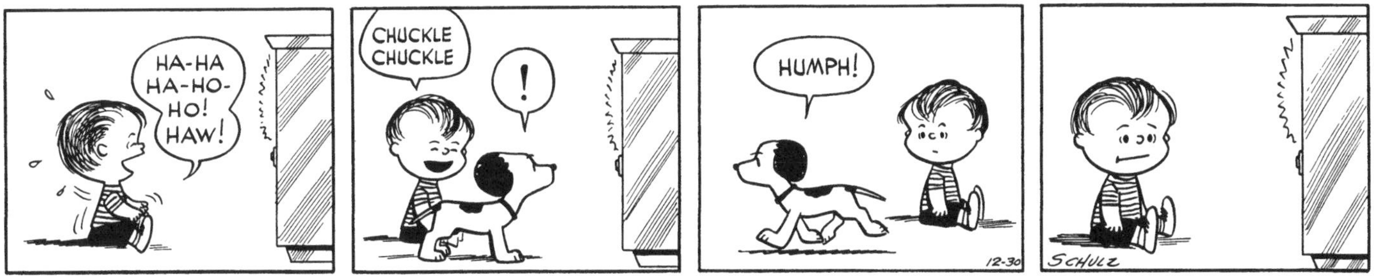
HA-HA HA-HO-HO! HAW!
CHUCKLE CHUCKLE
!
HUMPH!
12-30
SCHULZ

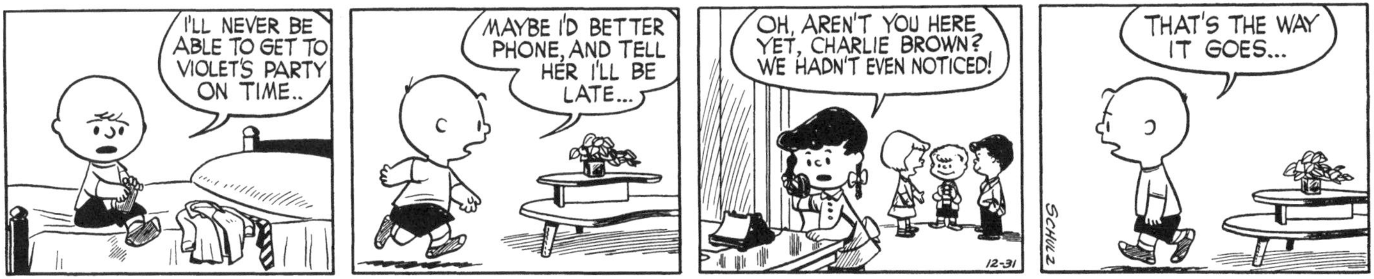
I'LL NEVER BE ABLE TO GET TO VIOLET'S PARTY ON TIME..
MAYBE I'D BETTER PHONE, AND TELL HER I'LL BE LATE...
OH, AREN'T YOU HERE YET, CHARLIE BROWN? WE HADN'T EVEN NOTICED!
12-31
SCHULZ
THAT'S THE WAY IT GOES...

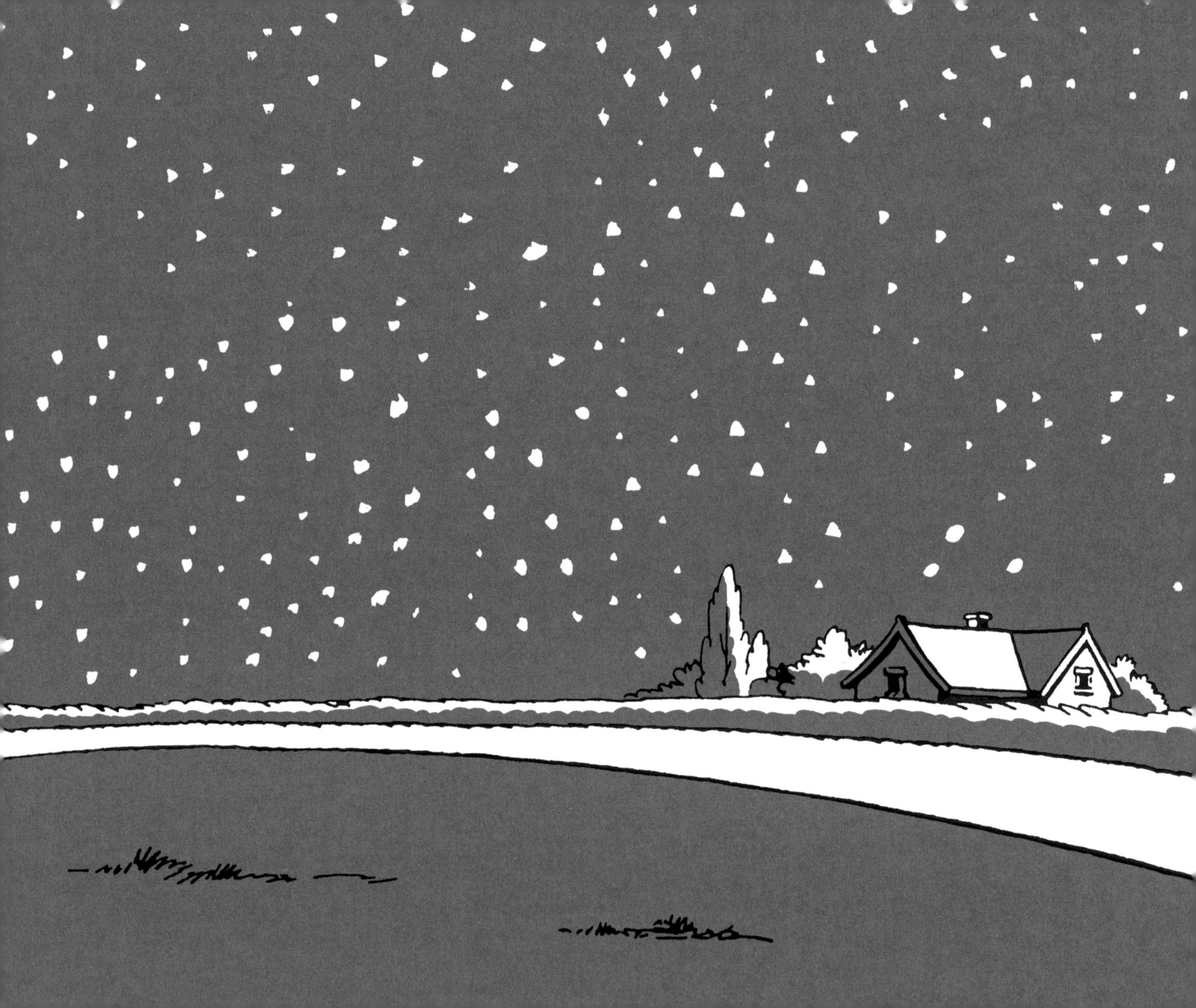

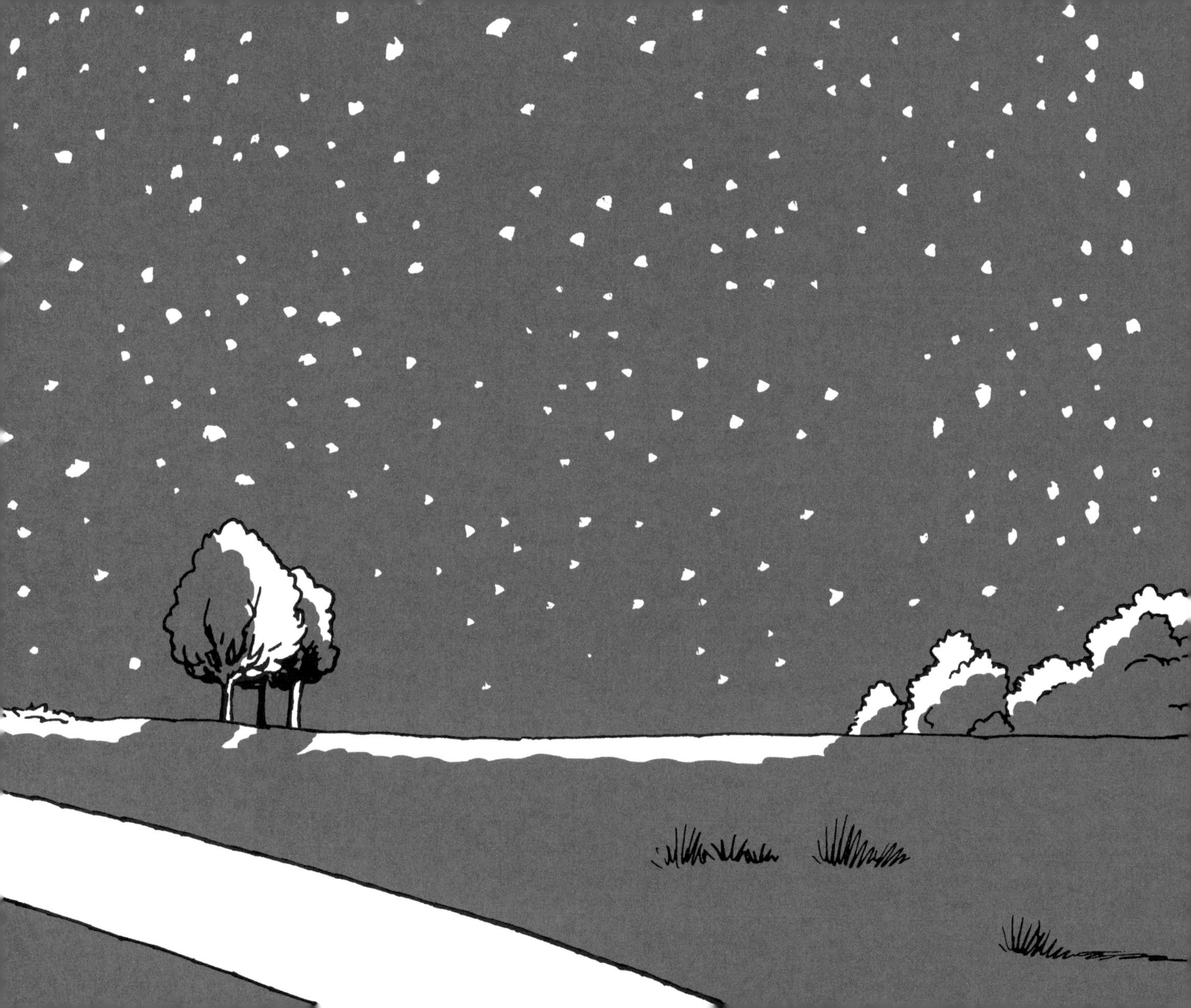

THE LIFE AND TIMES of CHARLES M. SCHULZ

On October 2, 1950, at the height of the American postwar celebration —an era when being unhappy was an antisocial rather than a personal emotion—a twenty-seven-year-old Minnesota cartoonist named Charles M. Schulz introduced to the funny papers a group of children who told one another the truth:

"I have deep feelings of depression," a round-faced kid named Charlie Brown said to an imperious girl named Lucy in an early strip. "What can I do about it?"

BY DAVID MICHAELIS

"Snap out if it," advised Lucy.

This was something new in the newspaper comic strip. At mid-century the comics were dominated by action and adventure, vaudeville and melodrama, slapstick and gags. Schulz dared to use his own quirks—a lifelong sense of alienation, insecurity, and inferiority—to draw the real feelings of his life and time. He brought a spare pen line, exquisite drawing, Jack Benny timing, and a subtle sense of humor to taboo themes such as faith, intolerance, depression, and despair. His characters were contemplative. They spoke with simplicity and force. They made smart observations about literature, art, classical music, theology, medicine, psychiatry, sports, and the law.

They explained America the way *Huckleberry Finn* does: Americans believe in friendship, in community, in fairness, but in the end, we are dominated by our apartness, our individual isolation—an isolation that went very deep, both in Schulz and in his characters.

A lifelong student of the American comic strip, Schulz knew the universal power of varying a few basic themes. He said things clearly. He recognized the phenomenal number of small things to which the big questions can be reduced. He distilled human emotion to its essence. In a few tiny lines—a circle, a dash, a loop, and two black spots—he could tell anyone in the world what a character was feeling. He was a master at portraying emotion, and took a simple approach to character development, assigning to each figure in the strip one or two memorable traits and problems, often highly comic, which he reprised whenever the character reappeared.

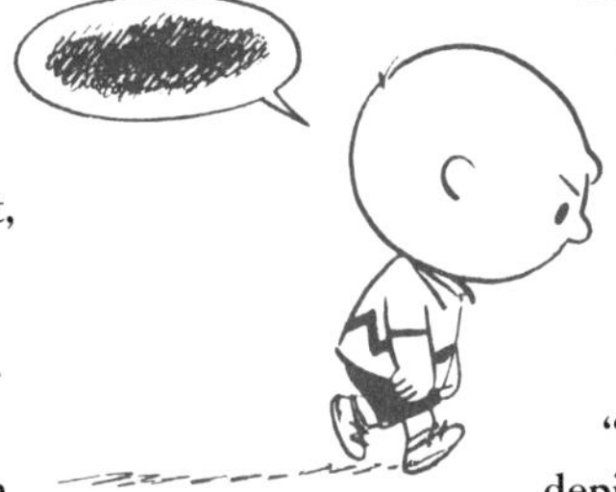

Charlie Brown was something new in comics: a real person, with a real psyche and real problems. The reader knew him, knew his fears, sympathized with his sense of inferiority and alienation. When Charlie Brown first confessed, "I don't feel the way I'm supposed to feel," he was speaking for people everywhere in Eisenhower's America, especially for a generation of solemn, precociously cynical college students, who "inhabited a shadow area within the culture," the writer Frank Conroy recalled. They were the last generation to grow up, as Schulz had, without television, and they read Charlie Brown's utterances as existential statements—comic strip koans about the human condition.

For the first time in panel cartoons, characters spoke, as novelist and semiotics professor Umberto Eco noted, "in two different keys." The *Peanuts* characters conversed in plain language and at the same time questioned the meaning of life itself. They were energized by a sense of the wrongness of things. The cruelty that exists among children was one of Schulz's first overt themes. Even Charlie Brown himself played the heavy at the start; in a 1951 strip, after prankishly insulting Patty to her face ("You don't look so hot to me"), Charlie Brown scampers away, relishing the trickster's leftovers: "I get my laughs!" But instead of merely depicting children tormenting each other, the cartoonist brilliantly used the theme of happiness—the warm and fuzzy happiness of puppies—as a stalking horse for the wrongness of things.

Peanuts depicted genuine pain and loss but somehow, as the cartoonist Art Spiegelman observed, "still kept everything warm and fuzzy." By fusing adult ideas with a world of small children, Schulz reminded us that although childhood wounds remain fresh, we have the power as adults to heal ourselves with humor. If we can laugh at the daily struggles of a bunch of funny-looking kids and in their worries recognize the adults we've become, we can free ourselves. This alchemy was the magic in Schulz's work, the alloy that fused the Before and After elements of his own life, and it remains the singular achievement of his strip, the source of its universal power, without which *Peanuts* would have come and gone in a flash.

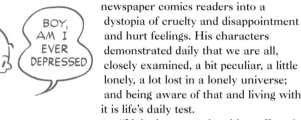

It's hard to remember now, when Snoopy and Charlie Brown dominate the blimps at golf tournaments instead of the comics in Sunday papers, that once upon a time Schulz's strip was the fault-line of a cultural earthquake. Garry Trudeau, creator of *Doonesbury*, who came of age as a comic strip artist under Schulz's influence, thought of it as "the first Beat strip." Edgy, unpredictable, ahead of its time, *Peanuts* "vibrated with '50s alienation," Trudeau recalled. "Everything about it was different."

A generation before *Peanuts*, the comics parodied the world. Schulz made a world. He lured mainstream newspaper comics readers into a dystopia of cruelty and disappointment and hurt feelings. His characters demonstrated daily that we are all, closely examined, a bit peculiar, a little lonely, a lot lost in a lonely universe; and being aware of that and living with it is life's daily test.

"Nobody was saying this stuff, and it was the truth," said Jules Feiffer, whose drawings in the late '50s, like Schulz's, were steeped in a new humor of truth called "egghead" humor. "Nobody was doing this stuff. You didn't find it in *The New Yorker*. You found it in cellar clubs; and, on occasion, in the pages of the *Village Voice*. But not many other places. And then, with *Peanuts*, there it was on the comics page."

Feiffer, the melancholy Jewish intellectual striking at the heart of life as we knew it, saw in Schulz a fellow subversive. Their styles and audience could not have been more different. Feiffer aimed for an elite, urban audience; Schulz was drawing for everyone everywhere. But their territory overlapped. In a Feiffer cartoon of the late '50s, a teenager enumerates the horror of middle age: getting stuck in a marriage, living in the suburbs, dying of boredom. A man confronts the teenager: "Why don't you just grow up?" The teenager replies: "For our generation a refusal to grow up is a sign of maturity." That was the message of *Peanuts*, too. Schulz was drawing the "inner child" many years before the concept emerged in the popular culture.

The *Peanuts* gang was appealing but also strange. Were they children or adults? Or some kind of hybrid? What would push real children to the breaking point, Charlie Brown handled admirably and without self-pity or self-congratulation. What would reduce children to tears in the real world was routinely endured in *Peanuts.*

In their early years, the characters were volatile, combustible. They were angry. "How I hate him!" was the very first punch line in *Peanuts*. Charlie Brown and his friends could be, as the cartoonist Al Capp said, "mean little bastards, eager to hurt each other." In *Peanuts*, there was always the chance that the rage of one character would suddenly bowl over another, literally spinning the victim backward and out of frame. Coming home to relax, Charlie Brown sits down to a radio broadcast whose suave announcer is saying, "And what, in all this world, is more delightful than the gay wonderful laughter of little children?" Charlie Brown stands, sets his jaw, and kicks the radio set clear out of the room. Here was a comic strip hero, who, unlike his predecessors Li'l Abner, Dick Tracy, Joe Palooka, or Little Orphan Annie, could take the restrained fury of the '50s and translate it into a harbinger of '60s activism.

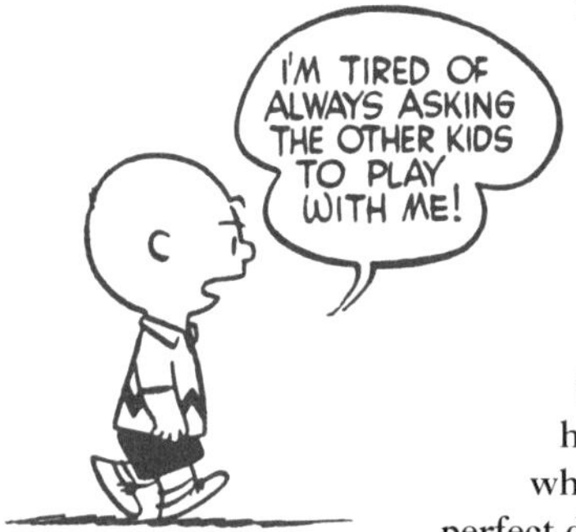
I'M TIRED OF ALWAYS ASKING THE OTHER KIDS TO PLAY WITH ME!

On the one hand, the action in *Peanuts* conveyed an American sense that things could be changed, or at least modified, by sudden violence. By getting good and mad you could resolve things. But, on the other hand, Charlie Brown reminded people, as no other cartoon character had, of what it was to be vulnerable, to be human. He was even, for a time in the '50s, called the "youngest existentialist," a term that sent his determinedly unsophisticated creator to the dictionary.

The experience of being an Everyman—a decent, caring person in a hostile world—is essential to Charlie Brown's character, as it was to Charles Schulz's. The quality of fortitude (one of the seven cardinal virtues in Christianity) is at the heart of Charlie Brown. Humanity was created to be strong; yet, to be strong, and still to fail is one of the identifying things that it is to be human. Charlie Brown never quit, which in the end would prove to be a perfect description of Charles Schulz.

Charlie Brown is a fighter, but a fighter in terms of pure endurance, not in terms of working out strategically how he is going to win. He simply endures; he stays longer on the baseball field than all the other kids. When the field is flooded in a downpour and only the pitcher's mound is above water, he remains. His strategy is simple: hang on. He does not go off, as Ulysses does, to seek and make a newer world. Charlie Brown never makes it new. Snoopy, an animal, makes it new. Snoopy is somehow or other always new. Real imagination is allowed only to the non-human character in Schulz's world. This tells us something: that the children are admirable for their human dignity and their lack of self-pity. Charlie Brown may feel sorry for himself but he gets over it fast. He is ennobled by how well he handles being disappointed. He never cries.

The moment when *Peanuts* became *Peanuts* can probably be marked at several spots on Schulz's 1954 calendar, but nowhere more clearly than Monday, February 1: Charlie Brown is visiting Shermy. He looks on, bereft, as a smiling Shermy, seemingly unaware of Charlie Brown's presence, plays with a model train set whose tracks and junctions and crossings spead so elaborately far and wide in Shermy's family's living room, the railroad's complete dimensions cannot be shown in a single cartoon panel. Charlie Brown pulls on his coat and walks home. Finally, alone in his own living room, Charlie Brown sits down at *his* railroad: a single, closed circle of track, no bigger than a manhole cover. But there is no anger, no self-pity, no tears—no punch line—just silent acceptance. Here was the moment when Charlie Brown became a national symbol, the Everyman who survives life's slings and arrows simply by surviving himself.

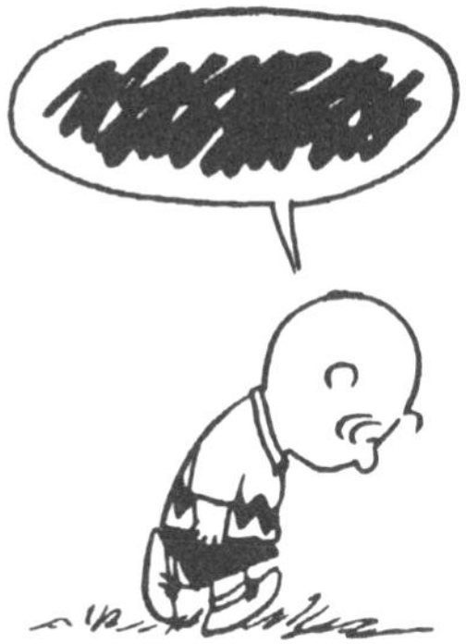

We recognize ourselves in Charlie Brown—in his dignity despite doomed ballgames, his endurance despite a deep awareness of death, his stoicism in the face of life's disasters—because he is willing to admit that just to keep on being Charlie Brown is an exhausting and painful process. "You don't know what it's like to be a barber's son," Charlie Brown tells Schroeder. He remembers how it felt to see tears running down his father's cheeks when his dad read letters in the newspaper attacking barbers for raising the price of a haircut. He recalls how hard his father worked to give his family a respectable life. By the fourth panel, Charlie Brown is so upset by his memories that he grabs Schroeder's shirt with both hands and screams, "YOU DON'T KNOW WHAT IT'S LIKE!!"

SCHULZ DID. A SHY, TIMID BOY, A barber's son, born on November 26, 1922, "Sparky" Schulz—nicknamed for the horse in *Barney Google*—had grown up from modest beginnings in St Paul, Minnesota, to realize his earliest dream of creating a newspaper comic strip. The only child of devoted parents, neither of whom had gone further in school than the third grade, Schulz linked the un-sophistication of his childhood home with the ideal of a dignified, ordinary life that he forever after tried to return to. "There are times," he wrote at fifty-eight, "when I would like to go back to the years with my mother and father. It would be great to be able to go into the house where my mother was in the kitchen and my comic books were in the other room, and I could lie down on the couch and read the comics and then have dinner with my parents."

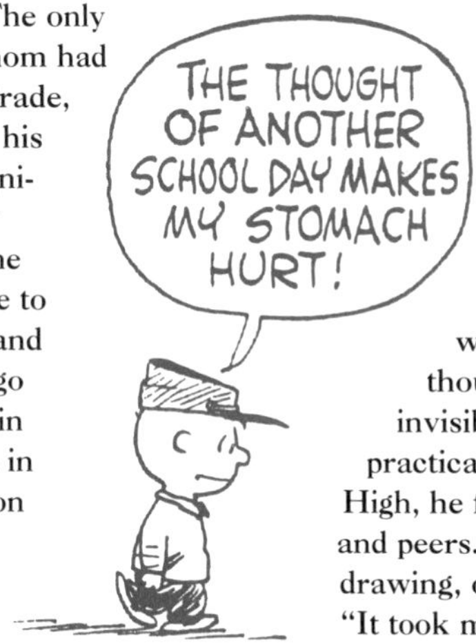
THE THOUGHT OF ANOTHER SCHOOL DAY MAKES MY STOMACH HURT!

But growing up was a dismaying process for Schulz. He felt chronically unsupported. "He always felt that no one really loved him," a relative recalled. "He knew his mom and dad loved him but he wasn't too sure other people loved him."

His intelligence revealed itself in the second grade. In a class of thirty-one pupils, Charles Schulz was singled out as the outstanding boy student. Two years later, the principal at the Richards Gordon Elementary School in St. Paul skipped Schulz over the fourth grade. By the time he reached junior high school, he was the youngest, smallest boy in the class. He felt lost, unsure of himself. With no one to turn to, he made loneliness, insecurity, and a stoic acceptance of life's defeats his earliest personal themes. At the same time, he possessed a strong independent streak and grew increasingly stubborn and competitive as life and its injustices, real and imagined, piled up.

As a slight, 136-pound teenager, with pimples, big ears, and a face he thought of as so bland it amounted to invisibility, he had few friends at school. In practically every thing he did at St. Paul Central High, he felt underestimated by teachers, coaches, and peers. No one ever gave him credit for his drawing, or for playing a superior game of golf. "It took me a long time to become a human being," he once said. "I never regarded myself as being much and I never regarded myself as being good looking and I never had a date in high school, because I thought, who'd want to date me?"

Sensitive to slights, he never forgot the rejections of Central High. To the end of his life, he remained baffled that the editors of the *Cehisean*, the Central High yearbook, had rejected a batch of his drawings. At the age of fifty-three, he made sure that a high school report card was printed in facsimile in a collection of his work "to show my own children that I was not as dumb as everyone has said I was." He projected the traumas of his adolescence far into adulthood—far enough, in the end, to see them become a crucial element in the universal popularity of his art.

Chronic rejection and unrequited love are the twin plinths of Schulz's early life and later work. Even when he had become the one cartoonist known and loved by people around the world, he could still say, with conviction, "My whole life has been one of rejection."

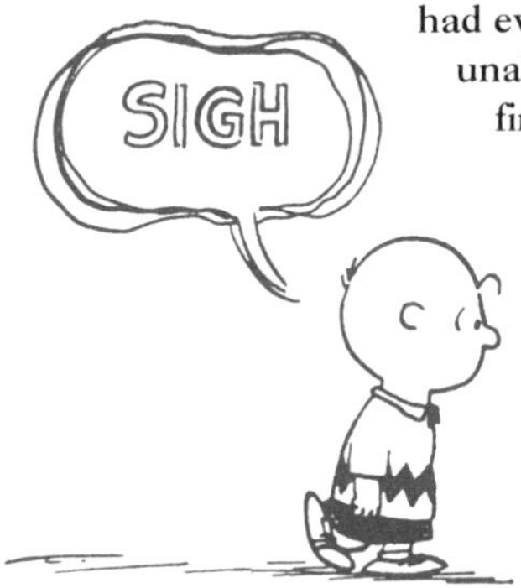
SIGH

As a young man he suffered deep loss. His mother's wrenching early death from cancer shaped the rest of his life. He was twenty when she died at the age of forty-eight in February 1943. Three days later, a private in the army, he boarded a troop train for Camp Campbell, Kentucky, and the war in Europe. The sense of shock and separation never left him. He survived World War II, as he had survived the Depression and the alienation of his youth, but the only world that had ever mattered to him—the secure home his parents had vouchsafed him—was gone, and for a time he had no hope for the future. His mother's death came to stand not only for her removal from his life, which would have been a cataclysm by itself, but also, because of the war, for Schulz's total separation from childhood and home. He would refer to it as a "loss from which I sometimes believe I never recovered."

Melancholy would dog him all his life, as would feelings of worthlessness, panic, high anxiety, and frustration. It wouldn't matter that he married twice, raised five children, and became the most widely syndicated and beloved cartoonist of all time, attaining success on a scale no individual comic strip artist had ever known. Success fell off him. He was unable to take refuge in its rewards. With his first wife and five children, he moved in 1958 to a paradise among the redwoods of Northern California, where for a decade the work of his pen and the peaks of his professional achievements coincided with the nation's upheavals. But Schulz knew better than anyone that he could never really become a sunny citizen of the Golden State. He found little comfort in fame or prosperity or the California sun. Pain gave him his core. "I think that one of the things that afforded Sparky his greatness," a friend would say after his death, "was his unwillingness to turn his back on the pain."

The private, quiet, depressed, Scandinavian part of Schulz's character was both the quality that made him completely different from any other comic strip artist and the trait that led him to struggle with himself and his creation like the tormented artist in a Henry James novel.

UNTIL 1965, SCHULZ PROVIDED UNCONVENTIONAL commentary in the national margins. He had no interest in taking a stand or in taking sides; his subject was the ordeal of individual experience. And yet *Peanuts* registered social tremors with seismographic accuracy. Schulz *was* topical, constantly illuminating up-to-the-minute questions and personalities: smut and gore in comic books [June 22, 1952]; nuclear testing and the H-Bomb [June 18, 1954]; excessive vigilance by the FBI [Oct. 30, 1956]; hazards of the jet age [Mar. 29, 1959]; Rachel Carson [Nov. 12, 1962; Feb. 19, 1963; Feb. 20, 1963]; the adoption of ZIP codes [Sept. 27, 1963]; prayer in schools [Oct. 20, 1963]; long hair and hippies [July 12, 1967; Nov. 1, 1967]; police brutality [Nov. 2, 1967]; teachers' strikes [Feb. 24, 1969]; Tiny Tim [Sept. 10, 1968]; love bead [Sept. 15, 1968]; the Vietnam War [July 1-9, 1970]; tear-gas at campus protests [July 7, 1970]; the rights of unborn children [July 20, 1970] all found their way into the strip. In *Peanuts*' first three decades of syndication, which happened to coincide with the greatest fomentation of social change in the United States since the Civil War, Schulz was the prevailing voice in mainstream newspaper comics on social change.

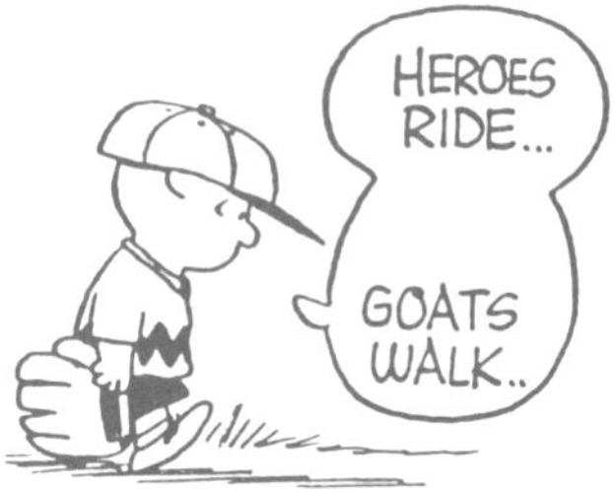
HEROES RIDE...
GOATS WALK..

Yet he personally remained apart from specific social and political causes, never joining the battle of ideas. He deliberately refused to settle the issues raised by the strip. He never made overt political statements through *Peanuts*. Having established a language that commented on modern ills, Schulz extended the area of doubt in modern life only insofar as he made it funny to doubt. But, as the '60s intensified, as the Vietnam War failed and nothing quite worked out, as the triumphal quality of American life modulated, *Peanuts* became a refuge. Schulz became the patron saint of people who were putting up with all they could take. Reading the strip was a peculiar mixture of utter forgetfulness, which created the spell, and at the same time, tremendous consciousness. *Peanuts* was proof that you were not alone when you woke in the middle of the night marooned with your failures, staring into the dark, worrying that the world had gone mad.

From 1965 onward, the strip skyrocketed. When Schulz's "bunch of funny-looking kids" appeared on the cover of *Time* magazine in April, *Peanuts* was embraced as the embodiment of the fundamental wisdom of the time. The strip and its characters had gone from being a campus phenomenon in the late '50s to a mainstream cultural powerhouse. Throughout the '60s and early '70s, the visual and verbal vocabulary of the strip was one of the only languages that kept both the younger and older generation fluent with each other. Schulz's phrase "security blanket," and his ideas about that most American of concepts, happiness, found their way into *Bartlett's Familiar Quotations* and *Webster's Dictionary*. The names and subversive attributes of his characters filtered into the counterculture of the '60s; the Grateful Dead's defiantly grubby organist, Ron McKernan, was nicknamed Pig Pen; another San Francisco rock band that formed in 1966 called itself Sopwith Camel. As American soldiers stenciled Snoopy onto their helmets and the Apollo 10 astronauts christened their command module Charlie Brown and their lunar landing vehicle Snoopy, Schulz left his imprimatur on the Cold War's highest and lowest moments—the race to put a man on the moon and the war in Vietnam.

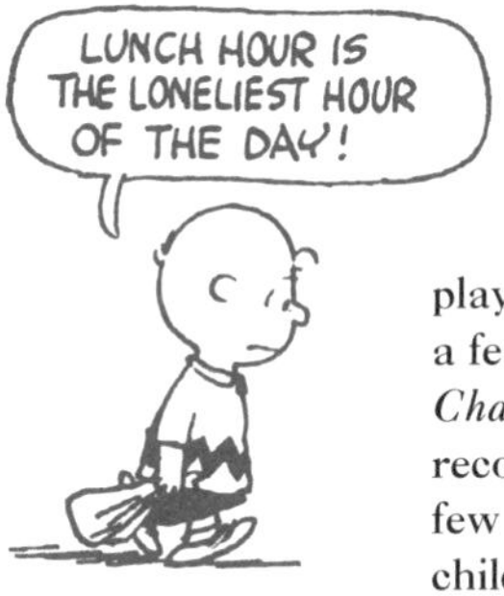
LUNCH HOUR IS THE LONELIEST HOUR OF THE DAY!

In 1969, as the nation teetered, Schulz soared to previously unknown heights of popular culture. One snowy night that December, when Schulz was forty-seven years old, some fifty-five million viewers, more than half the nation's television audience, tuned in to the Emmy-award-winning animated television special, *A Charlie Brown Christmas*, the popularity of which confounded network executives who had predicted that its cartoon format, melancholy jazz score by Vincent Guaraldi, and simple retelling of the Nativity story from the Gospel of Luke would alienate the public. That same night, a musical, *You're A Good Man, Charlie Brown*, was playing to sold-out houses on Broadway; and a feature-length animated film, *A Boy Named Charlie Brown*, was setting attendance records at Radio City Music Hall; every few hours, six thousand more parents and children would form a line outside the "showplace of the nation." More than one hundred fifty million newspaper readers were following the daily and Sunday editions of *Peanuts*, while in bookstores *Peanuts* collections swamped the bestseller lists, eventually selling more than three hundred million copies in twenty-six languages.

Peanuts had acquired a life beyond itself. Long-suffering Charlie Brown, exuberant Snoopy, philosophical Linus, domineering Lucy, talented Schroeder, narcoleptic Peppermint Patty became revered figures in Japan, beloved in England, France, Germany, Norway, Italy, and known by sight in seventy-five countries throughout Europe, South America, Africa, Australia, and Asia. The *Times of London* called them "international icons of good faith"—not surprising for the creations of a cartoonist with a Dickensian gift for characterization. As more and more people fit real life into the context of the comic strip, Charlie Brown and Lucy and Linus and Snoopy acquired an explanatory character as well as a descriptive character. Where Americans in an earlier generation might have analogized themselves to Scrooge or Pip or Little Nell or Miss Havisham or Uriah Heap or Bill Sykes, now the *Peanuts* characters explained people to themselves and provided a widespread idiom for struggles in life and love. At all levels of society *Peanuts* had a profound and lasting influence on the way people saw themselves and the world in the second half of the 20th century.

Schulz's achievement was singular and planetary. An artist, a storyteller, he was now a worldwide industry, too. This had never happened to a newspaper cartoonist before. The new markets that *Peanuts* was dominating in stage, television, film, book, record, and subsidiary forms, simply hadn't been open to newspaper comic strip artists in 1950, when United Media had given Schulz the chance to dream his dream. On that one night in 1969, he reached a larger, more diverse audience than any other single popular artist in American history. What was more, *Peanuts* was single-handedly expanding an industry that would revolutionize worldwide entertainment into the next century. In the late '60s, for the first time in the book trade, booksellers started to sell not just *Peanuts* books but also sweatshirts, dolls, and an increasing array of paraphernalia that bore the image and form of the characters in the books—an old idea called "licensing" that *Peanuts* products would turn into a global phenomenon.

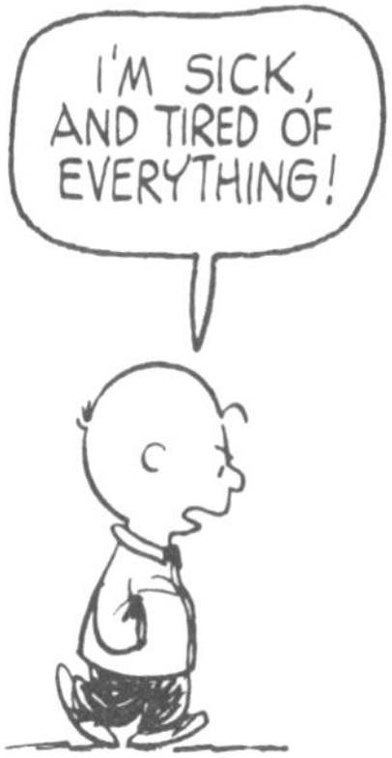
I'M SICK, AND TIRED OF EVERYTHING!

USING A CROW-QUILL PEN DIPPED IN INK, SCHULZ drew every day through the next three decades. He always worked alone, without a team of assistants. For a self-doubting perfectionist—Schulz referred to himself as a fanatic—the strip cartoon was an ideal form: the cartoonist's relationship to the world is self-limiting. The strip cartoonist can get up, go to work, draw his daily panels, and go to bed at night feeling he's done his bit. At the same time, Schulz had a conflicted sense of duty. The unprecedented obligations of his new role as world-famous cartoonist kept him in a state of constant anxiety and dread. He loved to be asked to go places and do good things and receive prestigious honors, but he hated to leave home and routine. He felt he should meet people and see the world, but he was increasingly phobic about travel. He panicked as he boarded airplanes, broke out in a cold sweat at the very idea of spending the night away from home. Safely at work in his studio, he loved receiving fan letters by the hundreds but resented the demands on his time. Perhaps because he refused so many requests for public appearances, he was unfailingly openhanded in his correspondence, answering scores of letters and special requests from strangers each day.

The condolences that flooded Schulz's office after news of his retirement from *Peanuts* and then crested over into his household after his death are dominated by a single refrain: *The handwritten response I received from Charles Schulz at a critical moment in my development changed forever the course of my life.* He influenced two generations of comic strip artists, standup comedians, and readers everywhere. But unlike other seminal figures of American mass culture in the 1960s and '70s—Marshall McLuhan, Buckminster Fuller, Andy Warhol —Schulz had no itch to be a teacher, a guru, a manufacturer of lesser artists. "I don't know the meaning of life," he once said. "I don't know why we are here. I think life is full of anxieties and fears and tears. It has a lot of grief in it, and it can be very grim. And I do not want to be the one who tries to tell somebody else what life is all about. To me it's a complete mystery."

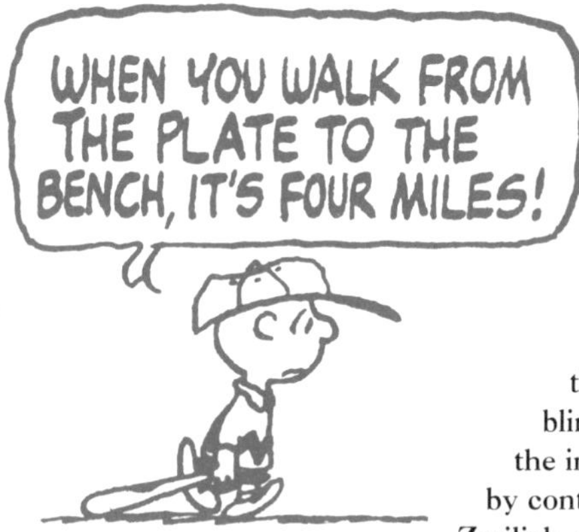
WHEN YOU WALK FROM THE PLATE TO THE BENCH, IT'S FOUR MILES!

He wanted only to operate from the extreme bottom right-hand corner of his own panels—where it said "Schulz." He wanted to limit himself to being that little scribble. If he could draw his four panels a day, sign himself "Schulz," close up shop and go home, all would be well.

Charles M. Schulz became highest-paid, most influential cartoonist ever. The only modern American comic strip artist to be given a retrospective at the Louvre, he was now in a class by himself. His characters cut a broad path across commerce and culture; Charlie Brown and Snoopy could go from being cartoon pitchmen for cars and life insurance, their huge heads and tiny bodies stretched across blimps at golf tournaments, to being the inspiration for a *Peanuts* concerto by contemporary composer Ellen Taafe Zwilich, premiering at Carnegie Hall. At the peak of Schulz's popularity, *Peanuts* captured three hundred and fifty-five million readers, and the merchandising of the brand created a franchise unlike any the funny papers had ever known, with the cartoonist himself earning from $30 million to $40 million a year.

He kept on drawing as he always had—17,897 strips by the end. He often said, "My main job is to draw funny comic strips for the newspapers." He didn't set himself up as a chaplain or philosopher or therapist to the millions. He made no statements about important issues. He sat on no commissions. He went straight on with his work, even though the world begged him to change from being a commentator for a minor constituency in the 1950s to a national observer who had a great deal to say to the world at large. He wanted to be no different than anyone else.

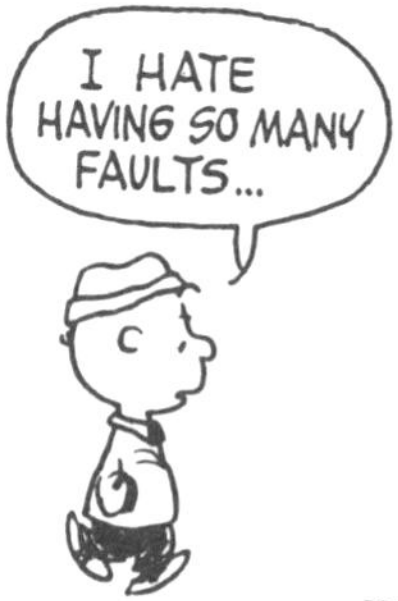
I HATE HAVING SO MANY FAULTS...

As part of his morning routine, he ate an English muffin with grape jelly and drank coffee from a Styrofoam cup, then sat down to his drawing table and the long, white Strathmore board with the five-inch by five-inch panels in which he drew the daily strip. "He attempted to be ordinary," said Clark Gesner, author of the musical *You're A Good Man, Charlie Brown*. He wanted to be what he thought he had always been—a regular person.

In later life, Schulz joked that he looked like a druggist. Genial, smiling, with straight white teeth and a head of silver hair, he dressed modestly in slacks and pastel golf sweaters. He stood a trim five feet eleven and a half inches and liked to sprawl after work in a big blue leather easy chair, his long legs pointing straight at the TV set. "People say 'Where do you get your ideas?'" he once recalled, "because they look at me and they think, surely this man could never think of anything funny." But smiling silver-haired druggists know the town pretty well. They have the common touch, they dispense daily doses of medicine to the melancholy people of Mudville, and they are the last to have illusions about what's really happening in people's lives.

He dreaded becoming a prisoner of success, perhaps because it meant he would lose control. "I don't want to attract attention," he said in 1981. "I've always had the fear of being ostentatious—of people thinking that these things have gone to my head." He didn't have any experience being a millionaire or a celebrity. He wanted to be free. When reporters came around asking questions about his success, he would reply, "Have I had enormous success? Do you think so?" He hated to talk about it. In 1967, he hotly told a writer, "*Life* magazine said I was a multimillionaire—heck, no cartoonist can become a millionaire."

Into the 1980s and 1990s, his fortune mushroomed. *Forbes* magazine regularly listed Schulz among the top-ten highest-paid entertainers in the United States, along with Bill Cosby, Michael Jordan, and Michael Jackson. He took little interest in accumulating money, gave millions away to charities, insisting always that he was the same old Sparky Schulz. At his drawing table in his studio at One Snoopy

Place in Santa Rosa, he drew with the same old pens, the same old nibs. He liked to say that he would stay at the desk until he wore a hole clean through it.

Schulz took professional pride in the achievements of the strip. But pride in one's work does not automatically override years of early disappointments to create pride in one's self, and Schulz struggled to the end of his life to believe that he himself was worthy of the respect and love his admirers showered on him. "It is amazing that they think that what I do was that good," he said in one of the last interviews of his life. His voice quavered and he seemed as if he might break down when he said: "I just did the best I could."

In November 1999, after a stroke put him into the hospital, doctors discovered that colon cancer had metastasized to his stomach. He had an operation to remove the cancer, and the doctors got most of it, but the stroke and the surgery robbed Schulz of the will to go on drawing. He couldn't see clearly, he couldn't read. He struggled to recall the words he needed. But all that might have been tolerable except that chemotherapy had begun to make him sick to his stomach, and the statistics for Stage-Four colon cancer gave him a slim twenty percent chance to live.

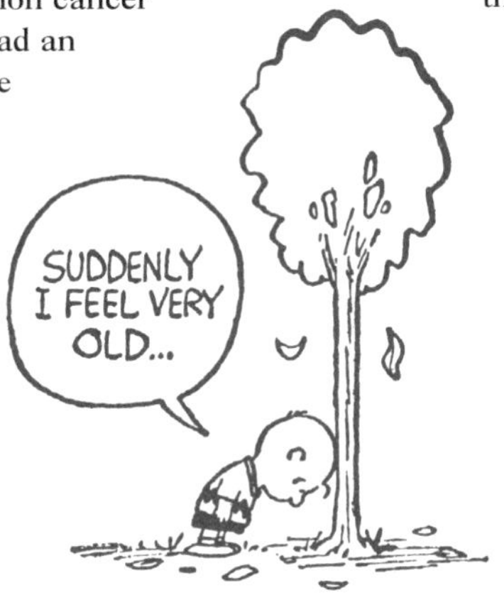
SUDDENLY I FEEL VERY OLD...

On December 14, 1999, at the age of seventy-seven, Schulz announced his retirement. "I never dreamed that this would happen to me," he said. "I always had the feeling that I would stay with the strip until I was in my early eighties, or something like that. But all of sudden it's gone. It's been taken away from me. I did not take it away," he emphasized. "This was taken away from me."

After nearly fifty years of drawing *Peanuts*, the world-famous cartoonist put down his pen in January, his vision blurred. Being a comic strip artist was all he had ever wanted. On February 12, 2000, a dark night of pouring rain in Santa Rosa, California, Schulz got into bed a little after nine o'clock. He pulled up the covers. At 9:45 p.m., just hours before the final *Peanuts* strip appeared in Sunday newspapers around the world, Charles Schulz died—his life entwined to the very end with his art. As soon as he ceased to be a cartoonist, he ceased to be.

David Michaelis, *author of* N. C. Wyeth: A Biography *(Knopf, 1998), is writing the first full-scale biography of Charles M. Schulz.*

AN INTERVIEW WITH CHARLES M. SCHULZ

This interview with Charles Schulz was conducted in late 1987 in Schulz's studio in Santa Rosa, California. It originally appeared in NEMO: The Classic Comics Library, *a magazine devoted to newspaper strips, cartooning, and popular illustration, in January, 1992.*

RICK MARSCHALL: *I wonder if you realize how deep an impact* Peanuts *has had on your readers.*
CHARLES SCHULZ: No, actually I'm very surprised. And I always kind of worry about it because I realize

that I'm in a medium where it's dangerous to stick your head out because there are so many people that simply don't read the comics and still don't regard it as worthwhile entertainment. There's nothing that annoys me more than somebody coming up to me and saying, "My nineteen-year-old daughter really loves your strip and she still reads it," because that's the audience that I'm really going for. And another thing that bothers me are the parents who come up to me with their two- or three-year-old child on their shoulder and say, "Look, you know who this is? It's Peanuts' father!" and the poor kid and I look at each other and the kid has no idea what the mother and father are talking about and it really bothers me. Beyond that, I kind of keep to myself and try not to think about that. When people say to me, "I really admire your philosophy," I literally and honestly do not know what they are talking about because I don't even know what my philosophy is.

MARSCHALL: *They try to read something into the strip.*

SCHULZ: Which is all right. I think that even minor art forms like this, as Robert Short tried to talk about in *The Gospel According to Peanuts*, do have certain truths in them, and I think that's important, and I think that people should be able to read whatever they want to into what they're looking at or reading. But as far as an overall philosophy goes, I'm really not sure what it is. Although I try to draw a gentle strip, I try to draw a strip that doesn't have any real cruelty in it, outside of things like Lucy pulling away the football. And it's not as insulting a strip as it used to be. Of course, I've gotten older, and I'm not as insulting as I used to be myself.

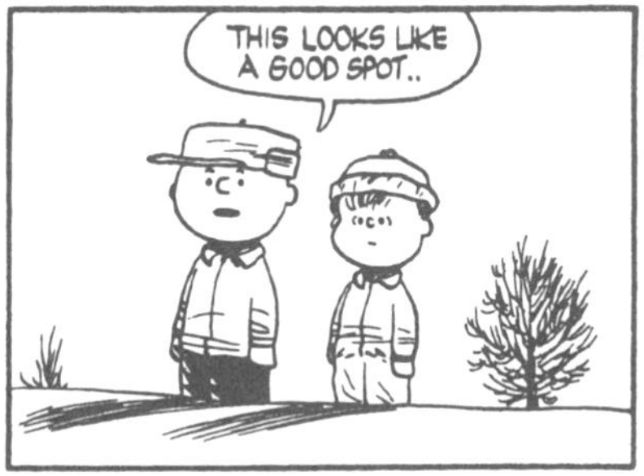
THIS LOOKS LIKE A GOOD SPOT..

MARSCHALL: *You don't consciously put your philosophy in it like Harold Gray did in* Little Orphan Annie, *but it's obviously a reflection of yourself.*

I'd like to ask about your background. I know you grew up in St. Paul. Your name is Schulz. Isn't that German? Do you have any ethnic flavor in your background, or has your family been here for many generations?

SCHULZ: My dad was born in Germany, but he was the only one in the family who was. Apparently, his parents went over on a year's vacation or something back to Germany, where he was born, but his brothers and sisters were all born in this country. My mother was one of nine children, and I always regarded myself really as being Norwegian, and not German. I think I was a little bit ashamed of being German, due to World War I, and always played that down. I never think about nationalities, and I know my own children don't think of nationalities: If you were to ask them what nationality they are, I think they are probably the first generation who would now say American.

My dad was a barber. I always admired him for the fact that both he and my mother had only third grade educations and, from what I remembered hearing in conversations, he worked pitching hay in Nebraska one summer to earn enough money to go to barber school, got himself a couple of jobs and eventually bought his own barber shop. And I think he at one time owned two barber shops and a filling station, but that was either when I was not born or very small, so I don't know much about that. But, of course, I was raised during the Depression struggle, which didn't affect me personally, because I don't think little kids are into what's going on. If you have pancakes for dinner, you think that's wonderful because you like pancakes. You don't realize that you're probably having them because your parents can't afford anything more.

But my dad ran a three-chair barbershop...

MARSCHALL: *Ran it through the Depression?*
SCHULZ: Right through the Depression. I know at one point he was seven months behind on his rent, but he told me years later it didn't matter because the big building where his barber shop was had so many empty spaces in it that the landlord didn't really care, as long as he kept up as much as he could on the rent. But I always admired him for being a self-employed person who loved his work. I remember his telling me several times that he loved to get up in the morning and go to work, and I think he was as totally at home in the barber shop as I am off doodling in my studio. Years later, I began to realize that a lot of this being at home in your place of work is not necessarily because you love it so much, but because you're secure there, and he probably had the same travel fears that I have. But he was incapable of expressing them and I knew about it, and I never had a chance to talk about these things with him. I don't know how much my dad made, but I never felt that I wanted anything. I had a baseball glove and a bicycle, for which my dad paid $24 and paid for it at the rate of four dollars a week at Western Auto. And we had a car. We never had a new car, but....

MARSCHALL: *Did you have friends whose families suffered through the Depression?*
SCHULZ: We never knew. You know, you're just little kids and you're playing cops and robbers and cowboys and Indians and you organize your baseball games. There was no little league at that time, so all of our baseball games were between neighborhood teams. We would make up our own teams and challenge another neighborhood. We literally did lose a game once 40 to 0, which is where I got the idea for Charlie Brown's string of losses.

The highlight of our lives was, of course, Saturday afternoons, going to the local theatre. We would buy a box of popcorn for a nickel from a popcorn shop a few stores down from the theatre and then we'd go to the afternoon matinee. My favorite movie, I still

remember, was *Lost Patrol* with Victor McLaglen. I loved those desert movies, which is why I like drawing Snoopy as the foreign legionnaire. We never went downtown to a movie to a first run theatre. I think first run theatres were about 35 cents. If we went downtown on Sunday night to a movie, it was always to a double feature where the theatre only charged 15 cents per person.

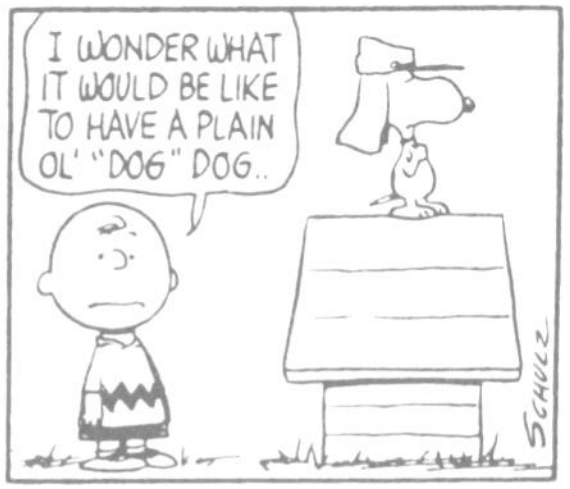
I WONDER WHAT IT WOULD BE LIKE TO HAVE A PLAIN OL' "DOG" DOG..
SCHULZ

MARSCHALL: *Was St. Paul in the '20s and '30s anything like Garrison Keillor or Jean Shepherd's stories about growing up in a mid-western town?*
SCHULZ: I don't know Shepherd and I've only heard four of the Keillor tapes, but that was different. He's talking about small towns. St. Paul is not a small town. I always thought of myself as growing up, really, in the city. So I always regarded myself as a city boy. I grew up on the sidewalks, not in the country.

MARSCHALL: *You were never tempted to make* Peanuts *a city strip?*
SCHULZ: I don't know where the Peanuts kids live. I think that, originally, I thought of them as living in these little veterans' developments, where Joyce and I first lived when we got married out in Colorado Springs. Now I don't think about it at all. My strip has become so abstract and such a fantasy that I think it would be a mistake to point out a place for them to live.

MARSCHALL: *Your backgrounds are pretty sparse, too. You've never committed yourself with tract homes or anything.*
SCHULZ: No, I've never been able to reconcile just how those backgrounds should be drawn, or even the interiors. I admire people who can do that well. I'm never quite sure how it should be done. I fight it all the time.

MARSCHALL: *Segar used to do that little roof just hanging a little bit over the horizon—every horizon. Speaking of Segar, I would like to draw you out a little bit on the strips you grew up with, the special favorites of yours.*
SCHULZ: Well, *Popeye*, of course. I could draw a great Popeye when I was a kid. And I could draw Mickey Mouse. I could draw the three little pigs, and, strangely enough, I used to like the black panthers that Lyman Young drew in *Tim Tyler's Luck*. You know, I was thinking about it today: When I was, I suppose, about 11—maybe 12, I'm not sure—I didn't really realize the value of drawing. I remember one night visiting some relatives who lived down in Stillwater, Minnesota or Hudson, Wisconsin. Our parents were talking and the boy, who was a couple of years older than I, showed me his loose-leaf binder. He had drawn some cowboys on the front of it and he was proud of them and I looked at them and thought, "That's kind of neat." And all of a sudden it occurred to me, I could

do that. Why hadn't I ever thought of drawing something on the cover of a loose-leaf binder? I started to do that, and, of course, when the other kids in my class saw me draw these things, then I had to draw them for everybody. It was a lot like autographing these days; it drove me crazy. So I didn't really know the joy at the time of drawing, or what you really could do with it.

And I remember, when I was about in the tenth grade, I think, in high school, one of the other guys in class, who was a much better student than I, had illustrated the essay that we were supposed to write. He had done some watercolors and the teacher posted them around the room. And somehow she found out that I could draw, and she said, "Why didn't you do that, Charles?" The reason I didn't do it was because I didn't think it was fair. I really thought that maybe me and a couple of the others were the only ones in the class who could draw and it wouldn't be fair to do something like that. And I was stunned that this teacher gave me a mild dressing down for not doing it. So it took me a long time to realize the value of drawing.

I'm always surprised at how few people can draw. Down through the years, there were never more than two or three people in any of my classes that could draw fairly well. And in my three years in the Army, I bet I never saw one person in any of the companies or platoons I was in that could draw better than I could—and I've never considered myself that good. There aren't very many people who can draw. I don't think you can learn how to draw. I think you can be given a few tips. Thinking about comic strips, you can learn a few things that can make your strip look better and give it a better appearance and all that, but I don't think you can learn how to draw, just like I don't think you can learn how to sing. Either you have a voice, or you don't have a voice. It's not learning how

PEANUTS
SOMETIMES I THINK I'D LIKE TO BE ALMOST ANYTHING BUT A DOG..
BIRDS ARE THE PEOPLE I ENVY THE MOST...

to play tennis or golf or anything like that.

MARSCHALL: *Did you ever use your talent for drawing as some sort of power over your fellow students?*
SCHULZ: No. Never.

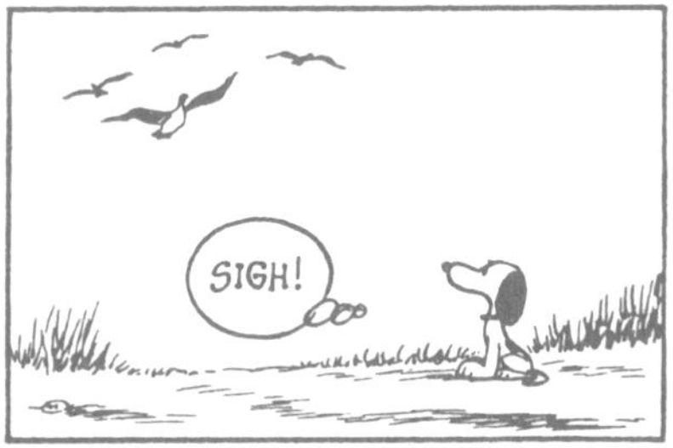
SIGH!

MARSCHALL: *I used to love to do caricatures of the kids who'd pick on me. They would walk into the classroom and they would see, anonymously of course, a caricature I'd done of them on the board. I thought it was a great power over them.*
SCHULZ: No, I never really liked caricatures and I still don't to this day. I never did caricatures. If somebody has a big nose, I'm sure that they regret the fact they have a big nose and who am I to point it out in gross caricature? So I don't do it. But, knowing how to draw has brought its moments of attention. I worked once at Northwest Printing and Binding as a delivery boy and office boy and one day, I drew a cartoon of the man who worked the big cutting machine and how proud he was when he got a new board to stand on. I was inspired, of course, by J.R. Williams and that type of down home type of humor. And I brought it down and showed it to him and, oh, he was so pleased with it and all the people that worked with him in the place came and looked at it. And, for the next hour, I got lots of attention and that made me feel good. It did demonstrate a little bit of this kind of power that perhaps you were talking about.

MARSCHALL: *You mentioned* Popeye *and* Tim Tyler's Luck *and I know you've written about being a fan of Roy Crane's. Were you drawn as a kid to the continuity strips?*
SCHULZ: I read them all. I liked every comic strip. *Skippy*, of course, was fantastic. Although I couldn't understand why [Percy Crosby] was so careless in his later years. He didn't even take the time to rule out the panels that were on the strip. That baffled me. There were a lot of things that baffled me when I was smaller which I didn't understand. I loved *Buck Rogers*. That was one of my favorite strips. Years later, I read one of the reprint books and discovered how terrible it really was. It wasn't a good strip at all. But it was ahead of its time and that puts some value into it, being ahead of your time.

Later on, as I grew older, in my last year of high school in the correspondence school, I became acquainted with some of the other great cartoonists and if that course did nothing else, it taught me to value good drawing in comics and good pen work. Clare Briggs, I thought, was wonderful and as far as writing, I always thought *The Bungle Family* was a great strip. And a couple of months ago, I spoke at a meeting or gathering here in Berkeley of some people who wanted to become syndicated and I opened my little speech by saying, "How many people have ever heard of Charles Payne? Raise your hand." Nobody raised their hand. I said, "Charles Payne drew *S'matter Pop*, and if you don't know *S'matter Pop*, frankly, I don't think I even want to talk to you." Because *S'matter Pop* is obviously one of the great strips of all time, beautifully drawn, and so funny. I like that and *Hairbreadth Harry*, I remember I loved *Hairbreadth Harry*. It annoyed me because Rudolph Rasendale was always so mean. And then, of course, later on, Al Capp came along with *Li'l Abner* and I loved *Li'l Abner* and then when Milton Caniff came along and put in the wrinkles where the wrinkles were supposed to be and shot all the camera angles and drew German Lugers the way they were supposed to look, it was a real revelation. There was nothing wrong with the way Chester Gould drew *Dick Tracy*; that was wonderful, too. But Caniff had this unique approach. As I look back upon it now, I don't think his strip was as witty as it could have been, but the drawing was marvelous. It was pure comic strip drawing, which we've never had quite enough of. It was marvelous. So those were all my heroes.

MARSCHALL: *Is there anyone else, maybe a certain period, whom you wanted to draw like?*
SCHULZ: I emulated Roy Crane when I was in my late teens, before I went into the Army. I tried to draw a strip which was similar to that and I used to observe downtown areas in St. Paul as I walked around delivering packages for these printing companies that I worked for—where would be a good setting for some action and I would try to draw it that way and my drawing was improving, but I had a long way to go. Then, after World War II, when I came home, Krazy Kat became my hero. I had never seen *Krazy Kat* up until then because neither one of the papers in the Twin Cities published it, so I didn't know *Krazy Kat*. But then it became my ambition to draw a strip that would have as much life and meaning and subtlety to it as *Krazy Kat* had.

MARSCHALL: *Your nickname is Sparky, and that's after Barney Google's horse Spark Plug. Is that because* Barney Google *was your favorite strip, or did you just get the nickname?*
SCHULZ: Well, I am told the day after I was born, an uncle, whom I never met [again] until I was 25 years old, came to visit my mother and me, looked down at me and said, "By golly, we are going to call him 'Spark Plug.'" Years later, I discovered that Spark Plug came

into the strip in the middle of the summer of 1922 and I was born in November, so apparently Spark Plug was an instant hit, in probably the most famous strip of its day. My mother and dad from then on called me Sparky. I was never called by them Charles. I was called Charles in school or other places, but all my friends and relatives referred to me as Sparky.

MARSCHALL: *Right from the start.*
SCHULZ: Right from the start, I was doomed. [*Barney Google*] was a great strip, you know, and I think that when Snuffy Smith first came in, it was wildly funny. I remember reading a reprint comic book of Snuffy Smith when he was first drafted. I used to just laugh at the things Snuffy said.

GARY GROTH: *Can you talk a little about the current state of the strip? Are there strips you like?*
SCHULZ: No. [Laughter.]

GROTH: *I know you're not wild about the current propensity for one-panel strips…*
SCHULZ: Yeah. It was a strange direction. I think Bob Thaves with his feature *Frank and Ernest* is good, and I suppose he was one of the first to do it, and that's perfectly all right. But now, I was looking at our own local comic page the other night—five features were

one-panel comic strips. And several weeks before that, six of them were just one long panel. I don't know. It puzzles me. Is it the shrinkage of space or what is it, but it's a bad trend. I don't think that you really build up a group of characters that way. And that's what a cartoonist is going to achieve. Something should be done about it.

GROTH: *Are you fond of Gary Larson's* The Far Side*?*
SCHULZ: Oh, yeah, he's good. He has a unique approach and he draws funny. I like the way the eyeballs are always close together. He draws funny animals and funny people. But I do resent that he is being labeled as the "new far-out humor."

GROTH: *Do you find the current state of the strips despairing?*
SCHULZ: I think the profession is heading in a strange way.

GROTH: *Do you have any theories as to why?*
SCHULZ: Oh, I suppose the number one problem would be space, that we just don't have space on which to work any more. A lot of the people don't know how to adapt to that space. And then, it's the following trends. One person does one thing and pretty soon, all syndicates are hiring people to do the same

thing. I think... I don't know if I should take credit for it or not, there seems to be a lot of what they call "sophisticated humor," with characters saying meaningful things, but in so many of them the character at the end does not say anything meaningful, it's just dumb. It just lay there. The person doesn't have the knack to do that kind of thing.

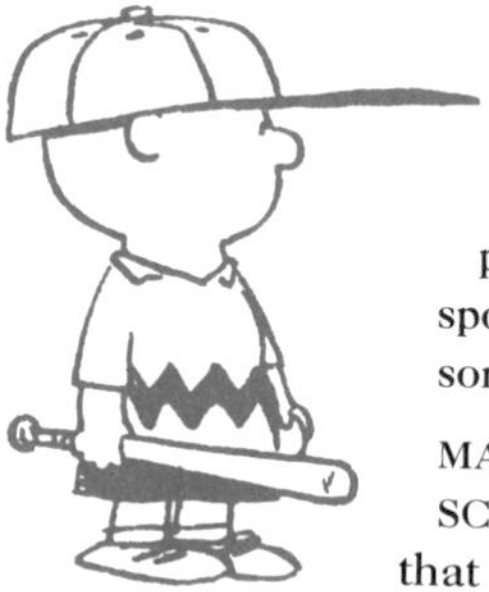

MARSCHALL: *Has the craft gone out of strips today? You have unique pen lines, thick and thin —I don't know what point you use, but it's like a fingerprint. A lot of cartoonists nowadays seem to think it's easier to use a rapidograph or a felt-tip pen or something like that. I don't think it necessarily reproduces better, and a lot of personality goes out of it.*

SCHULZ: But if you use that kind of pen, you have no thickness at all. If you use felt pens, the lines are just thicker, that's all. Of course it's quicker—you don't have to dip in—but I was a great student of pen techniques back when I worked at Art Construction. My friend and I used to do what we called Bart pen demonstrations. The author of the original cartoon course was Charles Bartholomew and he used to send out what he called "Bart pen demonstrations," which was a little card that had three sets of three pen lines, very thin, medium, and thick, all done with the same pen. And my friend and I used to practice making those when we had nothing else to do. We used to see if we could do three sets of perfect pen lines with the space between the pen lines narrower than the line itself [laughter]. It was like the surgeon practicing with his scalpel. So, I became really pretty deft with the pen. Now my hands shake and that spoils some of my pen techniques, but sometimes, I can still do it.

MARSCHALL: *That's characteristic, too.*

SCHULZ: No, [laughter] what is funny is that when they try to get someone helping with the licensing or something else, they copy my work and they copy this shaky pen line and say, "Gee, that's nice. How do you do that?" I don't do it on purpose – my hands shake. [Laughter.]

GROTH: *I was wondering what you thought of Walt Kelly's work.*

SCHULZ: I thought near the end, it became boring. I loved the older work and I bought every *Pogo* book that came out. I bought the comic magazine and I read it and I was influenced by it, and I would imitate his way of talking in it, the same way as when I was a kid, I would imitate Al Capp's hillbilly way of talking. But near the end, it got so wordy that I would buy the books and read the first few pages of it and just couldn't get through it. It wasn't funny any more. It's always a shame when people get so caught up with trying to give out their messages that they forget they have to be funny and entertaining. But he sure could draw. I only got to meet Walt once. I just said a few words to him one night at the Reuben Awards. I never really got to know him.

GROTH: *I was wondering if you paid any attention to the underground comics of the late '60s.*
SCHULZ: I stopped reading comic magazines years ago. I got so totally bored with them, with the super-heroes, all the muscles—the drawings all looked alike, and I just never read any of them. I never read any underground comics. What was strange about them was they pretended to be so different and they all turned out to be the same. They all used the same vulgar expressions and things. I got acquainted with a few of them from the Bay area and I said, "You guys pretend to do something so great and think what we're all doing is so bland, but actually, what I'm doing is infinitely more difficult than what you're doing. I'm drawing something that is good, but is clean and decent and I'm not bothering anybody and I'm not hurting anybody." And I said, "I defy you to do that." They draw the same dirty pictures, with the same dirty expressions and pretty soon, they're all alike. What's so great about that? I admit that some of them are good—Crumb is good—but that has never interested me. Besides, you get back to spirituality. I've always been very grateful for what has happened to me and I think it would be ungrateful of me to use whatever sensibilities I have for wrong. So I've always been very careful about that.

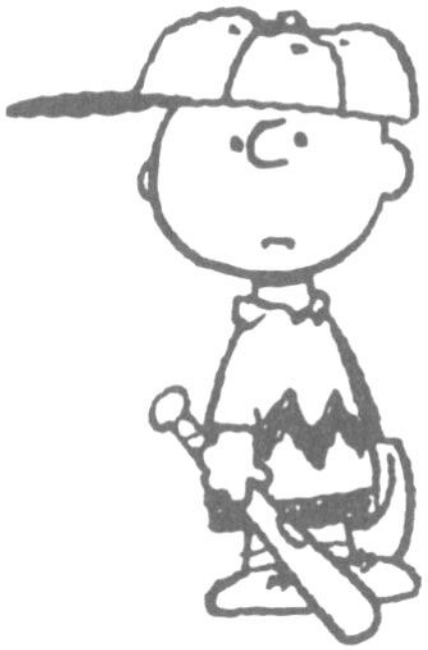

GROTH: *Were you familiar with Harvey Kurtzman's work?*
SCHULZ: Oh, sure, sure.

GROTH: *Did you like it?*
SCHULZ: I'm just familiar with it. A lot of them are wonderful. And the guys who used to draw for MAD magazine were sensational. Boy, some of them can draw.

GROTH: *Are you at all familiar with Carl Barks?*
SCHULZ: Oh, sure. But I never saw them when I was a kid, and I don't know why. I never read any Barks.

GROTH: *Did you read comic books when you were a kid?*
SCHULZ: Oh, I not only read them, I bought every one that came out. I had the original first *Famous Funnies* that came out. Some stupid friends of mine tore the cover off it and it disappeared. But I had it for years. I used to buy *Tip-Top Comics* and I can still remember the day when Superman came out in *Action Comics*. I took it over to a friend of mine and we thought, wow... I knew this guy had something. The drawing was nice to look at. It wasn't as....

MARSCHALL: *It was half cartoon.*
SCHULZ: It wasn't as slick as the latest Superman. But it was fun to look at. I knew that—boy, this guy really had something.

GROTH: *Did the EC comics leave any impression on you?*
SCHULZ: What would that be?

GROTH: *Well, of course, MAD comic books. They had also published Harvey Kurtzman's...*
SCHULZ: By then, I had stopped reading them. My own kids read Archie comics and that was about it. But I used to buy the Big Little Books, I bought every Big Little Book that came out until I got overwhelmed by them. I was the librarian in my neighborhood because the kids would come over and borrow my Big Little Books and my comics magazines [laughter]. All of my Big Little Books got lost in the fire in my dad's apartment.

MARSCHALL: *You've said that a lot of Charlie Brown's school experiences come from your school-age experiences.*
SCHULZ: Oh, yeah. It took me a long time to become a human being. I was regarded by many as kind of sissyfied, which I resented because I really was not a sissy. I was not a tough guy, but I was good at sports. I was a good baseball player. When I was fifteen, I instantly became a good ball-player. I was good at any sport where you threw things, or hit them, or

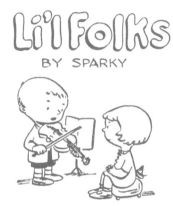

"DO YOU THINK I COULD HAVE HAD ANYTHING TO DO WITH THE DEATH OF BEETHOVEN ? "

caught them, or something like that. I hated things like swimming and tumbling and those kinds of things, so I was really not a sissy. We never had the chance in those days to do some of the athletic things we wanted to because the coaches were so intolerant and there was no program for all of us. So I never regarded myself as being much and I never regarded myself as being good looking and I never had a date in high school, because I thought, who'd want to date me? So I didn't bother. And that's just the way I grew up.

I was telling somebody, I think it was just yesterday, that it wasn't until I came back from the war that I really had self-confidence, because I went into the Army as a nothing person, and I came out as a staff sergeant, squad leader of a light machine gun squad. And I thought, by golly, if that isn't a man, I don't know what is. And I felt good about myself and that lasted about eight minutes, and then I went back to where I am now.

MARSCHALL: *You've said it, and Al Capp and I guess a lot of text humorists have said it: "The basis for humor is pain, suffering, or humiliation." You can intellectualize about that now, but when the strip started, did you see that as a formula?*

SCHULZ: No. When my strip first started, it was so totally different from what it is now that I don't even know what it was when it first started. I had experimented with many different types of features. I used to get on the train in St. Paul in the mornings at breakfast on the train and make that beautiful ride down to Chicago, get there about three in the afternoon, check into a hotel by myself, and the next morning I would get up and make the rounds of the syndicates. My first few trips, I really didn't have enough to show them and only one man treated me nicely. I met him years later and we talked about that and I was able to express to him my appreciation of how polite and nice he was, because some of the other syndicate people were very rude and most of them didn't even let me in the door. But as my work improved, I began to sell this thing called *Li'l Folks* to the St. Paul [*Pioneer Press*]. While I was doing this, I was also working at the art instruction correspondence school, drawing funny little figures, and I developed this three-panel strip which was unique in that what happened in the story was an incident that was only a couple of seconds. And so, when I sent in the panels that were finally accepted by United Features, I hadn't...

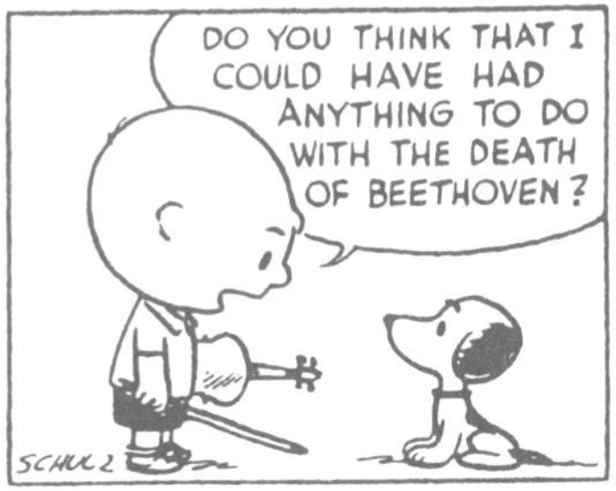
DO YOU THINK THAT I COULD HAVE HAD ANYTHING TO DO WITH THE DEATH OF BEETHOVEN?
SCHULZ

MARSCHALL: *Excuse me; it was a panel? It wasn't a strip?*

SCHULZ: It was unique. This was something that nobody knew about, and it annoys me that the editor lost my original submissions. For years, he kept promising me he'd send them back and he never sent them back and somebody had them someplace and I would love to know who has them. Either that, or they got thrown away.

But I was looking for an angle. I figured if I'm going to break into this business, I've got to do something that is a little bit different. I had developed this very simple style of drawing and I took all of the best ideas that I sold to the St. Paul paper and I re-drew them in a panel format. I took *Grin and Bear It* as my size to pattern after and, instead of drawing one single panel, I drew one above the other: I figured I'll be smart, I'll give the editor two cartoons for the price of one and this will be a good sales gimmick. So I sent it in and they were really good and I was very proud of them. And this is what the syndicate editor finally said to me: "We kind of like it. Would you like to come to New York and talk about it?" So, when I went to New York, I brought along a half dozen of these comic strips that I had been working on that I have been telling you about, which were really unique...

MARSCHALL: *These were two tiers?*
SCHULZ: The panel was two tiers. It was called *Li'l Folks*. And that's what the syndicate editor saw in my submissions. But then when I went to New York, in person, I brought along these other things because I wanted to show what other things I could do. And they opened up that package while I was out having breakfast, and decided that they would rather have a strip. And then, [laughter] like syndicate people do, they began to fiddle around with it. The sales manager said, "How about if we make it even broader in its appeal and we have one little kid strip at the top and a teen-age strip at the bottom?" So I thought about it and said, "Oh, all right, I have to do what they tell me." So I did that and they really didn't care for the teen-age thing. And then they said, "We'll just have the kid thing," and then... I'm kind of lost now, as I tell this story, but somewhere in there, they decided that they'd rather have a strip, and right then was when they made this fateful decision that it was going to be a space-saving strip, which I have resented all my life. Now it may have gotten me started, but I'm not sure, so I had to overcome the fact that I was drawing a space-saving strip under the title *Peanuts*, which was the worst title ever thought up for a comic strip. It's totally ridiculous, has no meaning, is simply confusing, and has no dignity—and I think my humor has dignity. Those are two things that have hung over me and I've resented my whole career.

MARSCHALL: *Thirty-seven years hasn't softened that?*
SCHULZ: No, no. I hold a grudge, boy.

MARSCHALL: *By "space-saving strip," you mean that it was reproduced smaller than the average comic strip?*

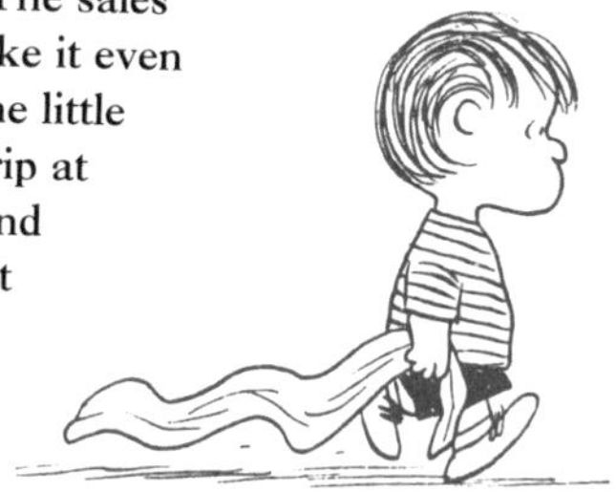

SCHULZ: It was reproduced smaller; it was drawn in four equal panels so that it could be run vertically, horizontally, or in a square, two below two. Now, the ironic part of it is, about a year later, they came out with *Twin Earths*, which was enormous in its size, and *Long Sand*, which was also enormous in its size. Then they told me that newsprint is kind of short and we're having trouble and we think having this as a space-saving strip will help. Well, you know where *Long Sand* is and you know where *Twin Earths* is. I've always been proud of the fact that quality won out over size and space.

MARSCHALL: *You've kept to that four-panel square format, though you don't have to now. [EDITOR'S NOTE: Schulz later converted the strip to three equal-sized panels and then began varying the panel size from strip to strip, a format that continued throughout the rest of the strip's run.]*
SCHULZ: I'm a great believer in loyalty. I'm not a believer in dictating to the newspaper editor how he

should run my strip. And I've had some papers with me now for 36 years and they have run my strip in the same spot all this time and who am I suddenly to say, "I'm too good to draw a small strip like this, I want more room, I want more space, I want more this or that." I believe in being loyal to these editors who have been loyal to you. And that's just the way I look at things. I don't want to break this agreement here and cause the editor to have to shuffle around everything that he's done and to change all of it.

GROTH: *How do you feel about [Garry] Trudeau's demanding more space [for* Doonesbury*]?*
SCHULZ: [Pause.] That he's not professional. He's never been professional.

GROTH: *How do you mean that?*
SCHULZ: I don't think he conducts himself in a professional manner in the things that he does.

MARSCHALL: *You're not just talking about the artistry on the strip?*
SCHULZ: It's his whole attitude toward the business.

GROTH: *You don't admire the strip.*
SCHULZ: [Shakes head.]

MARSCHALL: *You just talked about the title* Peanuts *and you've written about that before Bill Anderson made a list of ten names and* Peanuts *was chosen. Do you know where he'd come up with that?*
SCHULZ: Well, he told me, a couple of years afterward, "I never saw the strip. Somebody came to me and said: We're gonna start a new kids strip and we need a title. Can you think of anything?" He said, "I wrote down ten ideas and one of them was *Peanuts* and that's what they took."

MARSCHALL: *Do you know where he got Peanuts from?*
SCHULZ: No.

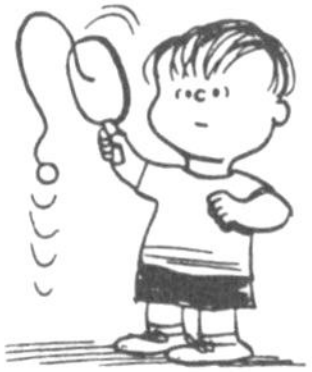

MARSCHALL: *He told me it was because thinking of a kids' strip, a kid's milieu, Howdy Doody was the hottest thing on kids' TV at that time and where the kids sat in Howdy Doody was the Peanut Gallery. That seemed logical to him.*

SCHULZ: But you see what bothers me. In the first place, it has no dignity. I don't even like the word. It's not even a nice word. They didn't realize that I was going to draw a strip that I think has dignity. I think it has class. But, of course, and I've said this before, when a young person goes into the president's office, what that syndicate president is buying is the potential of this young person. He's not even buying the work that he is looking at, he's buying the potential ten, 20 years down the road, and how does he know? They didn't know when I walked in there that here was a fanatic. Here was a kid totally dedicated to what he was going to do. And to label then something that was going to be life's work with a name like "Peanuts" was really insulting.

Now we'll go to the next step, which is that little kids are never called "peanuts" as they said they were. They never are. The only "peanuts" that are referred to are insignificant; something with no color, or else it might be the nickname of a ball player or some little kid. And I said they're going to confuse Charlie Brown with the name *Peanuts*. "No, no, no, no," they said. "No, no, it's just a catchy name that will attract the editors." So, what happens the very first year, I begin to get letters saying, "I love this new strip with Peanuts and his dog." Oh geez! That aggravates me.

I never mention [the name]. If someone asks me what I do, I always say, "I draw that comic strip with Snoopy in it, Charlie Brown and his dog."

MARSCHALL: *You've never pictured adults, parents or otherwise, in the strip. Maybe once or twice you've had the hand of an adult at a magazine counter or something like that. Was that something you set out to do?*

SCHULZ: Oh, I never thought about it at first. It was the way I drew the characters, they filled up the strip and I drew them from the side view. The type of humor that I was using did not call for camera angles. I liked drawing the characters from the same view all the way through because the ideas were very brief and I didn't want anything in the drawing to interrupt the flow of what the characters were either saying or doing. So there became no room for adults in the strip. At one point, I think, years and years ago, I drew a whole bunch of adults in a gallery where Lucy was playing in a golf tournament, which is something I never should have done. But it was an experiment.

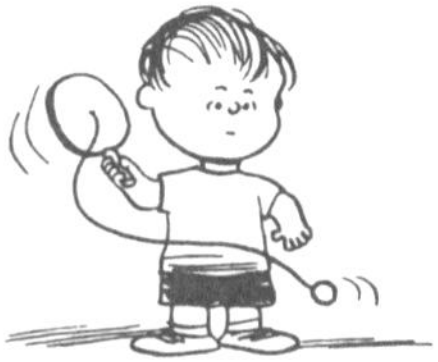

MARSCHALL: *In the background…*

SCHULZ: Yeah, in the background. I drew these adults. I never should have done that. And then I used to have off-stage voices, which again was simply because I didn't know how to handle it. Now, the strip has become so abstract that the introduction of an  adult would destroy it because you can't have an adult in a strip where a dog is sitting on a dog-house, pretending he's chasing the Red Baron. It just doesn't work. So, it's taken all these years really to learn some of these things. You make mistakes, but fortunately it's a medium that allows for mistakes if you recognize them right away. It's possible—I think—to make a mistake in the strip and without realizing it, destroy it. My best example, I think—and this will surprise you—I think Eugene the Jeep was a mistake. I think Eugene the Jeep took the life out of Popeye himself, and I'm sure Segar didn't realize that. I realized it myself a couple of years ago when I began to introduce Snoopy's brothers and sisters. I realized that when I put Belle and Marbles in there it destroyed the relationship that Snoopy has with the kids, which is a very strange relationship. And these things are so subtle when you're doing them, you can make mistakes and not realize them. You've got to watch that very carefully. What made Popeye great was that he solved all his problems by whopping somebody, but then by having Eugene the Jeep be able to predict the future and do all of these things, I think, was just the wrong direction. And once you go there, it's almost impossible to pull back. I think the Jeep was a great idea, but it shouldn't have become as dominant as it became.

MARSCHALL: *It introduced a whole lot of other fantasy characters.*

SCHULZ: The same with Superman. Superman was destroyed on several levels. In the first place, a comic strip cannot appear in its original form in too many areas because then, the tension goes out of it. You cannot have a daily strip going, a Sunday page going, *Action Comics* going, another Superman comic book going, a movie going. You can't have all these things going because he can't be damaged in one area and be undamaged in another. There are too many things going on at the same time. Now, Superman was great until he began to be able to see through things and fly. Superman shouldn't fly; Superman should jump. So they made a lot of mistakes.

MARSCHALL: *Before we leave the first period of your life, when you took the correspondence course, was it a federal school then, or…*

SCHULZ: Yes. It was the federal school. I was sitting at home at night and I used to draw on the dining room table. I had to push back the beautiful tablecloth my mother had made, put the newspaper down, and draw. I remember I fooled her one time. I brought a magic inkblot and pretended the inkbottle had fallen over and she came rushing in and I said, "Mom, look." She screamed and ran out to get a dish-towel. When she came back in, then I laughed—great sense of humor.

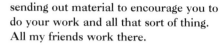

She came in one night and she said, "Look here in the newspaper. It says 'Do you like to draw? Send for a free talent test.'" So I sent in and a few weeks later, a man knocked on the door and it was a man from the correspondence school. And he sold us the course.

MARSCHALL: *They went door to door?*
SCHULZ: Yeah.

MARSCHALL: *Did you ever finish the course?*
SCHULZ: Oh, sure.

MARSCHALL: *I don't think I've met a cartoonist who's had the Famous Artists course who actually finished one. They thought the world of them, but...*
SCHULZ: I may be wrong, but the percentage of people that finish the course was very low, because it just takes a lot of drive to do this on your own at home. Now, this is a good course, and they were all good instructors, dedicated people. They were always sending out material to encourage you to do your work and all that sort of thing. All my friends work there.

MARSCHALL: *And you worked there, eventually...*
SCHULZ: After the war, yeah...

MARSCHALL: *Correcting the students?*
SCHULZ: Yeah. See, I was afraid to go to art school. I could not see myself sitting in a class with thirty other people who could draw circles around me. It just didn't interest me. So I didn't do anything after high school. I had a couple of jobs. And then, of course, the war came along, and that was the turning point for all of us. I remember visiting the service club one Sunday afternoon and seeing a show of originals of gag cartoons that had been in *Colliers* and *The New Yorker* or wherever they were, looking at them, and admiring how beautifully drawn they were. And before that, when I was still a teenager, drawing some kind of adventure strip, my mother noticed in the paper that there was a show of originals in the downtown library. We went down there that after-noon, and I walked around the room and I saw Roy Crane drawing boats in the water, then went home and took all of my work and tore it up and threw it away and started over again.

I knew I had a long way to go. But I used to go over then to the correspondence school, which was in

Minneapolis—although I mailed in all of my lesson work—I didn't even have the nerve to take that over in person, although we were allowed to do it. But then later on, after I got my diploma and graduated, I used to take my comic strips over and I would show them to an older man named Frank Wing and he used to draw this thing called *Yesterday*. He was a great believer in literal drawing. He could draw beautifully and he tried to encourage people to draw from life— you know, if you have to draw a shoe, put a shoe down on the ground and learn how to draw a shoe. You can't draw a cartoon shoe until you learn how to draw a real shoe. And he would look at my work, but he couldn't really tell me what was wrong with it and I used to say, "Well, look at *Popeye*. He doesn't draw real people." He never could explain to me why *Popeye* was good. And that always puzzled me.

MARSCHALL: *Did he really think it was?*
SCHULZ: Oh, yeah. He liked *Popeye*, but he couldn't tell me what marvelous quality was there. So, later on, after I got a job, he used to sit with me and we used to laugh and joke about things and talk about comic strips and stuff. But I learned a lot from Frank Wing.

MARSCHALL: *You sold gag cartoons to the* Saturday Evening Post *and, am I right, no other magazine?*
SCHULZ: No, nope…

MARSCHALL: *That's incredible—I mean, just starting out…*

SCHULZ: The [other magazines] just didn't buy the things.

MARSCHALL: *Yeah, but if you're going to sell to some magazines, it's going to be* This Week *or* American Legion *or something like that. The* Post *is the cream of the crop.*
SCHULZ: I did it all wrong. I drew this little cartoon of a boy sitting out on the ends of a chaise lounge, with his feet on the little stool. Then I finished it up and just sent it in all by itself.

MARSCHALL: *As a finish…*
SCHULZ: Yeah. I'd been sending things to other magazines. And I came home—I used to get mail from my dad's barbershop, when I lived in an apartment around the corner and upstairs. It said, "Check Tuesday for spot drawing of boy on lounge." So, I put it away. My dad and I went out for dinner that night, as we usually did, and I said, "I got a note today from

the *Post*. Gee, now I understand that. They're going to send me a check on Tuesday. I thought it meant I should check the mail on Tuesday, they were going to send it back." And, sure enough, that Tuesday, I got a check for $40.00 and it was my first sale, my first major sale. I had been selling cartoons, *Li'l Folks*, to the *Pioneer* for two years and I had been doing lettering for the Catholic comic magazine *Timeless Topics* for several years.

MARSCHALL: *That was located...*
SCHULZ: That was in St. Paul. I used to letter the whole comic magazine by myself: I would letter it in French and I would letter it in Spanish and it seems to me once I lettered the whole thing in Latin, sitting in my kitchen at night. I didn't know any of those languages, but they gave me the translations. I loved it.

MARSCHALL: *Did you do any other drawings for them, maybe fillers?*
SCHULZ: Once, I sold them two pages of little gag cartoons, four to a page, called *Just Keep Laughing*. He was going to run them regularly and then, after the second one, he said, "No. The priest that runs the place doesn't like it, so I have to tell you we don't need any more." And then, one day, I had done a special rush job for them. I went down after work, picked up these pages, went home, lettered the whole thing, and had it down there the next morning for him and as a show of gratitude, he let me do a four-page story and that was the only thing I ever got to do for him. You know, I saw him last year down in Santa Barbara and we reminisced about this.

MARSCHALL: [Showing Schulz some old roughs from his collection.] *After you made that initial sale to the Post, did you then start submitting roughs like these...*
SCHULZ: Yeah. Where are those from?

MARSCHALL: *I think I got them from Jim Ivy.*
SCHULZ: Yeah, but where would he get them? You know, David Stanford sent me some Xerox copies of things like this several months ago. Where did it come from? Because if they are *Post* submissions, they should have been sent back to me: I mean, they were rejected.

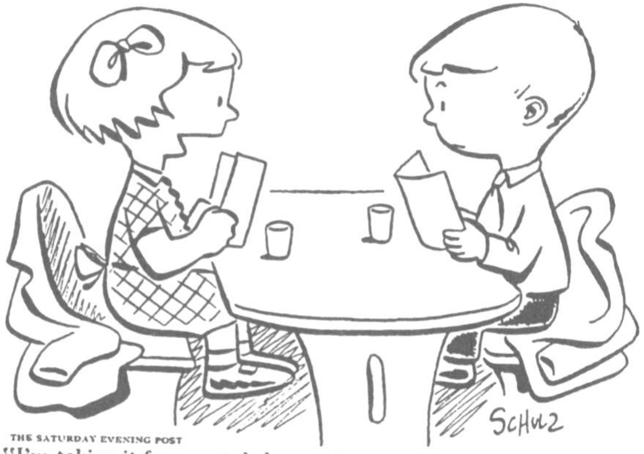
SCHULZ
THE SATURDAY EVENING POST
"I'm taking it for granted that you're very anxious to impress me!"

MARSCHALL: *And if they'd been bought, they would have been sent back with notes on them or something.*
SCHULZ: No matter what... But they weren't bought. Isn't that weird? Better keep them. So, I sent in ten every week and over a period of two years, after a couple of years, I hit a terrible slump. You know, John Doly was kind enough to tear off little notes and clip them to each cartoon and tell me why he didn't buy it. I've never met the man, but I've been told that he was very kind that way and very considerate of cartoonists. And then I began to get on track and I made most of my sales using the gimmick of little kids using something the way it shouldn't be, like they were playing football on the bed and one of them said, "We're close enough. Let's try for a field goal!" and the bedposts were the posts. And in another, they were going to have a race down this long davenport and the davenport was made to look like a racetrack. In another one, they were playing hockey on top of the birdbath. I've had Snoopy do that now for years. That was the kind of idea I sold.

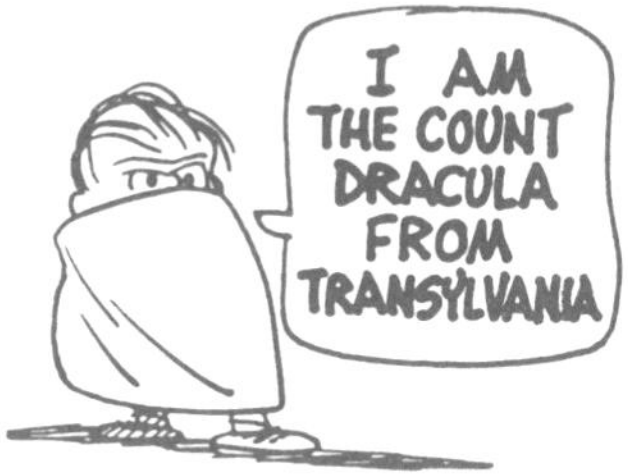
I AM THE COUNT DRACULA FROM TRANSYLVANIA

MARSCHALL: *Props?*
SCHULZ: Yeah. And the first good line I thought up was one that was jotted down on the wall over there. Somebody permafaxed it for me; it was a girl standing in front of a desk talking to a guy and she says, "We're taking up a collection for one of the girls in the office who isn't getting married or leaving, but feels that she's stuck here for the rest of her life." I think that was my breakthrough of doing something that was reasonably literate. Anyway, I sold fifteen over a period of two years, and then I sold *Peanuts*, and when I went to sign the contract, I said, "Would it be all right to continue to submit ideas to the *Post*?" And he said, "No, I don't think you should, because an editor who buys your strip usually buys your name and your work and we think he should have exclusive use of your work." That was all right by me. I wanted to draw a strip. I couldn't stand that freelancing and that bitter blow of opening the envelope and seeing a note that said, "Sorry, nothing this week." It was so crushing.

MARSCHALL: *Well, it's got to be like baseball players, when a successful ball player fails two out of three times at the plate. No matter how much you sell to the magazines, most of the gags are rejected.*
SCHULZ: Right. And I never got into the real professional pattern, which you have to do, I think. You have to have a lot of markets and be very practical about it. I never got that far in it. I just sold the strip too quickly so I never became a real gag cartoonist.

MARSCHALL: Peanuts *really was the renaissance—do you agree with this?—of the intellectual strip. Growing up,* Peanuts *played a large role in my not being embarrassed about using big words in front of the other kids, and the Beethoven thing made me interested in Beethoven and Mozart. Do you agree with that definition of the strip? Did you have something like that in mind when you started the strip, or was this just a next generation* Skippy?

SCHULZ: I didn't have anything in mind. I was just drawing. [Looking at promo brochure.] This came out later, though. See, Violet didn't come into the strip for at least a year and Schroeder didn't come in for over a year. [*EDITOR'S NOTE: Actually, four and a half and seven months, respectively.*] I never did figure out how to draw Schroeder's hair. Why did they buy that? That looks terrible.

MARSCHALL: *But it's marketed here as a little kid's strip.*

SCHULZ: Yeah. Well, I've fought that all my life, too. And I fight it with licensees today. I don't draw for little kids.... Well, I draw for myself, which is who I think we all draw for. We draw for ourselves and hope that people like it. But the licensees keep driving it down for little kids. We did the first television show, *A Charlie Brown Christmas*, we did the best show we could do and what happens? We win an Emmy for the best children's animated show of the year. We didn't draw it for kids. We drew it for grown-ups. I just draw for myself, and draw it as well as I can. I'm not pretending to be modest. I know I'm not an intellectual. I don't even think I'm very smart. I really don't. I think I'm witty and I think I know how to skim the surface of a subject and take out enough for me to use and to make it look like I know a lot about the subject. You really don't have to know much to be a cartoonist. So if it's an intellectual strip, I've never really even thought about it. I'm glad. I never thought about it, but I did want to draw something that was good.

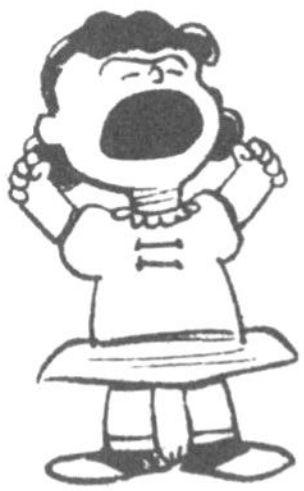

MARSCHALL: *Comic strip history breaks down into the pre-*Peanuts *era and the post-*Peanuts *era. It seems to me one of your main contributions is a technical construction of the strip. You started with a small cast of characters in the beginning, and then it got large. You drew them all with very, very strong personality traits, and then established a lot of premises and a lot of situations for them to fit into. So many strips before that were basically situational, "What are we going to do next?"—or humorous continuity. Since you established this type of strip—large cast, strong personalities as opposed to situations—virtually everything since that has come down the pike has been in that format;* Doonesbury, *certainly.*

SCHULZ: Few people give me credit for having started this, but I think a lot of them don't realize that I did start it. I think, too, they used to say *Peanuts* has brought humor back into the comics page, because there is no doubt that, during the war, we had a lot of adventure things, and gag strips and humor strips had virtually disappeared. I think the great tragedy is now we have lost the continuity strip. We've lost, especially, the humorous continuity strip. They're all turning into gag strips, they're all saying what they think are meaningful statements—they're not meaningful at all; they're just dumb. And that's a tragedy, too. A lot of it is due to the shrinking of the size. Poor Al Capp would die if he had to draw at the size of these things these days. Now, we have this terrible trend, which has just suddenly burst upon us, of the one-panel comic strip. I don't know where that's going to lead.

MARSCHALL: *It's cheating.*

SCHULZ: And boring. Not only that, but it's robbing a creator of a chance to develop a group of characters and some good situations. Now, I like what you said before, the way you expressed that about from the characters, we went to certain situations, and I think this is the key to the whole thing. I created Beethoven's birthday, I created Linus and his blanket, I created the pursuit of the Red Baron, I created the pulling of the football, I created the Great Pumpkin— all of these, these are the things that make up a comic strip. You can't sit down and say, "I think I'm gonna draw a comic strip and this will be my main character." The main character has nothing to do with it. What you really need are the situations and that's where you should start. Nobody wants to start with that. They want to start by thinking up a character, which will be a good gimmick and will make good plush toys. That's the wrong direction.

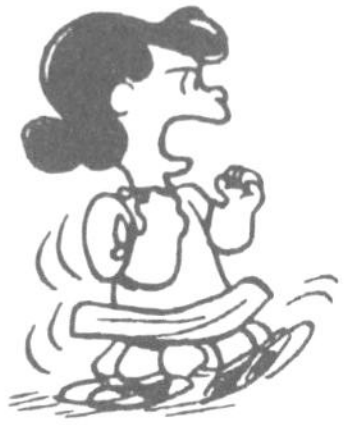

MARSCHALL: *More strips today start out based on animated TV shows. Seventeenth on the list is, "Oh, yeah, let's do a comic strip to base this thing on." It's not based on it.*

SCHULZ: It's interesting too: you mention animation. Animation doesn't make good comic strips. Animated characters are drawn to revolve. They're drawn with a slick brush line and the eyes and nose and ears, everything placed in a rubbery way, so that the character can revolve and do certain things. That kind of drawing does not fit in the comic strip page. The comic strip page has drawing, which is a scratchy pen technique. Usually, in some of the great old strips, the characters are only drawn from a couple of different views. Popeye was usually drawn from the left three quarters or the right three quarters. When you turn him into an animated character, he has to become rubber and it doesn't work. Bill Melendez and his animators had a terrible time with the *Peanuts* characters. Fortunately, we're in semi-animation, and it works. I told him, "This is just a cartoon. Don't worry about making it so lifelike. They don't have to turn if you don't want them to, just have them flip from one spot to another. That's all

right. It's still a cartoon. We're not trying to do *Snow White and the Seven Dwarfs.*"

MARSCHALL: *You once said in the development of character, "I don't think the cartoonist can show a character. He's got to expose a character, maybe, through situations and explain it as you show it."* *When Snoopy started thinking, that told more about him and the things you had him do. Did that just evolve, too? Snoopy didn't think at first.*

SCHULZ: No, he didn't think. He actually barked and ran around on all fours and was just kind of a cute little puppy, and I don't know how he got to walking, and I don't know how he first began to think, but that was probably one of the best things that I ever did.

MARSCHALL: *Linus and the blanket: was that just—*
SCHULZ: My own kids all had blankets, so that was something I observed. And I said many times that I was glad I did because I know if I hadn't done it Mort Walker would have come in with it a few months later for sure. Since then, I've seen other comic strips with blankets, and they've used the same ideas I had already drawn. In fact, lately, I'm beginning to see ideas in comic strips, which I drew twenty years ago, which makes me happy to know I beat these guys. But I remember being beaten by J.R. Williams by

thirty years, and I was beaten by Gus Arriola by ten or fifteen years, so that happens. But I do see people using ideas, which I've done a long time. Well, it's just a pattern of thinking; I don't say that it's stealing. I know it's not stealing; it's just a pattern of thinking.

MARSCHALL: *The sincerest kind of flattery.*
SCHULZ: Yeah.

MARSCHALL: *Okay, we mentioned Snoopy and the blanket. Charlie Brown evolved. He was almost like a wise guy, at the beginning?*
SCHULZ: Yeah. Little by little the characters begin to fall into place. I think there is a similarity to the lead characters in a lot of scripts. There is one simple char-

acter who is kind of innocent. He's not too strong in his personality; if he were, then he would dominate the strip. He's the one that holds everything together, and it's the other characters who have the unique personalities. He can't be a terrible character, but he has to be somebody that you like that holds things together. And that's what Charlie Brown is there for. Although, sometimes I think I should use him more—but I've got so many characters now that it's difficult to know who I should use the most. For a while, I received a couple of letters from somebody that said, "Don't use the dog so much. Get back to the little kids." I never pay attention to letters like that. But maybe he was right: maybe I was using Snoopy too much. I'm always trying to be selective. I'm always trying to do different things. And I always wanted to have some girls in the strip, which is why I have drifted more toward Peppermint Patty and Marcie.

There is something else here which is worth mentioning, I think, which again it's important towards building personalities and characters, in that Peppermint Patty calls Charlie Brown "Chuck." She's the only one in the strip that does that, where Marcie calls him "Charles." Everybody else calls him "Charlie Brown." Those are the little things. If you have enough of those little things, then I think you take on some kind of depth. I'm not a believer in funny names. I think a funny name is fine for one gag or one idea, but I don't think people are going to laugh at that funny name every day. You can't count on that. That's why my strip doesn't have many funny things like that in it, where you're trying for that extra laugh all the time.

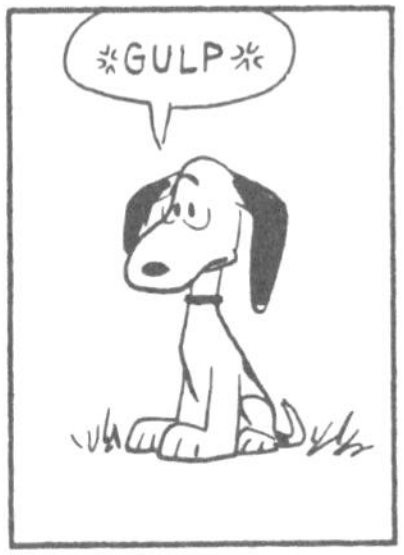
GULP

MARSCHALL: *In that vein, were you planning for the April Fool to take off like the Great Pumpkin did?*

SCHULZ: No. That was just a one-time strip. I didn't even like the way I drew it. I like the Easter Beagle. For a long while, I wouldn't do anything on Easter. I'm very sensitive to not offending anybody and I thought I shouldn't do anything with Easter. But then I thought, "Oh, the heck with it. It's fun—the Easter Beagle," so I did it anyway.

MARSCHALL: *My next question was going to be about Robert Short's two books [*The Gospel according to Peanuts *and* The Parables of Peanuts*]. Do you think he went too far in analyzing the strip?*

SCHULZ: Well, I don't know if he really analyzed. I think what he was really trying to do was use a comic strip as a springboard toward some kind of spiritual ideas. Robert's a great guy. We didn't even know each other when he wrote the book. I think the book had been out for a year before we finally met, but since then, we've become close friends and we love being together and talking about different things. I think he likes to just draw little spiritual thoughts from everything that goes on in his life and it occurred to me *Peanuts* was providing some spiritual jumping off place. Now I know it didn't come off that way, but I know that's what he was intending. The book was never mine and it was never

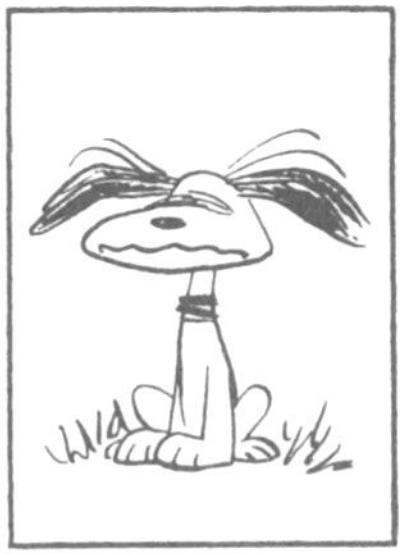

meant to be my idea. That was part of the original agreement that, sure, he can use the strips, but it's not my writing.

MARSCHALL: *It's his interpretation. You just talked about readers being offended—you've probably gotten complaints when you've used Scripture, which you have more than any other artist.*

SCHULZ: I think I've done more authentic scriptural strips than anybody. I hate cheap spiritual innuendo. I hate strips showing the kid praying, talking about what mean things he did in the daytime. I just despise that kind of thing. I'd like to think that mine was done on a better level than that. I'm a reasonable student of the Scriptures, a typical mid-western scholar. I think I use the Scripture very well in the strip in ways nobody else has ever thought of doing it, or would have the nerve, or even has the scholarship to do it. I'm proud of that, and also very sensitive to it. I've always done it in a nice way, never offensive. I was amazed when we put out the book called *The Beagles and the Bunnies* that we had enough to fill out the whole book. I never dreamed of that.

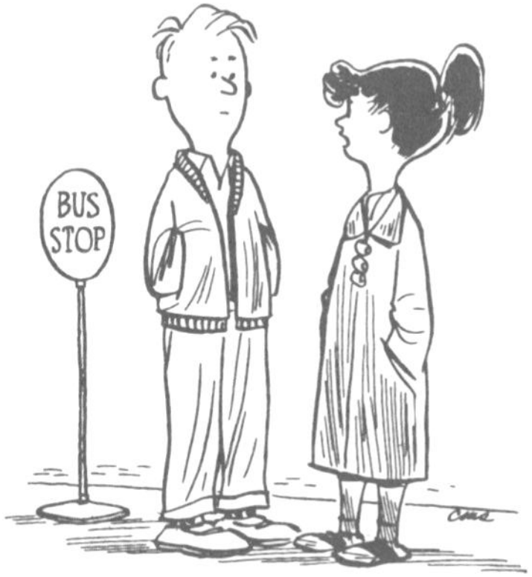
BUS STOP
"I wish you wouldn't always refer to our dates as 'fellowship'!"

MARSCHALL: *You're a committed Christian?*

SCHULZ: I think I'm becoming a secular humanist [laughter], but I don't want to get into that.

MARSCHALL: *I've heard that term applied to you. Did I read once that you were a lay preacher?*

SCHULZ: Oh, well, I was very active in the church group right after World War II. We were all in our twenties and we went to Sunday morning services. We went to Sunday evening youth meetings—although we weren't really youths—we went to Sunday evening services and Wednesday night prayer meetings and we were all very dedicated to the church. And now and then, I might be asked to speak on a Sunday evening. I have even spoken out on street corners, which I never should have done. I would never do it again because I no longer feel I'm in a position to tell anybody anything, so I don't do it. But, anyway, I did all those things and it was a good group; they were nice people. I still have contact with a few of them and I'm in contact with the minister, who is now retired. We studied the Scriptures and discussed them avidly. That's where my background for all of those biblical things comes from and I have an honorary doctorate from Anderson College, which is the Church of God College.

MARSCHALL: *When you go from your knowledge, or maybe you turn to Proverbs or some of those parables, you don't do it in a subversive way to get a point across.*
SCHULZ: I'm never grinding an axe. I'm never doing it to teach anybody anything, very seldom. Maybe if we looked through them I could point out a few where I might be trying to say something against hypocrisy, I really don't know. It's hard to say overall. It's just that certain phrases pop into my mind and I think that would be funny, so I look up the Scriptures or else I remember a Scripture and suddenly, I find something comes into my mind, a certain way of using it, that's all.

GROTH: *You said something earlier that I thought was potentially fascinating, that you were becoming a secular humanist?*
SCHULZ: Well, I don't go to church any more. I taught adult Sunday school class in Minneapolis and came out here to a local Methodist church, but I never became a Methodist. They were just a nice group of people and they were all quite educated. I enjoyed the class and I did it for about ten years. Finally, I just ran out of things to say and it became an effort to do all the studying. Besides, this business of always having to think of something gets to you after a while. It got so that I could never be invited to

"I think I've made one of the first steps toward unraveling the mysteries of the Old Testament. . . . I'm starting to read it!"

a banquet without having to get up and say a few words. I have to think up a daily strip and I have to think up a Sunday and I was drawing youth cartoons for Church magazine and trying to think of a Sunday school lesson and studying and oh, gosh... Finally, after a while I just had to say, let somebody else do it, because I just don't have any more to say. So I haven't been back to church.

GROTH: *Is there a sense that you're questing for...*
SCHULZ: [Laughter.] No, I'm not questing for anything. I don't know anything, frankly. I think it's all a total mystery. I have no idea why we're here and I have no idea what happens after you die. My class wasn't one so much of teaching as it was just getting people to say things. I know I led them through the Bible verse by verse four times and each time, I would learn something more. I was not at all anxious to teach them what I thought about.... Every now and then, someone would say, "Well, what do you think?" and I would say, "It doesn't matter what I think. I just want to hear what you think and get you to talk about these things and actually read the Scriptures instead of saying, 'Well, I've heard about that in this or that.' "

MARSCHALL: *An awful lot of people haven't.*

SCHULZ: Oh, I know I know. I don't even know what secular humanism is. Have you ever heard of the book, I'm sure you have, *I Never Promised You a Rose Garden*? I know the author very well. She asked me what I believed. I said what I thought I believed in, and she said, "You are a secular humanist, that's what you are," and I said, "I am?" and she said, "Yeah, that's what I think you are." [Laughter.] But she's a marvelous lady.

GROTH: *Was there ever a time when you questioned your religion?*

SCHULZ: Well, it's not a matter of questioning... My religious thing all started, it must have been a matter of gratitude. I was brought up Lutheran, but my dad liked to go fishing on Sundays, so we almost never went to church. I was never really brought up in church. But my mother was extremely ill with cancer when I was just turning twenty. She was just coming out of the hospital. She suffered terribly. I used to wake up at night and hear her down the hall crying in pain. It was a terrible time. I got drafted as soon as I turned twenty and I had to report. I got to go home a couple of weekends as they were deciding what ought to be done and one Sunday night I was home, she was so ill. I was saying good night to her to her back and she said, "Well, goodbye, Sparky. We'll probably never see each other again." It has to be one of the most heart-breaking things in my life. It's bad enough to get drafted, but to know that your mom will die. She was only 48. And sure enough, she died the next day. Then I came home from the funeral and the next thing I knew, I'm back with the army on a troop train and I'm traveling through the night with a bunch of guys I've never seen before in my life without knowing where I'm going. And I started going to church just out of a feeling of gratitude that I survived all of that. I felt that God protected me and helped me and gave me the strength to survive because I could have gone off in all sorts of wrong directions. I always felt that I was helped to live through those three years and come home because I never got shot or anything.

I knew about this Church of God—my dad and I used to go now and then—but one night, it was a Wednesday night, I was feeling very lonely and I knew they needed a new sign out in front of the church. It was a very poor church, so I walked all the way down several miles through the snow to the church. I told the minister I would make him a new sign if he wanted me to. He was a great man. I made a lot of friends there. That's how it all happened. And then we came out here and my

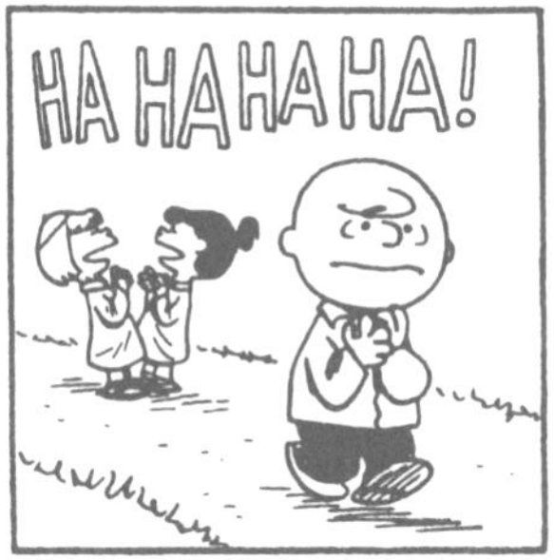
HA HA HA HA!

first wife didn't care much about getting involved in the church once we got out here, so we sort of drifted away from it. But now I've ended up with one daughter becoming a Mormon and going to England as a Mormon missionary [laughter]. We've become very close because of it; even though I don't like Mormons. I think that it's drawn us close together, we can talk about the scriptural things that she was never interested in before and she has a fine husband. My family has gone in all different directions, but they're all good kids.

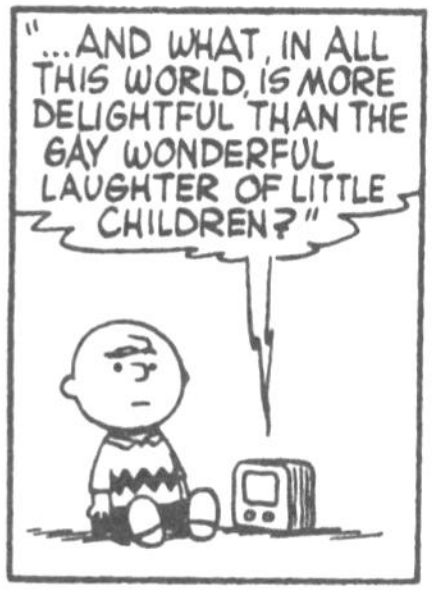
"...AND WHAT, IN ALL THIS WORLD, IS MORE DELIGHTFUL THAN THE GAY WONDERFUL LAUGHTER OF LITTLE CHILDREN?"

MARSCHALL: *We talked about continuity. It seems to me that one thing that could revive the newspaper comic strip, the humor strip, would be the return of humor continuities. And you use them. How do you plan them? Do you know the ending before you start, or do you just let it run and surprise yourself when it comes to an end?*
SCHULZ: I never have any idea where I'm going with it and I discovered something, which is why I don't think—and I suppose I'll always offend somebody someplace—I don't think you can write a comic strip on a typewriter. I think you're robbing yourself of the ideas that come from drawing, so what I'm more interested in is a good, standard, day-to-day group of ideas, which is more important than where the story goes. I'm doing a story right now and I have no idea where I'm going with it, but I'm very interested in trying to make each day funny. If you think of an overall story, you're liable to end up with a weak strip on Tuesday and Friday or Saturday and I don't want to do that. I'm more interested in making each day as funny as I can. I don't know, maybe I've had some stories run five weeks, five or six at the longest. I haven't had any lately. They're awfully hard work and you have to have time to think about them. But I do agree that some kind of stories and strips can bring the reader back so he doesn't want to miss the next day's strip. It's very important in building circulation.

MARSCHALL: *You've got characters with neuroses—Charlie Brown with his inferiority complex and Linus being insecure and Lucy kvetching and all that. Does anyone advance the observation that you have done sort of Yiddish humor in WASP clothes?*
SCHULZ: Not really. I have become a fairly good friend, through the mail, of Leo Rosten. He sends me all of his books, and I think *I'm the Captain* is one of the greatest humor books ever written. Otherwise, I don't know much about it.

There is one thing I do resent. I resent the fact that when we talk about America's great humorists, comic strip artists are never mentioned, not even the great people that draw for the *New Yorker*. Where's George Price?

MARSCHALL: *A couple of characters—Frieda and Faron. Are you a fan of country music?*
SCHULZ: I was. I'm not a fan of any music any more. It's very personal, but when Joyce and I were separated and divorced, and I was living alone and I was very unhappy, and I was separated from my children for a few months there, I couldn't stand to listen to the radio or any music. So I stopped listening to music and I really have not gotten back into it. I used to love country and western music. The whole business of Charlie Brown and the red-haired girl came from listening to a Hank Williams song. I was home alone one night listening to it and it was so depressing that it occurred to me that I would do something with Charlie Brown and the little red-haired girl and that's how it all started. [Laughter.]

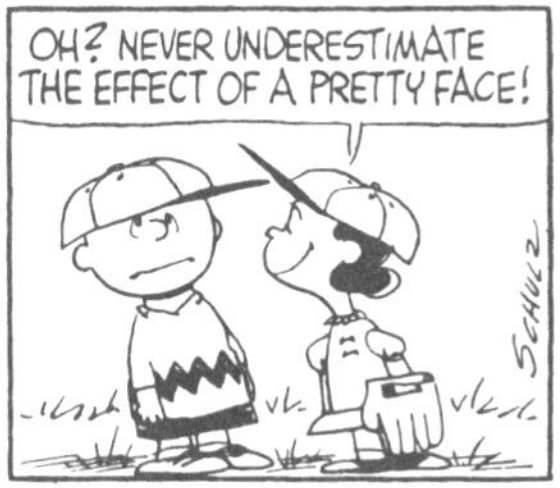
OH? NEVER UNDERESTIMATE THE EFFECT OF A PRETTY FACE!
SCHULZ

MARSCHALL: *You'll never show her, right?*
SCHULZ: No, and I think it was a mistake to even show her on television, but you make a lot of mistakes when you do a lot of media. But I could never draw her into the strip now. You reach a point where the reader has already drawn her. And you could never live up to the way the reader has drawn her in his or her imagination.

MARSCHALL: *Was that a temptation because of the animated format, or...*
SCHULZ: I'm not good at drawing pretty little faces. That would be the number one fear. I could probably be tempted into drawing her, if I could draw a real knockout of a cute little girl, but I don't think I could. So I don't think I will. I like the little face on the girl that keeps telling Linus, "Aren't you kind of old for me?" Even that face was a struggle to draw.

MARSCHALL: *You named Woodstock during the Woodstock era. Were you speaking of your readership, or did you just hear the name and think it was neat?*
SCHULZ: I had been reading the *Life* magazine article about the Woodstock festival and I had the little bird in the strip. It was a she and she was Snoopy's secretary and I was doing secretary jokes quite often so then I thought Woodstock would be a good name for this bird and also, it will get the attention of these people that liked that kind of thing. Suddenly, she was not a secretary; she became Woodstock, the boy. [Laughter.] It just happened. But that's what's good about a comic strip—you can just do it.

MARSCHALL: *Have licensing and merchandising or reader reaction ever influenced you to do things with characters and storylines?*
SCHULZ: No. There are a lot of temptations and that would be easy to do, but I've never drawn anything

with the thought that it would be good for licensing. I've never even emphasized a certain character because I thought it would be important. Right now, it's very tempting because we're working on this movie, starring Spike, and it's very tempting to push Spike in the strip just to give him more attention, so that people will be ready for him. I don't think I could do it if I wanted to because I can't think of that many ideas for him. But I like drawing Spike in the desert and I love drawing those rocks and the cactuses. [Laughter.]

GROTH: *Do you impose a substantial amount of authority over how your work is licensed?*
SCHULZ: Well, I have control over everything. My contract gives control. They can't do anything without my okay and I can do anything I want, as long as it does not destroy the property.

GROTH: *Are there certain ways that you would not want your property licensed, that you would veto?*
SCHULZ: Yeah. They're always dropping it down to make it too childlike and I don't like that. But I just can't get around it. Now they're coming out with the Snoopy quarterly magazine, which will be for very small children. But they promised it would be good quality. They're the same ones that put out Muppets magazine. It's a good outfit, I guess. They came out and visited us last week. Well, what do I care? [Laughter.]

GROTH: *Do you ever feel like you're losing control?*
SCHULZ: No. But I'm getting old. I'll be 65 in November. And I wonder what is happening to me? Someday, you're going to be old. [Laughter.]

MARSCHALL: *Does that mean you're thinking of withdrawing to the strip and letting other people pay attention to the merchandising? That doesn't show in the strip. I mean, you have introduced new characters.*
SCHULZ: Oh, no. No, the only reason that licensing keeps getting bigger is the fact that it's simply more popular now. United Features, which never even had a licensing department before, suddenly had this enormous licensing property and we had people devoted exclusively just to looking at other companies and finding licensed properties and things, which we never did. Everything we ever did came to us, really. We never went out and sought anything. So now licensing is very big, but I'm involved with it only to the point where I want to see it done as decently as possible.

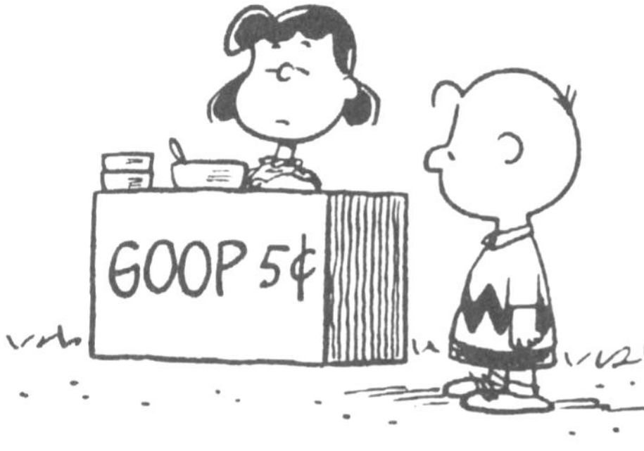
GOOP 5¢

GROTH: *I have a couple more questions I would like to ask you. One thing I am curious about is if you are a politically oriented person.*

SCHULZ: No. I was brought up Republican. I saw Herbert Hoover get off the train in St. Paul when he was running for re-election. And I saw Eisenhower once when we went to Minneapolis and we all stood out on the street... but I was very taken by Wendel Wilkie when I was young. I was calling myself an Eisenhower Republican, because he was the first person I ever voted for that got elected [laughter]. Gosh, you know, for twenty years we were under Democratic rule. Twenty solid years and then... But I sold a cartoon because of Dewey losing that morning. When I came back to Art Instruction that morning, of course Truman had won and some woman came in who had voted for Wallace. She still was glad Dewey had lost. Somebody said, "How did you sleep last night?" I said, "Oh, I sleep well enough at night, it's living during the day I find so hard," and I sold it to the *Saturday Evening Post*. So I figure I got $80.00 out of the election anyway. But I've never been involved in local politics or done anything. I've met President Carter and President Reagan. He called me on the phone when I was recovering from surgery, which was quite flattering.

GROTH: *Do you have any loosely defined political leanings?*

SCHULZ: No, no, I don't even want to get into that. It's the same as the religious thing. I'm not especially fond of all political cartooning. I think a lot of it is irresponsible. These guys write about things they really don't know anything about. They leap on the bandwagon the day after something happens and draw things that aren't even true. And some of them are terribly petty on both sides. I've had troubles with them in times past with them using my characters. Only one time in maybe thirty some guy drawing for one of the Chicago papers was using my characters for something the exact opposite of what I believed in. It reminded me of Bill Mauldin and his suit against the *Los Angeles Times...*

MARSCHALL: *Conrad?*

SCHULZ: Conrad. Yeah: because he used Willie and Joe in a cartoon in a way that offended Mauldin without asking him.

GROTH: *One of the remarkable things about the strip is that there are no perceivable ideologies.*

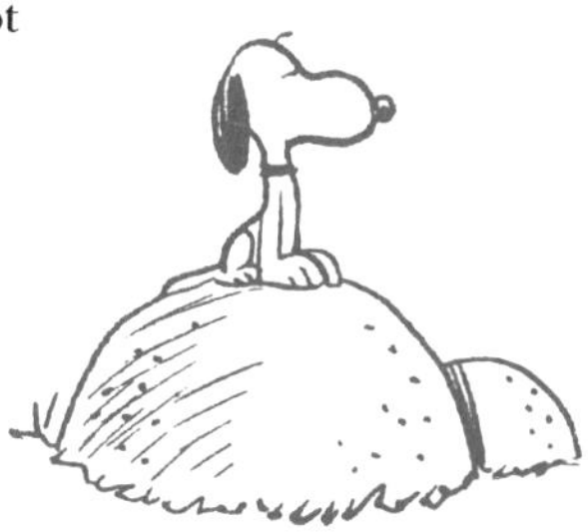

SCHULZ: [Laughter.] Sort of a wishy-washiness...

GROTH: *No, no, not at all... It's really remarkable, because there are so many shrill ideologies.*

SCHULZ: Well, I do think about it. I really don't want to offend people and I don't think it's necessary. I think

it can be funny and remain kind of innocent and yet I don't think you have to be sugary sweet or stupid.

GROTH: *This is a sort of cliché question, but I'll ask it anyway: Can you tell us what you think the future or potential of comics is?*
SCHULZ: Depends on the editors. I don't think we have any choice. I think we're totally at the mercy of the editors and whatever they're going to do with these comic pages. And if it keeps up the way it's going now... I think there are good futures for a lot of people. I know they're buying all sorts of new things and all that. I don't think it's necessarily going to produce great new superstars. And I'm not just talking about just making a lot of money: I'm talking about somebody really great. Obviously, *Calvin and Hobbes* is one that seems to have the opportunity to do something really great and I don't know if it will or not. It's difficult because of the space you have.

GROTH: *Do you think that the new formats coming out, such as book-length comic books, will have some...*
SCHULZ: I don't think comic books have anything to do with it, do you? Oh, do you mean the reprints of comic strips?

GROTH: *No, I'm talking about the new formats that are being published.*
SCHULZ: I haven't seen them.

GROTH: *Have you heard of Art Spiegelman's* Maus?
SCHULZ: Oh, sure, sure.

GROTH: *That's the sort of thing I'm talking about, because you get away from the space restrictions and the editors.*
SCHULZ: Yeah, yeah. But I suppose, again, that they're at the mercy of the publishers and the distributors and it's a whole different profession; it's something that is totally foreign to me. What I think is a pity is something like that can't be transferred to the comics page. The newspapers won't even listen to this, but the potential is there and I think there's a lot of great children's book illustrators who should be in the comic pages, but are not.

GROTH: *Have you resisted the temptation to take a vacation?*
SCHULZ: Quit for a year? So far I've resisted it.

GROTH: *But you've had the temptation?*
SCHULZ: I never thought I would, but the last few years, all my friends are retiring and I'm beginning to

wonder if I hadn't wasted my life. Yeah, wait 'til you're 65 or 64.

MARSCHALL: *You mean that literally?*
SCHULZ: Mm-hm. Not that I don't think I've done as best as I ever could with what abilities I have. I'm very happy and I've done more than I've ever dreamed I would do. Things have happened to me that I never dreamed of, and so I'll die content, as far as that goes. But there's still a big world out there that I don't know anything about and I'm married now to a woman who loves to travel and I'm thinking, Gosh, maybe there is more. And of course, I'm not very well educated so maybe I should get back to school and learn how to speak French or something like that, or go to Cambridge. There are just so many things that I could be doing.

And after you've had heart surgery, too, and were on the brink of dying at 58 and you begin to wonder, then, too. How do I know when the arteries are going to close up and bang, it's all over. Do I just want to sit here and just draw another daily strip?

MARSCHALL: *Sparky, you did one of the tenderest—that's the only word I can find—continuities you've ever done after that. It was different than other things, but it wasn't out of step with the strip.*
SCHULZ: That was where Charlie Brown was in the hospital?

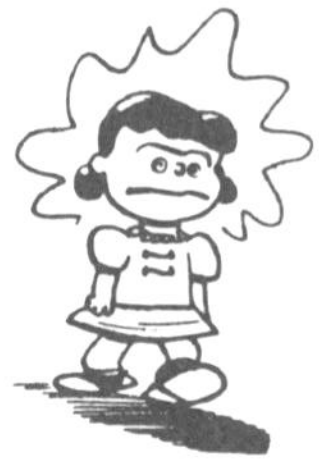

MARSCHALL: *Yes, and it was like a composer shifting to a minor key for a while. You survived a quadruple bypass?*
SCHULZ: Yes. That's like what I was telling you about coming home from the Army and suddenly, I'm a man, you know. I've done this and I'm feeling good about myself. I thought, "Boy, I don't want to go to the hospital, they're going to saw my chest open. I'm not that brave. I don't want to go anyplace. I don't want to do anything. I don't know if I can stand this." But I remember my kids saying, "But you'd better do this, dad, if you want to play tennis and hockey again. You'd better do it." And I went to the surgery and they explained what they did and they said, "It doesn't hurt when they saw your chest in half. It doesn't hurt at all." Well, [my wife] Jeannie and I thought about it for a couple of months. So I did it and I thought, "Boy, if I do this, I'll really feel good about myself." But that first night in the hospital, when they take you in and they take away all your clothes and you've got to take a shower and they come in and give you a pill, I thought, "Do I want to do this?" I've gotten on airplanes and I've gotten off before the plane has taken off because I didn't want to travel, I've backed out of things for years. I said, "I could get my clothes now and I could go home. I don't have to do this. I could go home and just take it easy and maybe survive, but I'll make a complete fool out of myself if I do

it and my wife will be ashamed of me and my kids will be ashamed of me." So I went to sleep and the next morning, it all happened. So I thought, "Boy, if I survive this, I'll feel great." But I'm still the same person now [laughter] that I always was. It didn't change me much. I still had the same fears I've always had. But if you don't have the surgery—I've talked to other guys—every time you go to sleep at night, you wonder if you're going to wake up in the morning. If you go away, if you go to New York and you're in a hotel room and maybe had too much to eat or something that night, your stomach is feeling kind of funny and you twist and you wonder, "Is this the night that last artery closes?" You can't live that way, which is why I decided to go ahead to do it. I've never put in my years that I promised that I would put in.

MARSCHALL: *Promised to whom?*
SCHULZ: The syndicate president, when he took over —see, I was ready to quit—we argued with the president for almost three years over what was going to happen. I said, "I want to own this thing. I'm tired of you selling Charlie Brown razor blades in Germany without telling me. I want to be able to do what I want to do and I don't want you doing anything but the strip. Either I get my way, or I'm going to quit." This guy, he couldn't understand it at all. "You make more money than everybody else. You want more?" I said, "Yeah, but I earn more, I've done more. You see, I don't want more money. I just want control so you guys don't ruin it." Well, fortunately, he retired. [His successor] came in and he and I sat down and within five minutes, he could see how sensitive it was. All I was asking is that they don't ruin it.

GROTH: *Mr. Schulz, if you were as militant about controlling the strip as that, why wouldn't you be similarly militant about newspapers running it large?*
SCHULZ: Because of what I said before: I don't think it's fair for me to dictate to the editors who are really my customers. And because so many of them, for so many years, like *The Chronicle*, run it in the same place for thirty five years now and suddenly, to force them to change the whole thing around just because I want more space, I just think that would be too egotistical.

But if it's something that I really want, I'll go for it. I never quit, too.

Rick Marschall *is a widely respected newspaper strip historian. He edited* Nemo: The Classic Comics Library *from 1983 to 1989; packaged many collections of classic strips, such as* Popeye, Little Nemo in Slumberland, *and* Polly and Her Pals*; and has written extensively about comic strips.*

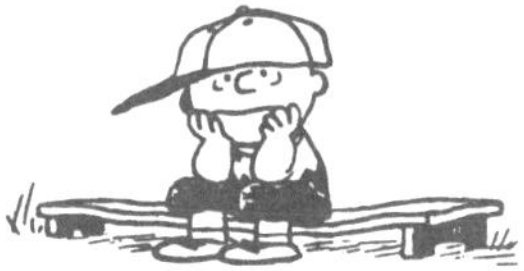

Gary Groth *is the co-founder of Fantagraphics Books. He has edited* The Comics Journal *from 1976 to the present, written about comics, and conducted interviews with over a hundred cartoonists.*

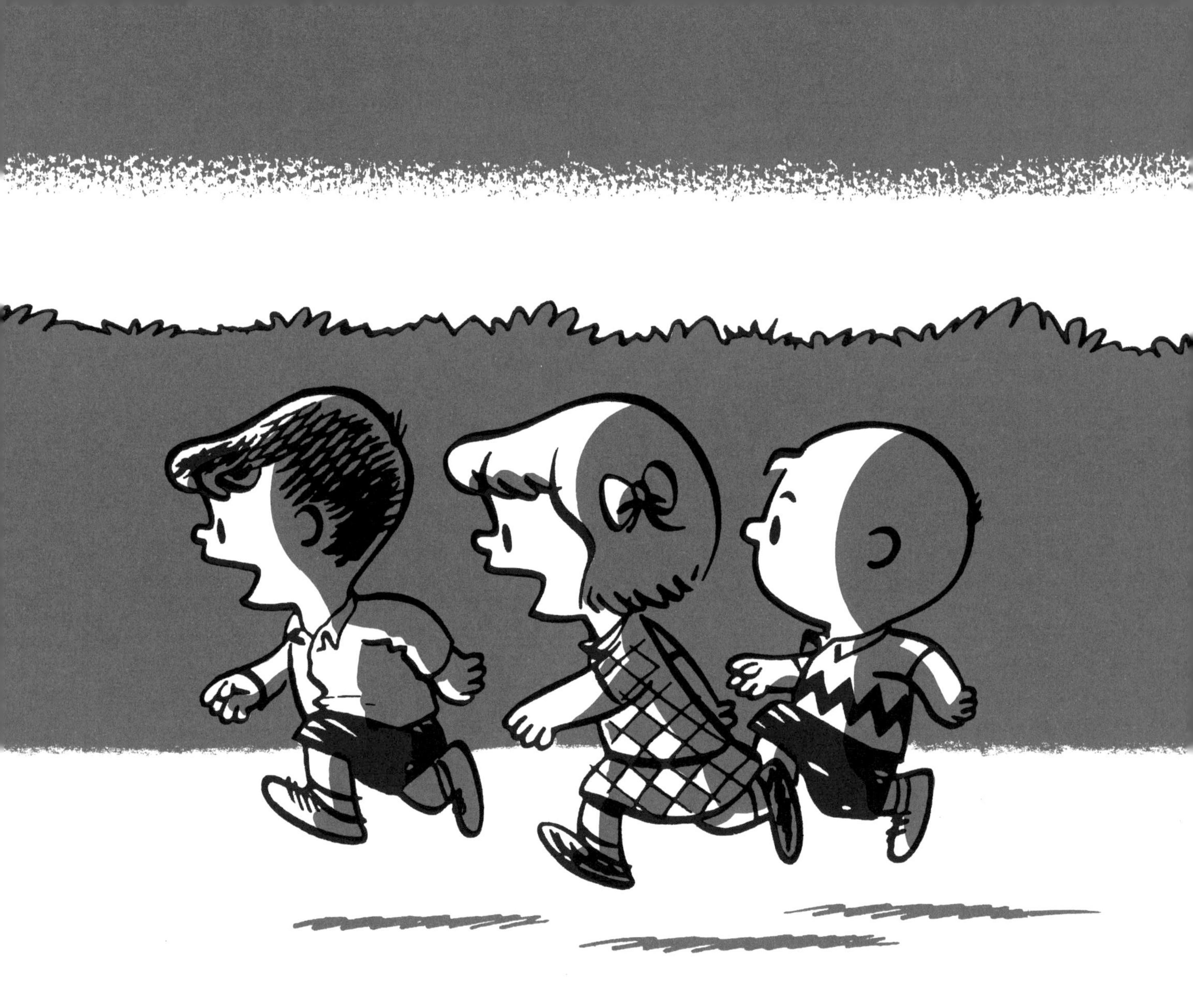

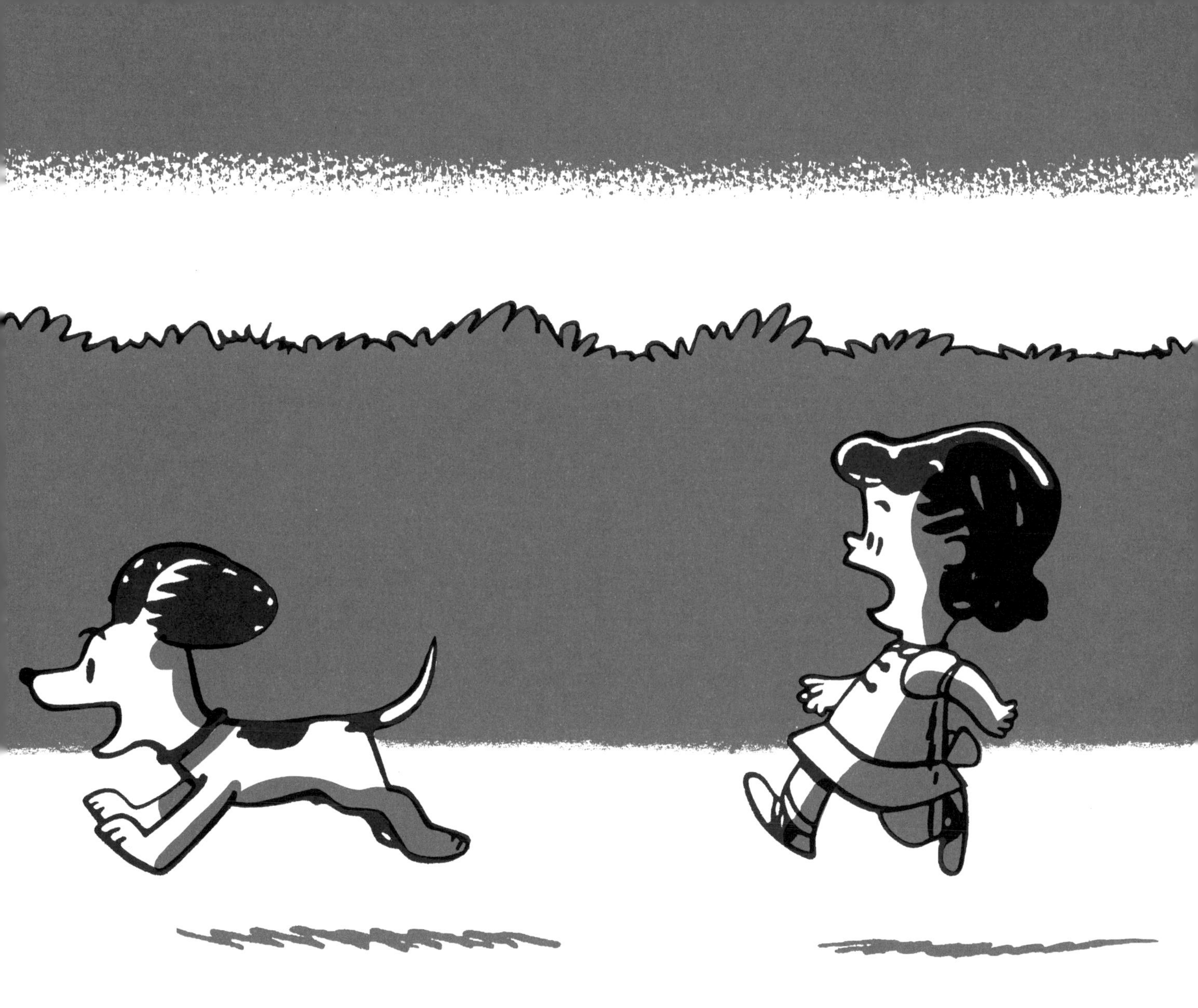

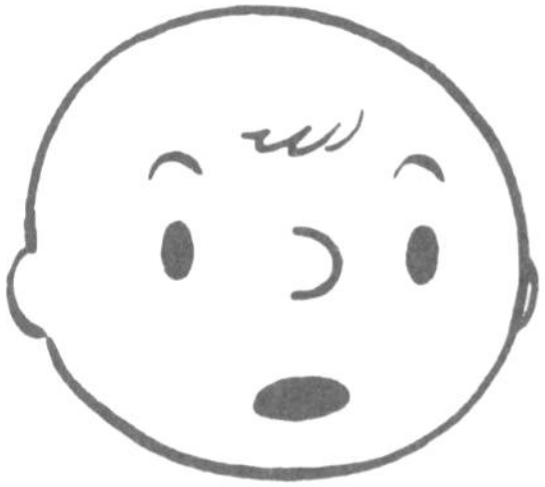

INDEX

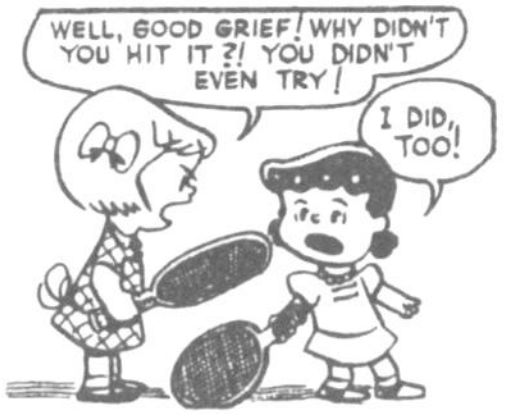

WELL, GOOD GRIEF! WHY DIDN'T YOU HIT IT?! YOU DIDN'T EVEN TRY!
I DID, TOO!

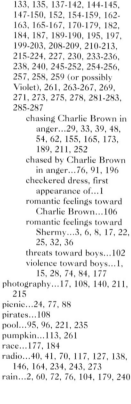

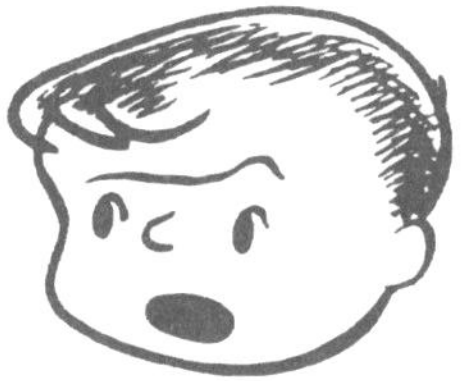

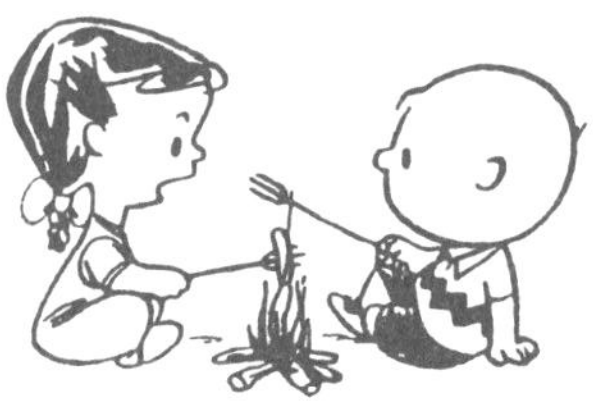

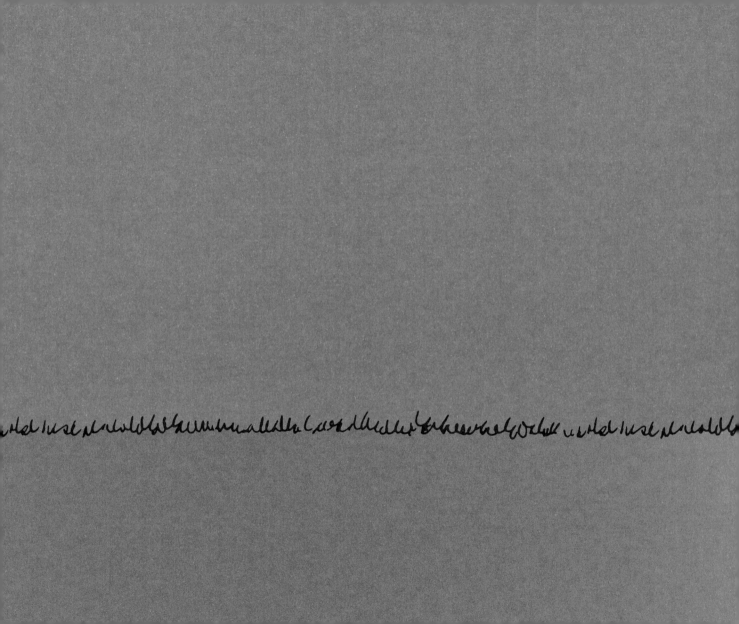

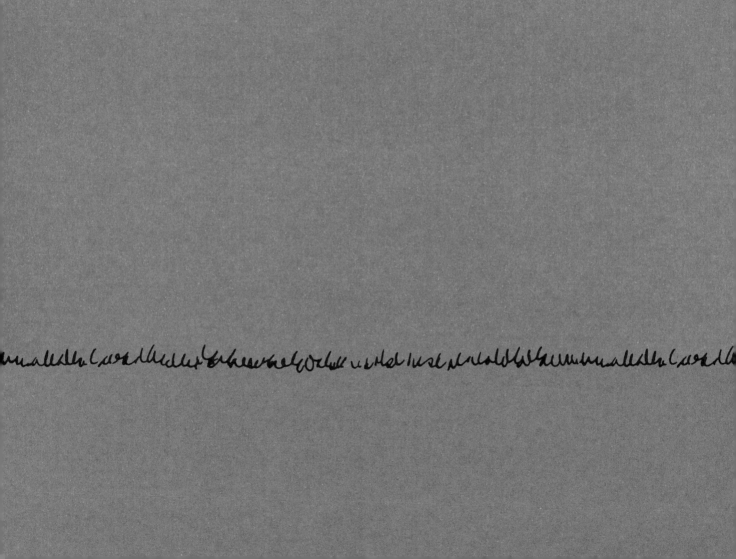

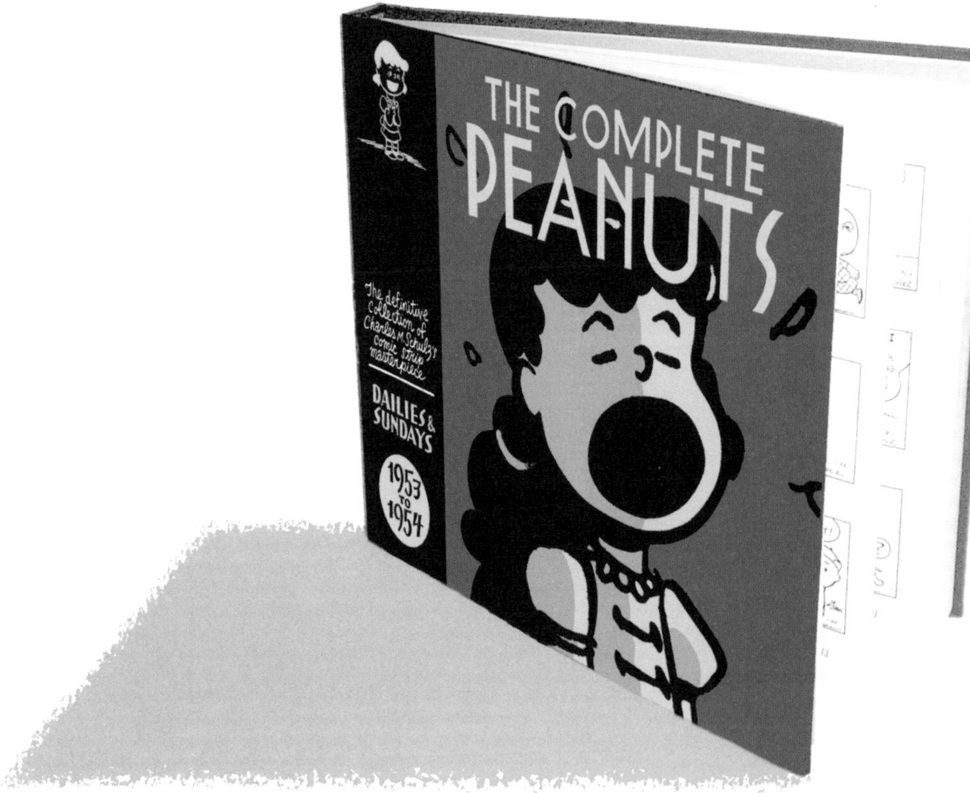
THE COMPLETE PEANUTS
The definitive collection of Charles M. Schulz's comic strip masterpiece
DAILIES & SUNDAYS
1953 to 1954

COMING IN *THE COMPLETE PEANUTS: 1953-1954*

Lucy initiates her one-sided flirtation with Schroeder… Linus's first thought balloon… Linus speaks… Charlie Brown loses his 10,000th checkers game in a row… the first rained-out baseball game… the "golf tournament" sequence with the visible adults… Linus acquires his security blanket… "Charlotte Braun's" brief career as a cast member… and the introduction of "Pig-Pen"!